IN THE SHADE
of the
MOUNTAINS

A History of the following School Districts:

Chedderville, Clear Creek, Crammond, Crooked Creek, Dovercourt, Hazeldell, (North) Caroline, Pineview, Ricinus, Shilo, South Fork, Wooler.

In the Shade of the Mountains

Elsie L. Stewart

"In the Shade of the Mountains" seemed to me to be a suitable name for our district History Book because we are so close to the mountains and are also the last settlement before reaching them. In my thinking we are truly in "the shade of the mountains".

© 1979
Serial Number 298365
Register 300
ISBN 0-88925-019-7
Published by
Ricinus — Caroline History Committee
Caroline, Alberta
T0M 0M0

Printed by
Friesen Printers
5720 Macleod Trail, S.
Calgary, Alberta
T2H 0J6
Head Office: Altona, Manitoba

Dedication

History Committee, Veva Rose, Mary McNutt, Sally Bugbee, Leah Rublatz

It is with great respect and sincere admiration that we dedicate this history book to the memory of Matilda Rose.

Without her notes as a reference and guide, many of the early day events would have been lost to us.

We who have edited, compiled, written, rewritten, corrected and gathered additional information have become well acquainted with the joys and woes of recording history.

We appreciate all the more, the effort we now know, that went into the work of those whose writings we have been priviledged to use.

To her we say "Hat's off" for the beginning of a worthwhile community project.

Dedication To The Pioneers

They came from all over
  From England, from France,
From Norway, from Sweden
  From Finland by chance.

They came from Ireland, and Scotland,
  From Kote and from Brae,
And from every State
  In the old U.S.A.

From Germany and Holland
  From the Ukrain and Hungary,
And brought all the trades,
  That their homeland knew.
There were Serbs and Grotes
  And Italians too.

They fought starvation
  And too many obstacles to tell,
    When illness attacked
  It was die or get well.

Not enough can be told
  Not enough praises sung,
Of those who carved homes from the
    wilderness
  When our country was young.

I've rejoiced in their triumphs
  I've shared in their tears,
I always will honor
  Those Old Pioneers.

— Guy E. Fay

Table of Contents

Foreword

Leah M. Rublatz

The inspiration for our book really must be credited to two people, Matilda Rose and Roy Devore. They each travelled many miles and interviewed many people, compiling considerable material concerning the early settlement of our area. Time, circumstance and finances did not permit them to complete or publish their works into book form, although Mr. Devore's work was published in a newspaper back in the 1950s. He kindly presented his original manuscript to the Village of Caroline for posterity and we have made liberal use of both Mrs. Rose's and Mr. Devore's writings, as has been noted elsewhere in our book.

Informative meetings between local residents and the publishers representative were held and our committee then came into being.

Since the committee was formed the four members have lived, eaten and slept with "THE BOOK". There have been many moments of frustration, equally as many of exhilaration on acquiring old photos, clippings and documents. Also many moments of hilarity during editing, proof-reading and the composing of captions.

It was decided to use the old school districts to organize our book into chapters. We have made posters, advertised in local newspapers, distributed brochures, pleaded, cajoled and mildly threatened to obtain additional material.

To those whose history's have been missed we apologize; to those who made pre-payments on books we are most indebted. Without their financial support the publishing would have been greatly delayed.

Overall it has been an interesting, informative and morally rewarding experience to have participated in this project.

We sincerely hope our readers will enjoy the results of our efforts and that our book will become a treasured possession of future generations.

Acknowledgements

Respectfully, Leah M. Rublatz, Secretary-Treasurer, Ricinus Caroline History Committee

The History Committee wishes to thank all those who have so graciously loaned pictures, documents and clippings; and to those who contributed histories and information for this publication.

To Mrs. Elva Mitten who contributed funds to give us a start. To the Caroline Golden Age Club who has sponsored us and enabled our committee to apply for a Provincial Government Grant from Alberta Culture and New Horizons. To the Community Clubs that donated money toward our cause. To our two typists, Veva Rose and Joan Dean. Our proof readers Mrs. Stella Clay, Mrs. Anna Demenuk and Mrs. Evelyn Benz. A special note of gratitude to Mrs. Sally Bugbee for her sunny nature, perseverance, and dedication — without her, I am sure our efforts would not have reached fruition. To Mary and Ted McNutt for the great part they have played in our work. To Della Milburn for the use of her home for meetings, and to the Caroline School Staff. To Vyla Johnson for our cover sketch.

Last but certainly not least to my husband Bill, who has been infinitely patient about late or completely missed meals and the inevitable disruptions in our household. He has encouraged and helped me in so many ways. He must surely have tired of the oft repeated, "I don't have time 'cause I 'gotta' work on THE BOOK."

As in all works of this nature there have been errors made in dates, the spelling of names, places etc. We beg the reader's indulgence for these discrepancies.

We offer this, the culmination of our combined efforts, to our readers in the hope that they will derive enjoyment and further their knowledge of our great pioneer families who settled this area. The hardships they endured have created many benefits for us of the present generation.

Our Native People

Henry Stellfox

The Butte in township 37-R-6-W-5 was a favorite camping place. Members of the O Chiese band of the Chippewas occasionally held their sun dance there. It was also the place where they went to gather Seneca roots and truffles called ground medicine by Indians and used for stomach complaints and drawing boils and carbuncles. Many white people, who have ploughed up samples of truffles (sometimes referred to as "mold") have mistaken them for Pemmican, because it so closely resembles dried Pemmican.

Old Jean B. Lagrelle, named thus by Father Lacombe, made his home at Caroline or at the Butte. He was half Cree, half Blackfoot. His father was Kie-Cut-Na-Wun, his grandfather Sa-Sa-Kan. Lagrelle's Cree name was Ko-Ka-Sic-A-Moo (hanging black cloud). His wife was half Cree, half Stoney, and her name was Pe-Po-Na-Sa-Usk. Jean B. Lagrelle died at 103 years of age. Their son, Joseph Lagrelle born December 29, 1873, is still living and a member of the Sunchild Cree band who signed the Treaty in June, 1944.

Joshua Saulteaux — Native family.

A family of Metis who use the name of Goodin, Goodau and Goodeye have for many years resided in and near Caroline.

A Stoney family, Joshua Saulteaux, members of the Lagrelle's their name originally being Crane, are descendants of the Crane family from Pigeon Lake and Hobbema.

This is a sketchy outline of the Indians one meets around the Caroline area.

House of Commons
Canada

As Alberta's 75th birthday nears it is gratifying for residents of respective communities to have the privilege of leaving a mark in the sands of time by having recorded the life story of our pioneers.

Their periods of joy and times of sorrow are indelibly inscribed in this book.

As time passes, those who peruse these pages will have the privilege of becoming acquainted with the true pioneer spirit.

GORDON TOWERS

Member of Parliament

To the Editor of the Ricinus-Caroline History Committee:

Jack M. Campbell, M.L.A., Rocky Mountain House Constituency

On behalf of the Province of Alberta, I feel honoured to bring greetings from the Provincial Government.

Congratulations to the organization who worked so hard to gather the material and finally get it into book form.

It is so important that we document the lives of our pioneers. In this way, future generations will realize how Alberta, with the dedication and foresight of these people, has grown to the prominence it enjoys in Canada today.

Grant MacEwan

Good for the Editor and Committee presently preparing a local history of the Ricinus and Caroline areas! In terms of lasting satisfaction, such a publication may prove to be one of the best community undertakings chosen to date. Such is the judgment of workers in other parts of the province.

A new and significant interest in history is sweeping this country and this generation. It has been strange — almost exciting — to watch. Most young people of my public school generation hated history. I was no exception and the reason was easy to detect. We were taught no Canadian history whatever. Canada was considered too young to have a history or the Canadian history was of no account. We received instruction in English history and only concluded that we wanted no more history.

But after being out of school for a few years, I made a couple of startling discoveries — at least startling to me. First I discovered the rich quality of my own Canadian history, especially Western Canadian story. It left me wanting more because I was left fascinated and charmed. And then the second discovery, that history — any history — has utility as well as charm. It can be useful, like mathematics, and citizens cannot afford to be without the benefits of the lessons of the past.

After all, history is simply the record of successes and failures, disappointments and triumphs, tragedy and humour from other years. History does repeat and the warnings and lessons from yesterday could help us tomorrow.

Local history is important, just as national and international history has something to tell us. Alberta has seen many local histories prepared, published and sold out since 1967. It is a mark of community pride and maturity when a district embarks upon such an undertaking. Caroline and Ricinus are now joining a group of Alberta districts dignified by the publishings of their proud past.

PIONEERS

They came from the earth's four corners
Driven on by the promise of land.
Up held by their own hard courage,
Not knowing a helping hand.

Some young, in their strength secure.
Others in uncertain middle years.
All in the clutch of a new land's lure,
With courage strong, quelling all fears.

Facing the future at all costs.
Turning their backs on the past.
Burning the bridges behind them,
Nor ruing whatever was lost.

Determined to strive and not give up.
A mark to make in this, their land.
To win this round, to drink their cup,
To love and honor, who held their hand.

The gleaming axe and the crosscut saw,
The whack and swish of the old broad axe.
As it hewed the logs so green and raw
To build palatial home or little shack.

The 'haw' or 'gee' as the horse or ox
Humped and strove to skid the logs
To the little raise, a home would stand
Just a short distance above the bogs.

The axe and the crosscut saw
Fell the mighty pine and stately spruce.
To build a cabin, fulfill the law
And tame the wilderness on the loose.

Raising a family of children,
Sending them off to school.
Trudging each day, their weary way
To be taught the golden rule.

A mother at home in her cabin,
Patched and sewed, made do,
To keep her family presentable
A pioneer tried and true.

Toil from rising to setting sun,
Blistered hands and aching back
Offset by picnic and family fun
Mountains of food, notice no lack.

Back to the washtub, axe or plow
From the wilderness, carving a home.
Brought from the old land the know how
Caring no more, ever to roam.

Bit by bit building a nation
A little here and a smugeon there.
Improving and bettering their station,
Building a home in this land so fair.

Here's to the toil, as each foot of land
Cleared by the early settlers' hand.
Paid for in sweat as he swung the grubhoe.
Paid with each stroke, each crunching blow.

Proud he had strength to do his share.
Tired, oh! So tired at the setting sun
Homesick, remembering his native shore,
But glad of the work, accomplished and done.

Here's to our fathers and mothers fair,
To their strength and their sacrifice.
To the years of toil and loving care,
A life well spent, a dream suffice.

Crackling in their caloused hands
In the tired backs, and seamed face
One reads contentment in their lands,
The woes and laughter of our race.

—Donald Cole

Roll of Honour

Vererans From the Caroline Area

W.W. I

Bell J.
Bell S.
Bell W.
Fleet J.
Garrison W.
Hobbs F.
Hobbs G.
Martin L.
McCoy A. E.
Smythe E.
Sorensen V.
Tose J.
Vandermeer H.
Willoughby W.
Wilson T. F.

W.W. II

Adair R.
Anderson H.
Armitage H.
Axtelle G.
Barby E.
Benz O. H.
Betts T.
Both L.
Bowers W.
Black S.
Blamire H.
Budden C.

Budden W.
Bugbee E.
Campbell R.
Campbell D.
Chapin T.
Chapin R.
Cooper H.
Dewey G.
Dial R.
Dix H.
Dix W.
Dolphin E.
Dolphin M.
Farris E.
Flynn P.
Franklin J.
Grieves S.
Hanson H.
Hazen D.
Hazen G.
Heck J.
Heck M.
Helm E.
Helm R. W.
Holt N.
Jackins D.
Jackins N.
Jamieson J.
Jennings N.
Kanten E.

Kanten W.
Kyler O.
Leavitt V.
Lynn B.
Mewha W.
McDonald W.
McColl R.
McLean F.
Milke H.
Motz H.
Motz O.
Motz W.
Moore A.
Mullen H.
Murray J.
Murray R.
Nicholson P.
Nicholson R.
O'Coin F.
O'Coin T.
O'Conner J.
O'dell Neil
O'dell Nels
O'dell Nelson
Ott E.
Patriquin H.
Pedley F.
Peterson A.
Pollard S.
Proudler D.

CANADIAN ACTIVE SERVICE

Roll of Honour

Radik J.	St. Denys C.	Willsie R.
Rickard H.	St. Denys H. J.	Williams B.
Reid W.	Stewart L.	Williams W.
Ross C.	Stewart W.	Wren P.
Rowles R.	Tose C.	Wren W.
Rhodes A.	Van Leest J.	
Shaurette R.	Weiss B.	

Veterans From The Chedderville-Dovercourt Area

W.W. I	**W.W. II**	
Clarkson T.	Anderson B.	May F. Jr.
May F.	Anderson C.	May J.
McArthur P. Sr.	Anderson J.	McArthur P.
McConnell D.	Howes L.	McKie J.
Smith L.	Lane H.	Schmelzer A.
Smith W.	Lougheed G.	Sinclair A.
Unwin G.	May F. Sr.	Soderburg A.
		Soderburg G.

Veterans from the Ricinus Area

W.W. I	**W.W. II**	
Clearwater, Vic.	Clearwater N. A.	Knorr H.
Cliff G.	Dunn W. C.	Knorr R.
Dean J.	Forster F.	LeCerf H.
Godley E.	Forster R.	Marvin W.
Godley P.	Frew D. E.	Rose S.
Godley R.	Justinen L.	Whittaker M.
Winchester C.	Kiser J. G.	

CANADIAN ACTIVE SERVICE

Chedderville

All Hallows Church at Chedderville

In 1940 during an air raid, "All Hallows on the Hill" — the oldest church in London, England was bombed. Under the west end, an arch of Roman tiles was found with a date going back to the year 680 A.D. It was from this church that All Hallows Mission at Chedderville was named.

A fragment of the bombed wreck was sent to Padre Moss, the Anglican minister at Rocky Mountain House, to be incorporated into the new church.

The credit for getting the church built and organizing the Chedderville A.C.W., goes to the late Padre Moss, our minister from 1947 to 1950.

The church was built entirely from donations and volunteer labour and the A.C.W.

The A.C.W. was formed November 23, 1948 with 13 members. Only three of the original members are with us today.

Mrs. Williams was elected President — an office she held for five years when ill health forced her to resign. Mrs. McArthur was the first Secretary-Treasurer — an office she held for twenty-five years. Meetings are held on the first Friday of every month at the homes of the members.

All Hallows Church at Chedderville.

Over the years, money has been raised in a variety of ways — catering to weddings and banquets, turkey suppers' card parties, garden parties, bazaars, bake sales, talent shows, serving lunches at auction sales and concession booths at local stampedes.

The money is used in many ways — donations to the Crippled Children's Hospital, Retarded Children's Hospital, Primates World Relief and Development Fund, Christmas tree fund, gifts for the past members now in nursing homes, fruit baskets to hospital patients and for the upkeep of the church.

Over the years, the members have worked diligently to serve the church and the community.

Chedderville-Dovercourt-Clearwater Club

In 1941 a club was formed called the C.D.C. War Workers. The main purpose of the club was to knit sweaters, socks, and mitts for the soldiers. The ladies would meet once a month at different homes often travelling ten miles or more by team and wagon, on horseback, or walking. Many parcels were sent to the soldiers. They would also send cigarettes and chocolates to some of the soldiers from our own districts. They held bazaars, raffles and teas to make extra money for these items and buy more wool.

After the war was over the club dispersed and then each district formed their own clubs and started working for the children's Christmas treats. Some of these clubs are still in operation.

Some of the members of the C.D.C. Club were: Mrs. Hattie Sinclair, Mrs. Emma Bert, Mrs. Edith Scott, Mrs. Bailey, Mrs. Vera Zengal, Mrs. Madeline Radau, Mrs. Riddle, Mrs. Clara Moberg, Mrs. Mary Hamilton, Mrs. D. Roover, Mrs. Gladys Zuberbier, Mrs. Maggie Clarkson, Mrs. Louise Soderburg, Mrs. Birdie Williams, Mrs. Bertha Williams, Mrs. Martin Hanson, Mrs. Elizabeth McArthur, Mrs. Albert May, Mrs. Fred May, Mrs. Marian Bancroft, Mrs. Barbara Hutchinson and Mrs. Mary McNutt.

Chedderville No. 3676

composed by Lorin Williams, Patricia Moberg and Carole Wilson

The first Chedderville School was one and one-half miles west of what is now the main road. The McNutt Brothers now own this land. It was built in 1917 and was later torn down by someone from Caroline. They then moved the school from North Caroline and another from Dovercourt in 1934 to the present location on the corner. These two schools provided education for all grades 1 to 9, until the older pupils were bussed to Caroline in 1959. However, only one of the schools is now used, for only grades 1 to 6 are now being taught there.

The present teacher is Mrs. Christien and the bus driver who has been driving over eight years is Mr. E. Della Costa, better known as Ellis.

Some of the teachers who taught there were: Ada French, Orville Kirby, Ivan Nelson, Ada McVeigh, Lenore Eversman, Helen Veal, Alta Russel, Mary Grant, Stella Ewing, Darlene Reighley, Margaret Shellian, Lula May Grieves, Phyllis Hunter, Minnie Scidoshie, Ruby Cunningham, Bertha Vessey, Anne Terrice, Mary Barnett, Gloria Robinson, Mr. Tuttle, Mrs. McKain, Mary Erdos, Ethel Skriever, Charlotte

Chedderville School Class — July 1928 — Teacher Miss Shellian: Back row — Lizzie McKie, Marjorie May, Fred Hodgkinson, Barbara Bancroft, Mary Robinson, Alec Hutchinson — 2nd row — Isy McKie, Alberta Williams, Donald Hodgkinson, Delena Hodgkinson, Charlie Hodgkinson, Jake McKie, Helen Spence, Rex Bancroft and Annie Spence.

Chedderville School Picnic.

Chedderville Baseball Team — Back Row — Albert Zuberbier, Howard Williams, Lawrence Williams, George Giffin — Front row — George Carlson, Rex Bancroft, Ed Pewonka, August Williams, Len Schafer.

Upham, Gwen Goldstrom, Louise Bowhay, Bill Lynn, Gladys Taranger, Sylvia Ulan, Beth Owen, Velma Rivers, Marion Nelson, Mr. Thomas, Mrs. Richardson, Mrs. Dailey and Miss Knight.

The Chris Anderson Family

Mr. Chris Anderson was born in Biersted, Denmark, in 1883, coming to Canada in 1907 to homestead twelve miles south of Seven Persons, Alberta, in 1908. Breaking was done a few acres at a time with a horse and walking plow.

Making a trip to Medicine Hat took a couple days going by horseback to Seven Persons and then by train to Medicine Hat.

In 1912 he married Gonda Van Maarion who had come with her parents and several brothers and sisters from Rotterdam, Holland, in 1910. They had a family of eight children.

After several dry years and crop failures, the government offered two free boxcars to any of the settlers that wanted to move their belongings north in hopes of better days, so the Andersons took advantage of this and moved to Chedderville, twenty miles south of Rocky Mountain House, in 1925. The land they lived on was the S.E.Q. 12-37-7-5. Here they stayed for three years, then moving to the Daley farm, eleven miles southwest of Eckville, and in 1930 they bought the east half of 15-38-3-5 on which Chris Jr. and wife, Lillian, still live.

Mr. and Mrs. Chris Anderson Sr. retired to Calgary in 1950 where Mrs. Anderson passed away in 1958 and Mr. Anderson in 1977.

Four of the sons served in the second World War. John who was in the navy, was lost at sea when the ship he was serving on, was torpedoed. Bill, who served in the airforce as a fighter pilot, was shot down over Germany. Charly and Carl were two of the fortunate ones to come back without injuries.

Chris stayed on the farm where he and his

wife still live. They have a daughter, Margaret, who, with her husband, Brian, and daughter, Kirsten, live at Bragg Creek. Margaret was a stewardess for Pacific Western Airlines for ten years.

Our son, Richard, has worked with the Weather Modification Board at Penhold for five years after completing his education at Red Deer College and U. of A. He lives at Sylvan Lake where his wife, Pat, teaches school.

Mary married Elvis Ross and she has a step daughter and a son. They live in Calgary.

Gonda married Earl Fair and he passed away around 1951. They had one daughter. Later she married George Humble and they live in Crossfield.

Lillian married John Rowles. They have a son and live in Calgary. Charly lives in Red Deer and is well-known in Central Alberta for his several business ventures. He married Laureen Rolston and they have one son and two daughters.

Carl worked for the city of Calgary for several years but is now retired. He married Helen Kylick and they live in Calgary.

Mr. and Mrs. Rex Bancroft

Mr. and Mrs. Bancroft came to Canada in the spring of 1913. We came right through to Calgary on the train and heard that a Mr. Sharman

Rex and Marion Bancroft loading bundles and Rex Jr. and Barbara on the wagon.

Rex Bancroft on mower and Mrs. Bancroft, Barbara and Rex Jr. standing.

needed a man and wife on his farm four miles out of Red Deer. He had a herd of Jerseys and we stayed six months. We made friends with Tom Clarkson, who had a homestead south or Rocky, so, while I went into Calgary to have my daughter, Barbara, Rex went and filed on a quarter near by. He built a shack and came back to Calgary to bring me home. The railway wasn't finished so we had to sit in a shelter and wait until a train came along. We arrived in Rocky near mid-night. There was no room in the Mount View Hotel so a man got out of his bed in a rooming house and said I could have it — imagine my feelings! Anyhow, I put my coat on the bed and we laid down thankfully. Next morning, walking down main street, a dead moose lay outside a shack and someone had cut the hind leg off and beat it (cheap meat). I wondered what kind of a country I had come to.

The winter of 1913 was beautiful; lovely chinooky days, no snow until way on in January. We soon got on to homesteading, putting up buildings with logs, etc. We were able to pick lots of blueberries in those days.

In 1918 our son, Rex, was born. We had to drive the twenty miles into Rocky, in the days of horse and buggy, and we never made it. At Drummond Creek, five miles out, the baby was born. My husband, Rex, tied the cord with brown thread in two places, bit the cord in the middle, and so all was well. It was never disturbed.

Around 1918 our school was built and our daughter, Barbara, started at the age of five. She walked the one half mile to school. The school was built on the School Section that was next to our land. For many years I boarded the school teachers and made many friends. Then being a seamstress, I made wonderful friends in Rocky and eventually went in and sewed by the day for $2.00 a day. I thought I was well off. I stayed with the Smiths for many years and went home weekends. After a while things got a little better, so I charged $4.00 a day. The Smiths moved out to British Columbia, and my one great friend, Mrs. Strong, asked me to stay with her, and I did. She was wonderful, and her family are still there and I visit them regularly. I kept up my sewing until I was over seventy, and I am climbing ninety now and still put the odd dress together.

I am living with my daughter north of our homestead.

Sterling and Iola Chappell

Sterling and Iola Chappell settled on the George Smith homestead on the north half of 9-37-6-5. They farmed and raised pigs.

They had one boy, Brian. He finished his grade five at Chedderville School. They left the farm and moved to Rocky Mountain House in June, 1960.

Brian and his wife, Virginia, went to Singapore in 1978, where his son, Ryan, was born.

Mr. and Mrs. Holender now own the farm.

Tom K. Clarkson

Mr. Thomas K. Clarkson homesteaded in the Chedderville district in 1912. He came from Sussex County in England with his brother, Bob. They resided on the half section 13-37-6-5, the land now owned by Joe Waite.

Tom enlisted in the Canadian Army in 1914 to 1918, returning to the homestead in 1919. He married Maggie McKie in March, 1924. They retired to Sylvan Lake in the early '40's. Mrs. Clarkson passed away in March, 1952, and is buried at Sylvan Lake. Mr. Clarkson moved to Gibson's Landing, British Columbia, in 1953 and lived there until his passing in September, 1970, at the Shaunessy Hospital in Vancouver. He is buried at F.O.H. Seaview Cemetery at Vancouver. He was one of the few Vimy men left. He

Anniversary for Meg and Tom Clarkson — cake decorated by Jenny Ankle.

was a Veteran member of the Sylvan Lake Branch Legion 212.

I am a niece of Mr. Clarkson — Isa Penner.

Donald and Helen Cole

In the fall of 1936, my father and a neighbor, Leonard Stout, and I borrowed a Model T Ford quarter ton truck and drove to Caroline to see the country. We had lost seven crops in a row to drought. We came to Mr. Sam Frazier's home on the Raven River, two miles west of Caroline on the south side of the road. He had been a close neighbor on the prairie at Czar, where we came from. We drove around the country with Claude Frazier as our guide. We liked what we saw; after the dry years on the prairie, the heavy crops of hay and grain looked good to us. I knew that, as for myself, I would have to go some place where wheat and combines were scarce, as the dust did not do my asthma any good.

In the spring of 1937, my younger brother, Gordon, and I put a tent on a hayrack and loaded a batching outfit. With a team of geldings and leading three horses, we headed west. Eleven days later on the morning of May 16, 1937, we pulled into Caroline. We camped south of Caroline a mile or so on some land owned by Mr. Harvey Langley. Then, announcing our presence to the Fraziers, we were invited to move to their place. We did, but within the week we rented a quarter section a half mile west of Caroline on the south side of the road and moved there. I believe this is where Steve Molnar lived until a short time ago.

Gordon went to work for Mr. Ben Harris and stayed over a year. I put in seventeen acres of oats, and due to fewer horses and smaller machinery, I found it quite a task, even after helping to put in six or seven hundred acres of crop on the prairie with up to sixteen horses strung out.

The summer of 1937 I put up hay for several

Tom and Meg Clarkson.

Donald and Gordon Cole — a "dirty Thirties Motor Home".

people as well as helping Jake and Opal Betchel put up hay and harvest some crop. I remember Opal pulling the hay in to a central location with a horse rake and Jake and I building a small stack. I enjoyed working with them and hope they enjoyed it as well.

In the winter of 1937 and '38, Claude and I hunted squirrels for a living for awhile. Then, as my father and stepmother had moved out to Caroline and were living with me, my father and I cut logs for Mr. Oliver Sr. the rest of the winter. Then my father rented what was known as the Wick Burns' place. It was across the Clearwater and north towards Chedderville. This land belonged to Mr. Harvey Langley also.

In the summer of 1938, I met Mr. Jake Vance who told me he had homesteaded on Prairie Creek. This was across the Clearwater River and northwest around ten or twelve miles. It was the N.W.Q. 22-37-7-5. In the fall of '38, together with a cousin and uncle, I moved up into that country and lived with them until the next spring. Then I moved onto Jake Vance's homestead, living in an 18 x 20 log cabin on the bank of Prairie Creek. The beauty of those flats and that small river have been a joy to me ever since.

That summer I broke up some flats and sowed it to oats. They sure produced a crop! My brother and I put in a good sized garden and spent the summer hoeing it, swimming and fishing as well

as building fence, etc. Gordon, it seems to me, worked some at a mill over on the Clearwater. This mill was owned by Mr. Gabler from up Strachan way.

In the fall, Gordon looked after the place and I went back to the prairie where I put in forty days on a combine and a header. Also had a little persuading to do concerning a girl I had left behind.

By the spring of 1940, I was raising a few saddle horses, using a colt out of a granddaughter of 'Man of War' as a herd sire. Many good horses from this fellow followed through the years. I rented the half section where I am now, from Mrs. Sarah Eddelstone who had lost her husband, Bill, that same spring of a heart attack. I put in some wheat and oats, and the crop was a good one. Mr. Howard and Lawrence Williams threshed it for us in the fall.

Helen Weddick and I were married that fall and we spent the first winter in a log cabin on Jake Vance's homestead. When we were married, Lawrence and Margie Williams went with me to haul Helen's horses back. On the way back, a boy with a load of straw pulled out kitty corner across the highway. There was no place to go and in trying to miss him, the truck caught the loose gravel and rolled. A trunk of wedding presents tied on top, lit right side up with a two year old colt standing straddle of it. Only one dish was broken.

Mrs. Eddelstone had wanted to sell us the place I had rented. I was not too enthusiastic about it, but we needed a home, so we bought it. Mrs. Eddelstone continued to live in her home for nearly nine years until sickness, and our need of more room forced other arrangements.

The years, some good, some bad, have passed too quickly. One good crop came to bless the couple of the wilderness, five girls and one boy. All have left on their own now; Winnifred married Herb Risto from Wetaskiwin. They are missionaries to the Maori and Island people in Auckland New Zealand. They have two girls, Joy and Grace.

Anita makes her home in Malawi, Africa, as a missionary to the dark people. She has a co-worker, Miss Isobel Duncan, formerly of Dapp, Alberta.

Beryl married a local boy, Ernest R. Wickins, and lives in the Dovercourt district. They ranch and farm and also raise a few horses. They have a girl, Connie, and a boy, Ronald.

Charlie, the only boy, is a welder and at present is manager of Prairie Welding, in Millet. He and his wife, Jackie, have one boy, Jason. Jackie is the youngest daughter of Mr. and Mrs. Bob Sharpe of Grande Prairie. Charlie and Jackie live at Millet.

Donna is married and lives northwest in the Everdale district. Her husband, Joe Davies, works for an oil company. They have one girl, Diana, and Joe has a boy and girl, John and Wanita.

Nadine works in the Foothills Hospital, Calgary, as a registered nursing aide at present. She is married to Kevin Cusack who is at present attending university and works for Gulf Oil.

The years have been kind. With an abundance of good down to earth neighbors, with the beauty of God's Country thrown in, and let us not forget the gift of our Lord and God, adds up to making life well worth the living.

Richard and Julia Dailey

Richard and Julia Dailey came from Cold Lake and bought the north half 8-37-6-5. It was Hudson's Bay land.

Julia taught school in Rocky Mountain House while living at Chedderville. They had four children, John, Ann, Jean and Ruth.

John is a history professor in England. He also taught in the States.

Ann is married to Jack Gill and lives at Pincher Creek.

The farm is now owned by Ruth and Jerry McLane who came from Didsbury and started dairy farming. They have four children, Lind, Laurie, Glen and Geraldine.

AN OLD COWBOY

When the last roundup is over
And has become history in a book,
What then for a fast riding cowboy?
Be he honest or a hard riding crook?

When the last open range is divided,
Cut up and fenced off by man's greed,
What then for the cowpoke and pony,
For saddle, chaps, spur, what need?

What then of the men of the ranges
Who know no other way of life?
What then 'till life's last chapter closes
All of this worlds turmoil and strife?
No more to see the red sunsets.
No more to ride with the wind.
No more to know the great freedoms.
Just an old, bowlegged 'has been'.

—Donald Cole

Jesse Royal Ditch

Jesse was born in Parkersburg, Iowa, in 1879. He came to Alberta with his friend, Charles Fogelsong, in 1908 or earlier and settled in the Chedderville area where he homesteaded the N.W.Q. 32-36-6-5. Later, his mother came to keep house for him.

Jesse remained a bachelor and was a good friend and neighbor to all. He had a lasting friendship with Charlie and Millie Fogelsong, both of whom he had known in Iowa. In 1946, after Millie had been widowed, first by Charlie in 1927 and then by George Bugbee Sr. in 1941, he went to live with Millie. He lived there until his passing in 1948. He had no other relatives in Canada but had five·sisters in the U.S.A. He is buried in the Pine View Cemetery at Rocky Mountain House.

Bill Eddelstone

Bill and Sarah Eddelstone came to this district in 1911 having previously immigrated from Blackpool, England, to Nanton, Alberta.

They farmed in the Chedderville district and south of Rocky Mountain House. Mr. Eddelstone

Mrs. Eddlestone.

was known as somewhat of a dealer. One time a neighbor's farm was sold for taxes in the thirties. This neighbor was away at the time, for some reason, and did not evidently realize he was going to be sold out. Mr. Eddelstone bought the land and when his neighbor came home he sold it back to him for what it had cost him.

A heart attack took him in the spring of 1940. Mrs. Eddelstone called for a sale on May 6, 1940. She passed away around 1949 having lived on the place until her passing.

Joe Error

by Donald Cole

Joe Error told me he was born in Syria. According to him, he ran away from home when he was eight or nine years of age. He never went back. At around age twelve, he shipped out of Bremen, Germany, as cabin boy on a freighter. After a year or two on this boat and visiting a good many of the world's ports, he jumped ship in Hong Kong. He said it was a very interesting place to a boy, but he nearly starved to death. One morning he was digging in a garbage can on the docks when a Canadian Captain spotted him and asked him how he came to be there. After hearing of the boys plight, the Captain took him on board and he became cabin boy on this boat.

Joe had had enough of boats and upon reaching Vancouver, he jumped ship again. He was in British Columbia for some years before the Immigration Authorities caught up to him. They were unable to prove where he came from and he was a man with no country. Eventually he received his Citizenship Papers and stayed in Canada.

He worked at various jobs and did some prospecting. Eventually he located a paying mine, but he took up some partners to help develop it and they ended up with Joe's mine. He sued, but lost it all.

Joe married a Miss Koples and when she passed on, he married another girl from Poland. Several children from these two marriages are still around.

Best of all I remember is drinking black coffee nearly all night with Joe. The coffee would lift your hair and take the bottom end off a spoon.

Joe's two-storey log house at one time was the envy of his neighbors. It stood on the N.E.Q. 28-37-7-5 and is still standing.

The children I remember are Steve, Minnie and Wesley from his first marriage and Ann, Bob, Elec, Joe, Steven and Paul from his second marriage.

Joe Error Sr. passed away in Vancouver.

James F. Hodgkinson Family

James Francis Hodgkinson was born on October 16, 1886, in Mayfield in the county of Stafford, England. In April, 1907, he married Rose Clara Pearson of Stafford.

Jim came to Canada in 1909, returning to England the same year. He later came back to Canada in 1914 to live in Calgary and Priddis, Alberta. While there, he hauled milk to Calgary for a number of years. In 1915, Rose and the three children, Frank, Ted and Fred, sailed for Canada.

In 1919 Jim moved his family north to the Billy Turner homestead, now the Dick Edmonson farm west of Elnora. They were on this place not quite a year. From there they moved to the Spence place north of Elnora, where the twins, Donald and Delena, were born in 1920 and Charlie in 1921. Their closest friends were the Camille Debucs and the Billy Ross'. It was for Mrs. Debuc that Delena was named. While on the

Mrs. Jim Hodgkinson, Don, Charlie, Delena and Fred.

Delena, Charlie and Don Hodgkinson, 1924.

7

Jim Hodgkinson.

Chrissie, Frank, Dell Hodgkinson.

Hodgkinson home at Chedderville.

place north of Elnora, the second son, Teddy, was lost due to burns. His mother had been sick in bed and Teddy was getting her a cup of tea when the fire he was starting with coal-oil, blew up in his face.

Pastures must have looked greener to the west because Jim, Frank and Lee Duft from Elnora first went out to Chedderville in the fall of 1924. Here Jim bought the southeast quarter of 23-37-7-5 from Lou Smith of Dovercourt. Their neighbors were to be Sid Smith to the east and later the Wilson and the Eddelstone family's to the south. The Clarkson's place was where the 'Big Rock' sits cornerwise from the Hodgkinson quarter.

In the spring of 1925, with the help of Mrs. Ernie Lusk (Della), Rose and the three youngest moved from Elnora to Chedderville. It was at this time that Rose sent a small spruce tree back with Mrs. Lusk and it was planted by Harold (Pee Wee) Segar as the head marker for Teddy's grave. Today this tree towers above all others in its peaceful setting in the Elnora Cemetery.

The schools in these years were open only until Christmas and again in the spring. The teacher for Cheddervlle School in 1925 was Miss Stella Ewing who later became the wife of Senator Donald Cameron.

The fall of 1926 saw Fred, Frank and Carl Beck drive twenty-eight head of horses out to Jim's where they held a one day stampede. Jack Cartwright was one of the riders. They traded a Model T car to Melvin Teskey of Elnora, for the horses.

In the winter of 1927 due to very hard times, Mrs. Hodgkinson with the four youngest children, moved to Mobergs logging camp northwest of the home place, then, in the spring of 1928, they moved out to Dan Bird's camp which was about two miles off Cow Creek Road, south and west of Rocky Mountain House. After part of the summer of 1928 spent cooking in the logging camp, Rose and the three youngest went back to the farm.

In the fall of 1928 Rose went to Calgary to stay. The children went to school at Glenmore School near Turner Siding which is now Haysborough. She took a job at Midnapore for a period of time. After Midnapore, they moved to a small house where the Glenmore Reservoir is today. When operations began on the dam, they moved across the road near the Polo Grounds and the Chinook Racetrack.

In the summer of 1933, Don and Charlie went back up to batch with their dad on the farm. In the spring of 1934, Charlie and Don put the crop in while their dad was gone to a bull sale. By 1936 the family were all out working and Jim stayed on the farm alone.

In 1937 Fred married Ivy Scarrott of Eagle Hill, Alberta. In 1938 Frank married Chrissie Michie of Lousana; 1941 Delena married Sam Melrose of Innisfail; 1943 Don married Kay Grisedale of Cochrane and in 1945 Charlie married Doris Cheek of Elnora. There are twenty-one grandchildren.

Over the years Jim made two trips to England and one to Australia. He lived on the farm most of the time until his death on March 6, 1968. Rose passed away in the Red Deer Auxiliary Hospital on November 2, 1968. They are now resting beneath the large spruce tree beside their son, Teddy, and grandson, Shane, who passed away in June, 1977.

Will Ives

Will Ives and his wife came to the Chedderville district in 1915 and filed on the S.W. 17-37-6-5. They came from South Dakota. They brought a large herd of cattle with them but the winter was severe and feed not good and they lost about two hundred head. They stayed for about three years. Mrs. Ives took sick and died with pneumonia, so the family went back to the States. They had five children, Willie, Ray, Neva, Mable and Keneth.

Kirstein Family

Paul Kirstein was born in Posen, Poland. He came to Canada with his parents and settled in Strasburg, Saskatchewan, in 1884. In 1900 he moved to Gleichen, Alberta, where he was a well known farmer for many years. It was at Gleichen he met and married his wife, Mary Rafferty, a school teacher.

Mary Kirstein was born in Ireland in 1880. She received her teaching certificate before coming to Canada. Their family were all born before they moved to the Chedderville district. There were four boys, Austen, Frank, Max and Ken. Three girls, Sheila, Doreen and Maureen (twins). The Kirstein family moved to the Chedderville area in 1934 to the S.W. 7-37-6-5 known now as the Gerald Haney place. They farmed there until their family were grown up. They retired in Calgary where Mr. Kirstein passed away in 1954 after a lengthy illness. Mrs. Kirstein passed away in Edmonton in March, 1964.

Mrs. Ives — mother of Neva Wilson.

Nora and Max Kirstein.

Billy Ives and sons Ray and Kenneth, Charlene Huber.

The Model T car built into a truck to move the Walter Korth family onto the Bill Robinson place.

Mr. and Mrs. Albert May.

Walter and Agnes Korth

Walter and Agnes Korth were married in February, 1934, and lived south of Sedgewick until the spring of 1938. Then they moved to the Chedderville district on the Bill Robinson Jr. farm with their three-year-old daughter, Caroline.

In the fall of 1941 they moved to the Sid Smith's homestead. At that time it was owned by Harry Wilson. They have lived there ever since.

They have seven children. Caroline married Russell Maxson of Stauffer and now lives at Armstrong, British Columbia. Marion married Gerald Gordon of Garth and now lives at Quesnel, British Columbia. Ivan and his wife, Elenor, live at Benalto. Ileen married Wendell Miller and lives at Markerville. Delbert married Judy Rudd and lives in Rocky Mountain House. Gordon and Lorraine live in Innisfail. Norman is at home.

When this was written they had twenty-one grandchildren and two great-grandsons.

Albert and Amy May

Albert and Amy May came from England in 1914 to Ontario where they stayed for a few years. Then they moved to Taber, Alberta, in about 1917 where Albert worked in the coal mines. The name of the mine was 'White Ash'. Albert didn't like the mines and it was too dry for farming so they moved to the Chedderville district in 1925. They bought the S.E.Q. 18-37-6-5 from Jim Melvin. Times were still hard and they had to do things like picking pine cones like the rest of the people and other things to make a living for their family.

Albert started an Illustration Station on his farm in 1927. It was under the supervision of Dr. Fairfeild and Mr. Everest. The fertilizer and lime had to be broadcasted by hand in those days and was not a nice job. In 1941 the station was relocated on the farm of Howard Williams,

Albert May's son-in-law, which they ran for many years until retiring to Rocky Mountain House.

Albert May ran the first post office in the Chedderville district then it was taken over by Albert Zuberbier, Albert May's son-in-law.

There was many a good old house party held in the May home. They retired from the farm in 1939 to Rocky. Amy May is still active at ninety-one years and is living in the West View Lodge in Rocky Mountain House.

They had five children, Gladys, Marjorie, Vera, Alberta and Sylvia. Gladys married Albert Zuberbier and they had two boys, Laurie and Roy. Laurie married Laura Evans and they have four children, Barry, Carrie, Shawna and Cheryle. Roy married Evelyn Greenwood.

Marjorie married Lawrence Williams. They had seven children.

Alberta married Howard Williams and they have two children.

Vera deceased at the age of four.

Sylvia married Art Soderburg and they had three children, Dennis, Jean and Earl. Dennis has one girl, Christina. Jean married Don Burdick and has four children. Earl is married and has two children.

L to R — Sylvia, Alberta, Marjorie and Gladys May.

Archie McDonald

Archie McDonald homesteaded in the Chedderville district on the N.E. 10-37-6-5. He worked his farm with horses and worked out to earn a living part time. He was never married. He retired and moved into Rocky Mountain House.

John C. McKie

by Isa McKie

The John C. and Maggie McKie family moved to the Chedderville district from Lethbridge in May of 1920 and settled on the half section of 18-37-6-5. They lived on the homestead until 1950, then moved to Sylvan Lake until 1962, then moved to Turner Valley. Dad passed away March 15, 1964, in the Colonel Belcher Hospital, Calgary. Mother moved to the Red Deer Nursing Home in 1971 where she still resides. They had nine children and thirty-two grandchildren, thirty-nine great-grandchildren and one great-great-grandson. Eskdale (Tye) McKie was born at Lethbridge May 13, 1913. He has two children and four grandchildren and resides at Caroline, Alberta.

Elizabeth Mary (Liz) McKie was born at Lethbridge November 29, 1914. She married Franklyn Stewart in 1935 and they had three children and five grandchildren. Liz passed away June 28, 1971, at Turner Valley where they lived from 1939 until her passing. They lost one son, Pat, in 1973.

Mr. and Mrs. J. C. McKie on their fiftieth wedding anniversary.

Kody Rae Christianson, 4 months old being held by his great great grandmother Maggie McKie, 87 years of the Red Deer Nursing Home. Kody's mother, Rhonda Christianson of Camp Creek standing on the left Shirley Bennett of Barrhead (centre) Isa Penner of Sylvan Lake. Taken at the Red Deer Nursing Home, May 15, 1978.

Five Generations — (clipping).

Peg, Tom, Nell and Jean McKie.

I, Isabella (Isa) McKie, was born at Culnaightrie Cottages, Scotland, May 5, 1918. I married Jake Penner in 1940. We have two children, three grandchildren and one great-grandson. We lost our son in 1974, and we now live at Sylvan Lake.

John McKie was born at Lethbridge on April 15, 1920. He was in the Armed Services from 1939 to 1945. Married in 1946, he now lives at Turner Valley and has five children and five grandchildren.

Janet McKie was born at Chedderville in 1922 and passed away at birth. She was buried at the homestead.

Peggy McKie was born at Chedderville on January 23, 1924. She married Sam Howes on May 4, 1944, and they have five children and eleven grandchildren. They reside at Dovercourt, Alberta.

Thomas Robert McKie was born at Chedderville on August 7, 1927. He was married in 1948 and had four children and two grandchildren. Tom passed away at Turner Valley on October 3, 1968.

Helen (Neil) McKie was born at Chedderville on March 22, 1929, and married Edwin Williams in November, 1946. They have eight children and seven grandchildren and now live at Turner Valley.

Alberta Jean McKie was born at Chedderville on January 8, 1931. She married Robert Castor on April 7, 1956, and they have three children and one granddaughter. Jean lives in Red Deer, Alberta.

John Moberg

The day I was born I didn't know who my parents or brothers were. I didn't even know who I was. As I grew older I started to answer to the name of Yohan (John) or Pety-kin-art. My Mother, Christina, told me she was born in Sweden where she married Arvid Moberg (Ed). Ed left Sweden for Canada in 1910 and settled at Greenwood, B.C. In 1913 my Mother followed with my five-year-old brother Sigfred. Brother Phillip (Philly-bume) was born at Greenwood.

Later the family came to Rocky and the Cheddarville area where I was born March 25, 1919. I was not the only one born there. Ahead of me was Bert (Elmer) and Ralph (Vinin-wing). Then came my sister Dorothy (Prairie Chicken), and last but not least sister Mildred May (Lindy). She was named Lindy because that was the year Lindberg flew the Atlantic. I was caught between four older brothers, and two younger sisters.

My dad later bought a quarter of land from Billy Strong further up Prairie Creek which is

The Ed Moberg family — Philip, Bert, Ralph, John, Dorothy and Lindy.

known as the Glacier district. It was here that Lindy was born, and Ralph still resides there.

Glacier school was three miles away. Most of the time we rode horseback, but there were days (weather permitting) when we made it by barefeet. As a rule school opened sometime in April and the weather was fairly nice. It closed when the weather turned bad in the fall. Swedish was the language at home, so we couldn't speak English until we began school — I'm not so sure I can speak it yet.

There was a family named Miels living quite close to the school. They had a collie dog that also came to school. We used to leave our lunch pails (syrup or lard pails) outside, and during class this dog could somehow manage to get the lids off our pails and have his lunch. We would advise the teacher, and she would tell us to go to Mrs. Miels and ask her to make us a new lunch.

Ed Moberg on Swan Lake in the early twenties.

When I got back, the dog still had the best lunch — my Mother's.

I have often told my children about the old bachelor who lived in the trees. He lived on the south side of Prairie Creek, and when the water was high he would take off his clothes, tie them on top of his head, and swim across — keeping his clothes dry. He also built a horse sleigh out of birchwood. It was built up off the ground on stilts so that if he had to cross any creeks which were not frozen, the things he might have in the sleigh would stay dry. When he came by our place on his way home from town he would always have a small sack of candies or other such delights. He had the right name for living in trees — Jack Eagle.

The first time I worked away from home — 1935 — I was sixteen years old. My brother Bert had an old Model T Ford which he drove to the Haynes district east of Red Deer. We worked there threshing until freeze-up. Bert sold the old car, so to save money we decided to ride the freight train to Rocky. The weather was well below zero F. We got on the tender of the steam engine where the coal was kept to feed the boiler, and so kept warm. We were so black when we walked uptown, a couple of boys we went to school with didn't even recognize us. Needless to say, we didn't stop to pass the time of day either.

My Dad acquired another quarter of land at Chedderville. As he had lots of feed and grain there he used to winter cattle and pigs there rather than haul the feed to the home place. He had a cabin built for that purpose, and it was here in Jan., 1941 that my brother Ralph found him passed away from a heart attack.

John Moberg and his mother and daughter Valarie.

There was no ambulance service in those days, so Phillip and I made our own. We borrowed a two-wheeled trailer and hooked it behind a Model A Ford. Between two shovels, a set of chains on the car, and pushing, we made it to the cabin. We loaded Dad into the trailer, covered him with a blanket and started back again across the field. At this point I want to mention that in January this country can be damned cold. It took about five hours to get to Rocky as the rest of the road was hardly fit for cars either. The whole incident will remain vividly in my mind forever. Our father was laid to rest three days later in the cemetery on Prairie Creek.

After working in a corn and sugar factory in Taber, and logging on the west coast I was finally attracted to Ricinus by a girl called Thelma Browning. We were married in February, 1943. We lived in a skid shack, moving it with the mill when necessary. I had become a sawyer for J. D. Spence and sawed ties for railway, lumber, etc.

We had the cabin at Phylis Lake once, and as the water in the Lake wasn't fit to drink or cook with — still isn't — we asked a boy who lived a half mile down the trail if he could bring some good water. He was only eight or nine at the time, but said "I'd be delighted to". The next day sure enough, he came down the trail with a goat hitched to a hand sleigh and a 5 gallon milk can full of good water. From then on he and the goat made the trip every other day. We paid him 25¢ each trip. Thanks for being such a pleasant boy and doing a good job Bill Turner. I wonder if Bill remembers the time I was setting up the mill for production, and he stopped to watch. He asked me if I chewed tobacco, and I said "Sure. Mr. Spence said if I didn't I could pack my turkey and get out". Bill looked at me and asked "Have you and Thelma got a turkey".

To augment my income I would guide in the fall, and work in the bush in the winter. In August, 1945 I bought NW 7-36-75 and SW 18-36-75 from John Clarence Millar. I paid $1500 for 219 acres of land, 1100 saw logs cut and skidded, a team of horses, five stacks of hay and a big garden.

In 1949 a lovely baby girl was born to us. We named her Valarie. She is now married to Wendall Hulberg of Rocky, and has two girls Kimberley and Shauna. Our marriage was not to be. In 1951 we went our separate ways, but we still remain friends.

In 1952 I met another young lady who became not only a sweetheart but a real friend. She is Thera May Hovis from the Butte district and Black Diamond. How well I remember when Thera and her brother Bud came to stay with me

John and Thara Moberg.

one spring. The weather was terrible and the roads worse. For nothing better to do, we would get in touch with a neighbor Jack Zimmerman. He worked for Dr. Banks who owned a small Ford tractor. I had bought one in 1948 and still own it. We used these as a mode of transportation to go to Caroline to pick up groceries. Before returning home we had to tipple a couple at the pub. On the way back, which was eleven miles, we would wager which tractor could do the best in the mud and water that was called a road. After losing the canned goods several times, the labels came off the cans. Later Thera (who became my wife in 1957) would say before making a meal "Anyone want to bet on what's in this can?" One time we lost the Star Weekly which we really looked forward to in those days. We went back and found it a half mile from home. Yes — we could still decipher some of it.

But things have changed a lot since then. Time, hard work, and raising a family of seven finally took its toll. After an illness of two years, Mother passed away in 1957 at the age of 69. She was laid to rest in Rocky Pine Grove Cemetery.

We sold SW 18-36-75 in 1965 to B. V. French, and retained NW 7-36-75 where we still reside.

A girl Alana Rae was born in 1965, and a boy Dustin John in 1970. Here we are in 1979. Alana is growing into a young lady, and she and Dustin are a lot of help to us. Mother and I are grateful as we aren't as spry as we used to be. At least now we have a hard top road and a better mode of transportation. The biffy still stands at the back of the house, but is of little use now. Thera doesn't have to guess what is in the cans, as it has been a long time since we lost any labels.

Edward and Esta Catherine (Mae) Pewonka

Edward Pewonka filed on his homestead in the Chedderville district in 1912, on the S.W.Q. 4-37-6-5. He brought his family to the farm in April of 1914. Between 1912 and 1914, he and his wife, Mae, worked on a farm in High River to earn a grubstake to go back to the farm. They lived in Innisfail one winter, returning to the homestead in April, 1914, to a roofless house. Mae was very upset as she had a four-month-old daughter, Evelyn, and an eight-year-old daughter, Josie, and it snowed that night.

Mrs. Pewonka had two daughters by a former marriage, Josie (Mrs. Josie Murray Ens) and Thelma (Mrs. Thelma Bean). Thelma was educated in Montana (1915-1918) while staying with her grandmother. Josie returned to Alberta and finished her schooling at Garth School west of Rocky Mountain House.

After returning to the homestead in 1914, Ed's father, Frank, homesteaded the quarter adjacent to Ed's. The Pewonkas spent the next few years clearing and breaking their land.

In the spring of 1918, Idella was born to the family.

In the year between 1917-1918, Ed purchased a stationary engine, grinder and wood saw which he mounted on a sleigh. He did custom wood sawing and grinding around the country. During the summer, people took their grain to the farm to be ground.

In the winter of 1920-21, the Pewonka family went to work at Revelstoke Logging Company (The Jack Pine); Mrs. Pewonka to cook and Ed to haul logs and ties to the log yard. They worked there for two years.

Evelyn and Idella got their schooling at the Chedderville school, going to school on horseback as they were five miles from the school. Josie attended Chedderville school the first year it was open. The teacher was Orville Dirby from Rocky Mountain House.

The girls eventually left home to homes of their own. Josie has three daughters, Glory, Lenore and Mildred, and two sons, Harry (deceased) and William. Evelyn McKinnon has two sons, Robert and Allan and one daughter,

Bill and Thelma Bean, May and Ed Pewonka.

Ann. Idella Whitesel has a son, Richard Federchuk. Thelma Bean, now deceased, has a family of four girls and one son.

In later years, Ed used his tractor with the Walsh boys' grain separator, to thresh grain from Butte to Chedderville and Ricinus. Ed and Mae Pewonka retired from the farm in 1951. Ed passed away in April, 1952, and Mae continued to live in Rocky doing some camp cooking and other jobs. She retired and moved to Creston for a few years, then returned to Rocky to live in the Westview Lodge until her passing in October, 1974.

Bill and Emma Robinson

Bill and Emma Robinson came from England to Canada in 1906 and settled in Nanton, Alberta. When they came they brought some horses along with them. Eighteen months later, Bill returned to England to get more horses to bring to Canada. Bill and a neighbor, Ed Smith, came to the Chedderville district and bought the N.E.Q. 13-37-7-5, in the South African Script in which a section cost $1400. Bill stayed with Mr. Hamilton until he built a house. In 1912 he moved his family out west. There was not much for roads in those days and you had to carry an axe with you.

Feed was very scarce and the stock had to be wintered out. Part of the stock was wintered at Stauffer at Mr. Gurnsey's and part up Prairie

Bill and Emma Robinson and daughter Elizabeth — now Elizabeth McArthur.

Emma Robinson and family on the farm.

15

Bill and Emma Robinson the second year on the farm in 1913.

Creek at Mr. Chesney's. That first year they lost many of their horses with poison weed.

They had to travel fifty-two miles to Innisfail for groceries by team and wagon. Bill had to go find work to keep the family. He got a job at Nordegg when they first opened up the coal mine and he was their first barn boss at the mines.

He formed the Chedderville School district and was secretary-treasurer for many years. He hired Mr. Thibedeau to build the school which cost $1100 including paint. That was in 1919 and it was used for thirty-five years and accommodated as many as thirty-five pupils. It was also used for dances and church services. Bill was also instrumental in getting a post office in the district. He was councillor for the municipal district of Prairie Creek for many years.

Bill and Emma had six children, Elizabeth, Emily, Bill, Rose, Alice and Mary. Elizabeth married Peter McArthur and they had four children, Marion, Charles, Jim and Peter. Marion married Jim May and they have two girls, Kathryn and Diane. Kathryn is married to Paul Chudic and they have two children, Lisa and David. Diane McArthur lives in Calgary. Charles McArthur is married and he and Gladys have two children, Bernice and Douglas. Bernice is married to Darrel Fay and they have three boys, Warren, Billie and Aaron. Jim McArthur married Pauline Prokop. They have two girls, Judy and Sheila. Judy married Robert Riddle and they have two children, Malinda and Kenneth. Sheila lives in British Columbia. Peter McArthur is married to Carol Purcell and have three children, Jan, Shannon and Rhonda. Rhonda is married to Cal Townsend and they have one girl, Shawntell.

Emily Robinson married Marino Cozzubbo. They have one girl, Lillian who is married to Frank Coulson.

Bill married Ruby Cunningham and they have two children, Billie and Rosalie. Billie is married and he and Irene have two children, Dorthy and Roger. Rosalie is married to Malcolm McGregor and they have two children, Carrie and Randy.

Rose Robinson is married to Lloyd Holditch and they have one boy, Dennis, who is married to Ellen Armstrong. They have two boys, Mike and Kenny.

Alice Robinson married Jim McDonald and they have two girls, Jean and Dorthy. Jean married Carl Haupt and they have two boys, Steven and Darren. Steven is married to Pat Marcenek. Dorthy McDonald is married to Walter Williams and they have two children, Gail and Terry. Gail married Keith Stuart and has two boys, Darrel and Neil.

Mary Robinson married Ted McNutt and they have four boys, Robert, Donald, Richard and Allen. Robert married Loraine Ouderkirk and they have two boys, Bradley and Bart. Donald married Beatrice Kirby and they have two boys, Kevin and Collin. Allen married Pat Kay and they have two children, Quenton and Kelty.

Vern E. Scott
by Edna Buck

Vern was born January 6, 1912, at Markerville, Alberta. In November, 1934, he came to homestead in the Chedderville district on a quarter of land located two miles north and one and one half miles west of the Chedderville store.

Vern and Lillian Scott and daughter Edna.

The Spence Story
By M. Hereford

In the early summer of 1924, my father, David Spence, mother (Nellie), brother Jim, sisters, Annie and Helen and I (Margaret) came to the Chedderville district, settling on the former Ollie Johnson place.

We had journeyed by team and wagon over the rough winding bush trails from Garth where Dad had homesteaded fifteen years before when coming out from Scotland.

We were blessed with many fine neighbors. Our closest were the Bancrofts, Mr. and Mrs. Bancroft, Barbara and Rex. They were extremely good neighbors and proved it in many ways throughout the years.

Kindly Granny Robinson was another fine neighbor.

In 1927 when my brother, Stanley, was born, Mrs. Bancroft willingly came to take care of my mother. Mrs. Jennie Ankle had a talent for cake decorating. Her beautifully decorated wedding cakes delighted many a bride — the three Spence girls included.

Other neighbors were Tom Hutchinson, Mobergs, Jake Vance and his mother, Clarksons, Mays, McKies and McArthurs to name a few.

The Chedderville School which all five of us attended over the years, was two miles away.

Times were hard and there was always a great deal of work to be done, but somehow there was time for visiting and social gatherings too.

The school Christmas concerts were one of the big social events. The school children produced a creditable performance — having been well trained in their acting skills by the teacher and Mr. and Mrs. Clarkson (fondly known as Uncle Tom and Aunt Mag). Mr. Albert May was always on hand with his accordion to keep the singing "in tune". After the concert Santa would arrive (he always sounded like Harry James) to distribute the gifts and candy bags, hanging from the huge Christmas tree. The ladies would serve lunch and then the dancing would top off a gala evening.

Everyone looked forward to the summer picnics too, families from all the surrounding districts would gather for an afternoon of fun, visiting, eating, races and ball games. In 1978 I had the pleasure of attending a Chedderville-Dovercourt picnic. It was nice to see that the old tradition picnics are still held — minus of course, the heavenly home-made ice cream and the lemonade made from real lemons!

In 1935 we moved down by Prairie Creek where Dad had built a log house on his homestead. It was a rather remote corner of the district and the trail leading into it was hard on

He brought with him a few cows and a team of horses.

He cleared his land by hand and when he grew a crop of grain, he hauled it into Rocky Mountain House by team and wagon to sell. He bought his supplies from Zuberbier's store at Chedderville.

In 1941 he built his own sawmill.

On January 17, 1942, he married Lillian W. Speight. That fall they moved to the "Plank Hill" west of Rocky Mountain House where Vern operated his mill. He served overseas in World War 11 from 1944 until he returned in 1946. He moved his wife and family to a house in Rocky Mountain House just across from the old telephone building, and then went back to sawmilling on the "Plank Hill".

The summer of 1948, he built a house this side of the overpass in Rocky Mountain House. Then in the spring of 1949 they moved to the Borstead farm north of Rocky Mountain House.

In 1951 he sold his homestead to Donald Cole of Dovercourt. In the spring of 1971 he sold his farm to Mr. Tom Yarschenko and moved to Enderby, British Columbia, where they have made their home since.

They raised five children, Edna (Mrs. Don Buck) of Rocky, Floyd and his wife, Carol, at Caroline, Rueben and his wife, Darlene, living at Enderby, British Colymbia. Karen and her family live at Caroline and Cindy at home in Enderby. They have ten grandchildren.

Jim Spence with Gerald Haney's team.

cars, as Helen's boyfriends were soon to discover.

Dad never owned or drove a car or any power driven equipment, always relying on his horses.

My parents left the Chedderville district in 1955, moving to Strachan to be near their daughter, Annie and family.

Mother died in 1956 and Dad in 1973.

Jim was for many years a timber operator in the area. He now lives in Calgary and works for Revelstoke Lumber Company. His two daughters, Doreen and Linda, are both married and live in Red Deer. He has five grandchildren.

In 1937 Annie married Marcus Gabler, a pioneer settler of the Strachan district. Marcus died in 1965. They had three sons and a daughter. Richard, a bachelor, still farms the original Gabler land, Ronald, Marlene and daughter live in Kamloops British Columbia. Robert, Heather and two daughters have their home at Strachan where he is employed at the Aquitaine Plant. Phyllis lives in Oakville, Ontario. She has two sons. Annie still makes Strachan her home.

Helen married Dennis Bruce and lives in Rimbey. They raised two daughters, Darlene and Gaylene who are both married. Darlene and Ernie Senic and two daughters live in Leduc. Gaylene and Carl Wine and daughter live in Bentley.

I (Margaret) married Jim Hereford. During the 1950's Jim was a Forest Ranger in the Clearwater and Strachan areas. We now live in Blairmore, Alberta, as does our only son, Douglas.

Stanley, the baby of the family, moved to British Columbia many years ago. He married Wanita McLean and had two sons and two daughters. Their eldest son, Gary, died in 1971. Karen, their eldest daughter, is married and has a daughter and a son. Dale and Lori live at home still, in Okanagan Falls.

Much could be written about the hard times and struggles experienced by the early settlers. The land they cleared, ties they hacked, roads they built, fires they fought and so much more, but space does not permit.

When we look around us and see the many comforts we enjoy today, we should be very thankful to them, for the contributions and sacrifices they made. Truly they were great people.

Gram Bancroft — that delightful pioneer lady, when recalling bygone days remarked, "Well we had strong backs, a sense of humor and Faith in God and somehow we always managed," That seems to sum it all up.

August Williams

August married a local girl, Ella May Marvin, from Ricinus on May 24, 1938. They now live in Calgary. They have five children, Judy, Louise, Billy, Robin and Cindy. Judy married John Vandermere and have three children, Judy, Billy and Tammy. They live in Calgary.

Louise married Rudy Bowolin and have two daughters, Karin and Robin. They live in Malakwa, British Columbia.

Billy married Lynn Cypperly and have one daughter, Kelly. They live in California.

Robin married Judy Christianson and have one daughter, Dawn. They live in Vernon, British Columbia.

Cindy married Henry Raj and haven't any children. They live in Calgary.

Albert (Jim) and Bertha Williams

The Williams family arrived at Chedderville in November, 1931, coming from the Lomond district where they had farmed for about three years. Before that they resided near Taber. There was Father, Albert James, Mother, Bertha Minnie, and four sons, August, Lawrence, Howard and Edwin.

When we left Lomond the government was assisting dryed-out farmers to relocate, and they allotted us two box cars. Jim rode with the box cars to look after our stock and other belongings on their way to Rocky Mountain House. The rest of the family motored to Chedderville in one small truck and a car with a trailer loaded with the remainder of our possessions. The roads were not very good in spots and it was a fairly slow trip.

We had farmed 2800 acres at Lomond and

Mr. and Mrs. Williams and family — L to R — Howard, August, Edwin and Lawrence.

came to a quarter section, S.E. 17-37-6-5, with twelve acres cleared that we purchased from Ed Clark.

While hauling our worldly wealth from Rocky, one Barred Rock hen rode all of the way to Chedderville on the spare tire carrier.

A mishap occurred on the Clearwater Hill while hauling some of our things out from Rocky with an old steel wheeled tractor, a high wheeled wagon and hay rack tied on behind. On the west side of the old bridge, just about to the top of the hill, the chain broke and back went the wagon and the hayrack over the bank. The binder that was on the rack, was broken to pieces, an old butter churn that rolled off of the load down into the bush, although cracked, came out in one piece, and a trunk full of dishes all remained intact.

We stayed the first few weeks with the Albert Mays' until we got settled in cabins for the winter, that were located on the banks of Mud Creek across from Archie MacDonald. While living there, we worked on a house built of logs. All of the buildings over the next few years were built of logs; the clearing done by the axe.

Some of our neighbors were the A. Mays (ran the post office), A. Zuberbier (ran the store), McKies, McArthurs, Hallocks and Robinsons.

Most of our good times were house parties and dances in Chedderville School and Dovercourt with music supplied by Mr. Frew, Leonard Hanson and other local talent.

The older three boys had finished school before we came to Chedderville. They worked for various people in the district, usually clearing, logging and choring. In the winter months they were kept busy keeping everyone with a good supply of firewood.

Edwin received most of his education at Chedderville and Dovercourt Schools, going as far as four and a half miles to Dovercourt. In the wintertime he used his dog, Bud, as a sleigh dog. The only problem was that there were too many rabbits, and Bud loved to chase them with or without the sleigh.

Times were hard in the 'thirties', but there were still lots of happy times.

Jim passed away in 1957 at seventy-two years. Bertha passed away in 1978 at age eighty-eight.

Edwin Williams

Edwin married Helen (Nell) McKie on November 4, 1946. They farmed the old McKie place and worked in timber in the Chedderville district until 1956. Then they moved to Turner Valley where Edwin owned and operated Ed's Transport. He sold the business which his son Dean had operated. At one time Edwin donated the land for the Dovercourt Hall. The hall is still there. They have eight children, Larry, Robert, Dean, Sandra, Wendy, Karen, Barry and Connie.

Larry married Wendy Walkemeyer and they have one daughter, Donna. Larry is an automotive mechanic in the armed forces and is stationed in Calgary. He is now a Sergeant.

Robert married Linda Davidson and they have two children, Tom and Angela. Robert is in the Communications Division of the armed forces and is stationed in Dana, Saskatchewan. He is now a Master Corporal.

Dean married Lynda Jones and they have two sons, Mark and Brian. Dean works with his father in their construction business and lives in Turner Valley.

Sandra married Rick Rishaug and they have two children, Paul and Dawn. Rick works for

Edwin and Nell Williams family — L to R — standing — Larry and Wendy and Connie. Front — Karen, Barry, Sandra. Sitting — Robert and wife Linda, Nell holding Tommie (Robert's), Edwin holding Mark (Dean's), Dean and wife Lynda.

19

Imperial Oil, Sandra works as a secretary in Calgary and they live in Turner Valley.

Wendy married Michael Wilhelm and they have twin daughters, Jeanna and Jennifer. Mike works for De Fehr Furniture and they live in Calgary.

Karen married Wayne MacKay and they have two children, Carrie Ann and Christopher. Wayne works as a dispatcher for Armstrong the Mover in Calgary. They live in Turner Valley.

Barry works for Sunburst Perforating Services in Brooks and is living in Brooks.

Connie is in her last year of High School and will be a licensed beautition upon completion.

Howard Williams

Howard married Alberta (Birdie) Evelyn May on February 14, 1939. They farmed in the Chedderville District and worked with the government on an Illustration Farm for 38 years. Then they sold the farm and moved to Rocky Mountain House. They have two children, Ray and Linda.

Ray married Carol Teskey and they have one daughter, Lisa. They now own and operate the Gateway Esso Carwash Garage and Celbee Automotive Shop.

Linda married James Fisher and they have three children, Michelle, Vicki and Jimmy. They farm west of Rocky and raise purebred Maine Anjou cattle.

Howard and Birdie Williams, baby Lynda and Ray.

Lawrence Williams

Lawrence married Marjorie Phyllis May on June 1, 1935. They homesteaded in the Ricinus district and then in 1938 they took over the store and post office and operated a sawmill gradually working their way back into farming as well. In their later years they moved to Rocky Mountain House where Lawrence worked for Bighorn Propane. He is now retired. They had seven children, Doris, Harold, Lois, Lorin, Ronnie, Phyllis and Dale.

Doris married Ralph Rosdal. They farm in the Everdell district and have two children, Debbie and John.

Harold married Shirley Dodsworth. He farms the old farmstead at Chedderville.

Lois married Dale Clearwater and they live on an acreage west of Rocky. Dale hauls propane. They also have a farm in the Everdell district. They have two children, Darwin and Lorina.

Lorin married Shannon Speight and they live in the Hardindell district. Lorin is a cat operator for Speight Construction and they have three children, Darin, Roxanne and Farron. They lost one son, Chad, at an early age.

Ronnie is married to Debbie Johnson and they live in the Everdell district. Ronnie is a cat operator for Speight Construction. They have two children, Kevin and Tammy. Ronnie has two daughters, Stacy and Amy, from a previous marriage.

Phyllis passed away May 16, 1971, and was laid to rest at the All Hallows Cemetery at Chedderville.

Dale married Crystal Kohtala and they live in the Tiami district. Dale also operates a cat for Speight Construction. They have one son, Newton John.

Frank and Harry Wilson

Frank and Harry Wilson came from Nordegg to the Chedderville district to farm on the N.E.Q. 24-37-7-5. and the N.W. 24-37-7-5. Their mother and sister, Gertie, lived on the farm for a few years, but returned to Nordegg where Mr. Wilson was employed.

Frank married Annie Lindburg from Ricinus and they had one girl, Pearl. They live at Alhambra. Harry and family moved away from the district after a few years.

Frank Wilson, early homesteader.

Albert and Gladys Zuberbier

Albert Zuberbier moved from Tabor in 1926 to the Chedderville district. Using dog teams, he and Albert May trapped through Swan Creek and Lost Horse Canyon area. On February 28, 1927, he married Gladys Amy May, eldest daughter of Mr. and Mrs. Albert May, in the Presbyterian Manse in Rocky Mountain House with the Reverend W. Irish officiating. The old manse is now located on the quarter south of the All Hallows Church. They moved to the old Eddlestone place where Don Cole lives now. They farmed here for one and one half years, however, due to many hardships they were unable to make payments on the farm and they moved to Mannville, Alberta, where Albert worked at breaking land. Lawrie was born in Mannville on January 17, 1928, and Roy arrived on October 20, 1930.

They moved back to Chedderville about one year later and operated the Chedderville General Store from 1933 to 1938. Dan Bird helped build the store. Albert and Mr. Albert May built a home made shingle mill. They used pine blocks for the shingles, which were boiled then sliced. Albert, Gladys and Art Schmelzer cut shingles for the Dovercourt Hall, Chedderville Store, Harry James and others.

In the winter Albert would haul cream and groceries with a four horse team and sleigh from Rocky. While operating the store he bought rabbits from neighbors for 2½¢ each and stored them in a sawdust bin. They were shipped and sold for 3¢ each to mink farms.

Albert played ball on the Chedderville Ball Team. Gladys made ice cream at the store and sold it at the ball games and picnics. In 1938 they left the store and went back to Mannville, returning in 1942 to take over Albert May's farm.

Lloyd Schmelzer, Albert's nephew from Winnifred, came for a visit, but decided to stay with the Zuberbiers. One Sunday while the family was swimming in the Clearwater River, he drowned. Art Schmelzer came to Lloyd's funeral. He also stayed with Albert and Gladys for ten years. He worked throughout the district threshing and cutting logs for Howard Williams and other neighbors. In 1942 he enlisted in the army and served in Holland and England, returning in 1947 to work at Howard Williams'.

In 1944 they sold the farm to Pete and Lizzy McArthur and they moved to Drummond Creek where he farmed. They moved to Rocky Mountain House and Albert worked for Traid Oil and seismic crews as camp attendant. He retired after many years of working for Skacdopole Construction on such projects as the Bighorn Dam.

Albert and Gladys Zuberbier, their two sons, Roy and Laurie and nephew Art Schmelzer.

Albert and Gladys Zuberbier.

Rex Bancroft and Albert Zuberbier.

21

Morrie Schmelzer, Albert's great nephew, spent summer holidays with Lawrie and Roy and in 1947 stayed and attended school at Clearwater. He became a permanent member of the family.

In 1959 Lawrie and Roy both married. Lawrie married Laura Evans of Strachan and has four children, Carrie, Barrie, Shawna and Cheryl. They farm at Chedderville. Roy married Evelyn Greenwood of Beaver Flats and they live in Rocky Mountain House.

In 1976 Morrie married Valerie Schmelzer and they have two children, Crystal and Treena and they reside in Rocky Mountain House.

On January 2, 1976, Gladys passed away after a lengthy illness. During his retirement, Albert continued to enjoy hunting and fishing until his passing December 30, 1978.

Clear Creek

Butte and Stauffer Districts
Clear Creek School

by the students at Clear Creek, 1920, Teacher Mr. Wm. Hobbs

To start this story we are going back thirty years to the time before the country was settled. At that time there were mostly Indians. There were some white men who were either trappers, hunters or traders. As far as we know the Hudson Bay Fort, west of Rocky Mountain House, was the first white settlement around here. It was built mostly of logs and stones and some iron was used. Mr. Andy Ross came in 1902, but he went to the States for a long time and just came back five years ago. Mr. Comstock came in 1905 and raised livestock and farmed. Others who came were Mr. Laybourne, Mr. Warren, George Fleming, Andy Fleming, Mrs. Tom Grosneck, T. Robinson, Mr. Mannsfield, Mr. Hankinson, Mr. W. Buck, Mr. Thorpe, Mr. McCoy, Mr. Leavitt and Mr. Metcalfe. They came in the years 1905, 1906, 1907 and 1908. By 1909 there were enough people for a school to be needed so they built the Clear Creek School. Mr. S. Ferguson was the first teacher. From this time on the area settled more quickly. In 1910 Mrs. Mitchell came to teach and she stayed at the Buck homestead. School was being well attended as people with families moved in. At this time the Carmichels were living where Pedersons are living now. George Sheilds was living where Budden and Coombs are living now. Budden and Coombs had homesteaded where Mr. Hoare is living.

We have had different teachers at the school. After the ones mentioned above were Mr. Scott, Miss McCallum, Mr. King, Mrs. Leavitt, Miss Ferguson, Miss Johnson, Miss Cook, Miss McKenzie, Miss Morrow, Miss LeBlanc and Miss Carswell taught for two years.

Some of the new settlers who have come are the Heares who settled east of the school along the Raven River. They bought cattle and horses and ranched as well as farmed. Mr. Hoare came to the district about five years ago (1920) from east of Didsbury. Frank Davis has been here about four years (1921). The Talentyres came in the spring. During most of the summer, Church services were held in the school. Among those who carried on the services were Mr. Wolframe, Mr. Murcell and Mr. Freak. For the last two summers, Mr. Thompson from Edmonton has been holding church services every Sunday. He came from Raven.

Within the last few years the roads have been improved greatly and a mail service from Rocky to Stauffer and Caroline was started. With the start that has already been made the district should go ahead and develop into a real agricultural community.

Clear Creek

composed by — Keith Leavitt, Curtis Bell, Garry Scown, Ricky Scown, Corinne Ceasor and Darlene Ouderkirk.

The Clear Creek school was built on the S.E. 19-37-5-5 in 1930. The Clear Creek School closed in 1960-61 and is now used as a community center. The first teachers were Miss Mary Ross, Mr. Leonard Willing, Mr. White, Miss Peterson, Mrs. Bert, Miss Golightly, Mrs. Tina McCabe, Mr. Kelly, Miss Mary Clancy, Miss Dot Clancy, Mrs. McGorman, Mrs. Slade, Mrs. Reiber, Mrs. Mary

Clear Creek School.

23

Stewart, Mr. Leonard White and Mrs. Harper. School fairs and concerts are held every year. These usually give everyone a good time.

Clear Creek School
by Clyde Comstock

The Clear Creek School was built on the N.W.Q. 24-34-6 in 1910 with Sam Ferguson as the first teacher. Later a new school was built a half mile south and two miles east on S.E. 19-37-5 around 1930. Mrs. Archie Slade was the last teacher in 1961 when the children were bussed to Caroline. In the beginning, school was held only part of each year during the summer months. It is impossible to name all of the teachers who taught in the school and even more impossible to list them in their proper order or in the years that they taught: Sam Ferguson, Mr. Scott, Mrs. Mitchell, Miss Johannson, Fred King, Mrs. Leavitt, Miss McCallum, Miss Stanford, Miss Nichol, Alice McKay, Myrtle Morrow, Mr. Kelly, Kate Carswell, 1923-25; Gladys Parker, 1928; Mr. Hobbs, 1925; Mr. Boyer, Miss McKenzie, Hattie Sinclair, Miss Kingsys, Mary Ross, Mrs. Archie Slade, Len Welling, 1937-8; Elsie Peterson, 1939; Mr. White, 1940; Phylis Bert, 1941; Grace Golightly, Ruth Arnett Moger, 1942; Dorothy Ryan, 1943; Tina Rizzo McCabe, Dorothy Clancy, 1952; Mary Clancy Stewart, Mrs. Archie Rieber.

Thompson's Trading Post was on the N.W. 17-37-5. It must have been deserted sometime around 1900. The bones of forty head of their horses were lying on the Butte Flat in 1906 as well as many buffalo bones. We heard the horses had died in a bad winter some years before.

This locality was quite open in 1906. The Indians claim that a fire burned off all the timber in 1865. The outlines of hundreds of big trees could be seen lying on the ground. The flat was covered with a good coat of grass, and stray stock used to be found there quite often. Andy Ross ran eighty head of cattle on it and was able to put up enough hay for them. The Butte Hill was a good place to climb when anyone was looking for his milk cows.

The Red River Cart trail entered township 37-5 near the southeast corner and went in a northwesterly direction up the north bank of the Raven Creek and down the Clear Creek to the Clearwater River about twenty-five miles to the fort at Rocky Mountain House. A buffalo trail crossed the flat from a point north of Clear Creek, southeast to Carr Creek, then climbed the bank and went on south-east. Along this trail were two big springs, one on N.W. 24-37-6, which flowed into the Clearwater River, and one on S.W. 19-37-5 which flowed east and formed the head waters of the North Raven River.

Every fall the prairie chickens would camp on the flat at night and in the morning there would be a big roar from the chickens as they headed for the timber to feed, the air would be full of them. They would light on houses, barns, fences and then go on. They also had several areas which they used as 'strutting grounds' in the spring and they would come back year after year. There were also countless partridges in the timber. In the spring the woods would be full of the sound of the roosters drumming. In October they had what we called their 'crazy season'. Odd ones would leave their home grounds and fly at random — they might be seen on the open flat or walking around the yard. Sometimes in cold weather they would borrow into a snow bank for the night. They generally made their homes in the willow and spruce trees. There were also what we called 'fool hens', they were of about the same size as the partridge but darker grey in color and had some red near their eyes. The partridge were white meat but the fool hens and prairie chickens were dark meat. There were always some deer around and the odd moose. The creeks and rivers were swarming with fish, mostly greylings, suckers and some bull trout. About 1911 the people began to come out from Red Deer with nets and that was the end of the big swarms. There were beaver dams in the creeks but the beaver had all been trapped out by 1906.

The Stony Indians used to come to Stauffer to trade, generally three families travelled together bringing pack ponies. In the fall they would come from Morley up along the foothills picking berries, hunting and fishing, then back to Morley for the winter. There are three Indian graves in this district, one a woman is buried on the N.E. 24-37-6, another grave is on the N.E. 3-37-6. They bought a head stone in Innisfail for

Clear Creek School class.

John Hunter's grave. It reads: "Born 1885, Died 1902". This grave is on the N.E. 13-37-6.

Earl Maddy used to travel back and forth from his trapline on the Ram River to Innisfail for supplies. His three pack ponies were named Nitchee, Buck and Red. He made one trip to Red Deer one winter for his supplies, a distance of almost one hundred miles each way, camping out on the way — one night it was sixty below.

Shorty Haven, Miller and Cline went west from here in October, 1906, to the Kootenay Plains prospecting. They had nineteen two-year-old ponies. Three years later, with one less, they came back and sold them. They saw coal around Nordegg but thought it was too far back for anyone to mine.

The first settlers moved up to Prairie Creek in 1907 and they had to travel to Innisfail for supplies and ford the Clearwater. One ford was along the south side of 14-37-6. One party waited for three weeks one summer for the water to go down so that they could cross. Some men were inexperienced and tried to cross when the water was too deep. At least three horses were drowned and two or three loads of supplies were lost. One time a wagon box floated off a wagon. Mose Rundell kept shifting his weight from one side to the other and managed to keep the box from overturning; one of the other men came up and grabbed the side of the box. Mose said, "Let go there damn you". The box floated out on a sand bar and Mose had saved everything. Another ford was two miles upstream known as the Pewonka Ford. Some people kept their teams pointed upstream while crossing, one team was almost lost doing this. If they crossed pointed down stream the team would have gone right across with the current helping it along.

* * *

Mr. Grossnic and his niece were stuck in a mud hole one day when Andy Ross rode up on his way home from Innisfail with a half empty bottle in his pocket. He said to Mary, "Help your uncle all you can, Mary," and rode on.

Mr. and Mrs. Jordan were both active in community affairs and always quick to lend a hand.

George Shields was an old lumberjack from Ontario. He used to like to take in the log drive down the Red Deer River each spring, and trap in the winter. Later on he raised a few cattle.

Mrs. Thom was complaining one day and she said, "The wind blew the tops off of their hay shocks to hell and then it rained on them".

Mazzina Leavitt was easy going and a friend to everyone.

Jack Edmonds was a lumberjack and saw filer. He was also an expert with a pole axe or board axe.

Thayer was hard working and breezy.

Layborne liked to trade and deal.

Jessie Jackson drove a four-up of oxen.

Billy Warren drove a team of oxen.

Curly Taylor was councilor for twenty years and always ready to lend a helping hand.

Rainy Garnsey, tall and slim, had one grey eye and one brown eye.

Mr. Doucommun picking berries in the fall when the 'no seeums' were bad, "From this eye I could see very little, from this eye I could not see at all". So much for the gnats.

In the spring of 1907 a threshing machine was pounding away on the farm of Will Comstock. It threshed forty bushels of seed oats. The machine was made from two pieces of wood fastened together with a piece of leather, it was called a flail. Later on a new model came out on the farm of Budden and Coombs. The cylinder was a piece of log with spikes driven in it and wooden bearings. It was powered by a home windmill.

It seemed like just about everybody came to the dances, usually held in someone's house. The floors weren't so good and it was crowded at times but people had a good time and came to see their neighbors. Two boys, Ray and Clair Edmonds, deserve to have their names mentioned for playing at so many of these dances. And the girls seemed so nice, then of course there was always a shortage of them.

The women used to do their share of the work and sometimes more than their share. They helped milk and make butter to sell for as low as fifteen cents a pound — whirling those barrel churns and wondering how much longer it would be before the cream started to break. A good many of the men who thought they were horsemen fell far short of being qualified. Some men fed well and then over drove their horses. A good many didn't even feed enough, and some people never got in a hurry until they got hold of the lines of a horse. Others seemed to think a horse was supposed to have sore shoulders or a

Edward and Florence Budden.

25

sore back, they didn't even know how to fit a collar and didn't care enough to learn. It should be said, however, that there were some fine horsemen in this country.

About 1905 a small crew of men stopped at Alex Stewarts homestead in the Diamond Valley district and had their dinner. The foreman said to Alex, "We're going out west to open up a timber limit and you had better come with us." Alex thought that was pretty lucky, a dollar a day for ten hours work and all the rest of the time to lay around and eat and sleep. By next spring he would have a nice little stake saved up. A few days later they were laying corduroy across a muskeg when Alex asked one of the men, "What does the foreman keep the old bum around for? He never does anything around camp and I believe he just goes out in the timber and lays around all day." The other man said, "That's Pettifer, he owns this timber limit and he's our timber cruiser every day and picking out a place for a mill besides blazing roads."

This limit took in the N.E. 28-37-5, most of section 27 and 34-37-5. It is almost an island with a lake on two sides and muskeg on the north. It is thought the fire of 1865 never got onto the island. Billie Wall was mill foreman for many years and when the mill was broken down, Billie would simply back up against the boiler and let someone else get it going again. At that time lumber sold for twelve dollars per thousand feet and good slabs were one cent apiece. One hundred logs a day was considered good going for two men with a cross cut saw. Sometimes in the evening there would be a square dance, the ones with a handkerchief on one arm would be the girls. Tail sawing was the hardest job and usually the youngest boy was put to work tail sawing.

The Buck Family

In 1907 Webster E. Buck, his wife, Beulah, son, Floyd and daughter, Nina, left Del Rio, Washington, and came by train to Alberta. They homesteaded at the headwaters of the North Raven River in the west part of the Stauffer (Butte) district.

Webster and Beulah lived in this district for almost forty years before retiring to Rocky Mountain House around 1945. Webster died there in 1948 and Beulah died in Lethbridge in 1968. Gladys, who was born on the farm, married George Tose. They had two sons, John and George. She died in 1944. Nina (Mrs. R. L. Earl) resides in Lethbridge. She has three sons, Melvin, Jim and Donald Cowie.

Floyd W. Buck married Katherine B. Howes on May 1, 1926. They first farmed the Butte flat and later rented the 'Gray Place.' In May, 1933,

the family moved to the present location which was Floyd's homestead.

The land had to be cleared by hand. First they built the house (which Katie still resides in) later adding a log barn, chicken house and big barn. Floyd and Katie cleared fifteen acres the first year. Their first crops were oats to feed the cattle and horses. They had five head of cattle, ten horses and two sows.

Like other homesteaders they grew most of their own food, supplementing their diet with wild meat and berries.

Floyd and Katie had six children, all are living except one son, Merlin, who died as an infant in 1934. The others are: Betty (Mrs. S. Oliver) of Rose Prairie, British Columbia, who has nine children and six grandchildren.

Donald (married Edna Scott) is on the farm and has three children.

Elmer (married Constance Conkey) lives at Lacombe and has three children and two grandchildren.

Elsie (Mrs. Virgil Fairbrother) of Edmonton has three children.

Edith (Mrs. R. J. Janiszewski) of Rocky Mountain House has two daughters.

For many years Floyd Buck enjoyed riding in the rodeos and stampedes such as Hale Lake. He also took great pride in raising pigs. His favorite pastimes were attending auction sales and writing letters to the editors complaining about the government. He died on November 5, 1974.

The Ed Clay Family
by Stella Clay

In 1937 Ed Clay and I were married in Red Deer. We went to live near Hale Lake where Ed had a farm. We had two children, Edna born in 1938 and Gene in 1940.

Previous to our marriage, Ed had carried on milling operations with different co-workers. They sawed for George Cliff and George McNutt among others across the Clearwater. They also sawed for Carl Boeken up the Raven Valley.

Ed and his partner, Fred Thomson, spent many years working on the Raven River where they bought a section of land from the Hudson's Bay Company. In the early days sawmilling was a not too profitable undertaking with the price of lumber $9.00 to $14.00 a thousand board feet.

For many years Ed continued farming in summer and milling in winter. Finally he took over the mill when Fred went to the Radar Station at Penhold. He and our son, Gene, continued working in the bush until Ed retired in about 1970.

Ed was very much an outdoors man. He enjoyed hunting and fishing. The mill land was a favourite fishing spot in those days and many people enjoyed fishing, picnicking and camping there. Ed also was a baseball player and in the early days played with a very successful Raven team. He caught and Roy Orcutt pitched for it. He also caught for the ladies' hardball team in those days. He played with the Caroline Softball team for a few years, but always reminisced about the years when they played baseball.

He was also one of a group of old-timers who acquired land at Hale Lake and started the Hale Lake Rodeo. At that time there was a real lake there so they added water sports to their good times.

When the war broke out, teachers joined up or went to other jobs connected with war work. I then went back to teaching. I taught Clear Creek (very briefly), Hazel Dell, North Caroline and finally came to Caroline where I remained until my retirement in 1971. Ed and I were able to enjoy several years of retirement until his death in December, 1976, in the Innisfail Hospital at the age of eighty-three. I still live in Caroline.

After graduating from Caroline High School, Edna cooked for her father at the mill camp for awhile. In 1958 she married Clarence Pengelly. They live on their farm southwest of Caroline. They have three children. Glen is at present working on oil rigs. Fay was married to Gail Dingman of Crammond in 1978. Ed is at the present time at home.

Gene worked in the mill with his father and guided in the west country for several years. He finally bought the 'Dewie' farm where he now lives. In 1972 he married Shelagh Winder and they have a young son, Jack.

Comstock Family

Caroline and William, with son, Clyde, came to Red Deer in October, 1904, from Los Angeles and lived on a farm until April of 1906 when they moved onto their homestead, the S.W. Q. 28-37-5. Before leaving the United States, Will had been a school teacher, a toll gate keeper, a lineman and a trolly conductor. He wanted to go someplace — he said "far enough away from a street car line so he would never hear another street car!" In 1911 Clyde homesteaded the S.W. Q. 28-37-5 and in 1917 he bought the S.W. Q. 24-37-6 and later acquired the S.E. Q. 24-37-6. In 1931 he married Miss Gretta Fitchett, a school teacher from Ontario. They had one daughter, Margaret Johnson, now living on Clyde's farm.

One afternoon Caroline walked up to the top of the Butte and wondered if there would ever be more neighbors living near her.

She made butter and sold it at Wests Store in Innisfail for many years. Will liked to pick

Caroline and William Comstock.

Clyde Comstock and his dog Mickey. Jack Bugbee and Major.

berries and to fish. The fish he liked to cook and eat by the stream. He also liked to hunt.

Clyde was eleven years old the spring they moved to their homestead at Stauffer. He walked from Red Deer and drove the cattle for his family and the Warrens, another couple from California. He was especially fond of horses and kept and rode horses until his death in October of 1977.

William Duncan

Mr. and Mrs. Duncan and family came to Alberta in 1931 from Swift Current,

Saskatchewan, and settled in the Stauffer area on N.E. 17-37-5-5. They had three children, Christina, Bill and Heather, whom are all married. Mr. and Mrs. Duncan lived on the farm for about six years, before moving to Calgary.

Mr. Duncan passed away shortly after moving. Mrs. Duncan moved to Penticton, British Columbia, where she still lives.

John Edmonds

John Edmonds abandoned Oregon in 1908, surrendering to the appeal of Canada's still untamed frontiers. Together, with his young family, he stepped down from the train to scrutinize this rugged new land.

His eyes beheld a knoll rising abruptly from a vast expanse of prairie wool with springs erupting beneath his feet. At once he was aware that a portion of these Butte Flats must belong to him. A claim was filed and his homestead, closer to the fringes than desired, became a reality — N.E. 12-37-6-5.

Come winter, the sound of frigid steel against crystalline timber rebounded in the woods as dawn approached and continued 'til dusk. John's expertise as a lumberjack was well known among the folks at Pettifers Mill. The trek home

Mr. and Mrs. John Edmonds wedding picture, 1897.

was begun only when the last light was failing, with one dollar for the day's toil. The lengthening of the days found John on a survey crew from the north of Nordegg to the head of the Clearwater.

Times worsened, and like many others he wandered in search of work to sustain his growing family. It became obvious that there would be no alternative but to leave his beloved homestead in the hands of his wife, Mae, and six youngsters.

Ray took upon himself the responsibilities of the family and farm in the absence of his father. Clair took to the open road and worked where he could always send money home to help.

Inheriting the love of old time fiddling from their father, young Ray and Clair Edmonds played for many a dance. No formal training but many an hour of practice atop the woodpile and the desire to make music.

Ray has moved but a short distance and still farms in the Dovercourt area today.

Clair and Ray Edmonds

They came in the Spring of 1908, young lads delighted with the idea of spending their first summer upon Butte Flats in a tent. With a first rate timberman for a father, it was not long before they found themselves in a snug log cabin, awaiting winter's grasp. Presently they were under the guidance of Sam Ferguson, Clear Creek School's new schoolmaster.

Ray recollects the day in the bitterly cold winter of 1914 when a stranger came to their door, needing a place to warm himself and tend to his horses. In the back of the horse-drawn sleigh huddled two small children, a boy six and a girl four years old. Her name was Valerie Helen Handkinson, and that was the first memory of the girl that was to become his wife.

Clyde Comstock was the nearest neighbor and they would do chores for him for that little "extra" that was always so desperately needed. With the chores finished the boys would practice the violin out upon the woodpile, with only each other to guide them musically. Many are the fond memories of playing for dances and benefits, for those that had become their friends and neighbors.

Clair left to seek his fortune south of the border, and Ray married Helen Handkinson in the fall of 1926. They lived on the old Rowlan T. Hankinson homestead, the grandfather of the now Helen Edmonds. The year 1928 brought them a son Charles, followed by their daughter Helen Mae in 1936.

The George Lewis homestead came available and Ray moved his family here in 1947 where he remains today. Clair is now retired and calls Summerland, British Columbia home.

Other members of the Edmonds family were — Jay deceased in 1974, Hazel living in Indiana, U.S.A., Claire lives in Summerland, B.C., Thelma deceased in 1979 and Jack now living in Quesnel, B.C.

Earl Godkin Family

In 1937, Earl and Bessie Godkin moved from Queenstown, Alberta, to what was then the Stauffer district and later became the Butte district. Armour and Eva Godkin and their daughter, Nora, came up at the same time. The fall of 1937 was very wet and they lived in a log house on the Tatham place while the men built two houses — a log house for Armour Godkins and a frame house for Earl Godkins. Wray McCallum, who had been living with the Godkins, came with the men to help with the building.

Later in the fall, the rest of the family moved up. There were several trips made to get everything here, with an old International truck — its best speed was twenty-five miles per hour.

Earl and Bessie had three boys, Gordon, Leonard and Ross. Gordon went through for a veterinary and practiced in Innisfail for twenty years, when he sold out and became a meat inspector. Gordon married Peggy Lee Mullen in 1953 and they have four children, Sharon, Alan, John and Patricia.

Leonard farms in the Butte district. He married Jeanette Phillips in 1961 and they have two boys, Dwayne and Brian.

Ross married Ann Lecerf in 1957 and they have three girls, Maureen, Verna and Arlene. They farmed in the Rocky Mountain House district until 1978 when they sold their farm and moved into Rocky.

On March 27, 1938, Mrs. Florence Budden passed away leaving eight children, the youngest a baby of four and a half months named Daisy. She lived with the Godkins until her marriage to Edward Kiem on July 8, 1959. They have six children, Gail, who married Dave Weaver, Karen, Sheila, Sandra, Dean and Kenneth. They live on what was formerly the Bert Jones farm.

Charlie Hankinson
by Kathleen Hankinson

Charlie and his wife, Winnifred, came up from St. Thomas, Ontario, to Red Deer in the spring of 1907. They lived there for a short time before coming west to the Stauffer area and settling on the N.W.Q. 9-37-6-5 where they lived in tents until they got their house built. The first of their six children, Gilbert, was born there in a tent.

Charlie ran the mail route from 1910 to 1919 between Stauffer and Rocky Mountain House. In 1920 they moved to Nordegg and Mrs. Hankinson ran a boarding house until 1921 when they moved back to Dovercourt. Mrs. Hankinson ran the Dovercourt Store for a few years.

Charlie passed away April 7, 1922, and Mrs. Hankinson in April, 1943. They are at rest in the Pine Grove Cemetery in Rocky Mountain House.

Names of their six children are Gilbert, Helen, Lorrain, Edna, Rowlen and Harold. Gilbert married Kathleen May and they live at Stauffer. They have three children, Jean, Douglas and Kenneth.

Helen married Ray Edmonds of Dovercourt and they had two children, Charlie and Helen. Charlie passed away March 29, 1976, and was predeceased by his mother in July, 1973.

Lorrain married Edna Coghlen of Rocky Mountain House. They live in Calgary and have four children.

Edna married Bob Ross of Rocky Mountain House and they had three children. After they were divorced, Edna married Ernie Robinson of Grande Prairie who is an exchange teacher. They are living overseas.

Rowlen married Verona Parks of Rocky Mountain House. They had two children. Verona was killed in a vehicle accident December 2, 1969. Rowlen passed away in November, 1976.

Harold married Ivy Baine (Dix) of Caroline. They live at Sherwood Park, Alberta, and have two children by adoption.

Rowlen Hankinson

Rowlen and his wife, Martha, came from St. Thomas, Ontario, in 1907 and homesteaded the S.W.Q. 4-38-6-5 at Dovercourt. Rowlen ran the Land Office in Rocky Mountain House for several years. They had four children, Mary, Susan, Charlie and Kenneth. Mary was married to Art Driscoll of Rocky Mountain House and they had a grocery store there for many years. Susan never married. Charlie married Winnifred Baker of Buffalo, New York, in 1907. Kenneth was a Railroad Engineer. Rowlen and Martha are at rest in the Pine Grove Cemetery in Rocky Mountain House.

The Heebe Boys
by Guy E. Fay

Lloyd, Floyd and Earl Heebe were nephews of Ren Sterns. Lloyd, and Floyd, who went by the name of Jim, came to Caroline in 1925. Earl came a year later.

In 1926 Jim filed on the S.E. Q. 28-6-5. This place had been filed on before by a man named Childs, who later abandoned it. There was a cabin on the place which the boys fixed up and made livable. They built a barn and did some improvements. In the spring they went out to work and while they were gone, someone stole the house, barn, a small shed and even the wood pile. Jim was so disappointed he never lived on the place again. It lay vacant until 1931 when George Hanson filed on it.

In 1928 Earl Heebe hauled cream, etc., from Caroline and Stauffer to Rocky Mountain House with a Model T. Ford truck that had solid rubber tires on the back wheels. It had no cab, just a seat in front. A real fresh air deal, but mud holes or rain didn't deter him. He seldom missed a trip. They all left in the fall of 1928.

William Hoare Family

by Edward Hoare

As a young man, William Hoare came to the Calgary district from Birmingham, England. For several years he worked on the railroad between Calgary and Shelby, Montana. At this time Calgary was a very small place, the stores and shops were small log buildings. He saved money and went back to Birmingham, only to find he did not like it there. After a visit he returned to Canada and took a homestead twelve miles east of Didsbury. There he built a small shack and barn and most of his land was broken with horses and a walking plow which meant a lot of hard work. The buildings were all destroyed by a prairie fire and he lost everything he had. Not to be defeated, he built another shack a little larger than the first and another barn. There was lots of good prairie grass so he cut and baled it and hauled it to Didsbury to sell.

As a small child, Martha Eleanora McCaig came to the Sieberville district from Parry Sound, Ontario. There she and William met and were married on July 5, 1911. By this time he had managed to build a house and they lived there and raised their family. They had Edward on April 22, 1912, Leonard on February 23, 1915, and on June 17, 1920, their daughter, Lorna, was born to complete the family. All were born in the Didsbury Hospital.

As years went by the crops were poor because of lack of moisture. Hope was fading for crops that would support a family. So once again William struck out to find something better. He came to the Caroline district in the summer of 1920 to find the grass nice and green. He had been told of a half section that was for sale so went to see about it. The place belonged to Cleveland Walrath, who, with three other Mormon families, had come out. One family stayed with him, one on the Jordan place and the other lived southwest of the Jordan place. They all moved to Edgerton after William bought the land. Ted Budden and Jack Coombs had homesteaded the

Mr. and Mrs. William Hoare.

William Hoare's children — Leonard, Lorna, Edward.

north half of section 36-36-6-5. It had taken them five years to put up the buildings, all logs. The barn was the largest in the area — the loft would hold most of the winters feed. The barn was on the east quarter and the house on the west. Walraths had put up another small house. It was July 20, 1920, when his purchase was final and William started preparing for the move, livestock and machinery was brought out first and hay was put up.

Mid October was a busy time at the home at Didsbury; packing was in the final stages. Everything was shipped by train from Didsbury to Rocky Mountain House. One big team of Clydesdales came on the train and the trip took all day. We stayed in the hotel overnight. Rocky was a rough little place, Indians, lumber jacks and coal miners were the main part of the population. The next morning we loaded more on the wagon and started out for our new home at

Caroline. It was a beautiful day and was a good thing for us too, as it was about twenty-two miles over rough trails. When we got to the Butte, the trail went to the southwest past that big rock on the hill just before we got to the Jordan place. There the road branched two ways, south to the Sawyer place and we took the one to the southeast through Grove's place. The trail ran through our land as there was a muskeg where the road should have been to the west. There was a trail from our place to the northeast to the McCabe place and on north to the Comstock place. The other trail went to the southeast toward the Edward Tose and Vandermeer places. The Cleve Nickolson family had been living on the Jordan place, then took a homestead a mile east of us across the line where there is now a good gravel road.

Mr. and Mrs. Edward Tose and son, George, were the first people to visit us in our new home. I was eight years old at the time and will never forget that day. There were about a hundred Sharp Tailed Grouse sitting in the trees around our yard and Mr. Tose shot some of them with his 22 rifle. After I was nine years old I could use the 22 rifle so in an hour the dog and I could come in with all the Spruce and Sharp Tail Grouse that I could carry. They would sit on the hay stacks and rail fences around the yard.

I had a small pinto pony that I rode to Caroline for the mail, and to school. The Clear Creek School at that time was three and a half miles north of our place. That little pony was a real pal and was always willing to go where I wanted. We would go to Caroline for groceries and he carried them home and would stand and wait while I opened and closed the gates. Some of the first boys I got to know were the Bugbees and Millers. A Mr. Jackson had the land that came up to the west side of the Butte hill, he wouldn't let anyone go across his land so someone made a cut in the side of the hill hoping to get a road cut through but had to give up as it was too dangerous. The cut was wide enough that my little pinto went up and over without batting an eye. To go around with the team we had to take the trail around the east side of the hill on the new land of Budden and Coombs on the southwest corner.

We had some bad years and good years too. The first year here we lost about fifteen head of our cattle from some kind of poison weed. After cattle were here a few years they either didn't eat the weed or became immune to it. Then it was just a matter of time until our big horses started to die with swamp fever. The smaller horses did not seem to get it but we had then to buy more horses. The soil was a heavy gray clay so was not very good. Years later we found out that we could get a fertilizer that would be of help to that type of soil. We used both limestone and fertilizer on the hay crop. We learned that by mixing timothy, clover and brome grass, it yielded better and helped to build up the soil.

Mr. Carl Anderson was the first man to move a threshing machine into our place with a Waterloo Boy tractor. We had a lot of trouble getting it moved in on that old bush trail as they cut through easily as the sod was thin and could not hold the heavy weight of the machine.

After we lived here a few years, it got hot and dry. I remember one summer the leaves turned yellow and brown on the trees. It was one of these dry, hot summers that the county decided to try and put a grade through the muskeg on the road west of our place. They got in a small grade and ditches on both sides. They also cleared and graded north to the Butte. But soon we got wet years again and then we could not get across where that grade was made across the muskeg. About the winter of 1928, Tom Roper, Frank Davis, Charlie Powers, Dad and some other neighbors got together with teams and sleighs and cut poplar logs which were long enough to cover the road bed and hauled them to the muskeg. They laid them crossways on the grade. It took a lot of logs to cover that quarter of a mile. The summer of 1929 the municipality got a dirt loader and a lot of dump wagons pulled with horses and covered the timbers across the muskeg and built up a grade about two feet high. This took a lot of work and most of the summer. In 1930 the municipality got a new cat and grader. It seemed like a big outfit then. The cat was a Monarch with a 75 horse power Allis Chalmers engine. The grader man could steer the grader because there were controls, the cat could go on the middle of the road and the grader could go off to either side. The cat was operated by Bill Neal. Mike Benz, Cliff Pollard, Steve Dutton or Frank Davis could have been grader man at the time. They graded the road from Caroline to what is now the Number 11 Highway between Rocky and Red Deer. The road looked good but it had no gravel so was terrible after a rain. I remember one time it took me five hours to get home from Rocky, as the road was almost impossible.

I quit school in the fall of 1927 and worked pitching bundles into a threshing machine at farms around the district. Then in the spring of 1928 I worked for Clyde Comstock at Butte and put in his crop. That fall I went out threshing east of Didsbury and worked for my uncle, Ed Liesemer. Wages were about two dollars a day. He had a big threshing outfit which took ten bundle teams to keep it going. We threshed for thirty days straight.

After the crops were all finished I went to the Technical School in Calgary to take a farm mechanics course which I finished in the spring of 1929. After that I ran my uncle's tractor putting in the crop and doing summerfallow and breaking. In the fall I ran tractor on the threshing outfit. I had a second uncle who farmed close by, Thomas McCaig. Between the two of them, I worked there for seven years and after the fall work was finished I would go back to Caroline and help my parents. We would cut posts and rails through the winter to sell.

The fall of 1929 I got my first car, a Model T Ford, the pride of my life. We went a lot of miles together in all kinds of weather and all kinds of roads. I did the repair work myself so I knew the car inside out. In November, 1949, it wore out. For years it ground all our grain. It was backed onto the power jack and put into gear. As the wheels turned they ran the pulley and turned the belt that ran the grain grinder.

A new hall had been built at Caroline and we had some real nice dances there. Paul Lamb's orchestra was very popular at that time and put out the type of music everyone seemed to enjoy. Young people cleared snow off spots on the lakes and rivers so they would have a place to skate. I liked to go skiing so would go to the Butte hill. It was a bit rough and steep, but a challenge.

When Mr. Tose shot the birds, I became interested in hunting. By the time I was fifteen, I was trapping coyotes and shooting squirrels and sold the skins. The coyote skins were averaging between ten and fifteen dollars which at that time was quite good. The squirrels were only about ten cents. I got some weasels for which skins I got about five dollars. Moose and deer were quite plentiful and I got my first deer when I was fifteen, since then there has only been about three years I didn't get my meat.

After Leonard finished school at the New Clear Creek School, he also went to work around Didsbury. He took a diesel engineering course and went to Salmon Arm, British Columbia, where he had a job. It was only a few days until he got polio which hit him hard. Mother went to be with him and after a few months he was transferred to the University Hospital in Edmonton. After spending seven years there he was able to get around with the aid of steel braces on his legs and crutches. He realized that the only work he would be able to do was a job where he could sit, so he took a watch repair course and went to Calgary to work. In a short time he had a small business of his own. While living there, he met and married Lavona Gillett on March 10, 1949. They lived in Calgary until moving to Carstairs in 1951, their son, Gary, was a small baby at the time. They rented a store on main street where there was living quarters in the back. His business grew quite fast with watch repairing and he sold jewelry too. Later he included the sale of health foods. Their children were Gary, born July 16, 1951, Loretta, born April 27, 1953, and Brenda, born February 8, 1959. In 1971 they moved to Breton where he bought a store on main street. After spending ten months in the hospital, Leonard decided to sell out on May 14, 1977. On July 19, 1977, he died.

My sister, Lorna, finished school at the Clear Creek school in June of 1935. She stayed around home to help as mother's health was not good. On April 22, 1938, she married Hugh Myson and they lived about two miles northeast of our place.

Charlie Powers came here from England and settled on the place Groves had. In 1935 Mr. Strum and family settled on an unimproved quarter across the road to the east of Powers' and north of us. They built a small house, but did not stay long. Later Alex Jakob and family came out from Calgary and settled on the Strum place. Then Ed Welsh and the George Dallas family came from Drumheller. Welsh took a homestead just west of us and the Dallas family settled on the half section where Stan Loomis now lives. There was a lot of good timber on that land so he got in a crew of men and took out about 15,000 logs. He got Mr. Tom Arnew from James River to move in his big sawmill. After we heard about his big mill coming in, we cut logs and hauled them from our place to the mill and later I worked at the mill.

I had decided by this time to stay on the farm so I sold lumber from the logs I had cut and bought our first tractor, a Fordson. It was not new but was an improvement over the horses.

The following very cold winter I worked for Russel McGrandle who had a sawmill on Beaver Creek south of Caroline. I worked for a dollar a day; guess I was lucky as a lot of men only got ten dollars a month.

The next few years I spent mostly around home and did some odd jobs such as help build roads. We had some heavy tamarack planks that we used to build culverts with. Being there was little money, the neighbors helped each other out in times of need. No one could pay wages as wheat was about fifty cents a bushel, oats about fifteen cents, a 220 pound pig about four dollars, cows were selling for fifteen to twenty dollars each.

When the war started, Dad's health was not good so I pretty well took over the farm, by 1942 Dad was to the point of having to stay in bed most of the time. I had been called into the forces. My health was 100% but there was no one to do the farming so they left me to work the farm. Dad passed away April 6, 1945, at the age of seventy years.

I will never forget 1945. It was a very wet spring, the roads would hardly get dry when it would rain again. The spring a mile south of our corner at times was almost impassable. Like for instance the 17th of June, the day Jessie and I were married, everyone came with team and wagon except for our minister, Mr. Griffin, who came from Raven. When he hit that mud hole at the spring, there he sat. I had to change back into my old clothes, get the team out and go and pull him out. It was kind of a rough start for a young Minister who was about to perform his first wedding but all went well in the end.

Mother moved to Calgary the following July and we stayed on the farm. Being just at the end of the war, the farm produce went up for a while, but prices soon went down again. The first machinery I bought was the Ford tractor, plow and cultivator. I sure enjoyed that rubber tired tractor after bouncing around on the old Fordson with steel wheels.

When they were building roads there were times when I checked gravel trucks. For three years I checked trucks. The last while was the worst. I had a five gallon bucket of wheat slip when taking it from the bin and it landed on my big toe, wow! Was that ever sore when gravel kept getting in my shoe.

We, like everyone else, had rough times, but the ones that stand out most in my thoughts are the crop failures we had. We lost about seven crops because of early frost, hail, too much rain and being snowed under.

We built up our cattle until we had mostly Polled Herefords. We raised Yorkshire pigs selling most of them as weaners but did finish out some. We got our last good boar from Shorty Carter.

In May of 1963, we got Tom Allen from Sundre to come in with his big cat and clear some land on our southwest corner. That was the first large clearing outfit we had on our land. Before that we did the clearing the hard way, mostly with an axe. There was still a lot of work piling up the logs and brush, picking roots and burning the brush.

My health got worse as time went on and in 1964 I was sick a lot. In July 1966, I had surgery and the Doctor advised me to quit farming. By that time we had just got the power, telephone and better roads. We sold our land to Ed Loomis on June 20, 1968. We bought a mobile home and by July we were moved into the Innisfail Trailer Court.

I spent forty-eight years on the farm. Our three children were born while we lived there, Marjorie, born August 19, 1946. Ella Mae was born November 30, 1949, and Trudy on September 25, 1958. Marjorie married Lorne Peters and they have two children, Michael and Holly. Ella Mae married Andy Gross and Trudy married David Quinlan.

After we came to Innisfail Jessie worked at the hospital for four years. I worked at Allen's Parkland Service for Allen Auld for almost four years. On February 15, 1973, we bought the business. At that time the name was changed to Innisfail Turbo Service. We both worked and Trudy helped a lot until she finished school. She worked full time until we sold our business on November 15, 1976. Our little gas business had grown to the extent that my health once again was suffering, so I knew it was time someone younger take a try at it.

Mother had been in failing health for sometime. She passed away on April 19, 1976 and was laid to rest beside Dad in the Pine Grove Cemetery in Rocky.

Sidney Perhan Jordan

Sidney Perhan Jordan was born February 29, 1867, at Otis, Maine, U.S.A. He moved to Minnesota in his young years and worked at whatever was available. He met his future wife, Josephine Sophia Reetz, who was born

L.-R. — Josephine, Kathryn, Irene and Sidney Jordan.

Mr. and Mrs. Syd Jordan.

33

September 14, 1872, in Kelnamarhine, Germany, near Hastings, Minnesota. They were married April 19, 1893, at Minneapolis, Minnesota.

Their two daughters were both born in Minneapolis Kathryn May on April 23, 1894, and Irene Marjorie on March 12, 1897.

The Jordan family went west to the State of Washington and lived near Spokane and later near Colfax where Mr. Jordan worked on a farm for a Mr. Hereford. The Herefords had a son, Bert, who was living in Alberta and the Jordans came to the Caroline district and homesteaded on the N.W. Q. 2-37-6-5, in 1909. A house and barn were soon built and land cleared.

His daughters grew up in this area and both married. Kathryn was married to George Leavitt on July 25, 1912, in Calgary. Irene married Thomas Wilson at Red Deer on March 14, 1918.

The Jordans stayed a few more years and disposed of their land and moved back to the State of Washington where they resided the rest of their lives.

Leavitt Genealogy

Mazzini Leavitt was born March 14, 1853, in Spencer, Medina Co., Ohio, one of eleven children of Lucius Luzern and Maria A. Leavitt, married Mary (Mollie) Sidener on December 3 1884. They had three children, George Dyer, born on March 16, 1886, Roy Frederick, born June 13, 1888, and Hazel, born May 20 1894, and passed away on September 15 1898.

In 1906 Mazzini and Mollie Leavitt and their two sons moved from Featherstone, Minnesota,

to Red Deer, Alberta, where they resided for a short period of time. In 1907 the family once again packed its belongings, and with an unbroken team of oxen which had to be guided by a man on either side, set out for a homestead near Stauffer, Alberta. Stauffer was not a town but a post office, and at one time, the Leavitts had the office in their home.

Less than two years after Mazzini and his family arrived in the Stauffer district, Roy Frederick was stricken with appendicitis and had to be taken to Red Deer in a sleigh pulled by a four horse team. On November 30, 1909, while in the hospital, he died of a ruptured appendix.

Mazzini Leavitt died on April 9, 1924, and Mollie on February 18, 1930.

George Dyer Leavitt was born on March 16 1886, and was engaged in various jobs during the time the Mazzini Leavitt family spent in Red Deer, at one time driving logs down the Red Deer River. Sometime after the move to Stauffer, George Dyer purchased four horses and hired on with the Railroad where he helped to build the grade for one of the lines which now serves Rocky Mountain House. He also broke some of the land on the Rocky Mountain House townsite. On July 24, 1912, George Dyer married Kathryn May Jordan, the youngest of two daughters of Sydney and Josephine Jordan who moved to the Caroline District in 1909 and later returned to the States around 1917. Kathryn's older sister, Irene Wilson, still lives in Rocky Mountain House and remains quite active. George and Kathryn had four boys, Frederick Vernon, born August 31, 1913, George Bernard, born January 28, 1916,

Mazzini Leavitt "catnap".

L.-R. — George, Vernon, Bernard, Clinton and Roy Leavitt.

Back row, L.-R. — Nanna Leavitt, Louise, Leah and Bill Cross, Kathryn and George Leavitt. Front, L.-R. — Roy, Clinton and Bernard Leavitt.

Clinton Merle 'Pat', born April 23, 1919, and Roy Jordan born March 8, 1922. George and Kathryn Leavitt opened the first store and post office at Butte, Alberta, and gave the district its name. George Dyer died on April 13, 1943, and Kathryn May on November 29, 1949.

Frederick Vernon Leavitt married Mary Elizabeth Maxson of Stauffer on December 15, 1941. They had four children, Donna May, born June 6, 1946, died June 9, 1946, Wayne Frederick, born June 16, 1947, died November 14, 1947, Lorrane Kenneth, born June 16, 1947, (twin to Wayne), and Patrick Dale, born March 17, 1955.

George Bernard Leavitt married Rosa Lee McKenzie of Stauffer July 28, 1936. He died October 13, 1970. They had four sons, Gordon Merle, born November 2, 1937, Calvin Arthur, born September 26, 1938, George Bernard, born April 21, 1945, and Thomas Kenneth, born November 4, 1950.

Clinton Merle 'Pat' Leavitt married Dorothy Marie Doll of Calgary, July 12, 1942. They had no children.

Roy Jordan Leavitt married Lorena Amy Maxson (younger sister of Mary Elizabeth Maxson) on July 8, 1944. They had five children, Maxine Eileen, born May 9, 1945, Patricia Marie, born October 5, 1947, Keith Jordan, born August 23, 1950, Brian Russell, born January 10, 1952, and Rena Joanne, born January 8, 1957.

The Leavitt brothers farmed together, ran a trucking service and continued the operation of the store and post office at Butte after their parents passed away. In 1948, Bernard moved to Rocky Mountain House with his wife and their three older sons where he took over the 'Modern Machine' business and lived until his death. Although the store and post office are now closed at Butte, and Vernon is semi-retired, Roy and Pat remain active in the farming business.

Lewis Family History

William John Rowland Lewis was born January 17, 1897, in Newport, Mon., South Wales.

He served in the 1914-18 war in the British Cavalry. After the war he came to Canada to join his father, John Lewis, who had come to Drumheller in 1910. William, or Rowland as he was better known, returned to Newport in the fall of 1923 where he married Doris Mae Hawen who was also born in Newport on January 17, 1899. They were married on January 18, 1924, and moved to Canada immediately after their marriage.

Rowland worked for Ralph and Ida Maxson on their farm south of Drumheller that summer and then moved to Wayne where he worked in and around the coal mines until 1935. During this time their daughter and two sons were born — Doreen, John (Jack) and Ralph. Doreen passed away in 1935.

In 1935 Rowland traded a Studebaker car to the Blackfoot Indians at Gliechen for five head of horses and went farming ten miles south of Wayne. The family moved to Butte on April 29, 1939, where they homesteaded. In 1942 Rowland joined the Royal Canadian Air Force where he served until the end of the war in 1945 when he resumed farming.

Rowland passed away October 31, 1961, and was followed by his wife, Doris, July 20, 1966.

Jack and Ralph both attended school at Clearwater. Ralph finished his schooling at Clear Creek.

Jack married Blanche Ross also of Butte, March 5, 1954, and moved to Sundre. They have three children, Lloyd in Calgary, Debora, and Keith in Sundre. Jack now lives in Bassano, Alberta, where he is in the trucking business.

Ralph married Thelma Taylor (Chick) of Stauffer on November 22, 1950. They have two daughters, Donna (Mrs. Clifford Christie) of Rocky, and Rita (Mrs. Dave Cumberland) also of Rocky. Ralph and Chick still farm the family homestead five miles northeast of Butte.

William John May

Mr. and Mrs. W.J. May and family came up to Stauffer, Alberta, from Lawson, Saskatchewan, on October 20, 1931, and settled on the S.W.Q. 19-37-5-5. They had five children, two girls and three boys. The oldest girl, Kathleen, married Gilbert Hankinson in 1935 and they live on the S.E.Q. 19-37-5-5. Florence married Dave Bourget and lives at Lantzville, British Columbia. The three boys, George, Douglas, and Gordon, live in Red Deer.

Mr. May passed away on December 18, 1932. They stayed on the farm for a few more years before moving to Red Deer. Mrs. May passed away on March 18, 1951.

Harold Ernest McCabe and Family
by Tina McCabe

"Go West Young Man," was the slogan that brought Harold and Minnie McCabe from Ontario to Alberta in the early 1900s. The Homestead Act stated that upon receipt of ten dollars in cash, and with the building of a liveable house and shelter for stock and the breaking of twenty-one acres of land, one could acquire a quarter section. Uncle George Shields, who was already in Alberta, persuaded the young couple to leave their home in the East, and come out West to fulfill the requirements of land acquisition and start a new life.

Harold Ernest McCabe was born in Peterborough, Ontario, on January 25, 1885. Minnie Eleanor Armstrong was born in Perth, Ontario, on May 16, 1885. They were married at North Elemsley in the County of Lanark, Ontario, on October 17, 1908. Shortly after, they set out for Alberta and moved to the Butte district to what was until recently, the Budden farm. While there, the Clearwater River overflowed its banks and flooded the Butte flats. Leavitts, at that time, were living high up on the hill to the south. McCabes waved a white sheet out of their upstairs window to let the Leavitt family know they were safe. That was the sole means of communition at that time.

Later they moved to their homestead a few miles south to land very close to the Butte and remained there; east half of section 12-37-6-5. Mr. McCabe was Secretary-Treasurer of the Raven Municipality from the time it was organized until his death in September of 1938. People came from miles to do business at the office which was located in the McCabe yard. Mrs. McCabe made tea on numerous occasions for visitors. Sometimes during the winter, when company came, she would be washing clothes. She would put the tub and washboard outside out of the way. By the time she returned to her washing, it was frozen in the tub. Mrs. McCabe would provide dinners for the council meeting members for thirty-five cents a head.

Mr. and Mrs. McCabe had four children. Harold, the eldest (known to all as Sonny), lives in Rocky Mountain House and owns and operates 'Modern Equipment Specialities' and 'Big Horn Propane.' He married Titina Rizzo from Coleman, Alberta, on December 27, 1944. Titina taught school at Clear Creek from March 1, 1943, until moving to Rocky in 1951. She has been teaching in Rocky since that time. Helen, the second child, married Douglas May from the Butte district on March 13, 1943. They moved to Calgary where Douglas was stationed during the war. When the war ended, they moved to Red Deer and remained there. They have one son, Larry, who with his wife, Heather, and son, Sean, also reside in Red Deer. Stanley (Paddy), who was born March 20, 1932, passed away November 3, 1972. Paddy joined the army when World War II broke out and was stationed part-time at Kiska in the Aleutian Islands. After his discharge, he worked at Swan Hills, Alberta, un-

Helen McCabe at Municipal Office.

Harold and Helen McCabe.

36

til his passing. Reginald was born on September 29, 1925, and passed away on March 18, 1966. He married Doreen Campbell of Byemoor, Alberta. They lived in Rocky Mountain House where Reg worked at Edward's Garage until the time of his death. They had four children, Richard, Brent, Greg and Karen all living in and around Stettler.

All the McCabe children attended Clear Creek School, always on foot except for Harold who rode horseback because he was the janitor at the school. The school was the social center of the community where Christmas Concerts, box socials and picnics were held. Country dances which lasted until the wee hours of the morning were the main source of entertainment for the community. Card parties were also held in the winter with each family taking turns at being hosts for the group. Tobogganing parties down the Butte hill were popular in winter for the youngsters. Harold, Stanley and Reggie, who were very musical, played for many of the dances. Harold played with Lamb's orchestra from Caroline for many years.

Some of the early neighbors were Mr. and Mrs. Comstock, Mr. and Mrs. Tom Wilson, Mr. and Mrs. Nicholson and Mr. and Mrs. Hoare. Mail delivered by horse and buggy or sleigh, was left in a box about one and one-half miles from the McCabe home. Later on, mail was picked up at Leavitt's General Store where groceries could be purchased. Everyone congregated at the store at mail time for a chat and exchange of news happenings.

Mr. and Mrs. Harold McCabe and sons, Stanley and Reginald, rest in the Pine Grove Cemetery in Rocky Mountain House.

A. E. McCoy

Albert Earl (Kid) McCoy was born at Pendleton, Oregon, and came to Alberta as a young man about 1909. He filed on S.E. 34-37-6-5 and lived there until he joined the army and served overseas in the first World War.

When he returned he bought the half section of 18-36-5-5 where he farmed for many years.

In the early twenties he married Mrs. W. Hankinson who had been widowed and they had two daughters, Winnifred and Winona. The girls grew up in the Butte district and went to school at Clear Creek.

Winnifred married Bill Shaurette. They had one son, Edward. Bill died during the early forties and later Winnifred married Donald (Scotty) Chapin and they had three sons, Donald, Lloyd and David. Scotty died as the result of a chuckwagon accident at the Calgary Stampede in the early sixties.

Winona married Bob Titford of Rocky Mountain House. They have three children, Larry, Allen and Barbara.

Albert Earl McCoy.

Winnifred Hankinson 1921.

Mrs. McCoy died in 1941 and Mr. McCoy in 1943.

Hugh and Lorna Myson and family.

Hugh Myson

Hugh Myson came to the Caroline district to work for the Vandermeer family. His mother, Mrs. Bryda Myson, and sister, Florence, moved out shortly after. Florence married Cyril Tose and Mrs. Myson lived in Caroline for several years. Her home was a gathering spot for the young people of the village where many lively evenings were spent around the piano. She moved back to Calgary in the late forties and came back again to her son's home. She was in ill health and spent the remainder of her life at a nursing home in Red Deer.

Hugh married Lorna Hoare on April 22, 1938. They had four children, Carol, Howard, Joyce and Eleanor. Carol married Chris Ayers and had four children, Brian, Norman, Diane and Darlene. She was divorced and is now married to Bill Leslie and lives in Calgary. Her eldest son, Brian, was married in March, 1978, and has a step-daughter.

Howard and his wife live in Edmonton where he is in the construction industry. They have four children, Deanna, Judy, Rita and Dale.

Joyce married John Lewin. They live at James River and have three children, Ronnie, Beverly and Donna Lee.

Eleanor married Bobby Shannon and has three children, Debbie, Shelia and Kevin. She was divorced and is now married to Ralph Pederson and lives in the Crammond district.

Andrew Ross

Andrew, better known as Andy, (by all who knew him), came up from Wyoming in 1902 and took up a homestead on N.W. 18-37-5-5 before this area was surveyed. He was a bachelor and a rancher raising around three hundred head of cattle on open range.

Sawyer History

George Sawyer was born in 1850 in Kingston County, England. He immigrated to Canada as a youth. He worked his way across the Atlantic as a crew member on a sailing ship and suffered from scurvy during the voyage.

He settled in Ontario and married a French Canadian girl, Matilda Drago, in Chatham, Ontario. They had a family of fourteen, some being born in Ontario and some in Minnesota, U.S.A., vhen they moved there. One of their sons, Clarence, was born on August 4, 1895, at Bemedji. The family moved back to Brandon, Manitoba. Mrs. Sawyer passed away and Mr. Sawyer was married a second time to Maude Collar.

While in Brandon, they owned and operated a store, which was traded for a half section of land north of Lipton, Saskatchewan. There were no buildings on the land, but there was a shallow well from which many neighbors drew water, as the only water available was seven miles distant. Money was borrowed for machinery and wheat seed. The first crop was poor — only about seven or eight bushels per acre and was sold for nine cents a bushel. The next year oats were planted and a better yield was obtained. Since building materials were hard to obtain a granary was constructed of slough grass and poles.

The price of oats at market was extremely low — seven cents per bushel, so the payments to the machine company could not be met and the land was lost due to foreclosure. Mr. Sawyer and Clarence then moved to Fort Quappelle to obtain work but remained only a short time. Then they went to Regina and camped out, where the railroad roundhouse is now located. There had been a cyclone in the Regina area, and some short term employment was secured there. They then moved on to Swift Current, where Mr. Sawyer got carpentry work on a church, and Clarence worked on the streets filling pot holes. Mr. Sawyer went to Calgary by rail, as the homestead land office was located there, and Clarence drove the team and wagon from Swift Current to Calgary — quite an undertaking for a thirteen-year-old youth. He camped along the way and slept under the wagon. He arrived in Calgary in due time, left his team and wagon at the stockyards and walked uptown to the post office where he hoped to find a letter from his father for further instructions. There was no letter waiting. He left the post office in a dejected frame of mind; wondering what to do next. Fortunately he met his father not far down the street. They were joined by Mrs. Sawyer and their household effects, in a short time, and came to the Caroline district in 1909 and filed on S.E. 2-37-6-5. The homestead was proved up in

Clarence Sawyer.

Marie and Hank Stainbrook and grandchildren.

1912. Their nearest neighbors, at that time, were John Trunell and the John March family.

They obtained their supplies and mail at the Langley store and post office.

Clarence volunteered for military service in 1916 and was inducted into the Sixty-Seventh Infantry Corps at Sarcee Camp, in Calgary, and transferred to the Forty-Ninth Infantry and was soon overseas. He was gassed during training overseas and suffered pneumonia as a result. He was returned and discharged in 1918. During the following years he worked at whatever was available. He and a companion looked for homestead land in the Peace River area but did not find suitable land and walked back from there to the Caroline area.

He cut mine props for the Brazeau Collieries, at Nordegg, and in 1925 obtained work as a cook on a forestry fire crew there.

In September, 1925, he was married to Olive Theresa Thibedeau. In the summer of 1926 he again worked for the Forestry as an assistant to Bill Shankland at Nordegg.

Clarence and Olive had two sons: Ray, born September 17, 1926, and Howard Earl Oliver, born September 19, 1936. Clarence continued in the Forestry Service and later became Ranger at the Clearwater Ranger Station.

Clarence was remarried in July of 1942, to Helen Forster. He was transferred to Pincher Creek as a game officer in 1946. He remained there until 1954, when he was transferred to Lethbridge.

Helen started to work for the Department of Lands and Forests in 1957, as a clerk typist and now works for the Department of Energy and Natural Resources. Clarence retired from game service in 1960 and then worked as a Commissionaire until 1965. They still reside in Lethbridge.

Henry and Marie Stainbrook

Henry Stainbrook was born at Parkston, South Dakota, on January 22, 1898. In 1905 he came by covered wagon, with his parents, to a homestead near the town of Tribune in southern Saskatchewan.

I, Marie Hansen, was born near Grafton, North Dakota, on February 20, 1901, and came with my parents to a homestead near Willow Bunch, Saskatchewan, in 1910. Willow Bunch was approximately one hundred miles from the railroad. The stores and lumber yards, etc., had to rely on teamstering to stock their places of business. The many shortages made shopping a problem, but somehow the settlers managed, and in a while the railroad came through and the farmers prospered.

In 1920 I came to Tribune to work in the Weyburn Security Bank where I met Henry Stainbrook. He was busy farming and playing baseball, curling and playing in the band. I also was interested in sports and we both liked to dance. In 1921 we were married and moved to the farm and gave our attention to farming.

In 1922 our son, Wilbur, was born and later in 1927, another son, Howard, was born.

By 1930 we had accumulated three quarter sections of land and were doing well. Then the drought came. It lasted for nine years. With it came dust storms, grasshoppers, army worms and extreme heat and howling winds. Nothing grew except tumbling weeds and Russian thistles. The Russian thistles tested out to be forty percent Epson salts, making it unsafe to walk within ten feet of the cow when bringing her in to milk.

In 1937 we gave up all hope of farming in Saskatchewan and abandoned our farm and moved to Stauffer, Alberta. We rented a run down farm with old log buildings and began farming in the bush country. Then we took a quarter section of C.P.R. land. Henry had no experience with working in the bush and did things the hard way. Wilbur helped when he wasn't in school, and Howard helped, but he was

Howard, Jean and Wilbur Stainbrook.

too young at that time. Our greatest ambition then, was to get a house built on our own place and move out of the old log cabin. On November 9, 1939, much to our delight, we moved to the new house, and on December 11 our daughter, Jean, was born. The new house was doubly appreciated.

Wilbur and Howard served in the armed forces during the Second World War. After Wilbur's discharge, he took up farming. He married Betty Johnson and they have three daughters, Joyce, Carolyn and Verna. Joyce married Darrel Holman they have one son, Dolan. Carolyn married Bud Jameson and they have two children, Michael and Sandy. Verna married Roger Smith and they have two girls, Tammy and Kim.

Howard married Nelda Ceaser. He took up mechanics and they live in Victoria. They have a son and a daughter, Cameron and Julie. Julie is married and has one child, Bladen. Jean married Don Van Kleek from Rocky Mountain House and they live in Kitimat, British Columbia, where Don teaches school. They have a daughter and a son, Lorinda and Mark. We now have seven grandchildren and six great grandchildren.

We sold the farm in 1959 and moved into Caroline where we have lived ever since, except for fifteen months spent in British Columbia. I find living in Caroline quite pleasant. I am a Pythian Sister and belong to the "Birthday Group" and the Golden Age Club and an art class where oil painting is taught. This keeps me occupied. Henry is happy as long as he is able to go boating and trolling for fish. We both enjoy a trip out to the mountains and admire the beautiful Alberta scenery.

Chas Taylor

The Chas Taylor family came to the district in the year 1905 and they homesteaded on the N.E.Q. 36-37-5-5. He built a log house which was used until a few years ago.

His son, Curly, came from Nova Scotia and worked in logging camps in British Columbia. He then came to the North Raven district where he settled and farmed. He blazed trails to help survey roads. He was a game warden; a councilor for the Municipal District of Raven and was on the school board for a number of years. He was also a great hunter. Once on his travels he came upon a bear and three young. He killed the bear with an axe.

Curly Taylor and Cyrus Clay started the first stampede at Hale Lake in 1920.

Curly married Louise Morgeau. Louise came to the district with her father, brothers and sister. They trailed sixty head of horses over the mountains from Windermere, British Columbia, to Raven. Many of the horses died after they arrived here.

Mr. and Mrs. Curly Taylor had a stopping house for people travelling to Innisfail to get supplies which was their nearest town. The Taylor children went to the school at North Raven. Curly also helped build the Raven Church and Mrs. Taylor and Mrs. Noa Heare stained the little church.

Mrs. Taylor was a midwife to the entire community and helped many in need.

Curly Taylor about 1910.

Louise and Curley Taylor.

40

Norman and Dolly Taylor.

Tom and Irene Wilson.

The Taylors had ten children, Sara married Mike Thomas and they had four children, Harold, Ernie, Earl and Iris. Norman married Dolly Lonto. They had three children, Myrna, Roger and Ardith. Lillian married Eli Cave and they had ten children, Vernon, Leona, Ken, Dale, Beverly, Gloria, Trevor, Calvin, Clifford and Darwin.

Jim married Agnes Syren and they had one boy, Gene. Lula married Joe Branson and they had four children, Leonard, Elery, Phillis and Louise. Mary married Marno Branson and they had three children, Twila, Sandra and Boyde. Alice married Walter Syron and they had two children, Joyce and Guy. Frances married Fred Molander and they had four children, Penny, Carol, Ronda and Harriet. Chick married Ralph Louis and they had two girls, Donna and Reta. Raymond married Alice Lacerf and had eight children, Chuck, Karon, Loretta, Danny, Larry, Barbara, Branda and Pat Lynn.

Thomas Flett Wilson

Thomas Flett Wilson was born in Milton Heights, Ontario, on May 8, 1893. He came to western Canada when he was fifteen or sixteen years of age. He worked, hunted, trapped and prospected in the Slocan area of British Columbia before coming to Alberta.

He and Irene Jordan were married while he was on leave from the army. Shortly after their marriage, he went overseas and served in battle lines of Belgium where he was wounded. After he returned from overseas, he and his wife settled on his homestead in the Dovercourt area.

Later, in the 1920s, they purchased land in what was then the Stauffer area on land of which the Butte Hill was a part.

Tom was a skilled blacksmith and though he never had a shop to do his work in, he helped many a neighbor by repairing their machinery and doing the work in his yard.

They continued to live on the farm and Tom passed away on August 7, 1963, in the Colonel Belcher Hospital in Calgary. He is buried in the Pine Grove Cemetery at Rocky Mountain House. Irene lived on their farm until 1966 when she moved to Rocky Mountain House where she still resides.

Crammond

Crammond School
Composed by Earl Graham

The first Crammond school (Ivan Graham's homestead shack) was moved in 1926 to the site of the present Crammond Community Center. The first teacher was Mrs. A. Barby who taught in the shack and in the school that was later built in 1926. The homestead shack is still standing and at present is a teacherage at the new Crammond School. When the old school, built in 1926, was closed, Mrs. McQuarry was teaching all nine grades. A four room school was built in 1956, half a mile north, on the S.W. 28-35. In 1960 grade 9 was moved to Caroline and in September 1962 grades 7 and 8 were also enrolled in Caroline. The school closed in 1965. All the children now are bussed to Caroline.

Crammond Teachers, 1930-1965

Margaret McFadyen — Nov. 11 - Dec. 22, 1930-1932; Walter Pendle — Feb. - June, 1930; William R. Sloan — Sept., 1933 - June, 1936; William R. Holeton — Sept., 1936; George C. Boorman — Sept. 1 - Dec. 21, 1938; V. A. Coleman — Sept. 5, 1939 - Dec. 22, 1939; James N. Nolty — Sept. 3, 1940 - Dec. 23, 1940; Mrs. M. E. Nash — April 15, 1940 - June 28, 1940; Charles E. Allen — Sept. 22, 1941 - Dec. 19, 1941; Mary Gladys Eddy — Oct. 5, 1942 - Dec. 22, 1942; Harold Rogers — March 1, 1943 - June 30, 1943; Ena M. Baynham — Nov. 15, 1943 - Feb. 29, 1944; Edith Stewart — May 17, 1944 - July 28, 1944; Mary M. Gordon — Sept. 10, 1945 - Dec. 21, 1945; Dorothy I. Reeser — Sept. 7, 1946 - Dec. 20, 1946; Miss M. Mayhew — Sept. 8, 1947 - Dec. 19, 1947; J. Alex Mercer — Feb. 4, 1948 - June 30, 1948; Arthur Buchanan — Sept. 1, 1948 - Dec. 22, 1948; Adele H. Murray — April 2, 1949 - June 30, 1949; Adele Froh — Sept. 1, 1949 - June 30, 1949; Hazel McQuarrie — Sept., 1950 - June, 1951; Dagny Dyrholm — Dec. 3, 1957 - June 30, 1957; Jean Severns — Nov. 13 - June 28, 1957; G. A. Carlson — Sept., 1957 - June, 1958; Moira E. Cole — Sept., 1957 - June, 1958; Betty Mannerfeldt — Sept. 2, 1958 - June 30, 1959; Roy Devons — Sept. 2, 1958 - June 30, 1959; Kathy Alstott — Oct. 18, 1959 - June 30, 1960; Edna Baughman — Sept. 1, 1960 - June 30, 1961; Joyce A. Scott — Sept., 1960 - June, 1961; James W. Smith — Sept. 1, 1960 - June 30, 1961; Gertrude Boyes — Sept. 5, 1961 - June 29, 1962; Tom A. Bowhay — Sept. 4, 1962 - June 28, 1963; Mrs. Edna Boughman — June 30, 1963; Edna Boughman — June 1965; Tom Bowhay — June 30, 1965; James W. Smith — June 30, 1962.

Pupils of Crammond School — June 1930 to June 1965 Ardus Looman, Bernus Looman, Mollie Wren, Lewis Wren, Joseph Fleet, Fred Dingman, Audrey Cook, Jacob Runham, Ruth Dingman, David Runham, Harold Runham, Mildren Fleet, Howard Cook, Violet Runham, Anita Rhodes, Ellen Cook, Wilbur Rhodes, Wallace Wren, Ray Womack, John Franklin, Alfred Anderson, Lawrence Wren, Marie Fleet, Pearl Runham, Donald Runham, Rosie Lamothe, Robert Hall, Kenneth McDowell, Glen Kanten, Ruth Gardner, David Graham, James Graham, Gordon Graham, Bruce Graham, Lyle Runham, John Cook, David Bunce, Florence Kanten, Milton Morrison, Oscar Kanten, Kathleen Hall, Doris Hall, Joyce McDowell, Lawrence Anderson, Leonard Kanten, Harry Rhodes, Wava Runham, Della Runham, Eddie Shenfield, Luella Lamb, Rubie Jump, Jessie Hazen, Alfred Orr, Lillian Lamothe, Letitia Bent, Fred Austin, Ray Mjolness, Merle

Crammond School children, 1940.

Mjolness, Georgina McDowell, Eileen Morrison, Marie Anderson, Grant Whitehead, Peggy Vickers, Norman Whitehead, Charles Vickers, Lawrence Whitehead, Florence Whitehead, Ruth Whitehead, Harry Fay, Ada Whitehead, Donald Crawford, Evelyn Morrison, Gerald Hall, Fay Crawford, Clifford Runham, Georgina McDonald, Francis McDonald, Arthur Lawther, Lloyd Lawther, Harvey Eggen, Peggy Lawther, John Eggen, Lula Graham, Merle Neal, David Shaght, Myrtle Buchanan, Dale Biggart, William Biggart, Jean Crawford, Twilla Hansen, Norman Nissen, Joseph Larsen, Roy Crawford, Ronald Eggen, Ruth Graham, June Lowther, Louisa Lindsay, Duane Neal, Rose Guidas, Bobby Guidas, Lorraine Larsen, Lawrence Larsen, Dennis Crawford, David Rhodes, Emily O'Coin, Lillian Rhodes, Adeline O'Coin, Albert O'Coin, James Mayhew, Mildred Mayhew, Loreane Miller, Florence Miller, Gillian Simons, Gloria M. Dingman, Sharon Hansen, Diane Jackins,

Larry Miller, Vera Neilson, Helen Neilson, Carol Buchanan, Myrtle Neilson, Eugene Abernathy, Dwayne Gordon, Andrew Buchanan, Larry Jackins, Francis Wren, Richard Becker, Darold Fairbanks, Leonard Becker, Jack Crawford, Gordon Wren, Lorraine Morrison, Melvin Hansen, Mona Arneson, Fay Simons, Mary Miller, David F. Runham, Gary Arneson, Grant Baldry, Kathleen Simons, Cameron Ottley, Micke Amulung, Peggy Baldry, Wendy Nevins, Charles H. Johnson, Sandra Carpenter, Barbara Talentyre, Wayne Wales, Ricky Carm, Gail Dingman, Karl Jackins, Richard Talentyre, Angela Talentyre, Phyllis Bjur, Linda Jackins, Larry G. Willsie, Doris Quast, Charles Hutton, Frank Hutton, Dianne Quast, Jacklyn Quast, George E. Miller, Helen Willsie, Lynda Olson, Jan Jackins, Dwayne Olson, Dennis K. Brown, Beverley Burk, Raymond Coderre, Linda Fifield, Earl I. Graham, Howard Scott, Carol Larsen, Jerry Saunders, Wayne Nevins, Carl Fifield, Sherry Hunt, Karen Jensen, Robert S. Brown, Larry R. Burk, Ormand Carpenter, Charlotte Fletcher, Terry D. Hunt, James

Kneesch, Judy Saunders, Leonard Way, Garry Burtch, Roland Coderre, Jacqueline Fifield, Carolyn Ritten, Marilyn Ritten, Allen Saunders, Connie Burtch, Doris Kappel, Duane Saunders, Kenneth Way, Wayne Baird, Donald Bowness, Brown Bernhardt, Keith Burk, Wayne Carpenter, Rita Coderre, Gloria Miller, Dennis Way, Dallas Burtch, Stanley A. Boye, Kenneth Boye, David Burk, Lorne Burtch, Jean Cook, Donald Fifield, Violet Fifield, Mervin Ritten, Ronald Rose, Noreen Baird, Delos Burk, Omer Coderre, Margaret Fletcher, Viola Graham, Lloyd Kappel, Rudolph Norgaard, Alice Orr, David Peterson, Michael Semaka, Freda Smith, James Bowness, John Lewin, Elizabeth Simington, Dolores Peterson, Stella Carpenter, Donna Jensen, Stansfield Morrrison, Mary Ann Hunter, Kenneth Youngman, Stanley Youngman, Carol Filgate, Terry Hunt, Richard Filgate, Peggy Baldry, Janet Boye, Donald Burk, Leslie Shannon, Janet Baldry, James B. Millar, Donna M. Runham, Sharon Wales, Ronald Bevons, Barbara Trottier, Cherry Ottley, Wolf Gerhard, Nancy Murphy, Mervin Ritten, Einar Sigurdur, Philip Burk, Kenneth Millar, Cecil Morrison, Homer Scott, Rodney Van Sprang, Susan Baldry, Kathleen Chanda, Layne McQuarrie, Barry Smith, Grace Metzger, Lora Strickler, Gilbert Bainton, Janice Rakestraw, Donald Smith, Frances L. Hunter, Ernest Morrison, Paulette Rakestraw, Roland Coderre, Elaine Hunter, Norma Hunter, Roger Smith, Candis Baldry, Dianne Brown, Fredrick A. Dingman, Charles Feddema, Daniel Jensen, May Miller, Margeurite Olson, Gary Rose, Homer Scott, Dwayne Chanda, Debbie Kubik, Roger Dube, Diana Dube, Donna Dube, Linda Burk, Delbert Dingman, Brian Pearce, Barbara Kubik, Richard Kubik, Stanley Phillips, Marvin Nelson, Barbara Phillips, Harry Strickler, Edwin Kubik, David F. Runham, Robert Saunders, Albert Dingman, John Feddema, Judith Hansen, Kathy Law, Norma Miller, Linda Ostergren, Michael Parenteau, Irene Peterson, Lyla Peterson, James Rose, Leora Smith,

Crammond School children — Fay Crawford, Ronnie Eggin, Lillian Rhodes, Merle Neal, Lulu Graham, Ruth Graham, Bobby Guidos, Joe Larson, Dwayne Neal, June Lowther, Louisa Lindsay, Jean Crawford.

Crammond School, teacher Bill Sloan.

44

Edward Miller, Allan Dingman, Dale McKie, Eileen Smith, Edna McKie, Bruce Baldry, Robert Day, Gerald Ennis, Wilbur Johnson, Valerie Hunter, Janet Lucas, Ann Scott, Sheila Stone, Roger Liegman, Lorraine Lohrich, Donna Sutcliffe, Edward Liegman, Yvonne Baughman, Mary Hunter, James Bowhay, Lorraine Cook, Gertrude Feddema, Robert Hunter, Darlene Peterson, Bonnie Smith, Alan Stone, Steven Kapty, Donald Bartell, Dawn Ballentine, Linda Harrison, Vera Randall, Shirley Harrison, Robert Bartell, Merdith Harrison, Yvonne Christensen, Marguerite Cook, Ricky Dingman, Peter Feddema, Debbie Law, Doris Lohrich, Donald Morrice, Sherry Feddema, Erich Bitsche, Brian Shepard, John Thomson, Melvin Matthews, Marlaine Matthews, Nora Millar, Sandra Pekse, Jacqueline Lampert, Dale Youngman, Daniel Jensen, Sharon Ennis, Erchard Steuer, Wendling Bitsch.

Memories of Crammond

by William R. Sloan

I taught the Crammond School from September, 1933, to June, 1936. I have many happy memories of those years.

The pupils at that time felt they were fortunate to have the opportunity of attending school. There were no discipline problems. I don't remember keeping anyone in. One day I thought a problem had arisen when one of the girls came in and told me that Fred Dingman had gone into the girls' toilet. I called Fred in and asked him about it. Fred said, "The door was open and the ball went in. The runner was going to third so I had to go in for the ball."

I batched in a building in the school yard which had been the school at one time. It was a very cold building. One night I left a kettle of water on the heater. The next morning the water was frozen. I told some that I had so many quilts on my bed, that I had to put in a book mark in order to know where to get in. I had running water at the teacherage. The only problem was that the running water was in the creek.

Jack Halls came to the district while I was there. Mrs. Hall asked how one could get a haircut. One man said, "Oh, most anyone can cut hair!"

I was fortunate in being invited out for many meals. This helped very much as I wasn't a very good cook.

I had the only radio in the district. One weekend I left it at Bert Rhodes' so the batteries would not freeze. On Sunday night Bert told me it was too cold to go to the teacherage. Also he wanted to hear another program so I gladly accepted his invitation. On Monday afternoon when I started to take the radio, Mrs. Rhodes told me to leave it where it was. Since the teacherage was so cold I decided it was best to board with them. I stayed about two months. When I offered to pay for staying, Mrs. Rhodes said the use of the radio was worth more than the board. I often put the radio with its two B batteries, a C battery and the wet A battery on a sleigh and visited neighbors.

Once Bert Mitten sold me three one pound boxes of chocolates for one dollar. I opened one box at Bert Rhodes and forgot to take the other two to the teacherage. The next afternoon I found a piece of two by six in one box. Sally (Miller) Bugbee was Rhodes' hired girl so I knew what had happened. She was worried when I told her I had sent the chocolates to my girl friend. She then brought out the chocolates she had taken for a joke. She felt better when I told her I had not sent the chocolates.

There was very little money in the district at that time. My salary was $500.00 per year, but that was more than the income of many. I used to help harvest in the fall to earn some cash so I could afford to teach. One winter many rabbits were traded at Mittens for food. The rabbits were very thick. One afternoon I shot forty-two in less than an hour.

Last winter when my wife and I returned from Hawaii, I thought the Greyhound bus driver resembled one of my Crammond pupils. His name plate said A. Anderson. Yes, I had recognized Alfred Anderson after forty-three years.

Mr. X. P. Crispo, the school inspector, came to my teacherage. He asked if he could give me some advice. He said he would spend Christmas alone in a hotel room as he had never married. I took his advice and was married that fall.

I taught the Raven School for four years, Red Raven for two years and then I taught at Dickson and Spruce View for thirty years. I retired in 1972 and continued to live at Dickson. We will be glad to meet former students at any time.

Carl Anderson Family

Carl was born in Dassel, Minnesota, September 17, 1880, and was raised there. He first came to the Crammond area in 1903, from Yellowstone Park where he had been working. He came to Bowden where he had some friends, either the Fleets or Rhodes. He rented a horse from them to ride out to the Crammond area to look at some land for homesteading.

When he was riding along the Schrader flats just south of George McCarthy's place, he came upon a large encampment of Indians. He tried to skirt around them, but they saw him and rode out to meet him. They were friendly, and took him into their camp where he had to stay for two or three days.

It was on this trip that he picked his homestead. He picked one for his father, Nels, and one for his brother, August, and then returned the saddle horse on his way back. When Carl was ready to take up residence on the homestead, having taken out papers on it, his back breaking work was to begin. Clearing the land and getting it ready for the plow was hard work and one could only do a few acres each year. He plowed his land with yokes of oxen at first then he went to horses. Some years later, he was able to get a Waterloo tractor which eased up the work a great deal.

Carl was married in Innisfail to Rosena McCarthy in 1924. Rosena was born in Aspen, Ontario, in 1904 and came with her family to settle in the Crammond area in 1918. They had three children, Alfred, Lawrence and Marie. The children attended the Crammond School.

Carl passed away in April, 1950, and is buried in the Raven Cemetery. Rose stayed on the farm until she passed away in March, 1975. She is buried in the Caroline Cemetery.

Nels August Anderson

Nels Anderson worked as a tailor in Dassel, Minnesota, and then for the army tailors in Yellowstone Park before coming to Canada with his three sons, August, Carl Alfred and Oscar Benjamin and a brother-in-law, Wolseth, in the year of 1905. They took up a homestead next to the Raven River.

It was that same year that a bad prairie fire went through the country. It was so smoky that they had to get on their stomachs to get a breath of air. It lasted about three days.

Nels August Anderson.

Aug. Anderson, 1915.

The Anderson family — Ella, Oscar, Carl, Aug., and Josie.

Nels had a threshing outfit with Dick Rhodes and used to go all over the country thrashing for people that needed help.

The brothers were musical so they held quite a few social gatherings at their log house.

Carl Anderson married Rosena L. B. McCarthy. In 1934 they bought a quarter of land four miles south of Raven River which belonged to Charles McCarthy (no relation to Rosena). Carl and Rosena had three children, Alfred, Lawrence and Marie.

Mr. and Mrs. Willard Axtell
by Gene Axtell

The new year of 1932 was a cold and frosty one, with temperatures ranging from twenty to thirty degrees below zero, which did not vary for months at a time. Mr. Axtell, his son, Gene, and Wallace Reese came into the area by sleigh and settled into the log cabin across the road from Clark Wren's place. They spent the first three months getting logs out and building materials for their house on the Raven River.

Mr. Axtell, Gene and Wallace bought C.P.R. land next to the Raven and on the Sundre road. In

Willard Axtel and Wallace Reese house building.

Barn Building for Willard Axtel.

the next five years the house and barn were built, and they fenced, cleared and broke land.

Mr. Axtell farmed there until 1947. They rented Curly Wren's farm for five years. It was 1953 when they retired to Caroline where they lived for many years. Mr. Axtell passed away in March of 1972 and Mrs. Axtell in January of 1975, both at the age of ninety-two years.

In the winter of 1932 the Caroline district was still much of a frontier area, sparsely settled, and large areas of land to be developed. Social activities were centered around the Caroline Hall and many school houses, not to mention many of the ranch houses where parties were held during the long winter months. But we enjoyed them with lots of visiting, games and dances.

I cannot help but recall the Innisfail road in those days, which we called 'Boulder Highway' — a long jarring experience not soon forgotten. In the first years, the Langley's freighted out groceries and goods by horse and sleigh, and it was a long, cold trip for driver and animals.

Below is a poem dedicated to Mr. and Mrs. Axtell on their sixtieth wedding anniversary:

The Ship of Marriage

We embarked on the 'Ship of Marriage'
Sixty years ago, Willard and Me.
He was the captain, I was the mate
As we sailed out on life's golden sea.

To Didsbury we sailed one fine morning
And there our first mooring was made.
I cooked for some boarders, while Willard
Was learning the carpenter trade.

We decided we'd like to try farming,
So to Crammond we came to reside.
There we entered the good 'Port of Friendship'
And many friends came to us on the tide.

We worked day and night on our homestead
We worked tho' it snowed and it rained
Till we sailed to the 'Cove of Contentment'
And the reward of achievement was gained.

We battled the rapids of sorrow
When the war took our son, Gene, away.
How we prayed that God would protect him
And bring him home safely some day.

When Gene returned home we were happy
Then we sailed to the 'Harbor of Joy'.
We were so proud and so thankful
For Gene is our only boy.

In Caroline now we are living
We have forsaken the billowing foam.
Our 'Ship of Marriage' is anchored at last
In a haven of 'Peace' and 'Home'.

Tonight we strolled to the hill top
And gazed on the sun's setting ray.
Our 'Ship of Marriage' of sixty years ago
Rests in the 'Harbor of a Perfect Day'.

Grace Hall

The Fleet Family

by Joe Fleet

My grandfather, Russell Fleet, was born in 1861 and grandmother, Eliza Ann Daily was born in 1860. They lived in Nebraska, where Dad and his two brothers were born. They came to Alberta in the fall of 1900 arriving in Calgary where they stayed for about two weeks. While there, Grandfather was offered what is now the Queens Hotel in trade for a team of his purebred Percheron horses. He declined the offer. They travelled on north to a place at the Lone Pine Coulee where they spent the winter. In the spring he filed on a homestead seven miles west of Bowden.

Dad, Eugene Edward (ED) Fleet, was born May 10, 1887, and took most of his schooling in Nebraska. He homesteaded a quarter of land in the Kevisville area where Maurice Robb now lives, and his brother, Jay, homesteaded the quarter east of it. Dad and Uncle Jay used to travel around the country playing for dances,

Eliza and Russel Fleet family — standing: Jay, Alice, Ed, sitting: Eliza, Russel, being held: Sadie, Jake, Ida.

Mr. Joseph Buchan family — standing: Florence and Nellie, sitting: Joseph, George, Mrs. Buchan.

Dad played the violin and Uncle Jay the jew's-harp.

In 1906 they moved to the Crammond area and Dad settled on the N.W. Q. 28-35-5-5 and Jay on the S.W. Q. 30-35-5-5. There had been a big fire through this area before they came leaving just a few of the larger trees standing, so for the first few years they wintered their livestock at Bowden.

In 1909 Dad's other brother, Jake, homesteaded the N.E. Q. 24-35-6-5 which is now my home. About this time, Dick Graham homesteaded the northwest quarter of that section.

Mother, Sarah Florence Buchan, was born in Ontario in 1893 and came to Alberta around 1904. When her mother died in 1906, she took her body back to Ontario for burial and when she returned, she lived with her brother, George Buchan, at Moose Mountain west of Bowden.

Mom and Dad were married in 1916 and I was the eldest of their three children. I was born in 1917, Mildred in 1919 and Marie in 1922.

In 1920 Dad sold our place to Roy Rhodes and bought Uncle Jake's place. This was the year that Grandmother Fleet passed away. Grandfather stayed on at their home until 1942 when he moved into an old folks home in Didsbury which was run by a friend of his. He died in 1944 and was buried beside Grandmother in the Bowden Cemetery.

Dad took his first crop off in 1923 and one day when he was moving a binder down the hill from the house, it hit a bump and threw him off in front of it. The horses ran away and the binder ran over him almost cutting his hand off. Mom and I got him to the house where we packed it in a pan of flour to try to stop the bleeding. Mom then went to Uncle Jays for help and he went to Fred Pearson's who lived where Jack Campbell

Ed Fleet family — Chester Miller and Marie — wedding day, Mrs. Sarah Fleet, Joe, Mildred and Ed.

now lives. Fred phoned Doctor Wagner in Innisfail to come out, by the time he got there Dad had lost a lot of blood. Bob Miller's dad drove him to the hospital in his touring car. Because of the loss of blood, the Doctor couldn't give him an anaesthetic, so he just had to grit his teeth and bear it while Doctor Wagner cut, trimmed and sewed his hand back on. He saved his hand and I think a lot of credit should be given to Doctor Wagner and those other fine doctors for the good work they did before the age of modern medicine and techniques such as we have today. Our neighbors stooked the crop and the Millers helped with the threshing.

In 1925 we moved to the J. R. Langley place across from the South Fork School. I went to school there for eighteen months and then we moved back to our own place again to help make up enough pupils to start a school at Crammond. Mildred was then old enough to begin school.

The school was a building purchased from Ivan Graham, 12 x 16, and it was moved to the site where the new school was built about 1930 and which is now being used for a community center. They added on an entry for boots, coats, etc. When they built a new school it was used for a teacherage, so it served it's purpose well.

Dad was a councillor for the Municipal District of Waterloo and served for thirteen years. He served a term of four years on the Crammond School Board as well. About 1930 he was a salesman for the Lionel Mill Clothing Company and for the Lacombe Nurseries, travelling most of the time on foot.

To help support the family when I was age thirteen and still going to school, I worked on Bert Rhodes' sawmill after school. The next spring I helped on a threshing outfit with team and wagon and earned $2.00 a day. I also hauled grain from the separator to the granary for $1.50 a day. Once a week during the winter, I would haul a load of rails to Caroline receiving $6.00 a load, and so we survived the hard times and misfortunes that we encountered along the way.

Mom died March 7, 1955, and Dad and I lived together until his passing in January, 1970. They are buried in the Raven Cemetery.

Mildred married Earl Johnson from James River in June, 1943. They have no children.

Marie married Chester Miller on October, 1940. They live in the Crammond area and have seven children.

Uncle Jay married Florence Pitts, a sister to Bert and Kelly Sheffield. She had two children from her former marriage to Bill Pitts and she and Uncle Jay had two children, Betty and Delbert. They moved to Fort St. John where Uncle Jay passed away.

Uncle Jake married Charlotte Scott, a sister of (Syd Scott who) lived where the Nesbits now live on Beaver Creek. They had two children, Dorothy and Alfred. They moved to Turner Valley and Uncle Jake died there. Aunt Charlotte lives in British Columbia.

Ivan Graham

I was born in Adair County, Iowa, on February 5, 1898, the second son of a family consisting of five boys and three girls. In 1905 I started school. The following year my family moved by covered wagon to Jefferson, Minnesota. We had to walk five miles to attend school. The first year in Minnesota was spent just surviving, as early frost had destroyed the crop. We burnt corn cobs for fuel and ate shorts (cleanings from flour).

About 1913 our family moved to Radison, Wisconsin. The school wasn't built until two years after we arrived but when it was built, we had to row across the river to reach it.

I hopped a train pulling immigration cars when I was seventeen. I travelled to Drake, North Dakota, as my older brother was there, and I was going to work with him. The journey took five days. I hid amongst the machinery the whole time and got off the train unnoticed. My family followed me to Drake several months later.

In 1917 I worked for the railroad as a section hand. After leaving the railroad, I worked as a carpenter. My family moved by covered wagon to Dunseith, North Dakota, the following year. I worked for farmers, stooking and threshing their crops. Two years later, my brother, Wilbur, Len Gilbert and his wife and myself, each of us driving a covered wagon, struck off for Canada. We crossed the border on June 2, 1920. We travelled as far as Bassano, Alberta, then stopped to find work. I worked for A. N. Maurer until fall, when Wilbur went to Washington. Then I took the train to Innisfail. From there I walked to Len Gilbert's home (where Fred McLean lives now) and looked at homesteads nearby. On my way back to Innisfail I had supper and rested for an hour at a stopping house on the Medicine River. Coyotes followed me the rest of the way back but I was too tired to run from them. I arrived in Innisfail about midnight and got on the train. In Calgary I filed on my homestead, S.E. Q. 34-35-5, and then went back to Bassano.

On November 2, 1920, I arrived at Len Gilbert's with my team and wagon, ready to homestead. On November 22, I moved into my homestead shack. I worked that winter clearing brush for George (Mac) McClarity and Mr. McCarthy.

In the fall of 1921, I went back to Bassano to sell my brother's team. I helped A. N. Maurer move to Winnipeg where I worked until the Christmas of 1922, when I went home to Dunseith. I returned to the homestead later.

To earn enough money to keep up my homestead, I threshed each fall for three years for farmers around Acme. I rode one horse there, and led the other. Since I had no money, I slept beside the road.

In 1923 I broke up some of the homestead with a walking plow. In 1924 I broke horses for Robert Miller just for the use of them. One horse would strike out or kick you whenever it could. In the same year, I bought my first car, a 1923 Star.

George McClarity and I broke some of the

Schrader flats for $2.50 an acre. We also put the crop in for two years.

In the fall of 1923 or 1924, Pinky Pitts (who had homesteaded in 1921) and I went to Rocky to cut wood with a hand-made swede saw. We slept in the wagon box the first night and started a cabin the following morning. The cabin had no door or windows and the roof was just poles and moss. Carl Lamb joined us about a week later.

About 1926 I went to Olds to work for a fellow named Hunter. He lived where the hospital is now. I fed his 500 head of cattle and 350 head of hogs.

I rented a quarter section of land one mile south and one mile east of Olds for three years. In 1928 I rented a half section near Didsbury and farmed both places. My first second-hand tractor which I purchased gave me so much trouble that I soon traded it in on a new Hart Paar. It cost me $1800.00.

In the late 1920s Art Lamb asked, on behalf of the school board, if my second homestead shack could be used as a school. It was used until 1928 when a new school was built. From that time, until the Crammond school was closed in 1956, it was used as a teacherage.

In 1929 I bought a half section in Didsbury. It was all willow so I broke eighty acres the first year. I bought a new binder that year to take my crop off. It started hailing as I made my first round of the field. I was hailed out for four consecutive years. Finally, I gave back the half section as I couldn't pay for it. I rented another place for a year and was living there when I married Anita Reese on February 24, 1932. She was born at High River in 1908. About 1915 she started school at Highwood School near High River. Her family moved to Longview in March of 1917. She walked one and a quarter miles to school. In 1919 her family moved to Didsbury and she attended Zella School until 1924.

Our first daughter, Lula, was born at Didsbury in November of 1933. Ruth was born at Didsbury in November of 1936, Viola in Olds of 1942 and Earl in Olds in May of 1950.

In 1933 we bought the Cook place, the quarter directly south of the homestead, and built a house so we could move the following year. I broke thirty-five acres with six horses that first summer. That same summer I moved thirty head out to the homestead for the summer and moved them back to Didsbury in the fall. When I drove them back I walked behind them all day and all night, covering fifty-five miles back to Didsbury.

In the spring of 1934, when we moved, we brought all the cattle out with us and lost forty-four head. They had been fed on oat straw and just went down and couldn't get up. I killed seven yearlings at one time with an axe.

Graham family — Ivan, Anita, Lulu and Ruth.

To help pay taxes on the land, one year I cleared the road allowance from the Cook place to Biggarts and used my tractor to pull a grader.

From 1935 to 1940 I was trustee on the school board.

Lula started school in 1940. She had to ride three and a half miles to school so we decided to buy the Wren place, the northeast quarter and south half of 33-35-5. Since we had Art Lamb's quarter already rented, I had between four and five hundred acres to seed. About this time we bought a W30 tractor. The first two crops yielded well and this helped pay for the land. We sold the Cook quarter to Ken Eggen in 1945.

The few roads that existed during those years were always in poor condition. We had a high wheeled IHC truck that came into use many times as ambulance and hearse. Mrs. Neal was ill once and it took five hours to go the twenty miles to Sundre and then we had to go another twenty miles to Olds to the doctor. Another time, after a rainy spell, an old fellow passed away. Since the roads were nearly impassable, Pinky Pitts and I volunteered to make a coffin, which was really a pine box. We wrapped the body in blankets and laid him in the coffin. We loaded it in the truck. Herman Nass solved the problem of keeping it there by straddling the coffin and saying, "Give 'er hell, Ivan, I'll hold it." We took off down the road. The 'hearse' and a Model T were the only ones that made it to the funeral. Everyone else was stuck.

I was councilman for the Municipality of Waterloo for ten or twelve years. The James River Bridge was built while I was a councilman. When the Garrington Bridge was opened, I drove the first car across with pioneers Claude Peterson and Willard Axtell.

Because help for threshing got so hard to get, in 1947 I bought my first combine, an IHC 82.

In 1948 we bought the Pioneer Store from Harris and Barby. Merle Reese managed it for a year until we moved to Caroline, when I ran it. In 1949 I moved the Mitten and Cross store across the street to its present location. We sold the store to Vance Braucht in 1952. We bought the school section the same year.

While we lived in Caroline we rented the farm to Cecil Wales for two years and then we hired Lawrence Bjur to work it. I also had a family from Holland staying on the farm, but they left after a few months.

After we sold the store I managed the Wrigglesworth Pole Yard for three years. There was a peeling and treating yard, a sawmill and a camp in the bush where the logs were cut. These enterprises employed up to seventy men. In 1955 we moved back to the farm and sawed lumber from the school section for a house.

I served on the Advisory Board in 1956 for the Local Improvement District number Ten with Fred Pekse and George Penney and was also on the board for the Rocky Senior Citizen's Home. For three years, I served on the first council in Caroline with Mayor Shorty Carter and George McLean.

In 1964 I sold the farm, which consisted of seven quarters with eight hundred acres broke. I kept twenty acres on the north east quarter of the school section, where we built a new house. I still own a quarter northeast of Caroline that I bought in 1968. I pastured cattle there during the summer and fed them on the twenty acres in the winter. In 1971 I had a heart attack and had to sell my cattle.

We purchased the Pioneer Store back from Vance Braucht that same year. Earl kept the hardware and grocery and Vern Larsen took over the Imperial Bulk Agency.

Lula married Constable R. G. Mills in September, 1959. He is now Staff Sergeant in St. Paul where they reside with their two boys and one girl. Ruth married Ralph Johnson in August, 1957. They have three children, two boys and one girl, and they farm norhwest of Caroline. Viola married Vern Larsen in September, 1960. They live on a farm northeast of Caroline and have two boys and one girl. Earl married Joy Tait in March, 1972.

Earl and Joy moved into our house in 1973 and we moved into his trailer in Caroline. My wife passed away on August 21, 1975. I am eighty years old now and still live in Caroline and work at the store every day.

The Hall Story

by Grace Hall

We came to Crammond from Carstairs in November, 1934, Jack and myself (Grace) and our children, Stuart at age eighteen, Kathleen, age thirteen, Doris, age nine, Robert, age four and Gerald at age one.

We had one team of horses, a wagon, sleigh and many tools. All of our household furniture, with the exception of electrical appliances, as I knew there was no power here. We had bought a quarter on section seventeen, but as there were no buildings on it we lived in a little log shack just south of the school house. November was so mild.

We were just nicely settled when it was time for the Christmas Concert. I had brought my piano with me so I took it across the road to the school house, where they held the concert and where the concerts are still held to this day, 1978. It gave the Halls the opportunity to meet the people of the district and we were surprised that there were so many living here, in fact there were more people here then, than at the present time.

We had to drive about seven and one-half miles to Caroline for our supplies and mail. We did all of our trading with Mr. Bob Mitten who had a young boy working for him whom he called 'Chick'. Mr. Mitten carried everything, groceries, nails and many other items and would take anything in trade — rabbits, squirrel skins, lumber, berries, eggs, etc.

At that time we had no gravelled roads, no snowplows for winter, so winter and summer the roads governed whether we went for groceries or made do with what we had. I remember one experience I had, going to Caroline. Mr. Art Lamb had a car so Jack asked him if I could go with him to get a few groceries. We left soon after supper, Mr. Lamb, Sidney Johnson, who worked for Mr. Lamb, and myself. We made good time until we reached what we called the Buchanan Flats, where the car dropped into a mud hole. The men dug and struggled but to no avail, we sat in the car until morning. In the morning we asked Mrs. Buchanan, who lived where Louis Johnson now lives, for a cup of coffee. She gave us a bite to eat and a cup of coffee. By this time it was daylight so we managed to get to Caroline and home before too long.

We had Church every second Sunday in the school house. The minister and his wife drove with a buggy or sleigh winter and summer, from the James River Church about ten miles. How they could keep warm in the bitter cold I could never understand. They always came across the road to our place to have a bite to eat and a cup of tea before they left to return to the James River Church. Mr. and Mrs. Purdy were surely two dedicated people.

The weather was quite mild up until Christmas night. Then it turned bitterly cold and stayed cold until the middle of January. We only had a cook stove that burned wood or coal but there was no coal here so we had to keep a goodly supply of wood on hand and feed the stove continually. We had only clothes suitable for town and they were much too light to withstand the cold, so Mr. Rhodes gave us an airtight heater and after that we were very comfortable.

In January, 1935, I was elected by the school board to serve as their secretary-treasurer, a position I held until it went into the Rocky Mountain House Division. At that time the board consisted of Art Lamb, Bert and Roy Rhodes, in years to follow, Mr. McClarity, Ivan Graham, Mr. Kanten and Mr. Womack. In 1935 and '36 Bill Sloan taught the school, followed by Bill Houlton in '37 and '38 and George Boorman in 1939. The first girl I met was Mrs. George Bugbee (Sally Miller). In about 1937 Bert Rhodes built a store across the road, east of the building where the Crammond Store now stands. That ended the long tiresome trips to Caroline.

During the winter of 1935 Jack and Stuart cut enough logs to have lumber made into a house. We moved into it in July though it wasn't quite finished. We were given a piece of land to put a garden in and in the fall I was astounded at the amount of wild fruit that was to be had for the picking — twelve different varieties. We had dug a cellar, so by the time November came I had the cellar full of fruit and vegetables. All we lacked was meat, but rabbits were plentiful so I learned to cook them in many ways. I made my own soap, baked my own bread, so our grocery bills were very low. Then I found that I could pick enough blueberries in one day to buy a sack of flour and a pound of tea. We bought Eckville flour at one dollar for fifty pounds. We couldn't afford coffee so didn't buy any. We bought skimmed milk from Mrs. Art Lamb for twenty-five cents a week, seven quarts, now skimmed milk is fifty cents a litre and seven litres costs three dollars and fifty cents.

In the summer of 1935 we broke up a bit of land, one and a half acres or so, and in 1936 we planted a huge garden and seeded the rest to wheat. My garden yielded beyond my wildest hopes, one hundred fifty bushels of potatoes alone. We had bought a milk cow from Mr. Dave Knight so we fed her potatoes all winter. I took care of my garden with a six inch hoe and the only time you could hoe was from four-thirty or five in the morning until about eleven. You could not hoe at night or in the evening on account of the mosquitoes. If you braved them and went to visit a neighbour in the evening, they would be sitting beside a pail with a smudge in it. Those pests lasted from May until the end of August, then at times a new batch would hatch and they visited you while you picked berries.

In 1935 I bought a hand mill. I got wheat from

Art Lamb, washed it, dried it in the oven, put the fine blade on my mill, ground up the wheat and I made brown bread, whole wheat bread and muffins. Then I put the coarse blade on and made porridge of it, so twenty pounds of rolled oats and fifty pounds of flour lasted quite a long time.

In the fall our wheat was frozen but Mr. Graham threshed it anyway. I had a weaner pig given to me so I fed it milk and boiled wheat and it grew to an enormous size. When I sold it I got sixteen dollars. I don't remember exactly how many pairs of shoes I bought with the money but I think it was four.

In 1935 Jack went to the prairie to work in the harvest field. He worked from seven in the morning until six at night, for a dollar a day. He went every year until 1939 when the war broke out. Then he got work here, stooking, threshing, etc. This money saw us through the winter.

By 1937 we had accumulated fourteen head of cattle and were shipping cream, but we made the mistake of getting too many head for the amount of feed we had, so that winter and spring we lost five head. We bought as much feed and chop as we could afford but there was no tame hay in the country, only slough, and it was all cut and none was for sale as each farmer needed it for their own use.

We lost one of our horses so Mr. Art Lamb gave us a horse to use until we could buy another. We bought a horse from Mr. Runham, later, one from Sidney Johnson and one from Albert Hill. Mrs. Fleet and Mrs. Art Lamb set some hens for me and I had a few hens given to me by a friend in Carstairs. By 1937 I had enough eggs for our own use and some to sell. Two dozen eggs at eight cents a dozen bought a pound of butter at sixteen cents. I never mastered the art of making good butter until years later.

In 1942 we bought land from Mr. and Mrs. Burwash, the northwest quarter of section eighteen. Then we were two and a half miles from school, Gerald was eight and Robert was eleven but they missed very few days. In August Robert was ill so we had to send him to Holy Cross Hospital in Calgary for an operation. He was in Calgary from August until November, and there was no medicare to pay his bill. We were getting two cream cheques a week, so we paid the doctor one cream cheque, we lived on the other, the next week the hospital got the cheque instead of the doctor.

In 1943 I worked in the store for Bert Rhodes in order to send Robert to school. In 1944 he had to go back to the hospital for another operation and we went through the same process of paying. In 1947 I was in the same hospital for an operation. In my days of being there, blood transfusions were not free so when I had to have them I was lucky enough to have friends who volunteered to replace the blood that was given to me so I didn't have to pay. The charge, I believe, was five dollars for each transfusion.

In 1948 we bought Mr. Art Lamb's place and in 1950 we bought the place we now live on, S.W. 19. By this time our milk cows had increased to seventeen and Jack and the boys milked by hand as we had no power. I couldn't milk so my part was washing and scalding nine milk pails morning and night and washing a huge separator every morning. Sometimes it was ten o'clock at night when I finished, they never finished milking and feeding calves until after nine, so they put in long hours too. In 1951 I got my first gasoline washing machine. I had a few hand machines but they were so hard to turn, I couldn't seem to get the clothes clean either, so I washed on the board for seventeen years. I still have my glass wash board.

In 1951 we bought our first truck, a light delivery. Jack bought it, but Bob drove it. In the '60s we got the phone and power in. I have all electrical appliances, water in the house, colored television, so there is nothing more to acquire.

As for my family, they are all married. Laura never has lived at Crammond as she was through school and working when we came here. Edith never has lived here but she spent perhaps a year or so with us. Stuart was here for a couple of years or so then he went to Tech in Calgary and took up the study of lumber and carpentry, etc. He went with the Atlas Lumber Company first and when they sold to Revelstoke he went with them and has been running yards, trouble shooter, estimator, etc. He retires on pension in April of this year. He is at Cranbrook, British Columbia.

Kathleen (Tiny) worked for her board for three years in Carstairs, got her grade twelve and married. She lives in Vancouver and works in the Post Office.

Doris got her elementary here and worked for her board in Dickson. She stayed with Mr. and Mrs. Herby Westergaard. Miss Gunderson and Bill Sloan and others were her teachers. Doris became a teacher and she taught at James River, Stauffer and then in Red Deer until she married. She lives on a farm six miles east of Innisfail.

Robert lives on the farm here on nineteen. We turned over the stock and machinery and land, but we kept the house where I now live at present.

Gerald went with the Wheat Pool when he was twenty-one and now lives in Calgary and commutes to Olds everyday where he is teaching a training course for the Wheat Pool at the College.

We have spent our twenty-fifth, fiftieth and sixtieth wedding anniversaries in the Crammond area. Jack died in 1975 at age eighty-one. I am eighty-four and have twelve grandchildren and eight great-grandchildren. We both worked very hard here, but we had a very rewarding life.

The Kantens
by Elsie (Kanten) Little

My father, Gilbert Kanten, was born in Minnesota in 1898, and my mother, Helen, was born in Norway in 1892. They were married in North Dakota, and left there to homestead in southern Saskatchewan in 1910. They lived and farmed there until the drought in 1929, and after three years of that, they decided to move. In 1931, Dad, Grandpa Kanten and Uncle Henry (Dad's brother) came to Alberta looking for land, which they got, so in 1932 we all moved to Alberta.

Dad came on the C.P.R. in a box car with a team of horses, some cows and a couple of calves and some other necessary things. A colt was born in the box car on the way, which he called C.P. He landed in Innisfail about the middle of May. I came with Uncle Henry in a car, such as it was, and Grandpa and Grandma Kanten, Henry and his wife, Hulda, and their baby, Colleen. We were on the road a week from Lisieux, Saskatchewan, to Innisfail. The roads were not very good and we ran into a lot of rain and muddy roads. We also had some car trouble. We got to Innisfail about the same time as Dad. We camped at the camp grounds there until the 25th of May.

On the 26th we started out from Innisfail to Caroline. Dad and I herding the cattle and Grandpa on a wagon driving ahead of us. What a day that was! Rain and sleet all the way the first day and it was cold too. We got to Jake Hansen's, at Spruce View, that evening. We were all soaking wet. Jake made supper for us, as Lena, Jake's wife, wasn't at home. She was out to a Ladies Aid that afternoon. We stayed there overnight and were the best of friends as long as they were there. The next day, the 27th of May, we trudged along the same way until we came to Dad's new place, which is three miles east of Caroline and one and a half miles south. We lived in two tents down by the bridge (Raven River) for a month until they had a house built. It rained just about every day.

In the fall, mother and the rest of the kids came. Ervin came in a boxcar with a few horses, machinery, furniture, etc., and landed in Innisfail on October 31. Mother came in a car with the kids; Uncle Henry had gone back for her. They landed at the farm on November 4, 1932. I say "the rest of the kids" as there are eight of us. Ervin was born in 1910, Elsie in 1913, Esther in 1915, Walter in 1917, Florence in 1921, Oscar in 1924, Leonard in 1927 and Glen in 1931.

It was pretty tough going those first few years. Dad had no money and everyone was pretty hard up. The first few years Dad worked in the fall for Bill Lewis; harvesting and threshing. Ervin also worked for Bill Lewis for quite a few years, and, of course, Esther and I also worked out. We didn't make much but at least we didn't eat up all the food at home. The winter of 1932 or 1933 I worked at Ed Kenny's in Innisfail. I got $7.00 a month which wasn't bad, but I really had to work too.

There was no land cleared when we came out here so of course Dad and the boys had to do that before anything could be planted. They cut logs and had them sawed into lumber for building. There were a few slab shacks built also.

As for money — there wasn't any! Mom made butter and could sell an odd pound at the store. She also picked blueberries and sold some and canned lots. She even killed rabbits and sold them to Bob Mitten. He used to have a pile of rabbits behind the store the size of a small hay stack. They were sold to the store for a few groceries, like tea, coffee, sugar, flour, salt — just the very necessary things.

I remember one time Dad got a cheque from the Grain Growers and he was so happy. He went to Caroline and ordered quite a few groceries. I guess he hadn't looked at his cheque too closely as when he went to pay for them, Bob said, "Gilbert, this cheque is for 45¢." All the time Dad thought it was for $45.00. Poor Dad!

We bought (or traded for) our groceries and things we needed at Bob Mitten's store in Caroline, and the mail came to Caroline as there was a Post Office. Mrs. Suhr had it for quite a few years. We used to ride horseback for groceries, etc., most of the time. The old hitching post was in front of the store.

We had real nice neighbors. Dick Rhodes and family were about one mile east; Vern Tricker and family were one mile west; right across the river was Willard Axtell and family. About four miles south, near Crammond School, were Wrens, Andersons, Lambs, Fleets, Runhams and two brothers of Dick Rhodes'.

Crammond School was the place we used to have basket socials, dances, etc., and everyone had a good time. We also used to have a lot of house parties which were lots of fun. There was quite a few, at that time, who played the violin, guitars, banjos, etc., so we never lacked for music.

It was the Crammond School where the four youngest children went. That was Florence, Oscar, Leonard and Glen, but I cannot name any of their teachers. We four older children went to Kanten's School in Saskatchewan.

Like I said before it was pretty slim picking

for Mom and Dad those first years, and a lot of hard work. And then in 1935 our house burned down. Just Mother and my youngest brother were at home. All they saved was the sewing machine and a violin. Then they had to start all over again.

In 1941 Walter joined the army. He was in the Kings Own Rifles, then was transferred to the South Alberta Regiment and was sent overseas that same year. He came home for Christmas in 1945. Ervin joined the army in 1942. He was in the third division of First Hussars (Tank Cor.) and was sent overseas the same year. He was wounded on the forty-ninth day of the invasion of France, and came home on a stretcher in September, 1944.

ESTHER was the first to get married. She married Edwin Hansen in 1934 and had three children, Twilla, Rodney and Karen. Twilla married Mike Keisler and has three children, Ronda, Katherine and Candice. Ronda married Chris Russel and has two children. Kathy has one girl and Candice has one child. Rodney married Eva Madkin and they live in California. Edwin passed away in 1971.

ERVIN married Bertha Stewart in 1950. They have no children and live in Caroline. ELSIE (myself) married David Little in 1940 and we have no children. David passed away in 1976. WALTER married Iva Tricker in 1941 and have two children, Kenneth and Deborah. Debby married Larry Kobza and has one girl, Nicol. They live in Red Deer. FLORENCE married George O'Brien in 1939 and have three children, Grant, Sharon and Patricia. Pattie married Lyle Jacobson. Florence and George live in Red Deer. OSCAR married Phyllis O'Dell in 1947 and have

Gilbert and Ervin Kanten, before Ervin went overseas.

54

The Gilbert Kanten family — back row — Elsie, Ervin, Florence, Walter, Ester — front row — Gilbert, Leonard, Glen, Mrs. Kanten and Oscar behind his mother.

three children, Carol, Penelope and Kevin. Carol married Wayne Ross and have one child, Jason. Oscar has one more girl, Fager, by a second marriage. Phyllis died in 1972.

LEONARD married Toots Peterson in 1950. They have five children, Sonja, Buzzie, Sidney, Alty and Nigel. Sonja married Clayton Haney and they have two children, Cody and Carmen. Sidney married Donna Katona. They all live at Caroline. GLEN married Rosalie Audy in 1952 and they had two children, Dwayne and Sandra. Dwayne married Susan Bingham and they have two boys, Peter and Paul. Glen is still on the farm, but Rosalie passed away in 1968.

Mother and Dad lived on the farm until 1952 when they moved to Caroline. Glen and Rosalie took over the farm. They lived in Caroline until Dad's death in 1964. He was buried in the Caroline Cemetery. Mother stayed alone until 1975 when she sold the house and moved to Autumn Glen Lodge in Innisfail. Mother joined the Ladies Auxiliary in 1953, and did a lot of work for them, like making quilts, crocheting, baking, etc. She still belongs to the Auxiliary and has a life membership. Ervin also is an active member in the Legion, and has been since 1946. Dad also belonged to the Legion up until his death.

Oh yes — Ervin also gave us all the first electric lights in Caroline. He started the lightplant and garage in 1947. Having the power certainly was a boon to Caroline. Then in 1952 he sold to the Calgary Power Co. but kept the garage until he retired in 1975.

Grandma and Grandpa Kanten had their home at Sylvan Lake. Grandpa died in 1945 and Grandma lived until 1963, to the age of ninety-seven years. They are both buried in the Sylvan Lake Cemetery.

Arthur Lee Lamb and Carl A. Lamb

Pauls's two brothers, Art and Carl, also came to the Caroline and Crammond areas. Art came in 1910 and homesteaded the S.E. Sec. 20-35-5-5.

In 1922 he married Fern Waddell. He owned and operated Lamb's Transport and Filling Station at Caroline and Art's General Store at Crammond in turn. He passed away in 1973 at the age of eighty years. He is buried in the Innisfail Cemetery.

Carl came to Canada about 1922 and made his home with his brothers. He played the violin in the band for a while, and returned to the States in 1928 where he still resides.

In 1971, Paul and Helen sold the Crammond farm and retired to the hamlet of Spruce View, Alberta. They have been very happy there, where Helen has a large class of music pupils and Paul is pursuing his favorite hobby of trapping.

Paul J. Lamb and Family

Paul was born in Indiana, U.S.A., in 1901, and came to the Caroline district in 1914. After spending some years working around the Olds and Eagle Hill districts, he filed on a homestead (S.E. Q. 18-35-5-5) which is now in the Crammond area. This was in 1919 when he was eighteen

Lamb's orchestra — Carl Lamb, Wilbur Cross, Oscar Anderson, Helen and Paul Lamb.

Helen, Louella and Paul Lamb.

Four generations: Standing — Bessie Reese, Anita Reese — Seated — Lillie Ennis, Marilyn Reese.

years of age. In 1926 he married Helen Ennis from Milk River, Alberta.

The homestead was their home for twenty years. The one bright spot in the few years after this, was the music. They formed a band to keep the farm going, as the depression hit us then. When the Caroline Hall was finished, a new piano was brought in. Paul, Helen, Oscar Anderson and Wilbur Cross played for the opening dance. The winter preceding the new hall's completion, Helen and the Anderson boys played in the Wooler School helping to raise money for the hall. In the 1950s their band broke up and they bought the south half of the school section, where they farmed for twenty years. In about 1950 Helen started teaching music and is still in the business.

Their daughter, Luella, was born in 1929 and attended Crammond School. In 1948 she married Alex Youngman. They have travelled extensively, doing missionary work. Luella spent some time in Gold Coast, Africa. They have a family of six children, and their present home is in Sicamous, British Columbia.

LILLIE AND BRICE ENNIS

In 1943 Helen's parents came and made their home with them. Helen's father passed away in 1944 at the age of eighty-four, but her mother made her home in the Crammond and Caroline areas until 1950. They are both buried in the Raven Cemetery.

Chester Miller

by Chester Miller

My father, George Miller, was born in Odin, Minnesota, in the year 1877. He took up a homestead two miles south and twelve west of Innisfail, arriving there by ox cart in 1901. He was a member of the Fraternal Society of Modern Woodsmen and helped build some of the log houses in the district, as well as the Cottonwood School, which he named. He also served on the local school board for several years. My mother was born August 3, 1883, in Dereham Township, Oxford County, Toronto, Ontario. My father and she were married at Red Lodge, in 1903. They survived many hardships as ours was a large family, consisting of three girls and six boys.

I was born in 1912 and first attended school at Cottonwood in 1919. My first teacher was Mr. Earl Blain, who was a resident of that district, and lived about two miles from the school. He later did clerking at the Marshal Wells store in Innisfail. My oldest brother was Roy, born in 1904. He came west to Caroline, in 1928, and worked for Jesse Sandborn on a sawmill for four years. He then bought a quarter section, the land on which I reside at present. In 1938 he married a widow, Mrs. Gladys Phillips, and they raised sheep on this place, until 1942, when they moved back onto my father's place where they resided until Roy's death from cancer in 1964. The rest of my surviving brothers and sisters are scattered about as follows. Charlotte Whitney (retired) lives at Millet, Alberta. Floyd farms at Bowden; Clarence at Enderby, British Columbia; Isabel Estey at Golden, British Columbia; and Fred is farming at Innisfail. My mother passed away July 4, 1977, at the ripe old age of ninety-three. I came west to the Caroline area in 1932, mainly because my brother, Roy, lived here and I really loved the country. I lived with Roy for several years and saw some pretty tough times. The main reason we survived was that the rabbits were very numerous in those days. We would shoot them in the winter time and when we got four to five hundred of them we would put them in a wagon box, hook the team up and take them

Sadie, Miller, Paul Miller, Charlie Woods, Granny Reid, Vi Wood, George Miller.

George and Sadie Miller, Isabel, Paul and Fred, 1931.

to Caroline where Bob Mitten ran the grocery store. He gave us three cents apiece in trade or two cents cash. When the rabbits got thinned out we would cut tamarack posts and take them out near Innisfail, by team and sled. There we sold them for a price range of three to ten cents for a seven-foot post, and to get ten cents, they had to be four to six inch tops. Then in 1938 Roy got the crazy notion to get married, so I had to move out or sleep three in one bed. Roy didn't think much of that idea, so I made a deal with a man by the name of Fred Kreisch, who had homesteaded a quarter section cornering the one my brother had, to the southwest, the S.E.Q. 4-36-5-5. The first winter there was really tough. I lived in a granary with only one ply of boards and tar paper. I was able to borrow a little cast iron heater, with one lid on top, from my nearest neighbor, Mr. August Anderson, who lived on the same section as I did. That spring he told me I could take a couple of his cows and milk them if I wished. I did, and that at least gave me a cream cheque so I could buy something to eat. I never did see the man I bought the land from, but he was very good to deal with. He owed about $200.00 back taxes and told me if I would pay the taxes and give him $700.00, I could have it on terms of $100.00 a year for seven years. Even at that there were, I think, two years that I couldn't make a payment of any kind, but he never complained. He lived at Kowichan Lake, B.C.

Then came the problem of breaking my land which had been broke by Mr. Kreisch, but had gone back to bush. I had an uncle, Fred Miller, who lived on the place that Roy Como has now,

and he loaned me his old John Deere tractor and breaking plow. All I had to supply was the gas and oil. I managed to break forty acres the first summer. The second winter I didn't want a re-occurrence of the first. Mr. Edward Fleet told me if I wanted to help his son, Joe, with chores, etc., I could stay the winter there, and guess who I met there — the girl that I later married, Marie Fleet. She was the second eldest daughter of Mr. and Mrs. Edward Fleet. We were married on October 29, 1940, at the home of the bride. We couldn't afford to put a dance on in a hall, so we had a little dance in Ivan Grahams' house and everyone brought lunch. We were blessed with seven children, five girls and two boys. Our oldest son, Larry, married Carolyn Schie of Innisfail. They live in Innisfail but he works for Stewarts Supplies, Penhold. George married Bonnie Bancroft of Dovercourt. They live in Olds and he is manager of Crown Mart in Olds. Loreane, our eldest daughter, married Gerald McGregor of Dovercourt, but has recently moved to Dixonville, Alberta. Our second daughter, Florence, married Fred Hamilton (school teacher) and they reside in Lethbridge. Our third daughter, Mary, married Edward Morton (mechanic) of Innisfail, and he works for Flint of Red Deer. Our fourth daughter, Gloria, married Rae Auld of Innisfail (truck driver). They reside in Coleman, Alberta. Our youngest daughter, May, married Dale Ennis of Caroline, and he works for Altana Gas and Oil.

We are real proud of our family and rightly so.

William (Bill) John Neal
by Lucile Neal

Bill was born in Havre, Montana, February 19, 1897. Mildred Lucile Neal (Harris) was born in Burlington, Washington, June 13, 1912. We were married January 5, 1933, in Innisfail.

Bill spent his life up to, and into his teens, in Montana where he received his education. He was a cow hand and he also broke horses. He went back to Montana for a few years after he came to Canada the first time.

He came to Alberta when he was seventeen years old with his parents, Mr. and Mrs. Thomas Neal. He had four brothers, Tom, Arch, Sam and Richard and one sister, Ruth. They settled in the Raven district where Mr. and Mrs. Neal farmed and raised their family.

Ruth Neal (now Mrs. Art Childs) lives in Rocky. She taught the South Fork School in 1919 and Shilo School in 1920. Some of the children she taught were Daisy Wyant (Harris), the older Art Bowers' children, Ray, Ralph, Catherine and Dolly, Jerry Vandermeer, Guy Eunice and Joy

Fay, Ernest and George Miller as well as some others who are gone.

Bill was a mechanic and worked at Innisfail, Claresholm and High River before I met him. He used to ride at the stampedes at Hale Lake and Finkles Grove. Finkles Grove was the land across south of Frank Heare's place (now Dean Dolls) in the thick spruce trees.

After we were married, we lived north of Caroline. Bill operated a caterpillar helping to build roads in the Caroline, Raven, Stauffer and Rocky Mountain House areas. Some of the men who ran the grader behind the cat were Frank Davis, Bill Cross, Howard Harris, Steve Dutton and Cliff Pollard. Tom McKenzie did the cooking and set up road stakes.

We then moved to the New Hill district where he did some farming and continued to run cat on road building to help keep the farm and pay expenses. The 1930's were hard times for everyone, Bill's wages were from thirty-five to seventy-five cents an hour. A five gallon can of cream, special, thirty-three test brought a dollar twenty-five, eggs three cents per dozen, a market size pig two dollars and fifty cents and a cow might bring ten dollars.

In 1939 we bought a quarter of land and moved to the Crammond area where we still reside. This place was really run down, buildings, fences, etc., and no well. We hauled water from a spring for the house and drawn by saddle horse. The two boys were two and five years old then and we were alone as Bill still had to work out to make money enough to build up our place and support the family. He worked for the Forestry running the cat at the Crows Nest Pass, Frank, Bellevue and around Corbin, British Columbia. Later he worked at the Raven Fish Rearing Station driving cat to build the first ponds.

When we could, we started farming; milked cows, raised chickens and pigs as a side line. We sawed lumber and later had a lath mill to make enough money to keep family and farm. Bill had papers to run a steam engine, which he did later on, for steam boilers for oil rigs.

We have two boys, Merle, born October 14, 1933, at Caroline. Duane was born July 7, 1937, at Innisfail. Merle was born premature, he was very small and fragile. We didn't weigh him at birth because he was so tiny it was a chore to do the necessary things for him, but we did weigh him when he was one month old and he weighed three and a quarter pounds. The Doctor said he wouldn't live as he could neither cry or nurse, but with the kind and loving care of a wonderful neighbor, Mrs. Thibedeau, and my mother in those first crucial days, he came through and became a strong and healthy man. He married Frances Evans of Caroline. They had six

children, but the first one, a boy, was stillborn. The other children are Wesley, Leslie, Heather, Russel and Rodney. Wesley married Francis Ankle and they have a little girl, Janette. Heather is married to Cal Caron, a boy from the Raven area.

Duane weighed five pounds two ounces when he was born, the nurses called him Peanuts and Jellybean, he was the smallest of the seventeen babies, all girls and he was the only boy in the nursery. Duane married Glenna Evans of Calgary but she was not related to Merle's wife in spite of them having the same maiden names. Duane has a farm, cattle and horses, his hobby is horses which Glenna and their three children, Patricia, Alex and Tom, also enjoy.

Bill and I are now able to relax and enjoy our family and hobbies. We help out when we can and when we are needed. Bill turns hides into rawhide and braids bridles, reins, hackamores, lariats and quirts, not an easy task but he enjoys it and spends hours working at it.

I do Reflexology and study Magnetics of the body, and also took courses in St. Johns Ambulance First Aid, cake decorating, stretch and sew and took driving lessons, all of this since my late fifties and I enjoy everyone of these projects. For relaxation I knit or play the organ. There are no limits to the things we can do when we are in or are approaching our Golden Years, if we have our health and well being to do so, and Bill and I are both quite well and are happy and we feel very thankful that we are so fortunate. We have had our tribulations in sickness, hard times and worries, but these things have helped us to appreciate the better things in life that we now enjoy.

Bill Pitts
by George F. Pitts

My father and mother came to Canada in 1906. Dad homesteaded eleven miles east of Carmangay, at Bowville, and we lived on the homestead until the spring of 1911. We then moved to the Talbert place on the Little Bow River and in 1912 we moved to Champion and lived there until 1916. We then moved to Kirkcaldy where we ran a restaurant for four years. In 1919 we moved up to Ricinus and 1922 we moved to Caroline on the Langley place east of the old store.

I, George F. (Pinky) Pitts, homesteaded seven and one half miles southeast of Caroline in the Crammond district. Dad and Mother lived with me until 1927 when they bought a C.P.R. quarter three miles south of my homestead.

There were four of us boys, Earl, Clarence, Wilbert and myself, George.

We had a good ballteam called the Clearwater

Mr. W. Pitts and son Francis (Pink) taken at the Patterson place at Ricinus.

Florence and George Pitts.

Beavers and I played from 1922 to 1926. The pitchers were Jack Bugbee and Martin Justinen. Catchers were Red Womack, Ed Pewonka and myself. First baseman was Wilbert Pitts, second baseman was Paul Lamb and short stop was sometimes Jack Bugbee or Martin Justinen. Third baseman was Bill Cross, right fielder was Elmer Hagsed, center field, Wick Burns and left fielder, Bill Justinen.

In 1927 I moved to Olds and played ball there. In Olds, Florence McNutt and I were married in 1942. Our son, Deryk, was born in 1945. In 1947 we moved to Nobleford and I did welding at Nobles Cultivator Factory for twenty-one years.

Deryk now lives west of Red Deer by Condor, and has a saddle shop at Blackfalds. He is married and has three little girls. We still live at Nobleford.

Bessie (Edith Rhodes) Reese

I was born in Minnesota, U.S.A. When I was very young my family moved to Fort Morgan, Colorado, U.S.A. After I was nine years old my family moved to Alberta, Canada. My father, Brice Ennis, and my brother, Harry Ennis, homesteaded about twenty miles east of the Town of Milk River, Alberta. I went to Milk River Valley School. After that I went to the sister of my mother and finished school; then taught school for two years. During that time my brother and his wife moved north, by covered wagon, with a herd of cattle. They settled about four miles east of Crammond, Alberta. When they had lived there about three years I visited them and met Roy Rhodes, whom I later married.

After Roy and I were married we lived on the N.W. Q. 28-35-5-5, which had been purchased from Ed Fleet and sold to the Rhodes'. Roy Rhodes had homesteaded the northeast quarter of section 28 and later purchased the Richard Rhodes' S.E.Q. of Sec. 28. The S.W.Q. of sec. 28 was Burton Rhodes' homestead.

While we lived there we had horses, pigs, chickens, sheep and cattle. We milked cows and sold cream in Sundre. We raised crops and hay. Our three children were born during the years we lived on the farm. They all went to the Crammond school until high school. Anita took grade twelve at Dickson, Alberta, and Harry never went beyond what he could get at Crammond. In June, when Wilbur was about finished with grade eleven and twelve and a business course away from home. Wilbur took grade twelve at Dickson, Alberta, and Harry never went beyond what he could get at Crammond. In June, when Wilbur was about finished with grade twelve, Roy was working under a truck and it fell down on him and killed him.

I tried to carry on the farm work, but it was too hard. A few years later, I married Wallace Reese. Three years later we moved into Caroline and constructed a house in which we still live.

In 1952 the Village of Caroline was organized. Mrs. Lillian Moger was the first secretary-treasurer for the Village. In 1953 I took over as the Secretary-Treasurer and kept this position for over twenty years, until the end of 1973. I was a Justice of the Peace for many years, and I was also Commissioner of Oaths until after I had retired.

Anita, my daughter, married Merle Reese. They lived in Caroline for several years and had a daughter named Marilyn. When Marilyn was educated in school and music she married Bryan Taylor. They now have two children.

Wilbur Rhodes, my son, taught school for several years, then took up work with the Meteorological Department and will be eligible to retire in a few more years. He married Frederica Jean Troupe while he was still teaching school. They have five children:

Dorothy Jean, who later married Jay Malcolm and Patricia Margaret, who later married Peter Collsen. The third child was Allan Roy Rhodes, who married Mona Vivian Courtright. The two youngest are still single, Jo Anne Rhodes and Robert William Rhodes.

Harry Lester Rhodes, my third child, grew up at Crammond, near Caroline. Later he married Ellen Kyler. They have three children: Deborah Louis, who married Fred Brigman; Darlene, who married Domenec Demarzo and the youngest is Kenneth Rhodes.

When I retired I had an insurance agency but later sold it to Harry McDonald in Innisfail.

Evan W. Reese Family
by Merle Reese

In the spring of 1938 my father purchased the S.W.Q. 15-35-5-5 from the C.P.R., better known to the people of that day as the Pitts place, who were the first settlers on the land. We fenced and put some buildings on it. After we had put the crop in at Didsbury, Dad and I gathered all the tools and equipment we would need to start our land breaking program at Crammond. We left Mother behind to milk the cows and do the chores while we were working on the new farm. We were joined by my brother, Wallace, who had first set foot in the district in 1931. It was no easy task to round up ten or twelve head of horses early every morning, to groom them well and harness. Wallace was the chief skinner. He could handle eight head very nicely on a Vanslack breaking plow while Dad and I worked at grubbing trees; clearing land for some years. By the first week of July we had approximately fifty acres broken.

Early in 1939, Dad and Wallace started to enlarge the house that was on the farm, in preparation for making the final move from the Didsbury district. I lost count of the trips we made with team and wagon over what we called the Sundre hills. It was a total distance of thirty-

Merle Reese and his mother in 1928.

Mr. and Mrs. George McClarty.

two miles, a big, long day both for horses and man. By the middle of the summer the last trip was completed.

The winter of 1939-40 Dad and I joined George McClarty as he had a considerable amount of logging to do. The job of hauling the logs to Burt Rhodes' sawmill and helping with the sawing was a new experience. By financial necessity we were forced to go out to Section 37 muskeg to cut tamarack posts and fence rails.

Evan Reese family — Mr. and Mrs. Reese, Wallace and Merle.

60

Merle Reese.

In May, 1941, I left home to join the Air Force and was discharged in 1945. Anita Rhodes and I were married on June 8, 1944, at the Raven Union Church. Anita is the daughter of Roy and Bessie Rhodes. The Rhodes family was among the early pioneers of the Crammond district.

In the summer of 1946 I opened a hardware store in Caroline. In February, 1947, my parents sold their farm and moved to Caroline, and Dad joined me in the hardware business. On July 24, 1947, our daughter, Marilyn, was born. Later I sold my interest in the hardware to my dad.

In the spring of 1950 we moved to Bowden, where I worked for Walter Sick for some years. For the last twenty-two years we have made our home in Calgary. On September 15, 1972, Marilyn was married to Bryan Taylor. They have two children and make their home in Calgary.

In tribute to my parents who came to Alberta in 1907, from the state of Montana and settled at High River as a pioneer family: they suffered their share of hardships and discouragements, but were able to provide a good home for their three children, of whom they were very proud. Mother's death was on November 16, 1954. Dad made his home, some of the time, with us, until his death on May 26, 1967.

Wallace Reese

I was born near Bozeman, Montana, on October 25, 1900. I was the oldest child of Evan and Emma Reese, who were both born and raised in Montana. In April, 1907, my father and mother moved to High River, Alberta, where my father had purchased land on the Highwood River (known as section 22) in the fall of 1906. He brought with him two carloads of settler effects, horses, machinery, household goods and furniture. On November 29, 1908, my sister, Anita, was born. I spent many hours as a child fishing in a creek on my parents place and also fished in the Highwood River. When I was eight years old I started school at the old Highwood School which was located four and a half miles from home. The first year my parents drove me to school. The next year I was able to ride a horse but had several gates to open and close on the way. Sometimes my saddle pony would refuse to go any further than the second gate and turn around and go home. I had a holiday from school on those days. In April, 1917, my parents moved to where East Longview is now, where my sister and I attended Big Hill School. We only lived a mile and a quarter from school, so we were able to walk. After my parents had moved to Longview and my sister and I were attending school at Big Hill, a teacher, by the name of Charles McKenzie, came to the school. He had previously been teaching at the Highwood School when we were there. We sure learned a lot from him. Unfortunately we only attended school for six months while he was teaching there.

In 1919 my father purchased a quarter section of land, twelve miles west of Didsbury, and after school was finished in June of that year, we

Marilyn Reese.

Bessie and Wallace Reese.

61

moved onto the farm. We were two and one half miles from school. My sister and I rode to school. On October 31, 1920, my brother, Merle, was born. I finished school in June of 1921 and worked and farmed in the Didsbury area, until 1931, when I purchased land from the Hudson Bay Company in the Caroline area known as the N.E.Q. 8-36-5-5. During the summer of 1932 and 1933 I broke up sixty acres on this land and fenced it, also built a house and barn on it. I farmed this and other land, until 1941, when I went to Didsbury to work for a year. During this time my brother had joined the Air Force and I came home in 1942 to help my father with the farm work. On June 27, 1945, Bessie Rhodes and I were married in the Kevisville Church. We lived on a farm in the Crammond area for three years. In 1948 we had an auction sale of the cattle, horses and machinery and moved to Caroline. In June of 1948 I started carrying the mail from Caroline to Dickson. This route was changed several times, becoming a daily mail in 1959. I retired from this work on June 30, 1977, with a total of twenty-nine years of service. I was presented with a plaque, on retirement, in recognition of twenty-five years service in the Public Service of Canada.

We started to build our present home in Caroline in 1948 and have lived here for thirty years. We've seen Caroline grow from a small hamlet, with a two room school, to a village of four hundred people, with a large school and a staff of twenty-six teachers. During 1961 my wife purchased a General Insurance Agency which we operated until June, 1975, when it was sold to Harry McDonald of Innisfail. I served on the council of the Village of Caroline from February, 1956, until October, 1971. In October, 1977, I was again elected to council and have been serving as Mayor since that time. I have been on the Board of Directors of Westview Lodge, Rocky Mountain Foundation, since it was opened in September, 1960. My wife and I are now retired and enjoy attending meetings of the Golden Age Club in Caroline. We have a large garden each year, which I get enjoyment working in, and it helps keep us busy.

Richard Rhodes

Richard Guy Rhodes was born in Blue Earth County, Minnesota, in 1884. His father and his mother, Mattie, moved their family across the States, to farm in Oregon and later in Washington. In 1905 the A. I. Rhodes family of three sons: Richard, Burton and Roy, and their three daughters: Ruth, Edythe and Effie, immigrated to Alberta, to farm west of Bowden. The climate in Alberta proved unhealthy for Ruth and it became evident that she must return

Home of Dick Rhodes, Arthur, Helen and Cecil Rhodes.

to the coast. A. I. Rhodes bought a small farm near Sheridan, Oregon. However, he and the boys had been bitten by the lure of Alberta, and returned, leaving the womenfolk in Oregon. The Rhodes men settled in what is now the Crammond District, and Burton Rhodes filed where the Crammond Post Office, much later, was established. Richard filed on the next quarter east.

The Rhodes' boys had the only threshing outfit, a separator and steam engine, in the area for years. They threshed all over the country, from Caroline to east of Innisfail and Bowden.

In the spring of 1913, John McCarthy of Aspden, Ontario, decided to immigrate to the west. He leased a cattle car on a train, for five cows, one horse and two stowaways (his son and daughter, Kryl and Marjorie). Marjorie cooked on their heater in the cattle car. One day the conductor heard John talking. He looked into the car asking John who he was talking to. John calmly answered, "me horse." John's wife and two younger daughters came later, with more cattle, in another cattle car. They homesteaded the land which is now William Biggart's: John on the west quarter and his son, Kryl, on the east quarter. Marjorie McCarthy often rode horseback to get mail and groceries, passing the Rhodes boys' home on her way to the old Caroline store. Always, upon her return, Dick would be waiting with a fine driving team hitched to a buggy or cutter. The saddle horse was led behind while he drove her home. In January, 1917, Marjorie McCarthy became Dick Rhodes' wife.

Soon after Dick and Marjorie's marriage, Dick purchased the Coon place, the S.W.Q. 7-36-5-5, which was their home for many years. Dick continued with his custom threshing, only now with Carl Anderson and his Waterloo Boy tractor.

Horses, being the principal means of farming and travelling — Dick purchased a dapple grey Percheron stallion named Dan, for $800.00, a con-

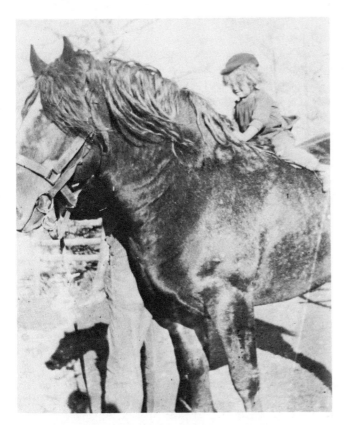
Dick standing and Helen on horse's back.

siderable sum in those days. Dan became the sire of many fine horses of the district.

Dick and Marjorie had six children: Arthur, Helen, Cecil, Dorothy, Lillian and David. The children all attended the old Shilo School, which was built in 1909. The first years of school were only during the summer months. They got an older neighbor girl to live with them and drive "Old Bird", hitched to a one-horse buggy, to school. In later years they rode horseback across country.

For a number of years Dick was trustee and secretary-treasurer of the Shilo School District. He built the school barn at Shilo.

Entertainment in those years was dances, ball games and picnics. Going to one picnic, a six-horse team was required, to pull the democrat across a soft spot in the trail.

In 1963 Dick and his wife retired to the village of Caroline. They sold the farm to their eldest daughter, Helen, and her husband, Harold Torgerson. Arthur and Cecil Rhodes reside in Victoria, working in the Naval Shipyards as electrician and machinist. Helen teaches in the Caroline School. Dorothy became a nurse and now lives on a farm, with her husband and family, at Athabasca. Lillian is a bookkeeper for an Oyen garage. David Rhodes works in Red Deer.

Richard Rhodes passed away in 1966, and was buried in the family plot in the Raven Cemetery, with his father, A.I., and brother, Roy.

Roy Rhodes

Roy Rhodes homesteaded the N.E. Q. 28-35-5-5 in the year 1912. He worked with his two brothers, Richard and Burton. They also had homesteads in the same section. Richard the southeast quarter and Burton the southwest quarter. Later they bought the northwest quarter which Ed Fleet had homesteaded. Richard moved away and Roy and Burton worked together until 1925. The Rhodes' brothers had a steam engine and operated a threshing machine and sawmill. They also had a herd of cattle that ran at large on the range in the summer. Horses were used to farm with and also to ride and drive. The roads were very bad.

Roy married Bessie Ennis in the year 1921, and lived on the northwest quarter of section 28. They had three children, Anita, Wilbur and Harry. The children all attended grade school at Crammond. Anita completed high school and attended secretarial school. She is married to Merle Reese and has one daughter, Marilyn, and lives in Calgary. Wilbur completed high school and one year of university. He taught school two years and later became a meteorological technician. He married Frederica Troupe and they have five children, Dorothy, Patricia, Allan, Joanne and Robert. Wilbur now works at the Vancouver airport and lives at Delta, British Columbia. Harry married Ellen Kyler and they have three children, Debbie, Darlene and Kenny. They live at Lillooet, British Columbia, and Harry is an engineer on the railroad.

Roy passed away in June, 1942, due to an accident. At that time he owned three quarters of section 28. They had a herd of cattle and raised hay and grain.

Roy Rhodes family — Bessie, Roy, Anita, Harry and Wilbur.

Ernest Runham and Family

by Violet Pekse

My father, Ernest Runham, was born in Victoria, British Columbia, in 1894. He moved to Bowden, Alberta with his parents in 1899. My mother, Sarah Fleet, was born in Alliance, Nebraska, and moved to Bowden with her parents in 1900.

As a young man, Pa worked around in several areas until 1914, when he and Mom were married. They moved to the Coronation area and lived and farmed there until 1924. Six of us children were born there and they had accumulated a nice herd of cattle and some horses. Leaving Coronation, they trailed the livestock, herding them along the way. The family and our belongings rode in covered wagons. When we reached Bowden, we stayed at Grandpa Fleet's for awhile. When we left Bowden we headed west to what is now known as Crammond, where we were to live with Uncle Jay Fleet for a time.

When we arrived at Uncle Jay's, Pa turned the cattle out to pasture. They used to go down by Beaver Creek to graze. Larkspur grew in abundance along the creek and Pa lost his whole herd except for two, from eating the plant. After that, Pa had to go out to work to make a living for the family.

We stayed at Uncle Jay's until Pa homesteaded the N. W. Q. 20-35-5-5 and got our log house built. The other five children were born here. This was not a good quarter of land, but it was home. Our neighbors were Ed Fleet, Jay Fleet, Red Womack, Paul Lamb, Clark Wren, Art Lamb, Bert and Roy Rhodes, McClarty, McCarthy, Pinky Pitts, Millers, Nellie Edwards and others.

By 1928 there were four of us children to go to school, but there wasn't a school close enough for us to attend; Pa got a job in Olds and moved the family there. I remember one summer while going to school. There was a mean bull on the open range and he used to chase us to school every day. He had a short plank hanging from his horns to cover his eyes, but it didn't do much good. He would toss his head, flipping the plank up so he could see where we were and then come after us. I don't believe we were ever late for school!

When Pa hurt his back on a job, he moved us back to the homestead. The people who had been fighting to get a school at Crammond, finally won out and so we took the rest of our schooling there.

We couldn't grow much on the pine tree quarter Pa homesteaded, so we lived off the land. We picked blueberries and cranberries and dug seneca root to sell. Pa knew the country so well we always had the best berry patches to pick from. We also cut timber to be sawn into lumber or shingles to sell or trade.

For entertainment we spent many evenings with music and song. Pa played the violin and Mom played the organ while the rest of us sang. Then there were parties held in the school and Pa and Mom supplied the music for dancing. There wasn't an organ or piano at the school so we would load up the organ on the stoneboat and take it. We moved it back and forth so many times that it wore out from moving it so much.

Our family and the neighbor children would have skating parties on McClarty's lake. We would all pile into a sleigh with heated rocks to keep our feet warm and off we would go. At the lake we built a big bonfire on the shore and with a lighted torch in hand, we would skate around the lake. Then there were the sleigh riding parties on

Back row — Ernest Runham, Jay Fleet, Richard (Dick) Graham — Front row — Ida Graham and Sadie Fleet.

The Ernest Runham family taken in 1937.

Ed Fleet's big hill. We would ride our sleighs, scoop shovels or cardboards down the hill at great speed, what fun we had!

Pa was an outdoor man and enjoyed big game hunting, fishing, and trapping and it added to our means of livelihood.

Around 1940 the folks moved to Bowden to take care of Mom's aged father, Grandpa Fleet, and the three youngest children finished their schooling there.

Pa and Mom had eleven children, Jake, Dave, Harold, Violet, Pearl, Don, Lyle, Wava, Della, Cliff and Ersel (Eileen). Mom passed away in April, 1963, and Dave in July of the same year. Jake died in February, 1967, and Pa in March, 1975. The rest of us are scattered around. Harold and Wava are at Mayerthorpe; Don, Della and Cliff at Mora, British Columbia. Ersel is in Calgary and Don lives in the Eagle Hill district and I, Vi Pekse, at Sundre.

We all have fond memories of our days on the old homestead. There were years of joy and happiness to compensate for the hard times endured by our hardy pioneers.

Mr. and Mrs. John C. Schrader

by Agnes E. Schrader

John and Anna Schrader and family moved from Moville, Iowa, to Olds in 1901. They took up homesteads twelve miles west of Olds across the Dog Pound. The family consisted of the parents and five children, John, Albert, Walter, Robert and Ida.

The boys and Ida attended Harrison School and this district became known as Harmattan.

Dad Schrader and his sons accumulated more land and built up a herd of Hereford cattle which were branded bar R.H. In early days they supplied the Great West Company with meat and other supplies and the Schrader home became a stopping place for many going west to the camps and also east to Olds or Calgary.

In 1912 the Ranch at James River was bought by the the Schraders from Graves and Addington. During the spring and summer, the cattle were pastured at the James, and in the fall and winter they were fed at the homeplace at Harmattan. If there was ice on the Big Red, the men brought the cattle by Sundre. It was quite a sight to see the six hundred head of cattle crossing the bridge and the bridge would really dance.

Dad and Mother Schrader have both passed away and are resting in the family plot in Olds Cemetery. Robert also passed away in 1918 and my late husband, Walter, passed away in 1970. Both are resting in the family plot in Olds.

Albert is residing with his sister, Mrs. Ida Sykes, in Calgary. John and his wife, Sadie,

Mr. and Mrs. John C. Schrader.

reside at James River and have three sons, John and Bob live in Calgary and Jim in Kimberley, British Columbia. Ida, Mrs. William Sykes, resides in Calgary. Her husband, William, passed away in 1969.

Walt and I were married in Edmonton in 1932. We lived on the farm at Harmattan until 1940 when we moved to the Schrader Ranch at James River.

Our son, John, (or Jack), was born in 1938. He attended school at Pine View, travelling by dog sled in winter and horse back in spring and summer.

Jack and Margaret Anne Fletcher of James River were married in 1960. Walt and I built on the three quarter sections at Crammond, moving there in the fall of 1960. Walt and Jack farmed the land at James River and Crammond until ill health compelled Walt to retire and he rented the land.

On December 28, 1968, we lost our home and part of the contents by fire. We lived in Sundre until we bought a trailer and came back to Crammond. Walt's health continued to fail and he passed away on July 7, 1970.

Jack and Marg reside on the ranch at James River. They have a family of three, Joanne, Eugene and Edward. The children attend school at Caroline.

I stayed on the farm at Crammond until 1973 when I bought a location in Caroline and moved my trailer there. When these self-contained units were completed in Innisfail in 1977, I sold my holdings in Caroline and moved to number 15, Poplar Grove Court, Innisfail.

Herbert Nelson Simons

Bert, Alice and their daughter Fay came to the Crammond area to live in August 1945. A second daughter, Kay, was born September 1945 in the Olds hospital.

They farmed the S ½-22-35-5-5 and the NW of 15-35-5-5 until April 1971 when they moved to Mission, B.C.

Both daughters attended the old and new Crammond schools, and the high school in Caroline.

Bert and Alice were active community members. Bert was secretary-treasurer of the Caroline Legion for two years and was manager of the Ball Team. Alice was secretary-treasurer of the Community Club and the Sports Committee. She was also C.G.I.T. Leader for three years.

Fay married Jim LeCerf. They have a son and a daughter and live in Eckville.

Kay married Lloyd Craig, has a son and daughter and they live in Wetaskiwin.

Bert died in 1973. Alice still makes her home in Mission, B.C.

Wren History
by the Wren Family

Clark John Wren was born in Hepner, Oregon, United States, on June 18, 1888. He homesteaded south of Castor, Alberta, in 1907 and, using oxen, broke up to four acres of land a day.

During his lifetime, he was married four times. In 1911 he married Maria Chute, born in Maine, United States, who lived in the Hanna District at that time. They had two children, Clarence (Curly) and Laurence (Pete). They farmed at Watts, Alberta. The marriage was short lived as Maria passed away in approximately four years and was laid to rest in the Hanna Cemetery.

Curly and Pete were left with Huttons (neighbors) while Clark roamed around for awhile, eventually ending up at his sister's home in Kooskia, Idaho. While there, he met Pearl Brown, born at Broken Bow, Nebraska, but at the time she was living with her grandparents at Kooskia. They were married at Grangeville, Idaho. They came back to his farm at Craigmyle where Lewis, Mollie (Doel) and Wallace were born. In 1923, due to Pearl's poor health, the family travelled for five years, going to British Columbia and from there, into the States. Living

The second Mrs. Clark Wren, Pearl and Clark.

The first Mrs. Clark Wren, Marie and son Pete.

Clark Wren and his third wife Adella.

in Washington, Oregon, California and Idaho, they stayed wherever Clark could get work. They returned in 1928 to Craigmyle, and the next year sold out and moved to Crammond, Alberta, where he bought the south half and northeast quarter of section 33-35-5-5. There was no land cleared, so the family lived in an old log house across the road.

Clark brought a 15-30 McCormick tractor with him, driven by Pete, which was used to pull one wagon load of machinery to Crammond. The other wagon, driven by Jack O'Connor, was pulled by a team, leading horses and a cow. Curly drove a '28 Chev one ton truck, loaded with belongings, and Clark drove a Chrysler car with the family.

Later that fall, in November, Pearl passed away in the Sanitorium in Calgary and was laid to rest in Burnsland Cemetery there.

Clark found it very hard to carry on by himself and was forced to seek a housekeeper. He inquired at the Unemployment Bureau in Calgary and found a very capable lady, Adela Franklin. She had her son, Jack, with her. The children attended school at Crammond. In March, the spring of 1930, Clark and Adela were united in marriage. This seemed to make the family complete once again. Adela was such a wonderful mother, and Jack was certainly a true brother, and fit right in with the family.

Clark bought a breaking plow and broke 180 acres that first year. He also did some custom breaking. People came from miles around and were amazed to watch him plow under trees six inches in diameter and twenty feet tall.

Times were hard, and logs were cut and hauled to Burton Rhodes' sawmill to be sawed and planed for houses, and other buildings and corrals on the farm. Clark and the boys cut tamarack posts which were hauled to Olds, and traded to Davey Brothers General Store, for supplies. In later years, many rabbits and squirrels were sold by the boys to Bob Mitten at Caroline. Clark purchased a threshing machine and did custom threshing in Crammond, Caroline and Ricinus.

Over the years, quite a large herd of cattle was acquired, and also pigs. He kept a stallion and raised colts, too, which were used for riding and work and occasionally, horses were traded. This was more or less one of his hobbies. He had one team of thoroughbreds which made a record trip to Innisfail in four hours and one trip to Sundre in two hours. During the summer, hay was put up from the numerous sloughs, on open land in the surrounding area, for winter feed. From ths Sundre corner south to Crammond, there were only a few settlers—the Rhodes brothers, Burt, Roy and Dick and the Anderson brothers, Oscar, Aug and Carl. Consequently, there was

quite a bit of summer range for the cattle (and the cattle thrived). Due to hard times, a lot of wild berries were picked and canned. Also a lot of pike were caught, mostly at Burntstick Lake, which made a nice variation from wild meat (which we had quite a bit of as hunting in those days was a necessity). The trip itself was a real holiday for the men and they truly enjoyed it. The women, meanwhile, were left at home to do the outside chores as well as all the fall canning, gardening, etc.

Clark was quite an athlete. He competed in sports all his life. At a fall fair in Caroline, he ran in a race for ages fifty years and over. He kept looking back to see where the others were, but won the race by quite a margin. He encouraged all the young people to participate in the ball games, rodeos, etc. He was manager of a team of young boys who were too young to play with the senior team, and later that summer the boys' team beat the senior team.

After the ball games, rodeos were held at the Wren farm each Sunday, where horses and steers were ridden. The cowboys received many a thrill and spill to the delight of all.

Student ministers held services in the school during summer holidays, which all enjoyed. Dances, box socials, card parties, etc., were held there also. It served as our community centre. Crammond Ladies Club made many a quilt to be raffled, to raise funds for the children's treats, given at the Christmas concert each year. Candy bags were given to all, and the people came from near and far to receive this annual treat.

Clark joined Technocracy at a meeting in Calgary in 1938 or '39 and became an active member in the Caroline area.

He sold the farm at Crammond to Ivan Graham and moved to Canoe, British Columbia, in the spring of 1940. Having taken horses with him, he obtained work for them skidding logs in the huge bush camps. Later he sold out there and

Clark Wren and his fourth wife, Margaret.

moved to Sicamous, where he obtained work in a pole yard on the lake shore across the road from the house. Adela took sick and passed away there, in the spring of 1945. She was laid to rest in the Armstrong Cemetery. He lived on there for awhile, later selling out and returning to Caroline where he worked for Wrigglesworth in the bush camp, skidding logs. In December, 1948, he met and married Margaret Lewis (born at Weston, Nova Scotia) and continued working at camp for a time. Again they moved to Canoe, where they spent a few years before returning to the Caroline area, eventually retiring in the village. Clark became very sick and they were obliged to move to Calgary. After a lengthy illness, he passed away January 17, 1964. Margaret moved from place to place, finally moving to the Autumn Glen Lodge in Innisfail. She was later transferred to the Auxiliary Hospital in Didsbury. While there, she fell and broke her hip. She passed away in the Holy Cross Hospital, in Calgary, on April 18, 1978. Clark and Margaret are laid to rest in the Caroline Cemetery.

CLARENCE (CURLY) WREN

Curly married Irene Dezall in 1937. They lived on the farm until 1947, when they moved to the Raven Rearing Station where Curly raised fish for the government, for twenty-six and a half years. He also served as trustee on the school board for nine years.

They had two children, Frances and Gordon. In 1961 Frances married Neal Collison. Neal worked on oil rigs until they moved to the farm, east and south of Caroline. They have two children Loran and Theresa. All in the family are active in sports. Neal, Loran and Theresa compete at rodeos. Frances curls and plays softball.

Gordon has worked for oil and gas companies since school days. In 1969 he married Corrine Ceasor and they have one daughter, Shelley. Now divorced, Corrine and Shelley live in Innisfail and Gordon lives in Trochu. He works in the Three Hills district for Amaco Gas and Oil Company.

Irene is actively involved with volunteer services in the community. Curly and Irene are retired now and live on an acreage at Caroline.

LAURENCE WREN

Laurence (Pete) learned to box during school days. At Caroline he joined the Boxing Club and competed in boxing meets at Caroline and surrounding districts. In 1933 he competed at the Provincial Finals at Calgary, taking second place in Welter Weight Division for Alberta.

In 1942 he joined the Air Force and served as aero-mechanic until he was discharged in 1945.

He then moved to British Columbia and married Margaret Peterson in 1947. They have four children, Denis works as a maintenance supervisor for Marathon Realty in Calgary. He married Valerie Toews in 1977. Lynette is a Department Head Councillor and teacher at South Peace Senior High School in Dawson Creek. Gayleen works for a stockbroker in Vancouver, and Verne is a crane operator for C.P. Rail. In British Columbia Pete worked at several different jobs. While working at Peterson Brothers, he drove truck, operated bulldozer and did mechanical work. Later he was employed by General Construction as welder-mechanic during the building of Roger's Pass. After that road was completed he obtained employment with the Department of Highways as welder-mechanic until he retired in the fall of 1974.

Pete and Margaret live on a hobby farm where Pete raises Appaloosa horses. He competes in shows, and has won ribbons and trophies. Margaret is an avid gardener and has also won in flower shows and fairs.

JACK FRANKLIN

Jack grew up in the Crammond district. He married Vaye Gardner and they had three children: Richard, Melvin and Debbie. Richard and family live in British Columbia. Debbie and Melvin and families live in Calgary.

Jack served overseas in the Army from 1940-45. He has worked for Standard Gravel Company for many years. Vaye taught music (accordion). They reside in Calgary, Alberta.

LEWIS WREN

Lewis married Ruth Dingman, in November, 1939. They had three children: Betty, Clark and Linda. They lived on various farms for the first few years, eventually moving to Caroline, where Lewis worked in Wrigglesworth pole yard for several years. After it closed down, they worked in various bush camps where Lewis was millwright and foreman, and Ruth cooked for the men. Lewis, like most men, loved to go hunting and was a good hunter. Ruth occasionally accompanied him. They were both active in sports and really enjoyed playing ball and curling, which they did together for many years. Ruth passed away in 1963 and was laid to rest in the Caroline Cemetery.

Betty married Duane Dingman and they have three children: Cindy, Darcy and Shawn. Betty taught school. Duane has his own business in oil construction. They reside at Swan Hills.

Clark married Gladys Alstott, and they have two sons: Marty and Darwin. Clark works for oil companies and they live on an acreage, west and north of Caroline. They enjoy outdoor activities, camping, hunting, fishing, riding and curling.

Linda married Doug Bancroft and they have two children: Tod and Sandra. They farm in the

Dovercourt district. They are active in sports also.

Lewis worked for Murray Brothers for several years, and while working in one of their camps, west of Caroline, he met Marcia Stanford who was cooking for the crew at the time. They were later married and now reside in Caroline. A few years later, Lewis bought a bulldozer and breaking plow and went into business for himself. He recently sold this outfit and has been working for Shell Service in Caroline. He has also been caretaker for the arena. They have two daughters: Wanda and Ester. Marcia enjoys doing macrame, ceramics and making quilts.

MOLLIE (WREN) DOEL

Mollie married Ronald Doel and they have three children: Ilene Bugbee, Kenneth and Loretta Kennedy. (Refer to the Doel History).

WALLACE WREN

Wallace grew up and obtained his education at Crammond School. He was active in sports and liked to hunt and fish.

He joined the Army and was in active service overseas, from 1942-46. He was wounded and spent considerable time in the hospital. Returning to Canada, he worked at various jobs in British Columbia, and in the Caroline area at lath and sawmills. At present he drives a taxi in Calgary.

Crooked Creek

Crooked Creek
by Dennis Brown and Stanley Boye

Crooked Creek school was built in 1911. The builders were Mr. Earl Benson, R. J. McKain, and other members of the community. The Crooked Creek number was 2231. The school was painted by Mr. and Mrs. E. Brown. It was white with green trimmings. The sign was painted by Miss G. Proud, the teacher at that time.

In 1940, the school was renovated by contractors from Rocky Mountain House. The school was raised and put on a cement foundation. Part of the old floor was removed and a new floor put in to overcome the hump which had developed over the years that the school stood. Even though many pounds were placed on the floor there was still a slight raising in the center. The school was lined with ten-test. A new chimney was built in front of the school by Mr. Sandberg. The stove was moved to the back of the schoolroom. Steps were built. The outside was painted cream with brown trimmings, while the roof remained green. The school remained this color until it was closed in 1956 when Fosiers moved it to their farm near Caroline.

The teachers of Crooked Creek were, Mr. MacDonald, Mrs. M. Madson, Miss Dagny Gunderson, Miss A. Crichen, Miss R. Moore, Miss Anna Donally, Miss G. Proud, Miss G. MacDonald, Miss Furleming (who came from High River), Miss Watson, Mrs. Lerman, Miss D. Hopkins Miss Corey, Miss Leismer, Mr. W. Sloan, Miss Ayen, Miss V. Haggerty, Miss M. Stronsmoe, Miss B. Vessey, Miss B. Silhs, Miss M. Taylor, Mrs. C. Brown, Miss Doris Hearl, Mrs. Vogel, Mrs. Mayne, Mr. C. Dahms, Miss Goldstrom, Mrs. Cliff Peterson and Mrs. Dyrholm.

The first pupils were Ethel Madsen, Maggie Hansen, Mary Hansen, Allen Hansen, Carlos Costella, Jim Costella, Ray McKain, Nellie McKain, Frank Roberts and Willian Roberts.

Sam K. Dixon and Mabel H. Dixon

There is no way I can write any kind of an account of this half section in the Crammond district without giving my wife at least half the credit for whatever was accomplished.

My wife, Mabel, and I were forty-two years of age when we purchased this south half of 26-35-5-5 from the Hudson's Bay Land Company. This was rather old to make a start at farming, but after going through the depression in towns and cities, we vowed that we would go back to the land if we ever became able to do so, and the opportunity was quite a while coming.

We were both born in June, 1904, Mabel in Velva, North Dakota, and I in Baldur, Manitoba. Although these two places are not so very far apart, it took twenty-seven years for us to do most of our growing up on farms in Saskatchewan, to finally meet and marry in 1931 at Melfort, Saskatchewan. I was operating a garage and filling station at the time.

This, of course, was in the depth of what we now call the Big Depression and most of the cars were gradually being converted to Bennett Buggies. This did not help the garage business any. We thought there would be a better chance in a larger centre so we moved to Winnipeg, Manitoba. The next six years held a lot of ups and downs, some of the ups were fair but some of the downs were very down. The best I can say about this whole period is that we managed to stay off relief. In 1937, I landed a nice job operating a repair bay in one of the larger filling stations, but when war broke out in 1939 and the Royal Canadian Air Force was calling for motor mechanics, I joined the 112th City of Winnipeg Squadron of the R.C.A.F. in August. We trained in Winnipeg for awhile and were sent to Ottawa in December and overseas to England in June, 1940.

Having had considerable experience as a motor mechanic, I was fortunate to receive fairly rapid promotions and eventually was commissioned as a motor transport officer in 1945. After serving in this capacity for a year I came up for repatriation and returned to Canada in 1946, having served in England for five years.

Upon returning to Canada I was given a choice of postings, one at Gimli, Manitoba, one at Yorkton, Saskatchewan, and one at Calgary. I made the wise choice of Calgary and have never regretted it.

Our thoughts, of course, immediately turned back to owning a piece of land. We still did not have all that much money but we were told that Central Alberta was the best mixed farming country in Canada and if we looked out west into the grey wooded soil area, there was land for sale quite cheap.

I was stationed at Number Ten Repair Depot of the R.C.A.F. in Calgary and as the time for my release was getting close, I watched for an opportunity to get up into this district or close to it. There was a garage advertised for sale at Dickson, so, although I did not intend to go back into that line of business when I got released from the air force, I came up to see what the place looked like. The owner, Hans Anderson, persuaded me to stay and work for him as a mechanic. Shortly after that, he sold the garage and the new owners asked me to stay and get them started. This was just what we wanted so I took the job and we spent our spare time looking for land. We finally settled on this south half of 26-35-5-5. My intention was to buy through the Veterans Land Administration, but upon applying, I found they did not buy raw land, and this was very raw — solid bush — poplar with a smattering of pine and spruce. It was Hudson's Bay Land, so we decided to buy it anyway, to leave money enough for a bit of clearing, etc. We took it on a lease option to start.

We got a few acres cleared and put up a little shack. I continued to work out and do what I could on my days off and holidays. I bought an old Hart Parr tractor and a twenty-four inch breaking plow and broke what land was cleared, then, working it down, we had a crop on it the next year.

When we started to get some grain off the land we started buying a few pigs and raising them. This caused more problems too, as we had no water and had to haul water for two miles from Crooked Creek. We bought a little Ford three point hitch tractor and hauled water in an old gas drum on the draw bar. Buildings were required too, so I found I had to go back to working out and my wife was left with the chores and farm work except for what I could do at nights, early mornings and days off. In spite of many red hot letters between us and the Hudson's Bay Land Company as to who was going to own the land after the next specified number of days, and there were many times when we never thought we'd make it, we paid it off in 1958 and had clear title to our half section. I

quit working out as a mechanic and took the job of post master at Crammond and operating the store for Mr. Art Lamb. I hauled mail from Crammond and James River to Sundre for three years.

We still only had seventy-five acres under cultivation and we knew that wasn't going to do much for us in our fast approaching old age, so I went to the Veterans Land Administration, which was now under a whole new staff for this district, and with no trouble at all, I got everything I asked for, with enough money to go ahead and clear the west quarter as well as purchasing a nice start of a herd of dairy cattle and a house.

After a few years, and doing quite well, I guess I must have been the weaker of the pair of us as I had a rather bad heart attack, so had to cut down on the work and sell the herd of cattle. We then paid off the V.L.A. and had clear title to the half section for the second time. We eventually sold the west quarter section to Stuart Machan, and we are still living on the southeast quarter. We have a fairly respectable house with all modern conveniences. We have all weather roads, even seven miles to paved highways, and a good vehicle to use on them. We think we are living in one of the best districts in one of the best provinces in Canada and that it has been worth all the blood, sweat and tears it cost to get here.

James Sydney Petersen
by Toots Kanten

Sydney was born August 31, 1898, in St. Paul, Minnesota. The family lived in Nebraska for some time, then moved to the Standard district in 1908 to take up farming. He attended school in Standard and it was at the same school he met the girl who would someday be his wife.

Her name was Clara Gladys Busch. She was born February 25, 1904, in Minneapolis, Minnesota. She moved with her family to Carstairs at the age of five. Her father was the elevator agent there, and when he was later transferred to Standard, Clara attended school there and met Sydney.

Sydney and Clara were married at Calgary on December 24, 1924. They farmed in the Chancellor district until 1938 when they moved to the Crammond district in June of that year.

Travelling in the back of their Model T Ford with the stock racks and top enclosed with binder canvas, were their nine children. Cramped and cold, they arrived in Innisfail and were given the nights lodging in the 3 Star Garage. Clara spread blankets in the back of a large truck box and put the children to bed.

After leaving a drought-stricken prairie,

Syd and Clara Peterson shortly after their wedding.

travelling west the next morning was a unique experience as they were soon in a rain storm that worsened as they went. They finally turned off highway 54, three miles east of Caroline, and were unable to go any farther. They walked the remaining distance to a vacant farmyard and stayed there for several days until the road dried up enough to travel. The then vacant farm is now occupied by Mr. and Mrs. Louis Johnson and family. They had only eight more miles to travel until they reached the farm that was to be their new home. The farm was formerly owned by Percy Buchanan and consisted of 160 acres, a two-roomed log house, a log workshop, a log barn, a quite good lumber granary and also an inadequate hand dug water well. They hauled water from the closest neighbor, Andrew Andersen, for a few years, and drove the cattle a mile to water until Syd hired Art Bowers and son, Ralph, to drill a well for them. The well was practically impossible to pump by hand so Syd had a little one cylinder John Deere engine do the job, and it pumped good water for many years until Calgary Power came to the district in 1954.

Not being used to brush and trees gave Clara many anxious days as she was afraid the children would become lost, and Jean did wander off into the dense brush but was found

when the little fox terrier took Syd to where she was.

It was on December 19 of the same year, while Syd was back to Standard for a load of wheat, that Clara gave birth to their tenth child. That morning Clara sent the children to school and warning the three preschoolers to sit on the couch and be good, she gave birth to a premature baby girl. She then got up and rekindled the cook stove fire to heat the house and warm water to bathe the incredibly small baby. When Syd arrived home three days later, he made a sling to weigh the baby on the weigh beam. She weighed two and one-half pounds. The family was saddened by the death of little Irene on March 15, 1939, after she contracted whooping cough.

The wheat Syd brought back was to be a lifesaver for the next two years. Soaked and boiled slowly into porridge and ground into flour, it provided good food for the family.

The family picked blueberries for many years for sale, and with the big garden, Clara canned at least 600 quarts of fruit and vegetables a year. With the milk cows and chickens they managed to eat quite well. Clara was fortunate to have a good treadle Singer sewing machine and was able to sew all the children's clothes. She loved to crochet and made mitts and hats for the children in that way.

Three more children were added to the family making it an even dozen. The children learned at an early age to tend the animals, milk cows, pick berries, weed and work the garden, make bread, sew and can and also helped mind the younger children. The key word to survival in a family of this size is 'share', and share they did, from half an egg each at times to the mumps they shared with Syd at the age of forty-two. The highlights of the year were the school picnic at the end of June and the Christmas concert. The children attended Crooked Creek School and they are:

Grace, married to Laurence Jensen. Laurence passed away in 1975 and Grace now lives in Innisfail.

Margaret, known to all as Marmie, married Fred Dingman. They have nine children and live at the Kevisville corner.

Joyce married Albert Peterson They lived many years in Innisfail and have now retired to a farm in the Garrington area. They have two sons.

Jim married Adeline Morrison and has worked for many years in the oilfields. They have seven children and live on an acreage in the Sundre district.

Christine married Leonard Becker in a double wedding ceremony with Toots and Leonard Kanten. Christine and Leonard live in Innisfail and have one son. Toots and Leonard live in Caroline and have five children.

The Peterson children in 1942. Back Row, left to right — Jim, Marmie, Grace (holding Dolly), Jessie and Joyce. Front Row, left to right — Christine, Jean, Ivan, Ida and Toots.

Jean, also known as Tiny, married Ralph Fisher. They have five children and farm in the Condor district.

Ida married Ken Law and has three children. Ken passed away in 1971 as the result of an accident. Ida lives on a farm in the Kevisville area.

Ivan married Myrna Wekved. They live at La Glace and have two children. Ivan owns an oilfield drilling rig and works around Alberta.

Dolores, known as Dolly Ann, married Eric McIntosh. They have three children and farm in the Kevisville district.

David, known as Teddy, married Lois Christensen. They have an oilfield catering business. Teddy has a daughter from a previous marriage.

At the time of this writing there are twelve children, forty-one grandchildren and eighteen great-grandchildren.

Syd and Clara were home bodies and did not care for travelling around. They devoted their lives to their family. Clara enjoyed crocheting, fancy work and house plants. Syd enjoyed gardening and flowers. They enjoyed the company of their neighbors and especially the company of their children, Sydney and Clara retired to Innisfail in 1965. Clara spent many years as a semi-invalid and passed away in 1972 at sixty-eight years of age. Sydney followed her ten months later in 1973 at the age of seventy-four years. Sydney and Clara are laid to rest in the Carstairs Cemetery alongside their infant daughter.

Dovercourt

The Dovercourt School

The Dovercourt School was built one mile east and four miles north of Ted McNutts. Some of the teachers were: Mr. Blikenstaff, Bill Lunn, Miss Nerlin, Tillie Glenn, Hattie McArthur, Mrs. Gray, Dagney Dyrholm, Miss McKenzie, Irene Thompson, Mrs. Peterson, Anne Terrice, Elsie Tighe, Helen Carol, Janet (?) Bardgett, Ida Rogers, Miss Pettis, Miss Watson and Miss Dimetri.

Dovercourt School — Lloyd Courtright, F. Soderburg, ? Leggett, S. Howes, L. Howes, Belva Napper, Ethel Leggett, M. Howes, Mac Napper, Art Soderburg, Jack Edmonds, M. Courtright.

Dovercourt School — Back row — Sam Howes, Art Soderburg, Norman Napper, Mabel Howes, Belva Napper, — Alexander, Frank Soderburg — Center row — Tom Hamilton, Maurice May, Thelma Soderburg, Raymond Spencer, Fred May, Evelyn Napper — Front row — Ida Hamilton, Mac Napper, Dorothy May, Jim May.

The Clark Family

The Tom Clark family arrived in the Dovercourt district in the summer of 1910 and settled on the N.W.Q. 1-38-7-5.

Thomas Henry Clark was born in Penitang, Ontario, on April 11, 1870, of Irish and Scotch parentage. In 1895 he married Sophie Schiltroth who was born March 20, 1877, in Chesley, Ontario. They settled in Little Current on Manitoulin Island where Tom worked in the lumber industry. It was here their four children were born, Emma in 1896, Lena and Blanche in 1904 and Charlton in 1907.

By 1908 the lumber industry in western Canada was booming and many eastern men of the woods began moving that way. 1909 saw the Clark family on the train heading west. They arrived in Red Deer where Tom had a job with Great West Lumber Company. They stayed there for nearly a year and the two older girls attended school. In 1910 they moved to Dovercourt in a democrat with all their goods including a piano, coming behind in a wagon. They stayed in a cabin on the Jensen quarter until their own house was built. Mrs. Clark was sure they arrived in God's Country when she saw the bountiful crop of Saskatoons available just for the picking. Soon after their arrival, work was begun

Dovercourt School 1929 — Back row — Art Soderburg, Mabel Howes, Lloyd Courtright, Marium Courtright, Leonard Howes, Sam Howes, Frank Soderburg — Front row — Edith Lane, Maurice May, Belva Napper, Thelma Soderburg, Dorothy and Fred May.

on the new house of log construction, poles and tarpaper for the roof — it was ready to move into by February. Blanche remembers that day very well, "Although it was cool, we had lunch outside under two poplar trees while the furniture was unloaded. Then we went into our own home." There was only an earth floor in the home and the linoleum intended for the floor was used on the walls to keep out the wind. Emma and Lena missed the great moving day as in the fall they had gone back to Red Deer to attend school. In order to afford to go to school, they worked as domestics after school for their room and board. This was common practice among girls who wanted an education in those days.

It was a great luxury they felt, to have all that land and a home too. But the home had not been built without any unforseen accidents. Early in the summer when the logs were being cut and peeled for use, Emma's draw knife slipped and she cut her knee badly. The gash was wide and deep and obviously needed medical attention, but no doctor was within reach so her mother took a needle and thread and after cleansing it carefully, she sewed it up and bandaged it. Emma did not peel logs for a few days, but soon was back to work. A very small scar was left, but it speaks highly of the resourcefulness of the pioneer woman.

The family was often left on the farm for months by themselves as Tom Clark worked in the woods around Nordegg as bush foreman in order to bring home some cash to improve the house. When a floor was finally laid, it was often used as a dance floor. The girls remember, not too fondly, scrubbing the floor with ashes regularly and for special occasions. Each girl was assigned so many boards to scrub and the competition was on — who could produce the cleanest boards?

When the two girls returned from Red Deer, the family was together and remained that way until Emma married Joe Bertagnolli in 1914. Mrs. Clark was very ill by this time and passed away in 1916. She is buried in the Pine Grove Cemetery in Rocky Mountain House. The three

Emma and Joe Bertagnoli on the Clark homestead.

children stayed alone on the farm until fall when they moved to Saskatchewan to stay with Grandma Schiltroth. Tom continued working at Nordegg until his death in 1925.

Emma and Joe remained on their farm across the river. They had four sons, Tom, Alex, Vern and Don, all still residing in the same area with their own families.

Lena and Lou Borley farmed in Nipawin, Saskatchewan, where they raised five children, Chet (deceased), Keith (deceased), Helen in Toronto, Lois in Carrot River, Saskatchewan, and Gordon in Flin Flon. Lena now resides in the Pasqua Lodge in Carrot River and entertains her guests with pictures and stories of her grandchildren.

Blanche married Wm. Fray, a C.N.R. engineer. They lived in Mirror and Jasper until 1949 when they retired to Kelowna. Bill died in 1968 but Blanche still resides in Kelowna.

Charlton became an engineer on N.A.R. and married Isabel Richardson. They had four children, Tom in Rocky, Mary in Valleyview, Don an engineer on the same line as his father and Ethel in Spirit River. They are all married and have families of their own. Charlton died in 1977.

The children of Tom and Sophie experienced many hardships as did all the pioneers, but when they used to get together, they remembered fondly the friendships and neighborliness of the 'good old days'.

Charlie Courtright Family

Mr. and Mrs. Courtright came from Oklahoma, U.S.A. in 1914. All the children but Lloyd were born in the States. They settled first at Sedgewick, Alberta.

Charlie homesteaded the S.W.Q. 2-37-7-5 in 1915, now Nellie Cole's. A son, Henry, homesteaded the N.W.Q. 35-37-7-5 across the road south, now P. Wylie's, also the N.W.Q. 2-37-7-5 adjoining the home place on the north, now E. Schockenmairer's.

Charlie and son, Jack, came from Sedgewick travelling with a four horse outfit, pulling a tent covered sleigh. The trip took five days. They landed at Bob Sinclair's, now G. Hayes, the night before Christmas, 1916. It was very cold. The next day they went on to the Bennett place, now J. Rauch's, staying there for the winter while they built a house on the homestead. This place is one half mile west of the old Dovercourt Post Office.

Their daughter, Lena, came in February, 1916. Mr. Bennett told Lena if she looked in the spring which stayed open all winter, she might find some canned fruit. She didn't think about it again until several months later when she was walking along the water course and came to the

Charles and Lucy Courtright.

L. to R. — Pearl and Jack Courtright — children — Violet, Bill & Irene.

spring. She could see something in the water and fishing around, pulled out several jars of fruit which were in perfect condition.

Mrs. Courtright and three boys, Harley, Dutch and Lloyd, came the first of April bringing the rest of the livestock, machinery and household things. They lived on the Culvert place, now E. Wickin's, for awhile in the fall of 1917. The road across the muskeg was one big bog. The house on Culvert's was built of logs standing on end in a circle. It was later destroyed by fire.

The summer of 1919, along with Herb Warren, they hayed along the Baptiste River. Herb stayed there for the winter, trapping and looking after Courtright's cattle and horses which they had trailed there. The Courtrights left the homestead in 1927 and moved to Leslieville where they bought a farm. They lived there for ten years, then moved to Vernon, British Columbia. They lived there for a few years until they passed away. They are both buried in the Kelowna Cemetery.

JACK COURTRIGHT and Pearl Speight of the Everdell district were married September 23, 1930, and moved to the Dovercourt district the next day, to the Tom Clark place, now E. Della

Costa's. Jack worked on the road south across the muskeg that was built in the winter of 1930-31. There was no snow that winter. Four children were born to them, two girls and two boys. Mrs. Fred Howes and Mrs. Fred May were the midwives in the district, bringing many of the district children into the world. The youngest boy died in 1941. Neighbors were very kind when the family was quarantined with scarlet fever. They brought milk, oven ready chicken and other food, leaving it on the doorstep.

Bill Courtright on farm at Dovercourt.

Jack and Henry Courtright on Dovercourt farm.

Marie and Louie DeRoover.

They left the farm in 1943, working at a bush camp the first winter for Vern Scott. Then they moved to Rocky where Jack built some houses and sold them. Pearl worked at the Deluxe Grocery Store, and for A.G.T. on the switchboard for four and a half years until it closed in 1962. They also owned the Riverview Store across the Saskatchewan River. They moved to Cow Creek in 1949 where they farmed until they built and started the Cow Lake store in 1971. Later they sold the store to Violet and retired. They live by the store where Jack is doing his leather work, making saddles and chaps and Pearl is busy with her knitting and bowling. She also works some days at the store.

Violet married Harley Holman. They had six children — three boys and three girls. They operate the Cow Lake Store.

Irene married Clary Klatt and they have two girls and two boys. They farm east of Caroline.

Bill is married and has two boys and three girls and lives at Rocky.

Henry, Harley and Lena all reside in Rocky. Dutch is at Victoria, and Lloyd at Enderby, British Columbia.

The DeRoover Family

Louie and Marie DeRoover came to the Dovercourt district in the early 1930s settling on the N.E.Q. 36-3t-7-5, now G. Hobbs. They came from Lethbridge where Louie had worked in the mines and Marie cooked for the Arthur Baalim family. This land had been homesteaded in 1911 by Bert Sinclair, and later lived on by Mr. Richardson. Mr. and Mrs. DeRoover had emigrated from Belgium to Canada.

Mrs. DeRoover continued with the Baalims and sent money home to Louie to buy horses and things needed on the farm. Louie cleared most of that quarter by hand.

Louie did carpentry work around the district. He worked on the Chedderville School in the early 1930s when the foundation was put down, and also on the Dovercourt School when it was widened in the middle 1930s.

Marie and Louie adopted two boys, Rollie and Joey. Rollie lives at Armstrong, British Columbia, and has several children. Joey lives at Sylvan Lake and has two children.

Mr. and Mrs. DeRoover sold their farm to David and Ellen Jaycock in 1960 and moved to the Albert Morton quarter on the east side of the road, now G. Skeels. It was known as the Andy Swales place. They sold out there in 1965 and went back to Belgium. They have been back for visits.

Mrs. DeRoover was a very kind and thoughtful person, taking food to people when they were sick. She passed away in August, 1977. Louie still lives in Belgium (1978).

Anna Hall
by Mariam Robb

Anna Bjornson was born in 1891 at Markerville. She is the eldest child of Bjorn and Margaret Bjornson. She took her schooling at Hola and area. Ed Hall, born in 1888, came from England to Canada to the Markerville area to look for work. He and Anna Bjornson were married in 1910 and they got a homestead in the Butte district.

Dorothy Hall, Thelma Soderburg, Gladys Hansen, Mrs. Soderburg, Mrs. Hansen, Marjorie Synge — 1936.

Mariam Hall and Leah Cross.

Anna endured may hardships, alone much of the time, with chores and young children. Ed worked in sawmills much of the time.

They had five children. Margaret, born in 1911, married Fred Fisher of Lacombe and had two boys and two girls. Edward, born in 1913, married Irma Ramsay of Ridgewood. They had four sons and one daughter. Edward passed away suddenly in January of 1977. Charles was born in December of 1914 and died as a baby. Mariam was born in 1916. She married Jack Shannon and had one son, Everett. Jack died in 1941 and she later married Morris Robb of Kevisville and had one daughter. Dorothy was born in 1918 and married Donald Craig of Butte. She had four daughters. Dorothy passed away suddenly in May of 1952.

Ed Hall passed away in 1920 and is buried in the Innisfail Cemetery. Anna carried on alone and the children went to Clear Creek School for a time. The going got so rough that she moved into town and worked out and kept her children in school. She worked at camps and in the fall she would go on cook cars for the harvest in the south.

She never liked town life so she took up a quarter section of land in the Dovercourt area. She lived there for many years and endured many hardships — such as getting feed in for the cows. She always had a few milk cows, pigs and chickens. She had really good neighbors and liked the district, but there were no decent roads and it was so difficult to get produce to market —

no conveniences whatsoever, and no hopes of getting any, so in 1942 or '43 she had a chance to get land at Butte. She sold her place and moved over there.

Anna will be remembered by her friends for her wool work. She used to sell wool balls for quilts — getting orders from as far away as Winnipeg. She used to spin her own yarn to make mitts and socks that she sold. The mitts and socks were well liked by men working in camps.

Anna Hall passed away in June of 1958 and is buried at Innisfail.

Gavin Hamilton

Gavin Hamilton came to the Dovercourt district in 1907 with his son, Linus, and son-in-law, Hugh Lee, and they homesteaded on the S.E.Q. 19-37-6-5.

He helped the early settlers and always had a helping hand for anyone in need, always remembering the help others had given him.

Gavin was a former resident of Wisconsin, Minnesota and Dakota and was a veteran of the Civil War.

He worked for Mr. Warehouser as a logscaler.

Gavin Hamilton passed away in Calgary at the age of eighty-two years, leaving three sons and two daughters. He was buried in Olds, Alberta, on August 21, 1911.

Gavoni Hamilton.

Back — Tom, Ida, Ann, Jim, Guy, Elsie — Front — Mrs. Hamilton, Arthur, Linus and Joe.

79

Hamilton family with Chris Jensen at far right.

Hamilton family.

Linus Hamilton

Linus married Mary Jensen in January, 1917. They raised five boys and three girls, Ida (Scott), Tom, Ann (Soderburg), Jim, Calvin (passed away in 1975), Joe, Elsie (Burk) and Art. Linus passed away in January, 1951, and was buried in Rocky Mountain House. His wife now resides in Sylvan Lake.

Jim Hamilton married Shirley Severs of Strachan on March 3, 1961. They have a family of three: Linda, born January 3, 1962; Steven, born February 1, 1964, and Kevin born July 28, 1968. They all go to the Caroline School.

Jim and his family took over the home place and have a large herd of dairy cattle. They are very active in the light Horse Association and have won many trophies.

Tom has a farm close by and had been one of the district's best log cutters. Calvin resided in Sylvan Lake. Joe is married, with a family of two, and resides on a farm in the Burnt Lake district, and works in a meat packers plant in Red Deer. Art resides in Camrose and works as a carpenter. He is married, with a family of three. Ida is married and raised a family of eight and resides on the old Burns place, straight south of the home place. Anne married and raised a family of three. They live in the district three miles east of the home place. Elsie is married and has a family of four.

Martin Hansen family while moving from Vulcan to Chedderville in 1934.

Martin and Gunhilde Hanson and Family
by Joanna Hanson

Martin was born in Yankton, South Dakota, the fifth child of a family of seven boys and three girls. Gunhilde was the third child of Andriane and Halvor Boe. They were married on July 2, 1904, in Park River, North Dakota. They had four children, Leonard, Alma, Gladys and Harlan when in 1912 they moved to Canada to the Vulcan area. There they had Violet, Margaret, Glen, Marlin and Opal adding to their family making nine in all.

During the depression years they decided to locate in the Dovercourt area, as they felt with four sons, there would be more opportunities for them. So in the spring of 1934, Leonard, Harley and Glen, with two six-horse outfits and one four-horse outfit, left the Vulcan area and started north avoiding the highways and using back roads. They had household effects, machinery, blacksmith tools, even a crate of chickens and a home on wheels with cooking and sleeping facilities — a different kind than the ones we have today. Marlin, riding his trusty horse, Jip, and herding twenty-five head of cattle, brought up the rear.

The grass was poor in April and water was often scarce for that many head of stock. One farmer, Hanson by name, west of Innisfail, kindly offered pasture and water one night, and in the morning, those prairie horses not knowing what a muskeg was, had walked right in. Three were drowned and a fourth, they were able to save by pulling it out with a team.

Harley was driving down the Ricinus hill when the brakes gave way on the wagons. The horses were sliding on their haunches when Harley whistled and the horses broke into a dead run. The wagons went careening wildly down the steep hill and half way up the other side with Harley hanging on and the others clinging to the top.

They arrived at the Adams place in May, a welcome sight even if the house was unlivable.

Mr. and Mrs. Martin Hansen and family — L. to R. — Martin, Violet, Glen, Margaret, Gladys, Alma, Harley, Opal and Leonard.

They soon fixed a granary, and on May 17 (Dad's fiftieth birthday) the others of the family arrived in Dad Hanson's 1926 Chev: Dad, Mother, Violet and Buster Burns and their five-month-old daughter, Vivian; Harley's wife, Joanna, and six-week-old daughter, Marlene, and Opal, with suitcases and luggage piled high. It was a hot dry summer and Dad and the boys pitched in to cut and haul logs from Lynus Hamilton's place to Dalton Urghart's sawmill on Jack Urghart's place where they squared them and built a snug 24' x 24' house. The floor was of poplar and by much scrubbing with soap, made a beautiful white floor. The floor had to be put down and nailed at once or it curled up like a corkscrew. Shingles from Boeken's shingle mill at Caroline, roofed it.

Harley and Buster both homesteaded and we lived on the Hank Smith place the first year. Harley and Glen cut mine props and hauled them to Rocky that winter. I'm sure it was fifty below zero many times. They had to walk to keep warm, but when they got to the Chinese Restaurant, there was always a huge platter of food and all the coffee they could drink, all for 25¢. The boys hauled lumber, etc., too. Buster worked at the mill.

In February, Buster and Violet had a boy, Kenneth. A week after the folks' house warming for the new house, Dr. Greenaway came to deliver the baby. This completed their family. Then Buster got work at Vulcan and they moved back there.

The feed was of poor quality and because our cattle were not climatized, we lost nearly all of them. Then the horses got sleeping sickness and more losses. Our last heifer drowned in a pothole. Our neighbour wanted five acres cleared and he would trade us a good cow for the clearing. Harley and Glen looked it over; it seemed to have quite a few open places, so those two green prairie boys, found by using teams to pull and sharp axes to cut, that cows milk was dearly earned.

Marlin and Opal started school at Dovercourt, the teacher was Irene Thompson. The mail and groceries were bought at Zuberbier's store at Dovercourt. We enjoyed the picnics, fairs, dances, school concerts and house parties. Mother and I joined the W.I. Leonard played the violin and Gertie Urghart had an organ for a time. Jack and Leonard would load up the organ in the sleigh and go to local schools and homes for an evenings fun. Opal could play at age thirteen, so she would go along too. One summer, Dad even umpired the baseball games.

There was always open house at the Hanson's, coffee for every guest; people were always welcome. Dad having been a barber, was always kept busy cutting hair while Mother made eats. Leonard and Dad soon had a blacksmith shop fixed up as they always did horse shoeing, plowshare sharpening, etc. Hanson's nearest neighbors were Bill Hardbottles and Digry Hutchinson. Soderburgs, Mays, Hamiltons, Helmers and Urgharts were close friends.

In the summers, we picked wild fruits, strawberries, blueberries, raspberries and cranberries. Mother loved to go with us, especially to pick saskatoons as they were easy to reach. Arthritis made her crippled at times.

When Opal was fourteen, her appendix ruptured and after Dr. Greenaway examined her, he took her to the Bentley Hospital for the operation. She was very sick and spent a month in hospital after which she had a drainage from her stomach which she dressed several times a day. It was almost two years before Dr. Stewart of Calgary operated and she was well again. She then finished her schooling and worked in her sister's beauty parlor in Vulcan. She married Lyle Christianson of Calgary and had two sons, Leonard and Herbie.

After Urguharts left, Leonard bought that place and he and the folks lived there for some time. He donated an acreage for a church and house on the south of the place, helping to build it too. Frank Wilson was pastor there for a time and the two families became good friends. In 1952 they sold out and moved to Calgary where Leonard worked at various jobs and often welcomed old friends from the Dovercourt area. Mother and Dad celebrated both their fiftieth and sixtieth wedding anniversaries with all of their nine children living, and able to be present with their many relatives and friends.

Mother died August 17, 1965, and Dad November 29, 1965, only thirteen weeks apart, Leonard died February 12, 1976. They are all buried in Mountain View Memorial Gardens, Calgary.

Harley Hansen Family.

The Harbottle family.

Harley and I lived for a time on the homestead. Soderburgs, Mrs. Hall and Dorothy were our nearest neighbors. Then we bought land in the Oras district, northeast of Rocky, and moved there.

Violet and Buster were in the oil fields at Longview and then Glen and Marlin found work there too. After Donna was born in 1938, we too, went to the oilfields. Harley roughnecked, derrick man for years, then on production. We bought a quarter in the Kew district and raised cattle, horses and feed. While there, our son, Dennis, was born. Marlene married Don Pearse of Calgary and had two sons, Byron and Barry. Donna married David Evans, a rancher in Millarville, and had three sons, Donald, Daryl and Cameron. Dennis married Patricia Cole of Calgary and had a son, Scott, and a daughter, Charlisa. Dennis is a steamfitter and works at Empress, but have their home in Medicine Hat.

Still having friends, we often go back to the Dovercourt and Rocky area to visit. Buster worked up to a driller then had his own trucking business. He and Violet are retired now and live in Calgary. Glen worked in the oilfields for a time then became a carpenter. Then he took up the pipefitting trade, and became a steamfitter working in Empress, but makes his home in Calgary. Marlin had a family of six children and is now in Calgary doing trucking.

Bill and Alice Harbottle

Bill and Alice Harbottle came to the Dovercourt district in the thirties. They settled on the south half of 28-37-6-5 now owned by John and Edith Umpshied.

Bill was a war veteran and had some after effects from the war. He loved to take pack horses and go up on the Brazeau along with a neighbor boy, Maurice May, and pan for gold. Maurice and some of the Williams boys worked for him on his farm. Bill and Alice had four children, Mary, Joan, Peter and Wesley.

Fred and Maude Helmer

Fred and Maude Helmer came from Red Deer to the Dovercourt district in the thirties to the N.W.Q. 20-37-6-5. Fred worked at hauling ties and other things in the bush besides working on his farm. Maude was active in the W.I. and other clubs.

They had three children, Murial, Mac and Alma. They left the farm in the forties.

Howes Family

Fred Howes was born in 1881 in Windsor, Ohio. He was married in 1906 to Emma Schlatter. She was born in 1875 in Hemburg St. Gallen, Switzerland.

Their children, Frieda and Katherine, were born in Ohio in 1907 and 1909. They then moved to Calgary by train where Albert was born in 1910. In 1911 they moved to the Dovercourt district. They homesteaded on the quarter where Keith Stuart now resides, on N.W. 31-37-6-5. They called their land the Alpine Ranch.

Perry was born in 1911 in Calgary hospital, but died as an infant of pneumonia. Fred (Lenard) was born in 1913 at home. Mabel was born in 1914 and Samuel in 1917.

They first got mail at Stauffer. For supplies they travelled to Innisfail by sleigh or wagon.

Mrs. Howes went to neighbors delivering babies and tending ill patients, as she was a registered nurse. Mr. Howes was a steam engineer for the railroad and this is what prompted his move to Calgary. Later, he decided to homestead. He and Floyd Buck were partners in a sawmill in the Prairie Creek district. He was a millwright for Connors on land near Cow Lake. Later, he worked on the first oil rig in the area as a steam engineer. He travelled as far as Norman Wells to make a living for his family.

The three older children, Frieda, Katy and Albert, first attended the Everdale School. They

Fred Howes family — L. to R. — Fred Howes, Albert, Mrs. Howes, Freda, Katie, Leonard, Mabel and Sam.

Fred Howes.

walked about three miles through the bush to get there, and for awhile they had to take turns going because they only had one pair of shoes between them. When Dovercourt School was started, they attended there. It was in a small teacherage on the Sinclair's place. Their teacher was Hattie McArthur (Sinclair). Later a larger school was built.

The older children went out to work and the youngest, Sam, farmed the land. Frieda worked in Calgary and never married. Katy married Floyd Buck and lives on a farm in the Butte area. They have five children, Betty Oliver, Elmer Buck, Don Buck, Elsie Fairbrother and Edith Janiszewski. Albert worked on the oil rigs and married Lily Wicks. They had one daughter, Marilyn Smith. Fred (Lenard) joined the army and married Tilly Mittenpergher. Lenard served overseas until he lost his leg in Artona, Italy, then he was an invalid at home. They moved to Calgary after his medical discharge. They had eight children. Alice, Shirley Brooks, Nonnie Howes, Lorne, Linda Runge, Andy, Carolyn Barkman and Sharon Brooks.

Mabel moved to Calgary to work. She later married Ole Lundsven and had one daughter, June Nicholls.

Sam married Peggy McKie of Chedderville

area. They have five daughters, Janet Doughty, Marie Stuart, Marlene Smith, Irene Woods and Colleen Minaker.

Emma Howes died in 1953 and Fred died in 1968, both buried in the Rocky Mountain House Cemetery.

Swan Iverson

Swan Iverson homesteaded the S.W.Q. 22-37-6-5. He was a very hard worker and was always willing to share with his neighbors. One day he was walking along the river and was mistaken for a deer. He lost his life.

The Jensen Family

Chris and Alice Jensen came to the Dovercourt district in 1910, homesteading the N.E. Q. 12-38-7-5, now V. Bertagnolli, and the N.W. Q. 6-38-6-5, now M. Radau.

They came to Innisfail by train from Pierre, South Dakota, and the rest of the way by team and wagon. With them were their three children, Mary, Madeline and Carl.

Chris cleared the brush off and broke the land with a team of horses and walking plow. Chris worked at Pettifor and McGrandle's sawmill. He also worked at Nordegg taking care of the mine horses. Mrs. Jensen worked at the top hotel for awhile. She passed away on the farm on August

Chris Jensen breaking land on homestead in 1912.

Mary Carl and Madeline Jensen.

Madeline and Arthur Lane.

Mr. and Mrs. Frank Joseph and their son George and his wife and their three children.

27, 1913, at the age of thirty-two years. Mr. Jensen passed away on March 29, 1939, at the age of seventy-eight years.

Mary married Linus Hamilton and they had nine children. Mrs. Hamilton is living at the Sylvan Lake Lodge.

Madeline married Arthur Lane and they had three children, Edith, Herb and Kenneth. They ran the Dovercourt Store and Post Office on the north side of the Clearwater River. Arthur passed away in 1932, Madeline stayed there to run the store and post office until she married Harry Radau in 1934. The post office was moved south of the river and Madeline continued running it. In all she had the post office for thirty-five years. Madeline and Harry had two boys, Neil and Benny. Neil married Jeannette Cannaday of Condor and has two children, Lorena and Jed. They farm in the Caroline area. Benny still lives on the home place with his mother. Harry passed away at home September 12, 1967, at the age of sixty-seven years and is buried in the Rocky Cemetery.

Carl married Gladys Davis of Brandon, Manitoba. They have five sons and five daughters and live at Enderby, British Columbia.

Frank and Hannah Joseph

Frank and Hannah Joseph homesteaded on the S.E. Q. 36-37-7-5 around 1910, coming from Ontario. Mrs. Joseph was Tom Clark's sister.

They had a son, George, who married and had three children.

When war broke out in 1914, Mr. and Mrs. Joseph Sr. moved to Nordegg where Mr. Joseph worked as a millwright.

George and his family moved to Alexo where George cut mine props.

Mr. and Mrs. Joseph are buried in the Nordegg Cemetery. George's family is in Edmonton.

Lars Krossenger

by niece, Inga Garrett

Lars was born at Valdris, Norway, February 5, 1878. He emigrated to Canada in 1924 with his wife, Mary, and their five children, Louie, Olga, Inga, Mary and Adeline. They came to Loyalist in Alberta and lived on a farm. They also lived at Veteran and Throne and as time went on, they lived on different farms in those areas.

After coming to Canada, they had four more children, Rhoda, Ole, Norma and Lorraine.

Times were hard in the 'hungry thirties' as everyone called them. Most of the places where they lived, there was poor land, poor crops and very little rain. Cow chips were used to heat the home and to cook with during the summer. For winter they hauled coal and wood from miles away using a team of horses. At times four horses were used, depending on how many miles they had to travel, taking over a week for a return trip.

The drought was as bad here as it was farther east. If you were lucky enough to get a bit of a garden, the gophers and crows would eat up most of the vegetables. There was really no way to grow a garden. It was so dry and the heat so intense that you couldn't haul enough water to do any good, for fear of running the well dry. The cattle and horses had to have water to drink.

People moved from one area to another hoping to find better land. They moved with horses and a wagon or a wagon with a hay rack on, taking their cattle along (six to eight cows). Chickens and a couple of pigs would be put in crates and carried in the wagon. If they had a buggy and an extra team of horses that the wife could drive, she and the children would ride in more comfort.

Uncle Lars and the family moved and lived at Coronation for a time. Inga was married and stayed in Coronation. She and her son, Ralph, still live there.

They, like us, heard there was better land and lots of moisture in the Rocky Mountain House area and that hay was plentiful. So Uncle Lars and his daughter, Mary, rode the freight train to Rocky Mountain House (Mary dressed as a boy) to look for a place to live. They found one — seven and one half miles east of Rocky Mountain House. They rode the freight back to Coronation.

The family all moved except Inga of course, and Rhoda who worked for some people by the name of 'Weeks' at Coronation. Louis was out on his own. They lived there for a number of years. The land had to be cleared to make larger fields. Using axes and grub hoes along with a team of horses to pull the stumps over with a stump puller, they managed to clear some land.

There were plenty of trees to cut and saw into firewood with which to heat their home. Gardens and crops grew well with all of the moisture from the rains and there was no end of clear, cold water for both man and beast.

Uncle Lars had a homestead in the Dovercourt area on which he had been clearing and building, hoping to move his family there. I remember him driving past our place on his way to his homestead. He drove a bay colored team

hitched to the running gear of a wagon, with just a couple of 2 x 12 planks for him to sit on. He built his house with logs and used some lumber as well. He travelled back and forth during the summer for a couple of years, staying two or three weeks at a time.

Aunt Mary never got to live on the homestead. After a lengthy illness, she passed away in 1938. The three children left at home, went to live with their brother Louie, in Calgary. Norma was four, Lorraine, six, and Ole, ten years old. They stayed with Louie and his wife, Nina, until they were out of school. Uncle Lars moved to his homestead and lived alone.

After I was married and had children, Uncle Lars used to stop at our place — we lived in 'Old Town' then. He used to play his mouth organ for my three children and they enjoyed the fast, musical Norwegian tunes. He used to play for my family, too, when we were small. Uncle Lars' family was quite musical. They made their own fiddles and wooden cases with fancy carvings on the lids. I have a fiddle and case that was brought over from Norway, made by my grandfather. I also have a wooden spoon with a nice carved handle.

Uncle Lars visited his sister in Rocky, Ingaborg Hagen, staying a few days at a time. He and Mom still had other relatives living in the old country. He always like to read the newspaper 'Norge' mailed to him from Norway so he could keep up with some of the old country news around 'Ron' in Valdres.

Uncle Lars passed away in the hospital in Rocky on May 13, 1956, and is at rest in the Pine Grove Cemetery.

Inga lives in Coronation and Rhoda in Calgary. Louie lived in Calgary, then in British Columbia. He passed away in 1975. Mary married and lived in Gull Lake, Saskatchewan, and passed away in 1965. Adeline, Olga, Ole and Lorraine live in British Columbia and Norma in England.

Uncle Lars was loved and is missed by his family and relatives and remembered by his neighbors and friends. I wrote this in his memory.

Hugh Lee

Hugh Lee came to Calgary with the Banisters when he was fifteen, when there was only the North West Mounted Police Barracks and two or three other places. He rode for George Lane, and on different ranches around Calgary. Later he joined the Mounted Police and went to South Africa during the South African War. He was shot twice and returned to Calgary in 1887. There he worked as a fireman and worked in a machine shop making boilers.

Lars and Mary Krossenger and children — Louie, Mary and Inga.

Later, he moved to British Columbia, around Armstrong, where he was a Provincial Policeman. After serving as a policeman he and Guy Hamilton went to the Cariboo, in Northern British Columbia, and bought the 59 Mile House Ranch and Stage Station.

In 1908 he married Guy Hamilton's sister, Ida Batho. They had one small daughter, Muriel, a step-son of fifteen, Harry, and one step-daughter, Vera, at age thirteen.

Hugh and Ida moved to Victoria, British Columbia, in March, 1909, where they bought Heel's Post Office and ranch at South Sanched. In 1910, they moved back to Alberta to live with his father-in-law, Gavin Hamilton. The next year, 1911, they moved to their own place — the Dovercourt Ranch, on the N.W. Q. 32-37-6-5, which was named after the estate in England where he was born.

They had the first Post Office in Dovercourt and sawed lumber for the settlers as they came in. He had the first threshing machine in the Dovercourt-Rocky Mountain House district. He had a large herd of cattle and horses, and was the first Justice of the Peace in the district. His wife was the first nurse, helping those in need which was very much appreciated by the early settlers. Hugh also helped with broken bones, etc., and advised that some patients be taken by buggy to Red Deer or Innisfail doctors, or he would ride to Rocky Mountain House to fetch a doctor back to the sick. One day Harry Batho rode horseback fifteen miles to Rocky Mountain House for a doctor for Mrs. Fred Howes in three quarters of an hour.

They held dances for the settlers in their home. The Lee family were the only ones who could dance at first, and they taught the others to dance.

Fred May

Mr. and Mrs. Fred May came from England in 1921 and lived at Taber, Alberta, for five years. In 1926, they homesteaded in the Dovercourt area on N.E. 30-37-6-5. Their first home was a shack with a sod roof.

Mr. May had served four years in World War I' where he received a military medal. When World War II broke out, he again joined the Calgary Tank Regiment and worked overseas for four more years. He now has nine medals.

Mrs. May worked for the Red Cross for twenty-five years for which she received a Citation of Merit. She also worked as a midwife for Dr. Greenway.

Mr. and Mrs. May had ten children — five boys and five girls. Maurice married Catherine Schnell from Everdell. They had six children, Eddie, Harvey, Ruth, Millie, Alice

The Fred May family — Back Row, L to R — Bill, Danny, Jim and Maurice. 2nd Row — Ruby, Frieda, Mr. and Mrs. May and Fred Jr. Sitting — Olive, Dorothy and Mary.

The Fred May family.

Mr. and Mrs. Fred May in the mail cutter.

and Stephen. Fred married Fern Hepburn from Three Hills and has eight children — Daniel, Wayne, Gwen, Ruth, Freddie, Brenda, Bonnie and Jackie. Dorothy married Rex Bancroft of Chedderville and had four children, Bob, Doug, Marion and Bonnie. James married Marion McArthur from Chedderville, and had two children — Kathryn and Dianne. Mary married Lloyd Loughead from Dovercourt and had nine children — Ronnie, Dwayne, John, Richard,

Maurice May feeding his pigs.

Cathy May pumping water and baby Harvey.

Melvin, Beverly, Norman, Alfred, and Barbara. Freda married Joel Dobbs from Georgia, U.S.A., and had four children — Daniel, Janet, Lusan, and Linda. Olive married Jim Bayford from Rocky Mountain House and have eight children — Donald, Nelson, Harold, Cameron, Sherry, Llyn, Dale and Jack. Bill married Dena McLellan of Rocky Mountain House and has four children — Billy, Rodney, Jo-anne, and Jamie. Daniel married Edith Padgant from Edmonton. They had six children — Gerald, Terry, Arnie, Cindy, Wendy and Darcy.

McClatchey, Tyler, Dickson

Tom McClatchey came to Calgary with his niece, Mrs. Bill Tyler and family and nephew, William Dickson and family, from the Hamilton area of Ontario in 1908.

In 1914 they all came to the Dovercourt district. Mr. McClatchey homesteaded the N.W.Q. 1-38-7-5, now H. Conkey. He was a bachelor. Mr. and Mrs. Bill Tyler and six daughters homesteaded the N.E.Q. 2-38-7-5.

Dicksons homesteaded about one mile northwest of Uncle Tom. They had two daughters, Grace, born in 1901 is now living in Winnipeg; Evelyn, born in 1904, lives in Bend, Oregon, and twin sons, Herbert and William Jr. were born in 1906. Bert passed away in 1967 and Bill lives at Rocky.

Bill Tyler was a railroad man and away from home a lot of the time, so he had a neighbor, Mr. Snell, clear his land for him.

Mr. McClatchey did all his own work; he had a nice house and out buildings. He left the district in 1925 along with the Tylers; they all went to Chicago.

The Dickson boys stayed on their place. William went to Bend, Oregon, where he lived with daughter, Evelyn, until his passing.

Hugh G. Napper and Family
by Belva Barber and Mac Napper

Dad came to the Dovercourt district in the fall of 1922 and purchased a quarter section which at that time was owned by a mortgage company, N.E. 38-7-5. This quarter was previously homesteaded by Herman Shaw, a bachelor, before World War 1. He enlisted and went overseas and when he returned to Canada he settled in Ontario where he originated from in earlier years.

We spent one more cold winter in the Orkney district which is about sixty miles southeast of Shaunavon, Saskatchewan. On June 5, 1923, we (Hugh Napper and his wife, Harriot, and the children, Norman, Belva, Mac and Evelyn) arrived in the Dovercourt district. This trip was made by team and wagon. Our new home was a small log house, one big room down and two small rooms upstairs. This place needed some repair so we spent several days at Mother's sister's home (Mr. and Mrs. Jack Rittinhouse).

The school in this area opened the first of April and closed at Christmas, so Norman and I started to school and our teacher was Miss

1926 — the Napper family — Mrs. Napper in door — L to R — Isobell, Evelyn, Mac, Belva and Norman.

Billy Rittenhouse, age 3. Isobell Napper, the baby sitter.

Harriett McArthur who later that fall married Ralph Sinclair. Our youngest sister, Isobell, was born October, 1924, on the farm.

The folks farmed until the spring of 1941 when Dad decided to rent to the Lougheed brothers. They had a farm sale and moved in June to Olds. Early in 1944 this quarter was sold once more to Mr. Jaycock. Mom and Dad made one more move; they came to Calgary in the summer of 1948.

Norman married Kay Carter and they had

Mom and Dad Napper and Kay (Norman's wife) after his death in 1942.

one girl, Ellen. Norman passed away May, 1942. I (Belva) married Cecil Barber and we had one son, Gorden. Mac remained single. He served in the Canadian Army overseas from 1942-1946. Evelyn married Glick Richardson of Seattle. They had one girl, Alice. Isobell married Kenneth Marsh of Vancouver and they had three children, Jeannie, Kenneth and Gary. Mother passed away June 2, 1966, and Dad June 15, 1967.

Alf Peach

Alf Peach came from England and homesteaded the N.E.Q. 20-37-6-5. His mother and sister came to visit shortly after the first world war. They didn't stay long and went back home appalled at the loneliness and primitive living conditions.

Alf worked clearing land for the Bertagnolli boys for three years. About 1922 he sold his quarter and went to New Zealand. He was a well educated man.

H. J. Smith, Mac McCrindle, Alfred Peach.

George Pearkes

Mr. George Pearkes homesteaded the S.E.Q. 6-38-6-5. He came from England with his mother and sister. They were all well educated. He joined up at the outbreak of the first world war, his sister and mother returning to England.

George Pearkes received a commission and won a V.C.

On his return to Canada he became a Member of Parliament. He also served in W.W. II. Later he was Lt. Governor of British Columbia.

The John B. Rauch Family

In 1928 John Rauch immigrated to Canada from Ebersbach, Germany, and worked on farms in the Calgary area. In April of 1930 he was joined by his bride-to-be, Berta Epple, from his home town in Germany. They rented land near Cochrane until 1933, but in order to get land of their own they decided to go homesteading. After some investigating, they decided to head for Rocky Mountain House area, so in June of 1933 their few belongings were loaded on wagons and their livestock was herded behind. One week later they arrived at their homestead, N.W. 3-38-6-5, in the Dovercourt district. A previous settler had built a small log house on the land and Rauchs lived in it until 1937 when a frame house was built. They stayed on the homestead until 1944 when they moved several miles west to the old Stevens place which is now farmed by their second son, John Jr.

John and Berta live close by on another quarter where they are semi retired. They have five children, all married with families; Evelyn (Mrs. Waldo Bertagnolli), Warner, John, Otto and Erwin and there are eighteen grandchildren. They all farm in the area except Erwin who lives near Innisfail.

The Rittenhouse Family

Johnathan M. Rittenhouse was born in South Cayuga, Ontario, December 2, 1873. He moved to Alberta in 1911 and spent three years in the Red Deer and Lacombe districts. He moved to Rocky Moutain House in 1914 and worked for various general stores until 1920. At that time he homesteaded the N.E.Q. 35-37-7-5, now D. Armstrong's Dovercourt.

John was a charter member of the Rocky I.O.O.F. Lodge and acted as secretary for many years.

John married Annie Isabel McNaughten in Calgary, August 9, 1921. They had one son, William. Annie McNaughten was born at Almont, Ontario, September 8, 1893, and moved to the Lacombe district in 1894 with her family. Annie loved horses and always rode and drove good ones.

John and Annie farmed until 1947 at which time they sold the farm and retired to Sylvan Lake. Mr. Rittenhouse passed away at his home in Sylvan Lake July 9, 1958, at the age of eighty-six years. Annie lived on in her home until the summer of 1976 when she sold the house and moved into the Sylvan Lake Lodge. She lived there until she became ill, and passed away in the Red Deer General Hospital August 17, 1978, at the age of eighty-five years. They are buried in the Sylvan Lake Cemetery.

William married Jane Leuella Herder of Sylvan Lake. They have four children, John L., David W. Brenda A and Jane E. They live at Camrose.

Herman Shaw

Herman Shaw came to the Dovercourt district around 1909 from a rocky area of Ontario. He homesteaded the S.E.Q. 1-38-7-5, now owned by H. Conkey. He left the district about 1916.

The Sinclair Family

Michael Herbert Sinclair was born in Dover, England in 1864. He married Eleanor Collins

Mr. and Mrs. Mike Sinclair.

Ralph Sinclair's mail truck Model T Ford about 1918 — in truck: Micheal, Elenor Sinclair, Rex Bancroft, Tom Clarkson, Rex Jr. and Barbara Bancroft — standing — Marion Bancroft, Lula Mac (Greives) Budverson and Alf Peach.

Stroud, five children were born to them. While in England, Mr. Sinclair was a fireman on the south-eastern railroad.

In 1906-07 the Sinclair family immigrated to Canada coming to the Dovercourt area, they homesteaded the N. E. Q. 31-37-6-5, now G. Hayes. However, it was not known as the Dovercourt area then. With Michael Sinclair having been born in Dover, England, and one of their neighbors, Hugh Lee, who came from Greencourt, they combined their origins and called their new home, Dovercourt.

The railroad had not come to this part of the country yet, so they travelled to Innisfail twice a year to purchase staples; buying large amounts of flour, sugar, raisins, salt, etc. The children always waited for their treat, a sherbet sucker or a small bag of candy.

After Mrs. Sinclair's passing in 1929, Mr. Sinclair moved to Rocky Mountain House and was a night watchman for the C.P.R. About 1933 he moved back to the district to live in his own house in the yard of his daughter and son-in-law, Louisa and Karl Soderburg.

One day when Karl and Mr. Sinclair were cutting logs, a tree fell on Mr. Sinclair, breaking his leg midway between his knee and hip. Medical skills were limited so the break never truly mended. He walked with a limp from then on and amused his grandchildren because he could always wiggle the break.

Michael Sinclair enjoyed playing his 'all button' accordian and entertained many gatherings at the homes of his families.

Mr. Sincliar passed away in 1948 at the age of eighty-four years. One of his homes is still standing (1979). It had been moved to the Bethany Gospel Mission Church yard in 1959 for a manse for the ministers. It is now a summer home.

The Sinclairs' five children were: Herbert, Walter, Ralph Albert, Louisa Maud and Reuben James. Herbert married Olive Corem. They took out a homestead, N.E.Q. 36-37-7-5, now G. Hobbs. He was a shoemaker in Rocky and Red Deer. They had six children.

Walter Sinclair took out a homestead. He married Maude Berton and moved to Edmonton. They have six children.

Ralph Albert Sinclair took out a homestead. He married Hattie McArthur and they adopted two children. Ralph operated the Dovercourt mail route and hauled cream to the creamery. They moved to Rocky and he was Secretary of the Rocky Mountain House Hospital for many years. Both are buried in the Rocky Cemetery.

Louisa Maud Sinclair married Karl Soderberg. They had four children. She filed a homestead, N.E.Q. 16-37-6-5, now W. Lougheed's.

Rueben James Sinclair enlisted in the Army and after returning, filed a homestead. Later he moved to Calgary. He married Jean MacCullum and they had four children.

George Edward Smith

Ed was born in Somerset, England. He came to New York State and worked there for awhile before coming to the Nanton district in the spring of 1905. Ed and Sid worked together, fencing, breaking land, etc. They worked out threshing and worked for ranchers and others in the busy seasons. Ed also worked out of the district at Gleichen, Golden and Lagan. Ed farmed at Dovercourt and Nanton travelling back and forth. He bought some pasture land northwest of his farm at Dovercourt later on.

Ed farmed in the Nanton district until 1946 when he sold and moved to Vancouver Island. He bought a farm near Sidney, British Columbia. Ed had many interesting yarns to tell of his experiences through the years. Ed passed away in 1962.

George Edward Smith.

Henry James Smith

Henry (Hank) Smith came to New York State from Somerset, England. He visited relations and stayed in the U.S.A. for a short time. He then

Micheal and Elenor Sinclair, Carl and Louisa Soderburg, Art, Thelma, Frank and Baby Gordon Soderburg.

came to Alberta where his brother, Sid, and family were living. He worked in Alberta for awhile then went to New Mexico to stay with his sister, Ann, and her small daughter after Ann's husband had passed away. Hank ran an Experimental Farm in New Mexico. Then Hank, Ann and Ann's daughter, Roberta, moved up to Alberta. Hank joined the Strathcona Horse Association in Calgary. Ann and Roberta lived in the Nanton district for awhile where Ann kept house for her brother, Ed.

Hank bought a farm in the Dovercourt district south of Rocky Mountain House. In 1921 he and his brother, Sid, started a butcher business in Rocky Mountain House. The chopping block was cut from a big Balm of Gilead tree. Hank ran the shop in town. The abattoir was out at Sid and Jessie's place at Dovercourt so the meat had to be hauled about eighteen miles in to the shop.

Hank married Darlene (Darrel) Reighley. Darrel had been teaching at the Chedderville School. Hank and Darrel and their two sons, James (Jim) and Robert (Bob), lived in Rocky Mountain House for a number of years.

H. J. Smith Meat Market at Rocky Mountain House.

H. J. Smith Cattle Truck — 1924.

Hank Smith Family.

Sid and Jessie sold their farm at Dovercourt and moved to a place about a mile south east of Rocky. A new house and abattoir, etc. was built there.

Fred Spoor came into the butcher business with Hank and Sid in 1925.

Later on Sid decided to go farming again and bought a place four and a half miles south of Rocky Mountain House. Hank and Darrel and their sons moved out to the place where Sid and Jessie had been living. Hank and Fred ran the butcher shop in Rocky Mountain House and owned and operated a butcher shop in Nordegg.

Jim and Bob were both in Air Cadets for awhile. Jim joined the R.C.A.F. in 1942. Bob and a number of other Air Cadets went to England on a tour about 1946.

Hank, Darrel and Bob moved to Vernon, British Columbia, in 1945. After living in Vernon for a few years Hank and Darrel built a house on their property by Lake Kalamalka. They moved there in 1952 where they have been living retired for a number of years.

Jim and his wife, Dorothy, moved to Vernon. Jim ran the Vernon Locker Plant. They retired at Vernon and have a boy and a girl.

Bob became a Medical Doctor. Bob and his wife, Margaret, and their two boys live in Victoria, British Columbia.

John Smith

John (Jack) Smith was born in Somerset, England. He came to Alberta in 1927 and visited relatives in the Nanton district and worked for awhile. In 1928 Jack bought a place southeast of Rocky Mountain House and visited relatives who were all living nearby.

Jack joined the army in 1940. He went overseas in 1941 and was on active duty in France and Germany. He came back to Rocky Mountain House in 1945.

In 1946 Jack moved to Vancouver Island. He worked at Campbell River for awhile. Jack has been retired and living in Victoria for a number of years.

Lou Smith

Lou Smith came out to the U.S.A. from Somerset, England, in 1909. He worked in New York State for awhile. He came to Alberta to his brother, Sam's, place west of Nanton arriving early in 1911 in an Alberta blizzard! After the weather had warmed up a bit, Lou and Sam walked up to Cayley and took the train to Red Deer where Lou filed on a homestead in the Dovercourt district. Lou and Sam walked out to their homesteads from Red Deer, about seventy miles. They spent the first night at Markerville and the second night at Stauffer. They arrived at their homesteads the following day where their brothers. Sid and Ed, were busy getting out logs for the houses, etc. Lou worked in the Nanton district for several falls. He worked for Bob Martin in the fall of 1911. The next four falls he worked for Walter Watt twice and Hughie Shaw twice. Late in the fall of 1915 he worked for a farmer south of Fort Macleod for about a month.

Lou joined the Army in December, 1915, in

Lou Smith — World War 1.

Red Deer. He obtained permission to go out to his homestead and make arrangements with his brother, Sid, to look after his cattle and horses or sell them. He reported for duty on January the second, 1916. Lou lost his right arm while on active duty overseas.

Lou married Ruth Brown in 1919 shortly after he was discharged from the Army. They lived in the Dovercourt district for a few years then Lou, Ruth and their son, Donald, moved to Rocky Mountain House. Lou ran a livery barn and was also an auctioneer. Lou, Ruth, Donald and daughter, June, moved to Vernon, British Columbia, in 1930. Two sons, Robert and Richard, were born in Vernon. Lou and Ruth went into the poultry business and operated the Avonlea Poultry Farm for many years. They sold the farm in 1967. Ruth passed away in 1968. Lou lived in Vernon for awhile then moved to Victoria where he now resides.

Lou Smith at his home built in 1911.

Lou Smith, Linus Hamilton, Harry Bethel — 1912.

L. to R. — Helen Hankinson, Don Smith, Rose Robinson, Ruth Smith and Alice Robinson.

Don joined the R.C.A.F. He was an Instructor there for some time. Don and his wife, Veronica, had seven children, six boys and one girl. Veronica passed away in 1969. Later on, Don remarried. Don and his wife, Marion, have a little boy. Marion has two children by a former marriage. Don works in Calgary.

June is married to Howard McLeod. They live in Vancouver. They have a girl and a boy.

Bob and his wife, Alice, live in Sarnia. They have two boys. Bob is in the oil business.

Dick and his wife, Ann, and their two children, a girl and a boy, live in Victoria. Dick is in the Forestry.

Samuel Charles Smith

Sam and his wife, Eva, came to the Nanton district from Somerset, England, in 1910. They bought a quarter section west of Nanton soon after they arrived. Later they bought the half section on the south and southwest of the quarter.

Sam and two of his brothers, Sid and Ed, took up homesteads in the Dovercourt district in 1910. Sam and Eva lived in the Dovercourt district for awhile. Part of the time was spent in building, fencing, clearing and breaking on the homestead and part of the time in farming at Nanton, sometimes travelling back and forth by team and wagon. They sold their homestead later to Sam's brother, Sid.

Sam and Eva were strong supporters of the Methodist Church and later of the United Church. Their flowers and vegetable garden were a beauty spot in the neighborhood. They had a son, Kenneth, born in 1917. Ken attended public and high school in Nanton and went on to Olds School of Agriculture. He joined the R.C.A.F. in 1940 and became an Observer before going overseas in 1941. He was a Flying Officer. Ken was on a number of operational flights before losing his life over Holland on the night of January 3, 1943. He was buried in Holland. The Dutch people have done a wonderful job of

Pilot Officer Kenneth Read Smith.

looking after the graves of Canadian boys and others who helped free their country.

Sam and Eva sold the farm in 1946 and moved to Vancouver Island. They bought a farm north of Victoria and farmed there for awhile. Sam passed away in 1951, Eva sold the farm and moved to Victoria. She passed away in 1965.

Sidney Swearse Smith

Sid and his wife, Jessie, and daughter, Mildred, came to the Nanton district from New York State in the spring of 1905. Sid and Jessie were formerly from Somerset, England. Sid and his brother, Ed, bought a half section of railway land west of Nanton. A house was built near the southwest corner of the place. The water had to be carried from Baird's spring, about half a mile. This lovely spring gushed out of the sand rocks near the Baird's house. The men would bring water from the spring in the morning but if Jessie needed more during the day she would carry her small daughter and the pail to the spring, get the water, and carry water and daughter back home. Range cattle roamed over the country at that time and were frightened and curious to see a woman and small child out on the prairie and would sometimes surround Jessie and daughter but never harmed them. It must have been a frightening experience for Jessie, though, who had lived in a town in England before coming out to North America. The men dug for wells but were unable to find water. The house was then moved up near the north end of the half section. A well was dug near the house and a good supply of water was obtained.

Some of the neighbors were Frank Wilsons to the north, the Thomas Johnsons to the northwest, Mrs. McLennan and son, Jack, Bill Stewarts and the William Robinsons to the west, W. D. Ransom on the south, Bairds to the southeast, William White and sons, Percy and Archie, to the east, the D. C. Williams to the southwest up the coulee which was named after them, the Alec

Jessie Smith, Darrel Smith and Eva Smith.

Campbells lived at the east end of Williams Coulee later on.

Sid and Jessie Smith worked at Geordie Greigs for parts of 1905 and 1907. Geordie Greig had a lot of good horses which Sid helped break and helped do the farm work while Jessie kept house. The threshing was done by horsepower machine. In the terrible winter of 1906-07 hundreds of cattle died and Billy Greig (Geordie's brother), and Sid skinned many and sold the hides for one dollar each.

Sid hauled the stones from Williams Coulee to Geordie Greigs to build the house which stands where John and Jean Greig live today. He also worked for others in the district at busy times of the year.

Sid and two of his brothers, Ed and Sam, homesteaded in the Dovercourt district in 1910. They spent part of the time on their homesteads building, fencing, clearing and breaking. Part of the time was spent on their farms at Nanton.

Sometimes the Smiths, or some of them, walked from Red Deer or Innisfail out to their homesteads with heavy packs on their backs. Sid later traded his share of the half section at Nanton to his brother, Ed, for Ed's homestead at Dovercourt. Sid and Jessie moved up to Dovercourt where they farmed and were also engaged in the butcher business. Sid bought his brother, Sam's, homestead and also a neighbors place. Sid and Jessie sold the farm at Dovercourt and moved to a place about a mile southeast of Rocky Mountain House where they lived for awhile. Henry Smith and family then moved out to this place from Rocky Mountain House. Sid and Jessie bought a farm four and a half miles south of Rocky Mountain House where they lived until 1946 when they sold the farm and moved to Vancouver Island. They bought a farm near Victoria and lived there until 1951. They then sold their farm and bought a place in Sooke,

Sidney Smith.

Ed Smith.

Mrs. Eddie Grant and Mrs. Sidney Smith — Laundry day.

Ed Smith, Linus Hamilton, Harry Bethel — 1912.

west of Victoria. Sid had many interesting yarns to tell of his experiences from his boyhood on through the years. He had a boat out at Sooke and enjoyed going out fishing. Sid passed away in 1956. Jessie lived in Sooke until 1971 then moved to Nanton. She enjoyed her flowers and going out to the old timers meetings and visiting. Jessie passed away in 1973.

William Smith

William (Bill) Smith was born in Somerset, England. When he came out to North America it is believed he came to New York State and visited relations there. Later on he came to Alberta and visited his brother, Sid, and family and worked in the Nanton district for awhile. He had a place in the Dovercourt district for a short time.

Bill joined the Army. He lost his life in 1917 while on active duty overseas.

The Soderburg Family

Karl Abel Soderburg was born in Helsingland, Sweden, in 1884. He came to Minnesota first, then came north to the Dovercourt area around 1914. He homesteaded two quarters, the S.E.Q. 21-37-6-5, and the N.W.Q 22-37-6-5, now L. Zimmer's. In 1916 he married Louisa Maud Sinclair. They had four children, three boys and a girl.

Karl was an avid hunter and fisherman and like most families of this time, they lived on wild game, birds and fish. One Season Louisa canned 390 quarts of blueberries in their natural juice — some treat!!

The Soderburg house was always full, with neighbors and friends who all enjoyed a time of dancing and singing. Those were the ' good ol' days' when there was always time for your neighbor. Many times Louisa would go to the chicken barn and catch a young rooster to make dinner for friends. The meals weren't fancy, but there was always lots of meat, potatoes and gravy! Mostly there was a kin feeling between all.

Threshing time was always hectic. Many bachelor neighbors came to share in the harvest. It was nothing to have to prepare a big meal for ten men plus the family of six.

Karl worked out in lumber camps in the winter, leaving Louisa with the milking, other chores and four small children. All the children were born at home with Mrs. Bill Young or Grandma Howes midwifing.

The roads were terrible, crossing through muskegs, etc. One story was told of a traveller who sank in one of these bog holes. A passerby came along and asked if he could help. The

Carl, Louisa, Frank, Gordon, Thelma and Art Soderburg.

traveller said, "Don't worry about me, I have a saddle horse below me yet!"

One of the big highlights as far as vehicles were concerned, was when they purchased a 1928 Chevrolet in 1932 for $175.00.

Karl bought two Guernsey-Jersey cross cows from Herb Warren, paying a "big price" for them. He paid $50 each. However, they were good cows and they built their entire herd from these two cows.

The Soderburgs retired to Sylvan Lake in 1954, but Karl kept up the farm for several years until they sold out in 1957.

Mr. Soderburg passed away in July, 1972, at the age of eighty-eight years. Mrs. Soderburg died in December, 1978, at the age of eighty years. They are both buried in the Sylvan Lake Cemetery. Their children are Arthur Cyril Carl, who homesteaded the N.W.Q. 16-37-6-5 now L. Helmer and J. Heikkinen's, before joining the army. After Arthur returned home he married Sylvia Grace May. They had three children, Arthur Dennis, Sylvia Jean and Kenneth Earl. Sylvia, Arthur's wife, died of polio in 1953. Arthur built a log house on his homestead. He left the district in 1966. He married Leona McNaught of Bentley in 1968 and they have two children, Margaret Irene and Allen Carl. They reside at Bluffton.

Frank Reuben married Betty Scott of Pine Hill. They had four children, Myrtle Louise, Dorothy Ann (deceased), Daniel Frank and Steven Carl. They live at Clive, Alberta.

Thelma Louise married Robert John Bioletti of Pine Hill. They have two children, Edith Louise and Robert John. They live at Centerville, west of Red Deer.

Gorden Roy entered the army and when he returned, he married Anna Hamilton. They purchased the Frank McCrinkle farm through the V.L.A. They are still living in the Dovercourt district. They have three children, Darlene Ann, Sharon Gail and Roy Lynn.

Andy Swales

Andy Swales came from Ontario in 1910 and homesteaded the S.W.Q. 31-37-6-5. He built a fine home. Andy worked in bush near Nordegg so was away from home a lot.

Andy was a cousin to Emma Clark Bertagnolli. He was married and had a daughter, Eileen. They sold their farm and moved to Nordegg.

Mr. and Mrs. Swales and daughter Eileen, 1910.

Jack and Gertie Urquhart

Jack and Gertie Urquhart came from Red Deer to the Dovercourt district in the thirties. The quarter they lived on was the S.W.Q. 20-37-6-5 now owned by Danny and Edith May. Jack and Gertie had four children, Audrey, Bill, Bernice and Wayne.

Jack operated a sawmill on his farm for many years and used a steam engine for power. He helped build the Dovercourt Hall and sawed some of the lumber such as stringers. Maurice May and his dad cut the logs for the floor joists and Jack sawed them. Jack also used to do

Leonard Hansen at Urqhart house.

Leonard Hansen plowing at Urqhart's.

blacksmith work and was always ready to give a helping hand to a neighbor. he was a great lover of horses and kept some real nice race horses. He operated a cream route to Rocky for many years when the roads were difficult to travel.

Jack loved to play ball with the rest of the gang. Gertie played the organ and Lenard Hanson played the fiddle for many a good dance in the Chedderville School.

They moved to British Columbia where they still reside.

Herb Warren

Herb Warren was a printer in the County of Lincolnshire, England. In 1905 he had to leave his trade because of ink poisoning. He decided to come to Canada and lived at Boissevain, Manitoba, until the spring of 1907 when he moved to Buck Lake, Alberta. He came to the Dovercourt district from Buck Lake about 1915. He settled on the Ed Perkes homestead, S.W.Q. 6-38-6-5, now S. Howes.

Herb trapped on the Baptiste River in 1919, also looked after some cattle for a neighbor. In the 1920s he worked in the mines at Nordegg and cooked for the forestry and survey crews. It was

Herb Warren.

Grizzly Bear attack.

The Wickins Family

Florence and Joe Wickins came to Alberta from London, England, in 1919. Dad had served with the Royal Flying Corps in England and France during the first world war. When he received his discharge, they decided to come to Canada.

Along with Mom and Dad were Winnifred, eight years, Doris, six and Stanley, two and a half. They settled at Huxley, Alberta where Evelyn and Tom were born. They farmed there until 1931 when they moved to Dovercourt by teams and wagons, settling first on the 'Lane Place', S.W.Q. 32-37-6-5, now Lyle Dorey's. Two more children, Phyllis and Ernie, were born there before they moved again, and for the last time, in the fall of 1933 to S.W.Q. 1-38-7-5. This land had been homesteaded before 1915 by Fred Culvert. Mr. Culvert worked on the construction of the railroad when it was put through to Nordegg in the early 1930s. People by the name of Gibson also lived on the Culvert quarter at one

while Herb was with a survey crew around Nordegg that he helped save a man from a grizzly bear. Three hunters had come up from the States wanting to get a grizzly. They borrowed some dogs from a man in the Nordegg area and set out. A grizzly was sighted, shot at and wounded but not killed. The bear attacked one man, the second man ran to Herb's camp for help. The third man stood taking pictures. Herb had one of the pictures that the man took. It shows the grizzly standing over a man sprawled face down on the ground, seven dogs barking viciously around them, and two men coming out of the bush with guns. Herb told us that they killed the bear and took the 'downed' man out to Rocky with horses and on to Red Deer by car. He lived to tell the tale. When the grizzly was skinned out, there were nine bullet holes in it.

Herb worked around the district and was always ready to give anyone a hand. He drove a fine team and worked on the threshing in the district. He loved fishing. It was while he was fishing down at the Clearwater River southeast of his place with a neighbor, that he had a heart attack and died. This was June, 1960; age seventy-four years.

Herb's brother, Richard, lives at the Cedars Villa Lodge in Calgary. He is ninety-seven years young (March, 1979). Richard homesteaded in the Rimbey area in 1908.

Mrs. Florence Wickins driving a four horse team, moving from Huxley to Dovercourt. The trip took four days.

time. Dad bought this quarter from a Mr. King in Calgary. Dad homesteaded the quarter joining on the west.

Times were hard in the '30s, so Dad travelled the country with a saw and grinding outfit pulled by a team of horses. He used a six horsepower stationary International Harvester engine to run the saw and grinder. It seemed that there was always stove wood that needed to be cut.

Of course Mom planted the usual big garden, and took care of it. There were no freezers then, so it had to be canned — also the meat. They had chickens to look after, cows to milk, cream to churn into butter — some of which she sold at Mr. Cony's store in Rocky. People used to ask for Mom's butter.

The weekly wash!! Water had to be hauled in and heated on the stove in a wash boiler and then hauled out again, saving enough of the rinse water to wash the floors. In the winter, Mom used to melt snow for the washing. Bake day — big golden loaves of bread, mmm! Can't you just smell it? It's something a person never forgets — coming in after school to eat fresh bread thick with homemade butter and jam on it. Isn't it funny how you can cook something that your mother used to make, but it never tastes as good!

When war was declared in 1939, Dad tried to enlist, but was turned down, so he went to Fort William where he worked in a war factory in the final assembly shop where he put the pnuematic systems in the Mark One and Mark Two Hurricane Fighters. He came back to Calgary in 1942 when Stanley, the oldest son who was in the Air Force, passed away. Dad worked in Calgary at the Ogden Shops until the end of the war. When

Tom reached eighteen, he also joined the Air Force. Mom kept the farm running with the help of the younger children while Dad was away.

In 1945 Dad bought a movie picture outfit and showed pictures in Central Alberta for a year. When he sold it he went back to farming until he retired to the Sylvan Lake Lodge in the Fall of 1969. He lived there until he became ill in June of 1971, and was taken to the General Hospital in Calgary. He passed away there on July 14, 1971, at the age of eighty-four years. Mother passed away at home August 28, 1965, at the age of seventy-seven years. They are both buried in the Rocky Mountain House Cemetery.

Ernie has the home place and married Beryl Cole of Chedderville in June of 1969. They have a daughter and a son.

Winnifred and her husband live at Airdrie. They have four daughters and three sons.

Doris lives in Vancouver. Her husband passed away January 8, 1979. She has a daughter and a son.

Evelyn and her second husband live in Calgary. She has one daughter from her first marriage. Tom and his wife farm at Eckville. They have four sons. Phyllis and Jack live in the district. They have two sons and a daughter.

Daulf Young

Daulf Young came from Ontario and homesteaded the N.E.Q. 35-37-7-5 in 1909. This quarter now belongs to D. Armstrong. Before he had a chance to prove up, the first world war broke out and he joined up and went away to war; he never came back.

Florence, Joe and Ernie Wickins in front of "The Chimneys" in Rocky Mountain House.

Daulf Young in 1909.

Hazeldell

Hazeldell

The Hazeldell school was built in 1939. It is now located on N.E. 11-37-5. The Hazeldell school was closed in 1958-1959. It is now used as a community center. There was an old Hazeldell school built in 1929 and is one half mile east of where the newer one is now located. The first teacher was Mr. Litebody, and this was the new school. The first teacher in the old Hazeldell school was unknown.

Christian (Peter) Roseth

by Edwin Roseth

Christian (Peter) Roseth was born and raised in Minnesota. He rented land in the Pollockville area of Alberta and farmed and worked in that area in the early 1900s. He met and married my mother, Rose Kathereen Thacker.

After farming there (his last years at farming), he put everything he had (money) into the crop he had planted. A terrible hail storm took their crop and all they had, so Mother and Dad left the farm and moved to Rosemary where Edwin and I were born. A sister, Goldie, was also born at Rosemary. Dad worked in and around that area and moved into the Raven district in 1930 where another member of our family was born in Innisfail, Gordon Walter Roseth.

Gordon, Edwin and Goldie Roseth.

Dad worked for various farmers until his death of cancer in, I believe, 1933, leaving my mother with three young children whom she raised by herself. She always made her home close to my Grandfather's and Grandma's. In the latter years, we moved onto Grandpa's farm east of Stauffer where Goldie, Gordon and I attended school at Hazel Dell.

I, Edwin, married Barbara Bremner and we had five children, Chris, Gene, Neil, Louise and Roger. Chris married Brenda Little. Gene married Bonnie Coley and they have two girls, Jamie and Jeanie.

Goldie Roseth married Gordon Hanna and they had four children, Dorothy, Lourie, Debby and Bruce. Dorothy married Devin Haines and they have one girl, Fairia. Lourie married Ray Germaine and they have two boys.

Gordon Roseth married Helen Tennant and they have two boys, Wayne and Rick.

Forrest A. Thacker

In 1928 I moved with my mother and dad,

Young people from Stauffer — back row — Ed (Cactus) McKenzie and Ralph Fisher — front row — Gordon and Edwin Roseth, Hugh McKenzie and Goldie Roseth.

Walter and Della Thacker, to the Raven district and took my education at the North Raven School where I finished grade eight.

The folks came up from Rosemary, Alberta, in a Model T. Ford car. My older sister, Ruby, and brother Leon, and I were so excited to be able to see the Rocky Mountains in the distance. We watched for hours to be able to top a hill and see what at! To young minds, this was a wonderful experience. The trip took us from six in the morning until midnight to reach Innisfail. Twenty was an average mile per hour, and what a thrill it was when Dad hit it up to a death-defying rate of thirty.

Coming from the prairies; a ten foot poplar was a big tree. When we got to Innisfail and climbed trees of thirty feet, it felt like we were on the Empire State Building.

After working for awhile in Alberta, I went to work in the sawmills of northern British Columbia. This is where I met my fiancee, Armen DeGrasse. We were married in 1939 and moved back to the Stauffer area. In 1943 I joined the Army and was gone for over three years. In 1947 my wife and I and our three small children farmed the half section of land a half mile south on the Sundre road. After three years, we sold and moved to Stauffer and bought land there, the S.W. 24-37-5-5, a mile north of the present Stauffer Post Office. For several years, we rented the half section from Art Buchanan on the corner of the Sundre road and Highway fifty-

L. to R. — Dad Thacker, Elaine Hollenbeck, Goldie Roseth, Gordon Roseth, Ron Hollenbeck, Edwin Roseth and Mother Thacker.

four. We always had a tender spot for the old-timers who struggled to make that country from bush land into the beautiful farms there are today.

We had two more boys born after we moved to the farm one mile north of Stauffer. Our family were as follows; Lillian, Albert, Forrest Jr., Terry and Bennett. In 1960 we quit farming due to ill health and have lived in Red Deer and Penhold where I retired.

Walter Thacker
by Forrest A. Thacker

My mother and father, Walter E. Thacker and his wife, Della, came from Omaha, Nebraska, in the early years of the 1900s. At first they settled in the Pollickville area of Alberta and they had eight children. Rose and Roy (born in the U.S.A.), Dewy, Verna, Carl, Ruby, Forrest

Armen Thacker and children — Forrest Jr., Albert, and Lillian.

Armen Thacker, Grandma Della Thacker, Leon Thacker, Verna Thacker, Ben Hollenbeck. 2nd row — Goldie, Edwin, Gordon, ?, and Rose Roseth, Grandpa Walter Thacker. Front row — Lillian Thacker, Ronald and Elaine Hollenbeck.

and Leon. After many years in the dry dust bowl of that Alberta country, we moved into the irrigation district of Rosemary, and then to the Raven district in 1928.

At first we stayed with Sam Niel. Dad had bought a quarter from Cyrus Jensen which he never farmed, so he rented land which was known as the Sam Miles place. After three years there, we moved a mile northwest of the North Raven School where Leon and I went to public school.

Again my folks moved. They bought land from the Hudson's Bay Company two miles east of the Stauffer Post Office as it is now. My father and mother were known as very hospitable neighbors and had many friends. Mother Thacker used to be called on many occasions to sit up with the dead who were, in those days, kept at home. She helped get them ready for burial. In those days they kept formaldehide on their faces to keep them from turning black.

Rose Thacker married Peter Roseth and they had three children, Edwin, Goldie and Gordon. Edwin Roseth married Barbara Bremner and they had five children, Chris, Gene, Neil, Louise and Roger. Chris married Brenda Little. Gene married Bonnie Coley and they have two girls, Jamie and Jeanie. Goldie Roseth married Gordon Hanna and they had four children, Dorthy, Lourie, Debby and Bruce. Dorthy married Kevin Haines and they have one girl, Fairia. Lourie married Ray Germaine and they have two boys. Gordon Roseth married Helen Tennant and they have two boys, Wayne and Rick.

Roy Thacker married Betty Sims and they have four children, Bobby, Ilene, Ronald and Donald. Bobby married Alice Austrige and they have two children, Lana and Lance. Ilene married Ted Chamberlain and they had two children, Bonnie and Jimmie.

Verna Thacker married Ben Hollenbeck. They had three children, Elaine, Ronald and Carol. Elaine married Bob Eodie and they had seven children. Ronald married Bev Cave and they had two girls, Carolyn and Ronda.

Ruby Thacker married Les Baird. They had three boys, Jack, Larry and Gordon.

Forest Thacker married Armen Degross and they had five children, Lillian, Albert, Forest, Larry and Ben.

Leon Thacker married Lidia Gerlutz and they had three children, Walter, Gerry and Valerie.

There were three sons overseas in the Army, Roy, Forest and Leon.

Dad Thacker had two strokes in 1941 and had to quit farming. So Mother and Dad moved to Condor where Dad passed away due to another stroke in 1945 at the age of fifty-nine years. Mother lived on in Condor a few years with Roy and Leon. She spent the last remaining years of her life in the West Park Nursing Home where she died September 11, 1968, at age eighty-two. Dad and Mother are buried in the Hespero Cemetery.

North Caroline

North Caroline School
Leah (Cross) Rublatz

North Caroline School opened April 8, 1936 in a log cabin on Walter Bowers' place, the NW 35-36-6-5. The first teacher was Miss Ruby Richardson from Bowden.

Some of the first pupils attending were Bill, Charles and Helen Benz, Joan Braucht, Leah Cross, Harry and Joyce Fay, Madell, Eugene and Curtis Harris, Otto, Harold, Martha, Irene and Evelyn Motz, Bill Stewart.

During June, July and August of 1938 the new school was built on the south end of the same quarter. It was a one room school, and in comparison with the old log cabin was a veritable castle in the opinion of we children who attended. It seemed so "BIG". It had two blackboards which were green. This was something our teacher had difficulty in getting through my thick head. As far as I could determine, if it wasn't black it should have been called a "green board". It had a hardwood floor and cloakrooms, and best of all "INDOOR" chemical toilets. This reminds me of a humorous anecdote related by Bill Mewha recently during the gathering of information for this history book.

Since Howard Harris lived directly across the road from the school, the Harris family did much of the maintenance of the school and grounds.

(North) Caroline School.

The chemical tanks of the toilets had to be emptied and cleaned periodically. On this particular occasion Howard was hauling the 'soupy' refuse away in open barrels with a team and wagon. The wagon wheel hit some obstruction and came to an abrupt halt — the refuse did not! The end result was that Howard was given a wide berth until the job was completed.

Other families moved into the district and the enrollment increased. Other children who attended the new school were Bill, George and Ernie Choukalous, Clarence Reddick, Raymond Blowers, Dean and Wallace Price, Miner Harris and Mary Pydroski. The teachers were Maisie Nyren, Jessie Hay, Grace Waldruff (Mewha) Polly Phillips, Lillian Perrault, Lillian Wright and Stella Clay.

The school was closed and the pupils were bussed to Caroline when the schools were consolidated.

Armstrong — Robert
by Helen (Dial) Mullen

Robert Armstrong was married to Ida Bohn. They moved from Bellingham, Washington to

The first North Caroline School: teacher Ruby Richardson, L. to R. — Joan Braucht, Eugene Harris, Madelle Harris, Curtis Harris, Helen Benz, — obsured — Martha Motz, Harry Fay.

Robert and Ida Armstrong.

Dorothy and Vance Braucht.

Dorothy and Vance and Joan Braucht.

Caroline district in 1913. The Ben Harris family came with them.

Mr. Armstrong settled west and north of Caroline. Mrs. Armstrong died shortly after. They had a son Charles and a daughter Mabel. Mabel married Ray Dial in 1915. Robert and son Charlie moved back to the States. None of the family are living.

Vance and Dorothy Braucht and Family

We came to Stauffer from Cochrane in May, 1931, and lived there for one year and then moved to Caroline to our farm, one mile west and two and a half miles north of Caroline, in April, 1932. We lived there for twenty years. Vance worked in the Oilfield for seven or eight years while we were on the farm. We sold out to Ivan Graham and took over his store in February, 1952, and ran the store for twenty years. We sold it back to Ivan Graham, his son, and son-in-law in July, 1971.

Since then we have been living in our home in Caroline. We have one daughter, Joan, married to Sam Nelson in 1950, a grandson married and living at Surrey, British Columbia, and two great-granddaughters.

Four Generations. Vance Braucht, Joan, Tucker and Angie Nelson.

Cross Family
by Leah Rublatz

Edwin Elmer Cross was born in the state of Iowa, United States, on November 19, 1868. Lillian Belle Blazier was born in Iowa on May 4, 1875. Edwin and Lillian were married on October 10, 1894, at Janesville, Iowa. Their only child, Wilbur Bruce Cross, was born in Bremner County, Iowa, on December 5, 1896.

The Cross family decided to come to Canada for several reasons, the main ones being that land was scarce and heavily settled in Iowa at that time, and they felt that Canada had much to offer. They also had friends already settled here. They immigrated to Canada in January, 1914, and lived briefly in Innisfail until March of that same year. Then they came to Caroline and stayed with John and Mabel March until the log house on their land was completed. Their second home was built in 1922 and a house warming for them was held that December.

Wilbur travelled with Art Lamb, by horseback, to the Lomond district, southeast of Calgary, in 1916, to obtain work. Wilbur returned to Caroline and homesteaded on the S.E.Q. 36-36-7-5 at the age of twenty-one. On February 10, 1920, he was united in marriage to Louise Matilda Thibedeau at Central United Church in Calgary. The young couple went on to the Great Falls area of Montana and worked on a ranch there for some months before returning to the Caroline district.

Mabel March, Dora, Vera and John.

Lillian Cross, Wilbur and Edwin Cross.

Edwin, Wilbur and Lillian Cross.

Tragedy befell the family in a two-fold manner in the spring of 1923. Mrs. Cross' brother passed away in Iowa and she and Wilbur and Louise journeyed back to Iowa by car. The distance was great, and they could not get there in time for the funeral. They didn't follow roads much of the way but took a direct route across the prairie in many instances. The trip was plagued with the annoyance of flat tires and they camped out with the most meager necessities along the way. They had only been there a short time when they received a telegram from Art Saunders, stating that Mr. Cross had suffered a ruptured appendix and was gravely ill in the Red Deer Hospital. They returned as quickly as possible but found they were too late and Mr.

Cross had died sometime during their return trip.

Saddened, but determined, they continued on with the development of their land. The now widowed Lillian Cross found work wherever possible and made her home with her son and daughter-in-law between jobs.

During the early 1920's the Cross' bought a Case steam engine and threshing machine. Wilbur wrote and passed his exam to obtain steam engineer's papers. Alec Brown and Mike Benz were two of the men who drove the water tank, necessary for the operation of the steamer. Louise also took a turn at being 'tanky' and on one occasion held down that job for three weeks due to one of the regular drivers being unavailable. During the winters it was used at various sawmill sets, one in particular being the Orcutt site in the Strachan area.

On April 14, 1927, a daughter, Leah Mercedes, was born to Wilbur and Louise at their home, and was delivered by Louise's mother, Mrs. Claudine Thibedeau.

The Cross' were a family of musicians. Wilbur's musical training began at age five on a miniature violin hand carved by his father from a pine board with the tail piece being made from a beef bone. The violin is a treasured possession of his family. He also played other musical instruments: the organ, piano, saxophone, clarinet and mandolin. He played for many dances in the community, first with his parents and later in an orchestra with Paul and Helen Lamb and Oscar Anderson.

In 1930 Wilbur purchased a Wallace tractor for farming and to operate the thresher. Leah much enjoyed the preparation of the threshing machine for the annual fall harvest as there were many grease cups in small secret places inside the thresher that were a delight for a small girl to fill, as well as the mysteries of lacing belts and watching how they operated on the flywheel

Wilbur and Louise Cross.

of the tractor, and the various pulleys of the thresher.

Wilbur did much custom threshing in the district until the fall of 1940 when the farm was sold and the family moved to Caroline where they operated the hotel for a year. In 1942 Wilbur went into partnership with R. W. Mitten to operate one of the general stores, Caroline Traders. It was originally built and operated by Hal Roach and stood where the Community Hall is now located. The business was sold to Ivan Graham in 1949 and later moved to its present location beside the newer Pioneer General Store. At present the old Caroline Traders building is being demolished. After the sale of the store business, Wilbur and Louise went to Calgary to work. Louise was housekeeper and Wilbur was desk clerk at Braemar Lodge, situated on fourth avenue, about where the new Greyhound Terminal is now located. Later, Wilbur worked at T. Eaton's as maintenance man and looked after the boilers used to heat the store.

In the early 1950's they returned to Caroline and bought the old Patriquin house. Wilbur took extension courses from Southern Alberta Institute of Technology to obtain a higher class of engineer's papers and subsequently worked for Brinkerhoff Drilling as boiler operator.

Lillian B. Cross passed away in November, 1952, at the Holy Cross Hospital, after suffering a stroke. Wilbur suffered ill health much of his later life and he and Louise spent the fall of 1955 and winter of 1956 at Mesa, Arizona, where the climate much improved his health for a short time. The remaining years of his life were spent at Caroline and he died on September 27, 1958, in Innisfail and is buried in Red Deer beside his parents.

Louise has continued to make her home in Caroline and worked for Vance and Dorothy Braucht in the Pioneer Store, until the care of her sister, Mrs. Dutton, who was an invalid for many years, came to take all her time.

The Cross family musical instruments — center violin hand made by Edwin Cross.

Louise still lives in the Village and enjoys reasonably good health. She takes great pleasure in her grandchildren and their accomplishments, and her two great-grandchildren.

Leah Cross

Leah was born at her parents' farm home, on April 14, 1927. She attended schools at North Caroline and South Fork, and took high school at Dickson while boarding at the Verbena Dorm.

She married Edward A. Betts, in Red Deer, in 1946. They had three children of this marriage: M. Prudence, born August 9, 1947; Edward E., on June 28, 1951, and Bruce M. on August 26, 1955.

Leah and the children moved to Calgary in 1959 where Leah attended Calgary Business College in the evenings to complete business training. She remarried in 1966, to J. William Rublatz at New Westminster, British Columbia.

Bill and Leah moved back to Caroline in 1971. Bill operated the Caroline Transport for three years, and both were employed for a time by the Village of Caroline, and are still making their home there.

Prudence Betts was married to Dave Hodgson in 1967 and lives in Calgary. They have two children, Christopher and Lindsey.

Edward Betts married Elsie Benz in July, 1978. They live at Seebe, Alberta, where Edward works for Calgary Power.

Bruce Betts lives in Calgary and works as a security officer.

Leah and children — Prue, Ed, Bruce.

Ben Harris Pioneer Family

by Lucile Neal

Benjamin Joseph Harris was born in Rockford, Iowa, October 1, 1877. He passed away at Kelowna, British Columbia, August 18, 1970.

L. R. Howard, Pearl and Paul Harris.

Pearl May Harris was born in Nashua, Iowa, June 18, 1880. She passed away November 30, 1964, at Kelowna. Both are at rest in the Lake View Memorial Gardens in Kelowna. They had three children, Paul, Howard and myself.

Paul was born at Bradford, Iowa, April 27, 1899. He married Mildred Orcutt and they had eight children, six boys and two girls. Mildred passed away at a young age and after his children were nearly grown, Paul married Clarice Pitts (Wyant).

Howard was born at Ionia, Iowa, August 9, 1901. He married Daisy Wyant and they had six children, three girls and three boys.

I was born in Burlington, Washington, June 13, 1912. I married William Neal (Bill). We had two children, both boys.

My mother used to play for Sunday School in "The Little Brown Church in the Vale", when she was a girl. Mom and Dad with my brothers moved to Burlington, Washington, from Iowa. Dad did carpenter work and was Sheriff for awhile in Whatcom County, Washington. He had a few hair-raising experiences at times.

Word was spread around about the cheap land in Canada, the land of opportunity, so Dad thought it a good idea to go and find out. He and his brother, Lou, a relative, John March, and a friend, Bob Armstrong came to Alberta in May, 1912, and filed on homesteads in the Caroline area. Dad's place was where Harold Brown now lives, his brother's is where Hazel Turton lives, Bob Armstrong's is where Vance Braucht used to live, now owned by Lee Pittendreigh, and John March's just north of Hazel Turton. They were all in line and on the same side of the road, only there was no road there then. After they filed, they returned to Burlington, coming back to

The little Brown Church in the Vale.

Harris Family — left to right — Howard, Pearl, Lucille, Ben and Paul.

The Ben Harris homestead 1913.

Paul Harris and Leo Leturnia.

Alberta in January, 1913, and built their houses of logs, each helping the other to build.

They had many hardships and lots of hard work too. I can remember Mom and Howard wrapping gunny sacks around their worn shoes, out digging potatoes after it had snowed. Paul and Dad were in the south country helping thresh grain to make a few dollars to buy clothes and groceries for winter.

Another thing I can remember, the mosquitoes, they were so bad that the folks used to build a smudge pot to drive them away while they milked the cows. They put mosquito netting over and around our beds so that we could sleep, but there was usually enough inside the netting that our sleep was disturbed anyway.

Dad used to run the steam engine and separator in eastern Washington called the Paloose Country before he came to Canada, and after we moved here, he used to go down to southern Alberta where he ran the steam engine on threshing machines and sometimes he ran the separator.

Dad used to be asked to build coffins for some of the people in the early years. He constructed the box, then Mom would line and cover it. When I got older, I used to help Mom with the covering, etc. A few times Dad conducted service and prayers and read some verses from the Bible for funerals that were held in the homes — there was no church at Raven yet in those days. Mom played the organ or piano, if there was one in the home, andled the singing and sometimes she and Howard would sing a duet or a solo. This usually took place in the winter time as it was too far for a minister to travel out here from Innisfail and impossible to get through the drifts by car. We didn't have a minister all year around as we do now, but a student minister came for the summer months only.

It wasn't all bad times, there were good times too. We had to make our own entertainment and people used to come to our house. Mom would play the organ, Wilbur and Mr. Cross played violins and Mom and Howard would sing. The highlight for me was to go down to Mr. and Mrs.

Pearl and Ben Harris.

The Motz family: Julius, Bill Anderson (friend), Harold and Bill Motz. — Middle: Mrs. Motz, Frieda and Otto. The small ones: Evelyn, Irene and Martha.

L. R. Bill, Julius, Harold and Otto Motz.

Thibedeau's place to hear their player piano, I will always remember it as being the most wonderful piano in the world.

We got our mail and groceries at Mrs. Langley's who kept the store and post office. I went to school at South Fork, my first teacher was Guy Mount, a returned man.

Mom and Dad sold the farm sometime in the 1940s; they lived up over the old store in Caroline for awhile. Then they drove back through the States and to Iowa to see some of the old familiar places and to see some of the people who were there, that they had known as young people. The little Brown Church was much the same as when they went to Church and Sunday School there those many years ago.

Mom and Dad bought a few acres of land at Rutland, near Kelowna, and that is where they spent their remaining years.

Motz Family

by William Motz

My parents, Mr. and Mrs. Leonard Motz, came to Canada in 1910 from Odessa, Russia. They first homesteaded at Piapot, Saskatchewan. In 1914 they moved to Leader, Saskatchewan, where I was born in 1918. I attended school at Leader, Gravelbourg and Golden Prairie, Saskatchewan. We moved to Medicine Hat in 1929, where I went to school until 1933.

It was the spring of 1933 when we moved to our homestead at Caroline. Our journey consisted of shipping, by rail, from Medicine Hat to Innisfail. The O'dell family made the trip with us. From Innisfail we travelled by team and wagon to Caroline. According to my recollection, this trip took about three days. We got stuck several times in mud holes with our high wheeled wagon and had to double up horses to pull us through.

I was married to Ruth Blowers in 1940. We lived in the Caroline district with our two children, Melvin and Esther, until April, 1944, at which time I enlisted in the army. I went overseas in October, 1944, and was discharged in

Ruth and Bill Motz.

April, 1946. After the army, we lived in Calgary, Vernon and Carstairs where I began buying grain. I was transferred to Trochu in 1949 where we lived until 1966. Our youngest daughter was born there in 1950. From Trochu we moved to Terrace, British Columbia, and returned to the Caroline district in 1975.

My sisters, Frieda Martin, Martha Lavis and Evelyn Landon all reside in Calgary. Irene Ross resides in Trochu, brother Julius lives in Edmonton, and my youngest brothers went overseas and are both deceased. My sister, Ester, and both my parents are deceased.

My three children reside in the district. Melvin married Noreen Weigum of Trochu. They have two children: Bradley and Teresa. Esther married Paul Ginther of Elnora. They have two boys: Kurt and Drew. Velma married Jerry Keeler of Terrace, British Columbia, and they have two children: Leah and Eleanor.

Clarence Reddick

by Annie Reddick

Clarence Reddick was born at High Point, North Carolina, U.S.A. in 1879. About 1906 he came to the Calgary, Alberta area and worked on various ranches. One large horse ranch he worked on was owned by Johnnie Hamilton. He homesteaded at Richdale, Alberta in 1911.

In 1899 I was born into the McKennie family at Singhampton, near Collingwood, Ontario. My family moved west to Medicine Hat, Alberta in 1910. My father was in the dray business and also worked for International Harvester Co. He decided to leave Medicine Hat in 1916. To make the choice of whether he would move to Pincher Creek and build a livery barn or go to Richdale to farm, my father tossed a coin. The coin was for Richdale, so we went northward.

In 1917 Clarence and I were married. We have three children, Marion, Lois and Clarence.

We worked hard and Clarence farmed the land well, but in the late 20's and the early 30's it got so dry we didn't even get our seed back. It

would look like rain, the clouds would roll up and a few drops of rain would fall, but the wind would get up and blow it all away. I shall never forget those terrible dust storms in summer and severe blizzards in winter.

One blizzard I shall not soon forget was in 1926. We had a good supply of coal in a shed not too far from the house, and a sudden storm came up. Clarence didn't dare try to go out for coal. We burned all the things in the house that we could burn — even some of the poorer furniture.

The house began to get so cold we knew we would perish by the time the storm would stop. Clarence said "We must take some blankets and go into the cellar". I was afraid of the salamanders or the spiders that I imagined might be there, but I knew I had to follow. Marion and Lois were little girls then. We wrapped them and ourselves in blankets and Clarence and the girls slept while I stayed awake the rest of the night watching the lantern light. When the storm subsided in the morning, there was a big snow bank over the doorway with only a space of about three inches above the door where you could see daylight. Clarence had to shovel out from the top down to get out for coal.

Not many miles from us a mother and her child perished in the storm. Her daughter was at the barn doing chores when the storm struck. The mother put a lamp in the window, and when her daughter didn't come soon as she thought she should, she took the child out with her to the barn. The daughter made her way to the house by going toward the light in the window, but the mother and child didn't make it back. They were found frozen to death the next day.

We left the prairie October 1933 and rented a place at Alhambra. A few days after arriving it began to rain, and it rained and rained. We said "Oh look at that rain! If only we could have had that on the prairie we would have had real good wheat crops instead of failures".

Clarence and Annie Reddick taken in 1917.

Standing L.-R. — Lois, Clarence and Marian. Seated — Mr. and Mrs. Reddick.

110

In 1935 we moved to the Frank Davis place S.E. 14-37-6-5 at Butte — now owned by the Follis family. During 1936-37-38 we rented N½ 21-36-6-5 from James Tobin, now owned by George Benz. In 1939 we moved to SE 26-36-6-5 — a Hudson's Bay quarter now owned by R. Evans. We were there for 7 years and had bad luck with quite a bit of hail during this time.

In 1946 we bought E½ 28-36-5-5. Clarence said "Now, this is it. I've rented land long enough and I'm not moving anymore". He began to work in the saw mills to pay for the place. Later, as my son Clarence became older, he took turns with his father working between the mills and the farm.

My son, Clarence, loves the farm and loves to raise cattle. My husband Clarence was a great horse lover. He raised horses all his life. He would spend hours curry combing and trimming his horses. He was still riding horseback after he was 90 years of age.

We began to build our first new home in 1970, and moved into it in the spring of 1971. Clarence passed away in March 1971 at the age of 91 years.

Marion married Courtland Pollard from Caroline. They moved to Penticton B.C. in 1946. Courtland worked in the saw mills while here at Caroline, and was a trucker in B.C. Marion worked for some time in the fruit cannery. Courtland is retired due to ill health. They have 5 children.

Lois married Mearl Petersen from Markerville. They first lived in Caroline, then moved to Calgary. He also worked at Cochrane in a sawmill with Russell McGrandle. In 1966 they moved to Surrey B.C. where Mearl worked at a plywood plant. He passed away suddenly from a heart attack October, 1973. Lois still lives in Surrey and works in Link Hardware. They have two married daughters.

I live with my son Clarence on the farm, and have certainly enjoyed living in this part of the country.

Arthur Sanders

by Guy E. Fay

In 1914 Art Sanders and his wife, Martha, emigrated from South Dakota and settled on the S.W.Q. 35-36-6-5 which his father-in-law, Moses Fay, had given Mrs. Sanders. They prospered until 1934 when Mrs. Sanders had a stroke, after which everything rapidly deteriorated. Without her guidance he was lost. In 1947 they moved to Rocky Mountain House. Mrs. Sanders died in 1952 and he in 1954.

George and Hazel Turton

George was born in Barnsley, Yorkshire, England. His forefathers were coal miners. He was the youngest of a family of eight and had four sisters and three brothers. His mother died of the first World War 'flu' when he was ten years old. He lived with one and another of his married brothers and sisters and knew no home of his own for many years. At age thirteen he went to work in the coal mines of Yorkshire.

His father was not too well and he and George came to Canada to stay with two married sisters at Russell, Manitoba. After staying a little over a year, it was back to England and home, and to the mines again for George. He worked at that until illnesss hospitalized him with kidney stones. One kidney was ruptured and he was a very sick boy for some time.

In 1927 his father died and George came back to Manitoba to his sisters. He worked for his brother-in-law for three years to pay back the cost of his fare from England. His third sister, Lydia, meanwhile had been sent out to Consort, Alberta, to work as a mother's helper on a farm there. She had met and become engaged to Jim Crawford. They were soon to be married and George was invited to be their best man.

So in 1931 he came to southern Alberta where he worked for ranchers and farmers until 1934. Tiring of the heat and dust of the prairies, George, Lydia and Jim came to the Crammond district to try their luck on their own farms. But times were hard and land prices were high so George eventually gave up his farm at Crammond and went to work for Art Sanders, helping to sawmill in winter and farm in summer.

In 1937 he met me, Hazel Bowers, and in October, 1938, we were married. We made a deal to buy the former Joy Fay homestead which was just across the road from the Sanders place and adjoining Ben Harris on the north.

We had a milk cow, but no other stock. We cleared our land by hand with axe and saw, using the wood for stove fuel. Life was a continuous struggle to get a start and pay for our place.

Gwen was born that fall, prematurely, at home. She came along well as she was strong even though she only weighed four pounds at birth.

George continued to work out part time while I kept the home fires burning, milked cows, shipped cream to Rocky and later to Markerville Creamery, raised chickens, sold butter and eggs as well.

With wild berries and canned garden produce we always had enough to eat. Many town people thought we were lucky, but they didn't realize how much work it all was.

Time passed and with the place paid for we were able to call our soul our own. With the advent of bulldozers, land was more easily cleared and tractors replaced horses.

In 1956 when the new schools were going up, George again worked out. This time for construction. He worked on Caroline, Spruce View, Crammond, Leslieville and David Thompson Schools. We sold our cattle, bought a small trailer, rented the farm and were off to the various school sites as life is too short to be spent alone.

In Rocky in the fall of '59, George had his first heart attack. He spent six weeks in hospital before he was able to come home. We moved back to the farm in 1960. We raised a garden, went fishing and sat in the sun. Eventually George regained his health and was able to farm again. I worked part time for a while in the Pioneer General Store.

In 1966 a movement was made to get the Caroline Boy Scouts going again and George put heart and soul into it. He had a very good Scout troup. It was something he had done as a boy in England. He took pride in seeing it done right. In 1967 the Scouts celebrated their 100th Anniversary at Camp Woods, Sylvan Lake. Many of those boys will remember that as a good week for all, as well as a good year. They went camping and on different trips both summer and winter.

In the spring of 1968 George again had to go to the hospital, a trip from which he was never to return. While there he had many visitors and had no time for boredom. He passed away on April 29, 1968, and will ever be remembered.

I continued to work in the store until I had to have an operation and was forced to discontinue work for a time. Later, after I felt better, I worked as cook's helper and cook on oil rigs for some time. Now I am back on the farm again with garden and yard work to keep me busy.

Gwen was married to Hans Rossen in 1959 and has four children, Shelly, Cindy, Chris and Darla who are almost grown up now. They live in the Valley View subdivision in Red Deer, raise a garden and a few chickens as a sideline.

Darla, fourteen years of age now, has two ponies and is trying her hand at barrel racing this year.

Chris works with his father on masonry construction and the two older girls are away from home on their own.

Pine View

Pine View

The first Pine View school was built in 1908 on the NW 19-34-5. In 1931, this old timer would have been lost if the Peterson boys had not succeeded in burning a good back fire around it. This guard kept the raging forest fire, which swept through the area that spring, from even scorching the old building. The old school house was taken down and part of it still lies beside the foundation. In 1952 this old Pine View school was replaced with a new one. This second school is now one mile north of the Crammond school. It is called the Church of Jesus Christ. This report was composed by Edwin Kubik and Richard Fifield.

Pine View School, 1944 — Back Row — Lorraine Oliver, Marjorie Fifield, Edith Oliver (teacher), Doreen Oliver, Eileen Fifield. Front Row — Kenneth Becker and Tim Oliver.

Pine View Pioneers
by Edith Oliver

In the year 1906, several families from Ontario ventured west to Alberta as they had heard there were many areas open for homesteading, so thought this would be a great opportunity to get land for farming and ranching.

Amongst those who settled in what is known as the Pine View district (deriving the name from the tall and thick standing of pine trees in this area), were the Gibb, Adair and Willsie families who were neighbors in Ontario. The Sam Adair family consisted of Sam Jr., Pearl, Ruby, Merle and Tom who were born in Ontario. Emily, being the youngest, was born on the homestead. In the Willsie family there was Oliver, Herman, Gordon, Ann, Reta and Earl. They were born in Ontario and Mary was born on the homestead. The Gibb family included Donald and Marjorie. Marjorie later married Dick Trelevan. They have lived for several years in Vancouver.

There was no school when these settlers arrived, but now there was a need for one. In order to have a school it was necessary to have six school age children. The first school in the Pine View district was built in 1908-09. Logs were hauled from the bush which surrounded the area. They were sawed into lumber close by and planed by hand. For the foundation, they were able to get rock and gravel from the Red Deer River which was also quite close by. The school was built by the settlers for little or no pay. Mr. George Willsie and Herman hauled the stones for the foundation with a team of oxen and Swan Starkane, who was a stone mason, built it. Mr. Walter Gibb, who was a carpenter, built the school, with the help of other settlers. He also made what furniture was necessary.

Some of the first pupils to attend the Pine View School were Sam and Tom Adair, Herman, Gordon and Ann Willsie, Donald Gibb and Fred Jennot. The first teacher was Harry Clark who later married and moved to Edmonton where he continued to teach. Shortly after, John Niddrie taught and Verda Johnson who later became John's wife, also taught. They moved to Edmonton. Other teachers were Dorothy Blakey, Ruth Livingstone, Elsa Gundersen, Dagny Gundersen, May Waterman, Granville Paton, Charlotte Peterson, Magna Stromsmoe and Jack White.

The people of the district elected three trustees and one of them was appointed secretary-treasurer. They looked after taxes and other bills as well as hiring the teacher. For a number of years Howard Squires and John and Elvin Oliver served on the school board.

The John Graham family homesteaded in the Pine View district. They had five children namely Fred, Erie, Belle, Alice and John. More children were born after they left the homestead. Mr. Graham owned a sawmill which he operated every winter. He employed several men, as in those days homesteaders had to work out part of the year in order to improve their homesteads. The women and children spent considerable time alone. All were kept very busy trying to make a living as there was no help in those days from the government.

Thomas Squires and his wife, Phoebe, came from Ontario on the same train as the Willsies, and Gibbs. They had a cafe in Olds for a short time before moving on to their homestead which was northwest of Gibbs about two miles. Their niece Naomi Barrowman, came out too, and lived with them. They were later joined by their son, Howard, and wife, Lizzie. Later, a son, Tom, and a daughter were born. Howard farmed the place for a number of years, then went back to Ontario a few years after his mother passed away. His father passed away before his mother. Naomi went back to Ontario too, where she and Howard both passed away several years ago. His son and daughter are still living in Ontario.

A couple of miles further west, lived Mr. John Oliver and family. They had lived near the Willsies in Ontario. Mrs. Willsie was a sister to John Oliver. Two sons, Edison and Wilbert (better known as Bill), came out west first and took up homesteads. John's wife, Euena, passed away in Ontario in 1897. His sister, Esther

Esther and John Oliver, 1910.

(better known as Auntie), lived with the family and took care of the younger children, Orville and Elvin. They came out west in 1910 and brought their belongings as well as three horses, in a freight car. As the horses had to be fed and watered, John and the boys rode in the boxcar to attend the animals. It was a slow and rough ride which they had. Auntie came out by train.

The Olivers lived for awhile with Edison on his homestead as he had built a small log house. They lived there until they could get a house built

John Oliver Homestead, 1912 — Bill, Elvin, Esther, John, Orville and Edison Oliver.

114

on the homestead. For a while Elvin attended school at Pine View. Orville enlisted in 1914. He won a couple of medals while in the service. He was killed in action a few days before the Armistice was signed in 1918.

Edison Oliver sold his homestead and went to southern Alberta to work. He later married Margaret Miller and they settled on a farm east of Bowden. They had six children. Beryl married Lloyd Ward and they had ten children. Orville married Phyllis Cowper and they had two boys. Crystal married Walter Perry and they had nine children. George married Jocilyn Hill and they had five children. Rae married Lillian and had one daughter. Orville, Beryl, George and Shirley live at Vancouver as well as their mother. Crystal makes her home at Creston, British Columbia, and Rae in Toronto, Ontario. Edison passed away in May, 1932.

Bill Oliver proved up on his homestead, but worked out in the winter time. He and Elvin worked for the telephone company for awhile at Coronation. Elvin returned in the spring to help his father with the farming. Bill went to Seattle and Montana to work. He married Ora Fortune of Didsbury, at Butte, Montana, and had one daughter, Jean. Ora died from the flu in the fall of 1918.

Auntie took care of Jean until she was of school age, then she attended school in Calgary. After graduating, she worked for awhile. She married Bill Saunders and they lived in Saskatchewan. About ten months after she was married, she died suddenly of pneumonia in August, 1941. Auntie passed away in July, 1930, and John Oliver in March, 1934.

Bill Oliver bought land in Warner, Alberta, about 1930. Here he farmed until retiring in 1965. He married Esther Johnson of Eckville about 1933 and they lived on the farm until his retirement when they moved to Victoria for a couple of years before moving back to Red Deer where they lived until Bill's death in November, 1974. Bill had been an active Alberta Wheat Pool

Delegate for a number of years, while farming at Warner. He also worked on the hail board.

Elvin worked at Claresholm and at Turner Valley. He later returned to the farm where he became a member of the school board and also councillor for the municipality for a few years. In 1931 he married Edith Lockard of Fort Macleod, Alberta. She taught school at Fort Macleod, Leslieville and Rich Hill before her marriage. They have three children. Lorraine married Bud Frieholt who was accidently killed while working in a garage at Rocky Mountain House shortly after their marriage. She later married Gilbert Hollingsworth. They live in the Rimbey district. Their family is Maurice, Marlene, Merlin, Maureen and Merletta. Gilbert has been engaged in trucking and has made several trips to many of the southern States, hauling cattle. Lorraine accompanied him when she could get away as she carried on most of the farm work.

Doreen married Lee Hollingsworth on July 9, 1956. This was her parents' twenty-fifth wedding anniversary which was celebrated at Leslieville. They have four children, Monty, Darcy, Angela and Rodney. They live in the Leslieville district. Lee is a battery operator for an oil company and Dorreen does his book work in his office at Eckville.

Tim married Louise Shatford of Claresholm. They have three children, Dale, Darlene and Darren. Louise taught school at Rocky Mountain House before her marriage in June, 1963, and for two years at Caroline after her marriage. They live on the Oliver homestead. Tim bought Bill's homestead and also land which was owned by his father. They are still living in the district.

Edith Oliver taught school at Pine View for six years before the family moved to Leslieville where she taught for twenty years. Shortly after Elvin and family left the Pine View district, a new school was built there about 1950. It was in operation a few years then the children were bussed to Crammond where a new school had been built. The school at Crammond was closed in about five years and the children were bussed to Caroline where they still attend school. The new Pine View School was moved to the Crammond district and used for a Mormon Church.

Elvin and Edith Oliver moved to Bentley in 1969 where Edith taught before retiring. Elvin passed away March, 1977.

The pioneers had many hardships to endure. Homes in those days were not built as warm as now-a-days and their only fuel was wood. One morning when Elvin and Edison Oliver were on the homestead, they woke up and their hair was frozen to their pillow. They had a small cook stove which they filled with wood to try to keep

Elvin and Edith Oliver, Lorraine, Tim and Doreen Oliver, 1941.

fire overnight. They put their sack of potatoes in the oven and in the morning they were frozen solid.

As everyone burned wood for heating and cooking, the men would each get up a wood pile by cutting trees and hauling them in. Then they would have a sawing bee and get the wood sawed into stove lengths. The women had quilting bees. In those days there were house parties and get togethers amongst the neighbors. Transportation was by horse and buggy or wagon in the summertime and by team and sleigh in the winter. People of the community looked forward to the Christmas concert which was held in the schools. The children all took part and often adults would put on plays which everyone enjoyed.

There was an abundance of wild fruit such as strawberries, blueberries and cranberries in the Pine View district. This is the only fruit they had. The whole family would go picking when the season came. Often they had to go horseback and carry the berries home in pails. Mounting the horse with pails of berries was not an easy task. I can remember taking the three children on the horse with me and carrying home two water pails of berries. Was so thankful to have such a gentle and faithful horse.

In later years after the ferry on the Red Deer River was in operation, people came for miles for berries. The ferry ran back and forth continually on Sunday, hauling berry pickers. Sometimes the pickers would be chased out of a good patch by a hungry bear.

The Red Deer River was quite a hazardous obstacle to people who had to get across it, before the ferry was in operation. Bill Oliver rode horseback to Bowden the spring of 1915. While crossing the river on the ice on his way home, the horse broke through the ice and he was unable to save the horse, but managed to save his own life. Bruce Kingsbury from Pine View

district lost his life in the river near Moose Mountain. He tried to cross the river on the ice on foot. The ice gave way and as near as I know his body was never located.

On another occasion, a car went off the ferry into the deep water and all that saved the occupants was their presence of mind to crawl out onto the roof of the car, where they were rescued.

In 1939 the August Christiansen family moved into the Pine View district. They were originally from Denmark, good community workers and always ready to lend a helping hand. Their family consisted of Victor, Anna, Elisa, Chris, Ester and Gordon. Mrs. Christiansen passed away in March and Mr. Christiansen in July of 1963. Gordon and his family are still living on the homestead.

The Claus Peterson family lived in the district for a number of years. They came up from the States. In their family there was Harold, Clifford and Gertrude who were twins, Albert, Reta, Arthur and Mabel. Mrs. Peterson passed away in April, 1960, and Mr. Peterson in October, 1965.

Bill Fifield and family lived on the Noye's farm for awhile. It was later sold to Mel Wilford who farmed there for a few years. They sold their farm to Walter Schrader and moved to Cranbrook where Molly, as she was known, passed away. They had one son, Jim.

To the east of Olivers lived Carl Aasted who came from Big Valley and homesteaded there. He was originally from Denmark. Several years after he homesteaded and bought more land, his sister, Jette, came out from Denmark and made her home with Carl. They live in Innisfail now, but often came back to the farm.

Other settlers who came into the district were Paddy Bruce, Billy Andrews, Walter Collier, Oliver and Ernest Desleppe and family, Avery Scott and family and Mrs. Elizabeth Becker and family. Few of the old timers of the Pine View district are left.

Ricinus

The Cairn

by Sally Bugbee

Through the effort of the late Mrs. Matilda Rose, a Cairn was erected in memory of the Pioneers who came to settle on the virgin soil of what was to become known as Ricinus. Most of them came from the United States and left there because of the drought stricken areas in which they lived, others left for different reasons but they all came with plenty of hope, faith and courage. When they arrived, they were filled with joy; here was lush green grass and lots of water, this was, for sure, the land of milk and honey.

They chose and filed on their homesteads at a cost of $10. A homestead consisted of 160 acres and each adult twenty-one years or over, could homestead only once in a lifetime. A time limit was set during which improvements had to be made such as housing, clearing and breaking land, etc., and had to be occupied part of the time each year. When the requirements were met, it was inspected and if it passed, you were issued a title as owner of the property.

It was a long hard climb but with back breaking labour and the sweat of their brow, they built their houses and cleared their land. There was so much to do and so little to do it with, no high powered machinery in those days, just their teams of horses or yokes of oxen, their own two hands and strong backs with which to do the work. They paved the way and smoothed the wrinkles for those who followed in their footsteps, to reap the benefit of their labours.

In consideration of these Pioneers, Mrs. Rose thought it only fitting that they should be commemorated in some way. The idea of a Cairn came to her when she was making tentative plans to compile their history. She approached her neighbors and some of the relatives of the pioneers with her idea of a Cairn and was met with a ready response.

A site was chosen on the northwest corner of the late George Bugbee's farm, and in May, 1961, about forty residents met to clear the ground and to dedicate it and to turn the first sod. Reverend Falk, minister of the Nazarene Church in Caroline, gave the dedication service and Mr. Frank Ankle turned the first sod. Mr. Ankle was among some of the early settlers, coming to Ricinus from South Dakota in 1911.

Mrs. Rose solicited the services of Rudolph Duerr to build the Cairn. The ground was tilled and the stones were hauled in readiness for the work to begin. A bronze plaque, engraved with the names and dates of the Pioneers, was put on order.

The expense of the project was paid for by donations from various people and from the proceeds of a bake sale held in Caroline and from the Pine Cone W.I.

When the Cairn was completed, an unveiling ceremony was held in October, 1963, with a crowd of people and honored guests attending. Mr. Erle Carr was master of ceremonies and each of the guests gave an interesting talk. The unveiling of the Cairn was done by Mrs. Frank Ankle and special tribute was paid and a bouquet of flowers was presented to Mrs. Rose by Neva Browning for instigating and organizing the building of the Cairn.

In conclusion, Mr. Carr paid special tribute to

Mr. and Mrs. Levi Bugbee at Ricinus Cairn.

the Wives and Mothers of the Pioneers who followed their men and shared their hardships, they were truly the backbone of the nation.

The Clearwater Forest
by Sally Bugbee
Research — Ben Schantz and excerpts from other sources

Control of crown lands, including forests, was vested in the Secretary of State in 1871 and transferred to the Department of the Interior in 1873. The necessity for conservation of the forest resources of the west was recognized in 1899 by the apointment of an officer known as the Chief Inspector of Timber and Forestry. This appointment is considered the beginning of the Federal Forestry Branch. When the Canadian Forestry Association held their convention in Ottawa in 1906 with Sir Wilfrid Laurier presiding, it was made known that it had been the practice to sell large western tracts of timber without any examination or cruising of the timber often resulting in the selling of whole watersheds. From this knowledge, Parliament passed a very important act respecting forest reserve purposes of which was cited as (1) the reserving of timber supplies, (2) the reserving of unsuited areas for agriculture so that they would not be homesteaded and (3) the preserving of the water level in streams by conserving the timber on upper watersheds.

A survey was immediately started extending from the United States border to the North Saskatchewan River. In 1910 a survey was made to determine the eastern boundary of the Rocky Mountain Forest. This reserve was then divided

Clearwater Forestry Gates — Bernice Oliver, Mrs. Bugbee, Irene Oliver, Sarah Bugbee.

up into five smaller reserves, one of these being the Clearwater. The boundaries were completed in 1911 and the Dominion Forest Service was formed. It remained under the Dominion until 1930 when the province took it over and it became the Alberta Forest Service.

These reserves had to be manned and so small cabins were built throughout the whole of the Rocky Mountain Reserve. A forest supervisor was placed in charge of each forest and ranger districts and fire patrols were set up in each of the five reserves.

A small cabin once referred to as the Cache, was built and located at the foot of the mountain near the Clearwater gap sometime between the years 1914-16.

It is said the first ranger here was Walter Bremner. He was followed by William (Bill) Scott who made his first appearance at the Cache with a Mr. Warren July 17, 1917, to help with a fire that was burning from the North

Ranger Bill Scott and ? at Clearwater Forestry Cabin.

Ranger Bill Scott and Mary at the Station.

Saskatchewan River to the Clearwater River. In late July, 1919, fire again broke out covering a wider scope and travelling southeast along the mountain range to the Clearwater River. One hundred men fought this fire under Forest Ranger Bradley, a local man from the Ricinus area. In spite of their effort, the rains came to the rescue and put it out. Fire fighters received 15¢ an hour at the time.

With the exception of a main station, rangers were hired on a seasonal basis. Their work consisted of blazing and cutting out pack trails and maintaining them, fire patrol and timber cruising. They were also fish and game wardens who were kept busy during the fall hunting season, checking hunters' camps and hunting licences and checking out their game. At the main stations, a daily report was made out for work done, weather, wind, temperature and precipitation.

A survey of the fire damage was done by Ranger Bill Scott and other rangers to estimate the loss of timber. When this was completed, work began on a basement for a larger building to replace the small Cache. Bill spent the winter here and with the help of Baxter Bean from Ricinus, enough logs were cut to build it. During the summer of 1920 the basement was finished and the cement poured for the foundation, and by 1921 carpenters Ed Steinback and Charles Wayman from Rocky Mountain House, had completed the building. It was two stories high, had a brick chimney, B.C. cedar shingles, windows, fir doors and trim. On the ground floor there was an office, kitchen, living room, one bedroom and a small anteroom for coats and boots. The upper floor had two bedrooms and closets. A ranger was kept year around from then on and they were given an assistant ranger to help with the work load.

As early as 1913, telephones were started and working in the Brazeau, Cold Spur and the Pembina Forks area. By 1914 Coleman and Gap Ranger Stations were on telephone, making seventy-five miles of line in the forest reserves. In 1926 a telephone line was completed between the Clearwater Ranger Station and the Base Line Lookout Tower.

Each month five days were allowed for the ranger to make a trip into Rocky Mountain House to take in their daily reports and to

Bill McAlpine, assistant ranger at Clearwater Station.

Ranger Bill Scott, Walt Richardson and ? building the Clearwater Ranger Station.

Completion of Clearwater Station.

receive new work orders. Groceries for a month were purchased and any other supplies that were needed. In those days these trips were made by horse and wagon or by saddle and pack horses, and were not always pleasant what with roads such as they were back then, often being axle deep in mud or deep snow to plow through.

In order to have better and faster control of outbreaks of forest fires, usually caused by lightning strikes or careless campers, a fire road

Harold and Ray Sawyer at the Clearwater Ranger Station.

was constructed beginning at the foot of Corkscrew Mountain where the old wagon road turned off toward the river. It followed the pack trail with some modification down on to the Seven Mile Flats. This was surveyed and dozed through by the forest rangers with Dick Knorr driving the cat. In 1948 the Eastern Rocky Conservation commenced construction and built what is known as the Forestry Trunk Road. New bridges were built along the way and a big one was put in across the Clearwater River leading to the Cut-off Creek area. Following this, campgrounds and kitchens were built along the way. This road links up with other main roads making unlimited travel whether for a fire or for the pleasure of the general public who wish to camp or to enjoy the scenery along the way, as well as for natural resources exploration.

The lookout towers have played an important role in the preservation of the forests down through the years since their inception. The first ones were built on a high elevation consisting of a small cabin for living quarters and a wooden derrick type tower with rungs that had to be climbed up on at intervals during the day for the purpose of spotting fires. They kept a lonely vigil and were allowed out for a period of three days per month only, unless a good soaking rain had fallen. New towers have replaced the old ones, modern in design and equipment, complete with radio telecommunication services between the towers and the head office in Rocky Mountain House.

Baseline Lookout Tower: Edith Scott and baby Mary.

Ram River Falls.

Uniforms were worn by the forest rangers for the first time in 1949, giving them an air of distinction suitable to perform their duty as rangers and game wardens.

A new ranger station and assistant house, garage and storehouse and a new barn was built in the early 1950s at the Clearwater, and a power plant was installed for electricity until the fall of 1960 when Calgary Power came through the area and replaced it.

A forestry training school was established at Hinton in 1951 in order to round out the knowledge of the rangers and field men, it is operating at full capacity.

Standing like a sentinel, witnessing all of the changes through the years and a link with the past, the old Clearwater Cache stands in a preserved condition, a credit to our rangers, God bless them all.

The following is a list of forestry personnel with apologies for any names missed or wrong dates.

RANGERS AT CLEARWATER RANGER STATION
1918 — Wm. Scott at Nordegg-Grouse Camp
1919 — Wm. Scott — Clearwater Ranger Station
1925 — Wm. Scott — joined by his wife Edith
1927 — Wm. Scott — Ranger at Clearwater, Eric Whidden Assistant Ranger — working out of Swan Lake Cabin
1931 — Wm. Scott became Headquarter Ranger and Timber Inspector until he retired August, 1936
1931 — Dick Englebritson — Ranger at Clearwater after Scott

1938 — Clarence Sawyer
1946 — Clarence Sawyer, Assistant — M. Verhaeghe
1948 — Jack Walker — R. J. Lyle Assistant; Dick Knorr
1951 — Harry Edgecombe; R. J. Lyle
1955 — R. J. Lyle, Assistant Gerald Stuart and W. Kay, Hank Chamney
1956-62 — Ted Loblaw, Vic Hume
1963 — Frank Jones, Assistant Frank Lightbound, Gary Schedmiller, Terry Turner, Don Harrison
Martin Justinen — first L/O Man at Baseline

FOREST SUPERINTENDENTS
A. G. Smith — Forest Superintendent — 1927-1930

Eris Huestis — Forest Superintendent — 1930-1932
Fred Edgar — Forest Superintendent — 1932-1940
J. R. H. Hall — 1940-June 30, 1950

T. Keats — July 1, 1950-October 30, 1955
N. Lind — Novemeber 1, 1955-March 2, 1956
R. G. Steele — April 1, 1956-June 30, 1959
G. A. Longworth — July 1, 1959-April 14, 1964
F. E. Sutherland — 1964-

Idlewilde Ranger cabin.

Ram River Ranger cabin — Terry, Helen, Bobby and Larry Mullen.

The Last Roundup

The Forestry held a roundup
Upon the River Tay.
The Rangers came from near and far
And Walker hauled the hay.

Maurice came from the Red Deer
On his Palomino Steed,
A horse known for endurance
And everlasting speed.

Jack Walker rode in on Nellie
A mare who liked to bolt.
He said he wouldn't ride her
Unless of the horn he had a hold.

Ronnie came in on Tony
And made a rugged tear.
He said he'd turn those horses
And never turn a hair.

Dick Knorr rode in on Corbet
Upon his prancing dun.
He said he'd catch that stallion
Before the day was done.

Jack and Dick came from the Bighorn
They rode in with horses four,
And said if these were not enough
That they'd go back for more.

The Brazeau east sent Ben
Who travelled fifty miles.
His horse was mighty awkward
But his face was one of smiles.

From the Meadows came old Harry,
On a horse known as Dan,
Who proved to be the toughest horse
That ever carried a man.

The wheel of riders gradually grew
Until we were short one cog.
Then Bill Winters from Moose Creek
Rode in on spotted dog.

For days they chased those Broncos
Through drifts of crusted snow.
We trailed them to the mountains
Or wherever they did go.

After five days of riding
Only seventeen were caught,
So the Forestry sent out Bloomberg
Who claimed he knew a lot.

Next morning at daybreak
Jack Browning called the crew.
We saddled up and headed west
But by two o'clock Bill Bloomberg was through.

For seven more days the chase went on.
Each night a band was caught,
Until thirty-five were coralled
On Bob Bugbee's feed lot.

This is the story of the last roundup.
The Forestry said it didn't pay
So go ahead and ask Mr. Hall
And see what he has to say.

Clearwater Beavers Ball Team
submitted by Paul Lamb and Pink Pitts

The players and their positions are as follows:

Catcher: Grover (Red) Womack
Pitchers: Jack Bugbee, Martin Justinen, Bill Justinen, Elmer Hagsted, Pink Pitts
First Base: Wilber Pitts
Second Base: Pink Pitts
Third Base: Wilbur Cross
Left Field: Paul Lamb
Centre Field: Elmer Hagsted, Pink Pitts, M. Justinen
Right Field: Elmer Hagsted or Pink Pitts
Short Stop: Wyck Burns

This team played many games in the surrounding districts and against teams from 'outside' — winning some — losing some, but always giving their opponents stiff competition. It should be noted that since there were so few players many played several different positions. Various anecdotes on the games played by these teams have been mentioned elsewhere in this history book and make interesting reading.

The Ricinus School No. 3148
by Sally Bugbee

Four acres of land on the corners of the north half of 23-36-7-5 were donated by George Bugbee Sr. and Willard Harness, for a school, each giving two acres from their respective homesteads.

Baxter Bean and some of his neighbors cut logs and hauled them to Thibedeau's sawmill which was set up on Fred Stewart's place, and were sawed into lumber. Carpenters Oliver and Bill Thibedeau built the school.

The school opened in July, 1917, with Mrs. Joe (Chrisie) Bean teaching twenty children between the ages of five and sixteen years.

The following year, Miss Ruth Slatt, from Rocky Mountain House, taught. The next year no teacher was available so Chrisie once again took over the teaching duties.

Like most country schools in the early days, Ricinus was not kept open during the winter months. In spite of the short terms, the children learned their lessons and passed their exams, doing as well as if they had gone for the full ten month period.

After Chrisie, the teachers came and went. There are no records left anymore and for that reason I have only a few names that I have

Back row — Nellie Clearwater, Louis Vincey, Vern Clearwater, Margaret Knorr, Jim Wilson — Front row — Irene Cliff, Ruth Chitwood, Dick Knorr and Margaret Marvin.

First Ricinus School Class about 1917 Back row — Bill Bean, Gerald McNutt, Smokey McNutt — Center Row — Chris Raynor, Theresa Bean, Della Stewart, Rose Bugbee, Gladys Stewart — 3rd row — Elva Burns, Mae McNutt, Willy Meekle, Doug Stewart, Bill Robinson, Bill McNutt — Front row — John Stewart, Florence McNutt, Bertha Meekle, Ted McNutt and Margaret Bean.

gathered here and there. They are: Allen Gilbraith, Francis Hayes, John Vanderburg, Nellie Kaiser, Ester Anderson, Mr. Peedie, Tom Cole, Miss Williams, Mr. Chute, Alma Sarc, Bob Pettie, Miss Wood, Bill Mewha, Jessie Limbough, Beth Owen, Gladys Novak, Mrs. Schmit, Mary Clancey, Edna Clancey and Betty Bean. Betty supervised for a short time in

Teacher Mrs. Limbough.

Ricinus School — Teacher Bill Mewha.

124

1952 and that fall the children were bussed to Caroline.

The school and acreage was put up for sale and was purchased by Mr. Art Reid, a former resident from the Bowden area. The proceeds went to the Ricinus-Wooler Community Association.

After a few years, Art sold this property to the present owner, Bill Turner of Sylvan Lake. The old school stands vacant except for about two months out of the year, but it served its purpose well.

Frank Ankle and a Model T constructed of various parts 1917 to 1926.

Frank and Jenny Ankle

by Guy E. Fay

Frank Ankle was born at Ailsa Craig, Ontario, on November 5, 1881. As a young man he moved to Miland, South Dakota, where he used to freight from Fort Pierre to Midland.

In 1910 he came to the Ricinus district, along with his mother, brother and two sisters and their families. In 1913 he married Jenny McKay, who was born in Glasgow, Scotland. She was a cake decorator and was known far and wide for her artistry. They had two children, Margaret and Jim. Frank was mechanically inclined and owned the first threshing machine on the west side of the river. He also operated a small saw-mill for years.

But Frank's first love was horses and freighting. Many a night he spent sleeping beneath his wagon, camping by the Medicine River on the road between Caroline and Innisfail. He also freighted for the Ram River Oils when he was in his sixties. They celebrated their fiftieth wedding anniversary on September 24, 1963.

Mrs. Ankle died on January 5, 1967, and Frank on October 22, 1976. They are buried in Caroline.

Frank Ankle and daughter Margaret.

Frank and Jenny Ankle on their 50th wedding anniversary.

The Barnes History
by Violet and Lou Noirot

William and Ione Barnes came to Kevisville from Calgary. In 1940 they moved to a bush camp owned by Raymond McKain. They lived in a tent until they built a log cabin. It was late in October and the tent was very cold so they were glad to get into the cabin. Charlie, the youngest, was two years old when they moved.

They were the first family to move there. Later other families started to drift in and in about two years there was Lillian and Garnett Gardner, Ralph Cave and his wife, Bob Long and his wife and Doug and Elsie Stewart. Eventually, LaCerf and McKain camps spread into one another and the camp became known as 'Slab Town'. An old bunk house was used as a school where a teacher, Ernie Forbes, taught. Later they built a log school across the road from what is now Cozarts' farm.

After leaving Slab Town, about two years later, they moved to Dezall and Hart's camp which was on the same quarter as what is now Thelma Montgomery's. They stayed there for five years, then lived on what is now Cozart's place. Ken Dezall owned it then. Then they moved down to the Ricinus area on the N.W. 31-36-6-5 where they lived for eight years. They moved to Penticton and later to Quesnel, British Columbia. William Barnes passed away on February 29, 1968, while visiting in McBride, British Columbia. Ione is still in Quesnel.

For entertainment at Slab Town, they had a dance once a month in a cookhouse, and also parties at Forsters. Several men, who worked in camps around the district, supplied the music. They also played cards and later some of the younger ones sent to Eaton's for several games to play in the evenings. These games were stored at the Barnes' house.

William and Iona Barnes had seven children, Franklin, William, Violet, Dorthy, James, Charles and Kathleen. Franklin married Dorothy McKinley. They live at McBride, British Columbia, and have five children.

Violet married Lou Noirot and they farm on the N.W. 25-36-7-5 in the Ricinus area. They have two children, Calvin and Wade. Calvin married Lleane Verhaeghe and has one son, Meryl. Wade married Wanita Wilson and has one son, David.

William married Veronica Kerrick and they live in Penticton. They have two children.

Dorthy married Chester Sands and they farm east of Rocky Mountain House. They have two children, Wendy and Stacey.

James (Jimmy) married Betty Kozak and they have three children. They live in Quesnel.

Chuck married Stella Murray and live in Valemount, British Columbia. They have three children.

Kathleen married Dale Webb and lives in Vernon, British Columbia. They have two children.

The John Baxter Bean Family

John Baxter Bean was born in Richmond Centre, State of Wisconsin, in 1874. When a boy of fourteen, he migrated to Shield River county in Montana with his parents to take up land. Here he worked and grew up to young manhood.

In 1902, he met and married Millie Brickner, who was born in St. Paul, Minnesota, in 1877.

Baxter worked on the Shield River Cattle Ranch for the next year or so, then Baxter and Millie moved to the State of Washington where he worked in the lime kilns at Evans. Their first child, a son, was born at Collville, Washington, March 15, 1904. They named him William. Their next move was to Superior, Montana, where Baxter worked on a mining claim. Here a daughter was born, Theresia Katherine, March 24, 1905.

They stayed here for about a year then moved back to Washington, where Baxter worked as a cooper (barrel maker) at the lime kilns. Here the third child, James Wilson, was born on June 22, 1908. In 1910, they moved to Bassano, Alberta, where Baxter ran a livery stable and blacksmith shop. A year or so later he changed to freight hauling. Here their fourth child was born on

Canadian soil, a second girl. They named her Margaret, born on August 21, 1911. That same year Baxter, restless once more, with two friends, Earl Warren and Hank Smith drove from Strathmore, Alberta, with team and democrat to the Len Bowers place on the Clearwater River, now known as the Ricinus District. Here two of the men, Earl Warren and Baxter Bean, filed on homesteads: Earl's being on S.E. Q. 36-7-5, and Baxter's on N.E. Q. 19-36-6-5, which Earl had bought from Ted Hensel to log. Bunny Brightman milled the logs for all the new settlers to build their new homes with.

The following spring of 1914, Baxter built a home to bring his family to live on their own land. It was the first piece of land of their very own. It was an early spring that year. The snow had gone by March 15. The first spring rain had come the night before and softened the ice on the river and creeks, and in crossing a creek the team broke through and nearly drowned on the way to the homestead.

That spring Baxter broke sod enough for a good sized garden plot. This they planted. Then he left to work putting in a crop on the old Jordon place in the Butte district. That fall his brother, Joe, and his wife Christie, came to settle on their homestead, S.E. Q 3.30 36-6-5. Joe Bean had a blacksmith shop on the homestead to supplement his income. Times were hard and people had to help themselves by working out and living on the game of the country.

Baxter and the neighbors cut logs and hauled them to the Thibedeau mill, which sat on the Fred Stewart place. These logs were cut into lumber to build a school on the north half of section 23-36-7-5. The school was built by the Thibedeau men, father and son, in 1917. In the winter of 1916 and 1917 all homesteads bordering the muskeg known as the Uncle John and Aunt Annie muskeg, were granted permission to cut

corduroy to build the road across the muskeg in order to pay their taxes. During the summer of 1917 the dirt was put on the corduroy. This road was quite a boost to the community. It saved over a mile of splashing through muck, mud and water, and became the best road to Rocky Mountain House at that time.

That same summer the Cattle Association was formed by the following people; Fred Stewart, John Bugbee, Vern Clearwater, Baxter Bean and the two Thibedeaus. They borrowed money from the Alberta Government to buy milk cows, the family men receiving $500.00 and the single men $300.00. This was the start of the Ricinus cattle herds. Now all began to do better economically until the winter of 1919 and 1920. Winter came early and lasted well into May. During the long and severe winter, the price of hay went up to $100.00 a ton, with much loss of stock. The next few years Baxter spent doing off the farm work to supplement the family income. In 1925, he moved the family to Rocky Mountain House where better schooling would be available for the two younger children. Baxter did smithy work in Charles Edward's Blacksmith shop. He later rented this shop while his eldest son, William (Billy), carried on with the farm.

The fall of 1926, Baxter had the misfortune of losing his wife. Millie passed away in the Innisfail hospital September 1st. Baxter continued to work in town until Margaret finished school. Later a gas light exploded, badly burning his hands and face. Now unable to do much, he stayed on in town until his hands and face healed. Then returning to the farm, he lived there until his death on May 3, 1938.

In the passing of Millie Bean, the district lost one of its pioneer nurses. Mrs. Bean did a lot of the midwife work and took care of many sick settlers.

The Baxter and Millie Bean children soon scattered to the four winds. Theresia Bean worked as a waitress for many years on the C.P.R. from the west coast to Bermuda. Later she went to Seattle, Washington, where she met and married Sam Smith. Theresia died in 1966 after a lengthy illness.

In 1928 James went to Olympia, Washington. He and his wife have five children, James, Kenneth, John, Patrick, and Margaret. The four boys are married and live around Olympia. Jim has retired fron his auto upholstery business and his wife, Rose, also retired as a nurse. Their daughter, Margaret, is a physical education instructor.

Margaret Bean went to Oregon to live with an aunt shortly after her mother passed away. She trained for a nurses career; and met and married Sam Petty. They live in Tucson,

Baxter Bean family. L.-R. — Jim, Bill, Milly, Margaret and Baxter. Missing, Theresa.

L to R — Bill and Thelma Bean, Pat Pattison, Margaret Bean. Front — Clifford and Christie Raynor.

Bill and Thelma Bean and family — Margie, Grace, Betty, Edith and Buck.

L to R — Paul (Whitey) Roeback, Christie Bean, Baxter Bean, Pat Pattison, Thelma and Bill Bean, daughter Margie.

Arizona, and have both retired now. Margaret was a nurse in Los Angeles for many years, and Sam was a captain for a transport ship.

William stayed in the district and farmed his father's homestead as well as his own. In 1927 he met and married Thelma Jane Scott from Kalispell, Montana. Billy and Thelma raised five children, four girls and one boy. The oldest, Margie, married Albert Jensen. They live in Rocky Mountain House where Albert is manager of the Smart Shop Clothing Store. They have three children, Thelma, Irene, and Dean. Thelma and Irene are both married.

Grace married Don Pearson. They live in Sundre, where Don is field manager for McGregor and Johnson Construction Company. This union has two children, Donna and Patricia. Donna is married. Betty married Lawrence Anderson and lives on a farm at Fosston, Saskatchewan. They have two children, Dwayne and Peggy. Dwayne is married. While visiting her uncle Jim in Olympia, Washington, Edith met and married William Dale. They have three youngsters, Don, Pat, and Terri. Don is married.

Their one son, Baxter, being plagued with asthma all through his youth, was the only one of Billy and Thelma's five children not receiving complete high school. At the age of eighteen he went to Calgary finding work with the Power Company for a number of years. Now he is a welder in Edmonton, and married a divorcee with two children.

It would not do not to mention that Billy and Thelma Bean were perhaps the first couple in this district to make the effort to give their children high school education. The girls went to Dickson High School, all finishing the four years. How this couple managed to scrape up the money for boarding them as well as tuition, no one has been able to figure out — doubt if they know either. This undertaking entitles them to honorable mentions, gladly given.

Billy too, always drove a nice team. He had a natural fondness and eye for good horses and took good care of them and his wagon. He also followed up his father and grandfather's interest in blacksmith work, kept a shop of sorts that saved many a trip to town for his neighbors.

Now Billy is gone. He passed away in July of 1967. A little more than two years after having one of those big heart valve operations. They retired to Sundre after the heart operation, Billy no longer able to do work except the very lightest. Thelma Bean passed away on February 26, 1974, after a lengthy illness.

Len and Della Bowers

Len and Della Bowers came to the Clearwater Valley from Midland, South Dakota, in 1906, in company with Charles Fogelsong and Jesse Ditch. They were to homestead one quarter and buy a half section of what was called 'Script Land' It was on the 'Script Land', north of half 10-36-7-5, that they put up their buildings.

When the other pioneers arrived in 1911, Len

128

Curley Fetterly, Len Bowers and Bill Scott.

Jack and Gladys Browning holding Dick, and Fred Stewart.

Len Bowers and his Indian friends.

and Della Bowers were running a sizable herd of cattle and horses along Moose Creek, an area that became known as the 'Bowers Flats'. Later, Inez Denton, who had lost her mother, came to live with Len and Della; the Dentons had been neighbors of the Bowers' in South Dakota.

Len Bowers was the proud owner of the first automobile in the district about 1917. In the winter of 1918-19, Della Bowers died suddenly of a heart attack while attending a community dance at the Wooler School house. After Della's death, Annie Ankle went to keep house for Len Bowers and chaperone Inez until Inez's marriage to George McNutt.

Len Bowers left Alberta in 1922 and was last heard of in Sandpoint, Idaho. He subsequently sold his farm to Harvey Langley, after harboring numerous tenants. The farm was sold by Harvey Langley to Doug and John Stewart in 1948. The Stewarts sold to Al Jacobson in 1961, and at the present time, Harry McKenzie lives on the original Len Bowers building site.

John Frances Browning

Jack Browning was born in 1900 in Pawnee County, Oklahoma and came to Caroline to stay in 1914. He attended the South Fork No. 1903 School. As Jack grew up he soon found the

Stewart family across the Clearwater River was a homey place to visit. Jack married Gladys Stewart in 1921. Gladys was the eldest child of Fred and Cassie.

They homesteaded four miles down the Clearwater river from where the store is today. Jack and Gladys worked the first year for a survey party, packing horses in the mountain area. Jack had started guiding and outfitting hunters by this time, and also kept working on his traplines.

In the winter of 1927 Jack and Gladys bought the Dick Godley homestead and moved there just across the road south of Fred and Cassie. There were three children — Arnold John (Dewey)

Gladys Stewart at first Clearwater. Bridge at Ricinus, 1918.

born in 1922, Thelma Mae in 1926 and Richard Gordon in 1928.

Jack was full of adventure and excitement, and at the out-set of his life in Ricinus country he had his full measure of living off the land making do with little in the way of comforts and conveniences.

In the course of his hunting trips into the hills of the west country he built up quite a herd of saddle and pack horses. When a survey crew came along looking for someone to pack them into some inaccessible region, Jack had the necessary equipment to do the job. Gladys helped with the packing and cooking. Over the years Jack took many notable people into the hills to get their trophy animals.

In the winter Jack made a good living on his trapline near the Clearwater Ranger Station. Besides the fur he also live-trapped several lynx and cougar. At that time there was a bounty on cougars and wolves as they were considered predators. Jack's hounds were well trained to run cougar and lynx.

One of the earliest trips was a scouting trip up the Ram and Clearwater Rivers with Ed Clay, Fred Stewart, and Doug Stewart. Young Doug and Jack took off on foot along the mountain tops scouting the country for game while the others moved the camp on, to the Clearwater valley. To their great confusion the fog rolled in and they were lost overnight. The next day they very shame-facedly found their camp. Since that time the canyon has been called "Lost Guide Canyon".

Jack Browning.

Jack started the Big Horn Rodeo in 1933. Many neighbors pitched in to make it a success. There were corrals, catch pens, chutes, Judge's stand and arena. At first a tent was used as a booth for catering to the crowd. The local bootleggers took care of the liquor situation. Later a dance hall was built with a booth added on. Gladys was a big help. She and her sister Della were in charge of the booth with the help of a number of community ladies.

Carl Boeken was announcer for many early years using a big horn. The Indians came in great numbers and camped west of the rodeo grounds. Jack always gave them a steer to butcher. They held a pow-wow, attended and enjoyed by white people and Indians alike. They added a great deal of interest and color to the early rodeos.

Jack dreamed up a pageant of the old days which was held at dusk and was called "The Burning of the Trapper". A rough cabin was built and put in the arena. Nat Jameson played the part of the trapper and came in with furs and traps over his shoulders. He went inside the cabin just as a number of Indians came riding in yelling and Ki-Yi-ing in a circle around the cabin. Jenny Ankle made a dummy trapper that was put in the cabin ahead of time. Then the Indians would set fire to the cabin. Suddenly the mounted cowboys appeared on the scene and attacked the Indians with blank shells in their guns and drove the Indians away. Nat Jameson always managed to escape through the back unobserved by the crowd who was sure he was burned alive. It was all very exciting. After a few years Thelma became Stampede Secretary, and Dewey and Dick helped in the arena and chutes. Dewey 'picked up' for fifteen years at this and other Stampedes.

Many dances were held at the Stampede Hall with the colorful names of Trappers, Outfitters, or Loggers Balls. In the mid 40's the Guide and Outfitters Ball started as an annual event, the first Friday in December in the Caroline Community Hall. The local outfitters and guides decorate the hall in western fashion with trophies, trees and packing equipment. This dance is still being held every year at the same time.

Jack had a very colorful personality and loved to entertain, be it rodeo, telling a story, playing his violin or harmonica at dances in the early days. As a story teller, real or fancy, Jack was able to keep his listeners spellbound. One of his favorites was a trapping story that usually took a long time to tell.

"I was on my trapline staying at the cabin tending my traps out on the Clearwater River. Walking home with my catch, late in the day I stopped for a rest — and by golly! there on my back trail was a cougar slinking along catching up to me. I headed for the cabin, but that cougar kept gaining on me. He made a spring at me and I just had time to duck down low in the trail and he over-jumped me. I turned and beat it back down the trail — so did the cougar. He made another big spring and over-jumped me again. I made a hasty turn back towards the cabin and the cougar was still watching me as I dropped over a hill. I stopped to catch my breath and waited to see if that cougar was still following me. Nothing moved, so curiousity got the better of me and I slipped back to peer over the hill. Well Now! there was that cougar practicing shorter jumps.

The Browning history would not be complete without mentioning "Huide" who has adopted our family and our country. Elliotte Huidekoper of Fort Collins, Colorado started hunting with Jack in 1948. Since then he has missed only two years of hunting, and is still hunting with Dewey at this time. Huide has donated to the Old Timers' Cairn, and also presented trophies at the Big Horn Rodeo.

After a fire destroyed their home in 1942 Jack and Gladys bought and moved to the Justinen place nine miles west of the Clearwater Store. They continued to raise cattle, trapping, outfitting and saw milling until Jack was killed in a car accident in the fall of 1960. Gladys has been in a nursing home in Red Deer for some years.

Dewey stayed at home working with his Dad trapping and hunting until 1945 when he and Tan Jameson bought the Ted Burwash place — now the Dr. Banks' place. He sold his half to Harold Jameson in 1946. Together Dick and Dewey bought the Browning home place SW 13-36-7-5. In 1947 he married Neva Hart. They continue to work at outfitting, trapping and raising cattle. They have three children — Wade who is married to Joan Prosser of Edmonton, has a son Jeremy and lives in Edmonton, Dena lives in Rocky Mountain House, and Kurt is still at home.

Thelma married John Moberg of the Prairie Creek area in 1943. They had one daughter Valarie (See the John Moberg story), and then separated. Later Thelma married Red Montgomery from Oroville, Washington. Red was a guide, cowboy and catskinner. He also engaged in trapping. They bought the old George McNutt S½ 10-36-8-5 where they raised cattle. Thelma and Red have a daughter Cinda who now lives in Rocky Mountain House, and a son Rick who lives at home. Valarie married Wendell Hulberg of Rocky, and they now live with their two daughters Kimberly and Shauna in the Taimi district.

Dick worked at home with his Dad for a few

Gladys Browning and granddaughter Valarie.

years guiding, trapping and working in the mill. He married Edna Ogilvie of the Wooler area. The first two years of their marriage they lived in a tent in the summer months in the mountains herding cattle for the Cattlemen's Association. In the winter he worked for his Dad in the sawmill. When Jack was killed Dick and family moved back with Gladys on the home place where they worked together until 1968 when Gladys' health failed and she sold the place to Dick.

Dick and Edna have four children — Gordon who has bought a quarter of land from his father, SE 19-35-8-5 — the old Siddon homestead. — Jed works and lives at home — Miles and Wanda are still in school and live at home.

The Bugbee Family
by Sally Bugbee

George Bugbee and his family lived at Amor, North Dakota. George's wife, Sara, died in October, 1913. They had five children, John, Rebecca, Florence, Levi and Rose.

After his wife's death, George had been considering a move and one morning at breakfast, he asked Florence how she would like to go to Canada. Since the housekeeping duties and the care of the younger children had fallen on her shoulders after her mother's death, she was ready and willing for any change.

John and Rebecca were both married and lived in South Dakota. John was married to Lillian Gillard and they had an infant named George. Rebecca was married to Irve Hartzell. As soon as they learned of their father's plans, they decided to sell out and join them.

They all spent the rest of the winter making

Dallas Heck, Jess Ditch, Florence Bugbee, George Bugbee, Sarah Heck, Lillian Bugbee, Jack Bugbee, Millie Bugbee, Bob and Lillian Moore.

preparations. By spring they had three covered wagons rigged up and a fourth one made with a flat deck to carry machinery to be pulled by a four horse team.

They left Amor May 10, 1914, the day before little George's first birthday. They had twenty-five head of horses, ten on the wagons and the rest of them loose, and were driven by Levi and Irve who rode horseback for the entire journey.

They reached the town of Olds, Alberta, without mishap in mid August, and although George had planned to go to the Peace River country they decided to try for something closer. So the next morning he took the train up to Red Deer and went to the land office there. He found there was plenty of available land in the Caroline and Ricinus area and so, armed with papers of land descriptions, he went back to Olds. They broke camp early the next morning with everyone anxious to end their long journey. Two days later they made camp beside the Raven River just south of Caroline.

The next day the men rode a few miles west and they came to the Clearwater River which they forded, as there was no bridge at that time. They met up with Frank Ankle, who was already established in that area, and with his help they selected their homesteads.

George filed on the N.W. Q. 23-36-7-5
John and Lillian the S.W. Q. 24-36-7-5
Rebecca and Irve the S.E. Q. 22-36-7-5.

Florence was married to the late Kirk Stewart in 1916 at the Melton Hotel in Rocky Mountain House. They filed and proved up on the N.W. Q. 24-36-7-5. To supplement their income they went to work at the bush camps at Harleck and Saunders; Florence cooking for some of the work crews and Kirk working in the timber. They had three sons, James, Richard and David, and all three served in the armed services in World War II. James and David were in the Air-

force and Richard with the Marines. Richard was killed in action at Tarewa in 1943.

In 1928 Florence and Kirk, along with their three sons, moved to the U.S.A. Kirk died in the 1960s and Florence lives in Crescent City, California, near her son David. Jim lives in Oregon.

Rebecca left Canada in 1917 and went back to the U.S.A. She and Irve had one daughter, Katherine, and then she had two more daughters from her second marriage, Sally and Betty. Rebecca, Katherine and Sally passed on some years ago and it is not known what became of Irve, but Betty lives in San Jose, California, with her husband Carmen Maruca and three children.

Levi trapped and worked with his father in the bush, etc., and then he filed on the S.W. Q. 32-35-8-5 and built a cabin on it but he never proved up on it. Later it was homesteaded by Mrs. Del Trimble and is now owned and lived on by Ivor Trimble and his family.

Levi went to work for Brewster as a guide at Banff and Lake Louise where he met and married Kitty Valelly. In 1929 they moved down to the U.S.A. They never had any children. Levi died in January 1970 at Wiemar, California. Kitty lives at Wiemar, and is nearly blind.

Rose went to live with the Charles Fogelsongs when her father and Levi went away to work. She lived with them for four years. Then she worked at Rocky Mountain House and Red Deer and then in 1925 she went back to the U.S.A.

She married an electrician, Louis Clausius, and they had one daughter, Lois, who lives at Santa Cruz. She is married and has two children, Randy and Wendi Strong. Rose and Louis are retired and they live at San Jose, California.

George and John and Lillian were the only ones who stayed. George married Mrs. Millie Fogelsong in January, 1932; Millie had been widowed in 1926. George had sold his homestead and came to live with Millie in her home. They farmed and raised a few cattle, horses and chickens until his death in 1941.

John and Lillian lived on their homestead for a time and then they moved to the east side of the Clearwater River. They bought the S.E. Q. 18-36-6-5, which was offered for a tax sale. They had four children, George, Sarah, Robert and Ernest. They took their schooling at the Wooler school. The Wooler School was moved to the west end of Caroline and after renovations it was made into a Catholic Church.

John trapped along the Clearwater and Raven Rivers and in 1922 he caught a silver fox, which netted him $128.00, which was a small fortune in those days. Coyotes sold for $10.00, but squirrels were of no value. To compare fur prices between now and then; at the Edmonton Fur Auction in February, 1978, squirrels sold for

Jack Bugbee.

$2.85, coyotes for $196.00, lynx for $515.00; yet silver fox sold for a mere $68.00. The fur trade like all other trades the world over can be likened to the ebb and flow of the mighty oceans, feasts and famines.

In 1919 a fire broke out in the Clearwater Forest and whether it was started by a careless human hand or a lightning strike, we will never know. It ravaged everything in its path and burned miles and miles of beautiful timber stands to say nothing of the loss of bird and animal life. Ashes fell as far away as Innisfail, a distance of more than sixty miles, and some days the dense smoke in the Ricinus and Caroline areas was so strong it stung the nostrils and throats of the settlers living there. Eventually it burned itself out, leaving a skeleton of ugliness and charred remains where once beauty reigned over all. Evidence of this fire can still be seen after all these years since; black snags still stand scattered here and there; and the trees, stripped of their bark from the fire, lying on the ground still sound and hard as flint; cured by the intense heat that sealed and hardened the sap and resin within the tree.

By 1923, the Clearwater Forest had become regenerated with virgin growth, and the big game and fur bearing animals were in good supply, and so the first registered traplines were issued in this area. John applied for one that had its beginning at the entry into the Reserve west of Caroline through to the Idlewilde summit with the Clearwater and Tay Rivers the boundary on either side. He held and trapped this line until his death in 1961. He was a Guide and Outfitter, a sawyer and mill wright, a papered steam engineer; he fired steam engines for both the threshing of grain in the east and saw-milling in the west. Last but not least he was an excellent sheep shearer and travelled many miles in the springtime shearing sheep. I can't remember the exact number of sheep he sheared on his record day, but he considered shearing 100 sheep a day was just an average day, and this was us-ing hand shears. In the later years he used electric shears some of the time, but he really preferred the hand shears.

In his younger days he enjoyed sports, and he joined the Caroline ball club. He pitched a mean ball with his south paw; he was left handed.

Lillian died in November, 1942, and was greatly missed by her family and friends. She kept the home fires burning and worked hard, she was always there to welcome her husband and sons upon their return from their various pursuits.

John's companions to share his last years, were his pinto horse, Pecos, and his little Terrier dog, Major. John died March 1, 1961. I am sure this article will bring back memories to many of you of a colorful man of the past.

GEORGE BUGBEE JR.

George was born at Amor, North Dakota, and was one year old when he came with his parents by covered wagon to Ricinus, in 1914. He followed in his father's footsteps for the most part. In 1921, at age eight, he went with his father and Mr. Kilgour, Fred Hart and his sons for his first trip to the big rock mountains on a sheep hunt. They brought out three rams, one goat, two deer and three grizzly bears. The fishing was excellent; every hole was full of trout.

In 1924 he started trapping with his father. There was no school in those days during the winter months, so he learned the art of hunting, fishing and trapping at an early age. In 1928, at age fifteen, he bagged a trophy Bighorn Ram with an old relic 25-35 calibre savage rifle. The sheep measured out 189⅞ inches, and was mounted by Charlie Fenterman.

He took up saddle bronc riding and in 1933, he rode in the first Bighorn Rodeo, owned and managed by Jack Browning and held at his ranch just west of the Clearwater bridge at Ricinus.

In the early 1930s he filed on the N.W. Q. 20-36-6-5 and built a log house on it where he batched until I came along. I first came to the Caroline area in the fall of 1934 where I was employed as a cook for Burt Rhodes and his saw mill crew. I cooked at his various camps until the spring of 1936, and in June of that year George and I were married. I was born and raised on a farm west of Bowden and my name was Miller before I changed it to Bugbee.

George guided big game hunters in the fall and we trapped in the winter on his father's trapline. We did this until the early spring of 1939 when we sold our homestead to the late Mr. Ray Dial for five head of horses and sixty dollars in cash, which was a fair enough price in those days. We kept our cattle and left them with George's parents. George had planned, when he sold out, to go to Jasper to start up an outfitting business. He took me and our small daughter, Joyce, to Bowden to stay with my folks until he got located and set up in Jasper. With the help of his brother, Robert, and a friend, Raymond Knorr, they got the pack string of horses lined out and headed for Jasper. When they arrived in Jasper they found they were much too early for the tourist trade; there was no work and they couldn't afford to stay and wait so they had no alternative but to turn around and come back. They had a few mishaps during the way there and back but nothing too serious; they had a lot of fun and enjoyed all the scenery.

Times were hard and we had no money but, worst of all, we didn't have a home either. However, since we still had our cattle, we were able to put them in the Bighorn Rodeo, and we made enough money for a grub stake. We then moved on to some government land, bordering the Clearwater Forest Reserve, where we exercised squatters rights until we could earn enough money to lease the land. We lived in tents all summer and were nearly driven to distraction from the mosquitoes. We had to keep smudge pots burning for ourselves as well as for our horses. I had never seen them so thick before nor have I since. We put the finishing touches to our log home in early October and moved in; what a blessed relief to get away from the mosquitoes and get a good nights sleep, for they were still going strong. We lived here for three years and then we bought the S.W. Q. 14-36-7-5 from George's Grandmother, Millie Bugbee, where we farmed and raised cattle.

In 1949 George shot and killed a world record brown grizzly bear while guiding an American hunting party. It was a case of necessity; the bear had made a kill and was prepared to defend it when he charged the party in no uncertain terms.

In July, 1963, we sold our farm and bought the

Record Grizzly Bear, George Bugbee and Ranger Jack Walker, 1949.

Boundary Service, eighteen miles west of Caroline. We operated that business until April 1966, and then sold it and twenty acres of land, keeping the remainder for our home and to farm.

In 1968 we ran a Junior Forest Ranger camp in the Clearwater Forest for the two summer months each year for three years; George as supervisor and instructor and I as cook. In the winter we trapped on the trapline that George had taken over from his father in 1961.

In September, 1970, we were involved in a tragic vehicle accident which claimed George's life. We had three children, Joyce, Karen and John. Joyce married Lawrence Pengelly in 1957. They live west and south of Caroline and have five children, Darryl, Dean, Brian, Keith and Kelly.

Karen married Lee Pittendreigh in 1958 and they live west and north of Caroline. They have a family of four, Laura, Keri, Dale and Jodi.

John married Ilene Doel in 1965 and they lived and worked in the oil fields at Swan Hills and Zama. They have two girls, Carmen and Michelle. After the accident they moved back here with me. He works the farm and has his own lath milling business and has the trapline which has stayed in the family for the past fifty-five years.

SARAH BUGBEE

Sarah married Austen Moore and they had two children, Lillian and Bob. In 1943 Sarah was married again, (after having divorced Austen), to Dallas Heck. They lived and farmed near Caroline until Sarah's death in November, 1970. Dallas then sold the farm and now lives in Caroline. They had two children, Joe and Prue, and they live in British Columbia.

ROBERT BUGBEE

Robert was a trapper, a guide and outfitter and owned a sawmill. He guided at Banff and Lake Louise for a time.

In 1943 he married a local Ricinus girl, Margaret Marven, and they managed the Tay River Ranch for the late Erle Carr for two or three years. Later they moved to Calgary and Robert went to work for Bannister Construction for several years. They had eight children, LaVerne, Roberta, Lynda, Deanna, Danny, Rocky, Smokey and Darla.

His marriage to Margaret broke up and in 1971 he remarried; he and his wife, Jean, make their home in Redwater, Alberta.

ERNEST BUGBEE

Ernest, the youngest of the John Bugbee family, led an uneventful life until he joined the armed forces in World War II. He enlisted in the early spring of 1943 and was given four months basic training in Wetaskiwin and two months ad-

Ernest Bugbee — Last leave at home before shipping overseas in W.W. II.

vance training in Calgary and then was shipped overseas. He was seriously wounded on July 17, 1944, in the Normandy Invasion and was hospitalized for several months and for him the war was over.

In May, 1945, he married Phyllis Hockwell from Farnborough Hants, England. Ernest was shipped back home in the spring of 1946, and Phyllis followed later in July, bringing with her their small daughter, Shirley, at age three months. They lived for a time on Ernest's father's place and there in 1948, their son, Richard, was born. In 1951 they moved to the S.E. Q. 15-36-7-5 and lived there until 1961, when they bought the farm originally owned by Clifford and Chris Raynor.

W. H. Burns and Family

by W. T. Burns

My parents were both born in Quebec and were of Irish and Scottish descent. They were brought up near the small town of Island Brook and later farmed in that district.

My father was married twice, the first time to Agnes Brown and they had five children, three boys and two girls. Neal, Dan and a baby boy who died in infancy, Nellie and Emeline were the girls. The first wife passed away in 1893. He married again in 1895 and to this union three children were born. Wycliffe on October 23, 1897, Wesley on November 17, 1900, and Elva in September of 1902.

When I was four years of age, my parents moved to California and they lived there for a little over a year. Then they moved to Eugene, Oregon, for a short time, then to Lebanon,

Oregon, and lived there for six years. Then they moved again back to Canada to Claresholm, Alberta, and finally to the Ricinus district. They filed on three homesteads in 1912, one for my dad, one for Dan and one for myself. We first rented land on the Flats of Butte and on the Gordon place to get feed for our cattle. We moved to the homestead in 1914 having then erected a set of buildings.

The homestead days were hard to make any headway, the clearing of land was very slow and very hard work. We were twenty-three miles from Rocky Mountain House and had very poor roads, especially when it rained. We had good neighbors and had many happy times together. My mother worked hard and made a good home for us and always a good meal was to be had for anyone stopping in. There were lots of blueberries to pick in those days and mother would pick them by the pails full.

Mother passed away quite suddenly with pneumonia in March of 1923, at the age of sixty-six years. It was said that she was the first white woman to die between the Clearwater and Prairie Creek. She was buried in Red Deer. My dad passed away in May of 1929, and Wesley died in 1924 in Rocky. Both were buried in Red Deer. Elva is living in Calgary and my wife and I are retired and live in Eckville.

In 1926 I traded the homesteads for land in the Diamond Valley district through Harvey Langley from Caroline. I moved there and married Margaret Frew, whose parents lived on the land cornering ours at Ricinus. We have three sons, Bruce, Stan and Robert. They all farm in Diamond Valley. We have now seven grandchildren and we enjoy going to the farm and to lend a hand when needed.

Erle and Barbara Carr

by Jack A. MacArthur

Erle and Barbara Carr lived near Ricinus from 1961 to 1976. Erle was born at Valentine, Nebraska, in 1893. His parents worked on a large cattle ranch in the sand hills. Those were the rugged days, in that country, where a hand gun was always carried and the children were brought up with a dirt floor in their cabin. There were no schools there. When Erle was eight years old, his father decided to move his family to Sunnyside, Washington. There they broke land and set up a mixed farming operation, and the children could get schooling. About 1913 they again decided to move and came to Grassy Lake, Alberta. A couple of years later, shortage of winter feed caused them to move their cattle north to Huxley for the winter. This is what brought Erle to Huxley. He liked the look of the district and decided to stay and set up his own farm there. He had to work out and do whatever he could to get started. It included driving livery, buying and selling hay, shooting ducks for the then commercial market, coal mining, etc.

Barbara Aronett was born near Glasgow, Scotland, in 1898. Life was not always kind. Before she reached her teens she was left an orphan. There were relatives at Alix, Alberta, and as she told the story, she left Scotland with a string and name tag around her neck for this new country. Her passage was paid and she had enough money to buy food for a week. She did house work and what she could for awhile, and then was able to take a business course. She then worked for a Mr. Larson, who had the creamery in Alix. She worked with him until he sold his business to the then newly organized dairy pool. She typed the contract and so claimed she had a hand in the very first deal of the now well known Alpha Dairy. By this time she had a brother working with the railroad at Huxley. While visiting him she met Erle Carr. They were married in June of 1918.

Erle now had his farm near the Red Deer River east of Huxley, and they rented more land and soon had a fair sized grain farm. In 1919 their first and only child was born, Margaret Anna (Marguerite). They took a great interest and part in community life and talked of the good times they had at the school concerts and dances, etc., where the babies were taken and put to sleep behind the piano.

Like the rest in the district they finally graduated from their Model T to a closed Durand car, and the Hart Parr tractor took the place of some of the horses. The elements also seemed to progress. The hail and the drought came more often, and by 1931 things were very serious.

There was an opportunity for them to take over a farm at Taber, Alberta. They decided to take it and moved with all of their belongings. This proved to be a very good move. This farm on the 'Great Snow Ridge', as the Indians had called it, was a good strip of land surrounded by poorer land. When it was found to be good, Erle was hired to break it up and then would rent it. In a few years they had one of the larger, privately run, grain farms in Alberta. In 1944 they retired and moved to Lethbridge.

Apart from his work, Erle seemed to have one great interest or hobby in life. This was wildlife — the hunting and conservation of same. Besides being active where he lived, by the late '20's he started taking an interest in the Caroline country and its big game hunting. The first guide I can remember them talking about was Jack Bugbee, who used to take them in to Seven Mile Flat with a Bennet buggy, and also would bring their game out. This went on for years. In later years there were other trips, with pack trains, going farther

back on game surveys and hunting, and we heard of the Jamesons and Brownings, etc. Erle had such an interest in that country. These hunting trips had other strange side effects. It was through the 1938 trip that I met his daughter, Marguerite, and we were married two years later.

In about 1945, Erle bought some land west of Ricinus, which they labeled 'The Tay River Ranch'. With the aid of Bob Bugbee this was operated for a few years and then their thoughts turned to just a summer cottage. This they built on an acreage just one mile west of Ricinus, in the early '50's. They enjoyed it as such until the spring of 1961, when they decided to make it their permanent home. They built onto it that year, and further the following year, making it into a very comfortable home with park-like surroundings. They were very proud of this and called it 'Edge of Beyond Cottage'.

After the Carrs' retirement from farm life in 1944, although they had much sickness, they still had more time to devote to community life. This they did through their 'Lodges', a little politics, and Erle's hobby 'The Great Outdoors' wildlife and conservation. He was active in both the Lethbridge, and the Alberta, Fish and Game. He also turned to a few other things to keep busy. He spent one year assessing land and several years in his real estate business. His main interest still being conservation of his 'Great Outdoors', he continued to work up in various branches, of Alberta Fish and Game, until February of 1956, when he was elected president for a two year period.

I think these next two years were the highlight in the Carrs' lives. They travelled con-

Barbara and Erle Carr.

136

siderably, aiming at visiting every local association in the province. They also attended meetings and conventions in the two neighboring provinces. Erle had many ideas of his own on conservation, the privilege of hunting, the protection of wildlife and their habitat. Many of these ideas he was successful in putting across, and getting them passed, in the Alberta Legislature. He didn't do this all on his own. Mrs. Carr travelled with him and was just as interested. She was a great help, especially at the social functions — so much so that by some of the other members of the association she was given the name of 'Mrs. Fish and Game'. This pleased her very much.

Life was quieter after this term of office was completed — their own health being an important factor in keeping it quieter. They enjoyed their home and their many friends and neighbors, visiting, and doing a little fishing and hunting when possible. They helped me in summer, with the resort at Pine Lake, until health would no longer permit.

On July 1 of 1965, they were grieved by the untimely death of their daughter, Marguerite. She left behind two daughters, Marlene and Beverly Ann (Leanne). Marlene, now Mrs. Ernie Reimer of Calgary, with a family of Beth, Andrew and Jeniffer. Leanne, now Mrs. Don Smith of Red Deer, has one son, Ellery.

Time went on, and with it Mrs. Carr's arthritis continued to get worse. Despite surgery, and much time in hospital, by the early '70's she wasn't able to get around much — not even to do much housework. Erle gradually took over doing the housework as well as the outside chores. He passed his eightieth birthday with having an open house for many of their friends. The winter of 1975-76 was bad, with first one of them, and then the other, in hospital. They could not keep up the work around the cottage, so in August of 1976, they very reluctantly sold and moved to an apartment in Innisfail.

This did not last long. In the spring of '77 Mrs. Carr went on to greener pastures, and in a little over six months, Erle followed.

I, Jack, their son-in-law, have written this from my memories of the stories, as they were told.

Jim and Mary Chorley
by Cliff Chorley

The Chorley family moved to a new home site ten miles southwest of Ricinus from Medicine Hat after the school term of 1934. The two oldest children of the family, Howard and Lucy, were married and stayed behind while the other six children, Clifford, Geraldine (Jerry), Eleanor

Elenor (Biddy) Chorley.

(Biddy), Theresa (Tubby), Jim and Peggy moved with our parents to our new home.

Our household belongings and livestock consisting of a team of horses, five cows and some chickens were shipped by rail as far as Innisfail and I (Cliff), (I was twenty at the time), travelled with the livestock in the cattle car. The rest of the family drove in a 1928 Chrysler touring car piloted by my married brother, Howard. Upon arriving at Innisfail the task of unloading our belongings onto the hayrack began. We were unable to carry everything so Dad and Mother sorted out what could be stored at Innisfail.

The journey west started with the team of horses pulling the hayrack loaded with our belongings and the five cows followed behind. It was a beautiful Sunday morning — my young brother, Jim (eight years), and my brother-in-law, Fred Lavoie, travelled with me and had the job of herding the cows on foot. The road west gave one the impression that you would soon go over the hill and then see some distance but there was always another hill ahead. Coming from the flat country of Medicine Hat, our new experiences were just starting.

Rain was something we were not prepared for as we slept under the hayrack and cooked our meals over a campfire. We camped at the Medicine River the first night, tired but happy to be on our way west. It started raining during the night and we had nothing over our belongings in the hayrack. Mother had brought along a roll of linoleum for her new kitchen which didn't survive the trip as that is what we used to protect our belongings and ourselves from the rain.

It required seven days of travelling to arrive at our new home. We were not familiar with travelling in the bush land and I had to unload some of our furniture along the way as the load was too heavy for the team. Dad made contact with our closest neighbor, Del Trimble, and made arrangements for him and my brother, Howard, to come and meet us with extra horses to assist us.

We finally arrived at our new home site on the Tay River, a beautiful spot. We spent the summer selecting trees and peeling off the bark for our new house. Del Trimble did the axe work while my job was getting the logs in place for the walls. We had lived in tents for two months and had eight inches of snow in August of that year. With all our discomforts that summer such as rain, snow, cold and frosty nights, we nevertheless enjoyed the heavy forest areas and the clear stream and the evening sounds of the Clearwater River. The big day finally arrived. In September we moved out of the tents. We were living in a house again and each one of us was very happy with our new home.

The next chore was haying which we did on the south side of the Clearwater River. Jerry and I had the task of haying. My dad stayed with us in an old house that Bill Winters had erected years before as they had wintered some cattle in that area. Following haying we built a barn for the livestock. My dad suggested that maybe we should haul the hay home before the river started to freeze that we would have a problem if we waited.

The only other neighbor we had was Wes Latem who was a guide and outfitter. I would help him when he required it. He invited me to go with him on a sheep hunting trip as he could use an extra hand. I was now faced with a big decision — to go on the hunting trip or stay home and haul the hay. Wes figured he would be gone at least two weeks and we were into September now. I guess I made a wise decision — Jerry and I hauled the hay. A few days later it started to snow and get colder, but we were ready for winter.

We were too far from a school so none of the children from the three families were able to attend.

For our supplies we travelled either to Ricinus or Caroline. As the car had been traded for supplies shortly after our arrival we travelled by team which was a long journey — ten miles to Ricinus or twenty miles to Caroline.

Our contact with the outside was mainly with

L.-R. — Jimmy Chorley, Chick Demenuk, Teresa Chorley, Elva and Howard Mitten, Cliff Chorley, ?.

people going fishing in the summer or hunting in the fall. During the winter months, the Bugbees or the Brownings would bring our mail or anything we required as they travelled back and forth to their traplines.

We left our home on the Tay in the summer of 1935 and settled in Caroline. My mother wanted to be somewhere near a school and able to get to a doctor if required as my father was in very poor health. Our stay in Caroline lasted until the summer of 1937. My dad felt we should move to Vancouver Island, so once again we packed our belongings in an old 1938 Chev. one ton truck and started for the west coast. Our journey ended the first night in Calgary where my dad passed away in his sleep.

The original group of Dad, Mother and eight children has decreased to just Mother and five of her children. My sister, Lucy, passed away in 1947 at the age of thirty-five of cancer. My brother, Howard, passed away in 1967 also of cancer — he was fifty-nine. My younger brother, Jim, died of a heart attack in Toronto in 1972 at the age of forty-eight. He was a broadcaster with the CBC.

My mother is now eighty-eight years old and lives at St. Anne's Nursing Home, 1220 Alberta Avenue, Saskatoon, Saskatchewan. Jerry (Mrs. Nate Jackins) is living on a farm outside of Centralia, Washington. Eleanor is married to Edward Dobish and lives at Kenaston, Saskatchewan. Teresa (Mrs. Nick Becker) and Peggy (Mrs. Pat Cassidy) are both living in Calgary and I and my wife, Jean, live in Devon, Alberta.

On looking back I value my experiences in the Ricinus-Caroline area and the friendships that were made there. I am grateful for each helping hand that was extended in our time of need and may God richly bless each one of you, your families, your homes and your loved ones.

John Clearwater and Family

John and his two sons, Vernon and Walter, came from Helena, Montana, in 1910 to homestead in the Ricinus area. John filed on the S.W.Q. 23-36-7-5 and Vernon on the N.E.Q. 27-36-7-5. Sometime later, another son, Vic, came to homestead on the S.E.Q. 27-36-7-5.

John and Walter moved back to the United States. Vic gave up his homestead and followed in 1927. This quarter was then filed on by Doug Stewart where he and his wife, Elsie, still reside.

Vernon stayed with his homestead and in 1918 he married Ada Cliff. They had three children, Vernon Jr., Nellie and Johnny.

Vern Clearwater Sr. with tree puller.

Vern Clearwater Jr. and Louis Noirot.

The mail came to Ricinus from Caroline before a bridge was built on the Clearwater. Vernon used to bring the mail across the river by boat and sometimes he, Jack Bugbee, Frank Ankle and Ed Godley walked to Caroline and packed the mail back on their backs to the river.

Besides farming, Vernon did carpenter work. He built a store for Arthur Lane at Dovercourt. He also dug seneca root and picked pine cones to sell, just like many of the homesteaders, to make a living for their family.

When the settlers decided to build a bridge over the Clearwater River, Vernon and Jim Spratt hauled the logs to the mill using horses and mules. Jim had homesteaded the land which was to become the home of the George Cliff family.

As the result of a flu epidemic in 1939, Vernon fell victim and died. Ada passed away in 1959.

Vernon Jr. married Velma Noirot of Ricinus and they had a son, Dale.

Nellie spent a few years in the armed forces and is married to Jack Roddy from Toronto. They have a son, Mark.

Johnny lives in Red Deer.

George and Edith Cliff
Sally Bugbee and Joan Dean

George Samuel Cliff was born May 31, 1893 in Stoke-upon-Trent, Staffordshire, England. After working in the CO-OP for several years selling quarters of pounds of tea, margarine, rice, etc. he became fed up and decided to emigrate to Canada. In 1910 he worked in northern Saskatchewan in the Turtleford and Meadow Lake areas with a surveying party. Later he moved to Medicine Hat.

May 15 1916 he enlisted with the 175th Battalion and served in France with the Second Field Battery in France. He had always been an amateur boxer, and was very proud of the fact that he had boxed several rounds with the world champion Georges Carpentier who congratulated him on giving a good fight. George carried in his wallet a picture of the two of them shaking hands. He received his discharge in March, 1919.

On board ship returning to Canada he met Mrs. Edith Ruth (Hibbard) Weldon who with her baby Ellen (Madge) was travelling to Medicine Hat to stay with her husband's parents. Her husband, Captain Leonard Weldon, had died of wounds in 1918. Edith had worked in a Munition factory making 18 lb. shells for cannons, and later as a Nursing Sister during the war.

George and Edith were married in Medicine Hat in 1920. For a time they worked together managing the dining room and coffee shop in a

Mr. and Mrs. George Cliff.

hotel. Later George worked for the Robin Hood Flour Mills. Their son George Jr. (Jerry) was born in Medicine Hat in 1920.

While George was in the army he became friendly with an American soldier from Kentucky named Jim Dean. Dean had a homestead on what is now the Dick Browning property. While on leave, George took Dean home to Stoke and introduced him to one of his sisters. The two were married and came to live at Ricinus. When he died she remarried and went to live in Toronto.

George had listened to Dean's tales of the wonderful west country, and after a visit he decided to move his family to a homestead obtained through the Soldier's Settlement. Several years before he had seen a picture on a calendar of a log cabin surrounded by trees and had fallen in love with it. When he saw the 1/49-36-7-W5, it had a similar cabin and he knew it was the place for him. He and Edith worked on the homestead during the summer months and returned to Medicine Hat to live and work during the winter. Their daughter Irene was born at Ricinus in 1924. In 1925 they returned to Ricinus to stay.

To make ends meet George worked for the Forestry Department in 1925 and 26 putting in mile posts from the Clearwater Boundary just east of the Ranger Station to the head of the Clearwater River and down the White Rabbit Trail. The miles were measured with the old fashioned link chains, and surveyors today say

that these mile posts are even more accurate than some measured with the more modern rigid chains. While he was with the surveying party George saw a small creek with a shining bottom. He took some of the shining pieces to have them assayed. He was sure he had found gold. Unfortunately it was copper which he considered worthless. Even so, he always had a dream of returning to the spot.

While he was away on these surveying trips life was hard and very frightening for Edith. She had had no experience with the wilderness. Before dark she would have wood and water in the house and then bar the door and let no one out until morning. One of her particular fears was that Jerry, who insisted on crossing the creek, would get lost or be eaten by a bear.

In 1927 their daughter Nellie was born. That year another change took place in the lives of the Cliffs. George started carrying the mail from the Ricinus Post Office to the Dovercourt Post Office. The post master Mr. Godley was not well, and George took over the hauling. The Government paid two dollars per trip. George used Godley's mule team and received one dollar. Godley got the other dollar. Since George was doing all the work that didn't seem quite fair, so later he got the two dollars, but had to use his own team. At first he had one mule and one horse. Then a team of horses. Finally a motor vehicle.

For over 23 years he hauled the mail, and for seventeen of those years he never missed a mail day despite rain, hail, snow or bitter cold. In true British tradition the Royal Mail had to go through — and go through it did. He figured that during his time with the mail he had travelled enough miles between Ricinus and Dovercourt to have gone around the world.

Besides the mail, Mr. Cliff also hauled cans of cream and brought back lists of groceries from the combination store and post office at Chedderville. He had many friends along the route. If in the cold weather some of the groceries he carried were perishable he would shout to the

Ricinus Postmaster George Cliff.

housewives to come to collect their purchases rather than just leave them by the mail box, and he would not drive on until they came.

During this time another son, Arthur, was born in 1932.

In 1942 George was appointed Postmaster of the Ricinus Post Office with Irene as his assistant. He moved the post office to his yard. George held this position until the Post Office was closed in 1963. It made no difference what time of day or night, or day of the week it was — if you went for your mail he was always willing to get out of bed or stop in the middle of what he was doing to get it for you. With his cheery greeting and wide smile, he was always the soul of patience and goodwill.

During the second World War, George received a citation from the National War Finances Committee for his part in the 8th Victory Loan. However, this did not mean as much to him as the watch presented to him by his friends and neighbours — the people on his route — when he retired.

In time Jerry took over the mail hauling, and was just as faithful and friendly as his father. Between them, they had nearly forty years of post office and mail hauling duties. When Jerry gave up the route in 1963, the community showed its appreciation by having a social evening and a gift of a watch.

Mr. and Mrs. Cliff stood together all their married lives. She was a kind and beautiful person. Many people had the pleasure of sipping her tea which was particularly good — especially when it was served in the pretty china cups of which she was so proud. Her cakes and cookies were well known. They should be — before the first war she was head cook for a titled family in the south of England. After a period of ill health she had a heart attack and died October 13, 1961 at the age of 68. Both she and Mr. Cliff will be remembered a long time for their kindness and love of children.

Jerry and Art still farm and live on the homestead. Like their parents, they are hospitable and kind to children. Irene married Richard Howard and lives in Rocky Mountain House. They have six children and eight grandchildren. Nellie married Bob Murphy. They have five children and eight grandchildren. Madge (recently widowed) married Fred Osterland. She lives in Ft. St. John and has four children and nine grandchildren.

Mr. Cliff lived on with his sons, cooking good meals and helping them when he could. He died from a heart attack April 23, 1972 just five weeks before his seventy-ninth birthday. George Cliff — one of nature's gentlemen.

Spoor and Esther Cole
by Donald Cole

In the fall of 1937, Mr. and Mrs. Cole shipped all their effects from Czar, Alberta, to Rocky Mountain House, Alberta. They drove the cattle and horses to their son's (Donald Cole) rented farm west of Caroline and lived with him that winter. In the spring, Spoor had rented a farm north of the river bridge, west of Caroline, in the Ricinus district.

A couple of years later, they bought a quarter section a half mile east of the Ricinus School. They lived there for some years, eventually going to Cloverdale, British Columbia, where Spoor died years later. His wife, Esther, remarried and later died in White Rock, British Columbia.

One day, when Dad backed his wagon into the Clearwater River, he leaned over to dip a cream can of drinking water, as there was no well on the Burns' place where he lived, and the lid rolled off into the river. It was thirty below and little snow and about eighteen inches of water, and Dad jumped in not reckoning on the very fast current. His feet were knocked out from under him and he was rolled over and over down the river. He said he nearly drowned before he could get his feet under him again. He had to be helped into the house as he was a block of ice.

Christie A. Connelly

We came to what was to later become the Ricinus District in November 1914, from Bassano, Alberta; having come to Canada in 1911 from Montana, U.S.A.

We had a railroad car for our household goods and stock from Bassano to Innisfail and were met there by Baxter Bean, my husband's brother, and a neighbor, Mr. Warren.

The first night we camped at the Medicine River. It was one of those cold frosty nights with a bright moon. You could see all around and rabbits were running everywhere, and two of them were in our frying pan for supper. What a treat!

The going was slow as the cattle were walking and we reached the north Raven the next night. We had partridge for supper that night and delicious it was to be sure.

The next morning it started to snow on our breakfast table. We got to Mr. Warren's place about three in the afternoon. The Warren place was just across the river from our new home. As we were fording the Clearwater River, I thought it did not seem like a very large river.

Baxter Bean had our logs all cut and they soon put up a log cabin (our new home), down on the south east corner of our quarter which was 36-36-6-5. That winter was a very happy one for all of us I think. As soon as our house was ready a

Christie Bean's log house which was built on flat land in the corner of quarter. Moved after flood of 1915 up to higher ground.

dance was in order. There was quite a crowd and as I remember the music makers were Mr. Cross and his son Wilbur. They sat up on a table away from the dancers. All winter there was a dance somewhere. There were quite a few at the old Wooler Schoolhouse, and later on Mr. Burns built a new house at the top of the hill where Mr. L. Scott lived, and dances were held there.

One night I remember so well. It was March 17, and Mr. Burns' birthday. Mrs. John Stewart had made him a birthday cake and presented it to him.

The spring broke with much rain, and in June, up to the 26th, it rained every day. The river got higher and higher. It had rained all day and the men put a stick in the water to see how fast the river was coming up. About six o'clock, a fellow we had stay in with us, came in from taking a look. I said, "Is it raising any?" He gave me an evasive answer and started for Baxter Beans. I looked out and saw a large stream of water coming past the house. The men got the cows and horses all together and drove them over onto higher ground. By the time we got ready to leave the water was coming on two sides of our log cabin.

Mrs. Baxter Bean, the children and I, spent the night at Mr. Reed's cabin, on the quarter just west of ours. The men went up river to see if they could help anyone. When the flood hit the John McNutt farmstead, Jack, as Mr. McNutt was called, went to get his horses to take his family to higher ground, but could not locate them quickly. The water rose so rapidly he could not return to his home and family on foot. Mr. Fred Stewart had started to build a boat. This, the men finished, and Mr. Clearwater, Jack Bugbee, and Jack McNutt started in to get the family. This was about four o'clock in the morning. They found the family on a very small island. Here Mrs. McNutt had put the children up trees keep-

ing watch lest they fall. By now the water was going down, so it was decided to take the family back to their home. The other two men came back out, but somehow they upset the boat. However they both managed to get home. That afternoon all the neighborhood was down to see them go in with horses to try and bring the McNutt family out on higher ground where they would be among their friends. Fred Stewart, Vern Clearwater, Jess Ditch and a few others, were amongst those to go in with horses, tailing horses to those they were riding. The water was so swift it nearly took the horses off their feet. This group was gone three hours and never did find the McNutt house. However the flood continued to go down, so they decided the worst was over. That night the Frank Ankles' kindly offered the Bean family food and shelter. The next day we went home. There was mud and pools of water everywhere. The Baxter Bean home was not touched, but ours was a mess. Water had been in about four inches high. In a tent where we had trunks and other things stored, the water went right through even into the trunks. My young turkeys were all drowned. Hens stayed on the roosts but one poor old setting hen drowned on her nest because she could not get off. We decided to change our building site.

Meanwhile there was talk of getting the school started, as some of the children had not been to school in a number of years. This was in 1915; the flood of which I have just spoken was in June 26, 1915. A year went by and no school. Finally in 1917 the school was finished. I applied for the post of teacher, as I had taught several years in the States and was granted a permit from Edmonton to teach.

It was a very interesting school, all were eager to learn. There were twenty pupils ranging from five to sixteen years of age. The older ones could read very well, but of arithmetic, history, grammar, etc., they had no idea.

We, the Baxter Bean children and I, drove to school in a democrat, seven of us altogether. One morning we were trotting along when all at once the front wheel rolled off into the bush. William quickly stopped the team and we had to walk the rest of the way. School was from July until Christmas that year, and the children did very well. We had a nice party and tree at the closing. The next year they had a teacher from Rocky Mountain House, a Miss Slat. It was the year of 1918. The following year I was home to put in time on my homestead, as my husband had deserted me and I was alone. The Ricinus School could not get a teacher, so Edmonton again issued me a permit. I taught from August until Christmas. By this time some of the older boys had decided they knew enough and were out working.

After I married Clifford Rayner February 5, 1921, we spent a great deal of time in Vancouver. He was a waiter in the Hotel Vancouver and I did waitress work too. We planned to fix up the place and get more land cleared on my homestead. We built the new house in 1926, and by 1930 we had about 75 acres of land cleared. Clifford stayed on the farm afterwards, but went to Banff Springs Hotel for seven summers, where I was in charge of the First Officers Dining Room. I was there the year the King and Queen came to have a rest at the Hotel on their tour through Canada. I saw them taking a buggy ride in a democrat drawn by two nice horses and driven by Mr. Brewster. When they went away, we were all allowed out in the court yard in our uniforms to say farewell.

When the Hotel was very busy I often worked in the main dining room and often we had a thousand people for dinner. The special trains coming in with tourists and the number of guests staying in the Hotel would be four or five hundred. Of course here one made quite a lot in tips. It was really wonderful working at Banff; one met so many really nice people.

Clifford and I loved our place and animals. We had lots of visitors from Calgary and entertained in our big room with parties of the Social Credit, our women's club and held wedding receptions. But good times cannot last. There comes a time of sorrow and one must abide by it.

Clifford was taken ill and died June 5, 1955. I sold the farm and bought a home in Rocky Mountain House where I kept roomers and boarders to help meet living expenses. I had some wonderful boys who worked on the oil and seismograph rigs.

I met Mr. Connelly; he was alone and so was I. We were married September 6, 1958. We are very happy, but the years are going much too fast and we are both living on borrowed time.

I cannot close my story without mentioning our mail men of that period, who braved floods, cold and storms to bring us our mail. At first it was once a week from Caroline and Mr. Godley was our mail carrier. In the flood, I mentioned previously, he lost the boat and mail bags and nearly his own life trying to ford the river — Mr. Clearwater who was helping him very nearly drowned too. For a time Ed Godley's brother carried mail. Mr. Cliff took over about 1928. The mail was coming then three times a week from Dovercourt. Mr. Cliff was ever faithful, never missed a day as I remember. Any errand one might have, he was ready and willing to do. We were fortunate to have such good men to carry our mail.

Many of the first ones who came have moved away or passed on. Among the most tragic deaths were Mr. and Mrs. John Stewart who died

Christie Bean (Raynor) on new breaking.

in a fire when their home was burned in the night.

We look back now and think how things were in our day: no bridge, no roads in their proper places, no cars and no store near. We wonder how we did it, yet we have opened up a beautiful country for future generations to enjoy.

Since this was written, Mr. Connelly passed away March 24, 1966. Mrs. Connelly is still active at the lodge playing crib and does embroidery work every day. She was ninety-two years old on Jan. 2, 1978.

The Bruce Cressman Family
by Buck Rickard and Sally Bugbee

Bruce was born in Ontario in 1889. His wife, Ella Garland, was born in Butte, Montana in 1896. When Bruce's father Sam came to Alberta, He settled in the high country around Cochrane.

I first met Bruce in July, 1919 when he was packing for the Raven River Surveyors. At that time, he and his wife and family were living in Bearberry where Ella had taken over the small store, mail hauling to Sundre, sorting and handing out mail. They had four children — Bruce, (Bud) Lyle, Donna and Roma.

Around 1927, Bruce purchased the S.W. Q-1-36-4-5 and homesteaded the S.E. Q-2-36-4-5 in the Raven area. He had a herd of horses that he brought from Bearberry. He added to these and started a rodeo string.

In 1936 Bud, Lyle and I gathered horses all spring to get them ready to take to the first Ponoka Stampede. We tried some of them out to test their performance, and if the truth was known, we may have pulled leather a time or two.

We started out with seventy-five head of horses and a chuckwagon hauling our camping gear and grub. When we got north of Gull Lake

Bruce would ask some farmer who was by the road "How far to Ponoka?" The answer was "Fifteen miles." We would go two or three miles and he would ask someone else and receive the same answer. Then he would ride up laughing, and say "By Gum Boys! we are holding our own. Still fifteen miles in."

Bruce trailed his horses to Stampedes as far as Calgary south, Peace River north, and both east and west of No. 2 Highway, for a great number of years. Bruce used to take part in some of the stampede events and in 1924 he won the Packing Contest in Calgary.

In his saddle bucking string he had the mighty bay gelding "Gavioda" that was never ridden. He had Old Tramp, Breezy, Powder-Foot, Kinkneck Jessie, Madam Queen, Tom Sawyer, Grey Ghost, Prairie Chicken, Susan Van Duzon, and big black Dynamo. For this string of horses, the pick-up men were Art Johnson on Roanie, and Doc. Pruitt on his Pinto.

In the bareback string, he had Black Rabbit, Orphan Annie, Tiny Tim, Fade'away, Birdie, Bambi, Slippery and Tom Thumb. He had several others, but these were among the best of the horses.

After separating from his wife Bruce married Lee Kiengersky at Whitecourt around 1935. They had six children — Jimmy, Harry, David, Gwen, Mary Anne and Dorothy.

In 1953, sometime after he had suffered a stroke, Bruce came to me to ask if I would take him to the Bird's Tail mountain in Montana. He went on to say that back in 1919 after the big blizzard, he and a girl, Hattie Deare, had moved a herd of cattle for her father from Okotoks to the Bird's Tail mountain. When they reached the Montana border they found they had to hold the cattle on the Canadian side for a month before they could take them across. They moved them back and pastured them north of the Waterton Lakes for the month. Then they continued the drive to their destination.

I complied with his wishes, and when we left Calgary Bruce was lost all of the way until he got north of Sims. We could see the Bird's Tail mountain from there. When we got south of Sims we crossed a cattle guard and saw a sign which read "The next twenty-five miles is the Deare Ranches" Driving on we came to a ranch house and there stood the old girl — Hattie Deare.

After a full and active life, Bruce died in 1959 and Lee in 1972. They are buried in the Raven Cemetery.

Bud, who was born in 1917, followed the Stampede Circuit for several years doing what he enjoyed best — Saddle-Bronc Riding. He was a good rider and put on a good show, winning many firsts during his career.

He married Louise Shannon from Kevisville and they had four children — Maxine, Doyle, Ivy and Gerald. Louise was killed in a car-train accident near Blackfalds in 1962. Doyle was killed in a logging accident in 1959. They are both buried in the Raven Cemetery.

Apart from Stampedes, Bud was in the lumbering business. When he retired he moved to Calgary from his home near the Clearwater Store. While in Calgary he learned hotel management. He married Rose Shannon and for a time she worked in Kresges and then joined Bud in the hotel business along with his two daughters, Maxine and Ivy.

With his partners, Bud owned and managed hotels in various places in Alberta. In later years he and Rose agreed to separate and Bud married again.

At the time of his death in April, 1978, he and his wife Muriel, and his daughter Ivy were operating the Victoria hotel in Olds. He is buried at Raven.

Lyle was a man who had a life of variety. He guided for Brewster at Jasper. He was a popular western singer over an Edmonton radio station. For a time he worked for the Forestry at Rocky Mountain House. Then he was on the town police force — first at Rocky Mountain House and then at Rimbey.

He married Evelyn Kerik in 1944 and in 1948 they moved to Caroline with the first two of their eight children — Birtris and Melvin. Those to follow are — Marvin, Roma, Velda, Cindy, Emory and Sandra. At this time five of these children are married, the other three — Marvin, Emory and Sandra are still at home.

After moving to Caroline, Lyle worked with Bud at his bush camp. He also worked in the Caroline pole yard for George Wrigglesworth. Failing health forced him into an early retirement, and in June, 1976 he passed away at the age of 58. He is buried at Raven.

Bud and Lyle's two sisters, Roma and Donna both died and are buried in the Cemetery in St. Albert. The mother of this family, Ella, passed away in Edmonton in 1965. She too is buried at Raven.

Dezall and Hart Story

In 1940 Ken Dezall and Ralph Hart set up a camp at the edge of the 'Big Timber' on George McNutt's homestead west of the Ricinus Post Office. They operated a tie mill and saw mill until 1947, employing from 15 to 45 men which added to the economy of the area.

Dances were held in the cook house and were enjoyed by the community. Marge Dezall, being a nurse, was often called on, for her services at

Dezall and Hart camp, 1941, in the 'Big Timber'.

the camp and surrounding areas, as the nearest Doctor was 30 miles away.

In 1947 the partners dissolved their partnership. Ralph went to Rocky Mountain House, where he built a garage. Ken Dezall

bought the Steed place and with Ray Mustard had an outfitting business.

Ken continued to operate the saw mill until 1949, then sold it to the Murray Brothers of Caroline. He moved to Devon, selling the Ranch to Dr. Banks of Calgary.

Dunn, Charlie and Bill

Our association with the Caroline, Ricinus Districts started in the fall of 1932.

My Dad (Charlie) and I (Bill), living at Priddis, south west of Calgary were harvesting and threshing in the Carbon area. We met some people there "Gibsons" and Norm Jennings who told us about the wonderful homestead land available west of the Clearwater. After threshing we decided to take a look and drove out in our 1925 Ford Model T Coupe.

We had been given a name to contact — Jack Browning, about five miles west of Caroline. We had been advised that he had a trapping lease on

Tony Rolfus at the Dezall and Hart camp, standing on a pile of railroad ties.

L. R. Charlie Dezall, Clyde Oper and Harvey Humphrey.

Mrs. Haney and neighbor Charlie Dunn.

a quarter section about two and a half miles north and two and a half miles west of the Clearwater Bridge west of Caroline. He was not too interested in this property and we managed to talk him into throwing it up. This land would then be available for homestead. This all took time but finally I received word that this land would be available for homesteading on such and such a date.

I could not take chances on losing out on this and must be first in the line-up when the Land Office opened in the morning. At this time I was working at a sawmill southwest of Calgary. The day before this land was thrown open for filing I left the sawmill late in the afternoon, planning to be in Calgary that night and be at the Land office first thing in the morning. I headed out across country for the highway as I had many times before. It was a snowy, windy, foggy afternoon. After some time I figured that I should be at the highway, but no sign of it. Quite some time later I finally decided that something was wrong. I headed up onto a high hill, and there in front of me was the Turner Valley oil flares. In those days they really flared. I had been walking in a circle to the right. I knew if I headed for those flares I would come to a road and eventually did. As it was a very bad night, there was no traffic and walking was getting very heavy. A few miles of this and I figured there was no hope of Calgary that night. I headed into a neighbor's and told them they had a guest for the night.

In the fall of 1933 I headed north with an axe, ambition and little else. I took the train from Calgary to Innisfail and caught a ride with Caroline storekeeper Langley and out to Brownings. I had him move me back to the homestead. It was getting late in the fall, so a shack had to go up quick and it did. 8 x 10 feet

poplar logs, squaw notched, sloped tar paper roof, no floor. The Homestead Act said "Live on it six months a year"; so I spent the winter there clearing some land. Groceries were packed in on the back from Caroline, Ricinus or Chedderville. It was a hard life but we did have our fun times. Dances at Ricinus and Chedderville schools, Caroline and Dovercourt halls, house parties at Forsters, etc. Browning had a small Stampede ground and hall.

I worked around the neighborhood when work was available, for Bill Robertson of Chedderville a couple of springs, a few months for Oscar Johnston of Caroline and on Thurbers, Nortons and Hart sawmills.

In 1935 my Dad moved onto the quarter east of mine. We managed to get a few acres broke, fenced the land and eventually proved up on the homestead.

I was in the army 1942-46 and was married in England.

On discharge I decided no more farming or lumbering — I was going to be a steam engineer. Then I got a job with Ram River Oils. After about a year I got a higher grade Certificate. I sold the homestead and moved into Red Deer.

Dad sold out a couple of years later and moved to Rocky and then to Red Deer where he passed away in 1971 at 94 years of age.

I moved to Edmonton in 1951 and obtained a First Class Engineers certificate and was employed as Chief Engineer until retiring in 1978.

We have five children and ten grandchildren.

We are really enjoying retirement — six months in Alberta and the cold six months in Arizona.

Charles Augustus Fogelsong
by Sally Bugbee

Charles came to the Ricinus district from Wisconsin, U.S.A., in 1908, and homesteaded the N.W. ¼ of 30-36-6-5, which is now owned by Don McNutt. Later he bought the S.W. ¼ of 14-36-6-5 and built a small log house on it. He had brought several horses up here with him but lost nearly all of them with Swamp Fever.

On April 21, 1910, he went to Red Deer, to meet the train carrying his bride to be from Iowa, U.S.A. Millie Findlay arrived in due time, and they were married that day in St. Lukes Church, with B. P. Alford and Clara Holstead as their witnesses.

In 1917, they bought the N.W. ¼ of 14-36-7-5 and built a two story, eight room frame house on it. For many years it was the most impressive house in the district. This house is still in use; it has a new roof and siding, is modernized inside,

Mrs. Charles Fogelsong.

and is now owned by Bill Gaw. Charles and Millie lived here until Charles' death in 1926, caused by an accident and followed by pneumonia. Charles had some of his land broken up by John Trunell and a team of oxen. Millie continued to live here with the help of George Bugbee Sr., and they were married in 1932. After his death, Millie stayed on until age and poor health made this impossible. She then moved over to her Grandson George's place, where he and Sally cared for her for two years. Then she moved to the Alfred Rose home for a time, then to the Three Way Hospital in Rimbey, where she died in April, 1956, at the age of ninety-one years.

Bob Forster

I was born in March, 1918, at Irricana, Alberta, where I lived for the first six years of my life, then in 1924 we moved to Calgary. In 1932 we moved to Ricinus and this is where the fun began! The fishing and hunting of those years was just a real paradise, the likes of which we'll never see again, so good in fact that my school-ing by correspondence was short-lived. However, the education I received in the bush those first years, I wouldn't trade for any university education. Some of this 'good' education, which was how to snare fish, was learned from Ed Godley, the local postmaster. This came in handy at times when the fish wouldn't bite, for in the 'Dirty Thirties' people had to live off the land. Lester Justinen and I spent a great deal of time together fishing and hunting, protecting their sheep from bears (cost the bears around nine casualties), taking over for his dad on the lookout (it's a wonder there's any rocks left on Base Line Mountain for the amount we rolled off), and cutting and splitting our family's winter supply of wood with Swede saw and ax — a week at each place. We weren't bothered with much traffic then, about the only ones who had cars were Wes Latem and Jack Bugbee. They both drove 1923 or '24 Dodges and we drove our Model T's for a year or so. The roads, if they could be called that, were just trails and if I could get to the store by the bridge in one hour, I had to drive like a maniac — which was the general opinion anyway. I'm certain none will ever forget the river hill by the bridge, sometimes it was so bad you couldn't even get down it.

I remember some of the people who lived in the area for awhile, then left again. There was an Englishman, a Mr. Woods, who lived on and took care of Ernie Crowder's place (Steed's in later years), he then lived with us for a few years before going to Calgary. Mr. Roach, who operated a store in Caroline for awhile, lived on Herman Suhr's place (now Cozart's). Across from Murphy's lived a Mr. Jackson, Charlie Snyder also lived with us for a couple of years. Whittakers lived on the Suhr place for a few years and Milo and I have kept in touch with each other ever since. A Mr. Watson was in the district for awhile, he used to sing and play his guitar — sort of a one-man band. To him I traded a horse for my first guitar.

Earl Jameson taught me what I know on the guitar and banjo. We later had a small band with my sister, Jean, at the piano and played for many dances around the countryside.

There were some severe hail storms that went through our area in the '30s. I remember one in particular in 1937 that happened on a Friday afternoon. The community had a picnic planned for Sunday at Del Trimble's and we made ice cream by using the hail stones which had been covered by at least a foot of debris knocked off the trees in the 'Big Timber'. Those stones were the size of turkey eggs and there were a lot of roofs to be repaired after that storm. Before another storm struck, I was busy cutting hay with a team of horses and mower.

The first stones that fell were few and far between but one happened to hit one of my horses in the middle of its back. They vacated the premises rather speedily with me going off backwards end over end. They went over a bridge and through a pole gate, then straddled a big tree. I took off as fast as they did for the house and after the worst was over, I found them standing in the barn with bits of harness hanging here and there. As for the mower, well, it was a complete write off — and no insurance.

The Clearwater River played a big part in my life, mainly because some of my timber berths were on the other side of it. This necessitated the building of bridges and boats. High water each spring usually washed out my bridge but when it reached its peak, that's when Jimmy Tobin and I would have some of our wildest boat rides. It gave us a nine mile run of pretty wild water down to the bridge. Here Mr. Simpson would be watching for us with some choice words meaning mostly that we were 'nuts', but we sure had fun. We did this many times without a mishap. Thank goodness.

As before mentioned, we built a sawmill. During the '40's I took over the entire operation myself and by this time the price of lumber had improved to about thiry-four dollars per thousand. Some who worked with me were Jim Tobin, Howard Thompson, Harold Rhodes, Dick Knorr and Bill Benz. We sawed fairly steadily until 1947 by which time the mill had been sold to Lee St. Clair, but I remained to saw for him until May.

In January of that year, I married Gertrude Slaymaker of Rocky Mountain House and we lived in a small house I had built there for us.

Bob and Gertie Forster — 1947.

Gertie had come from Barons in southern Alberta to the Rocky area in 1937, then moved into the town in 1939. She worked for Goods at the telephone office for two years and as a clerk in Killick's Drug Store from 1941 to 1947 and part time for two years after we were married.

From Ricinus we moved to my parents farm at Dovercourt, helped to put in the crop that spring, then moved to Charlie Poulson's at Strachan where I sawed for him at his mill for a year. In May of 1948 we returned to the farm and I built another sawmill as there was a lot of timber here to be sawed. By that fall we both moved back to Rocky and worked for Killicks unti the spring of 1949 when I started carpentering and building houses. We remained in Rocky until March, 1950, when again we moved back to the farm and have lived here ever since. For the next twenty-seven years I built many houses in Rocky and surrounding district and around the Caroline district. Five years ago I quit the building business, purchased Allan Doyle's planer and went back into the lumber business.

Gertie and I have raised six children. Joy is married to Chris George of Winchester, England, and lives there. She is a horticulturalist, having taken two years of studies at Olds College. She worked at Hilliers Nurseries for some years and Chris still works there. They have one son. Ken took two years Agriculture Mechanics at Olds College and has for seven years worked for Big Country Machinery at Drayton Valley.

Colleen also completed her studies in horticulture at Olds College and is presently employed by Highfield Developements at their tree farm at Edmonton. David is presently employed as an automotive parts man in Drayton Valley. Joan is in her second year of horticulture at Olds College. Doug is taking grade eleven at Caroline School and will also enter Olds College for an agriculture mechanics course.

Job Forster Family
by Bob Forster

Job Forster was born in Shropshire, England, in 1870 and came to Canada in the late 1800s. At first he settled in Manitoba. Here he married and three children, Carl, Orval and Ruth were born to them. Mrs. Forster was not well and after coming to Alberta she passed away.

Helen Barclay Fleming was born in Perth, Scotland, and as a young woman, emigrated to Canada. She came directly to Calgary where she was employed as a hotel cook. On August 31, 1908, Job and Helen were married in Calgary. They lived in Irricana where Job (mostly known as Joe) worked for the C.P.R. as a water well

Mr. and Mrs. Job Forster — 1947.

driller. While doing this work, it was not uncommon for him to walk eleven miles to work in the early morning, work all day, then walk home again at night. During his employment by the C.P.R., he was also called upon to do repair work on the steam locomotives. While living in Irricana they had four children, Gordon, Fletcher, Bob and Helen. In 1924 he moved his family to Calgary. Here then daughter, Jean, was born. Joe was also a carpenter and in Calgary he plied this trade.

By 1932 times were very difficult in the city so in March of that year, he purchased a half section of land at Ricinus, formerly owned by Charles Winchester. The home quarter was N.E. 12-36-8-5 and the north quarter was S.E. 13-36-8-5. He and his family left Calgary in two Model T Fords and as many belongings as they would hold. The rest of the household goods and a year's supply of food were to be brought by truck, however, this one broke down around Innisfail and Herman Suhr had to go and get it for them in his old Federal truck. The weather was fairly good that spring up 'til May 11 when it started to snow. By the 13th, two feet of snow had fallen. This didn't cause much inconvenience since few people had cars, travelling was done on foot or by horse. I can remember that we made some skis to get about on and while out on the road (actually just a trail then) we saw that Mr. Roach had gone by on his horse and had left two furrows alongside made by his feet. In about a week the snow was all gone again.

Not all the children came out to live on the farm. Carl, Orval and Ruth remained in Calgary where they married and made their homes. Gordon stayed a couple of years on the farm helping there and working at logging in the winter. He also worked in the store for Mr. Roach. This

store was the old Pioneer Hardware Store that was torn down in 1978. At that time it was on the north side of main street where the hall now stands. Then he returned to Calgary. By the following year Joe got interested in sawmilling so he and Bob built one. Incidentally that mill is still being used. At that time lumber sold for eight and nine dollars a thousand feet which wasn't very profitable even in those days. Money was very scarce in the thirties and everyone pitched in to make a living. The boys, Gordon, Bob and Fletcher, hunted squirrels and rabbits. The squirrels sold for anywhere from three cents to thirteen cents a hide and the rabbits went for fox meat at four cents each. Joe did carpenter work around Caroline and Raven.

In 1935, when the Social Credit Party was campaigning, meetings were held in their old log house almost every weekend. These usually turned into great social evenings with the business being dispensed with quickly, then dancing to music supplied by Nat and Earl Jameson on their banjoes with some help from the Forsters.

Mrs. Forster was kept very busy throughout those years keeping the household running smoothly. Wild game and fish were plentiful and the surplus would be canned. Also wild berries would be picked and canned each year. She also knit all the socks for the family and could read a book and knit at the same time. Still she found time to teach Helen and Jean to play the piano.

In 1939 a new house was built out of eight foot logs. These were sawed in half lengthwise and placed upright. This house is still in use today as the main house on the Bar XL Ranch. In the early '40s, Joe did more carpenter work and worked with Mr. Roger Rose on several occasions. In July, 1946, he sold the farm to Lee St. Clair and they moved to a farm in the east Dovercourt district, eight miles north of Caroline. This was the S.E.Q. 35-37-6-5, and had been homesteaded by Armour Godkin. Joe fixed up the log house there and they lived in it until 1954 when he and Bob built them a new house. Here they spent their remaining years. Both were quite active, taking care of a few cattle, helping occasionally on the sawmill, sawing up fire wood, taking his grandchildren for rides in a cart behind his garden tractor and at various times tending pigs, ducks, turkeys and chickens. They especially enjoyed growing and tending a good garden which, on account of frosts, was impossible to grow at Ricinus. Joe was still a great walker. In his sixties he walked from Calgary to Ricinus in two and a half days and even in his eighties was a familiar sight walking three miles to Leavitt's store for groceries and carrying them back home.

Standing left to right — Fletcher, Gordon, Orval, Jean. Seated left to right — Helen, Ruth, Bob.

After a long and generally healthy life, Mrs. Forster passed away in April, 1963, at eighty-two years of age. Joe passed away in April, 1966, at nearly ninety-six years of age. Both are buried in Calgary.

Gordon Forster married Mary Hart from Blackfalds in 1938. For many years he worked for Union Tractor in Calgary and then for Standard Gravel. About this time he purchased land at Crossfield and farmed it as well. Several years ago they moved to the farm to live. They have two children.

Fletcher Forster married Jean Dietrick in 1939. He had worked at logging, sawmilling, hunting squirrels and rabbits, harvesting in the Markerville area and working on the lath mill for Roy Miller. About 1943 they moved to Calgary when he joined the air force. After discharge from the service, they went to Rockyford to farm, then to Morrin where they farmed for a number of years before returning to Calgary where he has since been employed as a mechanic. They have four children.

Bob stayed on at home and with his parents moved to the Dovercourt district. He married Gertrude Slaymaker of Rocky Mountain House in 1947 and they have six children.

Helen married Clarence Sawyer in 1942. He was the Forest Ranger on the Clearwater. They moved to Pincher Creek and then to Lethbridge where they still reside.

Jean was in her first year of school when they moved to Ricinus and as the nearest school was at least seven miles away, she took her schooling by correspondence. In 1945 she helped with cooking at sawmill camps, then she went to Calgary and worked in the Bay and Eaton's. In 1947 she was married to Ben Maser of Medicine Hat and

they have one daughter. They still live in Calgary where Ben works for the C.P.R.

E. Frew and Family
by Margaret (Frew) Burns

Mr. Frew with his wife and family, left Airdrie, Scotland, for Canada in July, 1913. They settled in the Evarts district where a brother of Mrs. Frew's had bought a farm the year before. They lived there for about seven years and had a hard time adjusting to farm life in the west as it was so very different to what they were used to in Scotland. However, they liked the country life and they learned to milk cows, make butter, bake bread, etc. One outstanding part of it all is that Dad regained his health. His lungs were going, and the doctor advised him to try living in Canada. He regained his health and lived to be ninety years old.

My mother's sister, Nellie Robertson, later became Mrs. Donald Blair. Donald homesteaded in the Ricinus district and he was the means of getting the Frews to move to the Ricinus-Chedderville districts. They spent many happy years there and had many friends. Mother loved it there and my dad was well known for his accordion playing and he entertained at many social evenings.

In 1948 they retired to Eckville and Mother passed away in 1959 and Dad in 1960. They had three sons and a daughter. James, the eldest, was married and had one daughter, Margaret, better known as Fairy, and when he returned to Scotland, Fairy lived with her Grandma and Grandpa Frew. James returned to Canada for his parent's Diamond Wedding, and he passed away in 1965.

John worked with his dad on the farm for awhile, then moved to Calgary and married Mabel King. They had five children. David also worked with his dad on the farm. He also moved to Calgary, and married Jean Wight and they had two sons. He retired to Vernon in 1976 and a short time later passed away with a heart attack. I, Margaret, better known as Peggy, married Wye Burns in 1926. Wye was also well known in the Ricinus district. We have three sons, Bruce, Stan and Robert. Fairy, my niece, lived with us until she got through school. We lived in the Diamond Valley district until we retired to Eckville in 1971.

The Godleys
by Sally Bugbee

One of the first families to come to Ricinus in 1906 was the Godleys. Mr. and Mrs. Godley and their three sons, Ed, Percy and Dick, and their

Ricinus Mail Carriers — Jack Bugbee, Ed Godley, Frank Ankle and Vern Clearwater.

two daughters, Blanche and Grace, moved here from Red Deer.

Five of them filed on homesteads, Mr. Godley on the S.W.Q. 15-36-7-5 and Percy on the N.W.Q 15-36-7-5. Both of these are now owned by Mrs. Gladys Murphy. Blanche filed on the N.E.Q. 15-36-7-5 and it is owned by Bob Murphy. Ed filed on the N.E.Q. 9-36-7-5 which in later years became the late Clyde Oper's farm. Finally, Dick homesteaded the S.W.Q. 13-36-7-5 and this became the site of the Big Horn rodeo grounds beginning in 1933 which was then owned by the late Jack Browning and which is now the home of his son, Dewey.

It was the Godleys who built and operated the first post office. Percy and Ed carried the mail from Caroline and then later from Dovercourt.

All three of the Godley boys served in World War I and Dick was wounded. Both Dick and Percy were married overseas, Ed remained a bachelor.

After his father died, Ed helped his mother with the post office and in later years, Dick moved to Calgary and Percy to California.

It is said that Mrs. Godley was a kind person who never complained and was always ready to

First Post Office at Ricinus and Postmaster Godley.

help her neighbors. On one occasion she was called upon for the delivery of a baby during a severe cold spell. She answered the call, but at the cost of losing the ends of some of her fingers when her hands froze. A final example of her courage came when she died. She was a victim of the most dreaded of all diseases, cancer, yet no one knew she had it until she died. She is buried in the Red Deer Cemetery.

Ed carried on with the post office. He was made a notary public and settled many a dispute. He was also on the Ricinus School board for a number of years.

At the time of his death in the late 1930s, he had a fine collection of guns and artifacts.

George Grunda
by Sally Bugbee

George came to Canada from somewhere in the U.S.A. He had left his wife and family. In 1921 or '22 he went to Horburg, west of Rocky Mountain House, and he lived and worked with Jim Stewart, cutting railroad ties, mine props, etc.

Sometime in the late 1930s he moved to the Tay River where the camp ground is now situated. There were a couple of buildings left there by the Chorley family who had lived there for a short time.

He started into the goat business and raised quite a few. He had no mode of transportation so he used to walk to the Clearwater Store for his groceries accepting a ride whenever someone was going his way.

He got himself a huge Great Dane, a very powerful dog but friendly, he named him Wanie. He built a dog sled big enough to haul his groceries and himself too; it was a huge contraption that would tip over easily. However, Wanie was able to pull the old man back and forth quite easily during the winter.

There were some sawmill camps in the big timber east of the Tay hills and one of the camps brought in some pigs to feed them the vegetable peelings and left overs from the cook house. Since Wanie was such a large dog, it took a lot of food to fill his appetite and he used to wander down to the camps for a hand out and whatever he might find. After the pigs came and after they had some little ones, Wanie decided to have some fresh pork so he took to killing pigs and so someone put a quick end to that. Wanie never returned to the Tay.

George then bought a grey horse he called Silver from Cleve Nickelson. If ever there was a gentle and faithful horse, Silver was one of them. George often used to ride him, and he drove him on Wanie's sled. The sled often tipped the old man over in the snow, Silver would stop and wait patiently until he got the sled righted and climbed in. When there was no snow, George bought a buggy with shafts, made for one horse, and Silver transported him safely back and forth to the store or into Caroline, turning out on his own whenever he would meet another vehicle, be it a wagon or a car, while the old man dozed along the way. By this time George had gotten two Terriers, Bob and Tiny. Bob was a very vicious little dog for his size, ever protective of his master and home while Tiny was a gentle little dog.

In 1946 Jack Browning stopped by one day to see how the old man was getting along; he found him quite sick so he took him to the hospital in Rocky Mountain House; he was never to return to the Tay. When he was well enough he was sent to St. Joseph's Nursing Home in Edmonton, and he died there that fall. To my knowledge he had no relatives in Canada and I think he was buried in a cemetery in Edmonton.

His assets were disposed of and Mrs. Raynor bought Silver and the buggy. He gave Chris and her sister, Jessie Limbough, the same safe transportation that he had always given to his former master.

Hallock History

by Belva Arich

Sarah Hall Hallock was born on December 31, 1896, in Illinois, U.S.A. In 1906 the family moved from Illinois to the Turtle Mountains in North Dakota. One year later they travelled with two covered wagons to about thirty miles south of Portal, North Dakota, where they lived until 1910, when the family once again moved by covered wagons to the Medicine Hat-Alberta

Virgil, Bill, Wilfred, Dan and Gordon Hallock.

area, where they had heard of great opportunities for farmers.

On May 22, 1915, Sarah married Wilfred Hallock who was born on June 10, 1892, and raised in Oxford County, Ontario. They rented a farm at Seven Persons, Alberta, where they lived the first three months of their marriage in a covered wagon. The first seven children were born there. A baby girl, Doris, died and is buried there. There was no wood in the area, so dry cow chips were used for the fires. Before the rains, the women and children would go out with large bran sacks and gather the chips.

In the spring of 1925 Sarah and Wilfred, with their six children, moved to the Chedderville district, spending the first night camped at the Riddle farm just south of Rocky Mountain House. All the children had whooping cough. The next morning they went on to the farm they had rented at Chedderville, to find nearly all their cattle in Mud Creek. It took all day to get them out and home.

Two months after their arrival, baby Wilfred died and is buried at Pine Grove Cemetery at Rocky Mountain House. They lived in the Chedderville district for twelve years where they lost a third child, Ida, at the age of thirteen.

Sarah and Wilfred had twelve children, the five youngest were born in the Chedderville district. All were born at home except the youngest who was born at the home of Mrs. Fleming in Rocky Mountain House, which was used as a hospital at that time.

In 1937 the family moved to the Ricinus district where the five youngest went to school. Two more moves were made one-half a mile each time. The second one was in 1940 when they quit renting and bought their first home where they lived until 1975. The youngest two started school from there. The school was closed about 1951 and Belva, the baby of the family, took her grade nine in Caroline.

The roads were very bad and a trip to Rocky

Mrs. Hallock — Jim, Goldie, Belva — her grandchildren.

would take the better part of a day with a team and wagon, quite often getting stuck.

Every fall the men in the district would get together with their teams, wagons and threshing machine and go from farm to farm to get the harvesting done. Sometimes the day would start about two or three o'clock in the morning to get ahead of the snow.

During the winter months, quite often Sarah and the younger children would have the farm work to do themselves as Wilfred and the older boys went to the bush camp to work. As times were hard, folks had to pretty well live off what they could grow and raise — grinding wheat for flour and porridge, butchering a cow or pig as the need arose.

The doctor lived in Rocky and had to travel by horse, or horse and buggy, to visit his patients, or he would have to walk some distance to get to them. In one case when he was called out, he had to climb over high windfalls to reach a young lad who had been clawed by a bear.

The children walked or rode horseback to school, often getting frostbitten in the winter months. The children took their lunch in thirty pound lard pails which they filled with blueberries on the way home. Wild berries were plentiful with as many as six hundred quarts of blueberries being put in the cellar in one season, along with strawberries, gooseberries and cranberries. About twice a year, a crew would get together and buck up firewood with the cross cut saws, and later with buzz saws.

During the war, about 1943, we would have army jeeps and lorries camp in our field on training missions. Ration books were issued in the 1940s for the purchase of sugar, gasoline, etc. During these years it was quite common to have men from the logging camps stop for meals. Christmas time, when many of the men were unable to go home for the holdiay season, we would have sixty or more for a meal, setting the table, clearing it and setting it again. They sang songs and played cards and games.

In the summer of 1944 we had several outside folks stay with us to pick berries. A couple of girls from Rocky were at our place and one of them had to make use of the biffy. We heard a lot of screaming and crying so went to investigate and found a couple of bats hanging just in front of her and a snake by the door. She wasn't concerned about her appearance as she came dashing out.

Although times were hard and no one had very much money, many good times were had. Everyone would climb into the hay filled wagons to attend a Christmas concert, dance, pie or box social or a community picnic. The hard work and worries were soon forgotten.

In May, 1965, Sarah and Wilfred celebrated their fiftieth wedding anniversary at the Dovercourt Hall with many friends and family joining them on this great occasion. In May, 1975, open house was held at their home to celebrate their sixtieth wedding anniversary. Although Wilfred was gravely ill, he did enjoy seeing good friends and family that came to have lunch and brought good wishes.

Late September, 1975, ill health forced Sarah and Wilfred to sell the farm they had grown to love so much. They bought a house in Rocky Mountain House where Wilfred died one month later at eighty-three years. Since the death of her husband, Sarah's granddaughter, Twila Visotto, went to live with her.

There are nine children surviving, thirty-five grandchildren and thirty-four great-grandchildren. Mary Heare lives at Ricinus with three children and eight grandchildren;. Vergil of Caroline has five children, and lost one, and has ten grandchildren; Vera Steeves of Rocky has five children, lost two, and has ten grandchildren. Gordon, of Fruitvale, British Columbia, has two children and lost one. Richard of Rocky, has six children and five grandchildren. Amy Kohnke, Taylor, British Columbia, has two children. Daniel lives at Grand Cache and has seven children. Joyce Visotto lives at Rocky and has three children and one grandchild. Belva Arich lives at Calgary and has two children.

Joseph A. Ham Family
by Walter E. (Gene) Ham

The Ham family, my father, mother, two brothers, one sister and my grandfather, also Joseph Ham, and I came to Canada and homesteaded in the Ricinus district in 1921. We shipped our household belongings, stock and machinery by train from Fort Benton, Montana, to Rocky Mountain House.

Dad worked for T. C. Powers General Store before we came to Canada.

We got our mail at Ricinus but traded at Dovercourt, also. After three years we moved to Innisfail where Dad worked on the road with his horses. My brother, William (Bill), was born while we were at Ricinus. My sister, Lillian, was born at Innisfail. My brother, Joe, and I went to school four months in the summer while we lived on the homestead. One teacher taught grades one to eight.

We moved to Turner Valley in 1927 where Dad worked in the oil fields. He lived there until 1971 then moved to Calgary where he died in 1972. My mother, Minnie, died in 1976.

My wife, Bernice Nichols, and I have three children, a daughter, Mildred (Mrs.) D. W. Shillenberg from Inuvik, North West Territories,

153

a daughter, Barbara, Mrs. Norman Chaput from Spruce View and one son, Warren, and wife, Janice, of Calgary.

We have four grandchildren, John Shellenberg, Robert, Matthew Chaput and Sarah Chaput.

Haney Family

by Nora Kirstein

Enos came from Minnesota, U.S.A., with his parents in 1902. He filed on a homestead in 1904 at Haynes, Alberta.

On February 17, 1910, he was united in marriage at Lacombe, Alberta, to Lula Hoppus. After spending several years around Haynes and Iola districts, they moved to the Ricinus-Dovercourt area.

Mr. and Mrs. Haney raised a family of five. Zena (Mrs. Huss) lives in Hespero, Erma (Mrs. John Lakeman) lives in Haynes, Nora (Mrs. Max Kirstein), Gerald in Dovercourt and Claude in Rocky Mountain House. We moved up to the Ricinus country August, 1936. When we left the farm at Haynes, we used a covered wagon loaded with bits of furniture and supplies. Gerald and I (Nora) rode on horseback and chased the cattle. A young lad, by the name of Howard Andrews from Manitoba, also drove a wagon with a mower and rake loaded on it. Each wagon was pulled by four horses. On some of the long hills, we would take a rope fastened to the saddle horn to help pull the wagons. There were very few cars on the road at this time. A bad hail storm had hit the district just a few days before we arrived. Feed for the stock was hard to find, but we managed to pull them through the winter. It was a lonely time for my mother as she spent a lot of time alone, neighbors were not very near to us. Dad, Gerald and I worked at whatever jobs we could find. Hunting squirrels, hacking and

Mr. and Mrs. Enos Haney and grandson Darrel Kirstein.

Gerald Haney family — Geraldine, Gerald, Birtris and Clayton.

peeling railroad ties or working in sawmills — the pay was very poor.

Dad loved the wilderness and in 1939 he got a trapline on the Ram River and Fall Creek. The men went trapping in the winter while Mom and I stayed home to look after the stock. Claude was still too young to go to school, as it was five miles on horseback. We lived in a log house for quite a few years. In 1947 they built a new house which they lived in until 1963. Then they sold the place to Cecil Gill and moved into Rocky Mountain House. Enos' health was poor and he passed away in February, 1966, at seventy-nine years old. Lula remained in town until she passed away in January, 1978, at the age of eighty-six years.

Mrs. Haney was a very cheerful person and an excellent cook. She could always set an extra plate at the table for whoever might come along. When she was seventy-two years old, she shot and killed a wolf that was fighting with the dog. At her eightieth birthday party held at Dovercourt Hall, she danced a waltz with her son-in-law, Max Kirstein. Enos and Lula Haney were Pa and Ma to all their grandchildren and most all the people who knew them. There were fifteen grandchildren, thirty-four great-grandchildren and three great-great-grandchildren.

L. to R. — Nora, Claude, Zena, Gerald and Irma. Front — Mr. and Mrs. Enos Haney.

The Fred Hart Family

by Neva Browning

My father Fred Alexander Hart was born near Miles City, Montana in 1883. Mother — Bernice Beebe was born in Miles City in 1890. They were married in 1910.

By 1913 they decided to move to Alberta with its open homestead lands as the range in Montana was being used up by sheep ranchers. After filling 2 boxcars with their stock, household effects and machinery they travelled to Red Deer. My oldest brother was 6 months old. Dad vividly recalled the train trip he took to Rocky Mountain House on the newly built railway, and how they watched with fascination the water oozing up through the ties.

They rented a quarter section from Web Buck on the Stauffer Flats, and in the spring bought SE 33-36-6-W5 from Bert Hereford. Their next door neighbors were the Mike Benz family. They sold this particular property in 1927 to Steve Dutton.

In 1915 they homesteaded the Tay River Ranch. A lot of work went into the building of the homestead. They milked cows and shipped the cream to the Rocky Creamery. The nearest neighbors were seven miles away at the Clearwater Ranger Station. The Stoney Indians travelled through and stopped to visit and traded moccasins and gloves for tea, sugar and flour. They travelled this way on their trips between Morley and the Kootenay Plains.

My family fell in love with the mountains and spent as much time as they could in them. Dad had a Big Game Guide License and outfitted from 1918 through to 1930. In 1919 Bill Cross and Dad had a very successful Big Horn Sheep hunt. We have Dad's sheep head, and Mrs. Cross still has Bill's.

Even in those days the Harts and the Brown-

ings were making deals. My folks bought a pair of Airedale dogs (Smokey and Roxie) from Jack and his Dad. Mom remembers the delicious biscuits Jack made for their dinner. He was about 14 years old at that time.

Dad shot a big bear that was killing calves. It came at two in the morning and got its fourth calf. Dad shot it with his 30 U.S. Winchester with one shot in the throat. We still have this gun as a keepsake.

The first road into the ranch was a survey trail and crossed to the south side of the Clearwater and back again above the mouth of the Tay River. With the help of Jack Bugbee they built a new road from the west side of the Big Timber, through the poplar hills to the ranch. Andy Kilgour brought the first car up to the ranch in 1920. It was a four cylinder MacLaughlin Buick.

Forest fires usually burned themselves out in the old days and in the summer of 1920 a big fire started by lightning near the Forestry Boundary. It burned right through to the Idlewild. The whole community rallied to keep the fire from coming back on our ranch. They plowed a fireguard from the Clearwater River to the poplar hill on the four mile flat.

My brothers could not resist the lure of the west country and came back to sawmill in the Big Timber. One of the first mills in the Big Timber in approximately 1938 was Ray McKain from Kevisville. In approximately 1940 Pete LeCerf moved a mill in. In 1942 Ken Dezall and Ralph Hart (Dezall and Hart Lumber) brought a big mill in and operated it until 1948. Elmer and Ralph Hart (Hart Brothers) in 1944 sawed in Northwest of the now Dick Browning place until 1948.

Dad served as councillor in this area for 4 years.

In the winter, Mother had to take the kids into Rocky Mountain House to attend school. This was a hardship for all, so in 1925 with regrets for having to part with their much loved homestead, they made the move to the Spruce View district. The original Spruce View School was on our land.

They farmed at Spruce View until 1948 when Mom and Dad retired to Cloverdale, B.C. and then to Winfield where Dad died in 1952. Mother moved into Kelowna and died in 1963. They are buried in Kelowna.

There were 5 in our family. Ralph who lives in McBride, B.C., Elmer in Heffley Creek, B.C., Marjorie (Mrs. S. Pollard) died in 1950, Doris (Mrs. Bob Boyden) died in 1974, and Neva (Mrs. Dewey Browning).

Big Horn Rams — Left, Bill Cross' — Right, Fred Hart's with Hart boys Elmer and Ralph.

Harry and Jessie James

by Harry James

I was born in Minneapolis, Minnesota, April

27, 1893, and with my parents moved to Dent, Minnesota. In 1906 we moved to Stettler, Alberta, and homesteaded where Halkirk is now, four miles north, and there we farmed, raised cattle and horses and opened up a coal mine. We shipped coal to all parts of Alberta and Saskatchewan.

It was at Halkirk that I met Jessie Spencer. Jessie was born at St. Joseph Island, Ontario, March 17, 1889, and in 1906 the family moved to where Castor is now.

We were married in Stettler on the 12th of November, 1917. We lived at Halkirk for two years and then we sold out and roamed the country.

In February, 1923, we moved to Rocky Mountain House and settled down. My brother, Lawrence, and I bought the shoe and harness shop but we didn't like it so we sold it and then started logging until 1927 when we moved to Ricinus on April 7 with a wagon load of furniture and trailed ten cows and ten horses. There were

lots of snow drifts, four feet deep, and mud up to the axles. We had to make several trips back to Rocky for machinery. That spring was very late, we didn't get the crop in until June and the leaves didn't come out until the 4th of June.

We found the neighbors to be the best in the world. George Vincey was our local veterinary, he fixed horse's teeth and did what he could for their ailments. Bill Bean was our local blacksmith, he fixed all broken parts. Percy Godley was our mail carrier, he hauled the mail from Dovercourt to Ricinus. Dovercourt then was two miles east of where the Dovercourt bridge is today and one and a half miles south, and the bridge at that time was two miles east and two miles south. George Cliff was the next mail carrier and he hauled the mail for a good many years, and we got our mail three times a week and he never missed a trip.

For entertainment we had dances, ball games, surprise parties and picnics with lots of good eats.

In 1936 I was voted in as councillor for the Prairie Creek municipality and what they had was no good for the district, so I worked to get it into the Improvement District and it is still in the I.D. and working good. I was on the advisory board for seventeen years with the I.D. I was on the Westview Lodge board at Rocky Mountain House for fourteen years and on the Rural Electrical Association for fifteen years.

Jessie and I are retired and living in Westview Lodge. I still drive my own vehicle and we are in reasonably good health.

Lawrence and Pearl James

Lawrence and Pearl James came to the Ricinus district in 1927. Two years later, they

Jessie and Harry James.

H. B. James house — 1969.

Pearl, Lawrence and Lawrence Jr.

Pearl and Viola James.

had a fire and lost their house. They then moved across the creek onto S.E. 6-37-6-5, and they proved up on the homestead in 1934. They bought a pig for fifty cents, and when it grew up they sold it for thirteen dollars. It cost ten of the thirteen dollars to file on the homestead, so they had three dollars left for groceries.

Lawrence worked in the lumber mills and bush camps and he also worked in the coal mines. Pearl was a cook for a good many years and one of the best.

They had two children. Lawrence married Ileen Korth and they had three children, Violet, Doug and Larry.

Viola married Gordon Hallock and they had three children, Lornie, Sherry and Curtis.

Lawrence and Pearl are now retired.

Nathaniel (Nat) Jameson
by Bubbles Jameson

Nat was born in London, Ontario, October 19, 1878, and came west to Lacombe, around the age of seventeen years. He was a carpenter by trade and a banjo player, he loved and played good music and entertained in various night clubs.

Leona Rusk was born in Iowa in 1882 and came to Alberta in 1897 by covered wagon with her parents. Nat and Leona were married in 1903 and lived in various places in British Columbia and Alberta before coming to the Ricinus district in 1936. He bought the N.W.Q. 17-36-7-5 which had been formerly homesteaded by Gus Raynor.

They had five children, Nathaniel, (Tan) Hyacinth, Cuthbert (Cuff), Earl and Harold.

Nat passed away in 1956 and Leona in 1969 and are resting at the cemetery in Lacombe.

Tan was born in Lacombe in 1905. He was a bronc rider and rode in the Calgary Stampede and various shows in the U.S.A. He married Ettie Hepburn while living in the Lacombe-Joffre area. In 1937 he and Ettie came to manage the Tay River Ranch, then owned by Henry Stelfox of Rocky Mountain House. They looked after Henry's cattle on the ranch and for a time they milked cows and shipped cream. They also guided hunting parties — doing this for a few years. Tan and Ettie parted and soon after Ettie joined the W.A.C.S. in Calgary. Tan, being at loose ends, left the ranch and bought the S.W.Q. 17-36-7-5 which had been filed on by Mr. Burwash in the early thirties. Then in 1947 he married Hattie Inman who came from Manitoba to Alberta some time before. By this time Tan was a licensed guide and outfitter and Hattie cooked on the trail for their hunting parties. They sold out later and bought the Tay River Ranch. Besides catering to hunting parties they started into the cattle business and raised a small herd of fine Hereford cattle. They had one son, Terry, who is now married and has two children. Terry and his wife, Helen, live on the ranch.

Tan passed away at his home in June, 1961, and is laid to rest in the Pine Grove Cemetery in Rocky Mountain House. Hattie lives at the ranch periodically.

Hyacinth was born in Lacombe in 1905. She participated in rodeo shows in the early days. She married Glen Furlong, a farmer of Lacombe.

Cuff was born in New Westminster in 1909. He was a guide and guided for Outfitters Stan Kitchen, Jack Hargraves and Red Craten at Jasper. He has been a resident of Vancouver and area for a number of years. He has one daughter from his first marriage.

Earl was born in New Westminster in 1911. Like his father, he was an excellent banjo player. He worked in the carpentry trade and also did some guiding. He married Hazel Bardwell of Sylvan Lake, they had two children, Gary and Gordon. They lived at various places in the Ricinus and Caroline areas and in Red Deer. Here, Earl had his own orchestra and his young son, Gordon, who had learned to play a bass guitar at an early age, joined his band.

In 1967 they moved to Nelson, British Columbia. They have a trapline and they do some trapping. Gary is married and has two children, and is a carpenter. Gordon is still single and works with Gary. Earl still plays his banjo and keeps active. Hazel is a writer and has also taken up photography.

Harold was born at Lacombe in 1919. He guided for his brother for fourteen years and when Tan passed away he took over his outfitting business. He lived with his folks until he married Bubbles Stelfox of Rocky Mountain House in 1948. He had built a log house prior to their wedding on his father's place and that is where they live. Bubbles became a trail cook for Tan until she and Harold started to raise a family. They have five children, Bud, Ralph, Ester, Jake and Joe. Bud and Ralph are both married.

Martin Justinen
by James J. Justinen

Martin William Justinen moved from Oloberg, Finland, to the U.S.A. when he was seven years old, with his parents. Martin and Violet Bocken were united in Holy Matrimony on December 22, 1917, in Chicago, Illinois, by Pastor Jonson.

Martin Justinen served some time in the U.S. Navy during World War I.

Martin and Violet homesteaded in the Ricinus district between 1918 and 1919. Their two quarters were about eight miles west of the Clearwater Bridge, on the north side of the river.

Martin and Violet raised six children: Lester William, born April 14, 1919; Violet Jenny, born June 12, 1921; Evelyn Ottley, born in 1923; James Joseph, born April 21, 1925; William Frederick born in 1927, and Virginia May, born on April 1, 1938. Virginia drowned on May 2, 1940, and was buried on the homestead, just east of the buildings, on a hill.

When Martin and Violet first moved to their homestead, the south low land was covered by willows which they cleared by hand. It was rich land for growing crops and garden vegetables, but due to the late springs and early frosts in the fall, the grain crops would freeze before ripening. However, hay grew well and so did potatoes, carrots, beets, turnips, cabbage, cauliflower, peas and parsnips. Turnips were grown by the wagon boxes to feed to the milk cows, and they were stored all winter in a large root cellar along with other vegetables. Raspberries and blueberries were the main fruits, and they were picked wild, one or two miles away. Violet canned from three to four hundred quarts each year.

Due to the failure of grain crops, sometimes Martin would go out to work in logging camps around Rocky Mountain House, or to Bashaw where he worked at different jobs. Martin was an ardent ball player and played ball for the Bashaw Ball Club. Because he was exceptionally good, he was paid to play at Bashaw. He also played for the Caroline Ball Team.

Martin acquired the job as Forestry Lookout Man on the Baseline Lookout, in 1929. It was a twenty-five mile trip by pack trail from the homestead to the lookout. Groceries were taken up by pack horses at different intervals. Sometimes Martin never saw anyone for two or three months. He had to cut all of his own wood to heat the cabin and cook with, and his water had to be carried from a mountain spring about one-half mile from the cabin. At times, when lightning strikes would start fires below the lookout, Martin would walk down with a shovel and an axe and put the fires out. It was a good one hour walk down and a two hour walk back up.

The animals seen around the lookout cabin were mountain goats, cougars, bears and moose, also ptarmigan and chipmunks.

Some falls, the snow storms would come up suddenly, and Martin would head home on foot. The wet snow would bend the branches over the pack trail, so he would beat the snow off the branches with a stick to let them spring out of the way. On arriving home he would be soaked to the skin and in no good mood, as he would have liked someone to meet him with a saddle horse.

After the lookout job the family raised sheep and logged the hilly area of the homestead, sawing lumber with their own mill.

In the early forties, Violet's health failed and she returned to Chicago to live with her sister, until she was well again. Later she took special nurses' training to care for the sick, elderly people in their homes. She worked at special nursing until the early seventies when she fell and broke her hip. She now lives with her sisters in southeastern U.S.A.

The homestead was sold to Jack Browning in 1943, and Martin also returned to Chicago where, in 1946, Martin and Violet were divorced. Later Martin moved to British Columbia, then to California and to Hawaii, later returning to California where he remained until his death on July 24, 1976, at the age of eighty-two years. It was the wish of the Justinen family to have the remains of Martin William Justinen cremated at the Chapel of The Pines, Los Angeles, and return to the area that he wanted to pioneer and build a new life. The area selected was on the Baseline Mountain, just north of the old lookout, between two knolls that have an abundance of mountain flowers every year. The day of releasing the ashes, there was a family service held at the bottom of the mountain. William Olson, son of the oldest daughter, gave the service and prayers. After the services, Lester and his wife; James and his three sons; Wayne and wife; Ann, Brian and Kendal walked up to the old Baseline Lookout cabin.

The Children

Lester went to school while staying with the Hart family east of Caroline. At seventeen, he worked at his Uncle Carle Bocken's lumber mill south of the Clearwater River and three and one-half miles west of the Clearwater Bridge. He later went home to re-build the old sawmill which was used for some years.

In 1940 Lester was drafted in the army and after one year he was discharged for medical reasons. He returned to Lacombe, Alberta, and worked at College Heights in their dairy and also in the furniture factory and drove their furniture delivering truck. Lester married Elsie Olson and raised one daughter, Shirley, and adopted one son, Harold. Elsie passed away with cancer and Lester later re-married. He married Violet Daniels, and they moved to Vancouver Island where they worked in a hospital. The hospital closed down, and they now work in a Winnipeg hospital.

Violet Justinen went to an old school one and a half miles east of the Clearwater Bridge, while staying with her Uncle, Carle Bocken. Violet took more schooling at Lacombe and later married William Olson. They raised two children: William and Jenette. They farmed at Lacombe, then moved to a dairy farm just outside Mission City, British Columbia. This is where they retired.

Evelyn Justinen went to school in Midnapore, Alberta, and stayed at Walt Shaws. Then she went to Chicago and trained for a Registered Nurse and worked at the hospital there. She married Charles Merritt and raised four girls. In 1968 she died in a car-truck accident.

James Justinen went to school in Calgary, while staying with Dr. W. S. Quint in 1937, and in 1938 he returned home due to Dr. Quint having a heart attack. He logged and sawed lumber and also shot squirrels and the furs were sold to pay for groceries. He left home at age thirteen, and worked for farmers at Lacombe and Midnapore. He then went to Rocky Mountain House and worked in a Ford Garage. In January, 1943, he enlisted in the Canadian Armed Forces for active duty and went overseas and was wounded in the front lines in northwest Holland, on April 21, 1945. He then returned to Rocky Mountain House and worked in the Ford Garage for eleven years and acquired a motor mechanic licence, a gas and electric license and auto body repairing license. In 1958 he rented space to operate an auto body repair shop, and in 1969 he purchased the property, shop and house, to operate a welding and auto body shop.

James married Ella Jean Marshall, on May 2, 1948, and raised seven children: Wayne, Wendy, Ernie, Brian, Tammy, Kendal and Twyla.

William Justinen went to school in Lacombe, then moved to Chicago and taught school there. He is now back, and doing carpentry work for the

Seventh Day Adventist Church. He is married and raised five children.

Some points of interest of the first days — Dr. W. S. Quint had the quarter east of Violet Justinen's quarter. Mrs. Quint was midwife when James was born. Mrs. Cliff was midwife when William was born and Mrs. Ankle was midwife when Evelyn was born.

Grandfather Bocken lived on the south side of the Clearwater River for many years, until his death at age seventy-five. He was laid to rest at the Raven Cemetery. Carle Bocken, brother to Mrs. Violet Justinen, also lived on the south side, and he operated a lumber mill. When the steam whistle blew at noon and evening it could be heard for miles around the Ricinus district in the mid-thirties. Carle and Jack Browning were quite close buddies around 1909, and they worked between Nordegg and Rocky Mountain House.

One had to ford the River as there was no bridge. Once a team and wagon were lost on the Tay River during high water.

Bear and cougar became plentiful in the late thirties. In the early thirties our dog brought home a small weasel and we fed it fresh milk and kept it for a pet for some years. It would leave in the spring and return in the fall, entering the old house by way of cracks in the floor. It would jump on the table and drink milk from a saucer, and also sit on anyone's shoulder while they ate. One evening in the fall of the early forties, Evelyn saw what she thought was our yellow cat returning. She followed it over the hill, behind the barn, and found it to be a large mother cougar with her two kittens. Evelyn retreated in short order.

All dates in this story may not be correct.

Phillip and Nellie Kiser

Phillip Kiser, eldest of John and Mattie (Stewart) Kiser's four children, married Nellie Graham on January 2, 1920, in Phillip, South Dakota. Phillip was nephew to Fred and John Stewart. Nellie Graham, at the time of their marriage, was teaching school in Phillip, South Dakota.

Phillip and Nellie had one son, John, born at Midland, South Dakota, in 1921. Phillip, Nellie and John came to Alberta to visit the Stewarts in 1934. They were so impressed with the area that they returned to make their home in 1936, leaving John with his uncle, Bob Kiser, to attend school in Montana. They first settled on the former Charlie Fogelsong homestead, later moving to the original Jim Dean homestead where they built a house. During the early '40s, Nellie Graham Kiser taught at the Ricinus School while Phillip farmed.

John Kiser was married in Great Falls, Mon-

Phillip and Nellie Kiser.

John and Mary Kiser and family — Sheree, Phil and Karla.

tana. He and his wife, Mary, had three children, Phillip, Carla and Sheree. John Kiser passed away at Great Falls in 1970.

Phillip and Nellie Kiser left Alberta in 1946 to take up residence in Forsyth, Montana. Over the years they returned to visit friends and relatives in the Ricinus district many times. Phillip Kiser passed away in Billings in 1973 and Nellie Graham Kiser died in Helena in 1977. They are survived by their three grandchildren and several great-grandchildren.

The Herman Knorr Family

Herman Knorr came to the Ricinus district from High River, in 1934, with Bert Marven. He bought the N.E.Q. 27-36-7-5 and then returned to High River. He sent their horses and some land working equipment back up with Bert Marven, who had taken land north of his. Then in May, 1935, the family moved up with a Model T. Ford.

In the latter part of June, Herman and his wife, Lillian, went back to High River for the summer, to fill a haying contract, leaving their eldest daughter, Lillian, in charge of the five younger children.

Herman and Lillian had nine children: Robert, Herman, Lillian, Ray, Margaret,

Evelyn, Dick, Jack and Nona. Robert never lived here, he joined the American Army and was killed in action, in 1945, in World War II. The five younger children attended school at Ricinus.

Herman Jr. homesteaded the N.W.Q. 27-36-7-5 in 1937, and stayed until the war years and then enlisted for four years. He was married in 1945, and lived at Dovercourt, then Dawson Creek, and is now living at Kamloops, British Columbia.

Ray worked on Government Geographical surveys from 1938 to 1940, before the war. He also worked on pack trains as cook, in Alberta and British Columbia. He is married and lives at Prince George and works in the logging industry between McBride and Prince George.

Jack lives at Aldergrove, British Columbia. Lillian (Mrs. Alf Mills) lives in Calgary. Margaret (Mrs. Myron Lawrence) lives at Sylvan Lake. Evelyn (Mrs. Walter Mueller) lives at Canmore, and Nona (Mrs. Don Richards) is at Ladner Delta, British Columbia.

Dick and his wife, Marie, lived at Kamloops, British Columbia. His work has mainly been in construction; driving cat, etc. At present he is working on the pipeline for the oil industry.

Dick, before leaving Alberta, joined the Forestry staff and was Assistant Ranger to Ronnie Lyle at the Clearwater Ranger Station. He was instrumental in marking out and dozing the road over Corkscrew Mountain, in the Clearwater Forest, which was to be used as a fire road in 1951 and is now one of the main arteries leading into the west country. Dick and his little horse, Corbett, had a short but interesting career in Forestry.

The Herman Knorrs had, as their first and nearest neighbor, Doug and Elsie Stewart. They moved from here to Dovercourt in 1946, and in 1968 Herman passed away and is buried in the Pine Grove Cemetery in Rocky. Lillian stayed on at Dovercourt for some time and then moved to Calgary, where she passed away in December 1977, at the age of ninety-four years, she is laid to rest beside her husband.

Wes Latam
by Reba Nelson

Wes and Del Trimble (cousins) bought the N.W.Q. 30-35-8-5, better known as the Tay River Ranch, from Fred Hart in 1925. Later Wes bought out Del's share.

Wes spent some time working with the forest rangers in the Clearwater Reserve and he was also a guide, and he did his share of chasing and rounding up wild horses. It is believed that these horses originated from Casey Bathoom's herd as he raised horses in the Reserve in the early days sometime after the big fire in 1919. Perhaps the Ball brothers and the Indians added to them.

Enos Hunter, a Stoney Chief and his band were a familiar sight in those days as they travelled back and forth through the Reserve.

In 1932 a move was made to remove the wild horses from the Clearwater Reserve. Wes took part in the roundup as he was interested in buying some of them when they were put up for auction. They rounded up some twenty odd head of these "wildies" and among them was a big black stallion and a very chestnut gelding which my husband, Sam, and my father, H. A. Langley, had seen on some of their trips back there and they hoped to attend the auction to try to buy them. When the sale was called they were both in the hills. However, they knew the date of the sale and I was sure that they would be there. I also knew that Sam didn't have any money with him so I decided to scrape up what cash the children and I could gather and take it to the sale for him.

The day of the sale I saddled up old Diamond early in the morning and started out. I caught up with Ted McNutt who was on his way to the sale, and he offered me a ride in his sleigh which I accepted, as Diamond wasn't one of the best saddle horses. The sale was being held at the Clearwater Ranger Station but we decided to stop off at Wes and Dorothy's ranch for lunch. After we had eaten, we left for the sale with Wes riding along with us. When we arrived at the station, there were some men already looking at the horses but they didn't seem to be too impressed with them. A ranger from Rocky Mountain House had come to be the auctioneer. I kept looking for my men folk to come but they never did show up. When the bidding started Wes bought three blacks, one was the stallion my father liked. Ted bought two black mares and a colt. Some of the other men bought some. I bid $3.00 on the chestnut and got her, then I bought a buckskin and a lovely little grey gelding for $5.00. The last ones to go was a bay mare that had a colt and a yearling with her. The auctioneer tried to sell them separately but couldn't get any bids so he offered them together. A man bid $5.00; I said $6.00 and got them. It was dark by that time and as any brands that were on the horses had to be vented, we decided to go back to Wes' place for the night. The next morning we went back to the Ranger Station. Some of the horses had their brands vented by the time we got there and Wes and Ted helped with the rest. By afternoon we were ready to move out. I led the bay mare and her two colts followed. Wes led the black behind his saddle horse and Ted tied two behind his sled. The bay mare had been well broke before she turned wild so she was no problem, but the rest had quite a time. We got back to Wes' ranch and Dorothy had supper ready. We again spent the night at their ranch and went back to the Ranger Station to get the rest of our horses the next day. Again it was night when we got back to the ranch so we stayed another night. The next day Wes helped us get started and he went as far as Forster's which was a big help. I finally got home with my six horses and I put them in the corral. When I was putting feed out for them, the buckskin took a kick at me. Fortunately I saw it coming and got partly turned away when he hit me, otherwise I may have had a broken thigh instead of a bad bruise. Sam got home about ten p.m. that night but he had already heard about my horses as he had met Wes on his way down.

This was the first wild horse sale held at the Clearwater. They had another the following year.

Wes and Dorothy just had one child, a girl, I believe her name was Dot.

They sold the ranch around the mid 30s, or later, to Henry Stelfox, and moved to Canmore. Wes was hired by a doctor at Canmore to guide tourists and take out fishing parties from the Gateway Inn, a short distance from the Banff Park entrance.

In the summer of 1939 Wes booked a fishing party; one was a famous hockey player, Tommy Anderson, and one was Harry Ellis from Red Deer and a manager of the Arlington Hotel. Wes found that he needed his horses that he had left behind when he sold the ranch. He got in touch with Sam and I to see if we would trail them down for him. We did this and also took some of our own down. Wes found that he needed an extra man for this trip to Mystery Lake and so Sam went with him while I stayed at the Inn and helped them there. Wes had the pack boxes all packed in the evening, but he forgot to put them inside. The next morning when he started packing up, he discovered a bear had already sampled some of the contents, a side of bacon was gone and a roll of balogna. There were claw marks all the way through six pounds of butter; I guess it could have been worse.

Sam stayed on with Wes the rest of the summer and I went back to the farm. When Sam was finished and ready to come home he sent for Sam Jr. to help him bring our horses home. We always remembered that summer as that was when World War II broke out.

The Latams stayed on at Canmore and little contact was made with them through the years. Wes was killed at Canmore when he was racing his horse up and down the street cowboy style; his horse fell with him and he was killed. I don't know what became of Dorothy and their daughter.

Peter LeCerf Family

Gustave and Marie Louise and their six children, Paul, Madeline, Marie, Pierre (Peter), Agnes and James came from Arras, France to Alberta in 1902 and lived at Frank. They were there when the Frank Slide took place. In 1905 they went back to France and in 1906 they returned to the Raven area to homestead the S.W. Q. 24-36-4-5. This land was about one mile north east of the Raven Post Office and store which was run by J. B. Johns. Thomas Berry Sr. moved them from Innisfail to Raven by mule team.

Having a few cows, they shipped cream to Markerville until the spring of 1911 when Gustave found employment in Edmonton.

Their son, Paul, died as a boy about twelve years old. Gustave died in 1928 and Marie Louise in 1938. They are buried in the Evergreen Cemetery. Madeline died in 1978. Marie lives at Sylvan Lake, Agnes at Victoria, British Columbia, and James lives at New Hill, Alberta.

Peter, working at various jobs, also hauled cream to Innisfail. In July, 1917, he filed on the S. W. Q. 3-37-4-5. That year, he and other farm boys were called up for the Army, but were exempted. In 1918 they were called up again and Peter took basic training at Sarcee camp near Calgary. In August, he was given compassionate leave and the following February, he received his discharge.

Peter went to Rocky Mountain House and hired out to W. (Bill) Allen as road monkey, but

he soon got hold of a broad-axe and began hewing ties. Jack McNutt and son, Gerald, and Dan Burns also worked at this camp.

In January, 1920, he purchased the quarter of land adjoining his homestead. He then went to work cutting telephone poles and tamarac posts with Ed Clay and Kid McCoy.

On October 30, 1920, Peter married Blanche Deberge who was born in Lille, France, in 1899. They settled on Peter's land and it was here that their eleven children were born, Henri, Marquerite, Louise, Jeanne, Charles, George, Alice, Genevieve, Yvonne, and last but not least in December, 1939, twins, Albert and Theresa, were born.

In the early years of their marriage, Peter improved his farm, getting it into production. For two years, he hauled cream with a team of horses for the whole community, twice a week. The trip was forty miles gathering and twenty miles back.

Peter purchased his first vehicle about 1932 and being a man of the horse and buggy era, when he came to the first gate, he called out "Whoa," but it didn't stop — it kept on going right through the gate. His daughter, Louise, was riding with him at the time and often chuckles over it.

In the fall of 1940, Peter had the opportunity of

Pete LeCerf family — 54th Wedding Anniversary.

162

Pete LeCerf lumber camp in "Big Timber", 1943.

Pierre LeCerf's cook-house in the "Big Timber".

working on a sawmill in the Ricinus area, taking his pay in lumber. This seemed made to order, for with the arrival of the twins, more room had become necessary and he could use the lumber to enlarge his house. As it turned out, he had to take the mill over. But this time nineteen year old Henri was capable of looking after things at home, so he moved Blanche and their three babies out to the camp west and south of Ricinus. Peter and three of his neighbor's boys had aleady built a cook house and living quarters and they soon had a bunk house built. These three boys, Jim Knight, Paul Hrdlicka, and Humford Holmgren, were the first three men to work for Peter. They not only worked for him, but they married his three eldest daughters as well.

Besides LeCerf, there were several logging and sawmill camps in the area known as the 'Big Timber'. To name a few, there were the McKain brothers, Hart and Dezall, Doug Stewart and Mac Dix. Wives and their families moved in too. A small log school was built to accomodate the children with Mr. Forbes from the Kevisville area, to teach.

Rough lumber selling at $15.00 per thousand feet, was sold to the Atlas Lumber Company and to Mitten and Mullen, storekeepers at Caroline.

Doug Stewart and Dave Kleen moved in a planer and as the price of lumber gradually rose, Peter was able to pay off his debts at the farm.

Finishing his operation at Ricinus in 1945, Peter moved his outfit to a large timber berth at Harleck, belonging to the W.T. Nance Company. Many thousand feet of lumber came out of the Big Timber at Ricinus.

Having to get the children into school, Peter and Blanche bought the nursing home at Rocky Mountain House from nurse Marie Stewart. As their family grew smaller, they purchased Harold Killick's house where they still reside.

If all goes well, they plan to celebrate their Diamond Wedding Anniversary of sixty years, October 30, 1980.

Chris Lonto Family

by Myrna Kissick

Chris came from Blind River, Ontario, in 1912, and in 1913 he rode for Pat Burns in British Columbia. In 1914 he came to the Ricinus district to trap and hunt. From here he worked for George Wallace Spurgion, who came into the Markerville area in 1897; they lived on the Medicine River Flats, which became better known in these days as the Spurgion flats. Mr. Spurgion raised registered horses.

Chris married Mable Spurgion in 1916 and they lived in the Markerville area for two years, then they moved to Spokane, Washington, where he worked in a round house for one year. At that time Mr. Spurgion passed away, so they came back to Markerville.

With Mable's share of her father's estate, they moved to Ricinus where Chris homesteaded the S.E.Q. 4-37-7-5, which later became the Enos Haney farm and is now owned by Cecil Gill.

Chris and Mable had two children, Dolly and Ira Wilfred. Dolly was born Octoeber 16, 1916, and Ira November 26, 1918. They lived here until the passing of Mable in 1929; Chris then sold out and went back to Blind River. He met his death by knife wounds at the hands of an unknown person in 1935.

Chris Lonto.

Janice Cross and sister Mable Lonto, 1917. Mable brought this horse to Ricinus.

Dolly married Norman Taylor in 1933. They had three children: Roger of Calgary, Myrna Kissick of Caroline and Ardeth Servatius of Edmonton.

Ira Lonto served in the Army during World War II, and after the war he worked in the mines at Kitimat. In 1952 he was killed in a mine mishap.

Dolly passed away in 1970.

Mrs. Janice Cross, nee Dolly Spurgion, the last of the Spurgions, helped me in making up the Lonto history. She is still hale and hearty and lives at Wabamun, Alberta.

The Bert Marvin Family

by Hilda Crook

I first met Bert in High River in 1929 soon after his wife had passed away leaving him to raise their five children — Ella, Bill, Peggy, Margaret and Charlie. Charlie was just an infant and his mother's parents, the Cyres, raised him.

Bert was a carpenter and had a job to go to and my brother-in-law, Jack Leckie, could work with him. Bert couldn't take the job without having someone to stay with his family. I had been keeping house for my brother, George Buckman, who had just recently married, so I was free to take over the care of Bert's young family.

Bert was able to pay my wages for only the first month as the carpentry work failed. He then got a job looking after some horses for $30.00 a month. Half of that amount went to pay for his wife's funeral and the other half was what we lived on.

Bert had a cow and some chickens and grew a good garden, so we managed. I varied our diet by making cottage cheese from the surplus milk.

Bert Marvin, Bill, Margaret and Peggy.

With cottage cheese I made small patties decorated with parsley to sell in the butcher shop. In exchange I took meat.

I had always wanted to take up a homestead, so in 1934 filed on S. E. Q. 34-36-7-5 in the Ricinus district. This quarter had been filed on before by Charles Birch who didn't prove up on it. It was then filed on by a Mr. White, but he too failed to prove up on it. It had a small log house and a garden when I took it over.

Bert traded his property in High River for a homestead quarter in the Ricinus area. This was S.E.Q. 15-36-7-5, formerly homesteaded and owned by Charles Denton and Olen Hardy. We decided to live on my homestead as there was no habitable dwelling on Bert's land.

A friend of Bert's, Herman Knorr from High River, loaned us a team of horses, wagon and rack with which we moved our chattels to Ricinus. Herman had acquired the quarter adjoining mine on the south but had not yet moved his family.

We had a tent so were able to camp along the way. Everyone kept their eyes open to spot a rabbit or bird to supplement our diet. One day we came to a farm where a man was thinning his garden vegetables. I asked Bert to stop the horses and went over to speak to him. He said I was welcome to any or all of the thinnings. I gathered them all up and took them to our wagon. I had brought along several sealers of canned meat and fruit, but didn't want to use them if we could do without. With what I gathered from the farmer and the small game, we were able to make the trip without having to open any of the sealers.

When we arrived at the homestead the log shack looked rather hopeless, but I soon changed it to a pretty place. I removed the only partition which ran across the middle of the house and hung Bert's lovely velour curtains across instead. Bert built four bunk beds at one end, two on each side. Bert and Bill slept on one side and Peggy and Margaret on the other. With the curtains pulled at night they had a bedroom, and with them open in the morning we had one big room. Ella stayed in High River with an aunt until we could get ourselves established.

There was another little shack a little way off. This is where I slept and did my art work and writing. I guess this is why I was so happy here — it was like my own home where I could pursue my hobbies.

Hilda Buckman and Margaret Marvin.

L. to R., Bert, Ruth, Oma and Roy Marvin.

Our supplies and mail came from a combination store and post office run by Ed Godley. The children loved to take a lunch and walk the six miles to the post office and then stop and play with the George Cliff children.

The Ricinus School was about three miles from us. It was a log building. It was not always easy to come up with a filling for the children's sandwiches. One time when I had some plain white beans cooked up, I decided to add some brown sugar and maple flavoring, mash them together and try it. When the children came home they said their sandwiches were sure popular. They went all around the school.

I remember one time when I cooked for threshers for Jim Sexton who was a bachelor. I gave them buttered turnips for a dinner vegetable. In spite of their sweet and mild flavor, they didn't go over so good. For supper that night, they had what they thought was pumpkin pie and were lavish with their compliments. They never dreamed the pumpkin was left over turnips from dinner. Neither did Jim until he asked me where I had gotten the pumpkin.

When there was a dance or something to go to, everyone went. There were no baby sitters in those days. One time there was a dance that we wanted to attend but Margaret didn't have any shoes to wear. We had sent to Eaton's for a pair but the parcel hadn't arrived so we thought we would not be able to go. However, I decided to make her a pair. I went out and gathered some birch bark and proceeded to make her a pair of sandals. She was to young to dance so she just played around with the other children. Her shoes withstood her activity and wore quite well afterward for a time.

Shoes and stockings were the only things that were store bought. Fortunately I was good at sewing so made all of their clothes. Bert had a sister who lived in the United States. She had a good job and dressed well. She often sent parcels of her used clothing to Bert. I would make them over for the children and sometimes I would take hers and make mine over for them. I was never ashamed of what they wore. They were as well dressed as any of their friends. We never went on relief at any time.

With Bert making improvements on my homestead and I raising his children, we made out pretty good. I used to cook for threshing outfits to help make ends meet.

As time went on, I went to Vancouver. There were always housework jobs for women to be had and I managed to get a good job. Later on I found work at Kresge's store. After working there for a time I was able to talk the manager into selling souvenirs that I would make. I came home and began gathering woodland material — pine cones etc. with which to make the

souvenirs. When I had a fair supply made up, I took them back to Vancouver where they went over big. I would then return home to start another lot and would spend long periods of time at home. This worked out fine as I had to spend a specified time living on the homestead in order to hold it and to be able to get the deed. Bert couldn't get work but he worked out the taxes which was a big help.

I still feel that our move to the bush country was a wise choice. It was no more difficult to make a living here than anywhere else in the 'dirty thirties'. We were all healthy and made our own enjoyment. We had plenty of fresh air and exercise. With rabbits, birds, our garden vegetables and wild berries, we lived off the land. We had trees for shelter when the north winds blew, and plenty of wood to keep ourselves warm. In fact, it was a good life, better than living in the dust bowl of the prairies from where we came.

The children were growing up and Bert moved onto his own place. Ella was married to August Williams of Chedderville. Bill joined the armed forces in World War II. Margaret married Bob Bugbee from the Caroline area. After the failure of her first marriage from which she had a set of twin girls, Peggy married Raymond Adair from Caroline.

Bert built himself a new house in 1943 only to have it burn down a few years later. He was not at home at the time, so everthing was lost. In the intervening years between then and when he died in October, 1960, he spent the winters in British Columbia and was back and forth for a time. He then sold his place and moved to Calgary to make his home with Ella and August Williams.

I married Fred Crook and we lived on my homestead for the next four years. When I proved up on it, I sold and we moved to Mirror in 1943 where I still make my home.

Fred passed away March 10, 1978, and in October I went to Australia for the winter. Having just returned, it has been my pleasure to write an account of the Marvin family and myself for your history book.

The J. J. McNutt Family

J. J. McNutt came in the fall of 1913 in search of land. He chose and filed on N.W. Q. 19-36-6-5. He stayed that winter cutting logs and putting up a place of dwelling for his family. The oldest of their nine children, George, had his twenty-first birthday the day they arrived, April 16, 1915. Met by Baxter Bean at Innisfail, the McNutt family made their way to Earl Warren's place on the east side of the Clearwater River. Baxter and Earl helped them across the river to their homestead.

The McNutt family came from southern Montana, U.S.A., and stayed two years at Bassano, Alberta, before coming to what is now the Ricinus District onto their homestead. Their livestock consisted of one old horse, Old Nig. Poor Old Nig had one sound foot and three sore ones. He was jet black in color and jack of all trades. They brought perhaps a dozen hens and no cows.

The first winter J.J. cut fence posts for their own use, and trapped fur-bearing animals for income as they brought no money with them. Lynx were plentiful. As there were rabbits by the thousands, Lynx, hunting food, found this to their liking. Lynx hides were worth around fifteen dollars each. A good trapper could catch quite a few in one season, a great help financially for those early settlers.

J.J. and son, Smokey (John), held one of the first registered trap lines on the Tay River for twenty or thirty years. George did not stay with the family much. He found summer work outside as added income to support the large family.

When school opened, six young McNutts attended.

The Flood

June 16, 1915, will be remembered as one of the most anxious times of the McNutt family's experience. The McNutt home was located between the Clearwater River and a creek flowing into the river, a location handy when it came to keeping the large family supplied with fish for the table, a much appreciated addition to their diet. Those who had known the area better felt it not a wise choice, and Mrs. McNutt, though a good swimmer, was anxious about being so near the river with eight children. The happy-go-lucky J.J. so enjoyed stepping out the door to catch fish, he gave no thought to the family's safety.

The Clearwater, ordinarily a bright clear stream with every stone and pebble visible, was now a dirty boiling spread of water, and it rose to the very brim of its banks. The rain still came down. Mrs. McNutt felt they should go out on higher ground. The happy, carefree J.J. said if the river overflowed they would have a boat ride to safer ground. In the meantime J.J. and the boys were busy cutting trees and began lashing them together for a float. The float turned out to be too short, and the water came up very fast. J.J., realizing his mistake, hurried to their nearest neighbors for a team and wagon. By now the water was so high on most of the flat that the team had to swim, pulling the floating wagon. They soon saw that this would not work and turned back.

Fred Stewart had a boat under construction and it was finished in a hurry. John Bugbee and Vern Clearwater made an attempt to reach the McNutt family, but the boat swamped, and had it not been for John, Vern would have drowned. This scheme was abandoned and rescue given up until next morning. By now, the settlement knew of the McNutt family's plight and they spent a most distressing night doubting that they would see Mrs. McNutt and her children again.

During this time, Mrs. McNutt took the children to the highest knoll they could reach. They soon were all soaked by the rain that continued to fall; fortunately the rain was warm. Laura, who had a strong voice, called out that they were still safe in hopes Mr. McNutt would hear. They had no knowledge that any one else had made attempts to reach them. The knoll had a number of large trees on it that they considered climbing if the need arose.

About four in the morning as soon as it got light enough to see, the men made another attempt to find the family. This time they used saddle horses, and the plan was to swim them in the deep channels. As these people were still somewhat new to this area, and yet not too well acquainted with the lay of the land, the flood waters had changed its appearance and they had some trouble finding the McNutt home and lost a good deal of time. Eventually the cabin was located and to their great relief they saw the family when they turned around upon hearing Laura shout that they were still safe. After a happy reunion and looking the situation over, they saw that the river was gradually going down. So they decided to go back to the cabin and they lived there another twenty-two years. Then they put up a new house on the west side of their quarter on a good north and south road. The river never again came up that high, although Mrs. McNutt had a number of anxious times while living on the original sight.

The McNutt Children

George, the eldest of the children, joined the Navy in the spring of 1918. He spent two and a half years in Uncle Sams Navy, and came back to put in on his homestead. Up to 1922 he worked for farmers on the prairie. On March 28, 1923, he married Inez Denton.

This couple had one son that lived to the age of twenty-two years and one child that died at birth. Inez did not rally after the birth and death of the second child. Actually, she and George had not been satisfied with her health for some time. It was some time later, that the doctor told them that she had Multiple Sclerosis, an incurable disease. With Inez, its progress was very slow and she lived many more years. It was during the 1930s that the full meaning of the disease hit her full force. She had started to hurry to the window to watch the crew, who had put in the steel bridge, leave, and found that she had to sit down.

167

The Jack McNutt family in the early days.

At this time, son Alvin was two years old and soon became a self reliant youngster, helping his mother whenever he could. Inez refused to give in to her illness and carried on as much as possible with her housework and care of her little family. As time went on she had to rest more and more often, still doing most of the housework. Gradually Alvin and George took over her work. It was not until 1948 that Inez, now unable to leave, became a bed patient. For many years George patiently cared for her needs.

Alvin died very suddenly on May 10, 1956, in Calgary a few days before he was to be married to Fairy Frew of this area. This blow, on top of Inez's illness, almost cost George his sanity. Somehow he gathered enough courage to carry on giving Inez the best care he was capable of until her death, January 20, 1962. Her funeral was held in a little Mormon Church just south of Caroline and she was buried in the Raven Cemetery.

George still lives on his original homestead, although the land has been sold to his nephews, sons of his brother, Ted.

INEZ

Inez married Eldon Maine, and they went to Spirit Lake, Idaho, about forty miles from Spokane. She had one son and two daughters, Eugene, Laura, and Geraldine. Eugene passed away in 1977. Laura passed away when she was quite young. Geraldine now lives in Seattle.

LAURA

Laura lives in Bellingham, U.S.A., married with one child, Bruce. Laura took nurses training in the Royal Alexandria Hospital in Edmonton. She began training at the age of eighteen and has nursed ever since.

GERALD (Boney)

Gerald, always called Boney, was the fourth child and married Blanche Noirot. They lived across the Clearwater to the south until the fall of 1948. Then they went to Fruitvale, B.C., near Trail where Gerald found work in a smelter. They have two girls and two boys, Lillis, Garry, Clayton and Darlene.

JOHN (Smokey)

Smokey also married, but this marriage did not last. There were three children, two girls and one boy, Juanita, Opal and Jack. They are all married now. Smokey worked for the Forestry out of Rocky Mountain House for some time. C.K.R.D. Radio Station once interviewed Smokey. His humor and language was such that it was the talk of the community for some time. He now lives with his daughter in Sicamous, B.C.

MAY

May McNutt married Erick Dolman. They have three sons, Bill, Wayne and Jim, all married. They lived on a farm east of Red Deer for many years. Now May lives in Red Deer.

BILL

Bill, the seventh McNutt child, married Margaret (Peggy) Cornett from Ontario. This couple have five children, Billy, Merlyn, Larry, Sherly and Patsy. This marriage broke up when the oldest children were in their teens. All are now married. This family now centers around Red Deer and Rocky Mountain House. Bill lives at the west coast.

FLORENCE

Florence, the eighth member of the tribe, married Francis (Pinky) Pitts. Of this union one child was born, a son, Deryk. They lived on eighty acres of land at Nobleford, Alberta. Pinky did welding for a machine company. They are now retired and live in the town of Nobleford.

TED

Ted, the youngest of a family of nine McNutts, married Mary Robinson of the Chedderville District, bordering on the north of Ricinus. They have made their home just across the road from what was Mary's father's home place. They have four boys, Robert, Don, Richard and Allen.

Robert married Lorraine Ouderkirk and they have two boys, Bradly and Bart. They live on the N.W. Q. 12-37-7-5.

Don married Beatrice Kirby and have two boys, Kevin and Colin. They live on the N.W. Q. 19-36-6-5.

Allen married Pat Kay and they have a boy and a girl, Quenton and Kelty. They live on the S.W. Q. 14-37-7-5.

Richard is not married. He lives on the home place on the N.W. Q. 7-37-6-5.

The McNutt parents retired to Red Deer in the fall of 1946. J.J. passed away in 1956 and Mrs. McNutt passed away a few years later.

The Jack McNutt family in later years — L to R — May, John (Smoky), Inez, Laura, Gerald, Mr. and Mrs. Jack McNutt, Florence, Ted, Bill and George.

The Joys of the San

Twas in the June of '54
They brought me to the San.
They took some pictures of my lungs
And then my grief began.

Dr. Ryder shook his head
As he peeked into the screen.
"John, you're full of bugs," said he
"That's plainly to be seen."

They sent me to Infirmary One
Commanded by Nurse Rose.
She tucked me in my little bed
And took away my clothes.

"Please don't take my clothes," I pleaded
"Can't you leave my pants and shoes?
I can't wear this little shimmy
With the back all hanging loose."

"You won't be getting up," said she
"This is a T.B. San.
For all the things you'll need to do
We'll bring you in a pan."

Then I sank back on the pillow
Thinking of the days to come
Wished I were back in Rocky
With a gallon of good rum.

My room-mate's name was Smithy
Another victim of the bug.
He said "Don't worry Smokey
They'll fix you with the drug."

Then from down the hallway
There came a mighty roar —
Such a noise from out of human
I never heard before.

As it echoed up the hallway
I thought sure the walls would crack.
Smithy laughed and said, "Don't worry
It's only Mrs. Mac."

"She's the night nurse in charge now
She's short but fair in size,
And be careful what you say
Or she'll blacken both your eyes."

The next morning after breakfast
Nurses came in by the score.
Some quite neat, and some were chubby
And some six feet or more.

Miss Rose came in last — smiling
And rushed over to my bed.
Patted me oh so gently, and pleadingly she said
"Relax and don't be nervous.
Just turn and face the wall.
This is just a little treatment
We must give it to you all."

Then she pulled my covers downward,
Put my rear end in full view
And the students gathered 'round her
As she showed them what to do.

"This is where you have to put it."
And she marked that little spot.
Then gave a demonstration
How a needle should be shot.

She took two paces backward —
Gave her arm a mighty swing.
Then I prayed to God in heaven
To take care of everything.

She came up very quickly,
Made my bedside in one bound,
And I felt my body stiffen
As she pushed the plunger down.

Rosie said "That's how you do it
You must throw it with some force.
A miss would be quite fatal —
It would cripple him of course."

"But we must take these chances.
You girls have got to learn.
So come in every morning,
And you all take your turn."

Mrs. Ault came in a 'grouchin'
With hot water in a pan.
She said, "I'm going to shave you.
There's no whiskers in the San."

There I laid and tried to take it
Forcing out a weakened grin
As the blood oozed from my cheek bones
And was dripping off my chin.

The things I said that morning
I wouldn't dare to tell,
But another day like that boys
And I'd sooner go to hell.

Dr. Mullen came to see me.
Told me all about the bugs,
And how they planned to kill them
By using different drugs.

169

They're tough as little devils
And have a coating slick as glass.
Streptomycin will not kill them
Unless you drink the P.A.S.

Then one morning just at rest hour
Freeman rushed in with a stare
And said, "Smokey! get up quickly
And get in this wheelchair."

I said, "Why the fuss and hurry?
I thought I was in the San."
She said, "Don't be so damned stupid
You're booked for the slaughter pen."

We sure weren't long moving
Not when Freeman's at the chair,
'Cause sh's big and plenty husky
She could push you anywhere.

She wheeled me to the entrance
And the nurse there helped us in
Freeman said, "You'd better watch him
For he's meaner than ol' sin".

Flanagan was there a-waiting
And she took me to the floor
Where the patients all lay gasping
That had been down there before.

In the hall I met Miss Wallis.
She showed me to my room
And said "Get in bed quickly
'Cause Mike will be here soon."

Big Mike came in a-snortin'
Threw a mask across his nose.
In his hand he held a schooner
And a yard or two of hose.

The things that happened later
'Tis better left unsaid,
But he washed me out aplenty
And sent me back to bed.

My room was full of doctors
A-waiting for to see
If my heart was plenty husky
And my blood was running free.

Dr. Boyd said, "You see John,
We thought it better that you knew.
We're operating on your shoulder
Where the bugs have eaten through."

Dr. Sturdy said "Don't Worry tho
we won't do you any harm
We'll just take a bone from your leg
And put it in your arm."

"When we get it packed in solid
And nail it with iron pins,
I'll roll you up in plaster
And bring you back again."

They all smiled very kindly
As they filed out of the room,
But I heard them tell nurse Wallis
"We want him down there pretty soon".

Miss Wallis came in quickly
Laying on that nursing charm —
And while telling me a story
Shoved a needle in my arm.

It's very sly the way they do this
As they hold you by the hand.
Saying you're the nicest patient
That they have here at the San.

Then nurse Trivitt brought my nighty
With the tie string up the back.
Parks put on my muklucks
That were long and plenty slack.

Clara pinned me on a bonnet
That was whiter than the snow,
And then they said, "Get on the stretcher
You're all ready. Down you go!"

Down there nurse Catton met me
Masked up like the Turks.
She said, "Slide on the table.
This is where you get the works."

Whatever happened later
I cannot tell about,
As someone cut the circuit
And both my lights went out.

I wakened back in my room.
Miss Argent held my hand,
Feedin' me that same blarney
That they all do in the San.

Now all I can say is
I'm still a-living'
Getting weaker every day.
Just a-lying here awaitin'
For the time to pass away.
I've drank P.A.S. by the gallon
And had needles by the score.
But the bugs just keep on chewin'
And I'm getting might sore.

Now dear friends, in this story
There is lots I dare not tell
But if doctors go to heaven
I hope I go to hell . . .

Mr. McNutt (Smokey)
written in the Keith Sanatorium

Jim and Della Milburn

James Henry Milburn was born at Frankburg, Alberta, on September 10, 1913, the eldest of Jack and Irena Milburn's four children. Irena Milburn died of influenza in the epidemic of 1918, after her death the three younger children lived with friends and relatives. Jim lived with his father, only staying with neighbors in the Fallen Timber district when Jack was away working. During his growing years, Jim worked at any job a boy could do, farm hand, ranch hand, logging and sawmilling. He found very little time for school. Soft spoken and slow

170

Mr. and Mrs. John Milburn and family — Pat, Ila, Jack and Jim.

moving, Jim had a gentle hand with animals and children. His great love was always horses and rodeo, and it was while following the latter in the 1930s that he met Della Stewart, second daughter of Fred Stewart, at the Big Horn Stampede.

Della Stewart was born in Midland, South Dakota, and received her first two years of school there, completing her schooling at Ricinus after the school was built. She grew up on her father's farm, a fine horsewoman and familiar with handling livestock.

During 1929-30 Della worked at the Melton Hotel in Rocky Mountain House with her aunt, Belle Vincey, and cousin, Phyllis. She returned home to the farm due to her father's illness and remained there until 1938 when she took a job as cook for the Altoba Oil Company. This was the first oil well drilled in the Clearwater area.

The Diamond drilling machinery was owned by a man named Joe Bush, the derrick was built of native timber on the location. They worked two twelve hour shifts, two men to a crew, so the entire operation employed not more than five men, including Mr. Bush. Della received $30 a month for thirty working days and considered herself very well paid.

Jim and Della Milburn.

On December 26, 1938, Della gave up her 'career' and married Jim Milburn in Rocky Mountain House. After Cassie Stewart (Della's mother) passed away in 1939, Jim and Della took over the Fred Stewart homestead. Della had one daughter, Jean, prior to her marriage, and on June 26, 1940 a second daughter was born to Jim and Della. They named her Ila Phyllis, Ila, for Jim's sister who had died as a small child, and Phyllis, for Della's cousin on who's birthdate the baby was born.

Jean attended elementary school at Ricinus and Wooler, then started High School in Caroline, staying week days with Doug and Elsie Stewart. In 1947 Jim and Della decided to move to Caroline as Ila was to start school that year. They rented the farm and bought property in Caroline, Jim went to work as horse breaker and trainer at the government horse ranch west of Sundre and Della took a job in Steve Dutton's butcher shop. In 1948 Jean completed her education at Red Deer Composite High School.

From July to December of 1949, Della operated the 99 Diner at Hartell in partnership with her brother, Franklyn Stewart; Jim continued at the government horse ranch; Ila attended school at Mercury and Jean worked with her mother at the Diner. After Della and the children returned from Hartell, Jim and Della sold the property in Caroline and in 1950 returned to the farm. There was a school bus running now and Ila could attend school in Caroline. Jim worked in the lumber industry, logging off the timber on the farm and working in the mills, he was also guiding American hunters for the various outfitters in the area. Though Jim worked long and hard during the winter, he could always find time to rodeo in the summer. Della kept the home place going with a small herd of cattle and some sheep, Jean began cooking in lumber and construction camps, and Ila completed her education in Caroline.

Following in her father's footsteps, Ila developed an interest in rodeo, and in 1959 married a rodeo cowboy, Cecil Gill from Gadsby. Cecil and Ila settled on the home place and Cecil began breeding beef cattle and sheep while Ila worked at the Pioneer Store in Caroline. Jim at that time was working as cat operator for McGregor-Johanson of Edmonton. On November 21, 1964, Cecil and Ila presented Jim and Della with their only gradson, Troy Darcy.

In 1968 Cecil and Ila separated Ila and Troy moving to High River. Ila later married Alan France who worked in the oil industry. Ila is now working at the St. George Hotel in High River and Troy attends school at Senator Riley High.

Jim continued in construction, though past the age for riding rodeo stock, he still found time to be a rodeo judge. At the time he became ill

171

with cancer in 1975, he owned and operated a house moving business in Sundre. James Henry Milburn passed away in the Sundre hospital on September 1, 1977, at the age of sixty-three and rests in the Sundre Cemetery.

Jean continues as a camp cook, still unmarried, and Della has accompanied her on jobs in the Yukon and the North West Territories. Della and Jean still make their home on the original Fred Stewart homestead where Troy joins them on all school holidays. Troy is the fifth generation in direct descent to live on N.W. 13-36-7-5.

Roy Miller
by Jean Forster

Mr. and Mrs. Roy Miller moved from Rockyford, Alberta, to the Ricinus district in 1933 bringing with them three of Mrs. Miller's six children, Jean, Lloyd and Eddie (Dietrich). They homesteaded on the land east of the Forster farm and operated a lath mill. After the sale of Miller's homestead, about 1946, Mr. and Mrs. Miller moved to Caroline where they became proprietors of the Caroline Cafe, with the help of Mrs. Miller's son, Bob, and his wife, Betty. They later moved to Calgary where Mr. Miller passed away in 1960. Mrs. Miller stayed in Calgary and after a pleasant and healthy life, she passed away on December 25, 1970, at the age of seventy-nine years. Mrs. Miller was born in Blue Island, Illinois, and Mr. Miller was born in Manitoba.

Jean married Fletcher Forster and they have four children. After a stint in the Air Force, they went farming, first at Rockyford for awhile, then at Morrin until 1963 when they moved to Calgary. Since then Fletcher has been a mechanic.

Lloyd served in the Army during the war and

Roy Millar house.

after his return from overseas duties, he went to Rockyford, Alberta. There he married Eileen Vaile and they have eight children. At present they live and farm in the Lomond district.

Eddie, the youngest and last to leave home, married Jeanette Hendricks of Rockyford. They have, since their marriage, farmed at Rumsey, Alberta, and have four children.

Mrs. Miller's eldest son, Louis, and wife, Kathryn, live in Montana. Bob and his wife, Betty, live in Calgary. Margaret married Jack Bickerton and for awhile they helped out at the lath mill, then moved to Rocky Mountain House for some years and then went to Calgary where they still reside.

Edgar Murphy
by Gladys Murphy

Ed's father, Merrit, and his mother, Leona, lived in Nebraska, U.S.A. They had eight children and lost one. Edgar is the eldest, then Orpha, Jim, Charles, Dean, Charlotte and Clara. Ed was born in August, 1888, and in 1909, at age twenty-one, he moved with his family, to begin ranching, at Purple Springs in Alberta.

Gladys Vera Hodgins, daughter of Robert Archie and Sarah Jane Hodgins, was born at Fort William, Ontario, in April 1900. There were three children: Garfield, who passed away at age nine, Bernice and Gladys. Of Protestant faith and originating from Ireland, the family moved from Ontario to Alberta during World War 1. They moved around frequently since Gladys's father was a steam engineer. This disrupted the children's schooling, as they changed schools often.

Ed and Gladys were married in Lethbridge. They lived in various places, and they had one son born in Taber, Robert Edgar. They lived at Markerville approximately two years before they moved to the Ricinus area, in 1935. There they bought three quarters of land from Ed Godley, settling on the S.W.Q. 15-36-7-5, the other quarters adjoining, the N.E.Q. and the S.W.Q. of the same section.

Ed and Gladys, with their son, Bob, farmed the land and raised cattle, horses and sheep. In later years Ed's health began to fail and in December, 1962, he passed away at the age of seventy-four. He was buried in the Pine Grove Cemetery at Rocky Mountain House. Gladys still resides on the farm.

Robert Edgar, (Bob), married a local girl, Nellie Cliff, and they lived at Ricinus for a time. Two of their five children, Robert and Dwayne, were born there. Later they moved to Grand Prairie where Bob was employed in oil field work. Their other three children were born there, Barry, Darcey and Terry. They moved from Grande Prairie to Rocky Mountain House for a short time before moving back to Ricinus where they settled on the N.E.Q. 15-36-7-5, in 1970. Their son, Barry, passed away in 1976 leaving his wife, Sandra, and two small children, Rhonda and Kelly.

Ed's brother, Jim, and Gladys' sister, Bernice, married and lived in Red Deer for several years. Jim worked on the construction of the Alpha Milk Plant, and after its completion he worked there. They had three children: Gladys and Doris (twins) and one son, Pat. Doris passed away at age five. Later they adopted two girls, Avis and Sharon, who took part of their schooling at the Dorm in Dixon and now reside in Calgary. Gladys married Clarence Sirr from Cremona. They have two children, Darrald and Lee, and live at Lumby, British Columbia. Pat is married and is a trucker and lives at Canal Flats in British Columbia.

Jim and Bernice worked in sawmill and logging camps in the Ricinus area and worked for Caroline Lumber. Jim worked in the bush, and Bernice cooked. They retired and moved to Vernon, British Columbia, where they both passed away, one month part, in 1977, and were cremated.

Lou and Ethel Noirot

by the Noirot family

Lou and Ethel came to Alberta from near Olympia, Washington, in September, 1924. We travelled by train through Vancouver to Innisfail where we were met by Sam Nelson Sr. with a truck. During the two hour stop in Vancouver,

Blanche, Lyla and Velma Noirot — 1924.

Mr. Noirot, Blanche, Lyla, Mrs. Noirot with Wanda, Lou and Velma — 1929.

Mother decided to get more lunch material. She walked uptown, found a bake shop and bought a big bag of doughnuts, cookies and buns. Because it was too heavy to carry far, she left it at the store to pick up on her return. She stopped a half hour later and tried to find the shop to retrieve her goods but never was able to find it.

From Innisfail we were taken to Mel Ferguson's farm where we set up a tent for the night. Vernon Clearwater took us by horse and wagon, fording the Clearwater River, to the home place in Ricinus. We arrived about one a.m. to find the doors, windows and wall board stripped from the big house. Horses had been using the house for a barn and manure was thick on the floors. Dad shovelled out a place to put our blankets down for the night, then started hunting for a spring because we were thirsty.

The first winter in Ricinus the snow was deep. Dad was away working, and one night we heard a dreadful noise outside the door. Mother got the gun and slowly opened the door to see a porcupine gnawing on the steps.

The children of Lou and Ethel Noirot were Blanche, born in 1916 in Washington, Lila, born in 1918 in Washington, Velma, born in 1921 in Washington, Louis born in 1924 at the farm in Ricinus and Wanda was born in 1929, also at Ricinus.

Lila was married in Rocky Mountain House in 1933 to Herbert Bailey and they had three children, Herbert Wayne, Dennis and Barbara.

Blanch was married in Rocky Mountain House in 1934 to Gareld McNutt and they had four children, Lillis, Garry, Clayton and Darlene.

Velma was married at Rocky Mountain House in 1945 to Vernon Clearwater and had one child, Dale.

Louis Noirot and his mother — 1938.

Wanda was married at Rocky Mountain House in 1950 to Harold Edgecombe and they had two children, Mervin and Mavis.

Louis Noirot was married at Rocky Mountain House in 1951 to Violet Barnes and they had two children, Calvin and Wade.

Our closest neighbor was Mr. and Mrs. Donald Blair who lived one half mile from our place. James Sexton lived one mile away — he was a bachelor. Mr. Esplin lived around one and a half miles from our place. Jess Ditch was another neighbor who lived close and used to ride over to our place and tell us ghost stories and play cards which was our only entertainment.

We all went to the Ricinus School which was two and a half miles away. We walked most of the time, but at times rode a horse. Some of our teachers names were Miss Williams, Miss Link, Mr. Vanderburg, Mr. Chute, Mr. Russell, Mr. Petie, Miss Haze, Miss Alma Sarc, Mr. Murphy and Bill Mewha.

Louis Noirot Sr. passed away March 14, 1948, and is laid to rest in the Pine Grove Cemetery at Rocky Mountain House. Ethel Noirot passed away August 4, 1972, and is also laid to rest in Rocky.

Harry Norton
by Irvin Palmer

Harry Norton and son, Lamone, came to the Caroline area sometime in the early '30s. It seems there was a kind of syndicate that had gotten together and started a ranch on the east end of Burnstick Lake, and they hired Harry to be the foreman. They had some Holstein milk cows and also some Clyde horses. Anyway, the ranching business didn't pan out, but in the meantime, Harry met Mary Lastikka, and they got married.

They then moved to the Raven Valley on the Carl Edward Boeken's homestead. Harry and Carl Boeken worked together in the shingle mill for one summer, then Harry got a mill of his own.

Harry had a team of light buckskins, named Bud and Chief, and also used Charlie Kimball's grey team. Harry owned a police dog named Rock, whom he claimed had never been beaten in a dog fight. It was about mid-winter, in this one case, and Harry had Charlie's team and sleigh and was going down a fairly steep hill behind Anderson brothers' homestead, with his police dog bringing up the rear. The Anderson Brothers had a couple of baying hounds that they used for cougar hunting on their trapline. As it happened, the spotted hound had been out baying that day and was on his way home when he came on these hot tracks! He must have thought this was his big chance, and was doing about 'forty' when, out of nowhere, Rock jumped right in front of him! Well, that poor ol' baying hound went into orbit! He did about six tail spins, and Rock thought he had been hit by a locomotive! By the time the hound gathered himself together, and saw he was lurking in 'death's valley', he lost his voice completely as Rock was closing in on him. All that saved him was that he was running for his life.

Another time, when Carl Boeken and Harry had their shingle mill, they had men working for them. Herb Van Hollen was one. Herb had never been beaten pulling on the broomstick — he could even pull two fellows at a time. Harry Norton had the same record. Nate Jackins was also there, and as sort of a 'sports promoter', he used every tactic in the book to set up a match between the two, he even got the loan of a broomstick! Who would be the winner? Twenty-five cent bets at that time were not common. But Alas, the torque on the broomstick was too great. Well, Nate knew where he could get his hands on a crowbar and was back in nothing flat, but Harry and Herb decided they didn't want to bend a good crowbar, so they called it a tie. With this, Nate gave up sports promoting.

Harry and his family moved from the Raven Valley to a small cabin five miles west of Caroline, on the south side of the road just before you cross the Clearwater bridge. From there, he moved his family to Bowden and started a barber shop.

In the middle fifties, or perhaps a little later, he moved back to Caroline, and he hired Claude Frazier to build him a new pool hall and barber shop. He and Mary ran this for a time and then they sold out. Soon after they went to Blackfalds where he ran a barber shop and pool hall.

Harry and Mary both passed away at Blackfalds, sometime in the 1960's. Lamone moved to California.

Dan and Adda Oper History

In the year 1900, Daniel Joseph Oper of

Leamington, Ontario, was married to Adda Levina Switzer also of Leamington. In 1902 they had a daughter, Tressa Lorena, who died at fourteen months. Around 1904 they moved west to Red Deer, Alberta, where they rented a farm. For extra income, Dan freighted coal by team and sled on the Red Deer River from Alex to Red Deer.

Around 1907 they homesteaded southeast of Three Hills, known as the Mount Vernon district. They built a sod shack and lived in it until they could freight lumber by team and wagon from Red Deer, the trip taking five days. Meanwhile Adda stayed on the homestead and milked their five cows.

They later were blessed with two sons, Donel Daniel, born August 3, 1910, and Clyde Hugh, born July 2, 1915. Later in 1930 they adopted a little six-year-old girl, Birtris Mary.

In 1933, on account of the long drought (known as the dirty thirties), they were forced to sell their home and they moved to Ricinus where they rented a farm from Harvey Langley of Caroline. There, Dan built a small grocery store. Later they rented the Ed Godley farm and moved into the old log house, which still stands.

Ricinus Post Office and Postmistress Birtris Oper and helper Ada Oper.

The Oper family — Dan Oper, Ada, Clyde, Olive Ventress, Anna, Vivia, Donald, Clyde's son Eon.

He also moved the store and later, as Mr. Godley became too ill to tend to the Post Office, Adda became assistant postmistress and they moved the office into the store building.

Dan, though quite crippled with rheumatism, was a very cheerful person. With a four-horse hook up and the help of his family, he managed to farm a section of land. He fed quite a number of cattle and also milked quite a few cows. The cream was hauled by team driven by Mr. Cliff, the mailman, to Dovercourt where the mail carrier picked it up and hauled it to Rocky. The freight, as I remember, was fifteen cents for a five-gallon can.

Adda was a very capable, strong-willed person. She had the ability to take an old house and fix it up to look just great. She raised a beautiful garden, chickens, and turkeys, and was a great cook. She also taught Sunday School.

Their son, Don, married Anna Anderson of the Wooler district, they have two daughters, Ventress and Vivia. Ventress married John Tose of Caroline and they have four children, James, Elaine, Johnathon and Jason. Vivia married Lawrence Oliver of Caroline and they also have four children, William, Patricia, Lenora and Charlotte. Don now lives in Portland, Oregon.

Clyde married Olive Cave of the Stauffer area. They had three children, Eon, Diana and Gary. Eon married Sharon Lees of Fernie, British Columbia, and they had two children, Jennifer Christine and Daniel Joseph. Diana married Harvey Wright of R.R. 2, Innisfail, and they have one daughter, Mary. Gary married Holly Nicick of Rimbey. Clyde passed away in 1970 following heart surgery. His son, Eon, passed away in 1976 as a result of a train accident.

Birtris married Gerald Haney also of Ricinus. They have two children, Clayton and Geraldine. Clayton married Sonja Kanten of Caroline and they have two children, Cody and Carmen. Geraldine married Dennis Ross of Rocky Moun-

Eon Oper.

tain House and they have two children, Carla and Judilyn. Gerald passed away December 26, 1977.

Mr. and Mrs. Oper also have two great-great-grandchildren. Dad, Daniel Joseph Oper passed away in Red Deer on August 9, 1957, at eighty years, and Mother, Adda Levina, passed away on March 5, 1969, at eighty-seven years.

Plane Crash In 1943
by Guy E. Fay

On March 22, 1943, a Royal Air Force plane crashed on the mountain west of the Ram River Oil camp. It was two o'clock in the morning and snowing. The sound of the motors woke us up. From the door of our cabin we could see the lights of the plane. We knew it was in the valley and too low and would surely crash. Immediately after the lights went out of sight, we heard the crash. I heard the door close on the bunkhouse where my dad was sleeping, so I went over to see if he had heard it. We decided that we couldn't do

Plane wreckage.

anything in the dark and to wait until daylight. As soon as it was light Mrs. Osterlund came over and she had heard the plane also. We called Joe and Olivine Ison. After some discussion it was decided that I would go to the Baseline Cabin and try to phone the Forestry for help, and the others would start looking. We tried to talk Dad out of hunting, as he was seventy years old, but he insisted on going.

I started out with our husky dog, Smokey. When he saw the way I was going he would whine and sit down. After two or three times I told him, "Go home, I haven't time to fool with you." I was really surprised as this was the first time he had ever refused to go with me. Instead of going home he caught up with Dad. He would start up the mountain and look back and whine. Dad said, "I figured the old boy knows where he is going, so I said, lead on Smokey I will follow." He led Dad up the steepest part of the mountain over the rock face but where the wind had blown the snow off. He would climb a little ways then look back at Dad and whine. As soon as Dad got to where the mountain leveled out, Smokey left him. After following him a little ways, Dad heard one of the air men call back to the others, "There must be someone around, here is a dog!"

There were three men in the plane and it's a wonder they were all alive. Flight Lieut Wright had a broken leg; Flying Officer Summerville was only badly bruised, while L. A. C. Allen Mills had a badly cut arm, a bad gash on his head and a broken ankle.

Joe Ison and Fred Osterlund soon joined them. It was decided to use a wing off the plane for a sled to convey Wright to camp, while the other two would try to make it down themselves, while Dad would go on ahead and try to intercept me so I could go back to Baseline Cabin and phone for a doctor. However, I had hurried back to camp to see if there was any news. Dad caught me before I got away. As soon as the Forestry got my call, Eric Widden and Doctor Greenaway left. They got as far as Hart and Dezell's sawmill camp. From there they brought them the rest of the way with the wagon. They arrived about four a.m. the next morning. On the trip out, they were met at the mill by the ambulance from Penhold Air Base.

The Ram River Oils
by Guy E. Fay

The Ram River Oils was the first oil exploration of any note in the district. In March, 1940, they started building a road into their site which was located on the S.E.Q. 3-37-11-5, twenty-six miles west and three and a half miles north of Caroline. Oil was struck in well Number Two, but well Number Three was a dud. Being a small

Ram River Oil Rig.

Crew for Ram River Oil, 1940 — Back Row: Norm King, Fred Osterlund, Jack Bugbee, Alec Walker, Frank Salter — Front Row: Pete Fay, Guy Fay, Jim Ankle, Oli Olson and Joe Ison.

Mrs. Anne Salter the day Ram River No. 2 blew in.

company they couldn't carry on, but all the development around their leases certainly proves how right they were.

Memoirs of Ram River Oils
Toward the end of the hungry thirties,
    Fed up with poverty, hunger and cold,
A few hardy souls started hunting
    For a share of Alberta's Black Gold.

There were no mighty D. Sixes or Sevens
    With bulldozers to build a road,
We had axes, swede saws and shovels
    And we back packed many a load.

We slept in the ooze of the muskegs.
    We worked in the cold and the rain.
We were thankful for one hour of sunshine,
    But nary a man would complain.

Mosquitos, bulldogs and deer flies
    Tormented us by night and by day,
We swatted, smashed and cursed them
    And sometimes we would silently pray.

At last we reached the point at the centre
        fork
    That was marked by Hahn and Johnson,
And rejoiced that after many a heart ache
    At least one victory was won.

Then the trucks came in with the equipment
    Over sidehills and steep moutain ridges,
Uncovered corduroys for many a mile,
    Mudholes and shaky pole bridges.

Our derrick was rough two-by-sixes
    Our machine was a Sulliven N.,
And all that we had for power
    Was an old Case Hundren and Ten.

We rolled down wood from the mountain side.
    We worked twelve hours a day.
We saw town once in six months,
    And many times went without pay.

It was May in nineteen forty two
    That the first oil was struck.
Old Number Two became nationally famous
    And we all rejoiced in our luck.

We were feted and treated like heroes;
    We were welcomed everywhere.
We forgot our cares and our struggles
    And our many days of despair.

Then we found public opinion is fickle
    When Three and Four proved just a dud.
Over night we were no longer heroes.
    They treated us like we were mud.

Those days are all in the past.
    Many of the gang are gone from life's
        toils,
Still I cherish memories of friends there
        so true
    In my memoirs of Ram River Oils.

Ricinus — 1938 to 1940

by Bill Mewha

While teaching in a school south of Czar, Alberta, I was pleased to receive a letter from Jack Stronach, Secretary-Treasurer of the Rocky Mountain School Division advising me that I had been placed in the Ricinus School for the following year. Besides being near my Normal School buddies I would be close to the mountains where I could hunt and fish any time I wished. A teacher friend, Len Willing, had written to me telling me that the blueberries were plentiful and one's income could be greatly augmented by picking and selling them in the area.

I arrived in Caroline on August 3, 1938, in an old Model A touring car which had certainly seen better days. Since I hadn't been fully paid at my previous school, ($450.00 per year) I was broke. Upon presenting my plight to Earle Farris, a clerk at Mitten's store, I came away with a tank of gas, a razor and some other personal articles. Earle and I later became very close friends in the teaching profession.

My first recollections of Ricinus included a stop at Jack McNutt's home. Wonder what they thought of the new teacher? I was rather amused to see Juanita, Opal and Jack McNutt peering out from the bedroom door to see the first man teacher they would have in many years. I was sent over to George Vincey's since they usually 'boarded' the teacher.

Vincey's proved to be a home away from home. I was well fed and even had a room of my own although I occasionally shared it with a nest of flying squirrels. One would have laughed at Louis and I swinging brooms at two a.m. in the morning trying to knock down those pesky night marauders.

My first day at school was a happy one. The students were most cooperative and helpful. How I wished in later years that I had had students as helpful and cooperative as those in Ricinus. Thelma Browning, Juanita McNutt and Margie Bean were three I will never forget.

Many amusing things occurred during my stay at Ricinus. I can recall Bob and Jim Rose pounding the 'stuffing' out of each other on the way home from school. Then there was Margie Bean who would have easily won the Calgary Stampede chuck wagon races so adept was she at rounding the curves on the way home. Cliff's swayback horse with Irene, Nellie and Arthur aboard, always brought a chuckle.

Christmas concerts were a highlight for both the community and me. Looking back I often wonder how parents stood three hours of recitations, monologues and skits. Parents are real sports. One fund raising project for Christmas treats stands out in my mind. We were having a masquerade and my costume was the straw man in the Wizard of Oz. We were having so much fun making the costume at Bugbee's that we forgot to show up until the evening was over. Believe me I wasn't too popular that night. To make matters worse, Dick Knorr touched a match to my straw costume, some say accidentally. What a way to end an evening!

Another highlight of my years at Ricinus was the fun the young people of the district had at Forster's. Following a short lecture on the philosophies of Social Credit by Mr. Forster, we spent hours doing tricks and stunts. These evenings were always followed by a lovely lunch served by the Forster family.

The six mile trip home, sometimes just in time to go to school, never seemed to bother anyone. Sometimes we met at de Hemptinne's where the thought of Seances, talking to the supernatural and attempts at raising a table with our fingers, made an exciting but spooky end to an evening. You can be sure that there was many a backward glance as we headed home those nights.

House parties every weekend made for pleasant times. Seldom did the parties end before five in the morning. All that was needed for a good time was a mouth organ, a violin and a banjo. So no one ever set out at those parties.

I was fortunate to be able to make frequent trips with Bob Bugbee to their cabin on the Seven Mile Flats. Many were the times we danced till the wee hours of the morning and then rode to the Flats where we put up hay for the rest of the day. Bob was a taskmaster who believed in work before play especially when it involved the local schoolteacher.

I developed a great liking for the hills from my association with Bob and Ernie. It wouldn't have taken a great deal of persuasion to have changed from teacher to guide and outfitter.

When the war came along I was able to join Raymond Knorr, Sammy Howes, Hugh Oliver and Dennis Brown in Red Deer where we received our Basic Training along with a bad case of the measles. Some of us went on to join the Service in later years.

Both Grace and I had regrets about leaving the school, the community and many friends, but a chance to be Principal at Markerville was too hard to pass up.

I still get a great deal of satisfaction when I think back about the good times we had in school and the kindly people who made life pass so pleasantly. Ricinus was good to me and I will never forget it.

Rose Family

by Sydney Rose

Alf and Matilda Rose were married in 1927, and I had been farming on the prairie south of Craigmyle, Alberta. This was mainly a wheat producing area, but they were more interested in mixed farming and livestock and always kept about ten head of cows and a few pigs. They also had about fifty ewes, for a few years. A series of dry years and low prices for grain (wheat sold for 20¢ a bushel in 1930) convinced them they should look for 'greener pastures'.

I had been going to school in Hanna and worked with Alf on the farm each summer. I finished school in 1931, and we rented another quarter and worked together.

An old friend, Mr. George Sterling, of Benalto, had bought two quarters of land in the Ricinus district at a tax sale, and when he heard the Roses were looking for a mixed farming district, he suggested we look over his quarters as he had decided not to go farming. In April, 1932, Alf went by train to Benalto and Mr. Sterling took him out to Ricinus. Alf liked the area, and between us we scraped up the then pricely sum of $300.00. He bought the S.W.Q. 23 and I got the N.E. 22-36-7-5. Alf's quarter had been homesteaded and proved up by Mr. Clearwater (grandfather of Sonny Clearwater). The place was fenced and about twenty acres had been cleared and broken. There was a rough lumber shack about ten by sixteen feet on the hill near the west side. Mr. Clearwater had returned to the States, and the land had not been farmed for several years, so the bush was fast creeping over the old fields.

My quarter had been homesteaded by a Mr. Green, and he had a shack dug into the bank in the pines not far from the southeast corner. Mr. Green had joined the army in the first World War soon after filing, so he was given the homestead without the normal clearing, fencing and residency usually needed to prove up. However, he did not return to the place after the war, and it was eventually sold for taxes.

In June, 1932, after putting in the crop in Craigmyle, we loaded up three wagons with machinery — a breaking plow, disc, harrows, etc., and with eight horses we set out for Ricinus. It took us five days, and when we left the Clearwater flats, to go north to our new farm, there was only a narrow wagon trail. We doubled up the teams on the wagons to go up the hills in the last half mile. The bush was so close that I couldn't walk beside, and had to ride the wheel team while driving the head team. We moved into the shack on Alf's place and recleared some of the brush which was coming up on the old fields, and broke fifteen acres in the southeast corner.

Alf returned to Craigmyle in July to put up some hay and work the summerfallow. An old Englishman, Harry Haywood, and I stayed and cut and piled bush on twenty acres on the north side of my quarter. Alf returned in August and we grubbed out the bigger trees on the clearing on my quarter, pulled them down with a team of horses, then cut them up and skidded them off and piled them for burning.

A younger brother, Dyson, who had been going to school in Hanna, also joined us for part of the summer. He rode up from Hanna on a bicycle — he made it in two days over mostly gravel and dirt roads. We were the only people living on that road in 1932. Doug Stewart was farming north of us but was not living on the place yet. Jack Browning put up hay on the Lonto place, but there was no one living there. On the road a mile east there was only Willard Harness, Jim Sexton and Mr. and Mrs. Blair. Our nearest neighbors were Mr. and Mrs. George Bugbee, on the flat south of Alf's quarter.

We all returned to Craigmyle in the fall, but in the spring of 1933 we again journeyed to Ricinus by wagons, bringing more machinery, and we put in the crop on Alf's quarter and fenced the fields. We then went back to Craigmyle to get the cattle and returned in early July. On this trip Alf and Matilda each drove a wagon, and I had a saddle horse and trailed twenty head of cows and calves, some of which we milked along the way. Their two boys also rode in the wagons, Jim was three and Robert was two years old. That trip took seven days.

Alf had filed a homestead on the S.E. of 22 in early 1933. That place had been homesteaded by a family named Steede, and they had built a log house and a bank-barn and had cleared fifteen acres on the east side of the quarter. However, they had left before proving up, and we moved into the old buildings. The bush had grown up in the yard and the afternoon we arrived, in the

Threshing at Rose's, Alf at feeder, Syd on stack, and Roger Rose stacking straw.

rush of clearing up the old house and moving in, Jim wandered into the bush and we couldn't find him. I rode around and asked the neighbors for help, and within an hour about twenty people were combing the bush north and west of the old buildings. A few hours later, Gladys Browning saw him walk into the old clearing over the hill to the west. We soon cleared the bush out of the yard and kept a close eye on the boys until they learned their way around.

In 1965 Alf was cleaning out some letters and showed me one which I had written early in 1934. I had wintered at Craigmyle and was preparing to head the last of the machinery, tools, etc. to Ricinus, with two wagons and six head of horses. He had written and asked if I had enough money to make the trip, and in my reply I had said, "I was O.K., I had $1.35!" And in those days we didn't have any credit cards either.

Our parents, Roger and Elizabeth Rose, were living in Hanna. Dad was a carpenter by trade, but in the depression jobs were scarce and wages low, and they decided to move to the farm also. Dad was sixty years old and very deaf, and we had to shout in his ear to talk to him. On a clear evening I'm sure the neighbors on the flat could hear us and probably thought the new family were a rowdy bunch. Dad and Mother arrived in October, 1933, and spent the winter in the old log house with Alf and his family. In 1934 Dad built a cottage nearby, and we also put up the first of three large barns. Dad considered himself as semi-retired, but built a house for Alf and Matilda and numerous implement sheds, granaries and work shops over the next few years. He also did considerable carpentry work around the district, continuing up until he was eighty.

Mr. and Mrs. Roger Rose — 50th Anniversary.

Alf and I continued to clear and break more land. At first it was all done by hand, but later we bought a stump puller from Ed Pewonka of Chedderville. This enabled us to cut the larger trees in the winter and haul them off by sleigh, and then pull the stumps in the summer without so much grubbing and root chopping. The only problem with the stump puller was that the toughest part of the pull always seemed to come just when the team on the sweep were scrambling across the tight cable! By the time I joined the Army, in 1943, we had about 130 acres in cultivation and were still farming it with horses.

In 1942 the work horses began to die off suddenly, from Swamp Fever, and Alf bought a steel wheeled Fordson tractor. His son, Jim, was quite mechanical and soon took charge of the tractors, and they were able to expand their operation.

After the war I went to work in Calgary at the B.A. Oil Refinery and was later transferred to Edmonton. I sold my quarter to Alf in 1948. He and his family continued to improve their operation, and in 1956 they won a Master Family Award. They later purchased three quarters of Hudson Bay land on Section 26, on which Norman, their third son, now lives.

My dad passed away at the farm in 1960, at the age of eighty-seven. He was fairly active right along, keeping up a large lawn, and his flower beds were lovely each summer. He split his own firewood until the last two years, and a month before he died he was up on the roof of his work shop, helping to patch up some leaks. Mother lived on the farm until 1963, then spent ten happy years in the Westview Lodge in Rocky Mountain House. In 1973 she moved to a nursing home in Edmonton and passed away there in early 1977, at the age of one hundred and one years of age.

Alf passed away in 1967. He had been involved in numerous projects. He had been showing fleeces at the Edmonton Exhibition, and at the Toronto Royal, and had won numerous prizes, including several Grand Champion ribbons. Alf spent a lot of time with his sheep — almost living in the barn during lambing season. His care paid off, as he usually had close to a 200% crop.

Matilda passed away in 1973. She was also involved in many community affairs and was the leader in erecting the Cairn to the old timers, two miles west of the Clearwater Store. During her last years she started writing the history of the community.

Jim and Norman farm in partnership — Jim living on the homeplace and Norman living just north on S.W. 26-36-7-5. Norman married Veva Brown of Caroline, and they have three children: Jo-Ann, Bonita and Brian.

The Alfred Rose family of Ricinus, winners of the Master Farm Award in 1956. Mr. and Mrs. Rose and their sons — L.-R. — Robert, Norman and James.

Bob is a stock broker in Calgary and married Ella Morck of Dickson. They have two children, Keith and Lyla.

Leslie Scott Family
by Ida Scott

Leslie's father and mother, Mr. and Mrs. William Scott, moved to the Markerville district from South Dakota in 1900. On May 22, 1908, Leslie Lloyd Scott was born at their farm. At the age of twelve years he went to South Dakota and stayed with an aunt to finish his schooling. He worked at whatever he could get to put himself through school and was successful, he graduated from grade twelve.

He farmed in South Dakota and Nebraska, returning to Alberta where he took up farming and sawmilling.

In 1905 Linus Hamilton came to the Dovercourt district where he took out a homestead. In 1913 Mary Jenson moved to the Dovercourt district and in 1917 Linus and Mary were married in Red Deer, February 4. In the fall of 1922 they had a baby girl (me) Ida Marjorie. I grew up and got my schooling at Dovercourt.

Scott children — Wendall and Arlyn.

Leslie and I were married June 15, 1939, and we lived on the homestead until 1940 when we bought a farm, the S.W.Q. 32-36-6-5 from H. A. Langley (the old Burns place) where we farmed and sawed lumber with our mill. We had eight children, Lloyd Marten, Hazel Marie, Marjorie Ann, Harvey Gay, Lila LaVerne, Wendell Lee, Trilla Bernice and Arlyn Merle.

Lloyd has his own trucking business at Sylvan Lake. Hazel married Werner Rauch and they farm at Butte, they have five boys. Marjorie married Allen Rutschke of Markerville and they live at Olds and he works for the Department of Highways. They have two children. Harvey married Shiela Darlington of Eckville and he worked ten years for the Alberta Wheat Pool there and now works for the Rapeseed Plant in Red Deer. They have two boys. Lila married Wally Kinch of Prince Edward Island. He is a mechanic in Taber and they have one boy. Wendell works for Penner Oil out of Caroline at present. Trilla is off to College in Rexburg, Idaho. Arlyn is at home and going to school.

We have also taken in several foster children. Leslie passed away on September 27, 1974, and I

Les Scott Family — back row — Marjory, Harvey, Ida with Wendall, Les, Lloyd, Hazel with Trilla and Lyla.

still live on the home place. I have four Cardinal children who have been with me five years.

W. Scott
by Mrs. Edith Scott

William (Billy) Scott started to work in Nordegg as a Forest Ranger in 1917 after being discharged from the army in consequence of being medically unfit from wounds received in action. He was transferred to the Clearwater in 1921 (not sure of date), and a Ranger Station was built. Billy, Walt Richardson, Herman Suhr and a few others helped. Walt was a Ranger at the Meadows (west side of Baseline Mountain) and spent the winters at the Clearwater Station where the forestry horses were wintered.

I married Billy in March, 1925, and went to live at the Ranger Station. We had a daughter, Mary, while we lived there. I started taking her on horseback with me when she was six months old, as I travelled with Billy when he went on patrol. We did have some pretty chilly trips at times. No cars came up then; everyone came with horses. Quite a few fishermen during the summer months and hunters in the fall. After hunting season we didn't see very many people. Jack Bugbee and Jack Browning came up and stayed with us over night once in a while as they were going back and forth to their trap lines west of the station. When they came they brought our mail from Ricinus Post Office which was about twenty miles away.

Billy had to report to the Forestry Office in Rocky Mountain House once a month to take his diary in and pictures taken of any building that had been done, bridges or corduroy work. We drove to Ricinus one day and to Rocky the following day. The next day was spent at the office making it too late to travel to Ricinus that

day, so the following day we travelled to Ricinus again then back to the Ranger Station, the trip taking us five days in all. We travelled by team and buggy in the summer and cutter in the winter, a long cold drive at times. Later, we got a car and left it at Ricinus. That way we cut two days off our trip.

In 1931, when the province took over the natural resources, Billy was transferred to the Provincial Government and moved to Rocky Mountain House where he worked as Timber Inspector. In 1932-33 he went back to Nordegg where he looked after the unemployed that were sent from Calgary and Edmonton to work on the building of the road west of Nordegg. This was pick, shovel and wheel barrow work. After that, he was back in Rocky again. I don't remember the year he was forced to retire owing to being crippled with arthritis. We had a son, Stuart William, after coming to Rocky. Some years earlier, we had bought a farm near Rocky. Billy passed away in March, 1946, and Stuart and sons, William (Bill) and Rodney, do the farming. I still live in the old house on the farm.

The James Siddon Family
by James (Mike) Siddon

Dad was born at Kincarden, Ontario, in 1886 and came west with his brothers, Frank and Albert, in 1904, at the age of eighteen years. His brother, Charlie, came later, then Grandfather Bob Siddon with the rest of the family.

They all homesteaded in the Westward Ho and Harmatten districts west of Olds. Grandfather worked hard on his homestead for two years, clearing land and tilling the soil, and in 1907 he planted forty acres of oats. In August a snow storm flattened his crop and so, feeling disgusted with the world in general, he packed up and went back to Bruce County, Ontario, where he still owned some holdings. After he cooled down he came back to his homestead, where he continued to live until his death in 1921. He was buried at the Westerdale Cemetery, east of Harmatten, along with Grandma, Uncle Albert and Aunt Bess. My mother is buried there also.

My mother, Mary McKenna, came west from Prince Edward Island, about 1909, to teach school at Harmatten — she taught at the Harison School. She and Dad were married in 1917. They had seven children: Marie, Howard, Wilbert, Nettie, Dorothy, myself and Nora in that order. Mother passed away in January, 1927, and Nora followed, soon after, in March of the same year. There are just two of us left from that part of the family, Nettie and I. Howard died in 1937, Marie in 1942, Wilbert in 1975 and Dorothy in 1976.

The early years were hard years. Dad sold his homestead at Harmatten and did a tour of

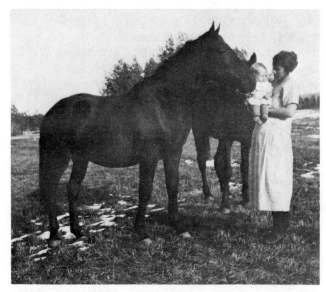
Edith Scott and Mary.

British Columbia, looking for greener pastures. He worked at odd jobs, one was at a logging camp at Tobe Inlet out of Powell River and then at Nelson where Wilbert was born. Then he came back to Harmatten where he rented a quarter of land and leased another quarter south of it. He took all the spruce off and had someone come in with a saw mill and sawed it into lumber. He must have made some money on this project as he bought a half section of land fourteen miles east of Didsbury in 1926. He plowed up the sod and sowed it into wheat. Then you know what happened to all the wheat farmers in those dry years? They all went broke! Then Mother died and Dad hired a housekeeper to help care for his family, Olga Nybo, who had just come to Canada from Denmark. They were married in 1928 and while they lived here they had three children: Olga Rebecca, Oda May and Elsie Margaret.

In 1931 the family moved back to Harmatten, to the land that Dad had rented before he went to Didsbury. This is where Uncle Charlie had lived and payed the rent on, for five years, and used for his headquarters as he too had sold his homestead.

Here, Dad cut poles and firewood and made sometimes three trips a week into Olds to sell the wood. While living here they had two more children: Archie Nybo and Anna Doreen, born at Olds.

Times were getting no easier, and after three years neither wood nor poles would sell. Dad had heard there was homestead land available on the south side of the Clearwater River, so he, Mel Eskrick and Howard Smith went to Rocky Mountain House and found this to be true. Since Dad had already filed on one homestead and proved up on it, my step-mother had to file on this one, as you could only homestead once. She filed on the S.E. Q. 4-37-7-5. At the same time they picked one for my brother, Wilbert, who was old enough to file on one. Howard Smith took one, a mile or so down the river. The Smiths did not stay long enough to prove up on theirs, and Wilbert took a look at the one they chose for him, but said, "It's not for me."

We moved late in June, 1934, after Dad and Dorothy had built our log cabin. Mel and Muriel Eskrick helped Collie, the dog, and I move the stock. In later years Collie and I had come to be among the best squirrel hunters in the west, and the last year that I hunted squirrels was the winter of 1941-42. With Collie's help I shot 900 squirrels. Prices had gone up some, and I sold them to Chester Simpson at the Clearwater Store at 24¢ across the board; no grading.

Dad and Ma and their family lived a good life in spite of the isolation at that time. There was no bridge across the Clearwater, so when you wanted to go to the store for supplies, or visit a neighbor, you had to ford the river; sometimes in the winter you could cross on the ice. Otherwise, you had to go all the way around at the back to get out; there were no roads, just bush trails and your only transportation was with horses, which were very dependable.

For neighbors, there were the Tan Jamesons, Del Trimbles and George Grunda. George Grunda kept a herd of goats and lived on the Tay River where the camp ground is now located. Prior to that the Chorley family had lived there. George had a big Great Dane dog named Wanie, who used to pull him by a hand made sled, big enough to hold him and his groceries, back and forth to the Clearwater Store during the winter months. Wanie used to stray from home and visit the sawmill camps in the big timber, where Hart and Dezall and the McKains had sawmills, for handouts. Being a big dog, he needed a lot of food, but he visited once too often. He killed a bunch of pigs which were kept at the camps and fed scraps from the camp kitchens, and so Wanie met his demise. George then bought himself a grey horse named Silver, a very intelligent animal. It was a familiar sight to see the horse pulling the sled, in the winter time, that Wanie used to pull. In the seasons when there was no snow, he pulled a one horse buggy.

Jack Browning used to stop there frequently to check on the old man, and one day he stopped and found him very ill, so he took him to the hospital in Rocky Mountain House. Later, he was transferred to St. Joseph's Nursing Home in Edmonton, where he died.

Our other neighbors were the George Bugbee's, who, for three years, lived across the river from us.

During this time Dad and Ma had three more children: Robert Nelson and Donna D., both born at Caroline, and the last one, Chester William, was born September 4, 1940, at Rocky Mountain House. Seven of these eight children are all living and well, but Chester died in a truck accident in October, 1961. He was buried in the Elnora Cemetery.

Bill Winters used to stop over at our place quite often on his trips back and forth from Olds to Cut Off Creek, in the Clearwater Forest Reserve, where he kept and raised horses.

Dad and Ma used to milk quite a few cows and Dad built a little house that he piped water through, to keep the cream sweet. They also kept butter and vegetables in there during the warm seasons. He hauled the cream down to the Clearwater Store once a week, where it was picked up and taken to the creamery in Rocky Mountain House.

Dad would put up tons of hay off of the Moose Creek flats, which grew lush and green, to feed his livestock in the winter. They also grew a large garden of vegetables, which always grew in abundance it seemed. There was lots of game around for their meat, and there was fishing in Moose Creek. If there is a shortage of fish in that stream now, they can blame me, as I took a lot of fish out of there in the 1930s.

In 1945, Dad sold the homestead to Bill Winters and they moved out to Elnora. Dad died October 12, 1948, at the age of sixty-two years and was buried in the Elnora Cemetery. Ma stayed on at Elnora for several years, and then she moved to Calgary. She spent some time in the Bow View and Bethany Nursing Homes, where she died in February, 1978, at the age of seventy-eight years. As was her wish, she was cremated, and her ashes were put off at Point Grey, Vancouver, British Columbia.

In 1976 I took a trip back to the old homestead, which is now owned by Dick Browning. A few of the old buildings are dilapidated but still standing. It is hard to recognize much of that country now with all the roads and seismic lines running here and there; oil sites and batteries. And now a bridge across the old Clearwater, built in 1977, joined by a gravel road that runs right by the east line fence of the old homestead, along with grazing allotments for cattle. It is so different from the way I once knew it, where there was peace and quiet, pure air and sparkling streams, where the moose and deer could roam at will in their solitude, uninterrupted by the noise of this mechanized era of drilling rigs and vehicles. I liked the old days best, but one can't stop progress.

Simpson's Mercantile
by Phyllis Burke

A.C. Simpson came from Calgary in 1938 to build a store at Clearwater bridge. Ches or 'Simmie', as he was known, had previous grocery experience having owned his own little grocery in Calgary about 1935 — on 617-5th Avenue, southwest, called 'Simpson's Grocery'. Previous to that he worked for Jenkin's Groceteria and then for Paulin's Biscuit Company. He bought a grocery store from Tom Hayhurst in Turner Valley and operated a thriving little business there for two or three years when he sold to young Tom Hayhurst, nephew of the former owner.

Ches was born in Nova Scotia. When he lived in Calgary as a young man, he took much responsibility in looking after his widowed mother. He met a lovely little Bank of Montreal secretary by the name of Kathleen Kilburn, who had come to Calgary from Saskatoon. It is of interest to note that she went to school with John Diefenbaker, former prime minister of Canada. 'Keenie', as she was known, was engaged to

'Simmie' for nineteen years before they could see their way clear to be married, as she had committed herself to look after her elderly father.

Walt Davidson, born and raised in Calgary, married Margaret Svee and subsequently moved to Sundre and operated a butcher shop in 1928. Later the family moved to a little farm on the west side of the Bearberry Creek, where they milked a few cows and delivered milk to a few families. At age six, their daughter, Phyllis, was Sundre's first 'milk man' using a little red wagon.

Ches and Walt knew Harry Norton who lived about a quarter mile north of the Clearwater bridge where he operated a small sawmill. Simpson thought it would be a good location for a store, so he acquired a piece of land from Norton where the store still stands.

In 1938 Ches and Walt undertook to build the store. With Walt's team and a slip they dug a basement 30 x 30 x 6 feet deep. With the help of a neighbor, they mixed cement on a sweat board and poured the cement by hand. They framed the building and then got Jack Davidson (Walt's brother) to head and do much of the work from there on. The whole project was completed in that one summer.

It turned out there wasn't enough business to support two families, so Walt would pick up jobs where he could. One of his jobs was fixing over Phil and Nel Kaiser's house, two or three miles north of the store. The Ricinus schoolteacher, Bill Mewha, was boarding there that winter and would get up early in the morning, jog to the river at the bridge, break the ice and take a dip. That was the time of the flu epidemic in '39. Bill didn't get a cold all winter and maintained it was this activity which kept him in good health.

These we remember as the 'good old days', but there were deaths and disasters too. Vernon Clearwater, along with several other older folks, was taken by the flu.

One winter evening a group of well wishers attended a birthday party for an elderly couple, the Stewarts, who lived about four or five miles north and east of the store. The guests having left around midnight, the Stewarts apparently banked the fires for the night. Early next morning, it was discovered that the log house was burned to the ground and Mr. and Mrs. Stewart had lost their lives.

Ches and Keenie were married about 1942. Walt moved back to Sundre with his wife, Margaret, and daughter, Phyllis, and opened the 'Sundre Meat Market'.

The Simpsons enjoyed operating the store for the eight years they were there. Art Lamb, from Caroline, did most of Ches' hauling, but he had to make special trips to Calgary to pick up a lot of items. The roads weren't the best in those days and many times mud and snow were some of the things that made his trips quite grueling.

After selling their store at Ricinus to Mr. and Mrs. John Cornish, they moved to Wimborne and operated a store there for about two years. When Ches' health became poor, they retired and moved to Calgary. Arthur Chester Simpson died in 1956, the result of a stroke.

Ches' widow, Gladys Kathleen Simpson (Keenie), now lives in Beverly Nursing Home in Calgary where she has been in poor health for the past four years. The store has changed hands seven times since its building, but is now operating under the name of Clearwater Trading and is still an important service to that area.

My recollections (Phyllis Davidson Burke) of living at Ricinus at Simpson's Mercantile and attending Wooler School, were those of happy years. The good rapport between girls and boys here was a pleasant change as there was much rivalry at the school I had attended. Three of us, Toots Dix, Sam Nelson and I, drove dogs to school in the winter and tied them in the horse barn. The dogs were amazingly strong. Mine was an Airdale, Cuffs. Toots had a big Collie-Bird-Dog cross, Rinty, and Sam had a small Collie, Ring. It was fantastic how Ring could pull him all the way to school, a distance of about three miles and quite a lot of upgrade coming and going. Occasionally his mother would have him go to Caroline from school and bring home fifty pounds of flour before supper. If these dogs met while in harness, there'd be a fierce fight. We'd have to keep enough distance between them so they couldn't catch up to one another. Out of harness they didn't pay too much attention to each other. When I'd stop my sleigh, Cuffs would back up and sit on the sleigh to get his feet warm. Ches had a red and white Pointer that was never to be tampered with so he wouldn't be spoiled for bird hunting. However, unbeknown to Ches, Pat, the bird dog, used to be lead dog on some of my excursions to visit Mrs. Ankle or someone on the north road, so we wouldn't be seen. Pat wouldn't pull much but he sure would travel and every once in a while would take off through the ditches on the scent of a rabbit or a grouse, so it didn't prove too successful an idea as barb wire fences used to get in our way.

Ernest Bugbee used to drive his dog to school too, but he lived only about a half mile away so hardly found it worthwhile. The teachers I had; Christine Monroe and Grace Waldroff boarded at Bugbee's. Another recollection I have of the good times is being invited to Mr. and Mrs. Jack Bugbee's for supper and Mrs. Bugbee cooked grizzly bear or mountain sheep steaks — whichever there were at the time, as I know both were fairly common for them, Jack being a great

hunter and guide. They were very delicious and was exciting for me and I can remember the family as being truly hospitable and friendly.

Toots Dix and I tried making travoises for our dogs in summer to haul cut wood for the stove. This was an idea I had and probably the only time I taught Toots anything. Usually she showed me everything that was to do with dogs or horses.

Fishing was pretty good in the Clearwater River, right beside the store and there didn't seem to be many fishermen. We didn't worry much about wardens. I remember one fall when the grayling were running, the big trout would swim in to a hole where the grayling were thick, and they'd all scatter. I snared three trout that fall that weighed four or five pounds. Some people think a trout can't be snared. When Wrigley's Spearmint gum used to have pink wrappers, I caught several fish with gum wrappers wadded on my hook. People laughed when I told them what I was using for bait.

Grace Waldroff, my teacher from Wooler School, married Bill Mewha, who taught at Ricinus. They are retired now and are living in Markerville.

We used to buy fresh milk and cream from the Jack Browning's, one half mile west of the store. Often I'd drive my dog up there or ride my horse, Kiddo. Vivid in my mind is that I'd try not to go at night because of the lynx they'd have tied up in their yard and in their hayloft. There'd be three or four sometimes. The way they screamed would scare me enough to keep me from loitering around there I can tell you. Once I watched Dewey get his thick moccasin rubber slashed by sharp claws as he stretched his foot toward one of the lynx to move it back so he could get the dish to feed it.

Just to the north of the store, Mrs. Norton's parents, the Lastikkas who were Finnish, had built a steam bath. We were invited to use this famous bath on numerous occasions. Some people would get into that bath house and steam for about an hour, then come right out into the cold and snow and not even catch a cold. I remember one night, the Bugbees, Chris Monroe (the teacher), Nortons, Ches and our family having lunch at the store after we'd all had a turn in the steam bath. My mother said we were probably the cleanest group of people in the country that night.

My husband, Dave, and his father, Fred Burke, also have fond recollections of the Caroline, Clearwater, Ricinus area, dating back to the late '20s. Mrs. Burke, a keen competitor, was a consistent exhibitor of sewing and baking at the Caroline fair. The family were ardent fishermen and visited Alford creek regularly, tenting there close to the road. They also visited the Frank Wilson's and recall picking blueberries by the washtub full — a tall story, but true.

At the time of this writing, January, 1979, Dave and I still live in Sundre. We have five children, the youngest fourteen years old. Dave's mother died in 1945 while he was still overseas. Following this, he and his dad, Fred, built and operated Burke's Hardware in Sundre until 1967 when Fred (now ninety-two years) retired and Dave embarked on a teaching career. My mother, Margaret, died in 1957. My father, Walt Davidson, and his second wife, Clara (nee Bramley), continue to be active and enjoy living here in Sundre.

Stewart, Ankle and Vincey Families

In the early 1880's, James and Ella Stewart moved their family of eight children from Decalb, Illinois, to Midland, South Dakota. They homesteaded in the Mule Creek district some eighteen miles from Midland. There were four boys in the family, Charles, John, Fredrick and Kirk, four girls, Jessie, Mattie, Hattie and Belle.

The Robert Ankle family came to homestead in the Mule Creek district in 1899 from Ailsa Craig, Ontario. The family at this time, consisted of the deserted mother, Annie, her eldest son, George, who was nicknamed Vincey and later adopted the nickname as a surname; daughters, Annie and Kathleen, and younger sons, Billy and Frank. The eldest daughter, Maggie, was married at the time to Arthur Tyler and she and her husband chose to remain in the east. On March 20, 1900, Fredrick Richard Stewart married Kathleen Lorinda Ankle in Midland; in the ensuing years, John Stewart married Annie Ankle Jr. and George Vincey (Ankle) married Belle Stewart. Charles Stewart married Marie Burke, a nurse, and Billy Ankle married Laura Walshire, a widow. In the year 1906, following a

(Grandma) Ella Stewart.

period of dry years in South Dakota, several of the Stewart-Ankle friends and neighbors moved to Alberta to take out homesteads in what is now known as the Ricinus district. Jesse Ditch, Charles Fogelsong and Len and Della Bowers filed on homesteads along the Clearwater River. On a return visit to Midland, Della Bowers' vivid descriptions of the lush green forested land convinced the Stewart-Ankle families that they, too, should move on to this wilderness paradise.

By 1911, when the move to Alberta had been decided upon, Fred and Kathleen (Cassie) Stewart had four children, Gladys Wynona, born December 23, 1900; Della Kathleen, November 18, 1903; Donald Douglas, December 25, 1905, and John Robert, June 25, 1908. Charles and Marie Stewart had one child, Ruth, born in the spring of 1908. The other Stewarts and Ankles were as yet childless, Frank Ankle and Kirk Stewart, unmarried, Frank living with his mother and Kirk with his parents.

In the spring of 1911, Fred Stewart sold his homestead on Mule Creek to the Heebe family, as of 1975 the Heebe's were still living there. George Vincey sold both his homestead and his livery stable in Midland, also both Billy and Frank Ankle sold their homesteads. Leaving their families with John and Annie Stewart in Midland where John operated a saloon, Fred, George, Billy and Frank loaded their household goods, machinery and livestock in boxcars and departed by rail for Alberta. Some time after crossing the Canadian border, they discovered two stowaways, Gus Lindberg and a man named Johnson, both from Midland, hoping to find homesteads in Alberta. On arrival in Innisfail in June of 1911, all but Johnson proceeded to load the wagons for the journey on west, Johnson left the company at this tine and was not heard from again. Gus Lindberg, however, continued on to homestead and later brought his family to join him.

The trip from Innisfail to Caroline, with loaded wagons and trailing livestock, took the better part of a week. From there they proceeded by saddle horse across the Clearwater to choose land near their friends. In order to file on their homesteads, they returned to Innisfail then by rail to Red Deer and the nearest land office. Their families then came by train to join them at Innisfail and once more the journey was made back to Caroline, this time by horse and buggy and taking only three days. For a time they camped where the Caroline Hotel now stands. The land at that time was owned by Joe Rockhill and had a small log cabin on it. The cabin was used for the preparation of meals; everything else was done in the open air. When the time came to move on to their homesteads,

186

now a distance of six miles, it took two days to reach them. Many times they were forced to use a block and tackle to move the heavily laden wagons through the mire. On reaching their respective homesteads, the families settled down to the business of preparing shelter for the winter and gathering feed for man and beast. The exception was Billy and Laura Ankle who moved back on the road to Innisfail to spend the winter with a family named Decker; the following spring they returned to Midland. Apparently some folks just aren't cut out to be pioneers! The Canadian segment of the families then consisted of Fred and Cassie Stewart and their four children; George and Belle Vincey; Frank Ankle and his mother, Annie.

In 1912 they were joined by Charles and Marie Stewart and daughter, Ruth. They homesteaded on the east side of the Clearwater and a little later the same year, John and Annie Stewart came, John and Annie's homestead was on the east side of the Clearwater and a little later the same year, John and Annie Stewart came, John and Annie's homestead was on the west side of the river, but a distance to the north of the main group. They were followed in 1913 by Kate Harness, sister of Annie Ankle, and her only son, Willard; they homesteaded a half mile northwest of Fred Stewart. Also in 1913, Ella Stewart and son, Kirk, came to Alberta after James Stewart passed away in Midland the previous year. Kirk filed on a homestead exactly one half mile north of Fred Stewart and built a home there for himself and his mother.

It was also in 1913 that Frank Ankle met and Married Jennie McKay, a Scots immigrant girl who had come to visit the Blair family. After Frank's marriage, his mother, Annie, lived with each of her children from time to time. In 1923 she suffered a stroke after which she spent much of her time with her daughter, Cassie Stewart. Annie Ankle passed away in 1932 at the age of eighty-five and she was buried in the Raven Cemetery.

In 1916 Kirk Stewart married Florence Bugbee, a local girl. After Kirk's marriage, Ella Stewart divided her time amongst her children, returning to Pierre, South Dakota, in 1930 to live with her daughters there until her death in 1934.

Donald (Doug) Stewart Family

I, Elsie Derbyshire with my mother, came to Canada in 1930 from Indianapolis, Indiana. For the first year we lived on the Winchester place, now Tommy Thompson's.

In due course of time, I met Doug Stewart (his mother had named him Donald Douglas, but most people know him as Doug). In 1932 Doug

Doug Stewart family — Virginia, Elsie, Ron and Doug.

and I were married in Rocky Mountain House and moved to his homestead, S.E.Q. 27-36-7-5.

In 1933 a son, Ronald K. was born and four years later a daughter, Virgina Lee was born. We stayed on the farm and son Ron started school at Ricinus.

Doug bought a sawmill and planer and we moved up in the 'Big Timber' country. We sawed lumber on Pete LeCerf's lease and later moved to Raymond McKain's timber berth where we planed lumber until the lease was finished. There was no school at this time, so a log school

Virginia and Ron Stewart.

was built along the road in the McKain timber lease and a teacher was hired, Mr. Forbes.

When Virginia was six, we moved to Caroline and later built a house. Ron and Virginia went to the Caroline School.

Doug and his brother, John, did custom planing in the surrounding country. The lumber business slowed down and Doug decided to take over the Purity Service Station in Caroline. We had this business for a number of years and then sold it and built a business known as the Stewart's Snack Bar. We operated this for sixteen years and sold it in 1977. In the meantime, we decided to return to the farm where we still live — trying to be farmers.

Virginia is married and has four children, Ross, Tracy, Shelly and David. Ron has been married and has two children, Charlotte and Boyd.

Franklyn and Lizzie Stewart

Franklyn Fredrick Stewart, youngest of Fred and Cassie Stewart's five children, was born August 9, 1912 and was the first white baby born in the Clearwater Valley. He received his education at the Ricinus school, passing his departmental exams after completing grade eight. During his teens Franklyn remained at home on the farm working with his father and brothers. He participated in the usual community events of the time — picnics, ball games and dances. It was at a dance at the Dovercourt Hall that he met Lizzie McKie.

Elizabeth Mary McKie was the oldest daughter of John and Maggie McKie of Chedderville. She received her education at the Chedderville School and went out to work, as, what was then called, a 'hired girl'. A hired girl's duties consisted of whatever chores the employer chose to assign. Anything from washing, ironing, cooking, child care and floor

Pat and Eileen Stewart, 1940.

scrubbing to cleaning barns and milking cows. All this was done for the princely sum of ten dollars a month.

On December 19, 1935, Franklyn Stewart and Lizzie McKie were married in Rocky Mountain House. They returned to Ricinus to begin their married life in a small log house Franklyn had built on the former Emery Davis homestead S.E. 23-36-7-W5. This land had been purchased by Franklyn's father, Fred Stewart, at a tax sale. It was during the years on the farm that Franklyn and Lizzie's first two children were born. Eileen was born Nov. 24, 1936 and Franklyn John, nicknamed Pat for obvious reasons, on March 17, 1939.

In September of 1940 Franklyn and his brother John decided to look for work in the oilfields of Turner Valley. Franklyn took a job at

Lizzie, Franklyn and Eileen Stewart, 1938.

Franklyn Stewart, 1937.

the Purity 99 refinery, and in December of the same year moved his family to Mercury, the housing area for Purity employees. On May 4, 1949 a third child, Gregory, was born to Franklyn and Lizzie. Gregory was, unfortunately, born a deaf mute. He had to be sent to special schools, first in Eastern Canada and then later in Edmonton. Eileen and Pat attended school in Mercury and later in the town of Turner Valley.

In April of 1952 the Stewart family moved to the town of Turner Valley where Franklyn owned and operated Sheppard Motors, the Dodge dealership and garage. During the time they lived in Turner Valley Eileen married a local boy, Sid Barker, who was a member of the armed forces. Pat also married Dale Hawks, a girl from Black Diamond. At this time Franklyn sold the farm at Ricinus.

Elizabeth Mary (Lizzie) Stewart passed away in the Turner Valley hospital in June of 1971 after a lengthy illness, and in November of 1973 their eldest son Franklyn John (Pat) passed away in the same hospital. Pat left two children John and Jody.

Franklyn sold Sheppard Motors in 1975 and returned to Ricinus. He purchased an acreage on the southeast corner of his father's homestead from his sister Della, and built a comfortable modern home there.

In 1976 Franklyn married a widowed lady from Barons, Frieda Newsham. Though it was Franklyn's plan to retire when he moved back to Ricinus, being healthy and active, he seems to be busier than ever before. He is much in demand as electrician, plumber, mechanic and general handyman. He is also an active member of the Caroline Lions Club.

Franklyn and Lizzie's oldest child, Eileen, has three children — Steven, Jamie and Christine. Eileen is at present living in Calgary. Gregory, the youngest, is living and working in Edmonton. Having surmounted his handicap, he has taken up the trade of upholstering.

Fred and Cassie Stewart

During the second summer in Alberta, on August 9, 1912, a fifth child was born to Fred and Cassie, Franklyn Fredrick, the first white baby born in the Clearwater Valley. Franklyn was born at home with Cassie's mother, Annie Ankle, serving as midwife. The nearest doctor was in Innisfail; it being impossible to cross the muskegs north to Rocky Mountain House, and doctors were not considered necessary for so natural a matter as child birth. Nor were doctors needed for the various axe and saw cuts, horse kicks and other pioneer accidents, and with the arrival of Nurse Stewart, Charles Stewart's wife,

Annie, salesman, Della, Fred, Cassie and John Stewart.

later in 1912, the community considered itself in the best of care. Schooling was also homemade until 1917; Fred and Cassie taught their children to read and write and do sums.

Entertainment was taken care of by the entire community getting together for card parties, picnics, ball games and dances. Fred Stewart and his growing sons were ever active members of the community, assisting in the building of the first school house and the first bridge across the Clearwater to Caroline.

During the early '20s, Fred and his sons ran a sizable herd of cattle. The boys cut ties and worked for the forestry, and for several years, the family owned and operated a small grocery store on the southeast corner of the home farm. In 1922 the oldest daughter, Gladys Wynona, married John Francis Browning of Caroline and within the year, presented Fred and Cassie with their first grandchild.

The oldest Stewart son, Donald Douglas (Doug), entered into a partnership with his brother-in-law, John Francis (Jack) Browning, in the Guide and Outfiting business which they carried on for some years, Jack eventually took over on his own. Doug filed on his own homestead and in 1932 married Elsie Maud Derbyshire.

Fred Stewart and Billy Ankle prior to 1910.

Fred and Cassie Stewart in 1920.

John and Franklyn remained at home, as did Della, with their father who was very ill with cancer. After a lengthy battle against the disease, Fredrick Richard Stewart passed away at home on June 3, 1933, at the age of sixty-three. He lies at rest in the Raven Cemetery.

After Fred's death Cassie carried on; times were hard and the family still needed her guiding hand. She took housekeeping and cooking jobs on the big farms in southern Alberta to help with the finances and was ever friend and mentor to her children and grandchildren. Cassie was also an active member of the community and was a member of the ladies club and was always ready to help a neighbor when needed.

In 1936 Franklyn Stewart married Lizzie McKie of Chedderville; they were to take up their married life on the quarter homesteaded by Emery Davis (see map) and purchased by the Stewart family at a tax sale. Then in 1937 John Stewart married Dixie Wilson, a local girl, and took up residence on the former Ham homestead also purchased at a tax sale. Cassie Stewart and her second daughter, Della, remained on the original Fred Stewart homestead until 1939 when virus pneumonia struck the small community in almost epidemic proportions. Cassie contracted the disease and passed away at home on February 2, 1939 at the age of fifty-five and sleeps beside her husband in the Raven Cemetery.

John and Annie Stewart

John Stewart and Annie Ankle were married in 1905 in Midland, South Dakota, where John owned a saloon in partnership with a man named Strootz. In 1913 John and Annie sold their holdings in Midland and moved to Ricinus to join other members of their families.

John and Annie homesteaded a short distance north and east of the main group. They built a

Annie Ankle and Della Stewart in 1920.

good sized home that was to become a gathering place for both social and political activities. It was at meetings in John and Annie's home that the Social Credit party was to get it's start in the community.

During the depression era in the '30s, Annie Stewart worked on the large farms in southern Alberta, cooking and keeping house. At such times John's niece, Della Stewart, and her small daughter, Jean, would come to stay with John and keep him company.

John and Annie Stewart were to stay on their original homestead until the late winter of 1940 when a tragic fire claimed both their lives. A neighbor riding by early in the morning, noticed smoke and went to investigate. He found John's body a short distance from the smoldering ashes, but no sign of Annie. Upon calling neighbors for assistance, and waiting for the ashes to cool, they discovered that Annie, along with the small terrier dog, had perished in the fire. What could be found of Annie's body was placed in the casket with John; the burial took place in the Raven Cemetery.

John R. Stewart

I was born in Midland, South Dakota, in June, 1908. I came to Canada with my parents, Fredrick and Kathleen Stewart, in 1911, settling

John Stewart at his trapper's cabin on Limestone.

John Stewart and the beginning of his herd.

Skip and Marie Stewart — "going hunting".

in the Ricinus district where my father homesteaded the N.W.Q. 13-36-7-5.

I received my education in Ricinus and after leaving school I worked for the Rocky Livery Stable for a short time. After that I spent number of years working for the forestry and also did some trapping and guiding.

In 1937 I was married to Dixie Wilson. We had two children, Norman (Skip) and Marie.

We moved to Turner Valley in 1939 where I worked in the oilfields for six years. I then went to Norman Wells, North West Territories, and worked on an Imperial Oil rig for a year.

I returned to Ricinus in 1945 and began sawmilling and planing with my brother, Doug, for about ten years.

Elsie Steel and I were married in 1954 settling on the North half of 10-36-7-5 where we lived for about seven years. We moved to our present quarter, N.E. 27-36-7-5, in the fall of 1961. We cleared the land, built our home and are now raising cattle and doing some farming.

My son, Skip, lives in Edmonton and my daughter, Marie, is living in Calgary with her husband, Sandy, and her two daughters, Stacey and Michelle.

Jack and Phyllis Stronach

Jack Stronach was born in Toronto, Ontario, September 19, 1907, the second of Jim and Georgina Stronach's five children. He was educated at Kinsella and Viking, completing his education at Camrose Teacher's College. His first teaching assignment was at Smokey Lake, from there he came to teach the Tiami School near Rocky Mountain House where he met Phyllis Vincey.

Phyllis Vincey attended school at Wooler, Ricinus and Rocky Mountain House. Until the time of her marriage to Jack Stronach on April 4, 1931, Phyllis lived with her parents and brother, Louis, working at both the Melton Hotel and the boarding house with her mother, Belle Vincey.

The first six years of their marriage, Jack and Phyllis lived in the teacherage at Tiami School where Jack taught. Their first child,

Jack, Bob, and Phyllis Stronach.

Sharon, Robert and Lyn Stronach.

Robert James, was born March 21, 1932, at Nurse Stewart's nursing home in Rocky Mountain House.

In 1937 the first school district office, No. 15, was opened in Rocky and Jack Stronach accepted the position of Secretary-Treasurer, moving his wife and small son to Rocky to live. Jack was to hold this same position for twenty years.

Jack and Phyllis' first daughter, Sharon Belle, was born on April 3, 1943, in the Rocky Hospital; the second daughter, Lyn Marie, was born January 9, 1951, in the same hospital. Their son, Robert, was educated in Rocky, completing his education at the University of Alberta in Edmonton with a degree in Pharmacy in 1956. He returned to Rocky Mountain House to work in Brownlee's Drug Store, which he eventually purchased. Also in 1956 Robert Stronach married Ruby Feys of Rocky, a divorcee with one son, Lee.

In 1958 Jack, Phyllis and their two daughters moved to Sicamouse, British Columbia, where they lived for three years. Jack then accepted a job with the school board in Spirit River, Alberta. Jack, Phyllis and Lyn moved to Spirit River; Sharon at that time was attending Mount Royal College in Calgary. From Spirit River they moved back to Bowness where Jack also held a position with the school board. After Bowness amalgamated with Calgary, Jack, Phyllis and Lyn moved to Herbert, Saskatchewan, where Jack took a position with the school board.

Robert James Stronach, only son of Jack and Phyllis Stronach, passed away in the Red Deer General Hospital in 1968 and was buried at Rocky.

After a lengthy illness, Jack Stronach passed away in Herbert, Saskatchewan, in November of 1971 at the age of sixty-four; his body was returned to Rocky where he lies near his son.

In 1967 Sharon Stronach married Lenord Mottus of Leslieville. Lenord and Sharon have four children, Stephen, Joanna, Tania and Alicia. They live in Vancouver where Lenord has his own consulting firm.

Lyn Stronach married Keith Berry of Compeer in 1975. They have one son, Dayman, and live in Saskatoon where Keith has his painting business.

After Jack Stronach's death, Phyllis moved to Calgary where she lived for seven years. In October of 1978 she moved to Caroline to be near her many cousins, and that is where she presently resides.

Herman Suhr

by Olive Dohlman

My father, Herman Suhr, came to Canada in the summer of 1918 and filed on a homestead two miles west of the Ricinus Post Office which was run by Ed Godley and his mother.

Our first impression of Canada, was bush and more bush and a little log shack with a dirt floor which we lived in for a year.

The family moved to Ricinus in June, 1919. We left Montana, the first part of May and arrived at the homestead the first part of July. We came by wagon and horseback, bringing about forty head of horses and cattle.

Our first winter in Canada was the hard one of 1919-20 in which we lost about half of the animals with swamp fever and lack of feed. Dad hauled straw and bundles from out by Innisfail, to see them through the winter.

In 1920, Dad built a four-roomed log house which was a big improvement over the little log shack.

We had very few neighbors. To the west of us was a family by the name of Charles Winchester. He was a retired Veteran from the first world war. He had married an English girl and brought her over as a war bride. We enjoyed her very much with her funny expressions and different ways.

In the spring of 1928, my folks moved to Caroline taking over the Post Office. My dad had a blacksmith shop which he ran with the help of Elmer Liedzen. He was with them for about eight years.

In 1946, they moved to Red Deer, taking Elmer with them. They lived in Red Deer until the spring of 1951 when they moved to Winfield to be near their family.

Their health was beginning to fail while they were in Red Deer, my dad had had a serious operation and it was quite a load for them to get around.

They celebrated their Golden Wedding in July, 1952. Dad passed away in October of that year. Mother passed away in April, 1953. They are both buried in the Mt. Clare Cemetery at Winfield.

Delmar Hill (Del) Trimble
by Sally Bugbee and the Trimble Family

Del's father, Andrew Hill Trimble, was born in 1846 at Carlton County in Ontario. In his early years he served in the Ottawa regiment and in 1870 he fought in the Fenian Raid (an attempted take over of the North West Territories by the United States), and was awarded a Fenian War medal.

In 1871 he married Cynthia Ann Wright, they had seven sons, Horace, Albert, Herb, Fred, Ben, Garnet and Clarence. Cynthia Ann died in 1889 and the following year Andrew married his first cousin, Lydia Trimble.

They moved to Alberta in 1890 and settled south of Calgary. After the crops were in, Andrew and two of his older sons, travelled on the old Calgary-Edmonton trail up to Red Deer where they found homesteads three miles south of Red Deer. After two years of living south of Calgary, they moved to their homesteads. Andrew helped to build the first log school at

Andrew Trimble.

Mrs. Andrew Trimble and son Delmar.

193

Springvale. He was a pioneer in the dairy business and was the president of the Ayrshire Breeders Association. With his second wife, Lydia, they had five children, Roy, Amy, Janie, Gladys and Del, the youngest, who was born in 1900. Andrew passed away in 1936.

Del enlisted in World War I at a too early age but he made it to England. A short time after his arrival there, he became ill, and it was then that it was discovered that he was much too young to engage in the war. They couldn't send him home and so he was made a bugle boy.

Sometime after the war and after he was shipped home, he came west and began work with the Dominion Forest Service in the Nordegg area. In 1925 Del and his cousin, Wes Latam, went into partnership and bought the N.E. Q 30-35-8-5, later known as the 'Tay River Ranch', from Fred Hart who homesteaded it in 1915. They both worked for the Dominion Forest Service. Later Wes bought Del's share of this quarter and then Del filed on the S.E. Q. 30-35-8-5, which is now my farm.

In the fall of 1929 Del was married to Taimi Antila who was born in Finland and had moved with her parents to the Oras district in the Rocky Mountain House area. Taimi filed on the S.W. Q. 32-35-8-5, which had been homesteaded but not proved up on by Levi Bugbee.

Taimi and Del had five children, Mary, the eldest, is married to Gordon Thomson. They have five children, Bob, Larry, Harry, Ellen and Richard. They live at Lumby, British Columbia. Lee, who was first married to Loraine Larson from Caroline, had two children, Roy and Brenda. Later, he married Mary Simpson from Fort St. John and they have one son, James. They live at Ross River in the Yukon where Lee has his own Outfitting business. Roy married Janet Jennings from Caroline, they have two children, Ronda and Gavin. They live and farm on the

S.W. Q. 14-36-7-5, formerly owned by George Bugbee. Roy also has his own Outfitting business.

Ivor married Louise Harms from Barrhead and they have two children, Marvin and Sheena. They live and farm on the land that was Taimi's homestead, they also own the N.W. Q. 19-35-8-5 They raise cattle and have a good sized herd. Larry, the youngest of the family, is married to Laura Svendson (Cave) who has three children from a former marriage, Monty, Cody and Tilde, and she and Larry have one son, Marty. They own a half section and live on the land which was homesteaded by John Trunnell.

There were many hard times and hardships for Del and Taimi raising their five children and living off the land, but there was plenty of wild game and fishing was excellent, cranberries grew in abundance among other wild berries. They grew a garden and kept a few milk cows and so they never went hungry, their children were healthy and strong.

For buildings there were good tree logs close at hand and Del became very expert in log building. With his sons' help, Del built a beautiful log house on the next quarter south of mine, for the late Gordon Henry, one of the founders of C.K.R.D. Radio Station, and which is now owned by Doctor Black who lives and practices in the United States, but visits here about once yearly.

Del did fine work, building much of their furniture, beds, tables, chairs, etc. I have three chairs that he built, they are sturdy and strong and one is of birch wood.

There were no roads, just trails cut through the bush and timber, fit only for horses, buckboards, wagons and buggies for several years. Trips were made to Caroline for groceries and mail, many of them made by Taimi and her children, taking all of the day and sometimes half the night. About 1937 a store was built by Chester Simpson and Walter Davidson on the bank of the Clearwater River, this shortened the distance considerably being able to get both their mail and groceries close at hand.

In those early days of coal-oil lamps and wood for cooking and heat, there were no comforts or conveniences that we now take for granted. Water was heated on the wood range and a bath taken in a round laundry tub on the kitchen floor. Clothes were washed by hand on a scrub board and the ironing was done with flat-irons heated on the range. Butter was made by putting cream in a three gallon crock and using a wooden dasher, churning it until it turned into butter. Bread was home made and baked in a hot oven. This always presented a problem in the hot summer days since the wood ranges were made of heavy cast iron that would still radiate heat

Roy, Ivor, Mary, Lee, and Larry Trimble.

Five generations on both sides of the family, Hilda Antila, Ronda Nordling, Roy Trimble, Tiami (Trimble) Lorinczy (inset), Anders Roy Nordling.

long after the fire was out, making the house feel like a bake oven itself.

In spite of having so little to work with, Taimi was a meticulous housekeeper and an excellent cook. How well I remember being there when she would take out steaming hot loaves of brown bread from the oven and minutes later sitting down and eating hot slices of buttered bread and drinking tea or coffee for lunch. She could turn out a roast of wild game that would make your mouth water.

Education was a big problem for the children living on the fringe of civilization until a little log school was built and taught by Mr. Forbes to serve the children of the families who were employed at the sawmill camps in the 'Big Timber'. The Trimble children attended school there until the camps closed down and then arrangements were made where by they went to school in Caroline.

Their neighbors were few since only five quarters of land with titles were taken up in those early days and then later, land was made unavailable to other prospective homesteaders with the exception of the Jim Siddon Family who homesteaded south of the Clearwater River on Moose Creek in 1934, and Doctor Greenaway from Rocky Mountain House who aquired a section of land about one mile north of Alford Lake which he later sold to Nick Chermansnok who set up a lath mill and logged it off before he sold it to the present owner, Tommy Thompson of the -XL Ranch at Ricinus. Jim Siddon sold his homestead to Bill Winters in 1945 and he had it for a few years and then sold it to the present owner, Dick Browning.

Their only neighbors for a few years were the Latams and the Chorleys, who lived where the Tay campground is now situated, but they never owned that land. After they left, it was vacant until George Grunda moved there about 1938. Henry Stelfox bought the Tay River Ranch from

Wes Latam and his sons, Buck (Henry) and Sonny (David), were there periodically. Then Tan and Ettie Jameson, along with Tan's brother, Harold, came to manage the ranch for Mr. Stelfox in 1935, who had added another quarter to it. In June of 1939 George and I, with our six month old daughter, Joyce, came to live on Government land near the gateway into the Clearwater Reserve, making the total residents of this area.

In 1960 Del and his sons built a Service Station known as Boundary Service, and the first gas served was pumped by hand until electricity made its debut into this area that fall. About this time Del's health began to fail, he made frequent visits to the Colonel Belcher Hospital in Calgary until his passing in November, 1962. Taimi is married to Gay Lorinczy, a farmer from Sylvan Lake. They are retired and live at Lumby, British Columbia.

Jake Vance
by Donald Cole

Mr. Jake Vance came to Rocky Mountain House in 1921. His mother, Sarah Vance (McCallister), came with him and made her home with him until her passing on a farm in the Ricinus district in the late thirties.

Jake came from a small place called

Jake Vance.

Pokohontas from across the Missouri River. He once told me his father had been a school-teacher.

He had been to Rocky several times, but this time he stayed. He told Nadine Cusak that when he arrived, Rocky was a livery barn across from the Mount View Hotel on main street.

Jake worked for Charlie Bruce quite a bit and also for Markus Gabler. While working for Mr. Gabler, a preacher came along and wanted to see how it was all done. He went to the bush with Jake to haul logs. The logs were decked out in large piles. Despite what Jake told him, he stood directly in front of one high pile when Jake broke it loose. If the logs had not been slow starting, they would have flattened the fellow.

Jake told of being alone in a logging camp on upper Prairie Creek, when a big black bear paid a call. Jake shot him in the back with a 38-35 and the bear ran into a tangle of trees. Jake could not see him, but kept the light burning the rest of the night. He found and killed him the next morning.

Another time on a place on Swan Creek, Jake woke up at night and in the bright moonlight he could see a big bear standing in front of a low window with just a screen on it, preparing to come in. Jake shot him through the screen, in the stomach. He could not find him and sat up most of the night.

At another logging camp, Jake had turned his team loose. There were 'soap holes' about, and one of his horses fell in. When he found him, only his head was sticking out. Gerald McNutt was nearby and he and Jake hooked a skid horse to the stuck horse, working him back and forth until they got him out. Then Jake hooked the horse up and hauled logs to warm him up, as he was nearly covered with cold mud and the barn was cold.

Jake tells about riding a saddle horse off the end of a bridge, across the Missouri River. The bridge had broke loose at one end and was under a couple feet of water. The horse turned a complete loop in the river and came up swimming with Jake hanging on for dear life. Jake could not swim, but the horse crawled out, a quarter mile down the river. When the livery man saw him, he said, "Where you been?" This was at Williston, North Dakota.

At one time or another, Jake owned ten quarters of land around Rocky, Alhambra and Caroline. He bought a lot of them at tax sales, and some from the municipality of Caroline. He bought Steve Dutton's old homestead and two quarters on Swan Creek. He generally took the timber and traded off the land. He never did farm much. He sold the homestead on Prairie Creek (N.W.Q. 22-37-7-5) to Roscoe Ettinger who

came from south of Wainwright. This man did not stay too long. He had one son, Edgar.

Jake was staying with Joe Error on Prairie Creek and had turned his team out with Joe's horses. One morning he could not find one of his horses. Both Jake and Joe could hear a horse nicker. They finally found the horse in the bottom of a sixteen foot dug well. They rigged up a tripod and a fellow near there hooked onto a cable with an old caterpillar tractor. The horse came out unhurt.

Jake was good with horses and I know of him driving some pretty snorty horses. He told me he had driven quite a few outfits of mules with a jerk line. I remember him best by his abrupt way of talking and being plumb full of business on Sunday. Jake was gruff with children, but I never knew a kid that did not like him. My own could get nothing better than having dinner with him. Jake sure liked beans. I batched some with him and he had a saying, "If I had of known you wanted potatoes, I would have had them on!" This rather upset me when I came in hungry.

At one of Jake's farms, I was cutting a good crop of wheat and he told me that in the spring he had planted a pail of potatoe eyes, willy-nilly in an old rotted down manure pile. So when I ran short of 'taters', I took a shovel and bucket and went looking. It was not a patch of potatoes — it was just one big hill of the nicest, mealiest taters you ever dug into. He never dug them.

He lives in an old folks home in Calgary and will be ninety years old in March, 1979. Jake always got up with the chickens and went to bed with the birds. There were a lot of old-timers lived that way.

George and Belle Vincey

George Vincey married Belle Stewart in Midland, South Dakota, where he worked for Standard Oil in 1907. George later owned and operated a livery stable which he sold when they moved to Alberta in 1911.

Belle and George Vincey and Louis in front, Robert Stronach behind.

196

During the first years in the Ricinus district, George and Belle worked at improving their homestead, at the same time operating a small grocery store on their property. On June 26, 1912, they became the parents of the first child born to the pioneers of Ricinus, a daughter, Phyllis Harriett. She was born in the nursing home in Innisfail and to commemorate the occasion, Phyllis Lake was named for her.

In the following years, George and Belle worked with the other members of the small community in building the school, roads and the Clearwater bridge. To augment their income, George also worked as a hostler for the mines at Saunders Creek and Alexo, Belle doing her bit by boarding schoolteachers.

In 1925 George and Belle adopted a brother for Phyllis. His name was Louis Harold and he was born in Edmonton, January 6, 1923.

George and Belle and the two children moved to Rocky Mountain House in 1927 where George drove dray for Jack Edgerton. Belle worked in the Melton Hotel, as did Phyllis, later they operated a boarding house.

Phyllis married Jack Stronach in 1931. George, Belle and Louis moved back to the homestead the same year. George and Louis resumed farming, George also carrying on with the trade of veterinary dentistry, and Belle once again boarded schoolteachers. George and Belle Vincey's home was ever a popular place for community gatherings, card parties and socials; it was one of the larger houses and George and Belle always made guests welcome.

In the spring of 1944, George Vincey passed away at the age of twenty-three and was buried in the Rocky Mountain House Cemetery.

George Vincey and Fred Stewart.

Belle Vincey.

After George's death, Belle and Louis rented the farm and moved to Rocky where Louis (nicknamed 'Spud') took up the trade of plumbing and pipefitting. They later sold the farm to Dewey Browning, and in 1949 Louis took a job at his chosen trade in Milk River, Belle going to live with him there. After a year in Milk River, Belle and Louis returned to Rocky Mountain House for a short time, then to Calgary to make their home near Louis' work. In May of 1960 Belle Vincey passed away in Calgary at the age of seventy-one. She rests beside George in the Rocky Mountain House Cemetery.

Louis Harold Vincey, unmarried, passed away in Calgary on June 15, 1978, at the age of fifty-five. As was his wish, he was cremated and his ashes cast on the original George Vincey homestead.

The Whittaker Family
by Milo Whittaker

Ernest Whittaker and three sons, Clarence, Vic and Milo, and daughter, Winnie, came to the Ricinus district in the fall of 1934 and settled on the old Roach place. A year or so later, another son, Ervin, and his wife, Lucy, and two children also arrived and spent the next two or three years in the district.

197

Like anyone else in those depression days, the family made a living by a little farming, hunting and trapping and working at whatever jobs were available. For some years they operated a sawmill, at first in partnership with Mr. Lang and then on their own.

When Mr. Whittaker's health began to fail the family left the district in the summer of 1940.

Frank Wilson Family

by Dixie Pennington

Frank and Marie Wilson were both born in Kansas and immigrated to Canada by covered wagon in 1917 — settling in the Acme area where they wheat farmed. Their three children, Dixie June, Norma Rae and James, were all born here. After farming there for several years they moved, also by covered wagon, to the Bearberry Valley where Frank made a living as a guide and outfitter.

In 1930 they moved on to the Clearwater area purchasing land on the Clearwater River approximately one mile down stream from the present bridge site. Frank supported the family doing some farming and guiding and outfitting.

They received their mail at the Ricinus Post Office and their supplies were bought at Langley's Store in Caroline.

The family's main sources of entertainment were picnics, dances and community get-togethers.

Dixie married John Stewart and they had two children, Norman Ray (Skip) who lives in Edmonton and works in the oilfield and Kathleen Marie who married Sandy Henry, and they have two daughters, Stacey and Michelle. They live in Calgary.

Norma married Elmer Park and they have four daughters, Dixie Lee, Leslie, Donna and Phylis, all residing in Nevada.

Jim married and has two sons, Ronald and Donald who live in Edmonton. Also there was a daughter who is deceased.

Frank Wilson passed away at Drumheller in 1968 where he is laid to rest. Marie, now eighty-one years young, resides in Nevada with her two daughters.

Harry and Polly Wilson

In the fall of 1909 Harry Wilson came up to the Ricinus district with his two sons, Kaywood and

Norma and Dixie Wilson.

Mr. and Mrs. Harry Wilson.

198

Mont, on a hunting trip. They came back in the spring of 1910 to homestead on the north half of 5-37-6-5. Kaywood homesteaded on the S.E. 5-37-6-5. They had a team of oxen and an old breaking plow which they used to get some land under cultivation, and also four head of horses. When they first came, they stayed with Linus Hamilton and his dad until they got their shack built.

In 1914 Harry enlisted and went overseas to the war. When the war ended he came back to live in Calgary where he worked for the Calgary Fire Department. He was captain. They used horses on the fire engines in those days. He and a partner, Frank McAra, started the Alberta Newspaper in Calgary. He was the first white man to discover and bring to light the dinosaur bones in the Red Deer Valley and reported it to the authorities in Ottawa but he wasn't credited with his findings.

Kaywood married Neva Ives in 1917. They went to the States and helped on the family ranch for awhile, then came back to Calgary where he

L. to R. — Kaywood and Neva Wilson, Mabel and Gus Huber, Ken and Jean Wilson — children — Carol, Kirk and Gloria and friend Karen Raby.

worked for many years with the Calgary Electrical Division. He then moved back to Chedderville in 1947 and lived until 1969, when he moved back to Calgary. He died in 1971. They had one son, Keneth. He married Jean Bowie of Claresholm and they had three children, Carol, Kirk and Gloria. Carol is married to Wallace Maurice and has four children, Christina, Tammy, Dion and Cheryl. Kirk is married to Shelly Martin and they have two children, Amanda and Clinton. Gloria is married to Wayne Searle and they have two children, Shannon and Tanya.

Bob Wilson was a brother to Harry. He bought the S.E.Q. 7-37-6-5 and the S.W.Q. 12-37-7-5 in 1908. He and his wife, Maude, stayed for a few years, then he went to the war. When he returned he stayed in Calgary. They had one girl, Muriel.

William Henry "Bill" Winters

by Sally Bugbee

Bill was born March 18, 1883, at Pine River Mills, California, a town founded by his grandfather, Isaac Henry Winters, a lawyer. Bill was educated there.

Times were hard and so Bill, with his brothers, Harry and Mac, gathered together a herd of horses and started out for Canada in 1907. After months on the trail they arrived in Alberta and Bill and Mac filed on homesteads in the Sundre area. A year later Harry filed on one and so they started ranching.

When war broke out in 1914, Bill and Mac joined the army with the 50th Battalion and were soon seeing action in France. Harry stayed to hold the ranch together and to look after their invalid mother and their father, who was going

Neva and Kaywood Wilson.

Bill Winters at his horse ranch on Cut Off Creek.

blind. Bill came home in 1918 after the war but Mac lost his life in France.

Bill never married and after spending some time ranching in the Poplar Creek and Bearberry districts, he decided to move his horses up to the Cut-Off Creek area in the Clearwater Forest Reserve, in the early 1930s, where he continued to raise and break horses to sell.

Bill made friends wherever he went and he became a legend in the west with his horses and the poetry that he wrote. He could keep you totally engrossed with true tales of his many adventures while in that area. He welcomed friend or stranger to his cabin on the Cut-Off, was a good host and an excellent cook and kept a good supply of food on hand. His door was never locked and he expected his friends to make themselves at home whether he was there or not. He was especially good at making sourdough pancakes and biscuits and kept his sourdough crock in good working order. It was always a pleasure when, on rare occasions, you could get him to recite some of his own poetry.

In 1945 he bought the Jim Siddon place on Moose Creek and used it for his headquarters for a few years, then he sold it to Dick Browning and disposed of his horses and went to live at Jim and Della Milburn's. He stayed a year with the George Bugbee's and then a few months at Ernest Bugbee's, where, in November, 1956, he suffered a stroke and was rushed to the hospital in Olds where he soon passed away. Thus ended the life of a very colorful figure and one of our early pioneers and a man whom we were all proud to call friend. He was buried in the field of honor, in the Olds Cemetery.

Shilo

Shilo School District No. 2188

Shilo School District was established by the order of the Deputy Minister of Education, D. S. McKenzie, effective May 26, 1910. Senior Trustee was R. F. Dial of Raven. The district was named after a place in Scotland and the school was built on one acre of land, purchased for two dollars from a Scottish pioneer settler, Mr. Davidson. It has not been moved from the original foundation of logs and stone. Water was carried to the school until a well was drilled in the 1930s. Pioneer settlers in the district were Mr. Kiem, Mr. Bowers, Mr. Rhodes, Mr. Tose, Mr. Vandermeer, Mr. Kliener, Mr. Devore, Mr. Coleman and Scott Bower, and were followed by many families in later years. Most school teachers boarded with nearby families and walked miles to and from school as did many children. The district was included in the Rocky Mountain School Division on October 16, 1937.

Industries and occupations were mainly farming, lumbering and trapping. Today extensive farming is carried on, present population is near one hundred sixty-two. The first teacher was Mr. Arden Litt, who taught Fred and

Arden Litt — first teacher at Shilo School.

Hugh Devore, Lulu, Glenn and Arthur Dial. Following are the names of other teachers and names of pupils who attended this school. Children now attend Caroline School, being bussed there since 1952.

TEACHERS
Miss L. Bibby
Miss Boles
Mr. William Boyer
Mr. A. Buchanan
Miss I. Clarke
Mr. Tom Cole
Miss Fingland
Miss Elsie Gunderson
Superintendent
Miss Helen Gunderson
Miss B. Knudson
Mr. MacDonald
Miss McCallum
Miss E. McDonald
Mr. William McIntyre
Miss Bertha McKenna
Mrs. N. Miller
Mr. Muir
Miss R. Neal
Miss C. Reavely

Centennial Picnic, 1967 and children who attended the Shilo School — Margaret Staben, Alma Vandermeer, Lorna Dolphin, Helen Katona (Stange), Hazel Bowers (Turton), George Bowers, Ralph Bowers, Jessie McColl, Gordon McColl, Henry Staben, Larry Grieve, Gerd Nanninga and Bill McColl.

201

Miss Alberta Russel
Miss Alma Sarc (Vandermeer)
Miss J. Siguardson
Miss Sophia Thompson
Miss Mable Wade

PUPILS

Dorothy, Dora, Raymond and Verna Adair; Velma Adrian; Harold and Thelma Armitage; Lawrence and Marie Andersen; Ruth and Jean Bennette; Charlie, Shirley and Donnie Benson; Beth, Stanley, Herber, John and Clara Black; Louise and Goldie Bower; Katherine, Ray, Dollie, Ralph, Ethel, Walter, Hazel, George and Everett Bowers; May Buchanan; Marjory and Rita Buchanan; Carol, Andrew, Myrtle and Faye Buchanan; Frank, Clarence, Nellie and Chloe Coleman; Molly, Billie and Jimmie Crate; Norton Crippen; Harry Dennis; Fred and Hugh Devore; Lulu, Glenn and Arthur Dial; Dollie, Ernie and Leona Dolphin; Lorna and John Dolphin; Bob Duffy; Cora and Albert Embleton; Harry and Joyce Fay; George and Leonard Fitchett; Esther Graham; Stanley and Larry Grieve; Milo Grubb; Clifford, Doris and Averill Hansen; Jimmy Harkins; Ruby, Wendel, Bernie, Kenny and Grant Harris; Elmo Head; Edward and Phyllis Helm; Ruth Hunter; Florence and Louis Johnson; Glen Kanten; Helen and Leslie Katona; Elizabeth, Ester, Frank and Edward Kiem; Joe and Peter Kliener; Walter, Donald, Edith, Barbara and Raymond MacDonald; Betty Mariglow; Gordon, William, Charles, Gertrude, Raymond, Blanch and Jessie McColl; Sam McIllwain; Annie, Lester and Dora Miller; Ward and Florence Montgomery; Lyle, Leroy, Verna and Lloyd Montgomery; Kenneth and Richard Montgomery; Swan, Bill and June Murray; Fritz, Gerd and Christa Nanninga; Gilbert, Raymond and Thelma Nelson; Roy, Mildred, Tom, Delbert, Donald, Bob and Marjory Orcutt; Fay, Iris and Max Redding; Arthur, Helen, Cecil, Dorothy, Lillian and David Rhodes; Mitchell,

The Shilo School children and teacher Alma Sarc, 1937.

Christmas concert at Shilo school — Christa Nanninga, Jessie McColl, Clara Black and Norma Stevenson.

Joe and Johnnie Roberts; Zulu and Ray Rowles; Henry, Margaret and Walter Staben; Herman, John, Marianne, Elisabeth and Irene Stange; Letty Starkey; Douglas, Dorothy, Norma and Butch Stevenson; Harvey, Cynthia and Clem St. Deny's; Francis Shaurette; Eva, Stanley and Harold Smith; Cora Taylor; Rene Thompson; George Tose; Carrie, Conrad, Gerry, Lena, Pete, Harry and Joe Vandermeer; Rosalie Vandermeer; Annie, Wilhelmina and Johnnie Van Leest; Wynne, Bernard, David and Mary Williams; Margaret, Leona, Donald, Emmett and Edna May Wise; Lawrence, Clarice, Daisy, George, Frank and May Wyant.

The Jack Black Family
Beth Thornhill

My Grandfather, Heber Chase Black, was born to Alexander and Margaret Black at Albany, New York on August 4, 1886. Alexander and his family had come from Scotland and when Grandpa was very young they moved to Utah to be near the Mormon Prophet. On September 24, 1894 Heber married Bethia Wilson whom he loved dearly. His son Lyle, and daughter Doris were born in Coalville, Utah. Grandpa made his living working in the coal mines.

In 1898 Grandpa and Grandma and their two children moved to Alberta (then the North-West Territories) settling a few miles from Cardston which was the Alberta settlement for the first Mormons. Jack (my father) was born at Mountain View, Alberta, and Aunt Zelma at Beazer, Alberta. They moved to Taber in 1905 and Aunt Adeline was born there. Grandpa

Zelma Murphy, Jack Black and Adeline Weaver.

Jack and Phyllis Black — 59th Wedding Anniversary.

managed the Golden West mine at Taber for eleven years.

Grandma had an attack of appendicitus in 1908 and did not recover. Grandpa was heart broken and turned against the church and life in general. He realized however that he had a big responsibility bringing up a young family without a mother. Aunt Doris became the mother and the family had many difficult times.

In 1923 Grandpa and Dad and family moved to Ranier to farm. In his youth Grandpa had learned irrigation and could help Dad with the farm. They farmed at Ranier until 1933 when they moved to Markerville. They were hailed and frozen out two years in a row, so in 1935 they moved to Caroline. Grandpa lived with us until 1946 when he returned to Ranier to live with Aunt Zelma.

He was still active in his late years and told wonderful stories to us children. He enjoyed gardening, fishing, hunting and helping others. He passed away at Brooks, March 9, 1954 at the age of 86 and is buried at Ranier.

John Alexander (Dad) was born February 16, 1900. He went to school in Taber. Phyllis May Neilson (Mother) was born to Neil and Rhoda Neilson at Vernal, Utah on May 2, 1904. She had two brothers, Wesley and Maurice. She came to Taber with her family when she was one year old. Phyllis went to school in Taber and she recalls the names of two of her teachers — Miss Freil and Mr. Archie Bennett.

Mom and Dad were married March 10, 1920. They had five children — Stanley, Bethia, Heber, John and Clara. Stanley and I were born in Taber. Heber, John and Clara at Ranier. Stanley, Heber and I started school when we lived at Ranier. While we were at Markerville we attended the Hola school with Jim Marshall teaching. It was here that Heber had rheumatic fever and was very ill.

Although times were hard, we always had something to eat — not a great variety perhaps,

but we never went hungry. Dad had some wheat ground when we lived at Markerville, and Mom (who could make very good bread) tried to make bread with it. Impossible! Then she tried making Johnny cake and behold! we had an edible bread.

We and Uncle Lyle's family lived in a two roomed house. Uncle Lyle had five children and with Dad and Grandpa and us five children it was bursting at the seams. Dad and Grandpa moved a granary to our side of the house and Grandpa and the boys slept in it. Even though they had a heater in it, it would get really cold during the winter.

In 1935 we decided to move to Caroline because land was cheap, game was plentiful and berries were free for the picking. Saskatoons, raspberries, strawberries, high and low blueberries and high and low cranberries. Times were very hard. Eggs sold for three cents a dozen (if you could sell them) — cream sent to the creamery was sometimes sent home — cows sold for ten dollars if you were lucky. Flour was $1.50 per hundred pounds. Dad traded seven cows for a radio and sold the radio for ten dollars. We arrived in Caroline March 20, 1935 and Uncle Lyle and his family moved to Condor.

Bob Mitten was one storekeeper in Caroline. He would take almost anything people had for groceries. He bought rabbits for three cents each. People hauled them by wagon or sleigh loads and traded them for groceries. Later Bob had a partner at the store named Howard Mullen. They were a blessing to the community. Langleys also had a store and did a good business. Mrs. Herman Suhr ran the post office. Mom said that when Stanley was in the army she always phoned Mom if there was a letter.

There were no fridges in those days, so meat, milk, butter and cheese were hard to keep. Meat was put in crocks covered by a brine and kept in the cellar. Some people had ice houses. They would cut blocks of ice and put layers of sawdust between each block. It would keep until summer. Ice cream was made with a freezer turned by hand — it was delicious. One Sunday Heber was feeling bad because he thought he hadn't had enough ice cream. The next day he made some himself from pure cream — ate most of it, and became sick. He says May Buchanan was sick too as she helped him to eat it.

We attended Shilo school — Miss Alma Sarc was our teacher. I quit school in 1935, and Stanley in 1938. Heber went until 1941, and Johnny and Clara until 1945 when we moved into the hamlet of Caroline. Mr. Forsythe was the teacher. Other teachers we remember were Jim Muir, Miss Sarc who married and became Mrs. Vandermeer, Mrs. Fred McKinnon and a Miss Clark.

Our good neighbour, Mrs. Bowers, was a very smart lady. She taught us how to pick berries and can them — how to raise a big garden and can the vegetables — how to make sauerkraut. Most of all, she taught us how to cope with the hard times. I remember her as a jolly lady who raised a large family and worked very hard. Her meals were something to enjoy and remember. She made her own bread, jam, jelly and everything else possible to make. She sewed most of their clothes and knit socks, mitts etc. for her family. Her family are all good people and wonderful neighbors.

Other good neighbors were the Stabens. They held Mom and Dad's 25th wedding anniversary at their place. They were always there when Mom and Dad needed a friend.

A group of men used to go west of Ricinus to hunt every fall. We used the fresh meat while the weather was cold and canned it when the weather grew warm. In those days you could get a moose, deer, elk and a bear all on one license.

Mr. and Mrs. Bowers and Dad and Mom used to go to the burn west of Ricinus by horse and wagon, and camp for a week picking and canning raspberries. It was hard work climbing over windfalls, dodging hornets and wasps, and trying not to get lost. They enjoyed every minute of it.

We had many good neighbors — Stanges, Keims, Harkins, Helms, McLeans, Nanningas, Weises, Montgomerys, McKinnons, Bill and Russell Smiths, McColls, Flatlas, Shannons, Grieves, Williams, Buchanans, Daulphins, McDonalds, Vandermeers, Johnsons, Van Leest and more.

For entertainment we had house and card parties. Sam Ennis and Bill McColl supplied the music. Many dances were held in the Caroline Hall with Ma Trainor being a favorite. Many local people played for dances as well. We used to gather at Bowers or Blacks on Sundays in the summer. We played horseshoes, baseball, or just sat in the shade of the trees and visited.

Mom and Mrs. Rod Campbell started the Legion in Caroline. Stanley served two and one-half years in the army — from Feb. 1943 to Nov. 1945. He was first stationed in the Aleution Islands and then was sent to England Holland and Germany just in time for the war to end. He served in the 2nd Division, 6th Field.

An Indian, Josh, and his family visited us often. Grandpa could speak a little of their language so they always came to visit when in our area. They lived for a time south of Caroline, but could be seen anywhere — working or visiting.

In early years the roads often became almost impassable from Caroline to Innisfail. Being half way between Raven and Caroline, our home was a favorite stopping place. One day Bob Mitten and George Langley, each driving a truck home from Innisfail, were stuck by Andy's store at Raven near Noah Heare's. Dad was a passenger and was helping them. It took all day to go seven miles. They had a 15-30 tractor and four head of horses pulling all at one time but they couldn't budge the truck. Mr. Heare anchored a stump puller to a tree and hooked it on the truck and pulled it through the mud. The men started in the morning and by evening only one truck was at Black's. They had travelled about five miles. The other truck was stuck at Mike Harkins corner.

Art Johnson was stuck one night and came in for help. Stanley crawled out of bed and pulled him out. It was raining and Stanley was soaked when he got back to the house. He was no sooner in bed when Art was back — he was stuck again. "Crawl into bed until morning Art. I was wet once and that's enough for tonight", Stanley said. The next morning Art said "Guess I'd better see how my passengers spent the night." A young lady and her child had been left in the car all night. Art hadn't mentioned them until morning.

Grandpa had a horse that he used to haul water for the house. The well was some distance away. If Grandpa had to pull anyone out he saddled the horse. One day a stranger came, so Grandpa took his horse and with difficulty pulled him out. The saddle was damaged from the pull but the stranger was invited in for a cup of tea. When he was leaving he reached in his pocket and handed Grandpa a quarter. Grandpa could swear up a storm when he was provoked, and the air was blue for awhile. If the man had just said "Thanks" it would have been sufficient.

Mom and Dad had the only radio in the area and everyone used to gather to hear William

Aberhart. I remember one occasion when several gathered to hear an important speech by Adolf Hitler. Dave Staben was there to interpret to us.

Don Parker, our neighbor at Markerville, came to stay at our house until his house and welding shop were built at Raven. He drove a car with a rumble seat, and many times when he took a drive he had several young people with him.

Bert Hadley also stayed at our house for awhile. Later he bought some land and built a house and outbuildings about two miles from us.

I can remember seeing reflections from Turner Valley Oilfields. At times the sky was quite red. We used to stand and look at it in wonder.

Dad was known as a "Wheeler-Dealer" and it helped in many ways to make a better living for us. Cliff Heale from Delburne worked with him. During the late thirties and early forties they made many deals throughout the country. After the war started times improved, and by the late forties everyone was better off.

At one time our area had eleven barb-wire telephones. They were really something. Dad also had an electric fencer. I can remember how they would laugh when some unsuspecting person was asked to touch the wire. It gave quite a jolt.

Wes Shanks used to travel the area with a stallion pulling a two wheeled cart. One day he reached our corner and Dad's black and white Shetland pony was on the road. The stallion was frightened and wouldn't move ahead until Dad caught the Shetland and led it away. Maybe he thought it was a skunk.

In 1935 Dad paid $200.00 for his quarter, and in 1947 he sold it for $2000.00. Mom ran the Caroline cafe until 1948. They lived here until 1970 when they moved to Valleyview. They farmed a homestead there until 1973 when they bought a pool hall in Big Valley. To date they are still operating the business with Heber's help.

Dad has a certificate from the Alberta Wheat Pool saying he is a founding member. He also has a Golden Jubilee Senior Citizen Award. Mom and Dad have a Golden Wedding Certificate from Ottawa and Alberta. Dad belonged to the Elks and the U.F.A. at one time. Mom belonged to the U.F.W.A. They celebrated their 50th Anniversary in 1970 with a supper for 140 guests, a dance and social evening followed.

In 1978 the Black family had a family reunion at the Westward Ho campground. One hundred and fifty people attended. They came from the United States, British Columbia and Alberta. Dad has two sisters still living — Zelma at Brooks, and Adeline at Kalispell, Montana.

Right to Left — Jack, Stanley, Wayne and Terry Black.

Dad is very proud of the fact that he has four generations of native born Albertans — Dad, son Stanley, grandson Wayne and great-grandson Terry. He has four generations in his other childrens' families, but they have boys and girls.

I, Beth, was born September 11, 1920 and married Bill Thornhill from Manor, Saskatchewan on June 30, 1942. We have lived at Markerville Caroline, Rocky Mountain House, Balzac, Turner Valley, Nanton, Langdon, Springbank, and in 1951 we moved to Calgary where we still reside. We have four children, William, Phyllis, Edward and James.

William was born in Innisfail April 4, 1943. We were living in Caroline at the time. It was spring and the roads were terrible. Heber went with us and had to go ahead breaking the ice so the car could get through. In a place or two, the water came in the doors. We left home at 6 a.m. and arrived in Innisfail about 1:30 p.m. We were fortunate to get to the hospital because the baby had to spend a month in an incubator. The other three children were born in Rocky Mountain House.

William is married to Lynn Meinerz from Milwaukee, Wisconsin. They have two children and live at Mossleigh, Alberta.

Phyllis married Jim Laing. They have four children and live in Calgary.

Edward married Judy Johnson of Kenora, Ontario. They have four children and live at Qu'Appelle, Saskatchewan.

James is single and lives in Calgary.

Brother Stanley married Margaret Kleiner of Caroline. They lived here until 1952 and are now living in Irricana. They have eleven children.

Wayne married Arlene Blomquist of Calgary. They have two children and live at Cremona.

Donald married Diane Charest of Golden, B.C. They have one child and live at Cache Creek, B.C.

Robert married Laura Wittif of Calgary. They have two children and live in Calgary.

Margaret married Doug Lewis of Cremona. They have four children and live at Cremona.

Marie married Emil Ward of Calgary. They have two children and live in Calgary.

Marilyn married Dave Chalmers of Calgary where they still live.

Douglas married Marlene Campbell of Calgary. They have one child and live in Calgary.

Dale is single and lives at home.

Beverley is single and lives in Calgary.

Bruce married Cheryl Kinch from Water Valley. They have one child.

Carrie attends school and lives at home.

Neil Heber born 1924, moved to Calgary in 1955 and lived in various places until 1973 when he moved to Big Valley to help his father in the pool hall. He has four children.

Johnny works for an oil company and lives at Rainbow Lake.

Linda has one child and lives at Salmon Arm, B.C.

John Wesley married Dorine Hutchinson. They have four children.

Donna is single and is an X-ray technician at Yellowknife, N.W.T.

Daryl married Gayla Andrews from Calgary. They lived in Calgary.

Terry is single and lives in Calgary.

Clara Doris married Bill Mayhew of Raven. They have an acreage at Big Valley. They have four children.

William is single and lives at home.

Barbara is married to Francisco Laisnez from Big Valley. They have two children.

Linda is married to Allen Benz from Caroline. They have a son Clayton and live at Caroline.

Larry and his wife Marion and their daughter live with his parents.

Art and Florence Bowers

by Hazel (Bowers) Turton

This couple were both born in the State of Kansas less than twenty miles apart, Art in Preston County, 1879, and Florence Mabel Reid in Pratt County, 1890. They were married at Taluga, Oklahoma, in 1907.

Shortly after their marriage they decided to 'pull up stakes' and move to Alberta. They and Art's brother and sister-in-law, Andy and Zaidee Bowers, travelled in 'covered wagons' from Oklahoma to Kansas and up to Great Falls, Montana, then on to Lethbridge, Alberta. From there they came by train to Innisfail and again in wagons to Raven where Andy already had land. By that time they had one child and were expecting another. Florence did housework for the

family's board while Art worked for various farmers to get 'their start'.

In 1912 they settled on their own homestead west of Raven in the Shilo district. Their family increased over the years to nine; Catherine, Ray, Dollie, Ralph, Ethel, Walter, Hazel, George and Everett.

Florence always raised an enormous garden and cared for her family. Art worked out in spare times for the railroad and at any kind of job available. He was a good blacksmith and many neighbors came to have him shoe their horses.

The Bowers home was a great gathering place on Sundays. Often with thirty to forty people there to play ball, eat home-made ice-cream and 'good old fried chicken'.

With all seven of the older children in school, there were many school lunches to be packed. Everyday would find bread in the oven for their lunches. The children attended the Shilo School and along with the Dials, Wyants, Devores and Stevensons, were some of the first pupils to attend.

Art farmed in the district for many years and invested in a waterwell drill during the 1930s. He and Ralph drilled many water wells around the home district, to the east of Kevisville, and Innisfail and even as far as Dovercourt and Rocky.

In the forties the farm was sold to Walter and the Bowers couple retired to Caroline where Ralph still lives.

Mrs. Bowers is a member of the Pythian Sisters Temple and Royal Purple Lodge of Caroline.

Art Bowers died in 1947. Mrs. Bowers stayed at Caroline for many more years. She is now eighty-eight and resides in the West Park Nursing Home in Red Deer. She is very alert and always ready for any company who drop by to see her. Arthritis has crippled her legs so she is in a wheel chair now. This is possibly due to the long hours spent in the blueberry patches which in earlier years were abundant. She would take four milk pails in flour sacks, two tied together in front and two in back on old Bess, her bay pony, and come home at night with all of them full.

These berries were canned for winter use, as well as sold to many town dwellers. Mr. Carl Morkeberg would pick up the cream for his creamery at Markerville and when he returned would bring back what Mrs. Bowers had ordered from the stores. Many times she bought all the winter staples (flour, sugar, etc.) with the proceeds of her labours. With the wild meat Art supplied, they managed to always have a full larder. In Art's spare time in the winter, he hunted and trapped.

Most of the family still live around Caroline except for Ethel in British Columbia, George in

Edmonton and Walter at Calgary. Ray passed away in the fall of 1978 and is buried in the Raven Cemetery beside the church which his dad, along with many other 'old timers' helped to build.

The Buchanan Family

JAMES ANDREW BUCHANAN married Myrtle Emily Doust in Nebraska in 1895. Their children are Blanche, born in 1897, Pearce born in 1899 in Minnesota, Laura born in 1901 in Gladstone, Manitoba, Henry born in 1903 and Arthur born in 1905 at Rossendale, Manitoba, Harvey born in 1908 in Belt, Montana, William born in 1911 and Rose born in 1918 in Lethbridge. The family moved to Alberta from Montana in 1909 and settled at Lethbridge until July, 1919, when Andrew rented a farm east of Innisfail, sending all he could put into a railroad car — cattle, machinery and household effects with three boys stowed away in the car to milk and care for the cows.

In 1920 he filed on a homestead east of Crammond, N.W.Q. 24-35-5-5. Bill, Rose and Harvey attended school at Crooked Creek, two and a half miles east of their farm. The teacher's name at that time was Miss Georgina Proud. Their first post office was at Kevisville and later the one at Caroline. They moved to Mayton, east of Olds, for a time around 1929. Then back to the homestead before purchasing and moving to the land west of the Sundre corner, S.E. 17-36-5-5, in 1932. Andrew sold the farm to his son, Arthur, in 1946 for $2500 and retired to Caroline. Andrew died at home on July 1, 1953, at the age of eighty-one. Emily died in the Innisfail Hospital in the fall of 1960.

BLANCHE PEARL BUCHANAN married Harvey Fillingham in 1914 at Lethbridge and moved to Wayland, Michigan, where Elmer and Irvin were born. She returned home for a short time in 1923 and cooked for a harvest crew in Trochu. 1923 was a tremendous year for wheat

Buchanan family: Percy, Myrtle, May, Mr. and Mrs. Andy Buchanan, Inez Redding.

and all available help was solicited from the towns for the harvest operations. Many hilarious incidents and accidents with 'greenhorns' are remembered. In 1928 Blanche returned home again with the two boys. She was remarried to Charles Ingram in Innisfail on May 23, 1933. Their farm was four miles east and two miles south of Crammond. Mavis born in 1937 married John Stone in 1956. They live west of the James River Store and a half mile south. Mavis has four children, Sheila, Alan, Sandra and Brian.

LAURA JANE BUCHANAN married Ben Redding at Pine Lake in 1920. Ben was a carpenter and built a house on the northwest side of the Sundre corner, lived there until 1939 when they moved to Innisfail and later to Vancouver. Their children are Faye, Iris, Max and Inez.

HENRY BUCHANAN went to Michigan to visit Blanche in 1924 and returned only once in 1928 on his honeymoon. He married Minnie Zwier. They had four girls, Mary, Barbara, Norma and Patty. Minnie was ill and bedridden for many years until her death in 1960.

ARTHUR BUCHANAN (1905-1975) took the first eight grades of his schooling in Lethbridge before the family moved six miles out of Lethbridge to make a fortune by planting wheat and harvesting it on 'spare time'! Wartime high prices were very enticing. Crops dried out for the next two years so a move was made to Innisfail area. The experience of milking cows on a train is remembered. The cows had been bounced around in a railroad car in July — nervous and tails were not clean and white. In 1921 the family moved to the homestead east of Crammond. Art helped build log buildings, cleared land by axe and team, gardened, picked berries and cut hay from sloughs and meadows for cattle and horse feed. In 1922-1924 he worked out harvesting, hewing railroad ties, digging drainage ditches at Dickson, working for Jim Daines Livery and Feed Stable in Innisfail and harvesting around Carstairs.

Arthur filed on homestead, S.W.Q. 24-35-5-5. He batched with Pearce on his homestead. They worked together at clearing and breaking land, sold tamarack and birch. He crossed the Red Deer River with Harry McKain when they had to chain the wagon box to the wagon gear because of high water. In 1926 he worked the entire winter for his father, Andrew, in trade for four big dictionaries. He abandoned the homestead in Bill's favor and went to Montana to help Grandmother care for ailing Grandfather, Joseph.

While in Montana Arthur finished high school and two years of teacher's training. He married Cecile Seek, June 7, 1933, in Belt, Montana, and moved back to Caroline in 1946 with four children, Carol, Andrew, Myrtle, and Faye. Jean was born in 1946 in Innisfail.

207

In 1947 Arthur began teaching at Shilo School, grades one to nine with about forty-five pupils. He became principal at Caroline in September of 1947. Mrs. Shaw opened school at the Legion Hall, grades nine to ten. Art taught school at Crammond in 1948. He resigned from teaching in favor of farming until 1954, then returned to teaching at Caroline. He left teaching at Caroline and sold the farm in 1962, moving to Sundre at this time.

Other children born to them were Roberta in 1947 in the Eckville Hospital, Ruth in 1953, Danny in 1955 and Joy in 1957.

HARVEY BUCHANAN married Ethel Coreyin in 1929 and lived on the land now belonging to Louis Johnson, N.W.Q. 9-36-5-5. Their children are Marjie, Reta, Harold, Jerry and Kenny. Harvey lived and worked in Caroline from 1933 to 1946. Bill and Harvey built the first pool hall — a two-storey building on the north side of main street. He owned jointly with Bill, the meat market that was on the corner where the hotel is now located. This meat market was later on the street south of the hotel and moved again next to the pool hall. In 1935 Bill sold his share of the pool hall to Harvey for $150 and the meat market was sold to Bert Blamire. Harvey and family lived for a time in the house where Mrs. Louise Cross lives now. Later he built a house near the present water tower. They moved to British Columbia in 1946.

WILLIAM CECIL BUCHANAN (Bill) was born in Lethbridge, April 12, 1911, and moved with the family to a homestead east of Crammond. He went to school two and a half miles east of the farm at Crooked Creek. He built the old pool hall and owned the Caroline Butcher Shop jointly with Harvey. Arthur turned over his homestead to Bill in 1927. This land was straight south of Dad Buchanan's homestead.

Bill married Gladys Adams in October, 1938. They spent one and a half years in Calgary while Bill had five operations and recuperated until the spring of 1941 when he helped with seeding at Oughton's in Calgary and harvesting at Harmattan. He moved on to Pearce Buchanan's place east of the Sundre corner in 1942 while Pearce rented Wise's land. Gladys cooked for John Fortman's sawmill crew across the road from the farm and Bill raised chickens and shipped eggs.

They moved to Caroline in March, 1945, with two daughters, Georgina, five years old and Marvina, one. They lived for a time in the old Langley Store building, then moved to their present land location where they built up a laundry business. They washed for the hotel and several sawmills and logging crews in the area.

Marvina was killed in a tractor accident in 1955. After finishing high school, Georgina attended business college in Calgary in 1957. She married Albert O'Coin in 1958 and they have four children, Kevin, Dwayne, Gary and Allan.

ROSE BUCHANAN married Don Montgomery in 1937 and lived 5 miles east of Caroline, for many years. They had seven children, Lyle, LeRoy, Verna, Lloyd, Bill, Howard and Robert. Rose died in 1961.

Pierce Buchanan
by Myrtle Buchanan

Percy Buchanan was born on July 27, 1899, in the state of Minnesota. At an early age, his parents, Mr. and Mrs. Andrew Buchanan, four brothers, Henry, Arthur, Harvey and William, three sisters, Blanche, Laura and Rose, moved to Lethbridge, Alberta. Here he received his education. Percy took army training for three or four months during the first World War, but never was shipped overseas as the war ended about that time. In 1922, they moved to Pine Lake where they resided for two years. In 1924 they took up homesteading in the Kevisville district. In the fall of 1925 Percy went to Carstairs to help with the fall harvest. There he met Myrtle May Corey and they were married on February 23, 1926. In the winter of 1926-27 they returned to Carstairs and on January 28, 1927, Myrtle May Buchanan was born, their one and only child.

In the spring of 1928 Theodore Corey, Myrtle's brother, took Myrtle and her daughter back to Kevisville, across the muskeg road, in an old Model T Ford. The muskeg was just like a bowl of jelly, and Theodore had to get out and push while Myrtle tried to drive. Talk about a nerve-racking experience.

In 1928 they moved to the Wimborne district

Top Row: 5 from left, Myrtle Buchanan, Andrew Buchanan, Pierce Buchanan — Middle Row: William Buchanan, ?, ?, ?, kneeling: Laura Buchanan, — Bottom Row: Harvey and Henry Buchanan — others unknown.

Percy and Blanche Buchanan with one of her sons.

hoping to buy land, but it was too expensive. They stayed in the district for two years, then moved back to the Kevisville district again.

In 1933-34 Percy and a few other Kevisville homesteaders built a corduroy road across the same muskeg mentioned above. Many an hour was spent putting this corduroy in. To cover the logs with dirt, an old fresno was used. It was pulled by horses, the poor animals! Today it is a gravel road.

Their closest neighbors at that time were Emil Brown, two miles away, Lorne Reesor, one-half mile away and Mr. and Mrs. Andrew Buchanan, Percy's parents, two miles away. Ray McKain, at the Red Raven Store, supplied them with groceries, but they had to walk another mile and a half to get their mail at the Kevis place.

Entertainment then was mainly house parties and Christmas concerts. With road building and walking those many miles it didn't take long to tire, so relaxation of the simplest form was to the best advantage. Sunday School was held in the schools on Sundays.

In 1934 Percy's parents moved from Kevisville to a farm in the Caroline district on to the S.E. Q. 17-36-5-5. In order for Percy and family to visit his parents then, they had to ride in an old lumber wagon. What a bumpy ride!

In the spring of 1936 Percy and Myrtle moved to his parent's home, three miles east of Caroline. In 1937 they obtained the quarter section east of the Sundre road, S.W. Q. 16-36-5-5. They farmed this until December of 1954. Percy suffered a stroke then and was unable to do work or to do farming. They moved to Caroline to a permanent residence at 5015-49 Street. The farm was rented out until 1957. It was then sold to Arthur Buchanan, Percy's brother.

On November 10, 1961, Percy passed away in the Innisfail Hospital. Myrtle still resides in their home in Caroline. She has attended the Nazarene Church for twenty-five years and has been Secretary-Treasurer for the Sunday School for seventeen years. Their daughter, May, married

Chris Staben on November 29, 1945. They also reside in the Caroline district.

Dial, Russell F.
by Helen (Dial) Mullen

"Russ" (as his friends knew him) was my grandfather. He came to the Caroline area from Goodridge, North Dakota in 1906. He filed on a homestead 2 miles east and 1 mile north of the present site of Caroline. He then returned to Goodridge, and the next year in 1907 brought his family back with him. The family (his wife, the former Sarah Branson, sons Ray, Glen and Arthur, and daughter Lulu) moved into an old cabin by Rounds Creek near Raven. They also brought horses and cows.

In 1908 Russ built a house on his homestead. Ray, Glen along with Carol, Loney and Sig Record helped him. Those were very hard years for homesteaders. They grew most of their food

L.-R. Glen, Arthur, Lulu and Ray Dial.

L.-R. Russ and Sarah Dial, Lulu and Ray.

209

and had berries and wild meat. The children went to Shilo school, but Ray had to quit in Grade 8 and get a job in order for the family to buy a few essentials including flour. I remember my grandmother telling me that she once had to sell the wash tub to buy some flour. Russ died in the Innisfail hospital about 1920.

In the years that followed Ray got a homestead 2 miles east of Caroline. Glen and Arthur went to Turner Valley and settled there during the oil boom. Lulu got her high school credits with much help from a Shilo teacher, Arden Litt. She then went to Edmonton and trained as a registered nurse at the Royal Alexandra Hospital. Grandmother Dial moved to Caroline (1 mile south of the present site) and lived in an old house owned by Harv Langley. She boarded the South Fork schoolteacher.

About 1925 Mrs. Dial married one of the district's most eligible bachelors — James (Jim) Leask who lived about a mile east of Caroline (the old Carter place). There were those who said that her home-baked bread got him. Later they moved to Innisfail and then to Calgary.

Jim was a wonderful man and was very good to Grandmother who became blind after they moved to Calgary. Some years later Jim died at the T.B. Sanatorium in Calgary. Grandmother Leask lived to be 93.

The only one of the family still living is Glen. He and his wife Juanita live near Ashville, North Carolina.

The Gardner History

by Fern Cave

Glen Gardner was born in Kansas in 1893. Etta Gardner was born in Missouri in 1893. They were married in 1912. In 1913 they moved to Dilke, Saskatchewan, where they farmed until 1918 when they moved to Carstairs, Alberta. In 1921 they moved to the Raven district, farming the Andy Bowers place for two years, then the Becktol place for two years before taking a homestead.

They were active in community affairs, and Mrs. Gardner was secretary-treasurer of the North Raven School District for twenty years. She played piano for Christmas concerts and church. They retired to Rocky Mountain House in 1957. They had thirteen children, two died in infancy and the youngest son, Glen, died in 1966.

The oldest son, Garnett, married Lillain Benson Cave, and they had one son and one daughter. They farmed, worked in sawmills in the west country and had a store and coffee shop at Condor, before moving to British Columbia where they have an orchard.

Cecil married Anne Miller and they had six children. Cecil worked on farms, mostly around the New Hill district.

Glenora married Harold Dix and they had two children, one son and one daughter. They lived in Calgary, where Harold worked for Standard Gravel.

Vaye married Jack Franklin, they had two sons and one daughter. Jack was in the army, overseas for five years. They live in Calgary, where Jack still works for Standard Gravel.

Helen married Tom Benson. They had two sons and one daughter. They farmed in the Caroline area and raised mink before moving to Red Deer.

Lewis married Lorraine Mae Smith; they had twin girls and one son. Lewis worked in Calgary at Ogden shops and later for a cement company.

Fern married Arthur Cave; they had two sons and lived in Red Deer.

Bud (James) married Edna Beatty. They worked in the Calgary area before buying a farm in Olds. They have seven children.

Joyce married Harold Smith, they worked around Calgary for three years, then bought the Herbert Hadley farm at Caroline. They had five children.

We lost our house by fire in 1934. The neighbors helped build a new one and kept some of the children. Mr. Gardner helped build the Raven Church in 1926. They got their mail and groceries from Mr. and Mrs. Walker who owned the Raven Store.

Raven River Ranch

by Charles and Edith Hall and family

Edith and myself are both native Albertans. I was born on a homestead twelve miles south of Seven Persons, Alberta. Edie was born in Calgary, but raised on a farm.

I am the eldest of a family of ten children. Edie was the eldest of a family of three. We have three children, Lois, Rita and Donald, and ten grandchildren, Lois has six and Don has four children. Lois and Don went to the North Raven School.

We came to the Caroline-Raven district from Calgary, where I worked as a tool maker in the Ogden shops.

We bought our present half section from Julius Callis. It had about twenty acres broken on it, the rest was timber and tamarack stumps. We have it all cleared and broken now. There was as much underneath the ground as there was on top!

We lived in two granaries pulled together, had five cows, three saddle horses and a few chickens, ducks and geese. We also had an old Chevrolet one ton truck.

The first winter was spent logging with a

swede saw and a skid horse. We cut enough logs for about ten thousand feet of lumber. After it was sawn and planed, we hauled it to Calgary and sold it for $16 per thousand feet. I could hardly sleep at night, my arms ached so bad. I was not used to such punishment as logging. All of our buildings were constructed of logs from the ranch. Bill McColl sawed the logs and Verner Neilson planed the lumber.

The first three years we were here, we were hailed out each year. One year the hail stones were as big as baseballs. They bounced about ten feet in the air when they hit the ground. They were solid chunks of ice. They smashed the one-inch rough boards on our roof and wrecked all of the shingles, but we saved the windows. It stripped the bark off of the west side of the trees, some of them died after that gift from the sky.

We had the best of neighbors who helped with the sawing of stove wood and haying; the Gardners, Berrys, Knights, Montgomerys, Mayhews and Mike Harkins.

There were no highways, power, telephones or gas in those days. What an unbelievable change from then to now.

The country was beautiful, birds and game were everywhere — coyotes, squirrels, procupines and mink. Drummer grouse and owls supplied us with their various songs and we just loved it.

We bought a few sheep from Mike Harkins and Edie asked Jack Bugbee if he would shear them, I believe there were six. Jack said he could shear that many without even getting out of his car.

We raised purebred Polled Hereford cattle for many years, and sold Polled bulls in this area.

I have driven a school bus to Caroline for twenty-five years and am still driving one. I have many young friends from bus driving. Mike Harkins used to say he set his watch by me when I went by in the mornings to school. When I first started driving, the roads were very poor, no gravel. In the winter I used to take a pail with some old rags and a little gas poured on it which I lit and put underneath the oil pan of the bus to get it started. I have driven many times when it was 45 degrees below zero F.

I think we live in one of the most beautiful spots in Alberta and Edie and I are very happy to be a part of it.

Harry Hansen Family
by Gladys Hansen

My husband and I and our three children, Clifford, Doris and Avril, left Calgary the first of September, 1935, riding in H. A. Langley's truck on our way to Caroline. We got stuck in a mud hole about half way to Caroline, so it was eve-

ning by the time we got there. We were invited to stay at the Langleys for the night as they had rooms above the store.

The next day we were able to get our tent up and got the stove going and began housekeeping in the tent. We got a house built on the S.E.Q. 24-36-6-5, one-half mile north of what is now highway No. 54.

I remember Mr. O'Coin Sr. bringing the lumber allowed us on the government scheme, to help people get started and become self supporting.

We were living in the house when the family on the quarter next to us decided to leave. We took over from them as they had a log house built, a dug well and some clearing done.

Clifford started school at Shilo, walking the three and one-half miles there and back. He used to go with the Williams boys.

Our nearest neighbors were the Williams east of us, Rogers to the west, and Bowdens were south of us. We visited back and forth.

Three more children were born to us, Harold, Howard and Marlene, all born in Innisfail.

Caroline was our post office and we traded at Langley's store for groceries. We didn't have a church yet in those days, but Mrs. Langley held Sunday School in her home. Student ministers would come during the summer.

I was born in England in 1901 and went to school in Calgary. I was married to Harry in 1928.

I took over the cafe in Caroline from Mickey Gainor in 1953 and had it about a year. I then operated the hotel coffee shop until 1960, when I moved to Calgary. I was in Calgary for about five years then I moved back to Caroline.

Howard died in a vehicle accident in 1959 and is buried in the Caroline Cemetery.

I have my own home on Harold's farm and am enjoying my life here.

Alexander Helm
by June and Al Helm

Alexander and Annie Helm immigrated to Canada, from Russia, in 1910. They lived in Calgary and then moved to Caroline in July, 1939. They travelled by rail from Calgary to Condor; then went overland by horse and wagon to their homestead, situated approximately six miles east and one mile south of Caroline, on a half-section of school land. The land is now the Bill McColl farm.

While living in Calgary, my father was employed in a lumber mill. However, during the depression years, with jobs few and far between, my father decided to accept the program offered by Government Agencies to secure a homestead. This turned out to be in the Caroline district.

Our neighbors at that time were Rudy Stange who lived on the South Raven River while across the road lived the Smith family. The Black family lived one and a half miles north on the main road.

Our mail and supplies were obtained at Caroline. The entertainment was limited, but there was usually a meeting of friends at a barn dance or house gathering. Music was supplied by the McColl family. We went fishing and swimming when possible, and any other leisure moments were spent around the children — playing cards, etc.

From the point of view of a fifteen year old boy, who was city bred, the homestead looked like a good place for a Boy Scout camp. Our farming knowledge at that time was almost nil — what we knew was prairie oriented. However with our brand new wagon, brand new scythe, our brand new walking plow, three prairie bred horses, one prairie bred Holstein cow and a few chickens, we set up our camp-site, which was boards in "A" design formed against a pole between two trees. This was our first shelter. From there we concentrated our efforts on constructing a more permanent shelter, and getting land ready for a garden, etc. The first land broken was done by the McColl family's steamer. From there on it was a matter of survival.

All of the Helm children were born in Calgary, except Katie, who was born in Russia. Edward, Phyllis, and I attended the Shilo School. Although I am registered as having attended Shilo, I really did not complete a full year as I was waiting for marks from Calgary, and ended up going to work instead.

The children who settled in Caroline were Daniel, Edward, Phyllis and myself. Other, older members of the family, were Katie, Pauline, Tillie and Ella.

I was married to Margaret Isobel Pratt on July 10, 1947, in Calgary. Margaret passed away in October, 1970. We had five children. Wayne was born in Calgary on July 24, 1948. He is married and has two children, Jason and Sarah. They now live at Alsask, Saskatchewan, where Wayne is stationed with Canadian Armed Forces. He is Sergeant in charge of maintenance of mobile vehicles.

Lesley Margaret was born in Calgary, on April 2, 1950. She is divorced now, and lives in Moose Jaw with two sons, Robert and Christopher.

Frederick Alexander (known as Rick) was born in Rivers, Manitoba, on October 27, 1951. He is married to Shirley Mahan and lives in Regina where he is Operations Chief at the Data Processing Centre of Co-operative Insurance Services. They have no children.

Edward John Melville was born in Rivers, on December 28, 1955. He married Debbie Canevoro. They live in Regina, where he is in the Internal Audit Department of Saskatchewan Power Corporation. Rick and Edward have both achieved the classification of Pipe Majors in the Highland Piping. They are both, presently, members of the Victoria Park Pipe Band of Regina.

Margaret (Peggy) Arletta was born in Zaviebruken, Germany, on February 11, 1960. She completed grade twelve and will be attending Saskatchewan Technical Institute in the fall, 1978.

I have been a member of The Moose Jaw Optimist Club for ten years, and also been in The Boy Scouts movement for ten years, both in Canada and Europe. I joined the Airforce, 1943 to 1946, and served in Western Coastal Command on coast patrol. I re-enlisted in 1948 and served until my retirement in 1973. I served in various operations from fighter command to transport and training.

Edward, Katie, and Tillie are now deceased. Mrs. Annie Helm passed away in 1968, and Alexander in 1969; they are laid to rest in Calgary.

The McColl Family
by Francis McColl

I was born in London, England, in the year of 1893. I was taken from my parents when I was four years old and was put in Doctor Bernardo's Orphanage in England until I was eight. I then came to Canada by boat and again was put in Doctor Bernardo's home for girls in Peterborough, Ontario.

While I was at Doctor Bernardo's home in Peterborough, I was sent to boarding school; you learn to milk cows and wash dishes and general house work. When I was old enough to earn wages they started me out on three dollars a month. I was still working out when I met my husband, Charles Henry McColl, in his home town in Westwood, Ontario. Charles McColl was born in Westwood, Ontario, on July 30, 1886. He homesteaded in the Swift Current District for ten years. He came back east to Ontario and married me on January 12, 1916. We came west to Stewart Valley, twenty miles north of Swift Current, where we farmed for six years. We were either hailed out or burnt out. We only had one crop in six years.

We were married one year when the family started to arrive. Gordon, my oldest son, was born March 15, 1917; two years later my son, William, was born on January 27, 1919; my third son, Charles, was born two years later on May 18, 1921. Very discouraged with our hardships of no crops, we moved to the Innisfail District to the

The McColl family and relatives.

Big Bend area, in the year of 1922. We moved all our livestock and belongings in March of 1922 and took up farming. We all took the flu after our long and hard move. The winter was very long and hard.

On May 19, 1923, my first daughter, Gertrude, was born, then two years later, on June 30, 1925, my fourth son, Raymond, was born.

My husband cleared eighty acres and grew pretty good crops, but he wasn't satisfied with this land and wanted to move further west. We moved out to the Caroline District in 1926 to the Shilo area just east of where the Shilo School now stands. There was thirty acres cleared on this place, so my husband and sons cleared up nearly all that place with brush hooks and brush cutters and horses; no push button stuff — all hard work. We had pretty good crops. While we were on this farm we had four more children. Violet was born on July 9, 1926, but she passed away at birth. Then Blanche was born on September 19, 1928. Two years later I had another son, Garnet, who was born March 30, 1930; he also passed away at birth. Two years later on August 30, 1932, Jessie, my youngest daughter, was born. All my children received most or all of their education at the Shilo School. Then in the year of 1934, we moved two miles north, where we are today. We had to start all over again. The land was all bush and we had to build a house and then we cleared some land. That is when the hardships started, we lost fourteen head of cattle just due to calve; there was something in the straw that year that caused it. We just couldn't save them. That was our only income. We had to go to Council to get some relief, but all we got was eight dollars a month.

But living then was not so high as it is now. The boys all went out to work, as well as Gertrude, my oldest daughter. My youngest son, Raymond, was called into the army on April 5, 1944, and was stationed at the Mewata Barracks in Calgary where he served as Batman for awhile, then he was sent to Barifield, Ontario, and received more training in Kingston, Ontario.

He never went overseas due to medical reasons. He was discharged from the army on April 21, 1946.

My husband passed away on September 9, 1962. Raymond took over the farm in 1961 before his dad passed away. I am still living on the farm. Most of my children are married and living in the Caroline district. Gordon is still single. William married Eva Smith on November 29, 1945, and raised a family of one boy and one girl. Charles married Betty Reesor on July 9, 1946, but has been separated from her now for some years. He now lives in Red Deer. Gertrude married Frank Rolfes on July 9, 1946, and she and Frank now live in Rocky Mountain House. They have no children. Raymond married Leone Gardner on June 23, 1961, and they have one girl. Blanche married Charles Benz on December 16, 1948, and raised a family of four girls and one boy. Jessie married Ray Sawyer May 6, 1950, but they are divorced now. Jessie and Ray had a family of one boy and two girls. Jessie lives in Caroline and Ray now lives in Calgary.

So with lots of hard work, perseverance and hardships we raised quite a large family and survived it all.

Fred McKinnon
by Mrs. Fred McKinnon

No one was more proud of his Scottish ancestry than Fred McKinnon. He was born near Aberdeen, Scotland, in 1908, moved to Vulcan, Alberta, where he farmed with his folks. In 1934 he married me, Miss Josephine Sigurdson, from Red Deer. I was teaching at the Shilo School and settled in that area for a period of seven years.

Four children were born, Diane, Ralph, and the twins, Ronald and Donald. All are married now. Diane is post mistress at Water Valley. Ralph and Ronnie are in the company, 'F. McKinnon and Sons'. If you watch television you may see Ralph's wife, Vera McKinnon, singing in the German Womens Choir. Donnie has a large dairy farm near Cremona. One more son, Lachlan, was born at Water Valley. He farms on his own.

We moved to Water Valley in 1941 where we bought a general store and have been there for thirty-seven years, farming, operating a treated fence post business, a coal and wood yard in Calgary and, of course, still in the store.

One of my most cherished memories of my teaching days was having a student at Shilo by name, Doug Stevens. Mrs. Vandermeer Sr. was his grandmother. Doug Stevens was always artistic and made a career of it. His cowboy and western motifs are very famous. The Emblem of the series of Stampede Dollars depict a different Western Emblem each year. Doug married a

Fred McKinnon. Mrs. Fred McKinnon — Teacher at Shilo School.

girl, Norma Cargo, whose mother had a small store near us many years ago. Small world isn't it? Alberta suffered the loss of a great artist when Doug Stevens passed away. Time takes its toll!

Fred passed away suddenly at home, June 28, 1978. He left his mark on many people as he was so well known through his affiliation with Masons, Scottish Right, Eastern Star and Charter member of Cremona Lions and his many business acquaintances. Two sons and myself still carry on the business 'F. McKinnon and Sons' and try to go on where he left off. Everyone has their own home in this district and hope to continue here.

Guy and Norma Miller
by Anne Gardner

My parents, Guy and Norma Miller, came to the Caroline area from Mission City, British Columbia, in the fall of 1928, to a farm a few miles east and north of Caroline.

Mom was to take charge of the Shilo School so she and my brother and sister came a couple of weeks earlier than Daddy and I. Mom and the other kids came by train and Daddy and I drove over in an old 1918 Model T Ford, arriving at our destination near the end of October. It took us a week to make the trip, which wasn't too bad I guess, everything taken into consideration, and I don't recall having any car trouble.

I don't know why Daddy decided to move to Alberta as he had a thriving Rawleigh business in British Columbia and did very well, but I suppose the urge to farm once more was stronger.

After getting ourselves established in our new home we soon began having visits from our neighbors from close by, Mr. and Mrs. Bowers, Mr. and Mrs. Crippen, Mr. and Mrs. McColl, Mr. and Mrs. Orcutt and many others. All were good

neighbors ready to extend a helping hand when needed.

We got our mail and our supplies here in Caroline as we could trade eggs, butter and blueberries for groceries, and this saved making long trips out for supplies. One trip I remember quite well, was one that Daddy and I made to Rocky Mountain House with a wagon load of cabbage that Mr. Killick had ordered to sell in his store. That was a pretty rough ride, that far in a lumber wagon across country. When we got cold we would take turns walking so we could keep warm. Then the horses decided that we could walk all the way, and they took off leaving us to catch up if we could. Daddy finally got close enough to climb on the back of the wagon and got them quieted down. We finally arrived home all in one piece about two a.m. the following morning.

The folks always raised a huge garden with all kinds of vegetables and this made it possible for us to sell produce to folks around Dickson and Markerville who had the misfortune to be hailed out several years in succession. Daddy was known throughout that area as blueberry Miller, cabbage head Miller, sauerkraut Miller and green peas Miller. The ripe peas he would thresh for seed and the broken ones he would sort out and sell for soup peas. In the summer of 1932, we picked and sold a thousand pounds of low bush blueberries, and somewhere in the neighborhood of five hundred pounds of cranberries.

Even though we all pitched in and helped pick berries, take care of the garden and make hay, we were never too tired to enjoy the association with our neighbors at the various house parties and dances that were held throughout the neighborhood, and we didn't need to be stoned out of our minds in order to have a good time. We were too busy dancing to that good old time music to have time for such nonsense.

Now maybe I should say that I came into the world in a little homestead shack at Truax, Saskatchewan in the fall of 1918. My brother, Les, was born in the winter of 1920 at Langley Prairie, British Columbia. I believe it's just called Langley now. My sister, Dora, was born in the summer of 1927 at Mission City, British Columbia. I'm the only prairie chicken. I started school at Pense, Saskatchewan, when I was five years old and Mom was my teacher. Even so, I was treated the same as the other pupils, if I needed to be paddled, I got paddled, and I'm glad I wasn't spoiled to the point of no return. Then when we moved to Alberta, Les and I both had Mom for our teacher for the first term here. We had Bill McIntyre next term. He was spoiled — used to throw books on the floor and jump on them, not much of an example to his pupils. We were sure glad when Mr. Liggett, our inspector,

Guy and Norma Miller, Annie and Lester.

gave him his walking papers. Following him, my last year at school, we had Mabel Wade, and I don't remember who Les' last teacher was, nor who the teacher was when Dora started school, but she got the rest of her education at the North Raven School after we moved, with Herb Stiles for a teacher.

In 1939 I married Cecil Gardner and we lived in the Raven area mostly. We had six children, Leone, Cliff, Lorna, Elwood, Portia and Linda Lucille (deceased at seven months). Leone married Raymond McColl. They have one daughter, Karen, and Raymond farms the home place a few miles out of Caroline. Cliff married Linda Russell of Caroline and they had three daughters, Deanna (deceased), Cheryl and Carol. Cliff (alone now) has the Caroline Auto Wreckers. Lorna married Ken Kissick and they have one daughter, Anna, and one son, Keith. They live on an acreage in the Hespero district. Elwood is single and is a driller on an oil rig, and has his own home here in Caroline. Portia married Everett Bowers. They have one son, Clinton, and one daughter, Lori Ann. Everett is our town foreman here in Caroline.

My brother, Les, enlisted in the army in 1942, and went overseas shortly after. He was overseas until the war ended, during which time he married, returning home in 1946. His wife and adopted son arrived in Calgary a few days later, and after spending a few days at the farm at

Raven, they left for Rossland, British Columbia, where Les lived until two years ago. He moved, with his second wife, to Chilliwack. While in Rossland, he worked at the smelter in Trail for twenty-six years, and is now in Civil Service and enjoying semi-retirement. My sister, Dora, married Bill Walsh. They live at Alix and have two daughters, Maureen and Wendy (both married) and one son, Tracy, still in school. They, too, are enjoying semi-retirement.

Mom and Daddy are both gone now and are sadly missed by us all. Daddy passed away on September 17, 1958 and Mom on October 18, 1977. They are both buried at the Raven Cemetery. Although at times the going has been rough and difficult, I have enjoyed my family, my folks, and my life and I hope to be around for several more years.

William Montgomery
by Florence Staben

William Montgomery married Charlotte Thompson, in 1901, in the U.S.A. They had a family of five, three boys and two girls. He moved to Alberta in 1914 and settled east of Innisfail. Later he took up homestead land in the Caroline district, the S.W. Q. 10-36-5-5, and later bought the N.E. Q. 3-36-5-5.

When we moved to Caroline, in April 1924, the roads were nothing but mud holes and corduroy. We had three wagons and a team for each wagon and, in the worst places, we had to put four horses on one wagon to get it through the mud. It took us four or five days to make the trip. We moved onto a rented place until Dad and the boys got a house built and some land broke, which was a slow job with horses. Most of the horses died from swamp fever, so at last we had to get a tractor. All three boys helped on the farm until they got married and got farms of their own.

Dad died in 1958 at the age of eighty-four years, and Mother died in 1968 at the age of seventy-one years. My sister, Lotus, married Tom Thompson before we moved to Caroline. Donald married Rose Buchanan. Douglas married Ethel Bowers and they are now living in British Columbia. The youngest boy, Ward, died in 1931 at the age of twenty-one years. I, Florence, married David Staben in 1930. He passed away suddenly in 1966 at the age of sixty.

The Jim Murray Family

Mr. Elias James Murray was born in Sault Ste. Marie on October 15, 1889. He was raised in Ontario and came west in 1908, joining his father, John Nicholas Murray, who was active in railroading and the mining business in the Drumheller Valley. Jim Murray operated his father's

James Elias Murray.

mine leases at East Coulee supplying the farmers with coal as far back as 1915. He served in the Canadian Army in World War I for two years. He filed on a homestead at Michichi Creek and became active in the cattle business.

In April of 1919, Jim married Jessie Dickson of Calgary. They settled in East Coulee where he built his first family home. He managed Whitlock Lumber, the first lumberyard in East Coulee. Mr. Murray was also employed by the Provincial Government as a relief foreman and supervisor of the Department of Highways in the 1930s. Their family of seven, Bob, Jack, Rachael (who died at eleven months), Swanie, June, Bill and Margaret (who died at birth) were all born in Drumheller.

In the fall of 1938, Mr. Murray purchased a farm in the Shilo district from Hugh Grieves. In the spring of 1939, the family moved to the farm where Swanie, June and Bill attended the Shilo School. Mr. Murray and his sons did custom farming and threshing for the next two years.

Mr. Murray who was always interested in logging, started cutting timber in the surrounding area. He then moved out to the Tay River in 1943 and set up a camp and sawmill. After several crop failures, Mr. Murray sold his farm in 1945 to Clarence Reddick and moved his family to the camp at the Tay. Mr. Murray logged on the Clearwater flats then moved to Brown Hill, just inside the forestry gates, where he logged for the next two years.

In 1947 Mr. Murray built a home in Caroline and moved to town. He logged in Swan Lake area until 1951 when he lost his mill in a fire. He then went into the office as bookkeeper for Murray Brothers who were also logging by this time.

In 1946 Bob Mitten who had a lumberyard in Caroline, took Bob Murray into partnership and formed Mitten and Murray Lumber. In 1948 Swanie bought out Bob Mitten, and Murray Brothers Lumber was formed.

Murray Brothers, always expanding, employed as many as ninety men (many of them local), during a winter, and had camps at Swan Lake, Burntstick Lake, Nordegg, Cut-off Creek and numerous parts of the Clearwater Reserve. Many loads of lumber came over the Cork Screw Mountain when the trunk road was a tote road. Murray Brothers built an office on the west end of town in 1952. Later, came a warehouse, garage and other buildings.

In 1952 Jim Murray drew up plans for the curling rink on land that was donated for recreation by Ivan Graham. In 1953 work went

The Murray Family — Jack, Jim, Bob, June, Swanie and Bill.

Murray Brothers mill in operation.

Jim and Helen Murray.

ahead due to the knowledge and enthusiasm of Ralph McParland and many willing volunteers. In 1954 the rink was completed, and those that had worked so hard were very proud of their project.

On Christmas Day of 1954, Mrs. Jessie Murray passed away suddenly at the age of sixty-one. Mr. Murray was on town council for four years and was Mayor for three years. He remarried in December of 1955 to Helen Harrison of Westward-Ho, a widow with no family.

In 1967 Bob sold his partnership to Swanie and in 1972 Swanie sold his sawmill equipment to Fisher Holdings of Rocky Mountain House. In 1978 Murray Brothers Lumber Yard was sold and all the buildings have been removed.

Mr. Murray retired in 1970 and spent his time with his family, especially his grandchildren and with gardening. He passed away March 19, 1978, in the Red Deer hospital at the age of eighty-eight.

Bob, the oldest son, joined the army in 1941 and served until 1945. He then worked in the coal mines in East Coulee and later took a barbering course in Calgary. Bob married Irma Massey of Calgary in 1943. They have two sons, Randy and Bernard. Randy is a building contractor and is at present in Innisfail. They have two children. Bernard works locally. In 1971, Bob bought the Budden farm which he sold, and now lives in Sicamous, British Columbia.

Jack joined the Navy in 1942 and served until 1945. He worked in the coal mines in East Coulee and later on oil rigs. Jack married Florence Johnson of Caroline in June of 1948. They have

two children, Karen and Gordon. Karen works for Alberta Government Telephones in Red Deer and Gordon is at present working on an oil rig. Jack moved from Caroline to Spruceview where he owned the pool room. He now lives in Red Deer and is a painter and interior decorator.

Swanie married Nellie Iannucci of Nordegg in 1948. They have two children, Don and Arlene. Don lives in Rocky Mountain House and has a son. Arlene lives in Calgary and has two children. Swanie operated his lumber business in Caroline and moved to Rocky Mountain House in 1966, where he is still active in logging in that area.

June married Gordon Johnson of Caroline in 1947 and they have lived there since.

Bill married Mary Boychuk in 1952 and they have two sons, Jim and Doyle. Jim lives in Calgary and has just completed four years of training in diesel mechanics. Doyle lives at home and is at present working on an oil rig. Bill still lives in Caroline where he has a trucking business.

Living in this area has been very rewarding due to many great friends and neighbors. So to those before us "Thanks". To the future generations "Good Luck!"

The Nanninga Family

Renko Nanninga arrived in Halifax, Canada, in May, 1930. He was born in Germany on June 4, 1897, and he grew up on a farm. He moved with his parents from the Province of Ostfriesland to Timmaspe in the Province of Schleswig Holstein when he was about fifteen years old. He married Magdalena Mehrens April 16, 1922, in Drogaspe. I, Magdalena Nanninga, came to Canada in September, 1931, with our two sons, Fritz was eight years old the day we went on the boat and Gerd was five.

When we arrived in Caroline, Renko had already purchased a quarter section of land from the C.P.R. located on the S.W.Q. 5-36-5-5. He had seven acres in crop and also had built a house

The Nanninga family — Renko, Magda, Gerd, Christa and Fritz.

217

and planted a little garden. On October 28, 1932, our daughter, Christa, was born.

We did not get to Innisfail again until about two years after we arrived here as we did not have a car. We all liked it very much here in Canada right from the start. Money was hard to get, but we never went hungry as we always had enough to eat. We raised a big garden and picked lots of berries, especially blueberries which were plentiful. We sold some blueberries to buy sealers. Renko always enjoyed the hunting trip in the fall and he usually brought home a moose to supply us with meat for the winter. We also enjoyed a meal of fish or a prairie chicken once in awhile. Besides this, we butchered a pig and made all kinds of sausages.

We also enjoyed the house parties very much. Every family brought something for lunch. We sometimes had about seventy people in our house.

We did not get a well drilled until about ten years after we came. We had to get water from a spring about a half a mile away. A few years went by before the men in the Shilo district put up a telephone line. It was a welcome link between neighbors.

One of our closest neighbors to the southeast was a bachelor by the name of Sandy Anderson who later moved back to Scotland.

Our oldest son, Fritz, married Effie Impey from Breton, Alberta, on October 26, 1949. They lived in Redwater for a short time. Fritz worked at moving oil rigs. They later moved to Edmonton where he bought a truck and worked for sixteen years hauling rigs. They now live in Slave Lake and managing the Slave Lake apartments. They have three daughters, Alice, Eileen and Nancy. Alice married Wayne Ptolemy on July 18, 1969. They have three children, Christine and Cynthia were siamese twins born on October 28, 1971. They were separated at the University Hospital in Edmonton in January, 1972. They also have a son, Calvin. Eileen married Tom Malone on October 7, 1972. They have two daughters, Tracy and Debbie. Nancy attended University last year.

Gerd married Mildred McMillan from Green Court, Alberta, July 2, 1952. They moved to Caroline in May, 1953, and moved back to Edmonton in 1956. Gerd trucked for awhile in the oil fields and also on transport trucks to the North West Territories. In April, 1961, they returned to the farm with their family, Garry, Gail, Robert and Daniel. James was born in 1964. Garry graduated from the University of Alberta. Robert married Doris Lohrich. They have one daughter, Carrie Ann. Robert has a farm at Raven, Daniel is a driller on a rig and James is attending Caroline High School.

I moved away from Caroline and lived in British Columbia for three years and returned to live in Caroline in 1968.

The Orcutt Family
by E. L. (Roy) Orcutt

My father, Miner Banks Orcutt, was born April 4, 1874, and mother, Effie Adelia Williams, was born January 26, 1881, in Ackley, Iowa. They were married in Minnesota March 29, 1900. They had seven children, E. L. (Roy), Mildred Ester, Thomas Raymond, Delbert Miner, Donald Lawrence, Robert Melton and Marjory Briones. The first five children were born near Wendell, Minnesota, and the last two in Alberta.

From here the family moved to Montana, near Conrad. After four years of grasshoppers and no rain, Dad decided to move to Alberta and so on a sunny day in October, 1914, Dad hitched the mules, Jenny and Molly, crossbreds from Montana broncho mares, and Jack to the lumber wagon that he had loaded with oats, bedding, grub box, water bag and a rifle. I bridled and saddled Jimmy, the pony, ready to ride. Tom and I, being the oldest boys, were going with Dad to Lethbridge where we would meet Mother, Mildred, Del and Don, who were going on the train.

We arrived in Lethbridge without mishap and met the family. Mother had purchased winter clothing at the Hudson Bay Store and Dad bought camping equipment, axes and more blankets, for which we were thankful; the beautiful Indian summer couldn't last much longer.

On the third day after leaving Lethbridge in our uncovered wagon, we pitched our tent in east

Roy and Mary Orcutt.

218

Mr. and Mrs. Miner Orcutt — Roy, Tom, Del, Don, Bob and Marjorie — 1942.

Calgary. We were to wait there until Dad and the C.P.R. land agent located our future home. After five days Dad came back enthused about the land he had bought from the C.P.R., seven miles from Caroline.

We left early the next morning and the third night we made camp on the north half of section 23 which was to be our home for the next twenty-two years.

Art Bowers, our neighbor, told us there was an empty log house on the Davidson place where he thought we could stay. Bod Davidson let us move in until Dad could build a house. The next day, I carved the date of our arrival to the Caroline country — November 2, 1914.

When we moved into the house, we filled the cracks between the logs with mud, moss and rags. Dad built bunk beds out of dried poplar poles with boards nailed on the bottom and sides to hold the hay and blankets. Dad borrowed an old cook stove and bought a sheet metal heater and some stove pipe. There was a nice spring east of the house where we got our water. It was my duty to cut wood for the stoves and the younger boys' job to fill the wood box which always seemed empty. We hauled large tamarack logs from the swamp and sawed them into two foot chunks with a large crosscut saw.

Rabbits were everywhere that winter; we had rabbit for dinner and then more rabbit for supper; we had rabbit fried, boiled and roasted. Art Bowers gave us some pork and we ground it up with rabbit for sausage, a welcome change. Thanks to the rabbit, partridge and oatmeal, we made it through the winter.

John Keim and Art Bowers helped Dad cut the logs for our house that winter. In the spring I helped build the large log house and we moved into it that fall. We planted a garden that first spring and Walt Williams, my mother's brother, arrived in Innisfail with a boxcar loaded with our household goods and livestock from Montana. Mosquitoes and horse flies by the thousands made their presence known, driving the horses and cattle frantic. We set piles of straw on fire and covered them with green grass and wet hay to make a fifty yard circle of smudges and the animals would take refuge in the smoke.

During nearly all of June, 1915, it rained. The north Saskatchewan River backed up into the Clearwater River and the Clearwater came down the North Raven valley. On the flats, the Raven, normally a small stream, was a half mile wide while on the road from Raven to Caroline, no bridge was visible as the water was above the railing.

Art and Florence Bowers were among the early settlers that homesteaded near Caroline in 1910. Other neighbors were the Keims, Mike Harkens, Scott Bowers (no relation to Art), Devores, Vandermeers, Dials, Davidsons and Rhodes.

At that time, many pioneer girls wore dresses made from flour sacks dyed with different colors. The boys socks were darned and darned again; overalls had patches upon patches. That was when we would look at our 'wish book', the mail order catalogue, until it was out of date and then it was transferred to the 'out house' until only the glossy pages remained.

A small lard pail with a bright green shamrock was a lunch pail much admired at school. We only went five or six months during the warm weather to the Shilo school which was built in 1910 and was two miles from our place. Hugh Devores' dad named the school after the Civil War Battle of Shilo. Miss Mary Fingland was our first teacher and she boarded with the Dials. Alta Russell, Ruth Neal, Bertha McKenna and Tom Cole also taught there. Many of them boarded with my folks. In those days very few pupils ever went beyond the eighth grade, the boys had to go out to work to help support the family. The summer I was fifteen I shocked oats at Scott Bowers' for fifteen cents an hour. That fall I helped thresh with my dad from daylight to lantern light west of Champion for $3.50 a day.

Our young people of today with electrical push button living can't begin to know the heartaches, hard work, hard times, trials and tribulation that the Pioneers went through to build the bridges and railroads, dig the tunnels and smooth out the rough places on the highway of life so that their children might have it easier.

Mother was never idle; she always did more than her share of work. She took care of the farm when Dad and I were away to work. She could harness the horses as well as Dad could, run the binder, stack the grain and do the fall plowing. Grandma Williams, who came to live with us, and Mildred did the cooking and housework. She had a big garden with all kinds of vegetables to can and store in the root cellar for the winter. She and Mrs. Bowers would take a team of horses with a wagon load of kids and go across the swamp to pick cranberries and blueberries. She would can over a hundred quarts and sell some of the berries in town for 25 cents a pound. She was barber, dentist and midwife for many of the neighbors around the neighborhood. One winter day she went fifteen miles in a snowstorm to deliver a baby girl when no one else would go. Ruth Blowers came twelve miles to get an aching tooth pulled. Mother was secretary-treasurer of the Shilo School District for eleven years and received $50 per year for her service.

We had dances, surprise parties, stampedes and ball games for entertainment. In the early days, dances were held in the different school houses — South Fork, Wooler, Crammond, Shilo, Raven, North Raven and Stauffer. Masquerades and box socials were a special delight, with the food boxes auctioned off to the highest bidder. The young fellows would gang up and make some guy really bid high for the privilege of eating supper with the new school teacher or the belle of the ball. The Orcutts and the Lambs had orchestras that played for many of the dances.

The Caroline Hall was built about 1925 with different people supplying the lumber, labor and other materials. My brother, Tom, and I selected good logs for the 2 x 10 floor joists in the hall. Rhodes and Womack sawed the logs at their mill free of charge. Many a delightful time has been spent in that old hall.

We had a good ball team; one game that I remember was when a team came from Milnerton, east of Innisfail, to play against the Raven team at the Hale Lake Stampede. I pitched the game, Ed Clay was the catcher and we got Jack Bugbee to play the outfield. When Jack came up to bat, he walloped a home run clear over the dance hall into Hale Lake and we won the game. Another time we picked a team of players that we took to the Sundre Stampede to play for the prize money on July 1, 1922. I pitched, two of the McKain boys from Red Raven, Ed Clay and Jack Bugbee played, I don't remember who were the other four, Ray McKain pitched one game. Jack was batting and I was waiting my turn when Jack knocked a home run at least five feet inside the foul line, away down among the Indians riding in the outfield. We were sore at the umpire because he called it a foul ball, but we won anyway about twenty-seven to eight, we received about $25 prize money.

When the depression started in 1929. Dad was farming 120 acres, most of it in wheat. Wheat prices kept going down until No.3 wheat sold for 19 cents a bushel and it didn't pay to grow it. With the depression eating up Dad's equity in the

Mildred Orcutt.

C.P.R. land, the folks sold out in 1936 and moved to Washington.

I had a farm one mile west of the log church at Raven and the South Raven River ran through it. I was married to Mary Spaulding June 3, 1937, and we had four children, Effie, Leroy Leslie, Emory Willard and Floria Rose. Effie died at birth and is buried east of the log church at Raven near my Uncle Jesse Orcutt and Grandma Emma Williams.

Reverend Lawrence Hoff and Reverend Nelson Woodroff held services in the Caroline Hall for the Nazarene Church about 1934 I believe. Mary and I helped the Jensens and Miss Thomas, as Pastor, to hold Sunday School and Church at 3 p.m. in the Wooler School.

I wasn't having much success on the farm and so in 1941 we too, decided to sell out and move to Washington. After leaving the farm, I was a pipe fitter for thirty-five years. I am retired now and do some writing.

Mother and Dad are both gone, Dad in 1942 and Mother in 1969. Robert Milton died January 1, 1970, and all three are buried in Olympia, Washington. My sister, Mildred, who was married to Paul Harris of Caroline, died in March, 1937, and she is buried near Yelm, Washington.

Partly taken from the 'Alberta Historical Review'.

Russell Smith

We came to the Caroline area on December 28, 1939, from the Pine Hill district, west of Penhold. I had a quarter section of land there which was very poor and rocky. I had to work away from home, for a farmer by the name of George Moore, to be able to make ends meet, for five years.

In September of 1939 we came out to Raven to visit my mother and father-in-law for two days. They told us George Ennis wanted to sell his farm and there was more adjoining land for sale. So, in November I bought his farm and we moved out in December. One year later I bought a quarter section of land from the C.P.R. This was much better land. We had good crops and there were lots of fence posts, rails and stove wood to get out of the woods in the winter months, to sell or trade for groceries and supplies.

Part of the summer months I worked for the Municipal District, improving much needed roads, in return to pay farm taxes.

We were fortunate to have close and very helpful neighbors. The Rudolph Stange family and the Alexander Helm family lived one half mile east of us. Roy Miller was our close neighbor, to the west of us, and Jack Black and Roy Duncan lived one mile north of us.

Herman Suhr was our postmaster in Caroline. We bought our groceries and supplies from Mrs. Langley's store for sometime, until Wilbur Cross or Howard Harris took over the store business.

Each Saturday night, through the winter months, the neighbors would take a turn at having a house party. Anyone who could play a fiddle, piano, guitar or banjo supplied the best of music, and the rest of us enjoyed dancing.

I was born October 28, 1898 in a log shack north of Innisfail, on a farm, which has been well known as the Daines' farm for years. My parents moved to several places as their family of nine were growing up; finally settling down on a farm in the Centerville district, north of Markerville.

I married Myrtle Ennis, January 7, 1924. We have three children: Eva, Stanley and Harold. They finished their schooling at the Shilo School. Stanley married Rose Johnson, from Caroline, on November 29, 1945, and they started farming the same year. Eva married Bill McColl from Caroline on the same day as Stanley and Rose, and they started farming in 1949. Harold married Joyce Gardner of the Raven district, on December 2, 1947, and they started farming in 1947. They still farm within two miles of each other. Stanley and Rose have five children; Harold and Joyce have five children, and Eva and Bill have two children.

My wife and I retired from our farm in April, 1956, and moved to Red Deer. I was then employed at the Red Deer Hospital until retirement, November 1, 1967. Myrtle passed away in the Red Deer Hospital, August 3, 1968, and was buried in the Innisfail Cemetery. On July 25, 1975, I was remarried to Alice McWade of Red Deer, and we are still living in Red Deer.

Chris Staben

I was born in Germany and came to this country in 1929. I went to work at Edgewood, British Columbia, for three months, then I came to the Caroline district and was hired by O. P. Johnson and did farm work for about three months. After that I worked in lumber camps and then I worked for Ray Dial as a well driller.

I bought the Flatla place in 1944, the S.E. Q. 21-36-5-5. I married May Buchanan in 1945. John was born in 1946 and Jean was born in 1948. Then I bought the N.E. Q. 16-36-5-5 in 1949, which was known as the Scott place. In 1952 I bought the south half of 12-36-5-5 which was known as the Sheffield place. I also bought the N.W. Q. 12-36-5-5. It was known as the Scott Bowers homestead.

John now has the home half section which is in the Shilo district. He married Valerie Chapin. Jean married Stan Boye and they live in the Kevisville district.

David Staben

Dave came to Canada from Germany in 1928. He worked as a hired man in British Columbia for a year then came to Caroline, and worked out for a year. He then settled on the S.W. Q. 14-36-5-5 in 1930 and married Florence Montgomery the same year.

Dave would go down to Turner Valley for gas with a half ton truck, with a bunch of barrels in the back. He would leave early in the morning and get back the next day.

They milked cows and sold cream for $3.00 for

Myrtle and Russell Smith and family.

a five gallon can, and that would buy groceries for the week.

Due to hard times he had to give up the place he was on and took a C.P.R. quarter on 15-36-5-5. This land was cleared with an ax, grub hoe and horses. Most all land work was done with horses as there was no money to buy gas. Later on, Dave bought more land and filed on a homestead.

Dave was a counsellor for the municipality of Raven for ten years, and a director for Calgary Power when it was first put in the rural districts.

Dave had a family of two boys and one girl. He passed away in 1966 at the age of sixty.

Rudolph Stange

Rudolph was born in Germany in 1904 and came to Canada in 1925. He worked on a farm at Ashmont, east of Edmonton, for two years at $300.00 a year. He then went to Edgewood, British Columbia, where he worked for three years on a dairy farm. Chris and Dave Staben later came from Germany and joined him there. In 1929 all three came to settle in the Caroline area.

Rudolph married Ernestine Mahrens in 1930 after she arrived from Germany. They raised five children and all are married. Herman is married to Patricia Bird, John to Helen Katona, Marianne to Rudolph Eisentraut, Elizabeth to Charley Taylor and Irene married Jim Ewan while she was in the air force.

Rudolph and Ernestine (better known as Anne to her friends and neighbors) worked very hard in the hungry thirties, and managed to give each of their children an education which wasn't easy when very little money was available in those days.

Dave Staben and Rudolph both had tractors

Ernestine and Rudolf Stange, Ranko Nanninga, Dave Staben.

and worked together, doing custom work and haying on shares.

In 1958 Rudolph sold his cattle and he and Anne made a trip to Germany. On returning to Canada, Rudolph went into the sheep business with the help of his two sons. They built the flock up to one thousand ewes. They owned eight quarter sections of cultivated and pasture land, seven quarters were fenced with hog wire which meant plenty of hard work and expense. Herman later went into the welding business and John stayed with his dad on the farm.

Rudolph sold a half section of land to his daughter, Marianne, retaining a life time lease on it. He built a house on one of the quarters which is the west half of 6-36-4-5 where he retired in 1968.

The Tose Family
by Cyril Tose

The Tose family, my parents, older brother, younger sister and myself, came to Canada from England and arrived in Calgary in April, 1908. My parents were born and raised in Yorkshire. I was born in Yorkshire in March, 1900. My brother, John, was two years younger, and my sister two years older.

Calgary wasn't too much at that time. I remember the first street car being unloaded — must have been around 1909. My brother, George, was born in Calgary in 1909, so we were a family of four children.

I went to the Old Alexandria School for awhile. I guess it is still there on 9th Avenue East. We lived on what was then Maggie Street. I think it is now 8th Street East. In 1910 we moved out east to some lots Dad bought, at that time called Golden Rose Park. We were some of the first out there — all open prairie. It is now owned by the city of Calgary. Dad worked at different jobs, once in the C.P.R. shops and in the Cement Plant in Exshaw. He got acquainted with Mr.

Ernestine and Rudolf Stange, Florence and Chris Staben, Dave Staben and Eric Harder.

Mr. and Mrs. Edward Tose seated — standing: Cyril, John, Florence and George in front, 1915.

Sawmill powered by steam, Tose's mill, late 1920.

Vandermeer who had taken a homestead at Caroline and he went with him to see what he could find. He got a homestead, S. W. Q. 30-36-5-5, presently owned by Mr. Rea. In 1911 we decided to move up here. Dad and my older brother stayed in Calgary; Mother, sister Annie, brother George and myself started out from Calgary with a single pony and democrat with a milk cow tied behind. Three weeks later we got here and set up a tent. We were sitting on top of the world — nothing but bush! We stayed awhile and went back to Calgary, leaving the cow with a neighbor, Mr. Dresser. It didn't take as long to get back to Calgary as it did to come up here.

Later in the year, about December, we decided to return to the homestead, so with a team, hayrack and wagon loaded with all the goods, we started out for Caroline. Mother, sister and younger brother went by train to Innisfail. We started out hoping to make it by Christmas, but the load was heavy and the roads or trails as they were known then, were tough going and the team was not the best in the west! Joe Vandermeer, about my age, travelled with us. We spent Christmas Eve in a big old barn a couple miles west of Olds. It was stormy, but there was lots of feed for the horses.

Travelling through the snow is not good travelling, but we finally made it to Bert Rhodes' with snow up to the hubs. We got some good horses from Bert. We ended up at Bert Dresser's where we had New Year's dinner. Herman Nass and Bert (both bachelors) were not used to the meat that Mother cooked with Christmas cake and pudding. They really stuffed themselves, but paid for it the next day.

After that we moved up to the homestead about a mile and a half and set up a tent. Next was the job of getting out logs for a house. Fred Hobbs whom we had met on the summer trip, got a homestead about the same time, (the place that Stan Loomis is now on), had a team of oxen

so they got logs out for both places. The oxen were slow, but sure. We stayed in a tent that winter and built the house the next year.

We had spare time in the summer and had several picnics down at the Raven River where we caught lots of fish. We also had picnics at the Raven River at what was then known as 'Finkles Grove' just west of the present Raven Campgrounds. There was an open space where ball games and foot races, etc., were held. There were just trails through the bush, but everyone came from miles around. There was a pole bridge across the Raven and when you got there when the water was high, you had to wait until the water went down before crossing, for the poles would be floating — so just camp and wait.

The next year, the men went to work at Calgary. The Hobbs' had a son, George, two years older than me. We had to go to the Raven Store for the mail, so we would hitch up the oxen and get there and back in three days — lots of fun! George (Judd as he was called) and I, had

Tose's outfit threshing on Elick Elickson's place in the 1920's.

223

the time of our lives. He is the uncle of George Hobbs who now farms at Ricinus. I believe he is now at Innisfail.

Our neighbors were Joe and Tom Roper to the west. Tom's son, John, still farms there. Vandermeers lived to the east and Russel Dial to the southeast. Russel's son, Ray, was well known at Innisfail. Hal lived at Raven and Robert has a campground west at Ricinus.

In 1914 or 1915 the mail started to come from Rocky Mountain House. Charlie Hankinson had the contract to haul it and my brother, John, worked for him. Charlie lived about half way to Rocky. He would get the mail and bring it from Rocky to his place and then John would take it from there to Stauffer and to Caroline. He would stay overnight at Harvey Langley's, one half mile south of the present town, and return the next day.

My brother, John, passed away in 1919. Mother passed away in 1924, my sister in 1938 and Dad in 1966 at age ninety-three years.

My sister married in 1918 to Edward Budden. They had a family of four boys and four girls. One boy, Cecil, was killed overseas in Germany in World War II. George Budden farms half way to Rocky and raises Angus cattle. Bill lives at Lacombe, Nellie and Bob are in California, Bessie is in British Columbia, Jane in Olds and Daisy farms at Butte.

My brother, George, married Gladys Buck and had two children, John and George. John is at present farming at Caroline and George is in the north country. Brother George is living about fifteen miles west and south of Caroline and is in the sawmill business.

I enlisted in the army in January, 1941, in the 5th Army Division Workshop R.C.O.C. and served fifty-seven months, almost five years. I returned home and was discharged in October,

1945. I served in the United Kingdom, Central Mediterranean and Continental Europe. I received the 1939-45 Star, Italy Star, France and Germany Star, Defense of Britian Medal, Canadian Volunteer Service Medal and clasp and the MID Oak Leaf.

In 1946 I married Mrs. Jessie Bertram and together we raised a family of all girls, all well adapted to the use of machinery from wheelbarrows to heavy machinery. Connie is interested in cows and pigs; Florrie at present is working on oil rigs, rough necking; Jessie is at Calgary and interested in horses; Linda is farming and in cattle and Celia is in Calgary at Mount Royal College as maintenance supervisor. We have twelve grandchildren.

The Vandermeer Family

Mr. and Mrs. Vandermeer came from Holland to Chesley, Ontario in about 1906. They moved to Calgary in 1909. They had ten children, one of which died in Holland. Mr. Vandermeer worked at the Cement Works in Calgary.

In 1911 Mrs. Vandermeer and the children came to a homestead in the Caroline area until Mr. Vandermeer was killed at work in Calgary. Mrs. Vandermeer put the younger children in the Convent at Midnapore that was run by Father Lacombe. She worked in the National Hotel making beds and doing floors.

In 1918 the family moved back to Caroline to

A good catch of fish — Cyril Tose, Edward Tose and John VanLeest.

L.-R. — Mary, Lena and Cora Taylor.

224

the Charles Hall farm which was called Sunnyslope Ranch. They had a few cows and horses.

In 1917, Harry, the oldest boy, joined the army until the end of the war. He joined with an army friend, Charles Taylor from Prentice, and went to California for three years. When he returned Harry helped the rest of the family to cut hay on sloughs in the area wherever they could to get enough feed for the livestock.

In the winter the barn burned down and they lost eleven cows and some horses. The family moved to Markerville for awhile until they could get a new barn built. The neighbors all helped with labor and material. Gerald, who was only eleven at the time, stayed with Cecil Birdikin at Markerville for the winter where he looked after Cecil's livestock and did other chores.

Joe got a homestead on what is now Walter McDonald's home. The price of the land was ten dollars per quarter — provided you could prove up on it. Then Joe and Harry went to work in the mines at Saunders Creek where they were both killed. Mrs. Vandermeer and the other children finished proving up on the farm and got title to it.

Mary had married Thurn Palmer and moved to California. They had eight children. Margaret married Andy Kliener from the Caroline area. They lived most of their lives in Calgary where Andy was a painter. They had four children. Lena married Charles Taylor and they homesteaded what is now Bernard Williams'

place. Charlie worked for 'Buzz' Herold for a number of years until they sold the farm and moved to Calgary where Charlie worked at the Brewery. They had two children.

Carrie married Charles McDonald. They spent their honeymoon via pack-horse along the Columbia Ice Fields. One of the horses fell in a crevice and was there two days before they could get him out with the help of a Forest Ranger. The other horse died from eating locoweed and they had to walk most of the way home.

Charlie worked in the mine for awhile, then moved to Chilliwack, B.C. for a few years. They again returned to farm at Caroline. They had five children.

Pete was an avid horseman. He lived most of his life in Calgary, working on the Pat Burns Ranch. In 1926 at the Calgary Stampede he became the World Saddle Bronc Rider. The Prince of Wales who was in the audience asked to meet him. He took his gold cigarette case from his pocket and offered it to the young cowboy. Pete said "I'm sorry Sir, I don't smoke". When the Prince returned to England he took Pete with him. At Windsor Castle he gave a command performance for the King and Queen. He was presented with a gold watch and belt buckle, and received a lot of acclaim in the British Press where they referred to him as "The Prince's Cowboy". He was killed in a car accident with his 4th wife in 1977.

Gerald remained in the Caroline area where he farmed and worked as a school bus driver, taxi driver, and bailiff for the sheriff. He married Alma Sarc who taught school at Shilo and Caroline. They had four children — Rosalie who married Marten Jorgensen of Olds — they have two children — John and his wife Linda and their two children live in Calgary — Bob who married Maureen Dean farms in the Butte district — they have three children — Ivan and

L.-R. — Mary, Charlie and Cora Taylor.

L.-R. — World's Champion Cowboy — Pete Vandermeer and Edward, Prince of Wales (center) the other man unknown — 1926.

his wife Sherry have two children and live in Swan Hills, Alberta. Alma died in 1969, and Gerald is now married to the former Fern Gardner of Caroline.

Conrad died at the age of twelve from a fall from a horse.

Times were pretty rough in the early years. Livestock froze to death and feed was scarce. Supplies had to be brought from Innisfail with a team and wagon until a store was built at Caroline.

Morris Williams Family

Mr. Williams was born in Bontnyedd, Caernarvon, Wales, in 1885. His father was a sea captain who lost his life when he went down with his ship, in the Irish Sea. His mother, whose maiden name was Brown, lived all her life in Wales where she died in her nineties.

Mr. Williams came to Canada in 1912, settling in Calgary. He served in World War I as an army medic, was wounded, and received the Military Medal for bravery in action. When the war ended, he returned to Calgary and became employed as a shipper with Plunkett and Savage, fruit and vegetable wholesalers. In 1921 he met and married Dorothy Irene Smythe of London, England, who came to Canada to climax a correspondence between the two, which came about through a mutual friend.

In 1934 they moved to Caroline with their four children and settled on a quarter section two miles east and one and one half miles north of the townsite. Times were hard and Mr. Williams and his sons cut posts to use as trade for farm machinery at one to three and one half cents a post. They picked blueberries in the summer in exchange for groceries, and when they did have beef to sell, they received one and one half cents a pound for it. The children attended Shilo School and helped with chores and farming the land. As Mr. Williams was not a mechanically inclined man, it was fortunate that the sons learned early to repair the old machinery which was constantly breaking down. He would shake his head in disbelief when they put all the parts together again!

To further supplement their income, Mr. Williams spent some years back in Calgary, working for the Royal Canadian Air Force at Number Ten Repair Depot. He worked extremely hard, and together, with his wife, produced a phenomenal vegetable garden, both in size and harvest — much was given away to needy neighbors each year. As well, they took great pride in their beautiful flower beds that surrounded the old log house.

In fact, the old house was the scene of many a house party over the years, with friends and neighbors helping by bringing sandwiches and cakes and supplying the music for dancing. In 1945 a reception for the enlisted men of the Shilo district was held there and over one hundred people sat down to eat. Ladies of the area had baked desserts of all sorts, and roasted chickens, along with all the trimmings. This dinner was followed by a dance accompanied by music of the guitar and violin played by the McColls.

The Williams' became very active members of St. Mary's Anglican Church in Caroline, and Mrs. Williams was also active in the Shilo Ladies Club as well as a member of the Canadian Legion Auxiliary.

On October 3, 1971, they celebrated their Golden Wedding Anniversary with an open house for all their family and friends. Shortly after, and in that month, Mr. Williams passed away at the age of eighty-six, and in 1975 was followed by Mrs. Williams also at eighty-six. They are interred in the Caroline Cemetery.

Of their four children, Bernard stayed on to farm the home place and property across the road. After serving in the Royal Canadian Air Force for four years, he married Mildred Mayhew of Raven. They have a son and daughter and one grandchild. The eldest son, Wynne, lives in Calgary where he owns and operates a furniture finishing business. He married Bessie Brown, daughter of another oldtime Caroline family. They have one son, two daughters and two grandchildren. Wynne was a member of the Royal Canadian Air Force during World War II and served in Canada for three and one half years. David, the youngest son, lives in Calgary and is employed by Gulf Canada Limited as a draftsman. He married Neata Hudgin of Cupar, Saskatchewan. They have one son and daughter. Mary, the only girl, is married to Vic Johnson. They have one son and live in California.

The Laurence Wise Family
by Leona (Wise) Friesz

My father Laurence Wise came with Grandfather Wise from Nobleville, Indiana, U.S.A. to Rockyford, Alberta. My mother Lucille was born in Silex, Iowa. She came to Rockyford also and met Laurence Wise. They were married in 1920 and lived on Grandfather Wise's farm at Rockyford until Grandfather passed away in 1933 and the farm was sold.

In 1936 we moved to Caroline area NW-23-36-5-5 known as the Roy Orcutt farm and now owned by Andy Machan. We moved by trucks with all our possessions including five milk cows, a team of horses, a few pigs, old 'Molly' our saddle pony, a shetland pony, dog 'Jiggs' and a buggy. Our house was a new four room bungalow with

Laurence and Lucille Wise.

Back Row L.-R.: Mr. Beck, Mort and Stanley Grieve, Stanley and Svend Beck. Front Row L.-R.: Laurence and Leona Wise, Mrs. Grieve, Mrs. Wise, Beth Black, Ray Bowers and Margaret Wise.

plain shiplap boards on the walls. I well remember the many hours spent chopping wood, carrying water and doing chores at the barn and garden.

When we came to Caroline my sister Margaret was fifteen years old and Edna Mae was three years old. Brothers Donald and Emmett were eight and six and I was thirteen. Mrs. Nellie Edwards who had been our friend for many years suggested we come to Caroline. She had cooked for Grandfather Charles Wise in earlier years. We spent many Sundays at her farm riding her saddle horse. One day Donald and I were riding under her clothes line. I rode away leaving him dangling on the line.

We drove to Shilo School which was near to the farms of the Staben and Flatla families. Here we met new friends — Keims, Bowers, McCalls, Blacks, Reddings, Murrays, Buchanans, Becks, Armitages, Grieves, Nanningas, McLeans, Williams and others. Our teacher was Miss Alma Sarc. Another teacher was Miss Clark. Sports

were softball, fist fights, snowballing, and passing notes in school. These years, known as the depression, make us appreciate the conveniences we have now.

Everyone was 'hard-up', and make-over and make-do was the guide line. We had meat once a week, lots of macaroni, Johnnie Cake, our own chickens and vegetables. In the summer we picked berries — hard work but fun too. Mother baked bread twice a week, and the cream we shipped bought the groceries. Margaret was a good sewer and was able to make over clothes that were given to us. Donald and Emmet wore bib overalls.

Edna Mae was our singer. Margaret and Donald played the piano, while I had fun with the guitar. During winter we had house parties, danced and sang songs with Doren and Madeline Wilson, the Murrays and McLean families. Our closest neighbors were Bowers, Armitages, Keims, Blacks and Murrays.

When we were ready for high school, Margaret went to Dickson and boarded at the Dormitory. I went to Rockyford and stayed with Aunt Agnes and Uncle Bert Erswell. Later Margaret worked for Nelson Brothers of Markerville. I attended high school in Innisfail and worked for my board at Oscar Lundgren's and later for the Krussell family. Our friends included Harold and Ken Rhodes of Markerville and the Savage boys from Raven. We spent some weekends back at Caroline. The second war was on and we saw many of our friends in uniform, and later go overseas.

The following summer I went to work on the farm of Mr. and Mrs. Noel Slack near Dalemead, Alberta. Here I met their nephew Alfred Friesz. We were married a year later in Innisfail, Dec. 17, 1942. When the Slack's retired we rented their farm.

In May 1942 Margaret married Harold Henrickson. Jobs were scarce, so Harold joined the army, trained in Ontario and went overseas with the Regina Rifle Regiment.

In the spring of 1942 my parents sold the farm

to Doug and Ethel Montgomery. Daddy worked in Atlee and Ardenode, Alberta as a Wheat Pool Agent.

We continued to farm at Dalemead and later bought the General Store. My father died in January, 1952, and Mother and the boys moved to Calgary.

Edna Mae married Roy Hahle of Carseland in 1952. They have three children, Glen, Brenda and Mark. Edna Mae and Roy now live in Calgary.

Donald married Ruth Haugen Nov. 1953. They have six children — Darlene, Valerie, Terry, Janice, Rickie and Lynn. They all live in Seattle, Washington.

Emmett married Lil Rogers Feb. 1955. They live in Calgary

In March 1963 we sold the store and moved to Calgary. Alfred has had health problems, and now works for Block Bros. Real Estate. We have four children — Sharlene who has three children, and lives in Calgary, Marvin who has two children and lives in Carseland, Gary is also married and lives in Carseland, Leslie lives with us.

Margaret and Harold live in Calgary and have one daughter, Linda. Mother will be eighty-two in June, 1979 and lives in a senior Citizen's Apartment in Calgary.

Looking back over the years, we appreciate good times and modern living. We shall always remember the good friends and happy times we had in the Caroline area.

The Wyant Family

by Daisy Harris

My parents, Alansing and Amelia Wyant, lived in Wisconsin. My brothers and sisters, Lawrence, Clarice, May, Daisy (me) and George were all born there. We had a half sister, Tessie, from my Dad's former marriage.

We left Wisconsin in 1910 and moved to Inverness, Montana, where Frank was born and where Tessie married Bert Yaple.

We left Inverness in 1914 to move to Alberta. Mom went back to visit in Wisconsin while the rest of us came to Innisfail. Tessie and Bert came along to mind us children in Mom's absence.

I remember the long train ride when we moved. My parents had bought May and I each a doll for on the train. The girls wouldn't let me play with mine because it had no clothes.

When we arrived in Innisfail, we lived there for two or three months and while there, we went to school. Dad came out to Caroline and bought the C.P.R. land south of the Shilo School. He started a log house and put in a lot of posts, he

Lansing and Amelia Wyant.

then decided to let it go and file on a homestead. This land is now owned by Leslie Katona.

I remember when Dad came for us in the wagon to bring us to Caroline. On the way, I asked him what kind of trees these were, he said they were pine trees. I didn't say anything, but I watched for pineapples all the rest of the way.

We lived on what was then Stevenson's place that winter, and then we moved on to a place owned by Charlie Hall, north of the Shilo School.

There were two Irish families living north of us and one of their little girls fell into a boiler of water and was badly burned. Mom used to go over everyday to dress her burns until they healed. Other neighbors that we had were Coberleys and Devores.

When we moved to our homestead, we met the Dial family who lived on a quarter south of us. Mrs. Dial was like a second mother to me, she was a very kind and gentle person. When Mr. Dial would drive into our yard, his first greeting was always , "Anyone killed or crippled?"

We moved to Rocky Mountain House in 1920 after the hard winter. We had no feed so we bought the black birch willow that Jim Leask had mowed off of his land before plowing it the fall before. It still had green leaves on it and we

Daisy, Frank, May and George Wyant.

B.R.L.R. — Curtis, Joan, Gene, Madell, Richard. Seated — Daisy and Howard, Patsy in front.

paid $5.00 a load for it. The horses were glad to have it. We didn't lose any stock, but they were sure thin.

After moving to Rocky Mountain House, Dad worked for the C.N.R. He died in 1929 at Nordegg where he had been transferred.

Lawrence had gone to Hythe, Alberta, where he homesteaded and lived until he died in 1931.

Clarice married Harley Cooper and they went to Florida.

May married George Sparks and they lived in Rocky Mountain House when they were first married. Then George homesteaded the farm where Hugh Oliver lives. Mrs. Charlie Brown of Caroline was a sister to George.

Frank and Mother moved to Hythe after Dad died. Frank married Violet Craeghton and they and their family still live there.

Mom passed away in Edmonton in 1956 and both she and Dad are buried in the Pine Grove Cemetery in Rocky Mountain House.

I married Howard Harris in 1924 and we had six children. Eugene lives in Drayton Valley. Madell lives on Pender Island in British Columbia. Curtis and Richard are both married and live in Kelowna. Joan is married and lives in Sylvan Lake. Patricia lives here in Caroline and is married to Rick Jones who is an oil driller. They have two children, Richard and Tammy Lyn.

South Fork

Church of The Nazarene

The work of the Nazarene Church in the Caroline area dates back to the 1930's. Honorable mention must be made in memory of Mrs. Cynthia Langley who held Sunday School for the children in her own home and also in rooms above her store. Several student and resident pastors from the church at Raven came out and visited and held Sunday School and church services in some of the homes and in the rooms above Mrs. Langley's store. Some of the early men were Laurence Hoff, Nelson Woodruff, John Therow and Rev. Fromberg. Many times they would stay at Mrs. Langley's and visit in the community.

Miss Olive Thomas came to Raven about 1938. As well as holding services in Raven on Sunday mornings she began to hold a Sunday School and service in the afternoon in the Wooler School house 4 miles west of Caroline. One of her helpers who lived with her and travelled with her was Mae Larsen (now Mrs. Ralph Lougheed of Benalto). They would ride horseback back and forth between Raven and Caroline.

From about 1941 to early in 1943 Reverend and Mrs. Carson Christiansen lived at Raven and

Original Caroline Church of the Nazarene built in 1949.

also continued the services at the Wooler School house.

From 1943-1945 Rev. and Mrs. Howard Griffin continued the services at Raven and Wooler School, and then extended their circuit to the Stauffer Hall. Their Sunday was a very full day having both Sunday School and service in the morning at Raven, Wooler School in the afternoon, and then an evening service at the Stauffer Hall. The road in those days left much to be desired for ideal travelling — especially in the rain. There was no gravel then.

There was not a pastor at Raven for a short time after Rev. Griffin left. It seems as though the services at Wooler School were dropped about this time. In May of 1946 Rev. and Mrs. George Wall came to Raven and also Caroline. They held services in Mrs. Langley's vacant store building which then stood on the corner lot where the Dept. of Highways Building now stands. During the mid-fortys students from Prairie Bible Institute came out and held Vacation Bible School in the Community Hall. They were the Misses Bertha Montgomery, Ethel Doan and Rosemary Kaiser. During the winter of 1947 Rev. Wall moved on, and the following

Nazarene Church in Caroline.

231

Church of the Nazarene, present building built in 1969.

spring Rev. and Mrs. Thomas Hermon began coming out from the Bible College in Red Deer. By this time the congregation at Raven decided that their numbers were few and that they would come and join fellowship with the Caroline group, so the Legion Hall was rented for services.

During the summer of 1948 Mrs. Cynthia Langley donated a corner lot, 2 block south of Main Street for a church building (the present church site). Donations of cash and labor were received from many people in the town and community for the erection of a church. It was the understanding then, and still is the policy, that the church be open for anyone who wishes to use its facilities for weddings or funerals. Construction of the first church began in August, 1948 with Bert Marchant as head carpenter and much volunteer labor. The two-roomed parsonage was moved from Raven and set on the same lot on the north side of the church. Two rooms were added. Rev. and Mrs. Tom Hermon became Caroline's first resident pastor. Dedication and official organization day was June 30, 1949 with 17 Charter members. 14 of these were by transfer from the Raven group. Six of this original number still remain here.

LIST OF RESIDENT PASTORS AT CAROLINE NAZARENE CHURCH

Rev. Thomas Herman — May, 1947 - June 30, 1950
Rev. James Watson — July 1, 1950 - June 30, 1951
Rev. Harold Hoffman — July 1, 1951 - June 30, 1953
Rev. Wolfe Grunau — July 1, 1953 - June 30, 1956
Rev. Norman Falk — July 1, 1956 - June 30, 1961
Rev. Russell Quantz — March, 1962 - July 15, 1967
Rev. Cecil Geiger — Sept. 1, 1967 - Oct. 21, 1973
Rev. Gerald Austin — July 1, 1974 - Apr. 30, 1976
Rev. Norman Ens — May 1, 1976

Facilities of the first building became inadequate as years went by, so plans were made to expand. In 1961 the lot just north of the church lot

was purchased from Mr. and Mrs. Wallace Reese who had formerly operated a grocery store on the site. The manse was moved on to a new basement on this lot, adding two more rooms and making it into a modern home.

November 11, 1968 after the Armistice Day service, work began to move the first church building off the property in preparation for erection of a new building. Head Carpenters were Richard Jensen from Spruce View, and Leonard Kanten from Caroline. Work went well with 'again' much volunteer labor. This sanctuary was dedicated May 4, 1969. 400 people attended. The church has always received with appreciation, community support, not only at times of construction but through the intervening years as well.

St. Mary's Anglican Church of Caroline

The first Minister we had in Caroline was the Reverend D.S. Pitts B.A. in 1952. Rev. Pitts was the Rector of St. Mark's Church in Innisfail and had been coming here for several years visiting the parishioners in their homes. When he suggested we start our own church we were enthusiastic. The Services were held in the old Legion Hall. The Legion did not charge for this.

The first Rector's warden was Mr. Don Bowden and the People's Warden was Mr. Proudler. Mrs. Elsie Bowden taught Sunday School, and continued to do so until she was 70 years of age.

Everyone was surprised and thrilled when more than two hundred people turned out for the first Mother's Day Sunday service.

On May 8, 1955 we had a visit from the RT. Rev. G. R. Calvert D.D. Lord Bishop of Calgary. He confirmed 6 adults and 3 girls.

The present church building was originally a school room in Caroline. It was purchased from the school Division in the fall of 1960 and was moved to the present site in the spring of 1961. It was remodelled by the Rector, the Rev. L.S. Thurston, and the men of the parish.

The altar and communion rails in the church were given during the incumbency of the Rev. Pitts by the Anglican Church of the Penhold Air Base, R.C.A.F. The organ was given to us by Mrs. Gilbert Kanten of Caroline. The Prayer Desk was presented to us by the parish of Bashaw.

The first service in the new church was held on Oct. 15, 1961. This was Harvest Thanksgiving Sunday, and the church was decorated with fresh flowers and vegetables. There were even fresh ripe strawberries (a great rarity in Caroline in those days) from the garden of one of the Parishioners.

May this building always be a place of Divine

Worship where people may give thanks and glorify God for His love and inesteemable gifts to all of us.

The Rev. Pitts left in Oct. 1955 and the Rev. Austin from Rocky Mountain house took his place on Nov. 22, 1955. Rev. Thurston took over on Dec. 6, 1959. The Rev. B.A. Rathbone came on Aug. 10, 1965. Our present rector Rev. A.H. Collier came Jan. 11, 1970.

St. Mary's true to its tradition of community service, has made land available for the new Senior Citizen's Drop-In Center. This will be a place where all the surviving pioneers living in this district and mentioned in this book will be able to meet and to enjoy themselves during the remaining years of their lives.

Community Hall

During the 1920's as more settlers moved into the Caroline area a small group of people with a great deal of foresight decided that a community hall was a much needed facility in the growing community.

A meeting was held at the Wooler School to try and organize the idea into an actual fact. From this beginning came the Community Hall.

It was operated on a shareholders basis. Most of the material was native lumber and all labour was donated. The major cash outlay was for the hardwood floor. The land was donated by Tom Roper with the understanding that the land should only be used for a recreational purpose.

The hall was completed in 1926 and the first dance was near Christmas of that year. An official opening dance was held in the spring of 1927 and as far as can be determined, the first wedding dance was that of Joy and Catherine Fay.

Over the years it has served the community very well. It has seen its share of joyous and sad gatherings of community residents. It was, on one occasion used as a clinic and temporary operating theatre where tonsils and appendix were removed.

School fairs were held in it, political meetings and courts have been held there. It has been used for Christmas concerts, amateur theatre, religious meetings and for funerals. Wrestling and boxing matches have been held there. It may be inappropriate, but it is certainly truthful to mention that it has seen many rowdy brawls in its day.

Interior of Caroline Community Hall.

Over the years it has been moved over and put on a basement. Modern heating and wash rooms have been installed and other modifications made. Most of these were done by members of Service Clubs of Caroline.

In recent years there have been some rumblings in the community that it has served its day, and is an "old relic" and should be demolished. It is the hope of the writer that the Community Hall will still be useful in some capacity in future years. It has a character all its own and has been an integral part of the community. It stands as a memorial to the men and women who recognized the need for it and who struggled so valiantly to bring it into being.

South Fork (now the Caroline School)

The Caroline school is now composed of the following districts — Caroline 1803, North Caroline, Shilo, Crooked Creek, Pine View, Crammond, Ricinus, Dovercourt, Chedderville, Clear Creek, Wooler and Hazeldell. The schools of Chedderville and Crammond of the present year 1962-63 have grades from one to six only.

The first school of Caroline was built in the winter of 1907-08 by Charles Lineham and George MacGrady. It stood one mile south of the Post Office on the south side of the Raven River. It was first called the South Fork School. The first teacher was a veteran teacher from Texas, W. H. Devore. Two adult pupils were Mr. E. Elingson and Mr. W. C. Browning.

TEACHERS AT THE SOUTH FORK SCHOOL

Miss Gawkie, 1918; Miss Nibister, 1919 for only two months; Miss Ruth Neal, 1919; Mr. Guy Mount, 1920, 1921; Miss Mary Waterhouse, 1922; Mr. James Fullerton, 1923; Miss Marie Edlund, 1924, 1925; Miss Blanche Olander, 1926; Mr. Hood, 1927; Miss Elizabeth Kaske, 1928; Mr. Bill Hackett, 1929, 1930; Miss Moe, 1931; Mrs. Anna Demenuk, 1938; Miss Priscilla Mewha, 1941, 1942; Mr. Earle Farris, 1942, 1943; Mrs. M. Shaw, 1944, 1945, 1946; Mr. A. Buchanan, 1947.

Below is an attendance Register for South Fork S.D. This we also think is a register of the first class taught by Mr. W. H. Devore.

South Fork S.D. No. 1803. Attandance for the Month of Feb. 22 to Mar. 19, 1909, W. H. Devore — Teacher.

Pupil's Register Number	Names of Pupils	Daily 1st week	5th week	Total Attendance
1	Rebecca Langley			20
2	Gussie Van Arsdale			9
3	John Browning			20
4	Tessie Browning			20
5	Hugh Devore			20
6	Fred Devore			20
7	Lulu Dial			12
8	Henry Baldwin			19
9	Merriet Baldwin			19
10	Esther Baldwin			18
11	Vilao Baldwin			11
12	Richard Lynum			20
13	Maggie Van Arsdale			8

Aggregate attendance for the month 218
Number teaching days school was open during the month 20
Aggregate days' attendance for the month 218
Average attendance for the month 10.9
Percentage of attendance for the month .... .83
I hereby certify that the above record of attendance is correct in every particular.

W. H. Devore
Teacher

Sunday School at South Fork School about 1915.

234

South Fork School.

Teacher Anna Anderson — Back Row: Gordon Johnson, John Radik, Maurice Miller, John VanLeest, Daisy Brown, Carmen Bingham, John Roper, Mary Radik, Margaret Johnson, Richard Bingham, Rose Johnson — Front Row: May VanLeest, Ellen Johnson, Earl Quinn, Florence Johnson, Marjie Buchanan and Edwin Tricker.

South Fork School in 1915. Gladys and Lincoln Langley, Cecil McFilemey, teacher Miss Fingland, Robert McFilemey, Myrland Hunter, Iris Gilbert, Howard Harris, John Browning, Ned McFilemey, Glen Dial, Myrtle Langley, Gussie and Maggie VanArsdale, Joy Fay, Hattie VanArsdale, Lillian Vetter, Eunice Fay, Violet and Theodore VanArsdale, Grace McFilemey, Arthur Dial, ?, Jess McFilemey, Clement Gilbert and Ruth Hunter.

South Fork Class in 1942 after the old school was closed — Building in background later converted to Caroline Legion.

Caroline School, class of 1949 — Back row — Merdie McGrandle, Everett Bowers, Howard Pittendreigh, Richard Harris, Mrs. Shaw (teacher), Leonard McGrandle, Robert Anger, Roger Taylor, Howard Mitten, Stanley Huffman — Middle row — Beverly McGrandle, Eileen Pittendreigh, Gladys Huffman, Virginia Stewart, Margaret Shaw, ?, Shirley Price, Edith Carter, Dorothy Chapin, Joyce Huffman, ?, Myrna Taylor — Front row — Arthur Shaw, Howard Hansen and Harold Hansen.

South Fork School — Back Row: Teacher Miss Moe, Dennis Brown, June Wilson — 2nd Row: Daisy and Bessie Brown — 3rd Row: Margaret Johnson, Doreen Wilson, (kneeling) John Roper, Gordon Johnson.

Caroline Grade Seven History Project

The story of Caroline is very interesting. We, the Grade Seven class of 1962-63 have chosen it as a project in Community Economics. We have collected our information from residents still living and from the article written by Roy Devore, published by the Red Deer Advocate of Sept. 29th to Oct. 20, 1954.

The following are the names of the students of the grade seven class for the year 1962-63; Curtis Bell, Stanley Boye, Dennis Brown, Thelma Budden, Edgar Bird, Beverley Burk, Corinne Ceasor, Irene Craig, Marvin Cressman, Roma Cressman, Kenneth Dezall, William Drummond, Ricky Fifield, Earl Graham, Bruce Hallock, Patsy Harris, Eric Hazen, Edwin Kubik, Keith Leavitt, Bard Keckie, Terry Leinweber, John Lougheed, Ruth May, Edna McKie, Patricia Moberg, Amber Moreau, Wayne Oliver, Muriel Standford, Allen Smith, Vinnie Tose, Marjorie Waunch, Lorin Williams and Carole Wilson.

Early Settlers in Caroline

In 1903, Andy Ross filed claim in the Butte district on the N.E.¼ 18-37-5-5, which is now Roy Leavitt's land. Also about the same time Mr. Knef filed claim on the S.W. ¼ 32-35-4-5, which is now Mr. Morrice's property. Leo W. Brooks filed claim on July 18, 1904 on the N.E. ¼ 36-36-5-5 but did not prove it up and it is now government land. Goodman Goodmanson filed claim on September 30, 1904 on the S.W. ¼ 28-36-5-5 but also did not prove up his land. This land is now owned by Mr. J. Vandermeer. Mel Ferguson claimed land in 1904 and died in 1961, living most of the years of his life in Caroline.

In 1906, Mr. W. H. Devore staked claim to 22-36-5-5 with his wife and three sons, Roy, Fredrick and Hugh. They lived in a tent until a house was built for them. This property is now owned by Mr. C. Standford. About the same time Mr. Comstock and his father settled at Butte. He drove the cattle out from Red Deer while his father drove the wagon load of possesions to their homestead. They found many arrowheads and Buffalo bones on this land so it is believed it was the scene of many buffalo hunts. Edwin Budden also came in 1906, to settle on N.W. 36-36-6-5, now the home of Mr. E. Hoare and family.

In 1907, Floyd Buck came with his parents to settle on 17-37-5-5 which Mr. Wilbur Stainbrook now farms. In 1906 or 7 Mr. Hagget staked claim on land three and one half miles west of the present village of Caroline. This land is now owned by Mr. Peters. Mrs. Peters is the daughter of Mr. M. Ferguson. Mrs. Graves is another one that we are not too sure about, she came in 1906 or 7. She homesteaded Mr. Walt Schraders'. Mr. Jackie Schrader now lives there. Ed Fleet came then also. He settled on the N.W. 28-35-5. He had his hand mangled when his horses, on a binder, ran away. Mr. Schrader also owns this land. Mr. Fleet was the first man to have a plow in the early days.

In 1908, Mr. H. A. Langley settled near the south fork of the Raven River where they opened the first store and post office and named it after their only child, a daughter, Rebecca Caroline Langley. That child, Rebecca Caroline, now lives at present in the village named in her honor but we now know her as Mrs. S. Nelson. Their early homestead is now owned by Mr. M. Steene.

Lynn Gilbert was a husky man with the ability to box, so it is believed he broke jail in the States and came here to homestead N.E. 32-35-5-5 in 1908. He left in about 1914 or 15 after aquiring a land title. He came back in 1920 with Ivan Graham and others. His wife drove one wagon while he drove another. Ivan Graham and his brother Wilbur Graham drove others. Lynn Gilbert held several boxing titles in the States. Mr. Fredrick MacLean now owns his land. Adam Lade came into this part but he didn't stay for long. Fredrick Kreisch was a light heavy weight wrestler. He never acquired a land title. Bill Gans, Ezee Zabber and Dick Agnow all secured titles but disappeared. These men were believed to have come looking for cheap land and a place to hide their past. Some of them came for furs and a quiet trapper's life away from the hustle and bustle of city life.

The Government and the C.P.R. advertised about the land between Calgary and Edmonton. This land was supposed to be the best land for miles around.

Their first homes were tents, underground dugouts, log houses and shacks.

The first lumber used in homestead houses was produced by a portable sawmill owned by Daniel McGrandle.

Fishing and Hunting

Some of the fish that were caught were graylings, suckers, trout, pike and perch. The province stocked the streams as early as 1941. From 1941 to 1950 there were 89,000 fingerlings, 171,000 yearlings and 538 two-year olds put into Alberta streams. They built a fish hatchery in the forties which was named the "Raven Rearing Ponds". Mr. Garfield Thompson was the first caretaker and Mr. C. Wren now feeds the young fish.

Most of the people only had a .22 rifle. Some of the animals they shot with these rifles were beaver, mink, muskrat, squirrel, rabbits, prairie chickens, partridges, fool hens, ducks, geese and weasels.

For larger game they used a repeating rifle but only a couple of people had them. They were the late Arthur Bowers, and the late William Womack. There was no wanton killing of game during the early days.

The Ox Age

The clearing of land, that was covered with poplar and willow trees, had to be done by ox and saw. Later, the oxen were used to remove stumps. This ox age began in 1902 with good sod turners like John Trunell, Bobbie Davidson and Carl Anderson. However, many men such as John Webb and others finally gave up — all going to work for wages.

Cemetery

In 1910 the Raven Cemetery was opened with Mr. J. Burgess as caretaker. The cemetery lies three miles west of Raven beside the Caroline Highway No. 54. Jack Ferguson's baby was the first person to be buried there. On July 30, 1912, the first adult to be placed there was W. H. Devore.

The Caroline Cemetery is a mile and a half south of Caroline where the first school was constructed. The village purchased the site in 1953.

It was opened in the year 1959 when Howard Hansen, a young man of Caroline, was laid to rest there after a car accident.

Anglican Church of Caroline

By — Kenneth Dezall and Dalene Ouderkirk

The Anglican Church formerly held their services in the Legion Hall every Sunday. They had Sunday School classes for the children. The Church bought one of the Caroline schools in 1960 and later moved it to its present location in the village.

Gas, Water and Power

In 1910 the first well was drilled. The drilling equipment was owned by a young Englishman Charles Hall and Arthur Bowers. Arthur Bowers soon had full possession of the equipment. After he died his sons Raymond and Ralph continued his work.

In 1954 water and power came to Caroline. There then were 17 wells in the village. The water system for the school was made to accomodate the 220 children that attended the school at that time. This system cost $5,000.00. In 1963 the sewage and gas were turned on, Jan. 30. There are water hydrants on the corners of each street.

The First Threshing Machine, Telephone and Automobiles

"Threshing Machine"

The Rhodes Brothers owned and operated the first threshing machine. The separator was hand fed and run by a wood-fired steam engine tractor. Each farmer gathered dry wood for the thresher in advance. The threshing crew was made possible by an exchange of work. They blew the whistle loud and clear to warn the next farmer in line that they were coming. But today combines have taken the place of many threshers.

"Telephones"

The first telephone service was in 1909 when Bert Dresser, an Electrician, brought a few phone instruments to the Caroline district. The party line ran eastward six miles to Richard Burdekin's homestead. They talked over the top wire of the fences. The telephone used a lot of dry cell batteries but it serverd for neighborhood news and "gossip". It also organized threshing crews, picnics, baseball games and other "social events". Some of that wire was taken up only recently by Mr. I. Graham of Crammond.

The first telephone office was situated in Wally Lundgren's Red and White Store in 1949. Mrs. Lamb was the first person to have the telephone office. The Red and White store burned on Feb. 14, 1956. The telephone office was then moved to its present locality in the private residence of Mr. and Mrs. Lundgren.

"The first Automobile"

The automobile records were not officially kept of the 1919 cars. It was a sputtering, coughing gas wagon which frightened horses, chickens and other things. The men who owned these early cars were Ray Devore, Clarence Kivett and J. F. Browning.

Stores of Caroline

Langley's had the first store in the Caroline area and it was located a half mile south of the village. They moved the store to the present site in Caroline in 1929. Mr. Merlynd Hunter took the post office from Harv Langley just before the Langleys moved. Hunter put the post office near the site of Lundgren's telephone office.

Herman Suhr opened a blacksmith shop near Russell's garage. About the same time Mrs. Suhr took the post office from Mr. Hunter. Mr. Steed and Mr. Mitten started a store where the hotel now stands.

The pool hall was built on the north side of the street near Lundgren's. Steve Dutton took over the pool hall and started the meat market. Mr. Roache built a store about the same time. Steed and Mitten then took over Roache's store.

A bakery started on the site of the post office. In 1937 Mr. Garrett built a hotel. Mr. Garrett also had the Imperial Oil dealership then. Mr.

The lot on which the hotel was built.

Tricker started a small store with oil and gas. Art Lamb established a service station and truck service.

Mr. and Mrs. Langley sold their store to Eisenstat who was better known as Izzy. Langleys started another store soon after. Howard Mullen took over Mr. Mitten's store which he called Caroline Traders. The Murray Brothers started a lumberyard in 1947. Mr. Eisenstat had to close down. Mr. Thorenson then took over the pool hall. Soon after the Lundgrens took over the meat shop and started a Red and White store. Russells then bought out Suhr. Mrs. Russell took over the post office from Mrs. Suhr.

Mr. Cross took over Mr. Mitten and Mr. Mullen's store, the Caroline Traders, but Mitten still had a share in the store. Don Dix built a cafe. Howard Harris and Al Barby bought out Mrs. Langley's last store. The Nazarene Church was

Main street in Caroline looking west about 1943.

238

Store built by Hal Roache.

then started. In 1942 the Treasury Branch opened in Caroline.

Mr. Walter Kanten bought the proprietor's share of Ideal Service from Mr. Tricker. It is now M. McGrandle's cat repair shop. George Wrigglesworth started a Pole Yard in Caroline with camps in the bush. Mr. Thorenson then sold the pool hall to Mr. J. Kissick.

Mrs. Craig (whose husband was a School Trustee) took the post office from Mrs. Russel.

In 1948 Mr. Ivan Graham bought out Harris and Barby's hardware and grocery store and Mitten then bought the cafe from Don Dix. Cross and Mitten in 1949 sold their store to Mr. I Graham who then bought the Imperial oil dealership from Black who had bought out Garrett earlier.

Mr. M. Reese who started a hardware later sold it to his father E. Reese. Mr. E. Reese then retired and sold it to his oldest son W. Reese. Mr. W. Reese made it into a combined hardware and grocery store. This stood where the Nazarene parsonage now stands.

In 1952 Vance Braucht bought out Mr. Ivan Graham's store. Mrs. Schlamp bought the post office from Mr. Craig.

The Caroline Lumber was then started. The owners were I. Graham, R. Braucht, Mr. Mitten, W. Kanten and M. Moger.

Mr. Vellner (who now owns Vellner Motors in Red Deer) bought it leaving Kanten and M. Moger out of the company. The Village of Caroline then built the curling rink along with a new skating rink. Walter Kanten then closed up the shop with Ideal Service. The consolidated school with buses came to Caroline in 1954. The Caroline Lumber closed down that same year.

In 1956 the Red and White store along with the pool hall burned down. In 1952 the Village of Caroline had the power installed. The Provincial Government had Highway 54 paved in 1960-61. The Catholics bought the Wooler School in 1954-55 and made it into a church. Another church is the Anglican Church. For this the congregation bought the first school ever built at the present site of the Caroline School.

Tricker's service station in Caroline.

Looking east on main street of Caroline.

In the year of 1960 Doug Stewart opened a burger bar on the east end of town just across from the phone office. Also in 1961 Vance Braucht opened Imperial Esso Oil and Gas Bulk Station. This is situated on the eastern outskirts of Caroline.

All of the following items happened in Caroline in the year 1962. Vance Braucht built a new addition to the Pioneer Store which now includes meat, groceries, hardware and a lunch counter. November was Caroline's big moment when Marie Morris opened a beauty salon in the Pioneer General Store. Also in the summer of 1962 Cash and Carry store was moved in from Kevisville by Drummonds. Caroline Utilities was started in the same year. This is service for plumbing and heating. The Caroline Supplies was started the same year. A Shell Service Station and garage is to be added in 1963.

The following happened in 1963. The hotel was remodeled inside and out. In May, the Chamber of Commerce was organized with Les Rhodes as the chairman. Caroline was the 186th locality to have one. Also in the same year the Provincial Government is widening and re-hard surfacing highway 54. They also started a new bridge across the Medicine River.

Roads

The roads in and around Caroline will be improved in the future. There are many rumors that highway 54 from Innisfail to Caroline will be continued as hardtop to Rocky. Although this is simply rumor it may be true. A railroad may be put in, passing through Caroline from Rocky to Sundre. All of this and a small airport may be found in and around Caroline within the next twenty-five years.

We, the grade seven class of 1962-63 have at

Main road east of Caroline (now Highway 54) as it was in the 1930's.

last completed our half-year project which in our opinion was very interesting and highly informative. May our future readers not criticize too severely our errors — spelling and grammatical — and may it provide for them as much enjoyment as it did for us. We would like to say thanks to the many people who so kindly gave us information on this project.

The following story was compiled and written by Roy Devore. We are greatly indebted to him for his reasearch and the manner in which the story has been written. He bequeathed his original manuscript to the Village of Caroline for safekeeping. We feel privileged to be able to include his work in our history book.

"The Story of Caroline"

The story of the Caroline country really begins at Raven, Alberta. It was here, at the Frontier Store and Post Office on the North bank

Hugh Devore.

of the Raven River, and one mile below the North and South Forks, that the pioneers, "Caroliners", came to buy their tobacco and beans, prunes, rice, ammunition, etc.

They walked. There were no horses in the Caroline country then, only a few oxen.

There were no roads, and along the route lay terrible tamarack swamps and muskegs heavily infested with a large population of mosquitoes to plague man and beast.

The early settlers were young men, and the blood of a pioneering ancestry coursed their veins.

Each had selected a homestead, and had a complete stranger been able to interview each man separately, all would have laid claim to the best possible quarter section in Alberta.

On August 15th, 1908 the Post Office of Caroline was opened in conjunction with a general store owned by H. A. Langley. The spot was given the name, Caroline, in honor of the Langley's only child.

The first mail-carrier between the points of Raven and Caroline was Mr. Carrol Langley, brother of H. A. Langley.

There was still no graded road — merely a winding trial. About one mile east of the eastern boundary of Township 35 Range 5 lay a formidable muskeg. By custom born of necessity all

that block of territory lying westward from here as far as the Clearwater River, and northward as far as the North fork of the Raven River, became known as "the Caroline country".

Most of the early settlers, however, located near the South Fork of the Raven.

Three survey parties figured in the mapping of the Caroline region. The first two were under Civil Engineer J. N. Wallace, the third was conducted by engineer A. E. Farncomb. Mr. Wallace's first report was submitted on October 31st, 1901, his second August 28, 1903. Mr. Farncomb's report was received in Edmonton on February 27th, 1904.

Be it remembered though, that while all three surveys were accurate and complete in every way, the seat of government was then located at Regina, Saskatchewan and the surveys were not approved and did not become legal until September 5th, 1906.

The early pioneers of Caroline were little different in charecter and purpose than those of most new countries. Most were from western and mid-western U.S.A. These may be said to have comprised three groups.

First: Those, who in an effort to better their condition, had responded to government advertising emphasizing the regions west of Olds, Bowden, Innisfail and Red Deer. These people had little or no means of learning that homestead lands then lay available East of the C.P.R. Calgary and Edmonton line.

Secondly: There were those whose feet naturally followed the adventure path, who yearned for remote places and who chose the more rugged road westward.

Finally: Those who wanted to hide their past and start a new life in a new country.

The two earliest homesteaders of Caroline were somewhat shadowy figures. First was Leo W. Brooks; he filed entry on the N.E. quarter of Section 36 Township 36 Range 5 on the 18th day of July 1904, but he did not return to perform his homestead duties and secure his title. There was no one in the region to see him come or go. He remains merely an entry in a large book in the basement of the Natural Resources Building at Edmonton.

Not far behind, came Goodman Goodmanson. But, as with Leo Brooks, his footsteps were unheard. On September 30th, 1904, Mr. Goodmanson filed claim to the S.W. quarter of Section 28, Township 36, Range 5. Had he remained, I would have become his next-door neighbor, but we were like "ships that pass in the night."

The early homesteaders were mostly bachelors. Among them were some real "characters". There was little Adam Lake, less than five feet, and whose sod house was built entirely underground; Lynn Gilbert, whose boxing

August Dilling.

Nellie Edwards,

ability and non-conformity brought no end of trouble to himself and others; Fredreich Kreisch, the light-heavyweight wrestler, who wrestled too well to remain longer than was absolutely necessary to acquire his land title. There was likewise "Bill" Gans, Ezee Zabler, and "Dick" Agnew who came, saw, and conquered by securing title to the land, then passed out the way they had come.

Arriving close upon the heels of the foregoing were the Anderson brothers, Carl and August. Carl is now dead, but August is the earliest pioneer now living in the region.

The first family of Caroline was that of W. H. Devore, his wife and three sons. They arrived in the summer of 1906 and pitched their tent on Section 22 Township 36 Range 5.

Roadmaking up to this time, and until some two years later, was merely a matter of road "cutting". Each settler, upon leaving the main trail, simply cleared his own road and corduroyed his own slough or muskeg.

The winter of 1906-07 settled down with a suddenness. The month of November saw the thermometer sink to 32 below zero. A heavy snowfall added to the rigor, but, undeterred new settlers continued to arrive. Some faced that winter unfalteringly in a tent with a sheet-iron stove fed with dry tamarack wood. Others sought shelter in the cabin of a neighbor while their own houses were being erected.

Almost all the lumber that went into the making of the early homesteader's houses was produced in portable sawmills owned by John McSuroy and by Daniel McGrandle.

The spring and summer of 1907 saw the first appreciable amount of sod turned. The "Ox Age" had officially begun; the age of "Buck" and "Bright", "Prince" and "Ben", "Tom" and "Jerry". The "Bullwhacker" had burst into full flower. John Trunell was good at it, also "Bobbie" Davidson. The late Carl Anderson was only fair. His profanity was too feeble to have much effect on the oxen. Then there were "Bulldog" flies to harass the oxen and try the souls of the drivers. It was not a pleasant profession.

The winter of 1907-08 gave birth to the social life of Caroline. One feature was the "Bachelor Banquets". Bachelors of the region would gather in accordance with pre-arranged schedule at the cabin of one of their number, to sit down to a Sunday dinner and eat as long as possible before getting up from the table. Frank Troyer almost always carried highest honors away. Most memorable, though, was the occasion when the company ate all the food that host, Arthur Lamb, had in his house. At the conclusion of festivities, 'Art', with no more money to buy food, locked his cabin, mounted his horse, and rode away with his ex-patrons, determined to live with whom he could for the remainder of that winter. Another feature of social life was the frontier folk-dances, consisting of polkas, schottisches, minuets, two-steps, waltzes, and quadrilles. These began at 8:00 P.M. and lasted until 8:00 A.M. Each lady brought a contribution to the midnight repast. There was no "booze", either government or of the "bootleg" variety. We were not very progressive in those days, but it was all good, clean wholesome recreation.

The Anderson brothers and Bert Dresser each owned guitars, J. F. Browning contributed a banjo, and by beating the bush we obtained two 'fiddlers'. The names of these latter are for the moment forgotten, but their services, I am sure, were long remembered. At these dances we invariably passed the midnight hat on behalf of our musicians. The invariable contribution was 25¢, bar one exception; one young gentleman who we will here describe as "Johnson", had brought in a $20.00 note from the "Outside", and consistently carried it on his person . When the hat reached him, Mr. Johnson would present his $20.00 for change. Since there was seldom half that much in the hat, Johnson danced free all winter long.

And yet, perhaps most memorable of all social activities during that year was the Caroline Literary Society, which, I fear, was most of the time none too "Literary". There were songs, prose and poetical recitations, and the occasional Mock Court.

Outstanding amongst all other features though, were our weekly debates. So convinced did the Caroline debaters become of their proficiency in this field, that a challenge was hurled at the neighboring community of Raven.

That challenge was accepted, a subject was agreed upon, and a site for the contest selected near the "Neutral zone" bordering the two communities. Raven's three debaters were headed by J. A. Armey, while the Caroline trio was captained by W. H. Devore. We had chosen several able judges to decide the outcome, and we were sure that a majority of them were good loyal judges, because their verdict was agreed upon before the debate had even got underway. The result was merely an increased enmity between the rival communities.

The shortage of money heretofore alluded to, might have caused extreme hardship to the early pioneers had it not been for a plentiful supply of game, and of fish in the Raven River. One could go fishing at almost any time and bring home fish. If you had a 22 rifle, there were myriads of snowshoe rabbits, prairie chicken, partridge and "fool-hens". If you had a high-powered repeating rifle, such men as the late Arthur Bowers and the late William Womack, might, (or might not have) told you of the availability of much larger game.

But the wanton killing of game unfit for use was virtually non-existent. One never saw a policeman, and game-guardians were seldom heard of.

Another natural resource contributed to the settlers survival during those early years. Small fur-bearers such as weasle and muskrat abounded. Also rumour had it that beaver were to be caught with a certain amount of specialized effort.

In the spring of 1908, Caroline community made its first contributions to the body politic. On April 15th, 1908, Local Improvement District 18-C-5 was established and the first organized effort at road building followed. This L.I.D. consisted of the four following Townships: Twp. 35 Rg. 5 — Twp. 35 Rg. 6 — Twp. 36 Rg. 6 — Twp. 36 Rg. 5, all of course west of the Mer. 5. The first Councillors were: Richard G. Rhodes, Arthur Gilbert, Melville Ferguson (chairman), and Wilfred L. Cone. The first Secretary-Treasurer was Thomas Forrest. The L.I.D. was enlarged by Order in Council of December 23rd, 1912 and re-named L.I.D. 342 with Mr. Cole as Secretary-Treasurer. Then again:

The Municipal District of Raven No. 342 was established by Chapter 49 of the Statutes of Alberta 1918, out of L.I.D. 342, and with J. E. H. MacCabe as Secretary-Treasurer.

Still later, on April 6, 1945, a Ministerial Order re-numbered it Municipal District of Raven No. 56 with offices at Rocky Mountain House, and with Mr. Jos. Chambers as the present Secretary-Treasurer.

During the latter part of the winter of 1907-08 two broadaxe carpenters, Chas. Lineham and Geo. McGrady, erected the South Fork school house. It was the first school in Caroline Country. It stood one mile south of the present school site and on the south side of the river.

On April 27th, 1908 the South Fork School District No. 1803 was established, and the man who rang the bell summoning the first pupils to their desks was a verteran teacher from Texas, W. H. Devore. Two of his students were very conspicuous due to their adult proportions. It was a

very happy relationship, and I am sure that if both Mr. E. Elingson and Mr. W. C. Browning were alive today, they would have nothing but kind words for, and pleasant recollections of, the first school teacher of Caroline.

Following are what we think are the minutes of the first school board meeting.
MINUTES OF SCHOOL MEETING OF
BOARD OF THE SOUTH FORK S.D.
July 10 — 1908
Meeting opened at 1:30 P.M.
J. F. Browning in the Chair
T. A. Van Arsdale Secretary
Motion made by H. Langley and seconded by T. A. Van Arsdale, that J. F. Browning be elected Chairman of the board.

Motion carried.
Motion made by H. Langley and Seconded by J. F. Browning that T. A. Van Arsdale be elected Secretary.
Motion carried.
Motion made by J. F. Browning and seconded by T. A. Van Arsdale that H. Langley be elected Treasurer.
Motion carried.
Motion made by T. A. Van Arsdale and seconded by H. Langley that the board draw up plans for school building also to correspond for School site.
Motion carried.
Secretary advised by Board to purchase one Ledger, one cash book, one minute book, also one Seal.
Minutes stand approved as read.
Sec. T. A. Van Arsdale
Chairman J. F. Browning

The Shilo School District to the East of Caroline was formed May 26, 1910, while Wooler School District No. 2976 to the West, was established May 25th, 1913. The school building in this latter district was finally moved into the village and added to the units of an enlarged school area. But the Shilo School House stands today abandoned, and seems struggling vainly to ward off the enveloping jungle of poplars and willows.

Grief and tragedy took their toll of Caroline pioneers. There was the eternal triangle which contributed its own share of the sadness. One homesteader, whose name eludes me now, succumbed to the loneliness and was found one morning wandering down the trail scantily clad, and permanently insane. Then there was young Conrad Vandermeer, 13, who went one evening in search of the cows. He was thrown from his horse and his body found the next day. There was Hughie Devore, 14, whose right hand was blown away by a powder blast while helping his father to dig a well. Then later along in the annals, 'Bill'

Womack and 'Dave' Knight lost their eyesight in an explosion of dynamite caps. W. H. Devore, respected by all, ruptured his heart while breaking sod with the oxen in stumpy land and died in great agony. Ed Fleet had his hand mangled when his binder team ran away; and Roy Rhodes was crushed to death beneath his farm truck.

From the outset the early homesteaders faced a formidable task. Most of the lands were covered with poplars and willows. There was then no heavy machinery for clearing purposes. It simply had to be done by hand work. There were some who clearly saw the difficulties; John Webb, for example, started to build his cabin, then giving his holding a second look, declared: "The first crop is far too heavy", and he walked back to Innisfail.

After the first two years, the cash assets of the greater number of the settlers was exhausted. Then it was found that the fish, game, fur, and wild hay did not go far when shared by an increasing number. This meant that many were forced during the summer months to go back 'outside' and work for wages. Result: the time farther removed when an income could be had from the homestead.

The first threshing machine in the Caroline country was owned and operated by Rhodes Brothers. The separator was of the hand-fed variety, and, needless to say, the engine was a steam tractor fired by wood. Each homesteader hauled up a pile of dry wood for this purpose in advance, and he also fed the threshing crew. This crew was made possible through an exchange of work. All grain was stacked before threshing. When one man's stacks were threshed out, and the separator coupled to the engine, the whistle blew loud and long, warning the next farmer in line that the threshers were coming. This allowed him time to beat the bush for a crew and for his wife (if he had one) to have dinner cooked and ready. Threshing was ever a gala occasion, second only to Christmas in its festive atmosphere. The only sad moment was when it came time to pay cash for the work done.

In 1910 the first well was drilled in the region. A young Englishman, Chas. L. Hall, had very little money but he did have a supply of promotional ability. He secured a well drilling outfit, and was joined by Arthur J. Bowers. "Art" was ever the handy-man at everything he undertook. Not many months had passed ere the machine came into Art's possession, and for many years he found water for the settlers. On his death, two sons, Raymond and Ralph continued in the work, and, I believe they are still so occupied.

The first telephone service was established in 1910. Bertram Dresser, electrician had brought a few phone instruments into the district, and others were procured later and set up until we had a party line running eastward six miles to the home of Richard Burdekin. Of course we talked over the top wire of the fences. The service consumed a lot of dry-cell batteries; but it served, not only for neighborhood news and gossip, but also to organize threshing crews, picnics, baseball games and other social events. It was really an epoch in itself.

Since auto records are kept no longer than five years, the name of the first licensed car owner in our midst is not available, but in 1919, coughing, sputtering gas wagons were seen carrying Clarence Kivett, Roy Devore, and J. F. Browning all at about the same time. They really frightened the horses and made the chickens flee for shelter!

Caroline has seen its share of political crusades and religious awakenings. Conspicuous amongst the early missionaries was the Rev. A. E. Barton, a polished English preacher, and who specialized in frontier missions. For the most part, however, we had student missionaries. These were lacking in lightning and thunder, and, I fear, not many souls, if any, were actually saved. Years later saw the widely supported crusade of the Nazarenes.

On the political horizon there rose at first the Liberals. There was then very little money in the treasury at Edmonton, and only so many political appointments to be made. Little emotion was connected with "Liberalism".

Conservatism (hold what you have) did not move forward rapidly. The people of Caroline then had little to hold on to, so the Conservatives never reached crusading proportions.

For a period of perhaps three years the Socialist Party carried on a fairly active organizational campaign. The late Chas. M. O'Brien M.L.A., and others, repeatedly toured the territory, but few Caroliners made any methodical study of social relationships. The movement was more emotional than realistic and passed to the vanishing point.

Then came the United Farmers of Alberta. Here indeed appeared a star to which any homesteader might hitch his wagon in all humility. The "Millenium" seemed at hand. After several years of U.F.A. Government nothing startling happened. Allegiance became lukewarm. It took only a couple of scandal stories to put the skids under the U.F.A. politics and to divert the electors of Caroline to greener fields.

Then, from out of a blue sky, fell "Social Credit", a combination of religion and politics. Here indeed was morality, justice, and liberation; an altar worthy of any sacrifice. The older residents were particularly happy. They would be able to still draw the Old Age Pension and have the new "dividend" for pin money. Today, after 19 years, the older people no longer dream about the 'dividend', and all of them seem striving to keep out of heaven just as long as possible, religious crusades not withstanding.

If I have passed over the political and religious phases of Caroline's history somewhat lightly, it is because of the pet personal theory that all of us would live happier, and perhaps longer, if we did not take such matters "too seriously".

Ever marching side by side with the problem of life during the pioneer days at Caroline was the problem of death. A last resting place must needs be provided. So in 1910 the Raven Cemetery was opened with Mr. J. Burgess as caretaker. It lies about three miles west of Raven and along the main Caroline highway. Jack Ferguson's baby was the first to be put there, while the first adult interment was that of W. H. Devore on July 30th, 1912. The cemetery is fast filling up now, and every several years it has been the self-imposed practice of your historians to wander anew amongst its mounds and headstones, and to see with his own eyes the growing number of old pioneers who have come there to rest. There are not many left, and their descendants will soon have a spot provided for themselves in the new cemetery to be opened near the Village of Caroline itself.

Among those who figured conspicuously in the early days were four family groups, each consisting of three sons. Perhaps they may deserve recording here. They were: Carl, August and Oscar Anderson; Richard, Burton and Roy Rhodes; William, Charles, and Grover Womack; Roy, Fredrick, and Hugh Devore.

For the first two years people travelling to Caroline store from the Past were compelled to take an awkward winding course to the south, while the legitimate route lay along the half section line. But where this bordered the homestead of Bert Dresser there lay one serious obstacle; a bad muskeg. There seemed but one solution: elect Bert to the L.I.D. Council. This we did in 1909, the muskeg was corduroyed, and the road made passable.

Previous to World War I, summer recreation in the region consisted almost entirely of frontier picnics. The stellar attraction at these events was the long awaited baseball game, Raven vs. Caroline. The boys were little practiced, and they were work stiffened. They would drop the ball far more often than catch it. These games were truly a hilarious spectacle.

The following episode (true or false) figuratively describes them: A passer-by enquired of one of the Caroline players: "What's the score?" "Twenty-four to nothing in their favour" came the answer. "Gosh!" exclaimed the stranger, "they're putting it over you rather badly aren't they?" "Oh I don't know" was the rejoinder, "we haven't been to bat yet. Wait 'til we get OUR innings!"

Following the war, however, a number of experienced ball players had settled among us. A four team league was established, consisting of the home club and those of Raven, Red Raven, and Markerville. There then developed a brand of baseball that compared very favourably with that played in such centers as Didsbury, Olds, Innisfail, and Rocky Mountain House.

Fishing had been another favourite recreation; but the tiny Raven River, at first found teeming with trout, grayling and suckers, finally fell victim to too many fishermen. It was then that the Provincial Government undertook stocking it with Loch Leven Trout. From the years 1941 to 1950, 89,000 fingerlings, 171,000 yearlings, and 538 two-year-olds were placed in the Raven's waters.

Also, and and finally, a fish hatchery known as Raven Rearing Ponds, with Mr. Garfield Thompson in charge commenced operations during 1942.

From the very outset, timber has loomed large in the economy of Caroline. In the early days, and long before the advent of motor-transport, the homesteader who had become hard pressed for ready money simply went to the nearest tamarac swamp where the best fence-post timber was to be found, and helped himself. Loading his sleigh with these heavy, green timbers, he would start out at the break of the following day for the nearest market: Innisfail. After travelling in subzero weather for four days, and paying stopping-house bills along the way, he might, with luck, return with a 50 lb. bag of flour and a 10 lb. bag of sugar.

When trucking became genral, timber then developed into a major local industry, and in spite of the ever increasing inroads upon the supply, the output is astonishing.

Much work is now done in the summer months, a task hitherto held impossible. This is particularly noticeable in Caroline's newest industry, the Wrigglesworth Wood Preserving Plant and yard. Telephone, telegraph, light and power poles are the chief products processed here. The "Osmose" chemical is made use of; only here, the process has been speeded up to a point where only five days are required as compared to the three weeks in eastern Canada. Lodge Pole Pines are used in place of the rapidly disappearing tamaracs. Four trucks are engaged in hauling these poles from as far as 30 miles to the westward. In 1953 the firm's wage bill ran into fabulous figures, $30,000.00 alone going for special trucking services. One hundred and twenty poles per day was the plant output and a crew of 32 men obtained employment in the plant and yard. These poles are transported by truck to almost all points in central and in Southern Alberta. Here is an industry that is really putting Caroline on the map.

The once rival communities of Caroline and Raven are rivals no longer. They have travelled widely divergent trails. The hamlet of Raven after half a century is a hamlet still. Time appears to have stood still for Raven, but for Caroline, time has marched onward with mounting changes. Once a hamlet of a store, P.O. and private dwelling, Caroline now spreads over an area of one hundred and sixty acres. It sits at the crossroads of the frontier. Northward to Rocky Mountain House there runs an all-weather highway. South to Sundre, and thence eastward to Olds, there extends a similar link with railway transportation. A fine wide highway connects with Innisfail to the east, while another road leads on westward across the Clearwater River, upward through the first range of foothills, and into the mountain fastnesses beyond.

The village of Caroline, soon to apply for village status, has a population of 320. This, and all that it implies, was made possible by motor transport; the nearest railway point, "Rocky", being 27 miles distant. It was a Mr. Suhr who took the lead in the transport business, but the greater portion of the hauling has been done by the Art Lamb Transport.

The original store and P.O. was moved north ½ a mile to the village's present site in 1929, and the original Postmaster left Caroline to live in B.C. in 1945. Mr. Suhr succeeded him in office.

I am relying upon the willing, though slightly fleeting memories of the villagers, for the following dates. Please do not shoot me if you are slightly misinformed somewhere along the line.

A hustling public spirited business man, Robert Mitten, established the first sizeable general store at the Caroline corners in 1933.

In 1937 Mr. H. Garrett opened the Caroline Hotel, and, at approximately the same time, the "Sharpes Picture Shows" made its bow. Both old and young then fell head over heels into 'Hollywood'. With the dying down of enthusiasm's first flame, the show business has travelled a hilly road, and under a changing management.

1938 saw Mr. Stephen Dutton open a butcher-shop and pool-hall. Steve proved himself a capable businessman until the increasing years and declining health forced him into retirement.

The opening of the Treasury Branch in 1942 filled a long felt need in the district.

Then the year 1947 brought a debatable piece of progress. The community was blessed (or cursed) with Govt. supervised beer. A place was made and provided where the "enlightened electorate" of both sexes could go, drink and forget their poverty, and "remember their misery no more".

The topographical elevation of Caroline is, to be officially exact, 3,499.52 feet above sea level.

There are 17 wells in the village, and a sanitary system is being built at the cost of $5,000.00 to accommodate the 220 pupils who attend the district school.

Up to the present Caroline has been very fortunate in not having a serious outbreak of fire. The volunteer fire brigade are keeping their fingers crossed. The extent of their equipment is none too comforting at the moment. It consists of a 40 gal. chemical extinguisher mounted on wheels, and a water-tank outfit capable of throwing a stream of water 75 feet.

There are 25 business houses in the village. The legal machinery is fairly complete. The village council is headed by a very capable mayor. As in most frontier towns and villages the mayor of Caroline has many extra duties thrust upon him. He is compelled to be several persons in one, but Mayor M. Carter is a very rugged man, and has a rugged sense of humour which enables him to stand up under his various duties without the aid of crutches.

His Worship, A. Proudler is the resident Justice of the Peace.

Broad-shouldered and broad-minded T. Beddingfield is the village constable. To assist him in his duties a brand new "bird-cage" has arrived and is open for business. Any unorthodox villager who has coveted his neighbour's chickens, or who has drunk exceedingly of Gov't. beer and then tried to emulate Rocky Marciano, will now be able to sit and patiently pay for his fun at the public's expense.

Since there is no law against an amateur historian becoming an amateur prophet, I prophesy that in the years ahead, the good, hard working people of Caroline, will not give such a fine administration very much trouble.

The Caroline country has been ever difficult. Life has come hard here. It has been rugged uphill road all the way. Many years ago there were people who made remark that white men should never have come here in the first instance.

Accomplishments, when viewed, are very eloquent. They have a language that is incorruptible. Caroline has won to these accomplishments in spite of the Caroline country! The credit is entirely due to the people who have lived here. They must have had what it took.

Here now, must end the story of Caroline. It has been told in the belief that if life is worth living it is also worth recording.

If I have dwelt over-long upon the hardships and struggles of the pioneers, then I have but vindicated that truism: "The things that we remember best, are the things that it were best to forget''.

If I have laboured the mention of the names of some, to the exclusion of others whose names deserve a place in the record, then I apologize for the oversight.

''To err is but human''. I can only assure the surviving pioneers, the present generation of Caroliners, and those other generations to come, that to them the foregoing humble effort is sincerely and affectionately dedicated.

el fin (Part One)

My Life In Caroline

by Earle Farris

The last week of July, 1936, Bob Mitten came to Coleville, Saskatchewan, and visited my parents and wanted to know what they thought about me going to Caroline to work for him in his store. They agreed to let me go so I hurriedly got ready for the trip to Alberta. Bob had his truck loaded with used machinery to take back to Caroline. The machinery was needed badly in the Caroline area because most people were very hard up during the depression. Mrs. Willsie, Jean Willsie and I travelled back to Caroline with Bob. I rode up on the back of the truck for many miles and when it got cooler at night, I

Earle Farris.

rode in the cab with the rest. We travelled all night arriving in Caroline in the morning.

My first impression of Caroline was one of amazement because of it's size. It consisted of Bob's store, Mrs. Langley's store, a hall and blacksmith shop which also housed the Caroline post office. There were several small houses and that was all. Although Caroline was small, I soon found it was a very busy little place especially on mail days and Saturday nights.

My first day clerking in the store was an experience I'll never forget. It was a general store with everything imaginable for sale. I recall my first customer was Ivan Graham, a farmer from near Crammond. He made some purchases and gave me a cream cheque to pay for the groceries. I was most embarassed because I couldn't make change, I was so green. Ivan gave me a bad time and I vowed I would never be caught that way again.

The hours of work were hectic — especially on mail days. Usually one could expect to be in the store anytime from six a.m. until midnight. The store became so crowded that there was barely standing room with customers waiting to place their order. Most people charged their purchases, and a record was kept in a large account book. Luckily we had the counter to separate the clerks from the customers. On mail nights, Bob, Elva, Whiskey, Chick and I put up groceries as fast as we could. The lighting in the store was by gas lamps, a hectic job to keep them in good working order. Invariably some would go out before the evening business ended and it was a mad scramble to fill them by flashlight and get them lighted again. It was several years before Bob purchased a Delco light plant. This was a great improvement over the gas lamps, but even then it proved hard to start at times or it would stop, and again the gas lamps came into use.

Business was so brisk that Theresa Chorley came to work in the store. She worked steadily until she and her family moved to Calgary.

Farmers brought in eggs and butter in exchange for groceries. Eggs were only 5¢ a dozen and butter 25¢ a pound. There were some excellent butter makers in the country and there were some terrible ones. One such customer, a bachelor used to bring butter about every two weeks. It was so rancid that you could smell it as soon as he opened the store door. Obviously this butter went directly into the back storage room and outside. All of the poor butter was packed in boxes and shipped to Calgary. I presume it was used to make soap.

Some furs were brought in by the trappers. Squirrel skins came in sacks; these had to be counted. They were greasy and smelly, but were essential to the business. Beaver and muskrat skins, some coyote and other skins graced our warehouse and were shipped off to Calgary to the fur actions.

Most days were spent doing the chores to get ready for mail days. Coffee beans came in 100 pound bags and had to be ground by hand and put up in pound bags. It was a great day when an electric motor did the grinding for us. Raisins, dates, coconut, sugar, salt, pepper — you name it — came in bulk and had to be weighed out by hand. One distrustful customer who had a phobia about being poisoned always sternly scrutinized the weighing and packaging of all his purchases.

Tamarack posts and lumber from the sawmills came in to be traded for groceries, clothes, gas and oil. All this had to be counted and recorded and credit given to the customers. I believe oil was one of the biggest nuisances because it all came in bulk and had to be measured out. Steam cylinder oil was the hardest to handle because it was so heavy. Number 90, as I recall, would harldy run out of the barrel. Imagine trying to get a gallon in the winter time with no light at night except a flashlight. It took a long time to fill a gallon container.

Saturday night was a big night in Caroline. It was a time to let your hair down and howl. The bootleggers came to town with their moonshine and homemade wine. Groups stood around the dark corners drinking. One ghastly wine I can recall was made from beets. Beet wine — imagine the flavor of that! But the nearest liquor store was Rocky, Innisfail or Red Deer and people didn't have money to buy the good stuff.

In 1937 Howard Mullen came into partnership with Bob. He bought out the Steeds share of the business. About that time Caroline began to grow. The Caroline Cafe was built by Don Dix, and served excellent meals prepared by his wife, Ivy. Not long after the hotel was built, Bob and Elva and family moved into it. Howard and I took over the living quarters above the store. I should mention that the Jamesons built a store front onto the store. This housed one bedroom and provided protection from the sun for the store.

I must not forget to mention the blacksmith shop and post office run by Mr. and Mrs. Suhr and Elmer. Mrs. Suhr kept a sharp eye on the post office and knew the events of the country side. She was very obliging because she always took the days receipts from the store. These had to be sent to the bank in Rocky Mountain House by money order. This transaction usually took place at night after the store closed.

Bathroom facilities in Caroline were limited and consisted mainly of the out-house at the back of the lot. The one for the store was no exception, it served the customers as well as the clerks in the store. It was a 'three holer' with no door so it was easy to be caught if you didn't make a lot of noise.

Sometimes for a break from the store, I would go out with the boys to bring lumber from the sawmills. The main ones were Boeken, Englund, Clays, Dezell and Hart. Most of these were located west of Caroline and the roads were a bog most of the way. A full day was required to make one trip because of the poor condition of the roads. I shouldn't call them roads. They were really trails through the woods.

Probably one of the most interesting jobs in the store was putting up supplies for the Guides and Outfitters. J. Browning, J. Bugbee and the Jamesons were some of the outfitters who dealt with us. It was a most interesting order and it had to be put up very carefully so it could be packed into pack boxes for the pack horses.

There was lots of entertainment around Caroline. One such was the Browning Stampede held on their place just west of the Clearwater Bridge. I saw my first stampede as I worked in the refreshment booth for Bob. The evening was spent at a wild and hilarious dance in the hall. Needless to say the 'moonshine' flowed quite freely at this big event. Dances were held throughout the country with orchestras coming in from Calgary and other large centers. Ma Trainer and her orchestra was one of the favorites.

In 1938 George McLean, Ray Sawyer, Deal Cooper and myself started up a small band called the Moonlight Rangers. We played at the various halls around the country, including Caroline. Softball was a favorite pastime during the summer. A ball league was formed by Rocky, Alhambra, Condor and Caroline and every Sunday games were played. The 'Urch Cup' was the trophy that went to the winning team. It was a proud day for Caroline when we won the Cup.

The story of Caroline would not be complete for me if I did not tell about the time I worked for Izzy Eisenstat. Izzy bought out Mrs. Langley's store. He used the store as headquarters for buying cattle. He used to go around the country to farmers places buying their cattle on the hoof. He would load them onto his truck and haul them off to Calgary. Harry Finberg was his partner. Well, Izzy owned the Langley store and one winter I did not work for Mitten and Mullen, so Izzy hired me. One of my big jobs was to clean out the cooler where the bulk cheese was kept. I soon discovered the whole place was overrun by mice, so I got mouse traps and set them in the cooler. I would check the traps every ten minutes or whenvever I heard them go off. The days catch totalled fifty mice in a little over three hours trapping.

Izzy was a good sport. He helped coach our

Caroline ball club 1938 — Back Row — Ron Stewart, Bob Willsie, Walter Kanten, Bill Ried, Howard Mullen, Hugh Grieves (manager), Izzie Eisenstat, Mac Dix. F. Row — Happy Pedley, Don Dix, Art Peterson, Bill Motz, and Earle Farris — when they won the Gus Urch Cup, 1938.

ball team and supported us to the full. He always loved to play jokes or pranks. One night a chicken raid was organized, the idea being that Mrs. Eisenstat and some of the other women around the cafe would cook the chickens for a midnight feast. I remember the group sneaking into Mr. Haas' barn to catch chickens. Well one chicken was caught. It squawked loud and long as it was being hauled away. It turned out to be the only chicken Mr. Haas' had on the farm.

During the time I worked at the store, I received $10 a month, my room, board and half my clothes. In 1939 I decided to go to Calgary Normal School, I had saved the $100 tuition fee. In spite of the war, I completed teacher training first year. My first school was Glacier, south and west of Rocky in 1940-41. The next year I taught Hardindell and in 1942-43, I taught in Caroline at the South Fork School which had been moved from one mile south into Caroline. From there I went to Dickson for one year and in 1944 to Benalto, where I was principal until 1963. I then moved with my wife, Janet, and two boys, William and George, to Mill Bay, British Columbia, on Vancouver Island. I was married in 1951 to Janet Staniforth of Evarts.

In January, 1979, forty years after I left Caroline, I revisited the old town and was absolutely amazed at its growth. To say the least I am glad to have been a part of the early history of Caroline during the depression years.

Any history of Caroline and district would not be complete without mentioning the government assistance given to families on relief during the Depression Years. Many families from Calgary and other larger centers were sent out to the district to take up homesteads. The homestead consisted of a quarter section of land usually with no buildings and no land cleared or broken for farming. Assistance consisted of a wagon, plow, various tools, a team of horses and a cow and $600 credit to last them until they were able to establish themselves. The $600 came in as a requisition for groceries, clothes and other supplies needed. They were only allowed $12 a month the first year and this was reduced accordingly every year for five years. It was a real struggle to make ends meet with that amount of money. Many times in putting up their groceries, a penny's worth of pepper was all that was allowed because the amount on the requisition could not be overspent. The main supplies consisted of flour, sugar, salt, yeast and a few other staples. The homesteaders usually came in once a month to shop. They had to be very frugal. Of course they were expected to clear their land and produce enough garden vegetables, eggs and butter to sell or trade for their well being. There were some who did extremely well on their farms while others packed up and left, returning to the cities as soon as their $600 was used up. By this time the war broke out in 1939 and money became more plentiful so they were able to return to the life they were used to.

The Caroline Hockey Team
by Bill Mewha

People today may be surprised to hear that in the early days, about the time that Mitten's General Store took in squirrel and rabbit skins in trade for groceries, Caroline had an excellent hockey team. It seems that about the year 1938 a number of Colville, Saskatchewan residents congregated at Caroline and became the nucleus of a widely respected hockey team.

The eight players, highly motivated by a love of the sport would haul the water from the raven for the rink situated where the present community hall now stands, by tanks and barrels until a fairly good ice surface existed. Supporters were many in those days. Hauling water in below zero weather tested out the stamina of supporter and player alike.

Players included Howard Mullen, Chick Demenuk, Nick Demenuk, Bert Mitten, Jack Morgan, Whiskey Willsie, Bill Mewha and Fred Scott who capably looked after the goal keeping duties. Charlie Dezall joined the team in the later years.

What a record this team established. The number of games lost could be counted on one's hand. It is to be remembered that Rocky wouldn't play the Caroline team and the New Hill goal keeper left the ice because the Caroline boys continually raised the puck too high for his liking.

Transportation was by the back of a truck. Straw and heavy blankets served to keep the players and spectators warm. It is remembered that at most games played away, the Caroline spectators far out numbered those of the local team.

Looking back one remembers Chick Demenuk playing a game three days after he had his appendix operation. No amount of persuasion would keep him off the ice. Bill Mewha still carries a scar on his face from an encounter at Raven. Howard Mullen's stick handling ability left opponents somewhat bewildered at times.

Hockey was played by those who loved the sport and were dedicated enough to put everything they had into it. Perhaps that's what made the Caroline team so well respected.

Ray Adams

Ray Adams came to Caroline in 1937 from British Columbia where he worked west of Prince George. He was originally from the States.

He bought the John Quinn quarter south of Caroline which was homesteaded by Mr. VanArsdale, the N.E. Q. 2-36-6-5. John Quinn raised purebred Aberdeen Angus cattle.

Ray Adams was quite humorous in ways. He was a large hog farmer, but usually let his hogs run loose. Ray passed away about the year 1964. He moved from Caroline to a home in Olds. He was always a bachelor.

Mr. and Mrs. Donald Bowden

Mr. and Mrs. Donald Bowden and daughter, Kathleen, came from Vulcan to Caroline in the year 1933. They settled on the Ray Dial place, N. E. 18, and lived there until 1947. They then bought eighty acres on S. W. 13 and settled on that piece of land.

Kathleen went to school at South Fork and later in Caroline. She married Alex Weiss in 1950. They bought five acres of land from Henry Thompson in 1954 and are still living there. They built a house and barns and always kept horses. Kathleen being a keen horse woman, took part in gymkhanas and horse shows. She has many trophies, ribbons, etc. Alex has been Janitor at the school several years. They have one daughter, Valerie. She is married to Jim Thompson and is living on a farm west of Caroline. Like her mother, Valerie is interested in horses and has several of her own. She, too, has won many trophies. They have one son, Dale. Dale likes nothing better than being placed on the back of a horse and with his mother holding on to him, to go cantering over the countryside.

Mrs. Bowden was supply teacher at the Caroline School for a number of years. She also taught school in England and there are many little stories she likes to tell, one of which is: The scripture inspector came one morning to examine the children. He asked them, "What is the meaning of the word confirmation?" One little fellow was very anxious to answer and this is his answer, "It's chemise and drawers joined together, my mother wears them!" Of course he could have been thinking of the word 'combination' instead of 'confirmation'.

George Breeding
by Guy Fay

The Breedings came to Caroline in the fall of 1918 and bought the N.W. Q. 25-36-6-5 from Fred Hobbs. There was George and his wife and two boys, Bill and Fred, also George's parents. The family left the country in 1920.

Charles Brown
by the Brown Family

Charles Brown and his wife, Dora, arrived in Caroline at the end of March, 1920. They brought with them six children from two to thirteen years of age, Charley, Myra, Alec, Ivy, Elsie and Den-

Charles Brown.

nis. Later two more girls were born, Bessie and Daisy. While in England, Charles studied organ and violin music and sang in a church choir. Dora was a milliner before she married.

The winter they arrived in Caroline was one of the hardest winters ever, and the old timers talked about it for years. Many cattle starved to death as the snow did not leave until May, and hay was very scarce. The Brown family stayed with Dora's mother and her two brothers (who came out in 1905) for two weeks on their homestead. Their homestead is now the home of Hugh Oliver.

Charles and family then moved to the homestead of Slim Furnish where they lived for two years. The Furnish homestead is now occupied by the Ford family (formerly owned by

Jack Heck). Then Charles homesteaded the old Matheau quarter N.E. 10-36-6-5, now owned by his son, Dennis. Charles built a house there and moved the family in 1923. This land was one mile west of the South Fork School, which they all attended. That school was torn down and the yard is now used as a cemetery.

Charles would take a team and rack, and go out harvesting in the fall and work in the McGrandle sawmill, and later the Thibedeau sawmill, in the winters to bring home a grub stake. He was secretary-treasurer for the South Fork School district from 1925 to about 1940 for a salary of $50.00 a year, and later for the Rocky Mountain School Division. He was remembered to have ridden horseback over twenty miles each way to attend a school meeting, and he didn't find riding a horse very comfortable. He also worked so hard for the school fairs for many years.

In those days there were no graded roads and no cars to speak of, so it was hard to get to town if someone was sick. The nearest doctor was in Innisfail.

However, they had good times with the hard times as neighbors often got together for a little dance and sing song and to play games. They would pick lots of wild fruit and catch fish, and in the fall the boys would go hunting which all helped to put food on the table.

Charles passed away in 1965 and Dora in 1967 and are buried in the Caroline Cemetery. They were pre-deceased by a son and a daughter in 1925 and 1932.

ALEC BROWN

Alec bought the half section to the south of his father's home from Ray Dial, which was first homesteaded by Louis Martin — S.E. 10-36-6-5, being his home place. He eventually bought land across the road to the east.

He met and married Margaret Doel who came to Caroline from the Consort area with her parents, brothers and sister. They have two

Dora Brown.

Brown children — left to right — Ivy, Bessie, Dennis. Front Row — Alec, Daisy, Charley and Elsie.

children, a son, Bob, who married Rosemary McCormick from Calgary, and they now farm the homeplace. They have one son, Ryan. Their daughter, Veva, married Norman Rose and they farm west of Caroline. They have three children, Jo-Ann, Bonnie and Brian. Alec and Margaret are retired and live in Olds, Alberta.

IVY

Ivy married Len McGrandle and they had three children, all married. Leonard Jr. teaches school in Red Deer. Melba lives in Forest Grove, British Columbia, and teaches sewing. Gary works for Imperial Oil and lives in Swan Hills.

ELSIE

Elsie married Howard Alstott on February 26, 1934, and moved to his dad's farm at Craigmyle. In August they moved back to Caroline with a wagon and team and one extra horse, trailing twenty-eight head of cattle which took ten days across country.

That fall they sold ten head of two and three year old steers for $98.00.

They had four children, Edwin, Dorothy, Gladys and Marlene. Edwin married Kathy Byrne, a school teacher, from Crowsnest Pass. They have four children, Wanda, Corrine, Barby and Johnny. Edwin has driven chuckwagon since 1968. He lives on the homeplace.

Dorothy married Albert Lucas from James River. They have two children, Janet and Joe.

Gladys married Clark Wren and they have two children, Marty and Darwin.

Marlene married Doug Lowry from Sundre and they have two children, Billy and Dustin.

DENNIS

Dennis married Fern Audy and they had two children, George and Janet. George lives at home and works out on oil rigs. Janet is married and lives at Kelowna where she works as a nurse. Dennis and Fern still farm on the home place.

BESSIE

Bessie married Wynne Williams on June 17, 1943. They live in Calgary where Wynne has his own furniture business and Bessie is a seamstress; makes anything from lawyer and choir gowns to complete bridal ensembles. They have three children, Colin, Faye and Joan. Colin is married and lives at Redwater. They have two children, Christopher and Dionne. Faye and Joan are living in Calgary.

DAISY

Daisy married Max Curp and lives in Guelph, Ontario. They have one son, Kevin. Daisy became a professional artist in many mediums.

Jasper F. Browning

Jasper Browning was born on June 15, 1861 at Liberty, Illinois. He married Anna Diana Miller July 19, 1884.

He was Sheriff of Pawnee County, Oklahoma, which bordered the famous "Cherokee Indian Strip". His wife died about 1904.

By 1906 settlers had crowded his free life style

Jasper and Warner Browning about 1908, en route to Alberta.

of hunting and trapping, so with four of his family of six — Mae, Tessie, Warner and John, he journeyed to Alberta by covered wagon. The two youngest girls Myrtle and Oma were left with relatives.

They ended their journey south of Caroline where he homesteaded on SE 2-36-6-5. In 1908 and 1914 they made the long trip to Oklahoma and back to Caroline.

Jasper carried on the long established Browning tradition of hunting, trapping and raising hound dogs. He held a registered trapline up Cutoff Creek for many years.

He was a lively entertainer — tap dancing and playing the banjo for dances.

In the 30's he moved to Nakusp, B.C., and died in Idaho at the age of 83.

John Bucko

John Bucko left Czechoslovakia for Canada in 1928. Years later, his wife, Elizabeth, and son, Andrej, arrived in 1948. This was the first time John saw his son. In 1939 John arrived in Caroline. He worked on McGrandle's planing mill in the northwest part of Caroline where the old sawdust pile used to be. Then in 1942 he bought the Shoemaker's Shop. In 1948 John and his son, Andrej, started working with Murray's Lumber Company.

Due to the depression in Canada it was hard for John to save any extra money. Farmers paid five dollars a month. Relief camps paid twenty cents a day — including clothes.

John and Elizabeth are still living just west of Caroline and Andrej and his wife, Marie, live at Caroline.

Mr. and Mrs. Maurice Carter
by the Hansen and Betts Families

Maurice Carter was born December 26, 1904, in Morcambe, Lancashire, England. Times were hard in England so as a young boy, Maurice delivered milk to many of the neighbor houses. Also during his years in England, Maurice was the 126 pound champion boxer of Lancashire. After his years of boxing, Maurice decided to go to Canada. To pay for his passage, he sold flowers and did garden work for the town people of Morcambe.

Maurice came to Canada in 1922 from England on May 1 on a C.P.R. steamship called the S.S. Montcalm. The voyage took four nights and four days to reach Quebec. From there he took an immigrant train to the west. It took five days to reach Calgary. The train travelled slowly and changed engines every four hundred miles. Since there were no dining facilities, the passengers left the train to quickly purchase supplies at each stop.

Maurice had little money, his worldy wealth consisted of one hundred and seventy three dollars. After seeing signs at construction projects stating Englishmen and Chinamen need not apply for work at the west coast, he decided to return to the prairies where the attitude to Englishmen was a little more friendly.

He obtained work at Nanton on a farm, driving eight mules. That job was a challenge for one so inexperienced. After a few years of being a jack of all trades, he decided to take the bull by the horns and start out for himself. He went to the Bowden area where he had an uncle, and then on to James River district in 1926, arriving in time to get in on the big depression which lasted all through the thirties.

Maurice then married Ellen Sharland Betts who had been previously married to Albert Ernest Betts and she had one child, Edward Albert (Ted) Betts, who was born December 16, 1923.

Ellen (Nellie) Sharland was born September 4, 1897, in Somerset, England. She came to Canada in 1907 with her family at the age of nine. There were eight children in her family. Her father worked for the C.P.R. at Medicine Hat. Nellie worked in Calgary and at a chocolate factory in Medicine Hat before her marriage to Albert Betts. They moved to the James River area and lived on a homestead for a short time before the dissolution of their marriage.

Maurice and Ellen Carter and her son, Ted, arrived in the Caroline district on Halloween night in 1928 accompanied by Arthur 'Toffy' Kemp. Toffy stayed with the Carters the first winter, but returned to the prairies to find work and lost contact with the Carter family for many years until 1973. He now resides in Armstrong, British Columbia.

The Carters arrived with a Modet T Coupe and a touring car, groceries, and a hundred

Maurice and Ellen Carter.

dollars cash. One vehicle was traded to the Blackhurst family at Sundre (Nellie's sister) for a team of horses. The other vehicle went to Mr. Brown for a cow and some chickens.

The Carters first home in the Caroline district was on the Palmer place, N.W. 9-36-6-5. There they had a log house and mostly homemade furniture. They later moved to the Langley place, N.W. 12-36-6-5, where they rented a house and Maurice worked for Mr. Langley. Next they moved to the Mel Ferguson place, S.W. 16-36-6-5, and farmed on shares. Later they moved to the Ray Dial farm, S.W. 20-36-5-5, east and north of Caroline. Maurice and Ellen were blessed with a daughter, Edith, in 1937. They moved to the Jim Leask farm, N.W. 18-36-5-5, and made their home there until after the second world war. After their son, Ted returned from the war, he obtained the N.W. and S.W. 18-36-5-5 through the Veteran's Land Act. They moved to the Bowden place, N.E. 18-36-5-5, and Maurice and Ted farmed the three quarters together until the early 1950s when they left the farm, purchased the Stan Grieves house and moved it to their acreage on the east side of the village of Caroline.

During the years they lived on the Leask place, the road, now Highway 54, had a notorious 'bog hole' and much of the spring and summer was impassable for cars and trucks. However, that did not completely halt traffic as travellers always knew they could count on 'Shorty' Carter to get them out of the bog with his good team, Pet and June, no matter what time of the day or night.

Life in the Caroline district changed during the Carters' lifetime. The hard times kept families busy preparing foods and preserving them. Hunting trips for the winter meat supply most often meant long trips by horse and wagon and on occasion they had to ford the Clearwater River six or seven times. Removing ice from the horses tails or rescuing loads from the icy water was not uncommon. Once a trail was opened into Swan Lake, families would take wagons and supplies and camp beside the lake, canning fish and berries on the spot.

Socials were a welcome break from everyday chores. Then friends would gather at the local schools. Everyone came and the little ones often fell asleep under the coat racks before the party was over. In those days people made their own entertainment. Getting to and from such events could be entertainment in itself especially if the horses bolted or the sled overturned.

When the late George Wrigglesworth started his pole treating plant in Caroline, Maurice was his foreman from 1945-1955.

The road systems gradually improved, but sudden storms still made some of them im-

passable. Travel to Innisfail could take more than a day in such conditions. Ted recalls on one occasion, when he bought chicks in Red Deer, and had to detour via Olds and Sundre due to an April snow storm.

Nellie was an active member of the community and for many years belonged to the 'Helping Hand Club'. Like all farm wives and mothers she helped with outside chores and found many enterprising ways to preserve farm produce and to beat the mosquitos during berry picking season.

When Caroline was incorporated as a village, Maurice was elected to council and became the first mayor and held that position without a break for fifteen years. He served as a member of council for over twenty years. Maurice was a 'jack-of-all-trades,' being a good farm hand, repairman, auctioneer, returning officer at elections and was often master of ceremonies at weddings and community functions and officiated on Santa's behalf at many Christmas concerts.

He raised registered swine between 1943 and 1972. He was president of the Curling Club, a member of the Elks Lodge from 1952 to 1975 which included two years as Exalted Ruler, eight years as Chaplin and two years as Leading Knight.

After the pole plant ceased operation, Maurice worked for Vance Braucht in the store and drove the gas truck delivering fuel and groceries to the remote areas to oil rig sites.

Maurice worked hard and long promoting Caroline and often was the driving force behind the progress achieved. Some of the highlights and events he took part in were: the celebration of the completion of Highway 54 to Caroline, October 21, 1960. In 1962 Mrs. Alma Sarc, at that time the oldest village resident, turned on the natural gas line for Caroline. In May, 1964, Maurice was host when the Post Master General, John R. Nickolson, was a guest of the village. In 1972 the Caroline Community Centre was opened. In 1974 Maurice represented the Caroline community at the offical opening of the new Red Deer River Bridge on Highway 54 to Caroline. Maurice and Ted surveyed the cemetery for the community.

In later years the Carter residence became well known for their collection of old ploughs, wagons, democrats, 'Bennet' buggies, threshers, etc.

Maurice and Nellie's two children, Ted and Edith, grew up in the community and received their education here. Ted attended classes at Wooler, South Fork and Shilo Schools. After school, Ted worked at the Palliser Hotel in Calgary with his father, Albert Betts. He served in the Royal Canadian Navy on the ships

H.M.C.S., Prince Robert and the Sussexvale. After the war he returned to Caroline to farm. He married Leah Cross in 1946. In the 1950s he sold his land and worked in construction; building schools at Caroline, Dovercourt, Rocky Mountain House, the new Crammond School, the David Thompson School at Condor, the Spruce View School and various other locations.

Ted married a second time to Jacqueline Norton and they lived and worked in Innisfail for several years, sold their home there and moved to Calgary where they now reside and Ted has continued in the construction trade.

Ted is an ardent fisherman and in the 1950s, fish were still prolific in the west country streams which could only be reached by rough trails. The effort needed to reach these creeks proved well worth while for Ted. In June, 1956, he caught his first 'big fish'. At the weighing in of that fish, he was narrowly beaten by Ivor Nordfors from Red Deer. Ted promised he would go back the next week and catch a bigger one. He did just that and held the record for largest Brook Trout for some years.

Edith Carter was married to Gunnar Hansen on September 4, 1953. Gunnar worked at the Wrigglesworth Pole Yard and later the young couple lived for a short time in Manitoba. They returned to the Spruce View area where they ob-

tained land and have resided ever since. Edith and Gunnar celebrated their Silver Wedding Anniversary in 1978.

In 1965 Maurice and Nellie made their first trip back to England. For Maurice, it was a great reunion with his eighty-three year old mother as well as his brother, Arthur, and other members of the family. For Nellie it was a time to re-walk the once familiar homeland in Wookey, Somerset. They made a second trip in 1969 and enjoyed it equally as well.

Nellie died on March 13, 1975 and is buried in the Caroline Cemetery. In October, 1975 Maurice made his third trip to England, this time with his grandson, Dwayne Hansen. Maurice was not well, though, and died at his home on November 23, 1975. He is buried beside Nellie in the Caroline Cemetery.

Maurice and Nellie are survived in Canada by two children, Ted and Edith, nine grandchildren, Prue, Edward and Bruce Betts; Dwayne, Charlotte and Patsy Hansen; Douglas, Dianne and Susan Betts and two great-grandchildren, Christopher and Lindsey Hodgson (Prue's children).

Shorty Carter and his wife, Nellie, will be long remembered in the Caroline community. He for his jolly, joking manner and his story telling ability; she for her kindness and dignity; and both for their ever willing readiness to help their neighbors.

Ted Betts and son Edward. This super fish, approximately ten and three quarter pounds was caught in the upper Stoney.

Poems written by Mrs. Carter:
We honour the boys of Caroline
  From farm and village neat
We miss you from our ball games
  And from our fields of wheat.

Many a sweethearts eyes grow dim
  Wives and Mothers hearts beat sore,
As we think of you boys fighting
  Far away on distant shores.
                — a sailor's mother

We honour the boys of Caroline
  Who went away over there
To do the right and take up the fight
  As your fathers did before.

Some will meet the cannon fire
  The shells will burst for some,
But you will do your best for Canada
  Whatever else may come.

We honour the boys of Caroline
  Who answered our country's call.
You did your best and now you rest
  Over there on those distant shores.
              — rest on in peace, rest on —

Tom Chapin

by Kathleen Chapin

In the fall of 1931 my husband, Tom, and I and our five children moved to Caroline. We had farmed in the Hand Hills for three years and never got a crop. So my husband and a neighbor, George Arnold, decided to go homesteading west of Innisfail. We fixed up a covered wagon for Mrs. Arnold, the children and myself. Mr. Arnold had a hayrack. We had seven horses between us. We also had two pigs and we butchered one for the road and hauled the other one along, with a few chickens, in a crate.

At Innisfail, my husband and Mr. Arnold rented two farms from Mr. Arnell, but when we reached Caroline, a fire had gone through both places and the buildings had burnt. So we travelled south of Caroline and found two other shacks. The men fixed them up and they put a make-shift barn up for the horses. The men were lucky as they got a chance to stack green feed for Mr. Tom Roper, and also got a chance to take out his garden on shares as Mr. Roper had the misfortune to break his leg.

The district we moved into had wonderful neighbors. Mr. R. T. Blowers, his brother, Jim, Frank and Dolly Blowers, Ruth and Grandma Lawson, Art and Isabelle Oliver, Maurie and Nellie Carter, Kathleen and Max Dix, Jake Betchel and Mr. Swanson. Coming to Caroline we met Mr. and Mrs. John Van Least. They lived five miles east of Caroline at that time. Mrs. Van Least took my son, Tommy, in (he was only three weeks old) and gave him his first real bath, as he had only had a sponge bath and rubbed in oil since we had left the Hand Hills. We had four other children, Clarence, who now lives in Calgary, Roy lives in Wayne, Doreen in Calgary and Tom in Stauffer. Don (Scotty) was killed in the chuck wagon races in Calgary in 1960. We had four more children in Caroline, Mary, of Westward Ho, Dorothy of Millet, Basil of Calgary and Roger of Caroline.

In the spring of 1934 we homesteaded down on the Raven River, eleven miles southwest of Caroline. It was a beautiful place — the scenery was out of this world. We also had some fine neighbors. Mr. Boeken Sr., Carl and Mildred Boeken, Austin and Sarah Moore, Mr. Clay's sister, Ina and Freddie Thompson, Mrs. Anderson and family, Mrs. Wies and family and Harry and Mary Norton.

In 1939 we decided to go home and see my family whom I hadn't seen since 1921. Dad and Mother, Mr. and Mrs. Dave Flynn, two brothers, Basil and Pat, and three sisters, Eleanor, Christina and Marie, came back with us in the fall of 1939. In the spring of 1940 my father and his family moved to Water Valley.

Doreen and Roy Chapin.

In 1941 my husband and my brother, Basil, enlisted and in 1942 went overseas. In 1943 my son, Roy and Pat, enlisted and went overseas. So I purchased the Miller farm one half mile east of Caroline. My husband and son returned in 1945, but in 1955 my husband lost his health and we moved back to Drumheller. I cooked in the Doctor Hospital for nearly ten years. Tom died in 1963 of a heart attack. I lived on there until 1974 when I moved to Calgary.

I had wonderful friends and neighbors at Caroline. They sure were good to me and Caroline will always be home to me.

Note: Since the writing of this history Kathleen Chapin suffered an illness and passed away in February, 1979 in hospital in Calgary. She is laid to rest at Drumheller.

The Demenuk Story

by A. Demenuk

My folks came from Denmark and settled on a farm near Olds, Alberta. I have three sisters and one brother all living in Alberta. I am the second oldest.

My father passed away in 1923, my mother in 1951. There was a brother who died in Denmark, a sister in New York, and a sister in Kevisville.

I was born in Olds in 1911. When I was a year old my folks moved to a farm at Dickson, Alberta. After farming there for three years, we moved to a homestead in the Kevisville area.

I went to school at Rich Hill until I finished public school. I attended High School in Innisfail

Anna Demenuk and Helen Mullen.

Chick Demenuk, Gladys Willsie, Bob Willsie.

where I worked for my board and room while going to school. That was in the "dirty thirties" during the hard times. I took teachers' training at Calgary Normal School in 1934-35. Since teaching jobs were scarce I did not get a job teaching for some time.

My first teaching experience was in the Pine Hill School District. I walked two and a half miles to school, and did the janitor work as well. I taught all the grades from one to eight and had thirty pupils.

In 1937 I came to Caroline where I taught grades one to nine in the South Fork School District for four years. These four years were my most enjoyable teaching days.

In 1941 I went to Innisfail and taught grade three for two years.

In 1943 I married Donald "Chick" Demenuk. He originally came from Coleville, Saskatchewan, and came to Caroline six months after Bob Mitten, in 1934. He worked for Bob Mitten in the store and also did some general trucking for him. He has been in the general trucking business ever since. The main trucking he does now, is the beer haul from Calgary to Caroline. The beer parlor opened in Caroline in 1946.

I boarded with the Mittens at the hotel and became acquainted with Chick. I continued teaching after my marriage since teachers were in such short supply during the war. I taught in different rooms and buildings in Caroline.

The South Fork School had been moved to Caroline. The first year I taught grades one to nine in the building which later became the

Legion Hall. I had forty-nine pupils. Inspector Barnes took pity on me and split the grades for the first time. I kept grades one to six. Mrs. Shaw took grades seven to nine. Later I taught grades one to three. For the last twenty years I taught grade one.

After forty years of teaching I retired in 1976. I am enjoying retirement, and Chick and I still live in Caroline.

Dial, Raymond R.
by Helen (Dial) Mullen

Ray (my father) got his homestead in the Caroline area about 1913. It was 2 miles east of the present site of Caroline (recently known as the old Bowden place).

He built a two-storey house and in 1915 married Mabel Armstrong. Ray had to take Mabel to Innisfail to have their first child — Helen. At that time there was no hospital there, so she was born at the Wm. Daines residence. Dr. Turner was assisted by Mrs. Daines who was a midwife. Their second child Harold (Hal) was born two years later. By that time there was a hospital in Innisfail.

Ray and family moved to Innisfail in 1918 where he made a living drilling water wells. Four more sons and a daughter were added to the family Robert (Bob), Richard, Jimmy, Melba and Lane.

Ray also worked at harvest time on the Indian

L.-R. Jim and Mrs. Leask, Mary Waterhouse and Ray and Mabel Dial.

"Chicken hunt" — Picture taken at Jim Leask's.

Reserve at Gleichen. He was one of the few men in the area who had papers to run a steam engine. During the "dirty thirties" the family was far better off than most other people. We had a hundred acre farm on the edge of Innisfail, and almost every farm animal you could name — horses, cows, pigs, sheep, goats, geese, ducks and chickens. We also had radios, a fridge and many other things that few people had.

This all came about because of the water wells that Ray drilled. He had to have enough cash to pay for the pipe, pump, repairs and gas, but the labour cost was all taken out in trade. A nickel in those days was worth far more than it is now. We were lucky — we had most of what money could buy. The children all went to school in Innisfail, and one by one went their own way.

Richard joined the R.C.A.F. at the beginning of World War II. He was in the ground crew and served in England. When he returned he married Audrey Graham. They moved to a farm and he worked as a guard at the Bowden Institute. Later

Ray, Mabel and Hal Dial.

Gordon Lindskog.

they moved to Red Deer and operated Dial's Car Wash. Then he went to work for Canadian Propane and is now in Smithers, B.C. with the same company.

They have a son Pat and two daughters Laurie and Karen.

Melba was also in the R.C.A.F. and was stationed at Claresholm and in Quebec. When she returned she married Gordon Davidson. Gordon was killed in a scaffold accident in Winnipeg. Melba and her four boys all live in Calgary where they have an import store. The boys are Bernie, Lane, Rusty and Alan. Little Jimmy, as we call him, died at the age of one of pneumonia, red measles and whooping cough.

Lane became a well driller and moved to Barons. He married Joyce Brooks and had 6 children. From Barons they moved to west of Sylvan Lake. Lane was killed about 13 years ago in a car accident at the amber light curve west of the Lake. The family, Sandy, Hal, Dixie, Jackie, Wesley and Jesse all live in the Red Deer district.

Ray's wife Mabel died in 1945. Ray later married Elsie Wear and had a daughter, Linda. Linda is now in Toronto and has majored in languages. Ray died in 1960.

The Doel Family
by Ronald Doel

My father, William Doel, was born at Bath, Sommerset, England. When he came to Canada he worked for awhile in Ontario. Later he came

Mr. and Mrs. Wm. Doel with winter wood supply.

west and freighted for the logging camps in British Columbia, and eventually, in 1909, he filed on a homestead north of where Sedalia is now located. He bought three oxen, a wagon and a walking plow in Castor, which was the end of the railroad. He drove them from Castor to the homestead. He built a sod shack and lived in it until the homestead was proved up and then built a lumber house.

My mother, Veva Emma Timms, came to Canada with her people, Walter and Wilhelmena Timms, in 1910, from Stratford-on-Avon, England. Her father took a homestead nearby.

Mother and Father were married in 1916 and lived on Dad's homestead. Four children were born there, George, myself (Ronald), Margaret and Madeleine. We went to Berryfield School and later on to Shannon Heights School on the prairie. Later on, in 1941, at Caroline, another son, Richard, was born. After many years of farming at Sedalia, battling the dust and grasshoppers got to be too much. My parents decided to look for something better. In 1934 with three teams and wagons and a small herd of cattle, we headed west. After three weeks of traveling we landed at Caroline on September 1. We settled on the N.W. Q. 31-35-5-5. In 1937 my parents bought the Calhoun place where my grandmother (Mrs. Timms) lived until her passing in 1966, and was laid to rest at Monitor, Alberta.

I remember how hard it was to look after the stock in this brush. We had no fences or corrals and it was no small job stringing wire around a quarter section. The horses, having been raised on the bald prairie, were sure scary in the bush. We had to finish building a log house and log barn before winter. We soon learned we had to have good traces, hame straps, singletrees and eveners to work with logs, stumps and trees. I remember Russel McGrandle let us have some lumber right away, and during the winter we hauled logs to the mill he and his dad had on

George, Madeline,˙ Veva, Mrs. Timms holding Richard, William, Mollie and Ron.

William and Ronald Doel.

Beaver Creek, straight south of Caroline. Lumber was worth sixteen dollars per thousand feet and cordwood was three dollars per cord. The cattle and horses did not do too well that first winter as they were not acclimatized and feed was scarce. A cow was worth ten dollars and a three year old steer was twenty-five dollars. When calving time came in the spring the cows were weak and we lost most of them.

The first forty acres we cleared with axes and a grub hoe. The horses were used to pull the big trees and pile them so they could be burnt. I remember breaking with the horses when the flies (bulldogs) were on. They nearly drove the horses crazy. There were loads of wild strawberries and Mother remembers hurrying to pick them before they got plowed under. We occasionally had our fill while resting the horses.

Sometime in the 1940s bulldozers and brushcutters came in thus making the clearing by hand obsolete. There seemed to be a lot more roots when the land was cleared this way.

The first few winters, there were a lot of surprise house parties. The neighbors would get together and surprise each other at their homes. They would take lunch along, and if musical instruments were taken we would have a dance. There were a lot of whist parties too. We had many neighbors. Tommy Orr, who came to the Caroline area from Ireland in 1928, first worked for Langleys when the store was south of Caroline. His sister, Betty, who came later, also worked for Langleys. She now resides at Kelow-

na, British Columbia. Her married name is Betty McPherson. Tommy later worked for various people making his home with us a good deal of the time. He spent several years operating a planer mill for Art Johnson. He passed away in 1967 and was laid to rest in the Caroline Cemetery.

Some of our closest neighbors were Dave Knight, Mr. MacBain, Mrs. Edwards, Terry Hastings, George Breach, the Norman Holt family and John Quinns family. Also Womacks, Fleets, Wilsons, Wrens and the Anderson and Rhodes families. Later on, Pedersons lived on the Quinn place and then it was bought by Ray Adams where he lived for many years. Bob Mitten moved to Caroline about 1933 and built a store on the corner where the hotel now stands. We traded almost anything there for groceries, etc., lumber, tamarack posts, rails and even bush rabbits. A lot of visiting was done on Saturday nights in Caroline, hardly anyone missed this. Mrs. Suhr operated the post office and her husband, Herman, had a blacksmith shop. Langleys had just moved their store onto the corner across from the hall.

In the summertime there were ball games at Crammond on the diamond in the middle of the school section. Also many dances were held in the school house there, and much of the music was donated by neighbors. Dances were also held in the Caroline Hall. Lamb's Orchestra supplied a good deal of the music there and other places and was good and really enjoyed by all.

In harvest time I used to go stooking and threshing to make a few extra dollars. Wages were from a dollar fifty to three dollars a day. The Wren family moved to British Columbia in the spring of 1940. That fall I went to British Columbia and worked in the logging camps. Wages seemed good at fifty cents an hour so I stayed until July of 1941, when I married Mollie Wren and we came back to Alberta. We worked at a sawmill on Beaver Creek that first winter we were married. Mollie cooked for the crew and I worked in the mill. Then in the spring we moved onto Dad's farm. It takes a long time and a lot of energy to hew a home out of this bush but having a good woman makes it a lot easier. We raised three children, Ilene, Kenneth and Loretta. Ilene married John Bugbee and lives west of Caroline. They have two daughters, Carmen and Michelle. Kenneth married Sharon Polnau of Leslieville and are presently residing in Red Deer where he is in the building construction business. They have three sons, Darin, Shane and Ryan. Our youngest, Loretta, married Timothy Kennedy whom she met at Calgary University. They have one son, Jesse, and are living at Judson, south and east of Lethbridge, where he operates the Alberta Wheat Pool elevator.

My brother, George, was here for about a year and then started trucking lumber out of the Winfield area. From there he worked on road construction as manager for McKelvie Construction Company, and from that he moved to Rosedale and, with three partners, formed the Fish Lake Sand and Gravel with ready mix concrete. He managed this until his passing in 1977. He married Pauline Rathgaber while still employed by McKelvie Construction. They raised five children. Two daughters, Georgette and Corinne, and three sons, Clifford, Alvin and Marvin. George was laid to rest at Drumheller.

Margaret married Alec Brown and settled on his farm near Caroline. They raised two children, Robert, who married Rosemary McCormick and farms his dad's farm, and Veva, who married Norman Rose and lives west and north of Caroline.

Madeleine attended school at South Fork until 1938 and later married Arnold Parks and resides in Calgary.

Richard, who was born here and attended the Caroline School, later attended the Institute of Technology in Calgary where he studied Aircraft Maintenance. He is now employed in Aircraft Accessories. He married Marilyn Rutherford of Calgary and they have three sons, Robbie and the twins, Doug and Steve. They now live on an acreage west of Balzac.

Father passed away in 1949 and was laid to rest in the Cemetery at Rocky Mountain House. Mother, after travelling to Australia twice to visit her brother, and England to visit relatives, still resides on the farm enjoying her flowers and garden.

Percy Doherty

Percy filed a mile west of Caroline on the north and west side of the road. He had an auction sale on May 1, 1925, and went back east.

Elick Elickson

Little is known of the home, family and early life of the late Elick Elickson. He was born in Norway on September 8, 1887, and came to Canada as a young man soon after the turn of the century. He took up a homestead one mile north of Caroline in 1907, where Angers now live. He broke quite a lot of his homestead with oxen.

In 1908 he went to school at the South Fork School to learn the English language.

He left this area only to work for brief intervals. Elick enjoyed dancing and attended almost every dance held in the Community Hall.

He was engaged to be married at one time and made many preparations for his forthcoming marriage, including the building of a new house and the purchase of a new car,. His fiancee had a change of heart at the last minute. Disappointed but determined, Elick carried on living alone the rest of his life. He passed away in the Innisfail Hospital on April 15, 1961 and is buried in Caroline Cemetery. The majority of his estate was willed to an orphanage.

A letter from a sister in Norway was found among his possessions and through that letter officials were trying to notify her and any other relatives. The letter was from Olga Ellingseth, Luster, Norway, and was dated May 5, 1956. That is the last and only definite information of relatives and their whereabouts.

Clarence Earl (Pete) Fay
by Guy E. Fay

Clarence E. Fay was born at Freebourne, Minnesota, on May 2, 1872. He grew up at Bonesteel, Nebraska. In 1902, he and his brother, John, started a livery barn in Gregory, South Dakota, which they operated until 1910.

In 1905 he married Jessie Hazen. On July 25, 1906, his first son, Joy, was born, and on January 4, 1908, a daughter, Eunice, was born.

In 1910 they moved to Hermosa, South Dakota, where I was born on April 24, 1911. We came to Caroline in 1912 where he lived, except for short periods when away working, until 1957. When I look back I realize how hard it must have been for Dad.

From 1918 on he had the responsibility of raising us three kids. Eunice married George Han-

L.-R. — Joy, Pete, Eunice and Guy Fay.

son in 1924, and Joy married Katherine Bowers in 1927.

I married Margaret Ankle on January 4, 1934. Dad was everybody's friend. When anyone was in trouble he was the first one sent for. There are many old timers in Raven Cemetery in coffins he made. He was a very generous man.

Dad died in Calgary in 1961, and is buried in Canmore. Joy died on his fifty-fifth birthday, and is also buried in Canmore.

The Moonshiners

The time of prohibition
    Many years ago
Was an excellent time
    For moonshiners to grow.

Wooden barrels were plentiful
    And could be bought for a little cash
They made a perfect vat
    For brewing the mash

With some yeast cakes
    And ground wheat,
Plus sugar, that's all
    A few days brewing then raw alcohol.

A secluded place in the muskeg
    They were likely to choose,
Maybe muskeg water,
    Would make better booze.

The A.P.P. were scattered and few
    And protection could be bought
With a bottle or two.

With no legal liquor
    Business was brisk
You purchased each bottle
    At your own risk.

Just one drink or two
    And you could cry like a loon,
God pity the man
    Who was poisoned on moon.

— Guy E. Fay

Moses Fay.

Moses Fay
by Guy Fay

Moses Fay was born in Quebec, in the hamlet of South Sutton, in 1834. He grew up there, and in his twentieth year he immigrated to the state of Minnesota, where he homesteaded.

He was drafted into the Union Army in the Civil War. After three years of service, he mustered out and moved to Nebraska where he resided for over twenty years, raising a family of five daughters and four sons. The youngest lad, Benny, died as a young boy.

In 1906 he moved to South Dakota with his young son, Clarence. In 1911, having heard glowing reports of Alberta from his grandson, Ren Sterns, he drove from Hermosa, South Dakota, with a team on a surrey, wintering in Montana, and arriving at Caroline in August, 1912. He was at this time seventy-eight years old. He homesteaded the S.W. 35-36-6-5, which he later gave to his daughter, Mrs. Martha Sanders. He was always looking for a deal of some kind, and at that time the dam was going in at Brooks and horses were at a premium, so he traded land that he had in Idaho for a bunch of horses, and made a deal with two brothers, by the name of Guy and Charley Coates, to bring them to this country and break them. They started out with one broke horse, and when they arrived in Caroline every horse had saddle marks on them, then they would harness them up and put a Flying W on them, and stand them on their heads until they learned to stop when they said, "whoa". Then they would take them to Calgary and sell them.

He returned to South Dakota in 1920 to live with his daughter, Mrs. Verily, at Centerville,

262

South Dakota. He was eighty-six years old then, and he died at the age of ninety.

Jessie and Frank Furnish
by Guy Fay

The Furnish boys were among the early settlers in the Caroline district. Jessie, or Slim as he was known, filed a mile west of Caroline on the south side of the road, and Frank filed on the quarter to the west. They were fiddlers and very popular at the early day dances.

In 1921 they moved to Carseland and later to Balzac where Slim passed away in 1949. Frank took him back to Coffeyville, Kansas, to bury him. Frank sold off their possessions and went back to Kansas to be near his relatives.

The Hazens
by Jessie Hoare

Frank and Ida Hazen (nee Ida Springer) as far as I know, lived in South Dakota or Idaho in the early years. Frank and his father were carpenters. The Hazens had four children, Emma, who married Frank Sutton, Jessie, who married Clarence (Pete) Fay, Charles, who married Aura Fitch from Sylvan Lake and Josie, who married Jim Clason.

For a few years the families had been wanting to venture north to Canada and in the spring of 1913 their dreams became a reality. Frank and Ida, along with Jim, Josie and family, son, Charles, and son-in-law, Pete Fay, started out with wagons with only what they needed for the trip, over little or no roads. It was a long trip and presented a lot of hardships but they made it finally to Stavely. (I think the Suttons stayed at Stavely where they had found a place to live).

The rest of the family continued north. I remember Pete Fay telling of stopping to ask directions to 'Calgeery'. He apparently had

Frank Hazen's family — Jessie Fay, Josie Clason, Emma Sutton, Charles Hazen.

difficulty getting the gent he was talking with, to understand where he meant. For some reason it was still 'Calgeery' instead of Calgary when he died. But anyway they got to Innisfail then on to Caroline.

At this time there were few people around, the post office was on the north bank of the Raven about half a mile south of the present town site and was operated by Mrs. Langley along with a small store. The Hazens and Clasons got a piece of land at the east of the Clearwater bridge, west of Caroline, and known as the Fleming place, (later occupied by the Bugbee family). Pete Fay homesteaded two miles north of the present town.

Now is when action took place, the women and children were left at Innisfail at the home of the Whitcomb family whom they had met on the first trip through. All the men went back to the U.S.A. to bring the rest of their possessions. Their return took longer as cattle and horses were driven and the wagons were heavily loaded. It was a busy fall for them, getting settled, they all stayed at the Hazen house while logs were got out and a house was built on the Fay place. The following years were spent improving the land making room for crops and gardens.

For winter entertainment there were card parties and dances. I'm not sure just where the dances were held but I think it would be in the Wooler area. It seems that when the children

Frank and Ida Hazen, 1937-38.

were tired they were put down on coats on the benches while the rest danced to music supplied by those who were fortunate enough to have instruments. Jim Clason played the fiddle and Charles Hazen played the mouth organ. The Furnish brothers played, but I don't know what, but everyone enjoyed the outings and it gave them the boost they all needed for the days ahead.

Times were hard trying to get started and not much to do it with. It was hours by team and wagon to get to a doctor and supplies that couldn't be got at the local store.

In 1916 Frank and Ida and the Clason family moved to Stavely where the men opened a carpentry shop which worked out real well as they were both top carpenters and could build almost anything from houses and barns to kitchen cabinets.

The Suttons stayed at Stavely, but the Hazens and Clasons after a few years moved back to Kerrywood, Idaho. There they farmed and the men worked as carpenters. It was while here that tragedy struck, two of the Clason girls were burned in a fire that left the family homeless, a third girl survived as her burns were less severe. Shortly after, the families moved back to Oregon settling around Salem and Portland. The Sutton family joined them a few years later. One of the Sutton boys was killed in World War II.

Meanwhile, Charles Hazen had married Aura Fitch from Sylvan Lake. They lived at Stavely also for a few years, returning to the Sylvan Lake and Pine Hill districts where they raised nine children; finally, residing in the Centerville district. Aura died in 1935 leaving several small children, one married and some were in school.

Charles Hazen's children — Dick, Ellen, Frank, Joan, Gene, Jessie, Harold (on chair), 1933.

Their children: Theodore married Dorothy Greene. They had eight children, John, Iva, Joe, Ted, Vera, Dwight and Eva. Ellen married Alvin Parker and they had five sons, Milton, Lorne, Ralph, Edwin and Gordon. They live at Spruce Grove, Alberta.

Dwight (Dick) married Marion Lepine from Renfrew, Ontario, near the end of World War II just before he was released from the armed forces. They have eight children, Judy, Ralph, Robert, Anne, Frank, Laura, Betty and Harold. They live near Renfrew, Ontario.

Frank died in 1941, but lived in the Centerville district while still alive.

Gene married Beryl Mass of Renfrew, Ontario, after serving several years overseas. They have four children, Randal, Brent, Shildon and Janice. They live at Kingston, Ontario.

Jessie married Edward Hoare and now lives at Innisfail. (See Ed Hoare story).

Joan married Ronald Toppin and now lives at Golden, British Columbia. They have six children, Lorena, Bud, Roy, Nina, Betty and Bertha.

Harold died in 1951 while working south of Sylvan Lake.

Iona married John Roper of Caroline.

In the late 1930's Charles Hazen returned for awhile during his father's illness, later moving back to the Caroline district. In 1945 his mother also died. In 1957 Charles died after a lengthy illness.

The Hecks
by Betty Heck

The Hecks originated from the Sunnynook, Alberta, area. Dallas came to the Caroline area in about 1934-35 and farmed on a rental basis for many years on several farms. He also worked in local sawmills. He married Sarah Bugbee, who had two children from a previous marriage, Lillian and Bob. Later Dallas bought land two and three quarter miles west of Caroline. Here they had two children, Joe and Prue, Sarah passed away in November, 1970. After a few years Dallas sold the farm and now resides in Caroline. Lillian and her family live at Langley, British Columbia. Bob lives in Caroline and Joe and Prue both live in British Columbia.

Marvin came to Caroline around 1935 and resided in the village in a little house he built, where later Mrs. Sarc lived until her death. He did general trucking for several years. One of the highlights in trucking was hauling piping to the well head west of Caroline in the Corkscrew Mountain area. There were sulphur springs near there, and the roads were very bad in those days. The hills were steep and trucking was quite an ordeal. The rig derrick was a wooden structure and of late there were remains still visible. Of course the roads in that area are much improved today.

Before the war, Marvin moved to Bowden, Alberta, and lived there with his wife, Arlene, until he enlisted. After his discharge of the West Coast Service he took up residence at Sheerness, Alberta, where he went into the trucking business in that area. There he raised a family of five children. Marvin has retired to Hanna, and his family all reside in that area.

Isobelle, a sister to the Hecks, married Arthur Oliver who is also a pioneer from the Sunnynook district. They lived south of Caroline on a farm. They raised eight children. Arthur passed away suddenly in 1951 and Isobelle passed away in 1974. The children, Leonard and Lawrence, live around Caroline, Colleen at Innisfail, Shirley at Vancouver Island, Owen and Vic are in various areas in Alberta, and Darlene passed away in the early '60s.

Jack came to visit with Isobelle and Marvin in 1935 and while here he worked at odd jobs in the lumber industry and at one time was cook at the Dan McGrandle lumber camp. There were many interesting events that took place as in those days you worked but the pay days were few and far between, so after a few years he helped Marvin with his trucking business until more attractive employment came along. He hired on as construction help when the building boom started and the war gave many a job. Hangers were being constructed at Penhold and Vulcan and his crew put the roofing on. He worked until one day it was his turn to enlist. After some basic training in Canada, he was sent overseas in 1942; he was in the Italian Campaign and on up through France, Germany, Holland and Belgium.

After his discharge he returned to Caroline and bought land one mile west of Caroline. In 1947 he brought out his wife, Betty, who had three children by a previous marriage. Here they farmed until their retirement in 1975. They now live at Salmon Arm, British Columbia. Walter Petersen is drilling in the Algerian desert and his family live on Mallorea Island. Gloria (Flower) lives at Edson. Keith lives at Kamloops, British Columbia.

The Bert Hunter Family

by Ada Sampson

The first of our family to come to Canada was Bert Hunter. He was born in Missouri in 1878 and moved to Lostine, Oregon, as a young man.

Ada Allen was born in Kansas and as a young girl, the Allen family travelled by covered wagon to homestead in the Lostine area.

This is where Bert and Ada met and married. Within a few years they had two children, Myrland and Ruth.

When homestead land in Canada was being advertised in the United States, Bert and Ada, on the advice of Bert's father, came to Alberta. The land they decided upon was two miles south and three-quarter miles west of Caroline. At the time of the move, Myrland was six years old and Ruth a baby.

Bert arrived first at the homestead, followed shortly by Ada and the children in November, 1911. Ada brought with her two box car loads of machinery and some horses from Oregon. The goods came by train to Innisfail and had to be transported by wagon to Caroline. At this time, the road was just a trail from the Medicine River west, so the trip out was a hard one.

Once the area became settled, their neighbors were the Jensens, Brownings, McFelemys, Nellie Edwards, Calhouns and the Hilemans.

Bert and Adas' marriage ended in divorce and years later, Ada married Mike Harkins. They lived at Nordegg for awhile, then returned to the Caroline area to farm. The farm was five miles east of Caroline and their neighbors were the Stanges, Blacks, Smiths and Keims.

Mike and Ada raised a baby boy, Raymond Dennis, born in 1935, better known as Jim Harkins. He still lives in this area. The farm remained in the family until 1968 when it was sold.

Mike died in February, 1970, and is buried in the Raven Church Cemetery. Ada died in November, 1960, and is buried in the Innisfail Cemetery. They were not buried together because of something Ada (my grandmother) told me when I was a young child. We were walking through the cemetery which was not kept up at that time, and she said to me, "If I am buried here, I will come back to haunt you!"

Myrland (my uncle) left the Caroline area to work in the Turner Valley oil fields. Later he farmed at Alhambra, then he sold his land and he and his wife, Irene, moved to Oliver, British Columbia, where they still reside.

Ruth (my mother) left the farm and moved to Nordegg where she married my dad, Walter Watson, coal miner and big game guide. I was their only child.

After their separation, Mom moved to Vancouver and became one of the first twelve Vancouver City Police women. She served on this force from 1947 until her retirement in 1960.

A few years after her mother died, Mom moved to the Caroline farm until it was sold. She passed away in April, 1971, and is buried in Canmore, where I live.

I was married to M. L. Sampson of Canmore in 1951 and we still make our home here. We have two daughters, Brenda and Sharon. Brenda has two sons, Mark and Bradley.

Chris Jenson

Chris Jenson had a homestead two and a half miles south and one mile west of Caroline. It could have been in the '20s when he homesteaded there. Chris's trade was repairing buggy and wagon wheels. He also farmed in the summer and worked in the mines in Nordegg in the winter. Sometimes they only ran two or three days a week so he didn't make much money.

One day Oscar Tress from a couple of miles west of Chris, was having trouble with his democrat tire rim coming off the wheel and passing him. What it needed was the heat and shrink treatment. Well, everything went well except the heat shrunk the tire rim too small — just wouldn't fit. No amount of hammering, words, etc., would do the trick so finally Chris rolled the whole issue off down the hill. To Oscar, this meant **war**! In the end they just went into Chris's home for a cup of coffee.

Chris had a white horse who could jump any fence in the country (riding or not). The horse ended up in the pound quite often because he was always into other people's feed stacks. He also had two other horses, a black and a brown. Chris was a frequent visitor up the Raven Valley and one day he came riding up on Brownie, leading Dan, his black, with a pack saddle on. He stopped at Carl Boekens for a couple of minutes saying he was going to 'Eatons' to pick up a 'C.O.D.' parcel on the salt lick at Wilds. (Wilds was an old sawmill sight about five miles up the Raven River west of Carl Boekens.) Well, about a week went by after that, when a lone rider showed up from the west on Brownie. No Dan, no 'C.O.D.,' just Chris with only one suspender holding up his running gear. He even run out of grub! Well, yes, he had made it to 'Eatons (a salt lick) right on time, picked up his 'C.O.D.' (deer), loaded it on his trusty horse, Dan, and was leading him with a shoestring when something went wrong. Dan spooked, and both horses and his·'C.O.D.' disappeared into the timber! Chris hunted and looked for them, but no luck. Carl listened to his tale of woe and told Chris to go home and get his horse bell, tie it on his saddle horse and ride back up where he had been. That did the trick, as his horse did come out of the bush but unfortunately, in the meantime, his horse had delivered the C.O.D. to another depot. Anyway, Chris rode off to the east again without his special C.O.D.

Chris also had a quarter section up by Clear Creek north of Caroline, but he couldn't keep up his payments so he lost it. He passed away in the 1950s.

Oscar and Mary Johnson

Oscar came from Fayette, Idaho, to Carstairs where he met Mary Dewhurst and they were married in 1922. Mary came from England with her parents at the age of eight years in 1911. Her parents had a dairy farm there. She got her schooling at Carstairs. Mary and Oscar lived on a farm in the Cremona district before moving to Caroline in 1923.

Gordon was born in Innisfail. They had a half section of land, Purebred Angus cattle and lots of horses and pigs. The stock ran on open range.

They had a family of four girls and two boys, Gordon, Margaret, Rose, Ellen, Florence and Louis. In 1927 Oscar brought Dave and Chris Staben from Calgary. They were over from Germany. They made their home around Caroline too. Our close neighbors were Jim Leask, Ray Dial, Fred Miller, Donald Bowden and the Grieves.

The children had most of their schooling at South Fork, one mile south of Caroline. Marg and Gordon started school in 1930 and went horse back three miles across country. Miss Moe was their first teacher. Louis started school in Caroline at the old Legion Hall with Miss Mewha as his first teacher. Rose, Ellen and Florence went there too. Ellen finished her high grades at Dickson. Florence took grade nine at Shilo, then went to Langdon for grades ten to twelve. Louis went to Langdon then back to Shilo after his mother's passing. He lived with Rose and Stanley. Oscar and Mary moved to Langdon in 1941 to another farm. Mary passed away May, 1946. Oscar moved back to Caroline until his passing in 1957. Florence passed away in November 1977. They are laid to rest in the Raven Cemetery.

Gordon married June Murray in 1947 and lives in Caroline. Gordon works with Skocdopole

Seated: Oscar and Louis Johnson, Standing: L. R. Ellen, Margaret and Florence, Rose — far right.

266

Mary Johnson holding Florence — children: Rose, Ellen Margaret and Gordon.

Construction. Margaret married Sam Ennis in 1946 and lived at Raven and Spruce View districts. They live in Caroline now. They have a family of four boys and one girl.

Rose married Stanley Smith in 1945 and lives five miles east of Caroline. They have four boys and one girl. The oldest son does the farming. Stan and Rose work out part time. Ellen married Fred Sicotte in 1948 and lived in Calmar and now in Edmonton. He is with the oil companies. They have a family of four boys and three girls.

Florence married Jack Murray in 1948 and lived at Caroline. They worked in sawmill camps. Florence worked at the Caroline Hotel, ran the lunch counter in the Pioneer Store and cooked for oil camps until her passing.

Louis married Evelyn Bird in 1963 and lives on a farm east of Caroline. They have a family of two boys and two girls. Louis farms and works for Don Beddoes Construction, now operating his own equipment.

Charlie Kimball
by Irvin Palmer

It was in the summer of 1934 when a grey team, pulling a wagon with a brown horse behind it, came up the Raven Valley. It was driven by Charlie Kimball, and it carried all his worldly possessions. Charlie was making his retreat from the grasshopper country, somewhere in the Killam area. Charlie homesteaded on the west

end of Burntstick Lake along side of a creek that flowed into the lake. Here a lot of his worries would come to an end! He would never get thirsty, he had a big swimming pool, fish to catch any time, lots of deer and moose, and if he should get lucky, duck or wild goose for Christmas. He had firewood to no end, and the little log cabin, about twelve by twelve, wasn't too bad to heat. Here he could really live off the land! There were some hay sloughs around, so he made hay coils in the summer and had all winter to haul them home.

After a year went by, Charlie realized that his diet wasn't quite complete, so he checked with his bank (an Old Chum tobacco can), and made a trip down to the Anderson Brothers and bought himself a Red Polled milk cow. Cows were kind of high — ten whole dollars! Later he bought a John Deere tractor.

Well, the years passed by and Charlie seemed to enjoy this kind of life, until old age finally caught up with him. Hopefully, from there he made it to the Great Happy Hunting Grounds!

David Knight

David Knight was born in Tennessee in 1881. He moved to Montana when he was seventeen years old. On June 12, 1909, he married Elizabeth Montgomery. They left there by covered wagon in 1910, bringing a herd of cattle with them. The journey took them three months.

They lived first northeast of Raven, but moved to Caroline in 1911 where he resided until he went blind. He lived with his daughter, Rose, for two years. From there he came back to Caroline to live with his son, Jim, until he had a stroke and passed away in 1954.

Dave Knight.

Reba, Harv and Cynthia Langley.

This Knight herd of cattle was brought from the U.S.A. in 1910 by trail.

Dave Knight family on his farm at Beaver Creek.

Harvey Augustus Langley

In 1906 Mr. and Mrs. William Comstock and Mr. and Mrs. Joseph Carral Langley came to Alberta near Bowden. In December that same year both families moved to homesteads west of the Raven Post Office. Joseph Carral Langley filed on the S.W.Q. 12-36-6-5. The Comstock family filed on a piece of land, but did not stay long. After Mrs. Comstock's death in 1908, William went back to Minnesota.

In December of that same year, soon after J. C. Langley moved to his homestead on the Raven, his brother, Harvey Augustus Langley, came for a visit, liked what he saw of the country and decided to stay. After looking the country over quite thoroughly, H.A. decided that the quarter north of his brother's suited him quite well.

It had been filed on though never proven up and H.A. filed cancellation on it. While waiting out the necessary length of time, he made an abode on the Eza Zobbler place, now the Jim Kissick place.

In March of 1907 Harvey Augustus Langley's wife, Cynthia, and their eight-year-old daughter, Caroline Rebecca (always known as Reba) arrived. Thus came about the beginning of the large part this family played in forming and developing a rural community and its way of life in an uninhabited parkland area of virgin soil.

Later that same spring of 1907, Mrs. H. A. Langley returned to Minnesota to bring their team of horses, a cow and their household goods. This necessitated being away one month and having to wait for a railway car to bring their settlers' effects. Special railway rates were in effect then to encourage families into new unsettled areas which were being opened for homesteading.

When Mrs. Langley arrived in Innisfail with their household goods and livestock, it still meant a good many hours journey by wagon to their homestead. In some places bridges had to be built and boggy places corduroyed along the way. At the North Raven River, Mrs. Langley herded the horses and cattle which belonged to various outfits, as a number of families had joined on the trek west. The men put a bridge across the Raven some distance upstream from the present bridge. The river was at high water at the time and they were not able to ford as usual.

During a very nasty snowstorm that spring, while Mrs. Langley was away, H.A. captured an eagle who had tried to dine on a porcupine and in the process got himself well infested with quills. H.A. saved the eagle and kept it as a pet for several weeks in a pen in one corner of the cabin. This naturally caused some upsets. While H.A. and Reba went to Raven for supplies and the mail one day, the eagle escaped from the pen. On their return, Reba was most annoyed to find the eagle loose and her little flannelette nightie in shreds; the eagle had eaten most of it. The Langley's bachelor neighbors were very interested in the eagle's welfare and contributed many tidbits to help feed the pet. Later the eagle's wings were strapped so he could not fly and he was put into a partially completed barn. One day, during the absence of the family, someone borrowed their pet and forgot to return it.

As soon as H.A.'s filings on his chosen quarter were completed, he took steps to get settled on his land. He had hauled lumber and put up a sloping shelter for the stove, then got busy putting up a house. The house at the time was built with a sod roof. Later the roof was raised to make room for an upstairs and as time went on, H.A. added a 'leanto' on the west, and still later, one on the east. This house still stands at this time, 1960.

Coyotes were plentiful and bold and they were blamed for the loss of several dogs from the settlement. When the Langley's acquired a beautiful collie pup from Mrs. Haggett, the pup was never allowed out of sight. She was named 'Gyp' and became Reba's constant companion along with 'Buck', a small buckskin pony. These three spent many happy hours herding stock before pastures were fenced. A bull calf, born that first summer, was a great pal of Gyp's and she never would bite him. One day, Mrs. Langley was bringing in the cattle and the yearling was particularly annoying. Mrs. Langley picked up a switch and said, "Now bite that calf!" Gyp gave her a nasty look, bit the calf once and went home. For several days Gyp was very cool toward her mistress.

H. A. Langley spent a lot of time showing newcomers around the country, helping them choose the better quarters still available for filing on. Among them were Mr. and Mrs. Haggett, Cliff Polard and John and Melville Ferguson. These men had all suffered from copper poison while welding for the railroad. They came in 1907. Mr. Hagett and John Ferguson died soon after coming into their claims. Mrs. Haggett lived and kept house for Melville Ferguson for a number of years.

On September 9, 1907, H. A. Langley and Mel Ferguson left the settlement on a trip to Innisfail. Just before leaving, he realized that there was a very small supply of cut firewood. A neighbor who happened to be there accepted the chore of adding to the supply of wood to do the women for three or four days. As the weather had been so very nice, Mrs. Langley did not think very much wood was needed and soon stopped the man. It was such a lovely day that Mrs. Langley and Reba decided to do the family wash and before noon put out the white things. Blueberries and cranberries were ready for picking and after lunch the two women took their berry pails and went across the Raven River to pick berries and visit Sade Langley. Picking was

good and soon all pails were full. They went home, canned the berries, finished the wash, did the chores (not many) and went to bed. About ten p.m. the wind began to blow and Mrs. Langley wondered why in the world a wind would come up and blow so hard so late in the evening, However, being very tired, they slept on and awoke next morning in no way prepared for what met their eyes. Eight inches of lovely fluffy white snow! Talk about shock! Everyone was utterly stunned! Had winter come? What could they do? Where were the men? Why had they ever left Minnesota? The whole community was in a state of shock. Charlie Baldwin, a neighbor, went over to the Langley place to see how the women had made out. As he stood in the doorway mopping his sweating brow from the walk, he exclaimed, "Judas Priest, ain't this awful, seven kids in the house and not a shoe on a foot!"

H. A. Langley and Mel Ferguson, on their trip to Innisfail, had camped on the Medicine River and crawled under the wagon to sleep. Being so warm, they left their boots by the wagon tongue and hung their pants over it. What a jolt to crawl out next morning and shake the snow out of their clothes! All's well that ends well! The snow melted quickly and a very nice fall followed. Perhaps the hint of what could happen helped hurry everyone into getting better prepared for winter than they might have been otherwise.

The first horses acquired by the Langleys were three mares, one a buckskin named Buck, a brown mare named Daisy and a beautiful dark chestnut called Topsy. Buck and Daisy raised several foals but Topsy never had one. Buck became Reba's saddle horse. Reba, Buck and Gyp spent many happy hours together and Reba shed bitter tears when Buck was killed by falling through a half poled bridge on the Lou Calhoun's homestead. She wept some more when Gyp died while she was away in high school at Innisfail. Daisy's first foal became Reba's first experience in veterinarian work. The foal ran into a wire fence and received a very bad cut across the chest. Reba doctored it faithfully and the wound healed safely with no ill after effects.

Many firsts to benefit the community were started by the Langleys. The first Sunday School and Church services were held in the Langley home. The Methodist Church sent a very sincere young student, Ernest Wilson, as the first minister. Others were Mr. Davis, Mr. Waring and Mr. Vernon Gilbert. Mr. Gilbert was also a schoolteacher.

The first binder to come to the district was used on a field of grain on the H. A. Langley farm. The first threshing machine to be used in the district belonged to the Morigeau brothers, Martin, Frank and Ed, from the Stauffer district. The brothers brought the machine to the

Caroline settlement to thresh for the Langleys. Bringing a big machine that distance over trails as they were then, was a mighty big job. They got stuck on the Eza Zobbler flat and the separator tipped over. A lot of time was lost setting it up and putting it in shape again for threshing. The crew was Martin, Frank and Ed Morigeau, Fred Howes and a cousin of the Morigeau's called Louie. It took about two weeks to bring the outfit to the Langley farm and do a field of about twenty acres. The power was steam.

The first gas-powered wood-sawing outfit came from Dovercourt and sawed stove wood on the Langley farm. This wood-sawing outfit was owned and operated by a man named Hugh Lee.

The first lumber sawmill to cut lumber in the vicinity of Caroline sawed for the Langleys too. The mill was owned by Mr. Dan McGrandle of Innisfail. The set was made on the Raven River and had previously been in operation on the William Comstock place, several miles down river on land now owned by the Stange family. Mrs. Comstock was an aunt of Mrs. H. A. Langley and mother of Mrs. Joseph Carral Langley. Mr. and Mrs. Comstock's daughter, Mrs. Ernest Foot, lived in the area for awhile. Her husband was an excellent violinist and provided the music for many a party while they lived here. He had a marvellous sense of humor and was liked by everyone.

Within a few years the Literary Society was organized. The society was a much appreciated means of getting together and enjoyed by most. Debates were popular with everyone, a cause of great merriment and very often quite enlightening. Recitations and songs were looked upon with favor. Mrs. J. C. Langley was quite an elocutionist and Mrs. J. R. Langley had a good musical background which was a big help.

The Joseph Robert Langleys came from Minnesota around 1909. J. R. Langley was the father of Joseph Carral and Harvey Augustus Langley. Mrs. J. R. Langley or 'Daisy' as she was called, was J.C.'s and H.A.'s step-mother and only a few years older than they were.

The Joseph Robert Langley family by second marriage consisted of Joseph Robert, Daisy (his wife) and six children, Bill Lincoln, Gladys, Myrtie, Alice and Merton, who were born here. They stayed until 1920 and then moved to Washington State. Gladys married, had two children and then died. The other children lived in various parts of Washington State. Joseph Robert Langley died in Washington many years ago. Daisy remarried but was widowed again. She died about 1950 at the age of eighty-seven or eighty-eight years.

The land on which the village of Caroline is located is the southwest corner of N.W.Q. 13-36-6, the northwest corner of S.W. 13-36-6, the southeast corner of N.E. 14-36-6 and the northeast corner of S.E. 14-36-6-5. At the time settlement took place, the quarters were homesteaded as follows: S.E. of 14 by Bine Vallier now owned by Steve Molnar after belonging to H. A. Langley for some time. The S.W. of 14 by George Bushnell. This too now belongs to Steve Molnar. The N.W. of 14 by Ren Stearn. He lived there until his death. His younger brother, Lou, spent many months with him. The N.E. of 14 was filed on by a Norwegian, Adam Tate. He was a great worker but did not stay long and sold his place to Tom Roper. The N.W. of section 13 was claimed by Joe Rockhill. This is the quarter where the Hotel now stands. The S.W. of 13 was taken by Ray Greer and now belongs to Don Bowden. Ray Greer's wife was a sister to George Bushnell. Her health was not good and she died very early leaving her husband to raise their two

Repairs by the wayside — Belle Langley and Cynthia Langley hauling the mail.

children, Ella and Curtis. After a few years he sold the homestead to H. A. Langley and moved to east of Innisfail.

Joe Rockhill was a tall slender man and his wife was equally tall and slender. He was a restless man and they soon moved to places more suitable to their type. The S.E. 13-36 was taken by Will Willoughby. The N.E. of 13 at that time was mostly swamp.

Mr. and Mrs. George Johns came from West Virginia. They homesteaded the N.E. of 12, east of the H. A. Langley's in the same section. His wife was ill when they came and steadily grew worse. She had tuberculosis and finally died in a tent at the Langley place. Mrs. Langley spent many hours helping Mr. Johns care for her. Soon after his wife's death, Mr. Johns sold his homestead to H. A. Langley and returned to his former home.

The Bine Valliers came when the Johns did. They had two children, a boy and a girl named Stanley and Ici. Mrs. Vallier had lost a hand. She was a gentle, kindly person. One baby was born the year after they arrived and only lived a few hours. Bine tried to improve his homestead, but without much success. H. A. Langley helped him with the improvements on the land, so he was able to get the title to it. Bine immediately sold the place to H.A and took his family back to the States, where Ici was married.

George Bushnell's sister, Blanche, and their mother, Mrs. Hilary, lived with George, Blanche was engaged to Ren Stearns for awhile but later she married Ephriam Bell and they left the district. George Bushnell sold out and went away still a bachelor.

The four corners, one mile west of the present site of Caroline, was called 'Batchelor's Corner' for a long time. George Bushnell did not live right at the corner, but Ren and Lou Stearns, Frank and Jess Furnish and Percy Doherty did. Stearns had the N.W. 14-36, Bushnell the S.W. 14, the Furnish boys had the S.E. 15-36 and Doherty the N.E. 15-36. Another bachelor had the N.W. 15-36.

The Furnish brothers lived there for a number of years and were grand neighbors. Frank was a wonderful violinist and many a lively party was held at their place. He played for the community dances as well. He was a left handed player but played a right hand strung violin. After quite a few years on their homestead, they left and went to southern Alberta where they lived in a cook shack on road allowances. However, for many years both Frank and Jesse came back every fall to go hunting west of Caroline. When hunting season opened they were joined by H. A. Langley and his son-in-law, Sam Nelson. Occasionally, Jim

Lewis from Oklahoma district near Innisfail, came along too. One season Paul Hess made a trip with them. Others to go were T. Pitts, George Picking, and Tom Still. On the way home from one of their hunting trips, a big pot of stew had been prepared. When they made camp, Tom, while the others were busy feeding the horses etc., took it upon himself to prepare the meal. After getting the fire going well, he put the stew to heat up and added some extra seasoning. Each of the men took a big serving, ate one bite and sat back watching each other. Finally Tom noticed this and said, "Hey, aren't you fellows hungry?" One of them replied, "Oh, it's a bit hot yet!" Tom fixed up his own plate and took a big bite and let out a yell, "No wonder no one is eating, I must have dropped the pepper can in!" He had in fact opened the big hole of the pepper can. Many a good laugh was had over that pot of stew. Most of this gang has gone on to better hunting grounds — Mr. Pitts, Jesse and Frank Furnish, Jim Lewis and later in October, 1960, Sam Nelson.

Mr. H. A. Langley, aged ninety-two in February, 1963, is still going strong. At present Mr. and Mrs. Langley live in Edmonton. Each year they make several trips to the Caroline district to renew old acquaintances. For the past two or three years the family holds open house for the H. A. Langley's on December 26, their wedding anniversary. There are five generations of the Langley family, the youngest member, a girl, is four years old.

During open house held for them in 1963, H.A. began recalling past happening before coming to Canada. He told how he had been a very shy young man and never really had courted Cynthia (his wife). He had been working for his father as hired man and Cynthia was working on the farm helping to care for H.A.'s three step brothers. Like most young men, H.A. had the urge to be on his own, gathered up a few things and started off. After he had gone a short distance he stopped, thought for a bit, then turned back. Cynthia, who no doubt had been watching, came out and H.A. asked her to come with him. Cynthia said "Give me a few moments to get some things," and off they went. With her mother's consent they were married.

They rigged up a covered wagon and started out. He found a job on the railroad and held a scraper for several weeks. Cynthia boarded some of the crew. When that was finished they got a job on a farm for harvest. The night H.A. collected his wages he was attacked by two robbers. He was riding a big black horse. The bandits ordered him off his mount. He pretended to obey but instead, kicked one of the thugs who had leaped at him with a knife. The horse lunged and he escaped safely.

Once more their few belongings were gathered into the covered wagon and they were on the move. This time to Bena, Minnesota, on to a homestead. They spent the next eight years there and Reba, their only child, was born. It was from Bena they came to Canada.

George Langley, youngest brother of H.A. from the first family of J. R. Langley (H.A.'s father) stayed with them while they lived at Bena. In 1919 George joined them in Alberta for a time but being in very bad health (arthritis) he went to Oregon and was gone for some time. When H.A. got word that George was worse, he went by car to Oregon and brought him home. George's health finally improved and he drove a truck and helped in the store. He became a general favorite around the country. In 1945 he was cooking for a road crew near Sundre and died of a heart attack while serving dinner. George was missed by everyone.

During one of Mr. and Mrs. H. A. Langley's visits back to Caroline, H.A. was standing on the banks of the Clearwater River watching bulldozers at work. The purpose was to change the river channel from the west side of the river bed back to the east side where it originally had been, as the constant wash against the bridge on the west side was doing damage to the pier. While watching this work, H.A. told about an incident in his life before there was a bridge over the Clearwater River. H.A. had come out with a load of bricks for the chimney of the Ricinus School, which was being built in 1917. He was driving a team of four mules. After driving into the river ford, he discovered his lead team rigging had somehow come unhitched. The mules went ahead fast enough to pull the reins out of his hands reaching the west side ahead. However, the pull of the water current on the reins had been enough to turn them and they stopped on the shore facing H.A. and the wagon. When the team and loaded wagon reached the steep slope on the shore, H.A. knew the young team could not pull the load up alone. So he stopped and carefully climbed down onto the pole, walked out on the pole between the young team onto the dry shore, caught the mules and found one single tree was gone. He tied the mules up, walked to Frank Ankle's, about a half mile, borrowed a single tree, came back and found his young team and wagon still waiting in the river. H.A. fixed up the eveners, hitched up the mules, walked back onto the load between the young team on the pole, picked up the reins and drove out of the river to deliver his load of bricks without a wet foot.

Langley House and Store — the beginning of Caroline.

The Store

The store was started in one corner of the Langley home in 1912 with one hundred dollars of supplies. By 1917 a big building was put up north of the farm house on the N.E.Q. 12-36-5. The upstairs was used for a community hall.

By 1921 the stock in the store was worth $8,-000, and the Langley's sold the business to Jim Lightbound. He could not manage it and in about 1922, H.A. took the business back. A good deal of hard work went into rebuilding and improving and Mrs. Langley, having resigned from the Post Office, attended to the store. At this time, Myrlan Hunter took over the Post Office.

When the Community Hall was built one-half mile north on the Adam Tate place, the Langley's decided the store should be there too, and between 1928 and 1929 they put up a small building and the business moved in, while the larger place was being moved up. Afterwards the smaller building was used for living quarters. This store the Langleys operated on and off until 1945 when they sold it and went to British Columbia for a number of years.

This admirable couple, both now in their twilight years, still stand straight and tall. H.A. must surely be over six feet and lean, Cynthia, too, is more than average height and slender, and like H.A. carries herself very straight and upright. The characters of both, portray dignity, charm and grace.

Since this history was written, Mr. and Mrs. Langley have both passed on, H. A. Langley July, 1965, at the age of ninety-five, and Mrs. Langley in May, 1973, at the age of ninety-four. They are both buried in the Caroline Cemetery.

Langley, St. Denys, Nelson

by Reba Nelson

Lately I have been introduced as the 'Grandmother of Caroline', rather a shock as I was only nine years old when the post office was named after me.

A collie dog, Gyp, and a buckskin horse Dad had given me when we arrived from Minnesota, were my constant companions. By the time Gyp was four months old she could be sent to bring in the cows from the pasture across the Raven River after Dad put in a foot log. She always seemed to know what was said to her. Mother was the only one who could scold her, anyone else and she would sulk for days. I have just now realized how much of my life has been mixed up with horses. I had my own saddle horse up until five or six years ago, a lovely black I rode to lead the Caroline Parade several times.

Being an only child I had to be both Dad's hired man and Mother's helper. I learned how to care for animals and tend their ailments and injuries. We had found a liniment called 'Horseman's Friend' and we used it extensively. I learned to cook at an early age. Not long before Frank Ankle passed away, he reminded me of the time many years ago when he and Len Bowers stopped by at our place, looked around, and asked for Mother. I told them that she was helping Dad hay and asked them what they wanted. They said they wanted dinner and I said that was alright, I could get it for them. He laughed about me cooking that meal when I could hardly see the top of the stove. I guess I always liked to cook and have done a lot of it through the years. I could write a whole book of my many experiences but that is not what this history book is intended for.

I attended school at South Fork through grade eight, a Miss Fingland put me through the eighth grade in about two months to get me ready for the governmental exams in Innisfail. I was taken there and left in a boarding house for a week, that was quite an experience for a lone country girl who seldom ever went to town, but I made it and passed. In 1915 I went to Red Deer to start grade ten. A girl from east of town and I batched together until her mother became ill and she had to leave. Then Annie Shields from Penhold came to live with me. The eighty-ninth regiment was training there and our teacher, who taught us math, was a patriotic man and he left us in the middle of the term. A lady teacher, who already had two or three subjects to teach, had to take his over as well, and it was hard to get it all in but most of us made it. The next two years I attended school in Innisfail. I managed to get through grade ten and half way through grade eleven when I quit school. It was there that I had become acquainted with Oliver St. Denys. After I left school I went to Calgary to work and I met him again. By this time he had gotten into the army which he had been trying to do but was always turned down. We were married in Calgary while he was in training.

On June 24, 1918, Harvey John was born, just in time for his father to see him before he was shipped overseas. The first postal strike hit right

Reba Langley and Cora Parcels, South Fork School.

Nick and Cynthia Maga and Georgina.

273

after his contingent shipped out and just before the cheques for the soldier's dependants were due. I have never approved of postal strikes since that time. Many of the soldier's families were in desperate need before the strike ended. My sister-in-law, Maggie Wilson, and I would have starved had it not been for an elderly merchant, whom we were well acquainted with,(he) let us have enough food to get by on. Maggie had a three year old son and a three month old daughter. Later Maggie went home to Innisfail and I went home to my folks in Caroline until Oliver came home in January, 1919. We then moved to Innisfail where Oliver worked at different jobs and then in October, 1919, Cynthia Mary was born.

Times were hard and money was scarce so I went home and worked for my folks for room and board. Oliver came out to the farm and then later he went to Rocky Mountain House and found employment running an edger in a sawmill. Our marriage was falling apart. Oliver got a mitt caught in a chain and lost a hand. He was taken care of by the compensation board but our marriage was over just before the birth of my son, Clement Merrill, on the 18th of March, 1921. Later I spent some time in Washington where I applied for a divorce and had to live there so long before they could start proceedings. Mother and Dad had taken us down to visit some of Dad's cousins and they took my children back to Caroline with them. I worked at several jobs and cooked on a sheep ranch during lambing and shearing time. I had as high as thirty men to cook for; the work was hard but the wages were good, I got $60.00 per month.

I arrived back in Caroline in July, 1923, and again worked for my folks. In August I met Samuel Nelson who was visiting his sister, Mary Lord. He went to work for my Dad and, on December 24, we were married. On June 18, 1926, our son, Samuel Langley Nelson, was born. He grew to be as big as my dad in his prime. For some six years after Sam and I were married, we moved from place to place, often on my father's land. We bought one place, put in a crop, got froze out and couldn't pay the interest, so lost it. Sam drove truck for the store and then bought one for himself and did very well.

In January, 1931, we bought a quarter of land for back taxes. This was during the depression and it was three years before we got a house built on it. In the meantime, we lived in a big log house on the quarter south of ours which was built by two Russian families. We were happy there. I still went three times a week to help my mother with the store and post office. She had the post office for twenty-five years or so and then Merland Hunter took it over for a short time — he and

Summer 1966

FIVE GENERATIONS

It is a very rare occasion when five generations can be brought together and the happy occasion shown above came about when Richard Wayne Maga arrived in the world. From the bottom to top are: Richard, Mrs. Cynthia Ann Langley, 87, great-great-grandmother; Mrs. Cynthia Mary Maga, grandmother; Mrs. Rebecca Nelson, 67, great-grandmother and Richard John Maga, 22, father. (Staff Photo)

274

Olive, then Olive's mother, Mrs. Herman Suhr, had it for a number of years. Herman was the village blacksmith.

We finally got some land cleared and under cultivation. The first year we sowed a twelve acre field into Ruby wheat and it went forty bushels to the acre. The children took part in the school fairs which were really great fun and they took prizes in lunches, candies, etc. They also used to take turns doing janitor work at school.

Things were pretty rough in those days trying to make a living off the farm and raising the children. In 1943 Sam started working for the Dominion Government Surveyors and I was hired to cook. In 1947, and for the next eight years, we spent every summer in the mountains west and north from Entrance and Jasper Park and we really enjoyed it. By that time we had a pack string of twenty-five horses and soon Sam Junior went into the outfitting business. We bought more land then, and started in to farm.

The children all got fair educations going to school at Wooler, Caroline and Shilo. Cynthia married Nick Maga and they had four children, Georgina, Norman, Delores and Richard. Delores passed away in March, 1971. She was married and had one daughter, Cleo Celest Brent.

Harvey served in World War II and while overseas he married a very lovely girl, Mary. Harvey is a licensed welder and has done well, but due to ill health he doesn't go out on jobs but he does some welding at his home in Blackfalds. They have two girls, Kay and Ray.

Clem joined the army and got as far as England where he was accidently shot through the shinbone. He was discharged and sent back home and was on crutches for several months. After Clem recovered from his injury, he married his childhood sweetheart, Rosie Odell. They had one son, Neil. They had a very happy life together until it's tragic ending, September 19, 1964, when Clem and his son went on a hunting trip near Onion Lake. They got caught in a severe snowstorm and were unable to start a fire when they missed finding their vehicle due to the storm. Clem died from exposure. He was laid to rest in the Caroline cemetery. Rosie lives in Edmonton and cooks in the C.N.I.B. She has raised Kevin Kanten, the son of her deceased sister, Phyllis Kanten. Neil is married to Mary Davy, they have two children. Neil has a responsible position at Michener Center in Red Deer where they live.

Sam Jr. is married to Joan Braucht from Caroline. They have one son, Tucker, who is married and is a long haul trucker and lives at Surrey, British Columbia. He and his wife, Lainey, have two girls, Angela and Yolanta.

My marriage to Sam was a happy one. He passed away October 28, 1960. I stayed on at the farm giving a hand to Sam and Joan in the busy seasons and taking cooking jobs at various places until just recently when I moved to the Senior Citizens Centennial Court in Red Deer, where I reside.

Dan McGrandle
by Len McGrandle

Dan McGrandle homesteaded in the Caroline district about 1911. Previous to this, he ran a sawmill at Caroline and Raven. About 1918, after which he moved his mill to Rocky Mountain House, he milled around Rocky until 1928 and then came back to Caroline to the homestead for a time. He started milling again with his son, Russell McGrandle. In about the early forties he sold the mill as his health was poor. He passed away in 1943. His son, Russell, passed away in 1975. One other son, Leonard, came to Caroline in 1936 and is still living in the village of Caroline.

Dan McGrandle sawmill.

275

Dan McGrandle.

H. Russel McGrandle
by Merdie McGrandle

H. Russell McGrandle was born in Arundel, Quebec, on February 13, 1905, the oldest son of Dan and Alice McGrandle. He moved to the Ridgewood district of Innisfail during the same year. Russell spent his early childhood on the family farm there. At the age of thirteen, Russell and his younger brother, Art, went to work for their father, Dan, hauling lumber from the sawmill at Raven to Innisfail. The boys, each driving a team and loaded sleigh, were able to make the one way trip in one day.

For many years Russell worked with his father in the lumber business. During the 1920's he was at Rocky Mountain House. The years 1933 to 1939 saw Russell operating sawmills in the Caroline area. During the summer of 1940, a mysterious fire completely destroyed the sawmill. The sawmill was never rebuilt and a change of style came into being. Russell then started a planing mill and retail yard in the village of Caroline. For five years the mill did customer planing for other sawmill operators. At the close of World War 11, Russell sold the operation and went to work for a local road builder.

In the ensuing years, Russell built many roads for the sawmill operators and government county roads.

It was while road building that Russell met with an industrial accident on a bulldozer. As a result he was in the hospital for a year and never really fully recovered.

For eight years Russell was millrite at a Cochrane sawmill.

In 1965 Russell and his family moved back to

Russel and Bernice McGrandle.

Caroline and he worked as town foreman for the village of Caroline from 1965 to 1972 at which time he retired.

Russell married the former Mary Bernice Oliver in 1935 and they were favored with five children, two boys and three girls. Beverley lives in Sundre and Treva and Donna live in Calgary. Eddie lives in Caroline and Merdie is in Red Deer. Bernice lives in Calgary. Russell passed away on March 4, 1975, after a short illness.

George and Mary McLean
by George McLean Jr.

George was born on Prince Edward Island in 1901. Mary was born the same year in Nova Scotia. Both families, the McLeans and the Patriquins, came west in 1912, the Patriquins to Edmonton and the McLeans to Calgary. At the age of twenty-one, George and Mary met and married in Calgary. They then moved to the Acme district and farmed for ten years.

In 1931 the McLeans came to the Caroline area, George, Mary and I, their son, George Jr. I was seven years old at the time, but I remember the move well. With wagons, grain for the horses, furniture and all our belongings, as well as ninety head of loose stock (horses and cattle). Our neighbors on the prairie, Emil and Lena Hester and their three children, Lela, Leonard and Glen, moved at the same time. Hesters had an old truck and were able to move some of the furniture and make two or three trips while we

276

George and Mary McLean.

moved all the stock, ours and theirs, at a much slower pace.

It was November and the nights were a bit frosty, sometimes water for the stock was hard to come by. Hardships were taken in stride and without too many problems, we made it to Caroline after dark, cold and tired.

Money was very scarce and Mary's brothers, Roy and Ralph, came out with us and worked for their board. There were no jobs to be had, and a place to eat and sleep was a good deal in the 'Dirty Thirties'. The Patriquins later settled on the quarter east of the Caroline Cemetery for a few years. We settled on the quarter section south of Caroline, now owned by Donald Bowden.

H. A. Langley's store — Harvey Langley, Cynthia Langley, standing in front of Mrs. Langley is George McLean Jr., Mary McLean, Mrs. Patriquin and Hazel, and Mr. Patriquin.

Fred McLean, George's youngest brother, came up from Seattle as a teenager, stayed with us and helped for a few years. He served in the army during the war years and worked on highway construction for a time, returning to the Caroline district in the 1950s and has farmed in the district ever since.

After renting land in the area for several years, George and Mary bought the Ren Stearns place, one mile west of Caroline. For many years McLeans supplied the few residents of the village with bottled fresh milk and cream. With grim determination, dedication and much hard work, George cleared and broke one hundred acres on his farm. In the years to follow, Mary worked at the Caroline General Store and George worked at Wrigglesworth's Pole Yard and later for the Department of Highways, but still farming all the while. In 1970 they retired and I took over the family farm. Mary passed away March 6, 1973. George is still active and very much interested in the farm at the age of seventy-seven.

When oil exploration became the big thing in Alberta in the mid 1940's, I hired on with Heiland Exploration. They were here looking for energy products as far back as that, and when they left, I went with them. While working in the Wetaskiwin area, I met and married my wife, Wanda, and we have one son, Terry. I later changed my vocation to highway construction, and for a short time in the '50s, made my home in Caroline again. This was during Terry's first few years of schooling. He had some of the same teachers I had. We later moved to Calgary, living there until our return to Caroline in 1971.

Fred Miller Family
by Sally Bugbee

Fred, my uncle, was born at Odin, Minnesota, December 8, 1880. He was one of a family of nine children, Joses (my father), Eliza, George, Emma, Fred, Luella, Jesse, May and Tony.

In 1901 his parents and sister, May, and brothers, George, Jesse and Tony, came to Alberta and filed on homesteads west of Innisfail in the Cottonwood district. His brother, George, was credited for naming this district 'Cottonwood'. They built a two storey log home which has weathered many a storm and was lived in until just a few years ago by Wes Gilgon, Aunt May's son. Through the seventy-seven years since it was built, it has been referred to as the "Grandma Miller's House".

The rest of the family stayed in the U.S.A. for a short time and two of Uncle Fred's sisters, Eliza and Emma remained there.

When Uncle Fred came to Canada, he homesteaded the S.E.Q. 16-35-5-5 in the

The Ambush — Fred Miller on horse — Chester Miller robber.

Crammond-James River area and lived there for a few years.

Sometime before 1920 he sold his homestead to Flora McClarty and then bought the S.E.Q. 13-36-6-6, one half mile east of Caroline, making this his permanent home where he cleared his land and farmed.

Bertha was born in England on May 11, 1881, and was raised there to adulthood and then came direct from there to Innisfail where she and Uncle Fred were married. She was little prepared to face the rigors of our harsh winters and to cope with the hardship of pioneering. I am sure her life here must have been difficult for her, being of delicate health and stature as well.

Their son, Maurice, was born April 22, 1926. He attended the South Fork School which was located south of Caroline where the cemetery now is. Uncle Fred, being an avid pool player, taught Maurice to play pool when he was barely able to see the top of the table. He became very adept at this and offered strong competition to his elders. On more than one occasion he would lock the door on his mother, when his father was away, and then run uptown to play pool, and more than once, he got his breeches warmed for his mischief.

Uncle Fred passed away November 10, 1938, at the age of fifty-eight years. Aunt Bertha and Maurice stayed on the farm until 1945-46 when Maurice moved his mother into the village of Caroline to live while he went away to work. He found employment in road construction in the Grimshaw and Morinville areas. Later, he became engaged to be married but a month before his wedding, he was killed in a motor vehicle accident at Morinville on October 6, 1951.

Aunt Bertha stayed on at her home in Caroline for a few years but because of ill health, she went to a nursing home in Red Deer where she passed away on March 3, 1959. All three are at rest in the Innisfail Cemetery.

Robert Miller

My mother and father came from Bruce County, Ontario, to the Grandview and Dauphin country, Manitoba. In 1904 they moved to the present site of Rosedale, Alberta. I was born on November 29, 1901, so I do not remember moving to Alberta. My father had his property moved by train to Gleichen, Alberta, then to Rosedale which is five miles southeast of Drumheller. He had bought an old log house to live in so he had the family moved to Rosedale. There were ten of us in the family, six boys and four girls.

It was all cattle country, then they had it surveyed for homesteading in 1907 but did not open it to be filed on until 1908. The railroad did not come to the country until 1912 as they had to cross the Red Deer River and it took about a year to put in the bridge.

The wolves and coyotes were so plentiful and I remember my sister telling me that when we first came to Alberta. The wolves howled most every night close to the buildings so we kept the lights burning all night. One morning they found a four year old steer that was killed during the night. The government and the cattle ranchers gave a good bounty on them. I remember my oldest brother, Bill, fixing up a bunch of poison capsules for coyotes. He used tallow to put strychnine in. The poison was furnished by the government. He put the poisoned tallow out where ever he could find old bones and the next day he went out with team and sleigh and came back that night with a box so full of frozen coyotes that he had to tie them on with a rope. Then his brothers and sisters all went to skinning and stretching coyote pelts. They got 50¢ apiece for stretching the hides on boards and Bill got $2.50 government bounty, and $2.00 apiece for the

Bob Miller

278

skins, so I learned how to skin coyotes when I was quite young.

The mange broke out in the cattle in 1906, so my father built a dip to dip cattle in. A number of others also used his dip. It was compulsory, according to law, that they had to be dipped to kill the mange. The mange seemed to work on the cattle the same as it does on coyotes — the hair all came off.

The winter of 1906-07 was a terribly hard winter for cattlemen of the prairie as a great many cattle were lost. My father had quite a few cattle and he got them all rounded up before the winter, so he did not lose any and he had lots of feed. He fed at what they called the Spring Coulee. It was well protected from the wind, but at the home place he didn't have much feed. The other ranchers' cattle drifted with the wind and stopped when they came to our home. A great many died there and I remember that almost every morning my sisters used to put the harness on an old work horse to skid the dead animals away from the barn door. My father knew who they belonged to and he would send word to them. I understood the ranchers had lots of feed but it was too stormy and cold for them to come and get them. They said it got down to 70 degrees below zero along the river where we lived.

I remember the big fire that started at Stettler, Alberta, and beat the train to Munson. There was a very heavy growth of prairie wool grass at that time. The fire stopped at the Red Deer River.

I remember when my mother, my brothers, Bill and Henry, and I were going to go to Bill's homestead six miles north of Rosedale up on the Michichi Creek. Henry was riding a horse and the rest of us rode the wagon. Henry said that he would stay dry and the rest of us would get wet, as we had to ford the River. We started off and came to the crossing. The wagon went into the river first and crossed first, but Henry's horse hit a big rock and it caused his horse to fall and it turned completely over. Henry hung on to the saddle horn and then let go. He managed to get to an island and stayed there until my father got there with a boat and saved him. There seemed to be a lot of drownings then.

I think it was 1911 that all the Miller family moved six miles north to Michichi Creek with all our cattle and horses. Every Sunday, some of the older members of the family would go out and see if the stock was still there. One day they came home and said there were four head of cattle short so my father went to Drumheller and told the police about it, but they could not find any sign of them. We got a letter from a rancher up at Stettler saying there was a steer with our brand on it and enclosed a cheque for $86.00. We knew pretty well who had taken them but we could not prove it.

Jim Murray, who passed away at Caroline, homesteaded the quarter that cornered my father's land. He built a shack on it and proved up on his homestead. I think it was twice that it blew down into our place and my father used to tell Jim to keep his darn old shack at home as he didn't want it — just kidding.

I remember the wet summer of 1915 and the creek and river were so high and the mosquitos were so thick that everyone wore a mosquito veil, and a few houses were washed away in Drumheller. My sister, Myrtle, and her husband, Ed Murphy, were living on a knoll and the Michichi Creek ran by their place. The creek got so high it had their place surrounded with water, so all they could find was the wagon box, so they got it ready, but the creek didn't come up any more.

In 1911-12 they had the stampede on my father's place and there was a very large crowd there. There were some very famous riders and famous horses there. It was the first stampede in that part of the country. They had lots of picnics on Bill's place as there was a very nice grove of trees on it. They had their picnics there until 1934, and they kept all the papers and garbage cleaned up very well and made sure the gate was closed when they left.

Bill joined the army in 1915. An officer gave them orders to hide, and about five of them hid in a shell hole and a German came along and threw a bomb in. My brother said he got wounded less than the rest but he eventually died a few years later from the after effects.

In July of 1918 my father went up to Caroline and bought a place four and a half miles south of

The Bob Miller Sr. family — back row — Mrs. Greentree (friend), Della, Bob Sr., Edith, Bill — 2nd row — Myrtle, Bob Jr., Henry, Mrs. Liza Jane Miller holding Annie and John.

Caroline. He bought John Montgomery's place then, and leased five and a half sections of grazing land and he got Bill and John Montgomery to fence it. In 1916 my father bought a 1917 Model T Ford. Some said it was the first car in that part of the country. He came back to get the family and his household things and brought Bill Montgomery to help chase the horses to Caroline. My father got a box car to send his household stuff to Rocky Mountain House. So when we got everything ready to move, my father drove the Model T and my mother, my sister, Annie, and my brother, Ernest, rode in the car and Bill Montgomery and I drove a good eighty head of horses. My father would go ahead of the horses to find a good place to camp overnight and he generally found a road allowance that was not used very much and would fence one end off. Bill and I slept in a tent by ourselves. One night we woke up with a start as we could hear the horses coming as fast and loud as they could, so we each grabbed a coat and started yelling. We saw what it was that was scaring them — a car with the lights shining on them. It looked like the horses were going to go right over the top of us, but they finally turned back. So we got to Caroline without anymore close calls.

The Caroline district was a very good fishing territory at that time. Beaver Creek and Beaver Lake were loaded with trout. My two brothers, Johnny and Henry, came up from Drumheller that fall so we went out to Beaver Lake to fish and we got the ice chopped away and my father started to fish first. He just dropped the bait in when a real big trout came and grabbed the bait. My father was so surprised that he dropped his pipe into the hole, but he pulled the fish out and it was 28 inches long.

It took a lot of work to clear land as there were no bulldozers at that time. When we got it cleared we used a walking plow to break it, then picked all the roots before we could disk it and get it ready for seeding. My father bought a half section of C.P.R. land and then more hard work started.

The winter of 1919-20 was a very hard winter, which started about October 12. We had plenty of feed but very few farmers did have. They say some farmers paid $60.00 a ton for hay and 25¢ for oat bundles. The winter lasted until about the middle of May. That spring my father bought nineteen head of cattle from George Palmer for $190.00.

In 1924 I homesteaded a quarter of land as George and Ernest were able to help my father. Then my work started — fencing and clearing land. So when the hard times started, I got a registered trap line for ten dollars. There would be about one hundred sections of land in my trapping territory, and I got a very good trail hound

Treed Cougar.

for treeing lynx. One winter Sunday in 1934, Bill Anderson came to see me. Toward evening on the way home he saw a track that he had not seen before so he came back and got me to see what kind of an animal it was. We decided that it was a cougar track and that was the first cougar track we had seen. So he went back and got their two tracking dogs and my brother, Bill, and I met the two Anderson Boys, Arvid and Bill, and we started to follow the tracks. When we got almost to Nels Swanson's, we turned all the dogs loose. The hounds followed the tracks close to Nels' buildings and the cougar had been laying close to the pighouse waiting for the pigs to come out. The dogs chased it east and treed it — I have a very good picture of it up a tree. I got about seventy-five cougar counting all the small ones, as I had that trapline for thirty-three years. There was far more money running a trapline than raising cattle. I had some close calls on the trapline. Once a grizzly bear chased me for awhile. But he did not want me very bad or he would've got me. He just seemed to be curious. Then one moonlight night a bull moose came down a hill after me. But I told the dog to 'sick 'em', and the dog turned him away.

My cabin on the trapline was about two miles from Hugo and Art Anderson's, who had traplines next to mine. I used to visit them about once a week and after a few years, I thought I should pay them for the meals I had eaten with them. When we figured out the cost, it amounted to 11¢ a meal. There were no frills in those days of the thirties, but we had plenty of good wholesome food, such as meat, rice, dried beans, cranberries, etc.

My mother passed away in 1937 and father in 1943. Eliza Jane Annie Miller passed away in 1969, George in December, 1969, and Ernest in 1967. Of ten children there is only myself left, and I am now at the Autumn Glen Lodge in Innisfail.

The Mitten Story

by Elva Mitten

Bob Mitten was born August 1, 1910, at Punnichy, Saskatchewan. I, Elva Willsie, was born June 1, 1914, at Kindersley, Saskatchewan. We were married October 4, 1933, at Kindersley. We moved to Caroline in October, 1933, and started business in our little store built by some of our friends from Coleville, Saskatchewan, where we both went to school and grew up. The store was built on the corner where the Caroline Hotel now stands.

We got to know about Caroline through Lyle Steed who lived at Ricinus. Their house burned down and they phoned Bob in Coleville, Saskatchewan, to use his light delivery truck to take the body of their daughter who died in the fire, back to Coleville to be buried where they used to live. When they returned the truck, they brought a load of wild blueberries from Ricinus back to sell and that's when we decided to build a store at Caroline. A country where you could pick wild blueberries and cranberries looked very good to us in the hard times.

Our first stock of groceries in the store was $208.00 which was all the money we had: We lined the shelves with boxes of cereal to make it look like we had a good stock. We had no bed and slept on a mattress on the floor in the back of the store which was our living quarters and had apple boxes and nail kegs as chairs. The store was open anywhere from 7 a.m. to 12 midnight.

Howard, our son, was born April 21, 1934, in Red Deer. Keith Steed was a partner with us in the store for awhile. Don Demenuck (Chick) from Coleville came to live with us in the spring of 1934 and my brother Bob Willsie (Whiskey), came to live with us in the fall of 1934. They stayed, drove the truck and worked in our store until they each got married.

Bob Willsie was in the Army during the second World War. We sent cigarettes and candy to nearly all of our boys from Caroline who were overseas and they all answered us in appreciation.

Elva and Bob Mitten.

Howard Mitten.

In March, 1935, we lost a son, Donald. He is buried at the Raven Church Cemetery.

Howard Mullen (Bob's school pal) came to be a partner with us in the store in January, 1937. We had now moved to a new store west of the Caroline Hall. We bought this building from Hal Roach.

Howard Mullen started the first hockey team in Caroline. There was no ice at first. They skated wherever they could find a piece big enough. Then they made a rink on the west side of the Caroline Hall. Some of Howard's players were Chick Demenuk, Whiskey Willsie, Bill Mewha, Charlie Dezall, Bob Dial, Bert Mitten and Jackie Morgan. They played at Leslieville, Horseguard, Markerville, Dickson — and never lost a game. Howard Mullen also started a ball team at Caroline.

In 1937 my sister, Gertrude, and her husband, Ralph Huffman, came from Coleville to Caroline. They had three children, Stanley, Joyce and Gladys. Ralph worked at the lumber mill.

Times were very hard in the 1930s; we used to buy frozen rabbits by the truck load and sold them to the mink farms for meat. We had a pile of rabbits at the back of the store that looked like a snow bank. The kids used to go and pick them from the pile and bring them back into us and we would buy them over again. This happened many times. One little fellow came in one day with a cat hide for us to buy so he could get some money to go to the show. We didn't want the hide, but we gave him 25¢ so he could get to the show in the

Caroline Hall. The next week all the kids brought us cat hides, so that was the end of the Caroline Cats!

Earl Farris came from Coleville to stay with us after we got the new store. He worked in our store for quite awhile and then went through for a teacher and taught school in Caroline. He taught Howard, our son.

Harry and Florence Garrett built a hotel on the corner where our first store was located. By the time they finished the hotel, Mrs. Garrett was sick and couldn't keep working so they sold the hotel to us for $1600.00 in 1938. The payments were sixty dollars per month. So we now had the store and hotel which kept us busy. The rooms were 75¢ for working people, travellers had to pay $1.00 and $1.25 for a room. Meals were from 50¢ for breakfast to 75¢ to $1.00 for dinner or supper. We could not get a bar room in the hotel until the war was over which was 1945, so we used that room off the hotel as a school room for awhile. Mr. and Mrs. Garrett moved to Calgary after having the Treasury Branch in Caroline for a good many years. Their daughter, Maisie, married Pat Godfrey in Calgary where she now

Howard Mitten and Maisie Garrett.

Bob Willsie (Whisky), Don Demenuk 1943.

282

lives. Both Mr. and Mrs. Garrett are buried in Calgary.

Anna Andersen came to live with us at the Caroline Hotel to teach school at South Fork. When Howard was old enough to go to school, I packed their lunches and they left hand in hand to walk a mile south to the school.

Bob sold his lumber yard to the Murray Brothers at Caroline. Howard Mullen went into the Airforce in 1942.

Mr. and Mrs. Wilbur Cross took over the hotel in 1941 for a year and we moved into a little house by George McLeans. After a year, we came back to the hotel. Mr. and Mrs. Cross were in the store with us from 1942 to 1949. We sold out of the store in 1949. We built a house in Calgary and moved there, but we didn't stay very long. We came to Red Deer in 1949 where we had the Mitten and Mullen Lumber Yard. We sold that and Mitten and Mullen went into the A & W Root Beer business.

In 1953, when Howard was nineteen years old and had a service station across from the Caroline Hotel, our daughter, Yvonne, was born May 4. Yvonne, now twenty-five, and Greg Roth, her husband, and their daughter, Aimie live in Red Deer.

Howard Mitten and his wife, Kay, are living in Red Deer. They have two children, Gladys and Wayne. Bob Mitten has an interest in the Arlington Hotel in Red Deer. We now reside at 3925, 43 Avenue, Red Deer.

When we first lived in Caroline, the roads were really bad. It would take us two or three days and sometimes more to go to Red Deer for groceries and drugs. We had a bunch of boys along to shovel mud or snow, and coming home, many times we couldn't make the hills for mud and would have to carry half the load up the hill and then put it all back on the truck again when we got to the top.

We never missed many dances in the country. We would all get in the back of a truck and have a real good time summer and winter. I used to make lunches at the hotel for the dances in the Caroline Hall. We would dance until 4 a.m. and then I would have to start making breakfast for the truckers back at the hotel.

The Molnars

When Steve Molnar landed in Quebec on June 9, 1928, from his native country of Romania (the area he lived in later became part of Hungary), he had no idea of the struggles and adjustments he would have to make. Before he left the old country, he knew his destination would be Calgary, Alberta, and that is all he knew about the country. The harsh prairie winters would be a great change from the mild climate of

Steve Molnar, Charles Brown, Lucy Molnar, Sam Hickman, Hilda Hickman, Alec Brown, Anna Demenuk, Daisy Brown, Shirley and Jean Hickman.

Romania where harvesting was done in June. Without knowledge of English, communication was difficult. Fortunately, he could speak some German.

He was strong and healthy. In Romania he had farmed and often he had to pack 100 kilos (220 pounds) of grain on his back and at the age of nineteen he could farm with a walking plow and horses. Some of the differences were that farming in Canada was on a larger scale with shorter growing seasons.

Steve worked for a farmer at Crossfield from 1928 to 1932 in a mixed farming operation. He was paid $25 a month. In the spring of 1932, Steve was hired by Billy Wise of Irricana to seed Marcus wheat. That spring they each put in 1000 acres of wheat driving twelve horse teams. When hard times hit, wheat plummeted from $2 a bushel to 35¢ a bushel.

Steve went into partnership with Sam Hickman in the spring of 1938. Sam was in mixed farming east of Penhold. In the spring of 1939, Bob Macadam, the owner of the farm, sold out. Steve and Sam looked around for two weeks for a farm to buy or rent. They had been to Caroline and had returned to Innisfail on a Saturday evening. They went to see Don Montgomery, the proprieter of a garage that Oscar Lundgren later owned. They asked him if he knew anyone who had a farm to buy or rent. Ed Chute happened to walk in the door and overheard the conversation and he said he knew of a place. The next morning, Palm Sunday, Steve and Sam accompanied Ed to Caroline. In Caroline, Ed took them to Mr. Langley's house. After dinner, Mr. Langley showed Steve and Sam a quarter section west of Caroline. They bought the quarter that day and farmed it until the spring of 1942 when Steve bought out Sam Hickman.

That fall Steve met Lucy Waselinko while harvesting at Irricana. They were married on May 30, 1943, and lived in a log house. In the

Bob and Gladys Robertson and Steve and Lucy Molnar and children.

spring of 1944 Steve rented the quarter to the east of the home quarter.

In the spring of the year Steve would go to Irricana to help Billy Wise put in his crop and he would earn enough to buy fifty pounds of binder twine and a drum of gas and then come back home to seed his small crop. In the fall he would help Billy thresh his crop. Steve did custom work around Caroline. He also had to clear and break his own land.

In the fall of 1947 Steve bought the east quarter. By this time Lucy was caring for two children as well as helping with the farm work. Steve was now busy doing his own farming as well as helping the neighbors. There were cows to milk, pigs to feed, chickens to look after, and all the other chores of a mixed farm. There were good years and bad years. There were many get-togethers with family and friends throughout the years.

Steve and Lucy sold the farm in the summer of 1972. That fall they moved to Montrose, British Columbia.

Katherine, the oldest, married Paul Sanford and they live in Granum, Alberta, and they have a daughter, Gayle. Elizabeth Gay married Larry Bailey and they live in Comox, British Columbia, and have a son, Lorne. Steve married Phyllis Mannerfeldt and they live near Rocky Mountain House, Alberta, and they have two daughters, Amanda and Tracy. Melba married Don McLacklan and they live in Montrose, British Columbia. Teresa is in grade twelve and lives with her parents.

Mullen, J. Howard
by Helen (Dial) Mullen

Howard moved to Caroline in January, 1937 from Coleville, Saskatchewan. He went into the Caroline Traders General Store with Bob Mitten. He and Bob were boyhood friends in Coleville. Howard had been born in Edmonton and moved to Coleville later. He was very active in sports and helped keep the hockey and ball teams lively in Caroline.

A few years later Bob Mitten took over the Caroline Hotel. Howard married Helen Dial and they ran the store. The store business in those days was something again. We took in eggs and butter (often not very fresh) in trade for groceries. Some farmers were covered for groceries, for months on the books until they could harvest their crop or sell their cattle. Indians came in to buy goods. They would often buy one article at a time and pay for it and continue this way until they had bought all they came for. It was hard to have regular store hours, especially on "Mail Day". This was once a week, when the mail came from Rocky Mountain House.

We lived above the store and many nights we didn't get upstairs to have supper until after ten p.m. Then rationing came. Customers had to have ration coupons to get coffee, butter, sugar and gas. In 1942 Howard sold the store to Wilbur and Lou Cross and he joined the armed forces. He joined the R.C.A.F. and trained as a pilot in Edmonton. He was stationed at High River, MacLeod, Quebec and Prince Edward Island.

Helen and Howard Mullen.

284

After the war in 1945 Howard bought a general store in Benalto from Alf Foster. He and Helen were there for two years and then moved to Eckville where they had 450 mink. The prices for mink pelts hit a real low in 1948-49, and we couldn't make a living.

Howard got together again with Bob Mitten and they bought Johnny Phelan's lumber mill in Red Deer. So the Mittens and Mullens moved to Red Deer where they still reside. Howard and Bob sold the lumberyard to John Mitten and Arnold Sherbino. Howard is now a partner in the A & W South, with Bob.

Howard and Helen have three sons — Larry in Edmonton, Terry in Edmonton, and Bob in Red Deer.

Memo: As I write this, just got the news that Howard and Kay Mitten's daughter Gladys (married to Doug Brookes) has a new baby boy "Adam". So the Bob Mittens are great-grandparents. Congratulations to all.

The Charlie O'Coin Family

In the spring of 1932, the Charlie O'Coin family moved to Caroline from Drumheller with a team and Bennett buggy and two saddle horses. They had to spend six weeks living in a granary east of Spruce View on the Snowdon place on their way to Caroline because of the heavy rains that spring. Eventually arriving, they stopped at Mel Ferguson's west of Caroline to visit the Tom Chapin family who had arrived earlier from Drumheller. They then moved on to the Lewis place, S.W. 6-36-6-5, which they were to rent from Mr. Lewis for the next few years. Charlie worked at Boeken's mill as well as carrying on a farming operation. Lizzie, Charlie's wife, with the help of Lucille, his daughter from his first marriage, renovated the old log house that was on the land, scrubbing, papering and white washing until it was quite livable. They planted a big garden, and traded butter and eggs for the needed supplies at Langley's Store in Caroline. They had three children, Albert, now working for the Department of Transport in Caroline; Adeline, living in Toronto and Emily living in Drumheller. The O'Coin family also lived on the Herb Riddle farm, S.E. 3-36-6-5, in 1936 and on the Langley place, N.E. 12-36-6-5, in 1937. Caroline School opened in 1939 on top of the hill south of the Raven bridge where the present Caroline Cemetery is situated. Albert started school that year. His first teacher was Anna Andersen now Mrs. Anna Demenuk.

The O'Coin family also lived north of Caroline on the Jacob's place, S.W. 1-37-6-5, for two years, (1940-41) before settling back on the Langley place until 1946. Edward and Floyd, sons from Charlie's first family, were away to war during this period. Floyd was killed in action in 1945 and Edward returned home to settle in Drumheller. Lucille married Albert DeKeyser and has also settled in Drumheller. Lizzie O'Coin died in the Olds Hospital in October, 1947, and Charlie died in Drumheller in January, 1968.

Edward Oliver Family

Edward Oliver was born near Carrickmacross, County of Monaghan, Ireland, on August 10, 1876. He came with his parents, four brothers and four sisters to Shelbourne, Ontario, sixty miles north of Toronto, settling on a farm in 1885. Edward left Ontario to come west in 1897. While working in Manitoba he met Annie Lougheed who had been born February 17, 1878, near Collingwood, Ontario. They were married November, 1900, and in the spring of 1901 they came to Alberta buying a quarter of land in the Lone Pine district, eight miles east of Didsbury.

Homesteading fever and prospects for more range for livestock, took them to the Sunnynook, Alberta, area in May, 1910. They moved across

Charlie and Elizabeth O'Coin and children — Albert, Emily and Adeline.

Edward Oliver home at Caroline, 1931.

country by team and wagon with three small children and another baby due in two months. They homesteaded S.E. 22-27-11-4 and lived in a tent until they could built a house with lumber and supplies teamed from Castor. The nearest rail was some eighty miles away. They acquired another section of land raising large numbers of horses, some cattle and hogs. One summer day in 1924 while Mother Oliver was baking bread, the house caught fire and burned down, destroying most of the family's belongings.

Year after year of drought caused crop failures so the family left and came to Caroline in July, 1931, purchased the S.E. Q. 22-36-6-5 from George Sparks, brother to Mrs. Charlie Brown. There were only twenty acres cleared and a small homesteader's shack which stood directly across the road from Daniel McGrandle's home and sawmill. In the spring of 1931 the Government had set up a plan whereby any farmer could get two boxcars free freight to move out of the dry area. The Olivers were among some of the first families to take advantage of this. Shipped to Rocky Mountain House were one team of horses, some cattle and the furniture. One of the first people Edward Oliver met in Rocky after arriving, was George Wrigglesworth whom he had known in Didsbury before 1910. Approximatley fifty head of horses, branded   Rt. Sh. were driven across country later that same fall. A clearing was made, the shack was moved and an addition put on near where the present house now stands. That fall a small barn and shelters for livestock were built. The first winter was very hard on the livestock especially horses, due to the change from dry prairie wool to the luscious grass of the bush land. Straw was hauled for many miles the first winter and stock were driven to the Raven River for water. Arthur Bowers drilled a well in January, 1932, which has supplied a never ending amount of good clear water all these years since.

We found all our new neighbors to be very friendly and some of the closest ones were Daniel McGrandle directly across the road, and John Trunell one mile to the east. Ren Sterns lived on the corner where George McLean now lives and the Charlie Brown family a mile south across the Raven River. Charlie Mason and the Frazier family were to the southwest and the O'dell family lived to the west. The Vance Braucht and Ben Harris families lived one mile to the north. A year or so later the Verner Tricker family moved into the log house on the Doherty quarter directly south of us, and the Chorley family to the place across the road from them known as the Jack Heck and now Willis Ford place.

Edward Oliver hired several Indians such as Joshua Saulteaux, Joe Yellowface, Whitecalf,

Redcalf, Swan and Gouda families to clear brush. Their tents were pitched on the land where they were working and the Oliver children were quite fascinated with their way of life as they had never seen Indians before. The Indians took eggs, meat, butter, flour, horses or cattle as well as cash in exchange for the clearing of land.

All through the depression years the Olivers always milked some cows, raised some hogs and kept laying hens. Edward Oliver was also a great horse lover. He loved to raise, break and drive them. He was always buying, selling or trading horses. Even though prices of farm produce were low in those years, the price of groceries and other necessities were cheaper. Annie Oliver kept records of where she sold eggs for 6¢ a dozen in February, 1934, raising to 7¢ and then to 10¢ later in the year, and cream at 14¢ per pound. A 100 pound sack of flour cost $1.75 (there were no 10 or 20 pound bags of flour in those days), and 20 pounds of rolled oats was 29¢. Men's denim overalls were $1.65 and a man's shirt from $1.00 to $1.20. You could buy 100 unsexed Leghorn baby chicks for $6.00. In 1934 a bunch of cattle were driven by saddle horses to Innisfail for the average of $11.00 a head straight through. Cows and big steers were sold to Harry Finnberg and E. Aisenstat. Bush rabbits were very plentiful and we, like many other families, shot them. In winter, rabbits were hauled with team and sleigh and sold to R. W. Mitten for 2¢ per pound. Weight of rabbits averaged from 2½ to 3 pounds. They were thrown in large piles and later hauled by truck to Calgary to the fox and mink farms. Two poeple could easily shoot enough rabbits to fill a double wagon box in a day. At that time squirrels were sold for 7¢ each.

There were nine children in the Edward Oliver family, Arthur, Edna, Hugh James, Irwin, Beulah, Bernice, Irene, William Hugh and Olive.

Individual family records for Arthur, Irwin and Hugh are in this book under their own names.

Edna married George Blake from Vancouver. George homesteaded N.W. 27-35-6-5 now owned by Denis Winder. The Blakes had one son who lives in Prince Rupert, British Columbia. George passed away in 1962 and Edna in 1964.

Hugh James passed away in 1906 at Didsbury at age six months.

Beulah married Carl Borgland from Stettler, Alberta. They live in Calgary and have three children.

Bernice married Russell McGrandle of Innisfail and Caroline. Bernice homesteaded S.W. 9-36-6-5 and sold it to Al Barbie, who sold to George Miller. John Hermann now owns this. (McGrandle history elsewhere in this book.)

Irene married George Griffith of Innisfail and Leslieville. They have two children and farm six miles south of Peace River town in Alberta.

Olive married Howard Thompson of Markerville district. They have seven children and they farm four miles east of Spruce View.

In 1936 Edward Oliver purchased N.E. 15-36-6-5 from Percy Doherty who had moved to New Brunswick.

In 1938 the present house was built with Harold Hembrow as head carpenter, and the family moved in near Christmas that year.

Edward Oliver passed away March, 1939, at the age of sixty-two years. Mrs. Annie Oliver and youngest son, Hugh, carried on with the farming.

In the later years Annie Oliver shared her time between the farm and visiting her daughters, Beulah and Bernice in Calgary, Olive at Spruce View and Irene at Peace River. Annie Oliver passed away suddenly in July, 1959, at eighty-one years. Edward and Annie Oliver are both laid to rest in the Raven Cemetery.

Hugh Oliver Family

I was born at Sunnynook, Alberta. I well remember as a young boy, arriving at Caroline. There were only about four buildings in the town. The general store, a two-storey building, was operated by Mr. and Mrs. H. A. Langley. The post office was run by Mrs. Ida Suhr in the front of her home. Her husband, Hermann, had the blacksmith shop. The two of these were on the lot where Caroline Motors now stands. The community hall stood on the corner lot east of its present location.

We had left the open prairie with it's drought, tumbling mustard, Russian thistle and dust storms where the sun was dimmed with dust clouds day after day. My father had come here in May shipping via freight to Rocky Mountain House. The rest of our family travelled in two cars arriving at Sundre in the evening. It began to rain, and we spent the whole night plowing mud, and arrived at Caroline at six o'clock in the morning, July 6, 1931. The half mile north from the main road was just a winding wagon trail in and out through the trees. The early morning sunshine seemed so bright, the sky so clear (no dust clouds appearing on the horizon) and everything was so wet and so green. We were fascinated with all the trees, every direction we looked there were trees, the grass was so tall and green and there were so many beautiful wild flowers. Our youthful hearts felt as though we had reached the land of paradise. I never, ever had to wear rubber boots before coming here, but they became a near everyday part of our wearing apparel, and still are to this day.

I enjoyed my few years at South Fork School and the many community activities as a young teen-ager. The community hall was the centre of amusement, as well as house parties in the winter. In the summer there were ball games and there was always fishing in the Raven River. We would walk or ride horseback everywhere we wanted to go, sometimes for many miles.

I farmed with my father until his passing in 1939, and then my mother and I continued on the farm.

In 1942 I married Audrey Sims from the Camrose area. We have two sons, Dwight and Dale. In 1945 we purchased the S.W. of 22 known as the Baldwin quarter, from Carl Borgland who had bought same from Floyd Frazier in 1934. In 1965 we purchased the N.W. of 22 from Charles Pittendreigh known as the O'dell quarter.

In August, 1967, Dwight married Donna Jamieson from Toronto, Ontario. They have two sons, Lorne and Michael, a chosen son, James, and a foster daughter, Mavis.

In May, 1968, Dale married Penny Leckie from Caroline and they have one son, Mark.

We are blessed to have our sons and their families choose to stay on the family farm.

In 1967 Dwight purchased the S.W. of 23 and Dale the N.E. of 22 from Leonard McGrandle.

We have raised range cattle, hogs, and have always milked cows. We first sold cream with the cream truck picking up the cans, then for seven years we bottled whole milk and delivered it to Caroline. In 1956 we built the first dairy barn replacing the original log barn which dated back to 1934. We then began shipping milk in eight gallon cans to Alpha Condensory Red Deer, with the truck picking up every second day. In 1968 we converted to bulk shipping of milk and the present dairy barn was built in 1974, with the bulk tanker truck coming every second day. We have seen a great change from the day of sitting on a stool milking a cow by hand to automation.

The future of this area could very well be that of major cattle feeding, made possible by high yielding forage crops fed as silage and by confinement of cattle. Confinement will become practical with the use of tower silos and automated feeding, and will in turn allow for total manure management, producing high value fertilizer. This area with its high rainfall, will then produce unheard of yields of forage and grain.

The isolation of the community is a thing of the past. It is no longer a two day trip to Innisfail or an all day trip to Innisfail or an all day trip to Rocky with team and wagon or sleigh. Since 1945 there has been a steady improvement in the roads from bush trails to graded dirt roads full of mud holes in rainy weather, to well gravelled and paved highways.

It has been a privilege to participate in community activities and I have always found the people of this area very friendly and co-operative. I have been past member on the organizing committees for the Rocky Rural Electrification Company when our community received rural power February, 1954, and also the Clearwater Mutual Telephone Company when we had our first telephones installed in 1961. It was interesting to have been local Poundkeeper for Stray Animals (1945-1977) sometimes tracing owners of livestock great distances. Being local trustee for Sub Division Number 2 for Rocky Mountain House School Division since 1960 is most interesting, and there have been many changes for the betterment of the education of our children. The process of centralization has been completed, and facilities at Caroline School have been enlarged several times with buildings and equipment.

Audrey and I have enjoyed being active in the Church of the Nazarene in Caroline. I am Church Treasurer and on the Board of Trustees. We were in the group of Charter members at the time of it's organization, June 30, 1949.

The Pengellys

by Almer Pengelly

I, Charles Almer Pengelly, was born August 4, 1896, in Rutherford, Ontario, and was the eldest of a family of ten children. I didn't like school, so I didn't get too far in the field of education.

I liked to work with horses, so I worked on farms and hauled freight from Dresden to Rutherford, a distance of seven miles, using an old horse and a democrat.

I worked for my uncle until I was old enough to go out into the world on my own. One of my first experiences was when another boy and I went to Detroit to look for work. We went to a hotel and got a room and left our suitcases there,

and then we went to an automobile factory. When we started back to the hotel, neither of us had looked for the name or address of the hotel. We walked and walked and finally I just looked up and said, "there it is!" We were lucky to be able to find it. I worked in the Gray Dart Automobile Factory, also in wheel factories, and then I gave a try at a white machine in a sugar factory.

In 1915 I came west to Melfort, Saskatchewan, for the harvest, and went back east that fall. When spring time came in 1916, I had the urge to come west again. I worked on farms until the spring of 1918, and that summer I went into the Army.

The flu of 1918 was very bad at Melfort. I had it and was very sick. My aunt said all that saved my life was water. She said it was a bucket brigade, water going upstairs and water coming downstairs. I got my army discharge in February, 1919, and that spring I came to Alberta. I worked on a large ranch at Brooks that had 80,000 sheep, 20,000 head of cattle and 2000 horses. I lived in a covered wagon and did my own cooking. I didn't know beans about cooking, and my first biscuits were made with flour, soda and water. You can imagine how hard they were.

The fall of 1919 was the beginning of the hard times. The ranch could have sold their ewes at $30.00 per head and in the spring, when we started to shear the sheep, wool was 65¢ a pound. One month later, when we finished shearing, wool had dropped to 16¢ a pound. The ranch hung on until 1922, when the bank sold them out for $2.50 a head.

I worked on farms in the summer and fall of 1921. I also mixed poison for grasshoppers at Blackie, Alberta.

I came to Caroline in 1921 and homesteaded the S.E.Q. 28-35-6-5. I had to go out to work at intervals to make a little money so that I could stay on my homestead.

In 1926 I hauled cordwood and props into Rocky Mountain House from about five miles

Almer Pengelly at a sheep camp.

The Almer Pengelly family — left to right — Clarence, Donald, Almer, Lawrence, Mrs. Pengelly, Margaret and Don.

south of there, using four and six horse teams to haul four cords a trip. I received $4.00 a cord; $16.00 a load.

There were three of us bachelors living on adjoining quarters: Bob Miller, Ernest Dean and myself. We made a bargain that the first one of us to get married was to receive $25.00 from each of the other two, and as each got married it was to be paid back. However, the other two remained single, so I was ahead of that game.

I married Annie Blowers, the second daughter of R. T. Blowers, on November 12, 1929. We had four boys and one girl! Clarence, Lawrence, Donald, Bob and Margaret. After the fourth boy came along, we said we would either have a girl or a baseball team, but the girl came along so we never tried for the team.

When it was time for the children to start school, the nearest school was six miles away, so we didn't send them until they were eight years old. Clarence went alone the first year, on horseback. He got along just fine, but the next year there were three to go, so they had to drive an old horse — they were too small and had lots of problems. Then we got a chance to go to Red Deer to take over my uncle's farm. The Springvale School was just across the road from the farm, so that would solve the school distance problem. So, in December, 1939, we moved out there. I farmed a half section of land, milked cows, and fed pigs, and I raised many calves that farmers gave me as they couldn't sell them. In addition to this we had 2500 laying hens. We delivered eggs in Red Deer and many were picked up at the house.

We trailed cattle back and forth from our farm at Red Deer, to my homestead at Caroline — we did this for about fifteen years. We had a big holstein steer that led the cattle back and forth. Many people remember him. He weighed 2300 pounds when I sold him.

Our eldest son, Clarence, was born November

L.-R. — Annie Pengelly, Mrs. Leask and Mary Sheppherd.

5, 1930, in Rocky Mountain House. After he finished school at Springvale, he stayed home and helped on the farm until he was old enough to go farming at Caroline. In 1958 he married Edna Clay, daughter of Ed and Stella Clay. They had three children: Glen, Fay and Eddie.

Our second boy, Lawrence, was born October 19, 1931, in Rocky Mountain House. He also took his schooling at Springvale. When he was finished school, he too, stayed home and helped on the farm, and when he was old enough he went farming at Caroline. In 1957 he married Joyce Bugbee, eldest daughter of George and Sally Bugbee. They have five boys: Darryl, Dean, Brian, Keith and Kelly; had they had four more boys they would have had our ball team.

Our third son, Donald, was born October 7, 1932. There was snow and it was quite cold, but we started out for Rocky Mountain House. We couldn't make very good time as the roads were bad and there were no windshield wipers on the old Ford. I would have to get out and wipe the windshield with a hand full of snow now and then. When we got to the corner by the old Clearwater School we knew we were not going to make Rocky in time for the event, so we stopped at the first light we saw. I asked if we could come in but they said, "No, we don't want any babies born in our house." However, Donald was born at their gate. We knew of an old neighbor a little farther on, so Annie had him inside the blanket, that she had around her, in her arms, until we got to this neighbor's place. We stayed there for the rest of the night, and the next morning Doctor Greenway came and took Mother and Babe to the hospital, and all was well. Donald took his schooling at Springvale and then helped on the farm until 1954, when he married Rose Gagnon of Red Deer. They had six children: Lee, Tod, Ann, Ruby, Gail and Della. Donald passed away very suddenly in April, 1969.

Our fourth son, Robert, was born on my homestead, June 16, 1938. He went to school at Springvale until the school burned down in 1949, and was then bussed to the River Glen School in Red Deer. After he finished school he helped on the farm until 1963, when he married Dorothy Towers, the eldest daughter of Robert and Katherine Towers of Red Deer. They have three children: Terry, Kenny and Sheryl.

Margaret was born in 1941 and started school at Springvale and finished at River Glen. She then worked at the Bank of Commerce in Red Deer. She married John Harder, the eldest son of Eric and Erna Harder of Caroline, in 1960. They have four children: Susan, Danny, Ross and Dale.

In November, 1945, I left Caroline to go on a hunting trip in the mountainous area west of Sundre, near the James River Ranger Station. There was about twenty-two inches of snow, and it was about thirty degrees below zero. A few miles from the Ranger Station I slid into the ditch. The road, such as it was, was treacherous. A short time after dark, Ranger Roy Wayent came along with a team and sleigh and took me to the station with him to spend the night, leaving my truck stranded. The next morning a local trapper and my old friend, Bob Miller, came along and told us about a three man hunting party, one of whom was lost. They were Oscar Kanten, Bill and Charles McDonagh — Bill was the one who was lost. Bob was on his way to hunt for him.

The Ranger took me back down to my truck and helped me get it out. I drove back to the Ranger Station, which took hours, but once I got there it wasn't long before Bob and the Ranger and the frozen man, along with his brother, Charles, came along. Three hunters had found Bill curled up under a spruce tree, and thought him dead, but a closer look proved he wasn't. His hands and legs and feet were badly frozen. They took him to their camp and then sent for Bob, with his team and sleigh. They gave Bill emergency treatment by soaking his hands in warm coal-oil, it was very painful but they were later credited, by Bill, for saving his hands.

When Bob got there they covered him with blankets and laid him in the back of the sleigh, along with his brother, and took him to the Ranger Station. I was the only one who was able to get a vehicle going, so I undertook the job of driving him to the hospital in Olds. Bill was placed in the cab of the truck, and Charles climbed into the truck box. It was a terrible trip, drifting snow and cold, no heater and no defroster and poor visibility. At times Bill would topple over on me, and I would have to stop and straighten him up. It took eight hours to make the trip into Olds, a distance of thirty-seven miles from where we started. When I came back over the road the next day, I couldn't see how I ever made it, especially when darkness fell, after we had just made the first four miles of our trip. He had to have both legs amputated, so he was transferred to the High River Hospital, but the hands had been saved. We were down to see him in 1976, at Cayley, Alberta. He has artificial legs and gets around very well. He is married, and is the father of three girls. He farms two sections of land. One of his daughters was there when we visited him, and she gave me her thanks, with hugs and kisses, for my part in the rescue, even though he wasn't even married then. Still, she realized how serious it was, and if things hadn't worked out as they did he might never have been her father.

It seems that I was forever in the middle of situations of one kind or another. Lawrence and Clarence had a young couple working for them,

and in September, 1959, I was at their place. The young woman was due to give birth, and while I was there the stork gave her his notice of arrival, and so I was going to take her back to Red Deer with me, to the hospital. It had been raining and the road was terrible. We got stuck several times and only got a few miles from home when we had to stop. She could go no farther, so we stopped at a farm house. She was worried about not getting to the doctor, but I told her not to worry, that if everything went alright I could look after her. Her eyes bugged out and she said, "Oh no, not you!" However, I did, and everything was fine; she had a bouncing baby boy. He grew up to be a fine young man, and in May, 1978, we were invited to his wedding.

In 1966 I sold the farm, at Red Deer, to Mervin Brett. As our family was all established at Caroline, we moved there in June. I am still interested in the farm here and have an interest in the cattle. With all the ups and downs, life has been pretty good to us.

Alexander and Mary Radik
by Mary Maty

My parents, Alexander and Mary, were both born in Czechoslovakia; Dad on March 16, 1890, and Mom on March 12, 1895. Brother John and I, Mary, were born there also; John, December 26, 1922, and I, April 15, 1925.

Dad came to Canada in 1927, and to Nordegg where he found work in the coal mines. He worked there until 1933 then came to the Caroline area. He purchased the S. E. Q. 34-35-6-5 from Mr. Langley which originally had been Mr. McFellamey's homestead.

After Dad got settled, he sent for us and we arrived in November. John and I enrolled in the South Fork School.

A year after we arrived, our house burned down. With the help of a neighbor, we built another log house.

Dad was able to buy a quarter of land from the government and together we all worked,

Alexander Radik.

Mary Radik and children John and Mary.

clearing it. We managed to clear twenty-five acres using picks and axes. We piled and burned the brush and sawed the trees into wood.

As well as repairing his neighbors' wagons and sleighs, he enjoyed building them. Those that he built, he sold, or traded for livestock or grain.

Mom enjoyed gardening and always planted a large one. In the fall, she would ship and sell potatoes and vegetables to some of the miners in Nordegg. She also enjoyed doing crochet work and embroidery in her spare time.

After finishing school, John helped Dad on the farm for a time, then he went to Nordegg to work in the mines.

When he became of age, John joined the army and served until the end of World War II.

After leaving school, I stayed to help Mom and Dad for awhile and then I went to Calgary.

Dad became ill and after several operations he passed away in 1944, and Mom moved to Calgary.

John married Dorothy Owen from Hanna and they make their home in Calgary. They both work for the school board and have three children, Linda, Mike and Donna.

When John got married, I asked Mom to live with me as she spent all her time with either John or I.

I married Peter Paul Planidin from Queenstown, we called him Paul. We lived in Calgary where Paul was in business with his brother, Sam. This business was called 'Planidin Brothers Grocery, Hardware and Furniture'.

Paul and I had seven children, Dennis, Robert (Bob), Frances, Phillip, Debra, Vicki and Pennie.

Mom gave John and I each a quarter of our half section at Caroline. John got the home place and I the other. John sold his, but I kept mine. There were no buildings on mine so Paul and I

bought the Milke quarter which joined mine, it had a small house on it.

Because of the business, we could only spend weekends and holidays on the place. Whenever it was possible for us to leave Calgary, we would bring the children and Mom with us and spent our time fixing it up. We enjoyed doing this very much and called it the \3P/ (Triple P half diamond).

Mom lived with us until she passed away on January 12, 1968.

Paul and I were looking forward to when we could retire, but he was stricken with cancer in 1972 and died on July 10, 1973. He had always donated a trophy to the Big Horn Rodeo, now the children and I donate one in his memory.

Sam and I dissolved the business in 1975. My children and I, then started up the 'Planidin Investments'. It is now managed by my boys, Dennis, Bob and Phyl.

In March, 1976, I married Mike Maty of Eckville. Pennie lives with us and the other children all live in Calgary.

Dave Richards

Dave homesteaded the S.W.Q. 22-35-7-5 sometime in the middle 1930s. He had a wife and family. He sold out during the early 1940s to Charlie Gill who farmed this quarter for sometime until he passed away with a heart attack at his home. Mrs. Gill sold out to Oscar Peterson. Oscar owned it for a few years then sold it to the present owner, G. Alexander and then moved back to Calgary.

Herb Riddel and Mickey Gainor
by the Dennis Browns

Herb was born in Ireland October 26, 1910, and Mickey was born in Quebec August 24, 1903.

When Herb came to Alberta, he worked for farmers in the Balzac and Calgary areas, helping with the harvest, milking cows and breaking horses. He worked on the Seebe Dam and for the Eau Clair Sawmills of Calgary, doing some of their river drives. On one drive on a hot spring day, he was thirsty so he drank from the river below the logs. A little while later when he was on the upper side of the logs, a dead deer came floating down the Bow and rested against the logs and he was not thirsty for the rest of the day. Besides doing this kind of work, he worked for the forestry for two years and in his last years of working out before he and Mickey settled down on his farm, he worked for Mannix Construction, first as a catskinner and then as their head mechanic.

Herb bought the Bill Clark place in 1943, renting it to Charlie O'Coin for about three years, then Dennis Brown rented it on a crop-share basis.

After Walter Kanten closed out his store in Caroline, Herb and Mickey turned it into a cafe and ran it for a few years.

Mickey was a pianist and played for many dances. She donated her time and talent to the Caroline School once a week until they were able to get a regular music teacher.

On the farm, Herb raised and milked cows and had pigs and Mickey raised sheep. Later, Herb quit the milk cows and went into range cattle.

Mickey was married to the famous all round sportsman, Dutch Gainor, who died after a long stay in a mental hospital in Oliver.

Herb began to have poor circulation in his legs so he had to give up farming and he rented the land to Roy Follis. In 1973 he made a trip back to Ireland to visit some relatives and to renew old acquaintances and to see his homeland once more.

Mickey passed away May 31, 1974. In 1975 Herb had a leg amputated above his knee. When he was well enough to leave the hospital, he was able to live at home alone with just a little help until 1977 when he moved into a nursing home in Red Deer. While he was there he had a stroke that has left him unable to speak. He is in the Dr. Richard Parson's Auxiliary where he was transferred after his stroke.

The Ropers

In 1908 Tom Roper and his two brothers, Joe and Alf, came to the Caroline district from Cumberland, England. They settled and proved up homesteads north of Caroline in 1910.

In 1911 Joe married Margret Stewart who had come to Innisfail from Paisley, Scotland. Joe was named to the office of Justice of the Peace for a time. In 1922 he took his wife and two daughters, Francis and Margret, to live in the Lacombe district where he continued farming and raising purebred Herefords. Francis and Margret went to school in Lacombe.

Tom remained in the Caroline district. He had married Rosina (Ina) Stewart in 1914. Rosina came from Paisley, Scotland in 1913 with her mother to visit her sister, Margret (Joe's wife). Tom served in the district in many ways, as councillor for the Municipal District of Raven. Many stories have been told of the problems, difficulties and even amusing experiences in attempting to build roads out of trails in those days. Man power and horse power meant just what it implies.

Tom was also active in the local fair for several years, both as a contributor and a director with three or four other people. In those years a prize list book was put out that contained eight to fifteen pages. It compared well with larger centers that had a thirty-page prize book. At that time, Caroline could also boast of a good-sized school fair in the late fall.

In 1922 Tom was named to the duties of Justice of the Peace. This job brought him in very close touch with the growing pains of the district as well as with the hardships of many, the joys of others and the frustration of the law officers in their duties. He saw the very real side of life in those times.

In 1925, with the community growing fast, the need of a Community Hall was felt. At this time, Tom gave the community one acre of land for the hall to be built on and for other community use. With a lot of hard work and time of men working together, as well as money donated and raised by other means, the old-timers of the district saw the hall become a reality in 1926. The village has grown up around the hall — the proud start for a community that many of these people and their families still call home. One of these families is Tom's son, John, and his wife, Iona, and their family. They still farm the land homesteaded in 1908 by Tom and Joe Roper.

J. C. Schafer
by Ivy McGrandle

Mr. Schafer and his sons, Conrad and Fred, came from Saganaw, Michigan. They lived in Saskatchewan for a short time then moved to Caroline.

Mr. Schafer homesteaded the old farm which is now owned by Dennis Brown. Conrad homesteaded the quarter on the north side, now owned by Gene Szulczyk.

When Mr. Schafer Sr. was alive he did all the baking. One fall, after his death, Conrad decided to bake some bread. From his point of view, it was a complete failure. He went hunting the next day and remarked that if he could get close to a moose and hit it with one of his loaves, he would not need any shells. However, the next day some very, very hungry hunters came along. He fed them some of his bread and they said it was the best they had ever eaten.

Fred liked to go to dances but Conrad was a home boy. They were good neighbors and always had a smile for everyone.

Mr. Schafer died before 1930, unsure of date, Conrad died in 1968 and Fred in 1977. All three were buried at the Raven Cemetery. Mr. Schafer's service was held at the old Langley Store.

Harvey John St. Denys
by Harvey St. Denys

I, Harvey John St. Denys, was born on June 24, 1918. I was raised and educated in the Caroline area. My schooling, such as it was, took place in Wooler, Shilo, and Caroline Schools. I can remember the first teacher I ever had, Mr. Fuller, who spoiled me, taking me to school on his back in bad weather. One of the other teachers I remember was Miss Bibbie. She taught me in her last term of teaching at Shilo, then left and wasn't heard of again. It was many years after the war, when I was signing in at the Colonel Belcher Hospital for some treatment, when a voice said, "Hello Harvey! Don't you remember me?" It was Miss Bibbie. She had taken up nursing after she quit teaching school and had served as a nursing sister during the war. She retired from nursing just shortly after this little incident happened, and I always jokingly said that I had chased her out of two professions, teaching and nursing.

In December of 1940 I joined the Canadian Army and was in the first Trade School ever run by the Army in Edmonton. The building was on 114 Street and Jasper Avenue, known as the Canadian Vocational Youth Centre. Civilians occupied it during the daytime and the Army had it in the evening. No one would realize it today, but that was the start of N.A.I.T.

Altogether I served five years in the Army, two of them in this country and three overseas. I enjoyed my army life and have no complaints on it. I served in such places as Caen, Compier Airport, Tille Comron, closing the Fallais Gap, Leopold Canal and the push to Neymegan and into Appeldoorn, and on across the Rhein. I had one leave in Paris, went back to the front, led two patrols across the Rhein and got my seven-day leave to England where I became engaged to marry Mary. Going back from this leave, I was crossing the English Channel when V-E Day was declared. The war was over. Without bragging I could mention that I served one of the longest known stretches of continuous front line service — eleven months. I went back to England and eventually married Mary on August 15, 1945. I came back to Caroline in November of 1945 to find everything changed. I made my home south of Caroline where Bowdens now live, and afterwards moved onto the farm which Mike Steene now owns. Mary came over here in May, 1946. Our daughter, Kay, was born on April 30, 1947. We left Caroline for a few years, 1948 to 1952, to live in British Columbia where our second daughter, Raye, was born, January 31, 1949.

Returning to Caroline in September, 1952, we continued to live and work there until the winter of 1961 when we moved to Red Deer.

Ren and Lou Sterns, a friend Ed Johnson.

L.V. (Ren) and Lou Sterns
by Guy E. Fay

Ren Sterns came to the Caroline district in 1907. He homesteaded a mile west of Caroline and the next year his brother, Lou, joined him. Lou was quite an athlete, such as a ball player and foot racer. Lou married Myrtle Dykes in 1917 and they went back to South Dakota.

Ren just used his place to spend the winters until 1928, then he stayed there steady. Ren died in 1948.

Jerry Stewart

Jerry was born September 9, 1907, at Armada, a small town east of Vulcan, Alberta.

Jerry's father passed away in 1930, then he and his brother, Walter, continued to farm the homestead until 1934. Their mother passed away in 1937 at Lobley, west of Olds where the family had moved. Jerry moved to Raven and his sister, Edith (Sis), came to keep house for him. After some time spent in farming here, he moved about ten miles west of Didsbury where he worked for a few years, then he moved back to Raven where he worked for Lou Johnson. In a few years he and Sis moved into Caroline and he worked for George Wrigglesworth in a logging camp for a number of years. After this he worked on the construction of the Clearwater and Spruce View Highway 54.

293

Edith Fay (Sis) passed away in 1960 and is buried in the Innisfail Cemetery.

Jerry then lived and worked for Hugh Oliver's on his dairy farm until 1974 when he moved into the Autumn Glen Lodge in Innisfail where he is enjoying a good home.

Since this was written, Jerry passed away February 5, 1979, and is buried in the Caroline Cemetery.

The Ogden Sweet - Agnes Lockhart Story

by Jack Campbell

Ogden and Malvina Sweet, their son Mark Sweet, and daughter Mrs. Agnes Lockhart arrived in Caroline from Oyen, Alberta on June 1, 1934.

They lived on what was the Calhoun place — now owned by the Ron Doel Family. Grandma Sweet passed away on February 16, 1935. The family then moved four miles south of Caroline on Beaver Creek. Their log house is now a barn on Bruce Nesbitt's farm.

Grandpa Sweet died on May 21, 1936. Uncle Mark was an avid hunter and fisherman and loved to play cards.

Aunt Agnes was a wonderful woman. She had to be to put up with her nephews and nieces when we arrived from Drumheller to spend the summer holidays.

In the late 30's my father built the Dallas house north of Caroline where Stan and Eileen Loomis now live.

I have many fond memories of good times and good people — Chris Jensen and his dog — Joe Little and his dog Captain O'Leary, — John Yaeger and Jack Stilwell.

After spending so many happy months in Caroline as a boy, it seemed natural that I would return. In 1960 my wife Maureen, our son Jeff, and Maureen's parents Carley and Leola Borwick bought the Nellie Edward's farm. The Borwicks moved to Calgary in 1965.

Jeff and his wife live just down the road.

Aunt Agnes passed away on May 11, 1944. Uncle Mark then moved to west of Elkton. He died on August 10, 1963. They are all buried in the Raven Cemetery.

The W. Verner Tricker Family

by Sally Bugbee

Vern Tricker was born in Barrie, Ontario, September 29, 1890. He came to Alberta in 1906 and in 1913 he homesteaded at Rhoden Ville (Swalwell), Alberta.

Rhoda Dawson was born in Stanhope, Haliburton County, Ontario, October 1, 1896. She came to Alberta in 1908.

Rhoda Tricker, Thelma Northcott, Janet Trimble, Ronda Nordling, Anders Roy Nordling.

Vern and Rhoda were married December 10, 1913, in Calgary and went to live on the homestead at Swalwell. While living there they had three children, Wilfred, Thelma and Edwin.

Things were pretty grim on the prairie so Vern built a butcher shop in town, to augment the meagre income from the farm.

Some time later, they moved north to the Westlock area. They didn't find it much easier to make a living here, but there was an abundance of blueberries — it was great blueberry country. It was here that their twin girls, Eva and Ivy, were born.

They moved back to the homestead again for a few years, but what with being dried out, they found they couldn't tolerate the incessant wind and dust storms any longer.

They bought some C.P.R. land two miles east, one and one half miles south of Caroline and built a log house on it. In the spring of 1931, leaving the prairie dust behind, they started out with a covered wagon, a topless Ford car, and drove a herd of cattle and headed west.

Their neighbors were the Mort Grieves', Gilbert Kantens, Paul Wilsons and Hoot Gibson.

For entertainment, there were house parties, horseback riding, ball games and swimming. They soon became acquainted with the people of the neighborhood.

They looked forward to getting the 'Free Press Weekly', it contained something for each member of the family. There were the comics for the children, serials and household hints for the womenfolk, farm news and market reports for the man of the house. When mail day arrived, eighteen gates to open and close between them and the post office at Caroline, was no deterrent.

The roads were often in such poor condition that sometimes they were almost impassable. Such was the case when Wilfred took sick with pneumonia in August of 1937. A plane had to be flown in to get him to the hospital in Innisfail, but the effort of family and doctor was of no avail. He passed away a few days later. His close friend, Fred Hedges, died about the same time. They were buried in the Innisfail Cemetery, side by side and on the same day, August 18.

In 1938, leaving Edwin to manage the farm, Vern and Rhoda and their daughter, Eva, moved into Caroline. Vern then built the Ideal Service Station and he ran it until sometime after World War II when he turned it over to his son-inlaw, Walter Kanten, who was married to their daughter, Ivy.

Vern passed away in 1963 after they had retired and moved to Red Deer. Rhoda and Eva came back to Caroline about a year later, stayed for a short time and then moved back to Red Deer. Eva passed away in 1975.

Thelma was married to Norman Jennings and they lived in the Caroline area. They had four children, Orsean (died in 1954), Audrey, Elvin and Janet. Norman served in the armed forces in World War II. He passed away in April, 1972. Thelma married Norman Northcott and with her second marriage, had four children, Helen, Marilyn, Terry and Ricky.

Edwin still lives on the C.P.R. land and he and Lee had four children, Gary, Dianna, Wilfred and Malcolm.

Ivy and Walter live in Red Deer and have two children, Kenny and Debbie.

Rhoda still lives in Red Deer and is now one of a five generation family; the other four are; Thelma Northcott, Janet Trimble, Rhonda Nordling and her baby boy, born April 4, 1979, Anders Roy.

Still in connection with this family, is yet another five generation group. They are Hilda Antila, Taimi Lorinzsky, Roy Trimble and Rhonda and Anders Roy.

John Trunell with oxen.

John Trunnell
by Irene Pittendreigh

John Trunnell was born in Glenwood, Iowa, U.S.A. He had two sisters, one is still living at Glenwood, his other sister passed away in 1977. In 1901 he was discharged from the U.S. army after serving three years in the Spanish American War. He came to Caroline in 1908 and took up a homestead. Most of his land he broke with oxen. My mother, Mrs. Bain, and he were married in 1935. They farmed until the early 1940's when they moved to Rocky Mountain House. Around 1952 they moved to Grimshaw to live with my sister. John passed away in 1956.

John Van Leest and Family
by Ann Wecker

John Van Leest was born in Holland on April 19, 1896. He married Maria Beekmans in Holland on May 5, 1920. Maria Beekmans was born in Holland on March 30, 1898. They immigrated to Canada with their baby, Ann, in October, 1922. They lived in Calgary where John found work in a garage for about five years, then moved to Airdrie where he worked in a garage for a year. They moved to Caroline in 1929 or 1930 where he farmed for about five years and then built a blacksmith shop. They lived there until Mrs. Van Leest passed away on February 23, 1938. She was buried in the Raven Cemetery.

Mr. and Mrs. Van Leest had eight children, three of these died as babies, the others went to school at Caroline, Shilo, South Fork and Bentley. Adriana (Ann) married Daniel Wecker in 1946 and lived on their farm west of Bentley. They have three married children, one daughter and two sons.

John married Nellie Pankowe from Musidora

John VanLeest family at the blacksmith shop.

in 1943 and they live in New Westminster, British Columbia where he has a barber shop. They have two married daughters. John served in the army from September 2, 1941, to 1945.

Wilhelmina (May) passed away in New Westminster in 1974. She was married to Ted Baumann from Medicine Hat in 1947 and was predeceased in 1951 when Ted met with a train and truck accident at Fort Macleod. He was buried in Medicine Hat. She married Stephen McRae from Morinville in 1955 and was predeceased by him in 1967, he was buried at Riviere Qui Barre. She was also predeceased by their first child, Kevin McRae, in 1960. He was one year old and was buried at Riviere Qui Barre. Their remaining children, Teresa and Mark McRae, are living in British Columbia.

Nellie married Gerry Austin in 1963 and lives in Weston, Ontario. They have two sons.

Mary married Harold Wilton in 1953 and they live in Bentley and have a son and a daughter. After Mrs. Van Leest passed away, Nellie Edwards took the three youngest children, Mary, Nellie and May. May wasn't there long but Mary and Nellie were with her for about six years.

Mr. Van Leest bought a blacksmith shop in Bentley in the spring of 1944 where his family joined him. Ann Van Leest got married and then her father went to Holland for a trip. He married Anna Beekmans over there in January, 1947, a sister to his first wife. John and Anna had three children and they got their schooling in Bentley and Edmonton.

Tony, the oldest son, married Margaret Kirchoff from Edmonton in 1971. They live at Aldergrove, British Columbia, with their three sons.

MaryAnn married Randy Platz from Edmonton in 1969 and they live in Edmonton with their two daughters and a son.

Mrs. Anna VanLeest, Tony, Maryann and Walter.

Walter married Linda Twoits from Edmonton in 1970. They live in Leduc with their daughter and son. Their son was named John after his grandfather, and like his father, is a chip off the old block — a true Van Leest.

Mr. Van Leest was a blacksmith in Bentley for seven years, moved to Edmonton in 1951 where he was employed with Cesco Welding until retiring in 1966. In 1973 they moved into Lacombe Senior Citizens Lodge. In 1976, after a fall, Mr. Van Leest went into Bentley hospital where he passed away from a stroke, February 1, 1978. He was buried in the Bentley Cemetery.

Over the years John loved to go hunting and fishing with his dear friend, Cyril Tose, who worked for some time in the blacksmith with him. Mrs. Van Leest spent time in the nursing home and Lacombe hospital until she passed away July 28, 1978, and was buried in the Bentley Cemetery.

Charles Vetter
by Guy E. Fay

Charles Vetter homesteaded just half a mile north of Caroline. In those days there was a real muskeg through that place. The Vetters built on the south west corner. The old buildings were still visible in the forties. He even had a corduroyed road out to where the main road is now. He was a great worker and drove three oxen. He broke all the land beyond the slough from his buildings, walking behind those oxen with a walking plow breaking at least 120 acres, besides breaking land for other people. He had one daughter, Lily. He sold out in 1917 to Joe Roper and went to the Peace River country.

Paul Wilson
by Dorne Wilson

We first saw Caroline on a sunny afternoon in mid-April, 1931. Dad had rented a place from H. A. Langley southeast of Caroline. We came from the Grainger district by team and wagon, herding some cows. We came by way of Sundre and the mud was axle deep. We were caught in a blizzard east of Carstairs and had to fort up in a granary for five days. There was very little wood in that area and it was very cold.

Dad was born in North Dakota in 1896 and came to Alberta in 1903. The family, including three children, travelled by covered wagon and settled in the Grainger district where they lived in a dugout for several years and two other children were born. Grandad Wilson also bought land in the Bearberry district and the family travelled back and forth between the two places. Grandad also did a lot of hunting and trapping there, this kept the family in meat.

Paul, Nona and Dorne Wilson.

My mother, Lenora (Nora) Lambrigger, was born in Nebraska of Swiss parents. Her father and grandfather came from Switzerland in 1865 and sailed from France to New Orleans, then up the Mississippi River to St. Louis, Missouri. During the journey the ship was holed on a snag in the river and the luggage, including all the money, was lost and they landed in America unable to speak English with nothing except the clothes they had on.

Mom came to Alberta in 1912. She and Dad met at her sister's house and were married in Calgary, Christmas, 1916. They moved to the Grainger district where I was born in 1917. Dad had an itchy foot and we moved back to Nebraska where they farmed and worked out and where June and Dorene were born.

In 1925 we received word that Grandad Wilson was very sick and came back to Alberta but were too late. The family were at the Bearberry place and the roads were too bad for them to get to the doctor and he died. The roads were in terrible condition and every low spot was a lake of mud. Finally, west of Sundre, we were bogged down until a group of riders pulled us out with lariats. I thought they were outlaws and then found out they were my uncles and cousins.

My folks returned to the Grainger home place and farmed that and other places in the district until finally being dried out in 1931. Dad decided to move to the Caroline area which, after the bare dry prairie, seemed to be another Eden. Several other families came from the Grainger district at this time, George McLeans and

Hesters being two of them. Vern Tricker, whose brothers were in Swalwell district, came a year later.

The first years were very tough with very little money, but everybody traded — work or wood, for groceries. We used to trade eggs and butter for groceries at Langley's store, eggs were worth three cents a dozen and butter about ten cents a pound. Five dozen eggs would buy a pound of coffee. I remember Dad saying that he had ten dollars cash all summer but we never went hungry. Dad was an incurable trader, would trade anything at the mere mention of anything. That's how I got my first guitar, which I still have, in a trade with Paul Harris. We lived on many places in the Caroline area, first a mile east of the cemetery which Marshall Holbrook now owns; for a time we lived where Don Bowden now is, and in the old log house which was on Steve Molnar's place, and for a while on the Calhoun place where Ron Doel now lives.

Around 1934 Dad undertook the job of moving the old store building (the old Pioneer Store which has just been demolished) from Harvey Langley's, now Mike Steene's, to the corner site in town. For the equipment he had to work with it was an incredible feat. He jacked it up, put skids under it and used only one team of horses and a block and tackle and a large log called a 'dead man', to pull against. He would skid it about one hundred feet, dig in another 'dead man' and move on. The job took a long time as it was a very big building and of course there was always something breaking, but money was scarce and much needed.

Dad used to cut fire wood and haul to the store and the Community Hall at a dollar a load which was usually taken in groceries and dance tickets at the hall. The hall was not yet on a foundation and was further east than it is now. Dances in the

L. Wise, Tommy Orr, Nona Wilson, Nellie Edwards, Mrs. Wise and Paul Wilson.

hall could be just as wild and wooly as today. Dad sometimes acted as unofficial bouncer as he was a big man, but goodnatured. I remember that one time Don Dix took exception to something that Dad said and took a swing at him, Dad moved and Vern Tricker, who was standing behind him, took it right in the mouth. Then the fur flew. The Stewart brothers kept things humming too. We could not always afford the hall dances so had parties instead. Neighbors gathered at different homes every week for cards and dancing. A bachelor, Bob Gibson, and I played guitar for the music. Some of the neighbors were Nellie Edwards, Doels, George McLeans, Don Bowdens, Hesters and Maurice Carter. We travelled by team and wagon, bob sleighs in winter, or horseback. Whatever the weather, we went with hay or straw in the wagon box and quilts and heated rocks for warmth. The only one who had to keep his head up was the driver although the team would usually follow the trail on their own. When the little ones got tired they would go to sleep in any convenient corner. It seems we had more fun than we do now.

Dad would occasionally haul grain into Innisfail for some cash. It would take a day to go and come back. One time we had a load in a Bennett wagon behind the Model T and at the Moose Creek Ranch the tongue broke and upset, spilling the grain into the ditch. We scooped it out and reloaded and carried on getting fifteen cents a bushel for all our trouble. I finished school at South Fork in 1932, the teacher was Mary Moe, a

June Wilson, Tommy Orr, Doreen Wilson and Wise children, 1936.

very good teacher. June and Dorene had Stella Dewey (Mrs. Ed Clay) and Anna Andersen (Mrs. Demenuck). Dennis Brown and I used to fish in the Raven during noon hour and get twenty or more in a short while. In fact fish was one of the main items in our diet in those days. Dennis and I used to get chased regularly by the game warden, Garfield Thompson, but I don't think he tried to catch us very hard. He used to stop at the house for a meal and we'd have fish but nothing was ever said. We also used to go west about fifteen miles to an old burn to pick raspberries, and later, blueberries. We'd camp out and canned the berries right there. Mail came in three times a week and everybody came into town to shop and visit around. The Post Office was where Russell's Garage is now. After leaving school in 1932, I worked out around Caroline. I herded sheep for Bob Miller's dad one year and earned enough to buy my first car, a Model T Ford, from Paul Lamb, for fifty dollars. I still have the bill of sale. I also worked for Vern Tricker and took lumber for wages and picked roots for Gerry Vandermeer and got a buckskin horse that time.

In 1939 we left Caroline, the folks went to Creston, British Columbia, and then moved back to Alberta where Dad joined the Army and then was on the Police Force in Medicine Hat and other places. In 1946 they were again in Calgary and then in 1949 they moved to Lillooet where they were living at the time of Dad's death in February, 1952.

Mom and June are still living in Vancouver and Dorene is now widowed and living in Sundre.

In 1939 I worked around Olds and Acme then went overseas in the Army in 1941, and was married to Eileen Barrett in October, 1943. From 1946 to 1952 I had a trucking business, then was an elevator agent until 1959 when we moved to Caroline. We rented a couple of years until finally getting our homestead southwest of Caroline where we now live. Our place was originally filed on before the first war, applicant unknown, who left to go to war and never returned. Then Clint Langley (Conrad) filed on it but couldn't get papers because of a name change. It was then a grazing lease until we discovered it was still open, proved up and finally got title. We have eleven children, five married, twelve grandchildren, one at home and the rest scattered in Alberta and northern British Columbia.

The Womack Brothers
by Marmie Dingman

There were five children in the Womack family, four boys, William, Fred, Charles and Grover (Red) and one girl, Sadie. They were all born in Lostine, Oregon, and got their schooling there.

Charles, William and Grover Womack.

Red came to Canada in about 1910 to join his brothers, William and Charles, who had come several years earlier to the district later known as Crammond.

In about 1930 William went back to Oregon and remained there until his passing in 1943.

Charles farmed three miles south of Caroline for several years before he sold his farm and moved back to Oregon. He loved hunting and fishing and it was on a hunting trip that he suffered a heart attack and died in 1967.

In 1923 Red married Edna May Dingman (nee IsBell). Edna and her two small children came from North Dakota to the Ricinus district to join her parents and brothers and a sister who had a homestead there. Her parents were George and Augusta IsBell. The brothers still at home were, Boon, Phillip, Paul and Robert and a sister, Nellie. A brother, Ted, and his wife and two small children also lived and farmed in the Ricinus area. Another brother, George, remained in the U.S.A.

George and Augusta moved to High River and remained there until their passing. Ted and his wife, Myrtle, also moved to High River with their children. They have both passed away but some of their family are still there.

Before her marriage to Red, Edna's two children were Fred and Ruth Dingman. She and Red had one child, a son named Ray, who was born in 1924. He married Lila Croston in 1951 and they have two children, Larry and Lorraine. They live in Calgary where Ray has an insulation business.

Fred had a twin brother who died at the age of two months from pneumonia. Fred married Margaret Peterson (Marmie) in 1945 and they have a family of nine children, seven sons, Gail, Allen, Albert, Delbert, Richard, Stephen and Jeffery, and two daughters, Gloria and Roxanne. They live and farm on the place that William homesteaded in the early days at Crammond. Three of their children are married and they have four grandchildren.

Grover and Edna Womack with grandchildren — Betty Lou Wren, Gail Dingman, Clark Wren.

Ruth married Louis Wren in 1939. They had three children, Betty Lou, Linda and Clark. Ruth passed away in 1963 at age forty-five.

Betty Lou is married, has a family and lives in Swan Hills.

Clark married Gladys Alstott and they also have two children and live near Caroline.

Linda married Doug Bancroft, they have two children and they live and farm at Chedderville.

Red passed away in January, 1957. Edna remained a widow and lived in Caroline until her passing in January, 1978, at the age of eighty-five. They are both at rest in the Raven Cemetery.

G. A. Wrigglesworth

by Esme Wrigglesworth James

George Albert Wrigglesworth (Dad to me) was born in Eau Claire, Wisconsin, on October 25, 1893. His parents had come from Ontario and would soon move on to settle between Olds and Didsbury in 1905. By the time Dad was ready for high school the family moved in to Didsbury and there his favorite pastime was attending the town council meetings.

From school, Dad went to Garbutt's Business College in Calgary where he took the six-month course in three months and stayed on to teach. Then came World War I and he enlisted in the Royal Air Force. By the time he had completed his pilot's training, earning the rank of lieutenant, the war was over, so he never saw action.

299

George Wrigglesworth and his mother.

When it came to being discharged he was the victim of official bungling. His papers were sent home with a C. A. Wrigglesworth and Dad had a year's paid vacation in England while that was untangled. Out of that came a marriage that would soon end in desertion, leaving him with me to raise (with the help of his mother) and depriving him of his son, whom he would see only once as a grown man.

We struggled through the depression in Rocky Mountain House where Dad was on the village council for several years. He was the agent for Massey Harris Machinery and Elephant Brand Fertilizer, a hog buyer and a trucker. Later, as a dealer in tamarac fence posts, he crisscrossed much of central Alberta on foot, drumming up sales. From that he worked into producing telephone and power poles and about 1947, that

business brought him to Caroline to be closer to the stands of lodge pole pine.

He set up his pole treating plant on the south side of the highway. This property is now the Department of Highways and Transportation and Maintenance yard. Dad was always an innovator and he had developed his own treating process in Rocky. He once asked for guidance from the company whose product he used; instead, they sent a team of men out to study his methods. In Caroline he perfected his technique, using steam to make the chemicals penetrate the wood. My husband had a few of those poles and after thirty years in the ground, they were still solid.

I believe Dad had as many as three logging camps going at once. All west of Caroline. He would never send a man out to camp without proper clothing. All too often he would send someone to the store to get outfitted at his expense and then the fellow would skip without even working off the cost of his clothing. Dad's generosity was one big factor in his perpetual money problems. Though many people earned a good living in his business, he had almost nothing for himself.

Dad loved being out in the timber. When he was over sixty he spent a night lost in the woods and thought it was a great lark. But, with a business that reached all over the south half of Alberta and into Saskatchewan, he was on the road all the time. I'm sure the irregular hours and meals were a big factor in the development of diabetes which, during the last year of his life, left him nearly blind. He coped with this handicap so well that it was only when he didn't recognize me until I spoke to him that I knew how badly off he was.

Although he struggled on with his business until a few days before he died, Dad was very

Gerald Haney skidding telephone poles for George Wrigglesworth.

Hauling poles to Wrigglesworth pole yard.

Stock pile at Wrigglesworth's pole plant.

sick for the last couple of years. I shall always be grateful to his secretary, Mary St. Denys, for her concern and care during that time. As Dad was always very careful to shield me from his worries, it was Mary who knew how badly off he was and saw that he got care. She also did her best to help me straighten out his affairs after his death.

Dad died in 1960 just a few days after his sixty-seventh birthday. He was penniless and hopelessly in debt but he left a priceless legacy of honesty, kindness, generosity and perseverance — and a host of friends. In his drawer I found several letters from parents, thanking him for his goodness to their sons who had worked for him. I am proud to be George Wrigglesworth's daughter.

Wooler

The Wooler School No. 2976

by Sally Bugbee

Joe Bell homesteaded the N.E.Q. 17-36-6-5 in 1908. As the settlers moved in, it became apparent that a school was needed, so he donated about four acres of land on the southwest corner of his property to be used for a school and play ground.

In 1913, meetings were held to devise ways and means of getting one built. The project had to be on a voluntary basis with everyone donating their time and work, as money was almost nonexistent. They elected a school board putting Melville Ferguson in as secretary, a post he held until 1951 when the school was closed and the children were bussed to Caroline. Ephram Bell was the secretary-treasurer and Joe Bell, Charles Stewart and Andrew Laidler were on the board.

Logs were cut and hauled to Dan McGrandle's mill and sawed into lumber. Oliver Thibedeau and his son, Bill, were carpenters and they built the school. With all of them chipping in to share the work, things went well. The mild winter was on their side and by spring of 1914, the school was built. Joe Bell named the school, choosing it from the Wooler district in England where he lived before coming to Canada.

The first year, school was held for only three months and for the next few years it opened when the weather warmed up in the spring and closed when it turned cold in the winter. The teachers boarded in homes near the school if possible, such as at the Charlie Stewart's, Sam Frazier's, John Helm's and John Bugbee's.

Some of the first children to attend school were Ruth Stewart, Jack and Edith Laidler, Edith Maine, Bill, Florence and Mae McNutt and Doug and John Stewart.

Since the school register was either lost, misplaced or destroyed, it is impossible to name

Wooler School.

Back row, L.R. Albert Hembrow, Don Proudler, Sam Nelson, Vivian Oliver. 2nd row, L.R. Tom Chapin, Cliva Helm, Leonard Ogilvie, Dorothy Proudler, Howard Helm, Doreen and Mary Chapin. Front row, Harold Ogilvie and Dorothy Chapin.

all the teachers who taught at Wooler, or the dates. The following is a list of the names I have been able to gather: Miss Bruebaker, Miss Gunderson, Seneth Moodie, Mrs. Bertha Miller, Syd Weller, Bill Hackett, Eileen Eilertson, Eva Beatty, Fred Miller, Miss Summerhaze, Jean Roy, Miss Brown, Beth Donaven, Willetta Donaven, Grace Waldroff, Mafelda Blassetti, Jessie Limbough, Beth Owen, Christina Monroe, Mrs. Hembrow, Lydia Seels, Nelda Ceasor, Gordon Godkin, Dixie Rohrer and Chester Dohms. Chester was the last teacher at Wooler, he taught from April to the end of June, 1951.

Like all country schools, dances and other forms of entertainment were held in the Wooler School. It was moved to the School grounds in Caroline, and used for classes for three years. After it was closed it was moved to the west end of Caroline where it has served the people of Catholic faith ever since.

The Wooler School

by Christina (Munro) Murphy

It was a beautiful day in late August 1939 when I first saw Wooler School. There it stood on a hill, with its playground partly surrounded by trees. I came to appreciate this location, for in winter the hill provided much amusement for the pupils and in spring break-up the snow quickly disappeared leaving a dry playground.

When I opened the door I stepped into a freshly cleaned classroom where grades one to nine had been taught for the past twenty-five years.

The Wooler District was formed in 1913 and the school built in 1914. In the years to come I learned that the school had served the community in many ways. It was here where meetings, dances, socials, concerts and church services were held.

The first event after the harvest was the Chicken Supper. This was put on by the women in the community to raise funds for the annual Christmas Concert. It was amazing how these women could organize and serve a delicious supper to so many, in a rural school house without the facilities of a kitchen.

The finale of any social was a dance. Local musicians supplied the toe-tapping music — square dances, polkas, waltzs, two-steps and schottishes.

Fall held another interest — hunting time for the Big Game. From the time the season opened until it closed there was a continuous stream of hunters with their pack horses, wagons and trucks all going west. As the school was close to the road, the pupils and I took great pleasure in watching the various outfits going by.

One frosty November morning I opened the school door and stepped into a warm cosy classroom. I was surprised to find that the wood and coal stove had a fire in it, and there on the grate were baked potatoes. I realized someone had spent the night there. In those days the school door was seldom locked. On the blackboard was a "thank you" note but no name. The little school on the hill had served as a lodging place for some weary hunters.

The boarding place for the teacher was at the home of Mr. and Mrs. Jack Bugbee. Their kindness and consideration made a new teacher feel at home.

Jack Bugbee was noted for his hunting and trapping ability. He was skilled in the knowledge of wildlife and their environment. On the living room walls hung some splendid trophies. The family, like their father, had the same interest and knowledge of hunting.

The Christmas Concert was the highlight of the winter season. From November to December box socials, pie socials, shadow socials and masquerades were a means of fund raising. The money provided Santa with a full bag of gifts and candy for the children of the district. These concerts were the combined efforts of parents, pupils and teachers. The classroom took on a Christmas air with it's decorations of streamers, bells and stars. The air was filled with the fragrance of pine and spruce boughs that decorated the walls. The Christmas tree stood in a corner near the stage. The pupils put forth their best effort in acting, reciting, dancing, drills and singing, making the parents and teacher proud.

That winter a great sadness came to the district when a type of pneumonia took the life of Viola Englund. The doctor from Innisfail was called, but she died before he arrived. The undertaker was miles away; the snow drifted roads made travel slow and difficult. The neighbors and local school board came to the aid of the family — they decided to use the school. I remember that dusky winter afternoon. I walked with the group in silence as we pulled a child's sleigh up the hill bearing the body of this lovely young girl. That evening a casket was brought to the school. The next day the Englund family, along with their friends and relatives, made their way to the Raven church. Here the funeral services were held and burial took place in the churchyard cemetery.

On Sundays, church services were held in the school, and one evening a week there was a Young People's meeting. This work was carried on by a young Nazarene missionary, Miss Olive Thomas. Through her ministry, Wallace Helm, then a teenager, was later to serve in the Mission Field in India.

Wallace was a fine student who brought honor to Wooler by winning the gold medal for the highest marks in the Grade nine Departmental Examinations in 1939.

Walking and horseback riding were the means of travel to and from school. Two pupils, Toots Dix and Sam Nelson had a unique way of winter travel. They trained their dogs to pull them on a sled to school.

The Wooler pupils were eager and willing students. The older ones were considerate and helpful to the younger ones. With their help and ideas a number of projects were undertaken. In the winter they cleared the snow from a strip of ice on the Raven River so they could enjoy Saturday afternoon skating. In the spring a ball team was organized and we would walk to Caroline to play against the other schools.

June was Field Trip month. Permission was obtained from the Inspector and Rocky Mountain School Division Board and we chose to take a trip along the Raven and Saskatchewan rivers. When it came to crossing the North Saskatchewan I was reluctant, for despite the shallowness of the river, I felt it would be too difficult for the younger children. However, the older boys and girls solved the problem. Sam Nelson, Don Proudler, Jim Tobin, Geraldine Helm and Arline Englund went in pairs to form a chair seat and carried the children safely across. They even carried the teacher. These students had a good understanding and knowledge of nature. That day I learned many new and interesting facts from them.

The last two weeks of June were devoted to examinations and completing Art, Penmanship, Note Books and other projects to be entered in the School Fair held the first of September at Caroline.

I am sure that the pupils of that year have met with success in life and have served with communities well in which they live.

The school house no longer stands on the hill. Like many of its pupils, it has moved from the Wooler district. In 1954 it was brought to Caroline to be used as an extra classroom. It still serves the community, but no longer as a school. It is now the Caroline Roman Catholic Church.

The John Anderson Family

by Bill Anderson

September, 1918 — Martha and John Anderson and family, Arvid, William, Hugo, Arthur and Anna, arrived in Caroline, Alberta, coming from Montana, U.S.A.

Arvid travelled with the livestock, machinery

Anderson Family — Back Row — Gertrude (sister of Mrs. Anderson), John, Bill, Arvid. Front Row — Helen (niece of Mrs. Anderson), Arthur and Martha.

and household goods in a box car, by freight train, from Montana to Innisfail, Alberta. The rest of the family came in the Model T Ford, camping out enroute.

The livestock consisted of a team of work horses, a saddle pony, two cows, a heifer and a small calf. For the trip from Innisfail to Caroline, they loaded the machinery and household goods in the wagon, put the calf in a crate tied on the rear end of the wagon box, and herded the cows along behind.

The first day was rather hectic getting loaded up and on the road and getting the cows to follow the wagon. They made it as far as the Medicine River that day, about eleven miles, and camped there for the night. The next day went a lot smoother as the cattle got used to travelling, and they made it the rest of the way to Caroline by evening.

Caroline, at that time consisting of a little store and the post office, was a little over a half a mile south of the present village. The store and post office, operated by H. A. Langley and family, was just to one side of their house yard where they lived. Andersons lived in a house on one of Langley's farms that first winter, about three quarters of a mile south east of the store.

After the family got settled in their temporary home, Arvid had to go back to the States as he was on leave from the Military Service. He was waiting to see if he would be called, as he was classified for limited service because of nearsightedness.

It was an open winter, mild and very little snow. John and son, Bill, did a lot of travelling to the homestead, (six miles west and two and a half miles south of the present Caroline), picking out a building site and looking for a place to dig a well, etc. Also they worked on the old wagon road making it a little better to travel on with the Ford — which, by the way, was the first car in Caroline, and at that time, the only one.

305

Early in the spring of 1919, probably in March some time, Arvid returned to join the family. When he arrived in Innisfail, he could find no way to get a ride to Caroline, so he took off on foot and walked all the forty, and a little more, miles without stopping anywhere, and arrived late at night very footsore and weary.

So went the winter, and late in April, 1919, they moved to the homestead. The grass was starting to come and things looked good. Then on May second came a snowstorm. By the time it quit there was about two feet of snow on the ground — no shelter for the cows — no feed! But about three quarters of a mile away was an old barn with only a flat roof with some old straw on it. Well, better than nothing, so Arvid, walking ahead to make a track, and the boys chasing the cows along, moved them to the old barn. They managed to get a little feed to do the few days it was needed, and walked over there twice a day to feed and milk the cows. Water was no problem as the Raven River was close behind the old barn.

Arvid filed on the quarter joining his father's homestead on the north, that spring.

Next they had to get a field ready to grow feed. There had been ten acres broken by the former homesteader, which had grown back to grass and a little brush, but was easy to clear again. So they got this broken with the old walking plow and three horses. The saddle horse had to help out in this operation. Then followed days of root picking before it could be disked and worked down for the seed. Seeding was done by hand-broadcasting it. It was not exactly a

bumper crop being rather late getting sown. It made pretty good green feed though; cut with a mower, raked, then cocked by hand like hay. But the worst was when winter set in the eighth of October, and covered the stooks so all you could see was a little hump in the snow. We had to dig it all out with a scoop shovel. It was a long, hard winter with lots of snow.

School was three and a half miles away. Transportation was provided by the purchase of an old cayuse to hitch to a two wheel cart brought along with the machinery. This did for a couple years, then later they rode horseback instead.

In the spring of 1923, (the spring the old two span wooden bridge washed away; one span washed down stream about an eighth of a mile), Bill filed on a homestead, the northwest quarter of the same section his father and Arvid had homesteaded. He sold it to Hugo and Art years later — where they still live.

In 1923 John developed health problems, and on the doctor's recommendation to try a lower elevation for his heart condition, he went to the west coast of Ketchikan in southeast Alaska where he had three sisters-in-law to visit. The change of climate did not help, he passed away in February, 1924, only fifty-four years old.

Bill went to Alaska in the fall of 1924 to Ketchikan. He worked in a sawmill and also tried fishing with his uncle-in-law the summer of 1927, but the salmon run was poor that year, so he did not do very well. He came back to Alberta for the

Art Anderson — 1949.

Hugo Anderson at his trapper's cabin on the Wilson.

306

Furs from Hugo and Art Anderson.

harvest in the fall of 1927 and then home to Caroline.

Arvid worked in the railroad tie camps west of Rocky Mountain House for several winters, hacking ties to earn a grub stake for the family, his last winter there was 1924-25.

The Andersons milked cows, shipped cream and sold beef for a living until about 1933, from then on it has been a straight beef cattle operation.

Hugo and Art acquired registered traplines on the James River in the Forest Reserve southwest of their home in the fall of 1933. They operated these lines every winter until the spring of 1943.

Hugo was called up for military service in the fall of 1943. He took his training at Wetaskiwin and Currie Barracks in Calgary in the Infantry. He was then posted to the Edmonton Fusiliers near Niagara Falls, Ontario, in April, 1944, doing guard duty along the Hydro-power canal until late in December. He then went home to Caroline on leave until Christmas, then back to Niagara Falls to catch a draft of reinforcements to Aldershot, England. Taking some retraining there, until February, 1945, he was sent to the front of Western Germany, to the Calgary Highlanders. He was wounded near the end of April in northwestern Germany. He was transported to a hospital in England until June and then was transferred to the Colonel Belcher Hospital in Calgary where he made a fair recovery, receiving his discharge from the Army at the end of October, 1945.

Hugo and Art bought Bill's homestead late in 1937, and after Hugo came home from the Army, they didn't do very much more trapping, only part time, as they had acquired a few cattle by then and so ended their trapping in 1953.

Anna married Don Oper in 1935, moving to their homesteads, the N.W.Q. 6 and the S.E.Q. 7-36-7-5, where Anna still lives. They had two daughters, Ventress and Vivia, both married and living in the district.

Bill married Hazel Rodtka in 1944. In 1950 they moved into Rocky Mountain House where they still live.

Martha (Mrs. John Anderson) died at home, April 30, 1954, at the age of seventy-six years.

Arvid passed away in the Red Deer General Hospital, after a short illness August 8, 1972, at seventy-five years of age.

Arvid's land and machinery passed on to Hugo and Art who operate both it and the quarter of land that they bought from Bill, where they still live.

The Bain Family
by Irene Pittendreigh

The Alex Bain family farmed at Nanton, Alberta, for a number of years. My sister, Ivy, and I were born there. In April of 1924, we moved to Craigmyle, Alberta, where my dad purchased a meat market.

In the fall of 1928 farming fever hit again. My dad sold his business and bought a farm four miles east of Craigmyle. The next year was the beginning of the dry years. We had come up to Caroline with some neighbors, to visit the Garrets. My dad decided this was the country for him, so when we went back we got ready to move. We got to Caroline on October 3, 1931. It wasn't long until we were settled on a farm again. But my father didn't live long to enjoy the change from the dust bowl, as he passed away

Mr. and Mrs. Bain and Beth Donovan.

suddenly on December 27, 1933. My mother is still living. She is ninety-two. My sister, Ivy, is married and has two daughters. They live at Sherwood Park.

Jake Bechtel

by Opal Bechtel

Jake moved from Harrington, Alberta, to Caroline in 1931 where he bought a farm, the S. E. Q. 9-36-6-5. Jake and I were married in 1933 and have lived in this area ever since. Having been raised on the prairie, I was not too impressed with the bush country. I was to change my mind, though, when I went back for a visit. The southeast wind blew steadily and the temperature dropped to -20 degrees Fahrenheit. I was sure glad to get back to the shelter of the trees, and neither of us have ever wanted to leave since.

Having no children of our own, Jake and I sort of adopted the children in the neighborhood. We have helped in any way that we could, to raise money toward their functions and projects.

The annual fowl supper was one occasion that we all enjoyed. The Christmas concert was another, the kids were always so proud of their efforts.

Back in the days of bed-bugs, do any of you remember them? I shall never forget our first night together when Jake and I were married. The next morning, I was welts from head to toe and that is when we had our first company, Maury and Nellie Carter. I don't believe Maury ever stopped teasing me. The following nights we slept in a tent until we could rid the house of those bugs. For many people, perhaps, it was a blessing when D. D. T. made it's debut, at least they got rid of the bed-bugs. The drastic results of its extensive use has taken its toll, affecting human, bird and animal life, as well as the environment. The bad qualitites have far surpassed the good that came out of its use, anyway the bed-bugs were taken care of.

Our first big production in social life was when we put on a three act play. It was portrayed as back in the nineteenth century. Maury and I were to be the servants getting ready to go out for the evening. I was to appear on stage in a pair of baggy bloomers like the ones women used to wear. I was also to wear one of those old bone corsets that laced up the back and Maury was to cinch me in, pulling the laces up tight. Thanks to Mrs. Langley, we found one of those corsets in some old stock in their store. Anyone who ever knew Maury can well imagine the performance he put on when he was lacing me in that corset; it brought the house down!

In 1939 we bought the N.E. Q. 9-36-6-5 from Mel Ferguson. With hard work and by burning it over, we finally got it cleared.

Jake served on the school board until the Wooler School closed and the students were bussed into Caroline.

Following his father's love for Shorthorn cattle, Jake started a herd of purebred Shorthorns in the late 1940's. This venture proved very successful.

One thing that we really enjoyed was raising ten pheasant chicks for the Fish and Game Association. These were to be released in our district in the fall. Besides us, others had some to raise as well. We kept ours in the hay barn and they could get behind the studding if they were frightened or if a stranger came along. Mr. Frazier was the only person who could come in and they wouldn't run away and hide, but he had to be very quiet when they were feeding. These birds are very smart. They proved it to me. One Sunday, I thought I would be a lady, so I put on a dress instead of the usual slacks. When I went to feed them no way would they come out to eat. I returned to the house and donned my slacks and when I went back, they recognized me and everything was fine.

When we turned the pheasants loose that fall, the hens always came back to feed and were tame, that first winter. The rooster was most ungrateful, we never saw him again. This was not a successful project for the Fish and Game; it is not the right kind of country for them, so they gave it up.

We sold our farm to Fred Malak in 1967 and moved into Caroline. Fred has a thriving dairy business and has done very well.

After moving into Caroline, I worked for ten years, first in the general store, then at the coffee counter and finally in the meat department. I enjoyed it very much, but we are now retired and keep ourselves busy at home.

Beulah Bell, daughter of Bill and Rasie Bell.

Joe Bell

Joe came from England and homesteaded the N.E.Q. 17-36-6-5 in 1908. Mrs. Bell was a sister of William Murray. Family are Billy (dead), Maggie (dead), Mary, Stan and Ephrem (dead). This is now owned by Gary Wold.

Charles Benz

Charles Benz was born in Rocky Mountain House in 1922. He lived with his parents, Mike and Mary Benz, who have farmed near Caroline since 1912. He attended North Caroline and Wooler Schools.

At the age of sixteen, he went to work for his father building roads for the municipality in the Rocky Division. In 1948 he was married to Blanche McColl who was born in Innisfail in 1928. She lived with her parents, Charles and Frances McColl, and attended the Shilo School.

Charles and Blanche settled on a farm near Caroline where they have lived for twenty-eight years. They have five children, Betty (Benz) Woof, born in 1951, now living in Red Deer; Linda (Benz) Johnson, born in 1952 and living in Lethbridge; Elsie (Benz) Betts born in 1953 and living in Seebe, Alberta; Albert Benz born in 1955 and working and Charlotte Benz, born in 1963, still living at home and attending Caroline School.

George Benz Family
by George and Eleanor Benz

George Benz was born at Strathmore, Alberta, October 28, 1918. He took his schooling at Wooler. Some of his teachers were Miss Beatty, Sid Weller and the Donovan sisters.

When he finished school he worked for Art Sanders and Oscar Johnson as a farm hand. He worked at various sawmills in the district, the Dan McGrandle mill, the Boeken and Englund mill, Art Oliver, Mr. Litke and Mac Dix.

He followed the harvests working for Elmer Johnson at Wimbourne. A good wage in those days was fifty cents per day.

George Benz hauling logs for Dan McGrandle.

George Benz at Wally's Lath yard.

He also worked for the Municipality of Raven on road construction, first with four horses and a fresno, later with an RD8 caterpillar and tumble bug.

Eleanor G. Flynn was born at Delorane, Manitoba, November 27, 1919. She was raised and educated in the Peterborough district of Ontario. She came with her parents and brothers, Basil and Pat, her sisters, Chris and Marie, to the Caroline area in the late fall of 1939.

The Flynn family lived the fall of 1939 and winter of 1940 on the Boeken land in what is locally known as 'Looney Valley'. The Flynn family moved to the Water Valley district in the spring of 1940 where Mr. Flynn had an acreage. He did carpenter work and had a feed lot as well.

George and Eleanor were married at Water Valley June 27, 1942. June, as we are aware is the traditional wedding month. It is also a month noted in this area for almost continuous rain and dreadful road conditions. It took George twenty-four hours to travel the distance from Caroline to Water Valley. "Woe betide the groom who arriveth late to his wedding," but in spite of all the muddy frustrations, George was able to be on time.

The young couple lived for a time at George's parent's farm and then went to work at Innisfail at the Hans Christie farm and later the Dennis dairy farm.

Their first child, William George, was born at Innisfail June 1, 1943.

They obtained an acreage a half mile west of the hamlet of Caroline and made their home there until 1960, when they purchased the N.W. Q. 21-36-6-5 where they now reside.

Over the years, George has worked at farming, helped to dig the basement for the first school built in Caroline; for Heiland Exploration, the first seismic company to operate in the district; for Mueller Construction Company as cat man on brush clearing and had his own sawmill for a time. He had his own caterpillar and hauled logs for Wriggleworth's camp. After the pole plant ceased operation, he had a gravel truck operation during the summer months and hauled lumber for Murray Brothers during the winter. For several years Eleanor operated the coffee shop in the Pioneer Store.

During the intervening years their family increased. Mary was born February 19, 1947; Michael on October 20, 1949; Allan on August 6, 1952, and Deborah on October 17, 1953. Their son Michael, passed away in June, 1966.

William married Barbara Houlton in 1963. They have two children, Brenda and Michael. William has lived all his life in the Caroline district and has worked for many years on oil rigs. He is presently farming and lathmilling.

Mary married John Black in November, 1965. They have two sons, Michael and Dale. John was raised in the Caroline district and took his schooling here. He works on oil rigs and at lathmilling. He and Mary live on an acreage north west of Caroline.

Allan married Linda Mayhew in February, 1977. They have one son, Clayton. Allan has worked on oil rigs and for an oil field safety supply company as a consultant. He lives on the N.E. Q. 21-36-6-5.

Deborah married Lance Tait on November 26, 1973. They have two sons, Aaron and Joseph. They live in Red Deer and Lance is employed as a tool push for Target Well Service.

Michael C. Benz

Michael C. Benz was born at Hastings, Minnesota, U.S.A., on May 1, 1892. He came to Saskatchewan with his father about 1903. They worked for Mr. Frank Jackson, who had a railroad contract to build rail grades on branch lines in Saskatchewan and Alberta. His mother and the younger children moved up to the Keoma district of Alberta, in 1905, and spent their first winter living in a tent. The next summer they moved onto land south and west of Strathmore and later to the Carseland district.

When the rail grades were finished, Mike worked with horses and slips and fresnos on the irrigation ditches around the Strathmore district.

In the fall of 1912, Mike Benz; Oliver and Bill Thibedeau came to the Caroline district to look for homesteads. They went back to Strathmore and worked for a time. Mike came back in the spring of 1913 and filed on N.W. section of 33-36-6-5. He married Mary E. Thibedeau on January 8,

Four generations — Oliver Thibedeau, George Benz, Mike Benz, William G. Benz.

1914, at Strathmore, and they came to live on their homestead in the summer of that same year.

Their first child, Louise, was born on December 21, 1914, at home.

They proved up their land and then moved back to Strathmore for a time, where their first son, George, was born on October 28, 1918. They came back to the homestead, and in October of 1919 they lost their house by fire. What household effects Mary and her father were able to save were stored in a woodshed. She and the two young children stayed with her parents until the material for another house was hauled from the Thibedeau's mill, which was then at Alhambra.

On February 21, 1920, their second son was born, Oliver H. W. Benz. Mike worked on the roads of the developing Caroline district, and at whatever other work was available, including the cutting of mine props for the Brazeau Collieries. Mary did much of the farm work, and on November 26, 1922, their third son, Charles W. was born. On September 12, 1924, a daughter, Helen, arrived; Frances was born on December 2, 1929; James was born on September 1, 1931; and their last daughter, Marie, was born at Rocky Mountain House on July 10, 1935.

During the war years, Mary and the younger children lived in Vancouver and Mary worked at an aircraft plant. Mike and the older boys carried on with the business of farming.

All of their family are married and live in the district with the exception of three daughters, Louise and Helen live in Vancouver and Frances lives in Rocky Mountain House.

Mike and Mary Benz Golden Anniversary — Helen Chwaklinski — behind the cake — Louise Bergren, Mike Benz, Helen Sawyer, Mary Benz and Clarence Sawyer.

Mike Benz suffered ill health in later life and passed away on July 20, 1977. He is laid to rest in the Caroline Cemetery. Mary lives at their home where she enjoys her gardening and still milks a cow. They enjoyed their family and at present Mary has twenty-eight grandchildren and seventeen great-grandchildren.

O. H. Benz (Bill)
by Evelyn Benz

Oliver Henry William, second son of Mary and Michael Benz, named after his maternal grandfather (Thibedeau), was given the nickname of Bill by his father who wanted one of his sons to carry on that name.

As with most of the boys of the pioneer families, Bill had many farm chores fall to his lot, and attendance at school of necessity took second place. The work at home was essential to life itself.

At times no classes were held at Wooler School, three and one half miles west of the present site of Caroline, because no teachers were available. However, when school was in session, roads and weather often proved to be serious barriers to attendance.

The early years left happy memories too though, swims in the Clearwater and Raven with brothers and friends, and of berry picking and fishing trips by team and wagon as far away as Swan Lake.

O. H. Benz, 1952.

Meuller brush cutting equipment — Meuller (foreman), Howard Alstott, George Benz, Elsie Alstott with Gladys and O. H. Benz, (Bill).

311

Bill spent the latter part of his teen years on his trap line in the Idelwilde area in the winter, and assisted the ranger, Clarence Sawyer, of the Clearwater Ranger Station with his work in the summer.

As time went on, Bill worked in the Wimborne area on a farm for Elmer Johnson, then trucked lumber in 1940 from Horburg to Rocky Mountain House for Charlie Edwards, founder of Edward's Garage and Lumber Yard, and operated a 'cat' in the Cochrane district, clearing land.

In November, 1942, Bill joined the army and, after basic training, became a member of the royal Canadian Artillery. At the end of the war in 1946, he obtained his discharge and again went to clearing land, this time in the vicinity of Caroline, and to seismic work.

He was united in marriage with Esther Thompson of Water Valley, Alberta. Tragedy overcame this marriage on a bitter February day with the death by fire of his wife and infant son, Alvin, while he was away at work.

In 1950 Bill, and Evelyn, who had moved with her parents, Sydney and Ethel Evans, to a farm in the Caroline area, were married and took up residence on the Thibedeau homestead, N.W.Q. 34-36-6-5. Bill continued his work with road construction with the municipality and with the Department of Highways on number 54.

A daughter, Terry Louise, was born to them in February of 1952 at Rocky Mountain House, and a son, Wayne Oliver, in August of 1956 at Fort Vermillion. A second son, Barry Michael, arrived in February, 1958, at Wetaskiwin and another daughter, Ethel Dianne, in September of 1959, at Rocky Mountain House.

Over these years Bill's construction work took the family to Vegreville, Innisfail, Alder Flats, Meander River and Peace River in the north, to Wetaskiwin, and then to Golden and Stoney Creek in British Columbia, where the Trans-Canada Highway was being built.

They moved back to Caroline in the winter of 1960-61 to the old homestead where they erected a new house and still reside, and have raised their family. The circle is not unbroken though, as Dianne is gone, lost at age fifteen in a car accident.

Since their return to Caroline, Bill has worked for the municipality again and for Edward's Lumber as mechanic until Dave Edward's untimely death, and has driven school bus four years. He then drove fuel truck for Imperial Oil and spent a year and a half in mechanic work at the Aquitaine Gas Plant at Ram River.

At present he is back with school buses, being mechanic for the Rocky Mountain School Division in Rocky.

Terry is married to Ken Williamson of Red Deer, a government engineering technologist, and they have their home in Leduc. Wayne has married Cathy Couture of Winnipeg, lives in Calgary, and is engaged in carpentry. Barry, who married Nell McBride of Caroline, resides in Innisfail and is on permanent staff for the town.

To keep them on their toes and to help fill in the empty spots, Bill and Evelyn have foster children with them now.

Frank Blowers

I was born at Clear Lake, South Dakota, August 6, 1904. I homesteaded S.W. 1-36-7-5 in 1927.

Frank Blowers on the binder and Dolly and Marilyn in the field.

I married Dolly Bowers of Caroline on the 16th of December, 1929. We have a family of seven, Raymond, Ralph, Wallace, Margaret, Loraine, Ronald and Marilyn. Raymond is unmarried. Ralph married Maxine Bilske. Wallace married Ange Gagnon. Margaret married William Hallock. Loraine married Miner Harris. Ronald married Lois Garella and Marilyn married Stan Carlson.

We farmed and raised cattle until retiring. We sold cream in the thirties for $1.50 for five gallons, $3.00 for market pigs and $15.00 for longhorn yearling steers. We would walk them to Innisfail to market.

R. T. and Maggie Blowers
by Frank Blowers

Mr. and Mrs. Blowers came from Clear Lake, South Dakota, to the Tees district in April, 1917, with their four children, Mary, Frank, Annie and Ruth. Annie and Frank attended School at the Nebraska School north of Tees. Mr. Blowers heard about the homesteads at Caroline, so he came and filed on N.E. 36-35-7-5 in 1919. They moved to their new homestead in 1920.

Lester Thompson, Bill Shepherd, Ruth Blowers, Annie Blowers, Frank Blowers and Dolly Blowers, 1929.

Carl Edward and Carl M. Boeken
by Irvin Palmer

Carl Edward Boeken was born in Illinois on March 18, 1859. He moved to Ellsworth, Kansas, in the year of 1863. When 1882 came, he thought that was his lucky year, as he married a girl named Otlillia Doring. This sweet fourteen year old could maybe be his only chance. Now this gal he married had no fear of dogs, for one thing. When they went for groceries at the corner store, the owner had a big police dog tied up at the back end along with a sign which read, "Anyone who can lead this dog out of my store shall be its rightful owner." Well, Otlillia did her shopping, gave the groceries to Eddie, walked back to the dog, untied him and three went out of the store instead of two. The storekeeper had no more guard dog and Eddie and Otlillia had a dog for protection.

By 1895 they had five children and decided to move to Michigan and in those days the only way was by covered wagon. En route to Michigan, the stork paid them another visit, this time a boy, Carl M. Boeken. The date was June 3, 1895, and he was the sixth of eight children. I would also like to add at this point the fact that Edward, while living in Kansas, never met anyone who could out box or out wrestle him. He could lift 500 pound kegs of salt into a sleigh with no problem.

In 1912 father and son, Carl Jr., decided to head north to the promised land, a land flowing with yellow golden wheat fields in southern Alberta. Well, as it turned out the first job they tried for they never forgot! As they were walking up the lane, the farmer's big black ferocious dog came down to meet them with flaming eyes and gleaming white teeth. If only Otlillia were there. Well, anyway, Carl Jr. was in the lead, but took up the rear quickly as the enemy came in to make the kill. He went for the jugular on Edward's throat but Edward quickly stepped aside and caught the opponent's rear running gear and gave him the 'alleyoop swing.' Old Blackie was just never quite the same.

At any rate, in the harvest job that year, they met up with Jack McNutt who was from west of Caroline. He told them of a place he had found in the Raven River valley about five miles west and six miles southwest of Caroline, and it was there that father and son put in their first winter. They built a log cabin, twelve by fourteen feet, with Jack helping them. In the spring of 1913 they filed for homesteads alongside of each other. In those days the government bet the homesteader ten dollars they couldn't make a living from the land — Carl and his dad won as they proved up their land. When Otlillia and the rest of the children moved up, Carl Sr. moved to the Bell place four miles west of Caroline. They later returned to the States and in May, 1918, Carl Jr. joined the United States Navy. When discharged in December, 1918, father and son again returned to their homestead on the Raven River. Carl Jr. worked for Dan McGrandle, who had a sawmill about two and a half miles up on the Raven River from the Clearwater bridge. He also worked for Chet Brierley at Rocky Mountain House, loading ties in boxcars. The ties were hauled in by horses and sleighs. Carl's brother-in-law, Martin Justinen, also worked there. Martin's job was driving a snatch team to help pull the loads of ties up a steep hill before they got to the loading place. Well, this one cold day (about forty below) the ties just stopped coming. After awhile one of the old Swedes, that drove a team came walking up with his horse whip wondering where that tow team had got to. "Carl," he called, "Just look over there behind the big spruce tree!" Sure enough, there was their tow man all humped over. Seems he had himself a novel and was right into it. Well, he had to read it sometime. But when the Swede snuck up and cracked that horse whip, that proved to be a better novel, and he never waited for ties again.

Carl M. got tired of being a bachelor, so on March 12, 1922, he married Mildred Huffman at Calgary. In the fall of 1922 they went to Forest Grove, Oregon, where Carl got a job as a faller, cutting trees. On March 25, 1923, Mildred and Carl became the proud parents of a daughter, Dorothy Lorraine.

Well, no place better to raise a family than on a homestead, so in May, 1927, they came back to sunny Alberta. As Red Womack would say, "Anyone that lies down on their stomach to take a drink from the Raven River, always returns."

In 1931 Carl'had another ten dollar bet with the government for a homestead two and a half miles from the Clearwater bridge on the Raven River. This homestead was south of Gerald McNutt's, along the sawdust pile of Dan McGrandle's quarter where Carl had worked. South and west of there lived the Anderson Brothers. Well, anyway, he lost this bet with the government, so it was one and one now!

Some people called the '30s the dirty '30s, but out in the west country they were the hungry '30s. Carl and his dad milked cows and shipped the cream with George Cliff of Ricinus, who ran a light horse express to Chedderville. From there the cream went to Rocky where a five gallon can of number one special cream (if you were lucky) brought a whole dollar fifty.

One of Carl's neighbors, about two miles to the southeast, was a homesteader bachelor by the name of Oscar Tress. Now Oscar didn't trust any 'pale faces', and in one case, when he left home to go harvesting south of Calgary, he made sure he would know if anyone came calling. He loaded up his moose gun, fastened it on a couple of chairs with a string leading from the trigger to the doorknob. Well no one seemed interested, and as it turned out, he was just about his own victim. One morning, Oscar mounted his noble black horse and paid Carl and his dad a visit. Oscar, thinking this might be a turn for the better, knocked and Carl opened up the old board door saying, "Good morning, Oscar. Come on in and sit up and have breakfast." No thanks," said Oscar, and he sits down and grabs up the funny paper to read up on Tillie the Toiler, Toots and Casper. Now Carl's dad was just starting to eat

his porridge, when 'chomp,' he bit right into a rock. Well the rock shattered, the jaw pained and the funny paper Oscar was reading, slipped a little. Maybe it was just as well that Oscar wasn't hungry. At any rate, there happened to be a second course for breakfast — hot cakes! The day before on the way home from the store in the democrat, the salt and the sugar had a disagreement as to who was the best, and they alternated! Well, the only syrup was what you made, and hot cakes were only good swimming in syrup. Carl's dad was the victim. What a disaster! Oscar had been half watching the events, and this seemed to be the last straw! Dropping the funny paper to the floor, he made his exit with a hasty "Goodday Cull." By the "howdy boys, what next?" was all that Carl could say. Needless to say, no more Oscar Tress for awhile. He went home to eat his own bannock made from cold water and flour and baked on the top of the stove.

As the winter wore on, the snow being quite deep, Carl and his dad were coming home, with a load of wood, when they saw this fellow walking in the ditch with just his head sticking out of the snow. Carl asked him if he would like to ride with them, but the fellow said, "No thanks, I'm riding my horse."

In the summer of 1934 Carl decided to move west to his first homestead on the Raven, and his dad moved back onto his old place. Harry Norton and his wife, Mary, and son, Lamone, were staying on the old homestead. They moved around the corner into the first log house that Carl and his dad built in 1912. That summer, Carl and Harry decided to go into the shingle milling business. But what were they going to use for power to run their mill? Well, they took a hard look at the Raven River, and yes, that would do the trick. Water power by means of a water wheel. They then took another look at the poor old Clyde team, Pete and Riley. Earthmovers! (What did they do to deserve this ill fate?) Two horsepower on a slip. As the summer passed, the dam took form and as the water wheel turned the shingles flew and a dream came true. But alas, what were the poor fishes going to do while the dam was filling up? They must have sent word S.O.S. as a fellow dressed in a green uniform showed up. The fish were here first and had their rights. So no more 'dam' for the shingle makers. At any rate, for history's sake, the Raven River had the first power dam — Boeken and Norton Incorporated. Carl then found an old Fordson tractor and they sawed shingles for the rest of the summer.

In the summer of 1934, Jack Browning put on a stampede. He had everything all lined up but had no loud speaker. How was his audience to know who was coming out of chute one or two, or who was riding Old Yellow Cloud or Thunder Head? Then Jack thought of Carl and an old tin horn, the two would do the trick. Carl was the announcer for the next two years. Jack McNutt, living a couple of miles away, said he didn't have to go to the stampede — heard it all anyway.

Fred Thompson and Ed Clay sawed logs one winter for Carl. Jack Orcutt from Chedderville and Herb Von Hollen from Stauffer hauled logs. Carl then went into partnership with Carl Englund on the sawmill and Mac Dix hauled logs with his black team. Mac had the best pulling team in Jack Browning's stampede. They used a stoneboat with rocks, and standbyers had a free ride for the extra weight. Jim Tobin had a brown team, Babe and Dick. He took up a homestead just over the hill south of Carl's dad's homestead. He logged there all one winter and hauled the logs to Carl's sawmill. Tom Chapin, one of the best horse skinners around, also hauled a lot of logs to the mill. His homestead was the first one you came to in the Raven Valley, then Carl's dad's, next was Carl's and Ted Von Hollen's was the last one. Ted had taken over the Sarah and Austen Moore homestead around 1934 or '35.

It was about this time, in the middle of winter, that rustlings for man and beast became very grim. Carl had been out hunting moose and he wounded a bull. Well, the bull moose started looking for a place to hide and took to the ice on a backwater strip on the Clearwater River and when Carl came into sight, the moose sort of sank out of sight. On the way home, Carl passed Chapin's residence, and feeling charitable, asked him if he would like a special 'water cured moose'. Well, Tom's team had to do some real scratching, but they did get that 'special water cured, ornery old moose' out. It was that same year that Carl and his dad sent eight Holstein cows down to Dickson for wintering — only two survived.

In October, 1937, Carl's dad passed away on his homestead. He was seventy-eight years old. Mike Benz made the coffin from rough spruce boards. The ground was frozen and the road extremely rough as the high wheeled wagon carried the remains to the Raven Cemetery. The total cost of the funeral was twelve dollars.

Lamming brothers of Rocky Mountain House, bought Carl's steam engine and sawmill. In the fall of 1939, Carl Jr. decided to go south again, selling his homestead to a fellow by the name of Mendze for $500.00. He left the first of January, 1940. Carl did some more logging, falling trees and sawmilling in Oregon. One day when he was falling a big tree, a wind came up and caught the tree and took it over backwards on Carl. All that

saved him was a hollow in the ground which he fell into as the tree fell. He suffered a broken hip which left him crippled for the rest of his life. He died in Oregon City on December 3, 1967, and was buried there. His wife, Mildred, lives with her daughter, Dorothy. Mildred, at the time of this writing, is eighty-eight years old. Dorothy married Jim Graham and has three children.

Entertainment was scarce in those early days but everyone made the most of what was available. Carl Jr., his father, and Jim Tobin were violin players and many 'rafter raising' house parties were held in the Boeken household.

Robert John Carroll

Bob was born at Walkerton, Ontario, in 1890. Bob, his mother and sister, Tiny, came to the Caroline area from the prairies in 1938. He bought the Carl Edward Boeken homestead, N.E. Q. 6-36-6-5. His mother passed away while living there.

He did no farming, but owned some cattle and horses. He bought feed from some of the neighboring ranches and hauled it home. One day while going for a load of feed, the sleigh upset. He was found the following day, frozen. It is believed that he died of a heart attack, December 22, 1955. He was survived by two sisters, Mrs. Keeler and Miss Edith Carroll.

My Days in Caroline
by David D. Craig

In June, 1947, my parents and I arrived in Caroline coming from Agassiz, British Columbia. In 1946 my dad came to Alberta to take in the Calgary Stampede, and, while spending a week in Calgary, decided to come to Alberta to settle.

I was seventeen years of age at the time, and, of course, a bit hesitant to leave my friends in Agassiz. However, I wasn't in Caroline long before I met and became friends with several boys my own age. I still remain friends with these same ones.

On mentioning our moving to this country, we were unable to get through to our quarter section (two miles west and one half mile south of Caroline) as the road was muddy — the 'Frazer Hill', as known then, was impassable for our car which was loaded with our belongings. Mr. Orcutt, thanks to him, came along and hooked up to our car with his Ford tractor and pulled us up the hill to our new home. My mother had a look at her new home and was somewhat disappointed after leaving a nice home in British Columbia, but she soon made wonderful friends and was loved by all.

My folks ran the post office in, I believe, 1949.

My dad passed away in 1950 and Ma and I were left with the job of running the post office. Neither of us had experience, but with determination, we soon mastered it. With the sum of $75 per month and another $15 per month for the building, we were able to just make it. Our friends of Caroline helped us in many ways.

The postmistress job got to be too much for Ma, and after a lengthy stay in the hospital, we gave it up. I worked at different jobs such as logging and sawmilling. In 1954 I took over a trapline which had been the Anderson's line on the James River. Lawrence Oliver had a line on the south side of the river and he stayed with me in my cabin. I must say at this time that I got to know one of the finest people that I ever met in my life — George Bugbee. I came stumbling up to my cabin cold and hungry, and there was this great hulk standing in my doorway with his homely grin. He had the cabin all warmed up and said, "I've buzzed up a little wood for you." That little wood lasted for three weeks. Other wonderful men I met were Art Oliver and Art Johnson.

I would like to end this attempt of compiling this by saying, "Bless you Caroline and district. I'll always remember you." My Ma passed away in 1976 and I now live in Victoria, British Columbia.

Ernest Dean

by Annie Pengelly

Ernest George Dean was born December 17, 1900, at Cape Tormentine, New Brunswick. The eldest of seven children, he attended school there and worked with his father, fishing for lobster in his spare time.

He came west to Winnipeg in 1919 and attended college there for awhile. From there he went to Hartney, Manitoba, near his Uncle Willis Stillman, and worked on farms. Then he came west to Carseland, Alberta, and worked on grain farms for a time. One day he was moving a family, by the name of Charlie Schnelle, to Fort Macleod. He was driving six horses and pulling two wagons, when his outfit was struck by a car, killing all three horses on the one side.

It was here at Carseland that he met Almer Pengelly. He persuaded him to come to Caroline and take up a homestead, which he did. Ernest homesteaded and proved up on the N.W. Q. 28-25-6-5.

He did some farming and raised a few cattle, putting up hay for them in the summer months. He also worked in the bush, cutting lath bolts, until his passing in January, 1970. He and Almer were life long friends; he was a kind man and loved children and they loved him.

The Dewie Family

by Stella Clay

When the Depression of the early thirties was at its height, many new families came to the Caroline area. One of these was the Dewie family consisting of Jack and Edith (Edealine) and their three sons, Chester, John and George. They came from Vulcan, Alberta, and bought the Smyth place. The next year the two daughters, Stella and Kay, arrived at the end of the school year.

After the dry, dusty bleakness of the prairie, this area with its plentiful rain and lush growth was very appealing. The farms were heavily wooded and meant years of back-breaking work in the days before the use of heavy machinery.

Among their neighbors were the Frazier, Brown and Pengelly families and Nels Swanson, Jake Bechtel, Ernie Dean, Bob Miller, Shorty McDermid and Fred and Conrad Schafer. Neighbors were very important in those days and these were very good neighbors indeed — always ready to help out in time of need.

Times were very hard, but although there was not much money in the country, most people raised good gardens and kept animals for milk, meat and eggs. The abundance of fish, game and wild berries added variety and with logs and wood plentiful for building and fuel, everyone managed very well. Jack Dewie's garden was always a source of good eating.

Almost everyone rode horseback or drove the well-known 'Bennett buggy' made from the chassis of the cars we could not afford to drive.

Entertainment, too, was inexpensive. Many very enjoyable evenings were spent at house parties where Claude and Mildred Frazier, Eric Harder and others provided music for dancing. The ladies brought lunch and anyone who could, entertained with songs.

After a group was organized that soon included most of the community, programs and plays were put on in the Community Hall. The hilight of the year was the Christmas concert put on by the combined efforts of South Fork, Shilo and Wooler Schools. The Dewie's were active in all these activities.

Church services were held in the Community Hall in summer with student ministers preaching. Mrs. Langley held Sunday School above her store.

I (Stella) became the teacher at South Fork School and taught there for four years. Those were four busy and unforgettable years. In 1937 Ed Clay and I were married in Red Deer. Our story is told elsewhere in this book.

Kay married Tom Park of Innisfail in 1933. They had a family of seven children. They lived on their farm near Innisfail until their deaths in 1962 within six months of each other.

My father died in 1938. The kindness of all the neighbors at that time is something we will never forget.

Mother lived on the farm for many years where she was busy and interested in all the doings of the farm. During the last few years she was in a nursing home in Calgary. She died in 1971 at the age of ninety-five.

Chester died in 1957 and is buried in the Innisfail Cemetery.

When war broke out, George enlisted in the Air Force. He was stationed at several places in Canada and later went overseas. After the war he came home and spent some time on the farm before going to Calgary where he still lives with his wife, Betty.

John lived on the home farm until 1968, when he died after an operation in the Foothills Hospital, Calgary.

The life on a bush farm in those days was hard work, but there were many pleasant memories of good times. There was also the satisfaction of being part of the progress in this relatively pioneer area.

Dial, Hal and Bob

Hal moved to Caroline from Innisfail in 1932 and farmed the old Bell place 3 miles west of Caroline. The farm was owned by Ray Dial.

Bob moved out to the farm a year later and Helen went to the farm to cook for them. Times were hard those years, but the friends and fellowship we knew in those years will never be forgotten.

Farming was hard and the conveniences in the old log house with its wood floors were very few. We washed with the tub and washboard,

L.-R. Richard, Hal, Ray and Bob Dial.

made butter in a barrel churn — no running water to wash the separator and milk pails. A hole in the ground was our cooler. The mattresses were filled with straw, and some of the beds were up on nail kegs.

Cliff Chorley and Earle Farris worked on the farm at times. Our friends from Caroline came to visit — two in particular came at any hour. Chick Demenuck and Bob Willsie (Whiskey) used to stop in, night or day, while they were hauling lumber. Sometimes they would go in the back room (our cold room) and slice wild meat and cook it by holding a pan in the heater. We all had to get up or be pulled out of bed, so there were times when we didn't get much sleep. They made up for it. They would leave us the canned goods left over from their trip. That was a treat!

Bob and Howard at the store often wondered how they ate all that canned food.

The old "Bell place" was the scene of many hair-raising occurrences. The "boys" used to shoot at mice that came in through a hole in the house. They would practice throwing hunting knives across the house from the front door to the back. Bob and Chick were the worst — Chick slapped a piece of chocolate pie with whipped cream across Bob's face one time, and they used to hang leftover pancakes on nails on the wall. A favorite way of waking whoever slept in the granary was to take the .22 and shoot at the discs beside it. A "miss" once sent a bullet into the granary and over Hal's head.

Then there was the time Chick cut all the hair off the mane and tail of my saddle horse. I could go on and on.

Cliff Chorley is now at Devon. Earle Farris is at Duncan, B.C. Hal married Marion MacDonald from Raven in 1939. Helen rented Don Dix's cafe in Caroline and a year later married Howard Mullen (see Mullen J. H.) who had the Caroline

Dial boys — L.-R. — Richard, Bob and Hal. Bob claims title of "Best dressed" with gunny sack trousers.

Bob Dial.

Traders Store. Bob Mitten had taken over the hotel. Hal and Marion then moved to four miles east of Spruce View. They bought the old Buzz Herold place. A few years ago they sold their farm and cattle and moved to Lavington, B.C. just out of Vernon. They are enjoying their retirement years.

Bob joined the R.C.A.F. at the beginning of the war and was posted overseas. When he returned he married Amy Klatt and lived in Innisfail. He drilled water wells for some time. They now live west of Caroline and have the Clearsprings Camp Ground. They have two sons, Robbie and Lennie in Red Deer and a daughter Shirley who is married to Franklin Daines.

Fred Dilly

Fred homesteaded the S.W.Q. 7-36-6-5 in the early years. He proved up on this quarter and then sold it to Prince Obolinsky of Russia who settled three Russian refugees on it. They had

escaped through China during the Russian Revolution. Their names are There Malashef, Oster Hanseff and Vishnia Koff. They lived here for about three years. The house they built is still standing and is an impressive sight, the logs appear to be in good shape. It is a two-storey building and was built for two apartments on the lower floor and was divided by a log partition, the upper floor was for one apartment. However, things didn't seem to work out for them so they left and went to Calgary from here. Sam and Reba Nelson lived in it while they were getting a house built on their property adjoining it on the north, then later they bought it, too.

The Dix Family

Malcolm (Mac) Dix was born January 16, 1884, in the central part of the State of Nebraska.

Kathleen (Morgan) Dix was born at Helena, Montana, during the 1890s.

Mac, Kathleen and her father, Thomas (Pop) Morgan, moved to Canada about 1909. They drove horses and settled for a time in the area between Olds and Eagle Hill.

Their first son, Harold, was born on December 31, 1912, at Eagle Hill. Wilmer (Bud) Dix was born January 22, 1914, at Eagle Hill. Donald was born April 10, 1917, at Olds. He had the distinction of being the first baby born in the Olds Hospital. Dorothy was born August 17, 1919, in Montana while her parents were on a visit at Helena.

The Dix family moved to the Caroline district in the latter part of 1919. Mac and Pop Morgan farmed and worked at whatever work was available.

The Russian house.

Gladys Browning and Bud Dix.

On January 28, 1926, their second daughter, Mildred (Toots), was born at Rocky Mountain House. Their daughter, Marie, was born April 12, 1935, at Innisfail. Marie was an extremely tiny baby and required careful and loving attention from all of her family.

The Dix home was an hospitable one and there always seemed to be plenty of food to be shared when unexpected guests arrived.

Mac was interested in promoting sports in the area. When tragedy or misfortune befell his neighbors, he could be counted on to organize a benefit dance or help in any way possible. He was floor manager at the Caroline Community Hall for many years.

Harold married Glenora Gardner and they had two children, Kenny and Donna.

Wilmer (Bud) married Eleanor Chorley. They had no children. Bud lives in the Vernon district of British Columbia.

Don married Ivy Bain. They had no family. Don now resides in the Rocky Mountain House area.

Dorothy married Nels Thomas. They had one son, Nels Junior. Dorothy lives in Red Deer.

Mildred married Cameron (Bronc) Allen and they have two sons, Carson and Grant. They live at Rocky Mountain House.

Marie married Sammy Sands and they have three children, Linda, Connie and Donald. Their home is also in the Rocky Mountain House area.

Mac Dix passed away in 1947 and Kathleen in the late sixties.

Merrill R. (Steve) Dutton
by Leah Rublatz

Steve Dutton was born at Cozad, Nebraska, August 5, 1884. He lived near Rosebud, Montana, and owned land there before coming to Alberta in the fall of 1919. He worked as a sheep shearer

Mercedes and Steve Dutton.

in Southern Alberta with a close friend, Frank Churchwell.

He homesteaded on the S.E.Q. 1-36-7-5, about 1920 and proved up on it. He worked at whatever was available in the district and at sheep shearing every spring.

He was married to Szirena Mercedes Thibedeau on July 27, 1936, and they moved to Nakusp, British Columbia. They returned to Caroline in 1938 and Steve operated a butcher shop and pool hall in Caroline for many years.

Steve was an avid fisherman and hunter. He enjoyed playing the violin and provided much entertainment at local dances, house parties and family gatherings. He died April 7, 1955, and his wife, Mercedes, continued living at their home until the fall of 1971. Then her arthritic condition became so severe that she was forced to spend the remaining two years of her life in hospital. She died December 15, 1973, and is buried beside Steve in the Innisfail Cemetery.

Carl Englund Family
by Sally Bugbee.

Fay Fitch married Carl Englund and they lived in the Peace River area for a few years. Viola and Clifford were born there.

Carl farmed for a time with Mr. Herbert J. Fitch in Centerville, Alberta, here Arleen, Edna and Stanley were born.

The family moved to the Caroline area and settled on the S.E.Q. 17-36-6-5 in 1934-35 and the children attended the Wooler School.

Carl was a sawyer and he sawed for Dan McGrandle and others and was adept at saw sharpening.

Their first-born, Viola, passed away in the spring of 1938 and was buried in the Raven Cemetery. The Englunds left Caroline in the late forties, 1948-49, and moved to the Vancouver area.

Both Carl and Fay passed away at Vancouver.

Melville Arthur Ferguson
by Mrs. M. Ferguson

My husband, Melville Arthur Ferguson, was born on a tea plantation in India, at a place called Burnie Bray, in 1883. His father, Donald Ferguson, was manager of the tea plantation. His mother was named Emma and they had six children who lived to adulthood.

Melville went to school in Scotland. All the children were sent home to their grandmother near Dundee as they came to school age. They all went through school and matriculated.

Melville and his older brother, John, became pattern makers. They made wheels for engines

319

Mel Ferguson.

Melville Ferguson and Mary.

and trains, etc. Melville and John came out to Canada and worked in St. Thomas, Ontario, for a year or so. In 1907 they homesteaded in Caroline. A couple named Mr. and Mrs. Hagget came out with them, and between them, they filed on three quarter sections. Before they came to Caroline, they stayed on a farm near Bowden for a few months to get a little farming knowledge. They had many experiences one way and another, I can't remember all the stories he used to tell.

There were no bridges between Caroline and Innisfail and they had to haul any freight by horses and wagons or sleighs. Mr. Harvey Langley and his family came to Caroline in 1906 and started the first store and post office. Melville used to help him haul freight. The district soon grew and a lot of new people came in. Horses were used for everything in the farming line.

I don't know when the first bridge across the Clearwater was built. It went out in high water. Nels Swanson was visiting at John McNutts and he had just got across on his way home when it broke out. John went out to work for awhile but he developed diabetes and died. Mr. Hagget also died. Mrs. Hagget, or Aunt Jane as she was called by everybody, died in 1936.

We were married on November 16, 1937. Mel

Reba Langley, Miss Hagget, Mrs. Jane Hagget, Melvin Ferguson.

used to take pack parties out hunting and fishing in his younger days. He worked very hard to get ahead, but his health failed. He died February 11, 1957.

Our daughter, Mary Jane, was born in April, 1940. She is now Mrs. Reg Peters and has four daughters.

Samuel and Myrtle Frazier
by Alma Frazier Orcutt

Samuel Frazier was born in Amity, Oregon, in 1869. Myrtle was born in McGraw, New York, in 1875, but moved to Corvallis, Oregon, with her patents. She and Sam were married there in 1896 and three sons, Floyd, Byron and George, were born to them. A few years later the family moved to Days Creek, Oregon, and Alma, Mildred and Claude were born there.

During the year of 1917, Sam was having health problems and the doctor advised him to move to an area where the altitude was higher One of his friends had moved to Canada and had settled at Czar, Alberta, on a farm. The adjoining farm was for sale so Sam went to look at it and then bought it. He sold the farm at Days Creek and the family moved to Czar. Sam and Floyd travelled with the livestock and other belongings in a freight car, but the rest of the family went by passenger train. They lived at Czar for about six years. George became ill with diabetes and died there. In 1923 they went to

320

Sam and Myrtle Frazier.

Caroline and moved on to the Larson place two miles west of Caroline. Myrtle's father, Orville Martin of Oregon, had previously been to Caroline and purchased property for speculation. He was very enthused about this area and had quite an influence on Sam's and Myrtle's decision to move there. Byron stayed on the farm at Czar and shortly after the family left, he married Lily Frost. They had four children, Art, Elsie, Lois, and Jim. He farmed for a number of years and then moved to Marysville, Washington, where he later died. Elsie, Lois and Jim still live in Washington but Art is at Drayton Valley, Alberta.

The house on the Larson place was small, but Sam, Myrtle and the family lived on it a few years until the house was completed on Sam's homestead. It was across the road from the Larson place. The new house had spacious rooms and many parties and dances were held there. Sam and Myrtle always enjoyed having company and of course the rest of the family enjoyed the fun and excitement too. Mildred and Claude often played the banjo and violin for these occasions. They also played at numerous homes and schools in the neighborhood. Times were hard and very few people could afford expensive recreation so parties and dances were welcomed by all.

As Christmas approached, box socials were usually held and the money obtained was used to buy gifts for the children of the neighborhood. The teachers and children spent many hours on programs so they could entertain at the Christmas party. Their efforts were appreciated by all.

The people who lived at Caroline during the

pioneer days seemed to appreciate one another and nearly everyone was there when needed in times of sorrow and also for the happy times. They decided that a community hall would be a fine addition to have at Caroline so the men donated their labor and a lot of the material, and completed one. Many of the dances, etc., were held there and most of the music was furnished by people in the community.

Sam kept cattle and horses on his homestead and managed to grow plenty of hay and oats to feed them. Gardens seemed to grow abundantly and Myrtle and her daughters canned many vegetables. They also canned wild blueberries, raspberries, etc. There was a root cellar beneath the house and vegetables were stored there for the winter months. The men of the family went hunting when the season opened and were many times able to get moose and deer. The Raven River ran through the place and at that time many fish were to be caught.

Floyd lived at Caroline for a few years and then he and his wife, Jean, moved to Grimshaw, Alberta, and farmed there. Jean had previously taught school at Czar and Caroline and she continued to teach until retirement age. They have passed away and are buried at Grimshaw.

Alma married Donald Orcutt and they lived on a farm about six miles northeast of Caroline. Three children, Shirley, Ronald and Gene, were born while they lived there. They moved to Marysville, Washington, for a few years and Darryl was born there. Myrtle visited them in 1939 and while returning home to Caroline, she became ill and was taken to a hospital in Spokane where she died. She is buried at Newport, Washington. About six years later, Don and Alma returned to Caroline and bought the Larson place. After three years, they returned to Washington and still live in Olympia where they settled. Shirley, Gene and Darryl married. Shirley has three children, Gene and Darryl have three and two children respectively. Darryl lives in California now, but the rest are in Olympia.

Claude Frazier.

321

Mildred married Lee Both and they lived for a few years on the old home place. They had one daughter, Lorna. Sam lived with them after Myrtle's death. Later they bought the Sanders farm north west of Caroline. They sold this place and moved to Blackfalds, Alberta. Sam had previously gone to Grimshaw where Floyd lived and he died there in 1955. Lee died in Blackfalds and after his death, Mildred has lived with Lorna and her family in Victoria, British Columbia. Lorna has four children.

Claude has been a carpenter for many years and has built many homes, etc., in the Caroline vicinity. He has always enjoyed fishing in the rivers and lakes there. He has remained a bachelor so has no family of his own, but all his nieces and nephews have adopted him.

Caroline has changed with the years and life is better for most of the people now, but memories of it during the earlier days are happy ones to recall.

George and Eunice Hanson

by Guy E. Fay

Hansons moved to Caroline in 1931 and filed on the S.E. Q. 28-36-6-5. They lived there until 1938. George spent most of his time trucking. In the spring of 1939 they moved to Parkland, Alberta, to farm. Eunice died March 22, 1940, and George on May 20, 1940. They are buried in the Stavely Cemetery.

The Harder Family

by Eric Harder

To the ones interested in reading stories of the early settlers. I would like to mention at the very beginning that I am a little at a disadvantage because my wife is, and has been, very ill and away from home — now, about half of the time and for that reason alone, it is hard for me to write free from the heart.

I came to Caroline from northern Germany (Holstein) in the spring of 1930. I worked as a young farm helper over there for nine years. Those days the young men did the field work with horses. My dream was to be my own boss someday, so I came by a slow boat, fourteen days over a very rough sea, to Canada. On the ship we were looked after fairly good, but the train trip was something else. Even the cattle had it better. We had nothing to eat until we got to Winnipeg, there my girl friend and I parted as she went by C.N.R. to near Regina to her oldest brother. I went west by C.P.R. to Innisfail where a friend took me to Caroline. I had no idea that our great country, Canada, was in this deep Depression. So I worked here and there around Caroline for very little and mostly nothing. I was lucky to find

Mike Harkins about six miles east of Caroline. They had a lot of roots and stumps to pick on a big piece of new breaking, but he told me, 'I have to talk to the 'Mrs.' as she is the boss.'' Well, that turned out in my favor and I had the job. After that I worked to clear ten acres for a very nice saddle horse. That was okay and the 'Mrs.' was a good cook and I never went hungry. I also learned how to speak English.

I bought a quarter section of land with very little clearing on it from a man named Ray Dial. This land was supposed to have thirty acres cleared on it, but they were what the old timers called 'homestead acres'. I could only find seventeen acres. I had a very good neighbor, Cliff Pollard, next to me to the north, that is three miles west and one mile north of Caroline. He told me a lot about their old homestead days, when there were only four families west of Caroline. They were Mel Fergusen, Ren Sterns, himself and Harvey Langley in Caroline who got the opportunity to name the first post office after his daughter, Reba (Caroline). This was supposed to be 1907 when Cliff Pollard homesteaded his quarter. I did a lot of outside work, too far to walk back and forth and all of it was clearing land, for some of it I never got paid.

In the meantime I heard from my girl friend, Erna, that she wasn't making it any better in Saskatchewan — three dollars a month when they paid her, so I wrote a very romantic letter of proposal to her, asking her to marry me and for us to try it together. That way I could work for a horse or a cow, a pig or anything, rather than nothing and she could be home looking after these animals and our so important garden. To my great surprise she accepted and so we got married on November 4, 1932. Here I want to add for the interested readers that from the first day of our marriage we never spoke one word of our mother tongue, we were proud of our newfound country and never regretted it. Canada to us is one of the greatest countries of the world.

For entertainment we had some great house parties, and danced to violin and guitar music, also accordion, harmonica and banjo. After the supper waltz and hearty lunch, the visiting parents wrapped their children in blankets and put them to sleep. Sometimes the party got a little livelier after that with some homebrew or a few stories. One thing I will not forget and it went deep to the heart, it didn't matter those days what country you came from, you helped your neighbor with whatever help he or she needed. I remember the year 1937 when our oldest son was a baby, I started out at four o'clock in the morning to take a few pigs to Rocky in my team and wagon. It was in May and I got caught in a bad wet snowstorm. It took me a long time over the muddy roads and I got home after midnight. While I was away, an Indian that was camped near our home came to Erna and explained to her that they had a sick baby, — needed some medicine; when Erna caught on, she had some 'root' medicine called Ginger. That man was so glad he couldn't do enough for her. He got her two pails of water from our well which was some distance from home. After that she believed her brother who told her once, "If you have an Indian friend, you have him for life," and my belief is that is what we need in our Government today. We have too many chiefs (dictators) and not enough Indians — too many 'yes' men. They raise their salaries first and then tell us 'old' ones how little to get by on.

With the help of a good old fashioned friend, Nels Swanson, we dug our well fifty feet deep to sandrock. Couldn't do no more? Yes I did; down in that deep hole I drilled twenty-eight feet through sandrock and got water that we used for many years. I used a heavy welldriller's crowbar. A heavy rain and hailstorm in July, 1943, washed that well out and the pump stood in the middle of a twelve foot round deep hole. These and many other memories are dear to us and maybe that is what holds us together. As I said in the beginning, 'alone' neither of us could have survived, but 'together' we made it and can talk about it. A few days ago we had our forty-sixth wedding anniversary and Glen and Roberta had their twentieth. I worked it in to have Erna home in that week and she told me the nicest thing any man would like to hear at such a time, she said with tears in her eyes, "I have no regrets." Over the years, when Erna was sick a lot, I kept my eyes and ears open; she helped me and it wasn't hard for me to make a nice meal, the way she would have even with a layer cake. This will be another of our many memories.

Our son, John, is married to the former Margaret Pengelly. Their children are Susan, Danny, Ross and Dale. Our second son, Glen, is married to the former Roberta Walker and their children are Robert, Roy, Tim, Wade and Sherry. Our youngest son, Richard, is married in Calgary to the former Nina Pennock with children Shawn and Charlene.

Our good friend and neighbor, Cliff Pollard, passed away in 1938. There is a lot more that I could write about that would make our great country a better place to live in, but only those people that started as low to the ground as we did would understand that, such as when your own country people take advantage of you.

John Harrison

John came from England and homesteaded

the N.W.Q. 17-36-6-5 in 1911 and left in 1913 to farm at Bowden. Now owned by Gary Wold.

John Helm Family
by Mrs. Madeline Helm

John and Madeline were married September 11, 1923. John worked for the Great West Saddlery in Calgary for several years.

In 1927 they traded their house in Calgary for the S.E. Q. 17-36-6-5, known as the Maine place, three and one half miles west of Caroline.

Their parents, having given them a team of horses, a wagon and rack, John loaded up their furniture, personal belongings and some groceries and started for Caroline, taking almost a week to get there. After getting things in order, he then walked to Innisfail and caught the train back to Calgary.

He brought his wife and their three small children to the farm in a Model T Ford. They left Calgary at four a.m. but didn't arrive until about noon the next day. It had been raining and it rained for the next three weeks, the roads were in a deplorable state.

The house on the farm was one of logs and it was old, built in the early 1900s. The roof leaked and Madeline used every container available to catch the drips. She did this for several years, everytime it rained, until they could afford to build a new one.

In John's absence, when he left to bring the family out, pranksters had entered the house and wasted a lot of their food supplies, something they could ill afford as there was so little money to be had in those days.

Madeline Helm and children.

323

John Helm family.

They raised a family of seven children, Wallace, Geraldine, Elmer, Dolores, Cleava, Oliver and Howard.

They worked hard raising their children, and through 'blood, sweat and tears' they cleared all of their land by hand, using axe and grub hoe. They hauled their water for eighteen years from the Raven River. As the children grew old enough, they worked on the farm too; there were no idle hands in those days.

Little by little they added to their holding and got their land into production. They milked cows, raised chickens, fed pigs, grew a garden and did a lot of canning of their vegetables and the wild berries that they picked.

The children took their schooling at the nearby Wooler School. They often boarded the school teachers at the Helm household.

There were good times too, such as the school picnic once a year, house parties, card parties and the annual Christmas Concert, and they had good neighbors.

Wallace served two years or so in the Air Force in World War II and became a pastor. He resides at Naniamo, British Columbia.

John and Madeline sold their farm in 1959 and retired to Calgary where they still live.

They celebrated their Golden Wedding Anniversary September 11, 1973, with many of their friends from Caroline attending. They are enjoying their twilight years as much as their health allows.

Harold Hembrow Family

Harold Hembrow was born in Somersetshire, England, in 1892, and came to Canada in 1905. Harold homesteaded north of Bindloss in southeastern Alberta in 1914.

Harold and Jessie were married in 1923. Jessie was born in New Brunswick. They moved to Vancouver where Harold worked as a carpenter on the grain terminals. The family later moved back to Alberta to Acadia Valley where they farmed.

The Hembrows moved to Caroline in the spring of 1936 buying all of section 8 from Mrs. Frazier who had inherited the land from her father. Mr. and Mrs. Harry Garrett owned and lived on the north half of 5 directly to the south. Jessie Hembrow taught school at Wooler for two terms during the mid 1940s.

In 1952 the Hembrows sold their land to Mr. and Mrs. Bill Evans and moved to Vancouver Island near Nanaimo. They built a house and lived there for some time, sold it, and moved to the mainland near White Rock. Harold built another house there and again sold it and moved to Summerland in the Okanagan. They are enjoying their retirement having built another home there.

The Hembrows have two children, Albert who was born in Vancouver, is married and lives at Prince George, British Columbia. Albert and Helen have one son who is in College. Vivian who was born at Caroline, is married, lives at South Surrey British Columbia, and has two children who have nearly completed high school.

The Hereford Family
by Wilma Hereford Balfour

In the summer of 1907 Bert Hereford came to Alberta from Colfax, Washington, and filed on a homestead along the Clearwater River flats approximately four miles north of the present Highway 54. A log house was built and made ready for his wife and young son, Adalbert, to join him, in February of 1908.

Their possessions were shipped to the nearest rail point at that time, which was Innisfail. This meant a trek of forty-eight miles by team of horses to their new home — forty-eight miles to the nearest doctor — forty-eight miles to bring in all their major supplies. What true pioneers

Bert and Anna Hereford, 1904.

these people were, who came to settle Alberta. Within a short time most homestead land in the Caroline-Butte-Stauffer area had been taken by people seeking a new life.

Bert Hereford, always a lover of fine animals, brought to Alberta a herd of Hereford cattle and several Percheron horses. Several set backs came to this pioneering family; the horses developed swamp fever, something that hit many imported animals and within a few months were dead. Some twenty head of cattle disappeared never to be seen again or any trace found of them.

In January of 1910 a long time friend of the Hereford family, a Dr. Pocock of Colfax, Washington, came to visit his friends and see Alberta, and to attend the birth of Bert and Anna Hereford's first daughter, Wilma.

1910 was a cold wet summer and with the loss of horses which were needed on the farm, this family moved to Innisfail where work was found. At this time survey of the C.N.R. right of way between Red Deer and Rocky Mountain House had commenced and work was available in 1911 on the grade for this railway line. This family lived a few miles east of Sylvan Lake during the summer of 1911.

Ted Hensel a brother-in-law of Bert Hereford's who had also homesteaded on the Clearwater River flats also found work on this C.N.R. right of way, but returned to Washington with his family in 1913. Another homesteader of this area was a brother of Anna Hereford's, Donald McGinnis, who left and spent the remainder of his life near Bellingham, Washington.

During 1912 and 1913 the family continued to live at Innisfail and a second daughter, Grace, was born in May of 1912.

The family returned to the homestead in the late fall of 1913, and many happy times are remembered by the older children. There was always time for a fishing trip or a picnic with the neighbors, and Sunday dinners. My mother was always recognized for her culinary art.

There was an abundance of wild berries and a great variety too. Blueberries, cranberries, raspberries, saskatoons and a high bush cranberry that made a delicious jelly were there for the picking and it was most important that these be preserved. A good supply of all these wild fruits was found in our cellar. Sometimes a blueberry patch had to be forsaken because a bear had taken over.

I remember many musical evenings and Sundays at our home and at the Ben Harris home. We had an organ and a violin. A young man by the name of Ed Morijeau played the violin and Howard Harris, who was probably in his late teens at that time, would sing many favorite

songs of those days with everybody joining in at times. These gatherings with the neighbors are memories I shall never forget.

In 1916 we two older children attended Wooler School. This school was on the north side of present Highway 54 and I beleive about three-quarters of a mile from the Clearwater River. School commenced that year in the summer and continued on to near Christmas. We had a wonderful teacher, A Miss Moody, and there were only five students, Jack and Edith Laidler, Ruth Stewart, Adalbert and I. Ruth Stewart later lived at Rocky and many will remember her mother, Nurse Stewart. Adalbert had previously attended school for a year in Innisfail; but here we got a thorough grounding in the Three R's.

In November of 1916 my brother, Jim, was born.

These were First World War times and in 1917 our school only opened for a very short time when the teacher, a Mr. Ferguson, joined the army. No replacement came for him so now we rode horseback to school at the South Fork School near Caroline. It was at this time work was commenced on the bridge across the Clearwater River at Ricinus. This is the bridge on Highway 54 and what a boon this was to the many settlers who had homesteaded on the west side of the River.

In the summer of 1919 our family planned to move to Rocky, but because the house we were expecting to rent did not become available until late fall, we lived in a farm home close to the banks of Clear Creek and attended school at Clear Creek until November when we moved to Rocky. I remember we children being taken up town before Christmas and being amazed that lights could be as bright as they were in the J. H. Killick store.

In January, 1920, the youngest son of this family was born. Winston will be remembered as

The Hereford family.

one of the late John Plathan's Band Boys. This band played in Calgary for the visit in 1939 of King George V1 and Queen Elizabeth to Canada.

Adalbert and I attended the school that later was owned by Mr. Henry Stelfox. A third room had to be opened that year, and Grace, in the junior room, was in a hall in the vicinity of the Eric Whidden house. Miss Ada Lent was the principal and I was in Miss Godkin's room. Sometime that fall, many of us saw our first airplane in flight. Miss Lent had school dismissed so we were able to see this unusual sight.

The family moved to Nordegg in November, 1920, where work was plentiful. This continued to be their home until 1926. In March, 1924, a third daughter, Edith, was born. When the family returned to Rocky Mountain House in 1926, this was their home for nearly twenty years, and when my father retired, he and my mother made their home at Sylvan Lake where their home was in a park like setting among a glorious array of flowers and shrubs. My father died in June, 1959, and my mother at the age of eighty seven in 1967.

Adalbert joined the Alberta Forestry Service in 1932 and continued in this field until his retirement in 1972. In 1935 he married Agnes Smith of the Prairie Creek district. They have two daughters. After retirement the Herefords continued to live at Coleman.

Grace Hereford and Walter Fisher were married in the Presbyterian Church in November, 1934, on the thirtieth wedding anniversary of Grace's parents. When Walter received his discharge from the R.C.A.F. he worked at Nordegg, going later to the new town of Devon, where he was a plant engineer at Imperial Oil company's plant, until his death in September, 1972. The Fishers have one son and two daughters. Douglas Balfour of the Strachan district and Wilma Hereford were married in April, 1940. Doug Balfour joined the R.C.A.F. in 1941 and was posted to Halifax. His wife and infant daughter joined him early in 1942. The Balfours also have a son. Douglas Balfour had

Bert and Anna in their garden at Sylvan Lake.

been Secretary-Treasurer of the town of Sylvan Lake for six years at the time of his death, October 1, 1962.

Jim joined the Royal Canadian Navy in September, 1941, but wasn't called to service until early in 1942 and served for the duration on the West Coast. In July, 1943, he and Margaret Spence of the Chedderville district were married. After the war they lived at Nordegg and in 1950 Jim joined the Alberta Forestry Service and after various postings including Grand Prairie and Hinton, they were posted to Blairmore and are presently living there. They have one son.

The first break in this family came, as it did to so many families during the war. Winston joined the R.C.A.F. in 1941 and graduated as a pilot in 1942. He was posted in Britain. He was killed in action in June, 1943, and is buried in Holyhead, Wales.

Edith, who after completing her high school, attended Alberta Business College in Edmonton, and was employed by the Assessment Branch of the Department of Municipal Affairs. She met an American soldier, Melvin Ollerman, and they were married in August, 1946, and live at Fond du Lac, Wisconsin. They have two daughters.

In February, 1960, I was appointed assistant Secretary-Treasurer of the Town of Sylvan Lake, and in November, 1962, after the death of my husband, I was appointed Secretary-Treasurer, and have worked continuously for the town until I retired in 1976.

The descendants of Bert and Anna Hereford were six children; there are ten grandchildren and sixteen great grandchildren.

Julius Kallis Family

Julius Kallis was born in Russia March 13, 1892 and came to Canada in 1904. Adeline Klinner

Bert and Anna Hereford's 50th Anniversary.

was born in Russia July 31, 1892 and came to Canada about 1904. They were married January, 1912 and lived in Beausejour, Manitoba, later moving to Alberta. Adeline Kallis passed away Nov. 1, 1925 at Redcliff, Alberta. There were 8 children — 6 girls and 2 boys. Margaret, Teenie, Ellen, Lenard, Henry, Violet, Lillian and Dorothy. Dorothy, the youngest, died shortly after birth.

Julius Kallis remarried July 31, 1925 to Amelia Spitzer who was born at Honey Grove, Texas, October 21, 1892. They lived in Redcliff, and later in Medicine Hat. In June, 1933 they moved to Sundre.

In 1937 the Kallis family came to the Caroline area. Julius and Amelia both took homesteads — N.W. 36-35-7-5 (now owned by James Knight) and S.E. 35-35-7-5. They had the misfortune to lose their home by fire shortly after coming here.

In 1940 they moved to Raven and purchased S.E. 18-36-4-5 from Roy Orcutt. In 1943 Mr. Kallis made a deal with James Knight of Raven who owned S.W. 18-36-4-5, for the Kallis homestead at Caroline. Later Julius Kallis sold to Charlie Hall and moved back to Sundre to an acreage on their daughter's place (Mrs. Ted Walle).

In the spring of 1965 Mr. and Mrs. Kallis moved into Mt. View Lodge in Olds. Mrs. Amelia Kallis passed away Jan. 1972. In August, 1973 Julius Kallis was married to Audrey Johnson and continued to live in Mt. View Lodge. Mrs. Audrey Kallis died Jan., 1978. Julius Kallis spent from Dec. 15, 1977 until June, 1978 in the hospital, and is now in the Dr. Fanning Extended Care Centre in Calgary.

Leonard lives in Edmonton. Teenie and Lillian live in Calgary. Violet lives at Olds, and Ellen at Rimbey. Margaret and Henry live at Sundre. Henry has operated Kallis Electric for many years and is now manager of Marshall Wells Hardware in Sundre, Alberta.

Jim Knight

Jim was born at Raven, Alberta, on August 26, 1921. He had his schooling at North Raven. In 1940, Jim went to work for Pierre LaCerf, west of Ricinus. Here he sawed lumber and ran the steamer. On June 9, 1942, he married Louise LeCerf. They moved to Raven in 1943, and lived there until their house burned six months later. In the fall of 1943, they moved back to the 'Big Timber'. In October of 1946, Jim bought the N. W. 36-35-7-5 from Mr. Kallis. In February, 1947, he also purchased the S.W. 36-35-7-5 from Mr. Litky where they lived until 1957. From there they moved to N. W. 36-35-7-5 where they still live.

During these years Jim sawed lath and lumber. In 1951 and 1952 he sawed lumber and

The Jim Knight family.

mine props on the burn at Burnstick Lake. In 1961 Jim moved his lumber talents to British Columbia, sawing lumber for Crestbrook Forest Industries in Parson, Canal Flats and Cranbrook. He returned home in 1963 and built his own lath mill and sawed lath for five years. After this Jim started working in construction and is now driving cat. Jim always raised some livestock, but now just has cattle and hay.

Jim and Louise have eight children. Marie, who has four boys and one girl, Kenneth, who has three girls and one boy, Leonard (not married), Donna, who has two girls, Jeannette has one boy and one girl, Dianne has one boy, Joan has two boys and Peter is still at home.

Adam Krause

Adam Krause was born in Poland and came to Canada in 1925. He settled in Calgary and moved to Caroline with his wife, Lydia, in 1933 and homesteaded the N.E.Q. 21-35-7-5. Among other settlers, Adam was termed as a $600 man. This was a grant the government gave out to help get them started on homesteads during the depression.

They returned to Calgary in 1940 and later sold their land to Mrs. Helen McCormick. In Calgary, Adam worked in a munition factory and later became engaged as a carpenter up until his death on October 22, 1966, and was a member of the Carpenter's Union.

Adam and Lydia had three children, one passed away at an early age, Jeanette Riske lives in Edmonton and Alfred Krause lives in Calgary. They had four grandchildren.

Andy Laidler

Andy came from England in 1910 and homesteaded the S.E.Q. 20-36-6-5. They had two children, Jack and Edith. They stayed until the fall of 1916 and then left to farm at Bowden. This place is now owned by Eric Harder.

Julius Litke

Mr. Litke homesteaded the S.W.Q. 36-35-7-5 in the early 1930's and he was termed as a $600 man. This was a grant the government gave to people to help them get started on homesteads during the depression. Mr. Litke sold this quarter in the 1940's and then he built a shoe repair shop in Caroline and ran it for a few years. He passed away while living in Caroline.

George Lougheed
by Ron Lougheed

Dad was born in Collingwood, Ontario, but was raised in Morden, Manitoba.

It was in the fall of 1936 that Mother and Dad, George and Lucy Lougheed, decided after twenty-five years of trying to survive at Sibbald on the prairies, that there must be a better place to make a living. Upon the advice of Dad's brother-in-law, Ed Oliver, they moved to Caroline. Dad rented the old Lother place.

In the spring of 1937, Dad passed away suddenly, a severe blow to Mother and us four boys. Through perseverance, good neighbors and a kind Uncle Ed and Aunt Annie Oliver, we survived.

We marvelled at the wonderful abundance of grass, crops and gardens, after being on the dry prairies. Mother kept house for us, Ronald and Arnold continued their schooling at Wooler School. Miss Grace Waldruff was the teacher. Ron and Arnold took an active part in the Caroline Boxing Club.

In 1942 we moved to Condor. Arnold went overseas with the R.C.A.F. He brought home an English bride, Joan Walton, they live in Edmonton and have three children.

Ralph married Mae Larsen of Bentley. He bought the Howard Mullen store at Benalto in 1946. He also operated a fertilizer business, which he has sold. They are now retired and are living in Benalto.

Bill and I stayed on the family farm. Bill married a Dewberry girl, Grace Hodgson, and they have five children. He was very active in school affairs and served on the Rocky Mountain School Division for several years and was instrumental in getting the David Thompson High School built. He passed away in 1968. I still run the farm and look after my gravel business.

Mother passed away in 1972 at eighty-eight years of age.

Charles Mason
by Sally Bugbee

Charlie was born in Yorkshire, England, in 1881 and was the eldest of a family of eight, he had two brothers and five sisters. His youngest brother, who participated in World War 1, was listed as missing in action and was never heard of again.

Charlie left his home in England in 1911 to come to Canada, living in Saskatchewan before coming to Alberta. When he came to Alberta he homesteaded the N.W.Q. 15-36-6-5 two miles west of Caroline in 1912.

Three of his sisters came to Canada also, Alice, to live at Peace River in 1920 and Nellie and Syble to Eastern Canada. Nellie worked in Montreal and in the Government House in Ottawa, later returning to England where she has remained and is now the age of ninety-two years. Syble stayed in the east from her first arrival to Canada in 1926.

Charlie was a bachelor, adding to the list of bachelors in the Caroline area. He was a butcher

George Lougheed family — 1936 — Back Row: Bill, Mr. George, Mrs. Lucy, Ralph — Front Row: Arnold and Ron.

Butchering Day — Ed Oliver, Charlie Mason, Hugh Oliver, Lloyd Lougheed.

by trade and was much in demand throughout the neighborhood.

In June, 1950, while working out in his woods one day, he slipped and fell breaking his hip. He lay out in the blazing hot sun for two days before he was found. Frank Cole from Innisfail came to visit Charlie on a business matter but didn't find him around, he did notice, though, that there were freshly purchased groceries on the table. He returned the following day and still didn't find him there, but he became alarmed when he saw the groceries still on the table undisturbed. He notified Hugh Oliver who organized a search party. Earlier Pat Flynn had seen Charlie's dogs out in the woods and so he directed the searchers to that area and that is where they found him suffering, not only from his broken hip, but from the torture of lying out in the hot sun for those two days. Steve Thorenson took him to the hospital in Rocky Mountain House where he stayed for several weeks.

When she heard of his accident, his sister, Alice, came from Peace River to visit him and contacted their sister, Syble, who was then living in Toronto. Syble came to Rocky Mountain House where she stayed for several days to be with Charlie. Later on she rented a house from grandma Oliver (Hugh's mother) and went there to live. She then made arrangements to have a new house built on Charlie's homestead. He was released from the hospital before the house was finished but they managed to get moved into it before the cold weather set in.

In June, 1951, their niece, Nan Sandham and her five year old son, Ricky (Richard), came from Yorkshire to live with them and to lend a hand.

Charlie passed away October 25, 1951, at the age of seventy years and is at rest in the Raven Cemetery.

Syble, Nan and Ricky stayed on and made their home there. They grew a large garden and also went into raising a small flock of sheep. Ricky went to school in Caroline and when he finished he went to work in the oil industry where he is still employed. He married Helen Barker of Caroline and they have two children, Kim and Jason. They live two miles west of the Clearwater store.

In February, 1976, Syble went to the Rose Haven Nursing Home in Camrose and is happy there.

Nan lives on at the homestead tending her sheep and enjoying her life here among her many friends.

Meilke

Mr. Meilke homesteaded the N.W.Q. 22-35-7-5 in the early 1930's but only stayed into the 1940's.

He sold this quarter to Paul Planidin who still owns it.

William Murray

William came from England and homesteaded the N.E.Q. 21-36-6-5 in 1910 and left in the spring of 1913 to farm at Bowden. His family are Nellie, Jack (dead), Betty, Mary and Don. Don resides in Olds. This land is now owned by George Benz.

Sam Nelson

Sam was born in Innisfail on June 18, 1926, and has resided at Caroline. He married Joan Braucht on November 4, 1950. They have one son and two granddaughters.

Sam was a licenced Big Game Guide for twenty-four years and a licenced Outfitter for nineteen years, retiring in 1970 to raise Polled Hereford cattle. He is now a Director of the Alberta Polled Hereford Association, also the Central Alberta Hereford Association. He was also president of Alberta Outfitters for three years.

He rodeoed for years in his spare time, picking up a few trophies along the way. He has managed local rodeos and was president, for a number of years, of the Rodeo Association. He was on the Alberta Tourist Council for three years. He is a director on the Rocky Mountain House Gas Co-op.

In August, 1973, Sam joined the Lions Club. He was 100% President in 1975 to 1976, Zone Chairman from 1976 to 1977, Deputy District Governor from 1977 to 1978, holds three District Governor's Appreciation Awards, holds A10 and 25 Visitation Pins for 1976 to 1977 and has a five-year perfect attendance record. He attended two International conventions, one in Hawaii in 1976 and Tokyo in 1978.

Samuel and Reba Nelson and son Sam.

The Odells

by Rose St Denys

Nelson Odell, my father, was a carpenter by trade, but because there was no work available in that field, he decided to take advantage of a government offer, which was to pay families eight hundred dollars to homestead. He and nine others set out scouting the country, and at last he filed in Caroline.

Thus the family gathered all we owned and began our move to the west country. Mother (Kate) and three of us girls travelled from Medicine Hat to Innisfail by train, where we met Dad (Nels) and the two boys who had brought up our household items, farm implements and a horse, by freight. In Innisfail we loaded a wagon and hayrack with all we owned, as well as a cow Dad bought, and headed out for our new home.

It took us three days to travel the forty miles as the road was only a dirt trail, full of ruts and holes and still wet with winter's snow. Another family, by the name of Motz, travelled with us and there were often times when we would use all four horses; from both families, to pull one wagon through some of the bad holes. When we did finally arrive in Caroline, there was only one store, a community hall, a post office and a garage of sorts. This was late on the day of April 21, 1933.

The Nelson Odell house with heavy insulation.

Our homestead was about three miles west of Caroline, and we had neighbors only about a mile from there. East of us lived Len McGrandle, south was Charlie Mason, and to the west, Pollards.

With the eight hundred dollars Dad had, we were able to buy farm tools and implements, two horses, a cow, two pigs and some chickens, and to build our house. Dad had to clear land for our house, and it was built from these trees; the finished product was a small board house not to be finished for a couple of years. Meanwhile we lived in a log shack about a mile out of Caroline.

All our mail and supplies we picked up in Caroline; mail from Rocky on Tuesdays, Thursdays and Saturday nights, and groceries and hardware from Langley's store.

For entertainment the community people held house parties, dances, picnics, skating parties and hay rides, and although there were no churches, Mrs. Langley had a Sunday School for the area children, held in the Wooler School.

Dad, Nelson Clifford Odell, was born in Oilsprings, Ontario, on June 1, 1888. Mother, Catherine Flynn, was born in Linlithgo, Scotland on March 15, 1889. There were seven children in the family, most of whom attended school in Winnifred, Saskatchewan, and later the Wooler School here. I remember our first teacher was a Miss Donavan from Innisfail and she taught for many years.

Mother was a midwife, so from the time we moved to Caroline she was busy nursing. Her first baby was born to Mrs. O'Coin, who had a baby boy. As well as maternity, Mother helped anyone with nearly any sickness that occurred, from the itch to pneumonia, and travelled in all weather in any vehicle. The nearest doctor was in Rocky Mountain House, twenty-five miles away and often was unable to come out because of bad roads. So Mother would go, often being ill herself.

Dad worked clearing land and putting up wild hay to sell, and he helped many neighbors.

Nelson Odell.

330

War broke out on September 3, 1939, and by the middle of September, both Neil and Nelson, brothers, had joined the Calgary Highlanders. Dad joined the army in March, 1940, and was sent overseas in May. Neil went over in the spring of 1941 and Nelson followed that fall. Because the army discovered Dad was older than he should have been, he spent his service in London, and they were all discharged in 1946.

NELSON

Nelson was born in Kincaid, Saskatchewan, April 21, 1918. He moved to Cardston and cooked in a hotel there. He met and married Pat O'Bray of Cardston in 1940 while still in the service overseas, then he rejoined the airforce in 1948. They had six children. Gloria, married to Leon Sellers, lives in the States with one daughter, Heather. Catherine married Bill Beaman and lives in the States. They have three children, Stacey, Sabra and Shae. Karen is married to Allen Hembrie and lives in Lacombe with one son, Jeffery. Patsy Ann is married to Eli Harper and lives in Manitoba with two children, Nathan and Gol Camille. Clifford attends University in Edmonton and Betty Jean still lives at home. Nelson passed away March 5, 1965, and was buried in Cardston.

NEIL

Neil rejoined the army in 1950 when the Korean war broke out and was discharged in 1951. He married Ruth Stocker from Taber in 1950, in Vancouver, and they have five children. Neil was born on September 1, 1919. Their children were: Carol Ann who lives and works in Vancouver. Nancy is married to George Cox and lives in Vancouver with one son, Michael. Cathi married Dave Masden and lives in Calgary with one son, Dion. Bob lives and works in Calgary and Kelly works and lives with a sister in Vancouver. Ruth passed away in November, 1967, and Neil in October, 1972. Both are laid to rest in Calgary.

ROSE

Rose was born on December 21, 1920. She married Sam Fakas in 1940 and had one son, Neil. She divorced and married Clem St Denys of Caroline in 1947, and lived in Edmonton. Their son, Neil, is now married to Mary Davy and lives with their two children, Michael and Vicki, in Red Deer. Clem passed away in 1964 and is laid to rest in the Caroline Cemetery.

RUBY

Ruby was born in Linlithgo, Scotland, on February 24, 1919. She married Vince Hickle and lives in Ray, North Dakota. Their one son, Neil, is married and lives in the States with two children, Theresa and Shelly.

PHYLLIS

Phyllis was born on September 3, 1922. She married Oscar Kanten in 1947 in Innisfail. They had three children, Carrol married Wayne Ross and lives on a farm near Caroline with their son, Jason. Penny lives and works in Edmonton and Kevin lives with Aunt Rose in Edmonton. Phyllis passed away in June of 1972 and is buried in Edmonton. Oscar has since remarried and lives in Utah with his wife and a daughter.

LOIS

Lois was born on April 17, 1924, and was married to Bill Legary in 1940. They divorced, and she remarried Vic Gamarch. They had two children, Terry, who is married to Ray Stevens, lives in Calgary with two daughters, Doris and Paula. Tim lives and works in Calgary. Lois and Vic are divorced and Lois now lives in Chilliwack, British Columbia.

Mother passed away in July, 1964, at the age of seventy-five and Father followed her in January, 1973. Both are buried in West Lawn Cemetery in Edmonton.

Although we had many hard times in the early settling years, there are many more good memories. The trip out was really an experience for us kids and early in the move, I cried to go back home; there was so much mud and cold. The first winter there was so much snow and the house was not finished, so it was really cold. We wondered if it was worth the struggle. But Father banked up the place with some three feet of hay and it was warm and fine after that.

I also remember well, on March 24, there was a huge picnic where we were staying. A tall boy kept pestering me for a drink, so I set the dog after him. Well, the dog took the seat out of Ernest Bugbee's pants instead of the tall boy. It turned out, the boy was Clem St Denys, whom I later married.

The Ogilvies
by Annie Ogilvie

Norman Ogilvie was born in 1911, taking all his schooling in the Lousana School. In 1930 he married Annie McGrandle of Innisfail whom he met while harvesting in the Innisfail district. During the hungry thirties, Norman and Annie rented land in the Lousana and Delburne districts until April 12, 1937, when they rented the Campbell place, now owned by Bill Wales two and a half miles south and one mile west of Caroline. It was a day both Norman and Annie remember well, as the east country was very dry and on arriving in Caroline, after coming through many mud holes between Raven and Caroline, found they were unable to get through to their destination on account of the road being impassable for a truck or car at the Raven River south of Caroline. So all their belongings were unloaded at Annie's brother's place, Len McGrandle. And with the aid of Len McGrandle, all of their belongings and machinery, what little they owned, was hauled by wagon and horses, taking four head of horses to pull the wagon through the mud hole.

On getting settled and working on the quarter, they had a heavy snow storm in May. This was very strange as they had never encountered this before, but were able to buy a couple of loads of straw for their stock which lasted them through the storm. In 1939 they moved onto the quarter section now owned by John Herman. This quarter section only had seven acres of broken land. So they spent a hard summer clearing and breaking more land. At that time the clearing was done by axe and swede saw. Their eldest son, Leonard, listening to their comments on the hard work, decided he might help, so he set a fire in the corner of the place and, it being a hot dry day, the fire soon spread. The children and Annie were alone and were really frightened (of course Leonard knew nothing about how the fire was started). In seeing the smoke, Jake Betchel and Lee Both came to the rescue and with their help they were able to save the barn and buildings. They knew nothing of how the fire was started until this history book got in the making, and Leonard recalled how he thought the easiest way of clearing land was by burning the bush!

While on this place, Harold and Alice Ann started school at the Wooler School. The children walked across country, crossing the Raven River on a log.

In 1942 they moved onto the Norman Holt place, three miles south of Caroline, now owned by Mr. Follis, the house is still there. They farmed it until 1947 when they moved onto the Ray Dial place, renting for one year and purchasing it the following year. With plenty of

Madeline Helm, Annie Ogilvie, Ada Proudler, John Helm, Norman Ogilvie, Albert Proudler.

hardships along with the good years, they were able to come ahead. Both Edna and Leona started school at Wooler School which was situated on their home quarter. The five children thought this was a great relief just being able to walk the half mile to school. Edna and Leona finished their schooling in Caroline when the government consolidated the schools, and the Wooler School was then moved into Caroline and was used as a school until it was purchased and is now used as a Catholic Church in Caroline.

Leonard, our eldest son, is now living with his wife, Ardith, and their family at Balfour, British Columbia, where they own a summer resort. Harold is farming and is living with his wife, Marie, and family three and a half miles west and north of Caroline. Edna, Mrs. Richard Browning, and her family are living on the former Jack and Gladys Browning farm. Leona passed away due to a motor accident on July 4, 1973.

In the spring of 1971 we sold our half section to Gary Wold and built a home in the village of Caroline. Danita Wilson, Leona's eldest daughter, is making her home with us and is going to school at the Caroline School.

Arthur E. Oliver and Family

Arthur Edward Oliver was born at Didsbury, Alberta, August 11, 1902. With his parents he moved to the Sunnynook area and grew up on his father's farm.

As a young man, he worked in both the Three Hills and Drumheller area as a mechanic and farm labourer. He was good in mechanics and was more interested in machinery than livestock.

Isabelle Violet Heck of Sunnynook was born April 17, 1911, and on December 8, 1927, she and Arthur were married. The first two of their eight

Cultivating potatoes on the Ogilvie farm.

children, Lawrence and Lenard, were born at Sunnynook.

In 1931 they moved to the Caroline area and in 1933 they homesteaded the S.W. Q. 5-36-6-5. Their other six children were born here, Shirley, Victor, Owen, Colleen, Darlene and Wayne.

For the next several years, Arthur worked at sawmilling and doing mechanical jobs. In the fall he would go back to the prairie for harvesting.

Arthur passed away in 1951 and their daughter, Darlene, in 1961.

Isabelle stayed on the farm and raised the last of their children. In failing health, she sold the farm and moved into Caroline, living there until her passing in 1974. All three are buried in the Raven Cemetery.

Irwin Oliver

Irwin Oliver was born June, 1908, at Didsbury, Alberta. He moved with his parents, Edward and Annie Oliver, to Sunnynook, Alberta in May, 1910. In June, 1927, he married Grace Campbell from Sunnynook. They came to Caroline in 1931 when the Oliver family moved, but went back to the prairie shortly afterward. Later, they moved back to this area, settling first on a place at Bingley, Alberta. Some time later, they came to Caroline renting the S.E. Q. 3-36-6-5 known as the Clark quarter, now owned by Herb Riddle. In 1939 Irwin purchased the N.W. Q. 10-36-6-5 and built a home there. He worked some with his father and brother, Arthur. Irwin also drove a truck on the cream haul for some time.

In 1945 Irwin sold his farm to Dan Hicks of Sunnynook who in turn sold to Mr. and Mrs. Donald Craig. Mr. Craig was postmaster in Caroline for some time until his death. The Craigs sold to Charlie Taylor, and Taylor sold to Fred Burlatoff. Eugene Szulczyk presently owns and farms this land.

Irwin and family moved back to Sunnynook and he worked for some time on the railroad section crew. He then took up grain buying which he worked at until retirement, living at Benton, Oyen and Richdale, Alberta. He passed away suddenly in June, 1973, at the age of sixty-five years. They have one daughter, Verda, married to David Gray, living on a ranch at Big Stone, Alberta. The Grays have two daughters and three sons. Irwin's widow, Grace, resides in Hanna, Alberta.

George Palmer
by Irvin Palmer

George Palmer sailed across the ocean from England when he was only fourteen years old. He paid his way by working on a livestock boat.

Coming west to Red Deer, he got a job working with the Great West Lumber Company. He then moved to the west country and took up a homestead two miles west of Caroline, south about a mile, and one-half mile west again. He was just south of Mel Fergusen's homestead. This was in 1912 or a little later.

In the year of 1919 he married nineteen year old Esther Boeken, who had originally come from the States. George had a grey team of mares, Vic and Pearl. The day they were married (in the middle of winter) George hooked up his team, loaded up some hogs to sell, and drove on the sleigh the forty miles to Innisfail. As time went by, they had three children: Irvin, Helen and Gordon.

The next move was to Cayley, south of High River. They rented land from George Coats of High River and took up prairie farming. In about 1931 the north country called again, and they moved up to Sylvan Lake. George died in 1944, at Sylvan Lake and is buried there. He was somewhere in his fifties. His wife went back to the States and is still there.

Charles Pittendreigh
by Irene Pittendreigh

Charles Pittendreigh was born near Aberdeen, Scotland, and came to Canada in 1927. In 1928 he moved to Craigmyle, where he worked in a dairy for his aunt and uncle. He worked for them for three years. In 1931 he helped move us to Caroline, Alberta. In 1933 Charlie and I were married and started farming. Charlie was quite a horse trader when he wasn't farming; he was always trading for something. Sometimes he would trade a horse and get a horse and cow, or machinery — almost anything.

Times were hard but they were good times in the thirties. There was always time to visit your neighbours. Every week there was a house party at someone's place. The ladies would take lunch and there was always someone who could play music, and we would dance until the small hours of the morning. I can remember Eric Harder playing for quite a few parties, on his mouth organ.

In the winter the men in our district would hunt squirrels, cut posts or cut wood, to make a dollar.

Charlie passed away on August 18, 1968. We had six children. John is married to Ruth Bird. They have five children, Donna, Kenny, Lynne, Kevin and Valerie. They live in Caroline. Howard, his twin brother, was married to Doreen Burdensky. They had no children. Howard passed away on January 27, 1977. Lee is married to Karen Bugbee. They have four children, Laura, Kerri, Dale, and Jodie. They

Charlie and Irene Pittendreigh, Don Dix.

also live at Caroline. Eileen is married to Gilbert Fald and also resides in Caroline. They have three children: Sharon, Bryan and Debra. William lives at Rocky Mountain House, and is not married. Norma is married to Robert Hope. They have one daughter, Shelly, and live at Alhambra, Alberta.

I lived in Caroline until 1970, and then moved to Innisfail. In October, 1977, I moved to an acreage at Rocky Mountain House.

Clifford Pollard Family

Clifford Pollard came to the Caroline area as a bachelor prior to 1910. He homesteaded NE 36-20-6-5, now owned by John Harder. He married Margaret (Maggie) Bell and they had four children — Courtland, Margaret, Stanley and

Marian and Courtland Pollard and their daughters Marie and Margaret.

Joseph. Maggie passed away giving birth to her fourth child in 1921 or 1922. Mrs. Ben Harris cared for baby Joe until Cliff was able to find someone to take charge of his home and family.

Mr. Pollard had several housekeepers to care for his children but none of them was satisfactory. Mrs. Alma Sarc then came and raised the Pollard children along with her own four. The two youngest Sarc children were Frank and Alma. Mrs. Sarc was a good homemaker and they all got along very well together. Mr. Pollard worked as road boss for a number of years.

Cliff Pollard passed away with pneumonia at his home in the fall of 1938.

Courtland married Marion Reddick from Caroline. They have five children and live at Penticton B.C.

Margaret married Frank Sarc. They have two children and live in Oregon, U.S.A.

Stanley is married, has two children and lives in Windsor, Ontario. He retired from the Ford Factory in Windsor.

Joe worked in many of the saw mills and for several farmers in the Caroline area. He is married and lives in the town of Ponoka.

Cliff and Maggie Pollard are both buried in the Raven cemetery.

The Albert Proudler Family
by Ada Proudler

We moved to the Caroline district the first of November, 1936, from Sylvan Lake, with our two children, Donald and Dorothy. As it took more than one truck load to move, the horses were taken first. It was a long hard trip as it had been raining, and the roads were almost impassable in spots. The truck slid off the road near Evergreen and the horses had to be unloaded to pull it back on the road. The team proceeded to Caroline under their own steam and made almost as good time as the truck. The furniture arrived with us on the next load, and we had better weather for this trip.

It was the first experience for the children in farm life and going to a country school. They attended the Wooler School, and their first teacher was Grace Waldroff.

Both Albert and I had been raised on the farm, so we knew what was ahead of us — hard work and not much money.

Albert was born in Glasgow, Scotland, and came to Ontario as a child. He and his younger brother enlisted in the Army during the first World War. His brother lost his life in France.

Albert was a steam engineer by trade and ran steam engines on the prairie for harvesting and land breaking. I was born in the district of Sylvan Lake and attended Melita and Kewsamo Schools. We were married in 1923, in Edmonton.

Ada Proudler cutting grain in 1944 at their farm.

Don was born in Minneapolis, Minnesota, and Dorothy in Sylvan Lake.

The land we bought at Caroline was purchased from Mr. and Mrs. Trenholme and was the N.W.Q 9-36-6-5. This quarter section of land was homesteaded by Mr. George Palmer. Our farming was done mainly by horses. The first tractor we bought was an old John Deere Waterloo, but it was heavy, slow and awkward and was not of much use except for breaking land and grinding grain. Later we purchased a Hart Parr tractor and grain separator which was used for threshing our own crops as well as the neighbors. Farming never really became mechanized for us until after the second World War.

The roads were always a concern when a trip further than Caroline was made, as it usually always rained when we were away, and the task of returning home would become almost impossible. I remember one trip we made to Red Deer. It was a beautiful day when we left home, but the clouds came up from the West and after a continuous rain we were all night and part of the next day getting home. We usually alerted the neighbors before a trip so the chores would get done if we didn't return.

Dorothy completed her High Schooling at Dickson, and then went on to Nurses training in Edmonton. During this time the second World War broke out and Don enlisted in the United States Army, where he served in the South Pacific until the end of hostilities. His unit liberated the prisoners of war from one of the largest concentration camps in the Phillipines.

In 1953 we built a house in Caroline and moved

Don Proudler.

from the farm to town because of Albert's ill health. He sold insurance and was Justice of the Peace until his passing in January, 1955. I carried on the business until 1961 when I moved to Red Deer. I have since lived in different parts of Canada.

Don still owns the farm but lives in Red Deer where he is supervisor of the Transit System. He married Barb Thomas in 1959, and they have two children, Steven and David.

Dorothy joined the R.C.A.F. medical branch

Captain Dorothy Proudler.

in 1957 and has been stationed across Canada, as well as in the United States and Germany. We both now reside in Victoria, British Columbia.

John and Alma Sarc
by Robert Vandermeer and Mrs. Oliver

John Sarc was born in Yugoslavia and Mrs. Alma Josephia Sarc was born in Germany. Her parents owned a large coal mine, and John was an immigrant miner. They had friends who were emigrating to the United States, and full of the spirit of adventure they decided to accompany them.

1906 — Alma and John Sarc with their two children Magdalene and Ralph, arrived in Cumberland, Wyoming from Westfalia, Germany to seek their fortunes. Frank and Alma were born in Cumberland.

1912 — As for many people in the United States, the lure of free land in Alberta brought them to Red Deer. In the spring with their trunks on the backs of horses, they pushed west for five more days to reach the Gaetz District. Here, they spent their first night in a school house. In the morning they loaded up again to head for their homestead.

Alma and John Sarc.

There were no roads and so they found themselves stuck more often than not. This meant loading and unloading all their belongings at every hole. They finished their trip with oxen, only to discover that the land they had chosen from a map was muskeg, and what wasn't muskeg was rocks. On the homestead near Evergreen they found a wooden hovel with a sod roof (10'x12'), complete with a trap door. The first summer was spent here. During that time John started to build a log house. He had special axes and hammers made by Mr. Bonc, a blacksmith at Leslieville. By winter the Sarc family was snug in a new house consisting of a kitchen, linen and pantry room, master bedroom, and children's room. With the help of a good neighbor Mr. Dornik (who supplied them with butter and milk) the Sarc's lived from hand to mouth on their garden supplies, a few pigs and a cow. During the following winters John worked in various mines. He walked all the way to Nordegg to find employment. Summers were spent breaking virgin land and draining muskegs on the homestead.

1920 — February 11 tragedy struck. He was asked to inspect the mine that had already been declared faulty, and was killed in the mine at Saunders Creek. He was buried on the farm at Evergreen, and later his remains were moved to the Raven Cemetery.

1921 — Alma Sarc moved with her family to the Pollard homestead west of Caroline. Margaret Pollard had died leaving Cliff with four children including three months old Joseph. By this time Magdalene Sarc had married Octave Morrigeau. She had five children, Harriet, Joseph, Ralph, Howard and Betty. She remained in the Stauffer District until 1946 when she moved to Calgary where she still lives with her second husband Arnold Vercammen.

1922 — Ralph Sarc moved to Windsor, Ontario where he worked for the Ford Motor Company.

1924 — Frank Sarc followed his older brother to seek employment with the same company.

1927 — The two boys returned to the Pollard homestead. Ralph soon went back to Windsor where he married the former Lorraine Bell. They had one son, William. Ralph died in 1972. Frank remained in the Caroline area working on threshing and road crews. Later he worked at the Herbert Paint Company in Calgary and at various ranches.

1934 — Frank Sarc returned to Windsor, fare obtained by working on a cattle train as an overseer — seven days to Toronto. One year later he sent the train fare to Margaret Pollard — object — matrimony. From Windsor they moved to Gladstone, Oregon where he found employment at Crown Zellerbach. He remained at the paper mill for twenty-three years. At the time of his retirement he was the strawboss in the color codeing department. Margaret and Frank have two daughters Shirley and Doreen. Margaret and Frank are still residing in Gladstone.

1930 — Alma Sarc began teaching school in this year and taught for thirty-seven years excepting for three when her children were born. She went first to Wooler School (which had been named by Joseph and Margaret Bell — they had come from Wooler in England and had named the school which was built on their quarter section). Alma then attended Normal School in Edmonton. After completing her final year she returned to teach the remainder of the school term at Wooler. She remained a teacher for the rest of her life. Her schools included Ricinus, Clearwater, Cremona, Shilo and Caroline. Alma Vandermeer was a hard worker and will always be remembered for her kindness to everyone. Alma married Gerald Vandermeer and they had four children, Rosalie (Jorgenson), John, Robert and Ivan. She died in 1969 and is buried in the Caroline Cemetery.

1944 — Mrs. Alma Sarc remained on the Pollard farm for sometime after Cliff passed away. In 1944 she moved into the village of Caroline to the Marvin Heck house which was one of the first homes built in Caroline. When natural gas service was provided to the Village in January 1963 Mrs. Alma Sarc turned the valve to start the flow of gas. She was accorded this honor because she was the oldest citizen in Caroline. She lived in Caroline until 1971 and was delighted in being Caroline's Senior Senior Citizen. At that time she was forced by ill health to go to the Autumn Glen Lodge. Her mind and sense of humor were sharp until the day she died — November 16, 1972 at the age of ninety-one. She planned her own funeral — even the hymns, and was buried in the Raven Cemetery.

L.-R. — Alma Vandermeer, Mrs. Sarc and Magdalene Vercammen.

Charles and Marie Stewart
by Ruth Stewart

My mother, Marie L. Burke, was born in Switzerland in 1880 and moved to South Dakota in about 1891. She graduated from the Souix Falls school of nurses. Later, she homesteaded in Stanley County, South Dakota.

My father, Charles Stewart, was born in Chicago, Illinois in 1886. They were married in Fort Pierre, South Dakota in 1907. I was born there in 1908 and was their only child, although father had a son in Arizona by a previous marriage.

Mother and I came to Caroline in the spring of 1912. My father was already here as was most of his family. He met us at Innisfail and we came to Caroline through the mud by a yoke of oxen.

We lived for several months with a bachelor, Mr. Larson. Then we moved into our own home on the S.W.Q. 17-36-6-5.

I remember when the Wooler school was being built because I adored Bill Thibedeau. He used to carry me around on his shoulder when he was helping his father build it. I learned to read and write before the school was ready so I had a head start.

I remember a young Dane, Valdemar Sorenson, who joined the army first thing when war was declared in 1914. He was killed immediately on arriving overseas. He left all his belongings to us with the understanding that we would send his pictures and personal things to his mother in Denmark.

Others I remember were the Stearn brothers — Louis and Renn. They were old friends of my father, as was their relative Pete Fay.

There were no children living close enough for me to play with. Laidlers lived a distance away, and after a few years they moved to Bowden.

We all rode horseback those first few years as the roads were very poor, especially in the bad weather. I remember a bad hailstorm we had one year. The stones were as big as my fist. All the grain was ruined.

We had quite a problem with water. We never did get a well, even though we tried witching and

Nurse Marie Stewart.

337

Dr. Greenaway

everything else. For years all our drinking water had to be carried or hauled in kegs from the Raven River half a mile away. Fortunately there was plenty of surface water in the sloughs that was suitable for washing, etc.

The wolves were thick those first years and I was forbidden to play out of sight of the house.

Mother was often called upon to deliver babies and to tend the sick or injured.

We moved to Rocky Mountain House in 1922 where mother set up a nursing home. Dr. W. H. Hill was in practice there that year, but there was no hospital. Later, Jessie Fleming also had a nursing home. Dr. Hill sold his practice to Dr. A. C. Greenaway about 1932 I think. Mother kept her nursing home for several years.

When a fourteen-bed hospital was built and opened in 1938, Dr. Greenaway and Dr. A. B. Blumes were the first two doctors, and the first matron was Miss Irene McRae. When Mother closed her nursing home she nursed in the hospital for a time.

Dad passed away in Rocky Mountain House in 1945, and Mother in Surrey, British Columbia in 1961.

I am retired and live in Burnaby, British Columbia and am happy to have contributed my bit of history to your book.

Nels Swanson

by Sally Bugbee

Nels was born in Osland, Sweden, December 26, 1889. When he was a mere boy, nine years old, he rescued a five-year-old child from a raging house fire. He gained entrance in and back out again through a window, carrying the child to safety. However, the child was fatally burned and died a few hours later. Nels had severe burns to his face and arms.

While in Sweden, Nels worked as a cabin boy aboard ship. He left his family and friends in 1909 to come to Canada. While crossing the ocean, he took out his naturalization papers to become a Canadian Citizen. On disembarkation, he travelled to White River in Manitoba. After spending some time there, he went to Nelson, British Columbia, where he found employment. He worked on a railway construction line where they used heavy explosives for blasting rock from the right of way. Because of the danger of this work, and because of some loss of life during the blasting, Nels decided not to work there for very long.

In 1912 he came to Caroline with his friend, Chris Jensen. He then took out papers to homestead on the N.W.Q. 4-36-6-5.

To the Indians, who often travelled through this area, Nels became known as 'Scar Face'. The reddened skin and the scars from his burns in Sweden, earned him that name. In time the sun and his healthful outdoor activity helped to fade the color until in later years it wasn't so noticeable.

Between working at various jobs, both within and out of the community, Nels made improvements on his homestead. He worked at haying and harvesting, and in 1913 took part in a river drive where they floated logs down stream for several miles to a mill site on the Red Deer River.

Eventually, having built a house and barn and by making the necessary improvements, Nels was able to pay the customary $10.00 and gain title to his land.

For several winters he worked in logging camps to sustain and build up his homestead.

One day, having left the door open, he saw four coyotes enter his barn. Sneaking up, he closed the door and then climbed an outside ladder to the loft. The loft had a pole floor and in his excitement, he fell through the poles to join the coyotes below. Trapped, the coyotes began an attack. Nels managed to grab a club of sorts with which to ward them off. To Nels' relief, one of the coyotes tore a board off the door and made its escape, the other three followed.

It was during the bitter winter and deep snow of 1918 that Nels had an attack of acute appendicitis. A trip to Innisfail by team and sleigh, or to have a Doctor come out, was not to be considered. Instead, he was taken to Marie Stewart, a registered nurse who lived near the Wooler School, a short distance away. The appendix had ruptured, but Nels was tough, and with the great skill and talent of a wonderful nurse, Marie pulled him through.

Nels worked on the construction of the Alaska highway from 1941 to 1943. One winter day he and a pilot, who was flying a small plane, crash landed. The pilot was injured, but Nels, scared and badly shaken, was otherwise unharmed. He made the pilot as comfortable as was possible and then walked several miles to find help. It is assumed he found help and that everything turned out fine for the pilot.

Nels was always active in community affairs and gave unstintingly of his time and money toward the community and school. For many years he was Santa for the Wooler Christmas program. He sang at local parties, visited his neighbors, and made all newcomers welcome to the neighborhood.

He married Pearl Audy from Drumheller on October 17, 1951, Thanksgiving Day, in the Nazarene Church in Caroline. This was a pleasant change for Nels after so many years of bachelorhood. Together they enjoyed visiting and playing cards. They helped to form a whist club in the community where they spent many pleasant evenings.

Fifty-five years after his departure, Nels made a trip back to Sweden in 1964 for a visit. He enjoyed it very much and saw several changes in that country.

After a full and active life to the end, Nels passed away September 25, 1974, and is buried in the Caroline Cemetery. Pearl sold the farm and moved into Caroline where she still resides.

Oliver Henry Thibedeau

Oliver Henry Thibedeau was born on December 4, 1862, at Conners Corners in the Tammiskimang District of Upper Canada, which is now the province of Ontario. His parents moved to Byetown (now Ottawa) when he was a small child.

In his early youth he worked on freight boats on Lake Michigan. He learned the trade of carpentry and also worked at sawmills in Wisconsin where he was married, on January 27, 1882.

His wife, Claudine Miller, was born on September 26, 1864. She was orphaned at an early age and lived with an older sister until her early teen years when she 'worked out' until her marriage.

Oliver and Claudine lived in the Shell Lake district of Wisconsin and all of their family were born in that state. They had five sons all of whom, but one, died in infancy. The surviving son was Francis William, born April 1, 1884, at Washburn, Wisconsin. They also had five daughters, Mary Elizabeth born March 23, 1896; Szerina Mercedes born January 19, 1899, at Shell Lake; Helen Victoria born April 17, 1901, at Shell Lake; Louise Matilda born on December 22, 1903, and Olive Theresa born April 4, 1907, both also at Shell Lake.

In 1910 the family moved to Strathmore, Alberta. Oliver and son, William, did carpentry

work on the Gleichen Reserve and built ranch houses in the surrounding area.

Oliver, William and Mike Benz came to the Caroline district in 1912 to look for land. Oliver filed on the N.E.Q. 33-36-6-5 and Bill filed on the N.W.Q. 34-36-6-5. That quarter had originally been filed on by a Mr. Rice, so there was a log house on it. They returned to Strathmore to work during the winter, and the next spring (1913) they returned to their land to make improvements. They started the construction of the Wooler School. The winter was mild and the work on the school was completed in early spring of 1914.

Mrs. Thibedeau and the four younger girls lived in Innisfail while the log house was tidied up and an addition was built on. The family moved out to the homestead on May 8, 1914. The trip was made by horse and buggy, with household effects coming in a wagon with a six horse team, as roads were very bad.

In June of that year, Oliver and Bill went to Nordegg to build the 'tipple' at the Brazeau Mine at Nordegg. The Thibedeau men obtained a sawmill in 1917 and cut much lumber in the area. They built the Ricinus and Chedderville Schools and also the Bill Robinson and Charlie Fogelsong houses which are still a landmark in the Ricinus district.

An anecdote of their carpentry days concerns the building of the Fogelsong house. There were of course several interested observers of the construction and many good yarns to be spun. The framing went up and two of the yarn tellers were so deep in conversation that they didn't realize the deviltry of Bill Thibedeau until they found themselves completely boarded in with doors and windows deliberately covered over. The two 'yarners', Fred Stewart and Vern Clearwater Sr., found themselves the subject of much laughter and razzing, but being the good sports they were, they waited for an opening to be made for their escape.

Another annal of the Thibedeau history con-

Oliver and Tina Thibedeau's home.

339

Crew at the Thibedeau Sawmill.

cerns the destructive Clearwater flood of 1915 and Jess Ditch — The younger girls were playing outdoors and Louise heard someone shouting in the barn. She called her mother who cautiously approached the barn and was told not to come in, but please bring some of 'Dad' Thibedeau's clothes, which she did. Shortly Jess Ditch emerged in the borrowed clothing and told his hair-raising story. He had tried to ford the river not realizing the terrible danger. One of his team had got its leg over the wagon tongue and both horses were drowned and the wagon box was swept off and overturned, with Jess being plunged into the raging current. He was tumbled and swept along to a small island where he was washed ashore. His clothes were torn to shreds but he had managed to save his money and some letters which he wedged in the branches of a tree and then made his way through the rest of the water and up to the Thibedeau barn in a severe state of undress. He was dried out and given food and drink. With Louise's help he caught a horse of Fred Hart's and returned to the island for his money and letters which he then took to Caroline and mailed.

The Thibedeau home was a popular gathering spot for the young people of the district, as they had a gramophone and one of the first player pianos.

Bill Thibedeau sold his land to his mother and left the Caroline area in 1922. He moved to

Mr. and Mrs. O. H. Thibedeau Diamond Wedding Anniversary January 27, 1946.

Spokane, Washington where he married and raised his family, three daughters and a son.

Mary was married to Michael Benz at Strathmore before the Thibedeau family moved to Caroline. Mercedes married Merrill R. (Steve) Dutton; Helen married William Bell; Louise married Wilbur B. Cross, and Olive married Clarence Sawyer. Oliver and Claudine Thibedeau continued living on Mrs. Thibedeau's land and celebrated their sixty-eighth wedding anniversary in the community. Mrs. Thibedeau passed away October 21, 1950, and Oliver then made his home with his daughter, Mercedes Dutton, until his death on November 24, 1953. Both he and his wife are buried in the Pine Grove Cemetery at Rocky Mountain House.

Their land is now owned by their grandsons. Oliver Thibedeau's homestead is now the home of Charles and Blanche Benz and Mrs. Thibedeau's land is the home of Oliver (Bill) and Evelyn Benz.

James Tobin
by Sally Bugbee

Jim came to Canada from Missouri, U.S.A. in 1916 and settled in the Centerville area. He was married to Lilas Jackson in 1920 and they had one child — James Beverley — born in 1925 at Evarts.

Mrs. Tobin died in 1928 and little Jimmy went to live with the John Fitch family at Centerville until 1933 when he came with his father to settle on the N.W.Q. 21-36-6-5 in the Caroline area.

Jim, like so many of us during the depression years, worked at whatever job he could get to make a dollar. Mostly he worked at logging and sawmilling as there were not many other choices in those days.

Much of this time Jimmy was left to fend for himself. I remember the first time I saw him. I thought he was just about the most adorable little boy ever with his big blue eyes and blonde curly hair. I felt a great tenderness toward him when I learned that he had no mother. He kept himself clean and was nicely mannered, and would get himself off to school in the mornings. I understand that he did very well in school too. I remember hoping, with his father away so much, that his neighbors would keep an eye on him.

When Jim Sr. left this area in the late 1940's, he went to Edmonton to live. He died in 1951.

Jimmy went to the Wooler school and when he was fifteen years old he went to work for Dan McGrandle in a logging camp. He spent the next few years logging and sawmilling. In the off seasons he did farm work and other forms of employment.

In 1945 he married Madell Harris of Caroline. They had four children — Lyla, Marlo, Lynda and Louanne. In 1949 Jimmy started in the oil field work. He began in Leduc and moved his family there.

He has been on nearly every phase of this type of work — from rough-neck to tool push and more. He has worked in Australia, Libya, Malta, and Arctic Islands and Venezuela. At present he is living in Edmonton where he works as a drilling supervisor for a consulting and engineering firm in the drilling business. I am happy that Jimmy has done so well, and that he has been able to see so much of the world.

He and Madelle parted several years ago and he married again in 1956. He has two sons from this marriage. His son Marlo died in 1972.

Jim Wiles

Jim homesteaded the N.W.Q. 7-35-7-5 on the Raven River in 1921. He lived here for about three years but never proved up on it. Belle Furguson, who owned a coal camp down on the Raven River, took it over and made the necessary improvements to prove up on it. She sold it to Edwin Alstott in 1956 and he still owns it.

Photos and Documents

Wooden bridge on the Clearwater washed out.

Ferry on North Saskatchewan at Rocky Mountain House.

First Clearwater Bridge, 1916 or 17 — Frank Ankle, Bill Bean, Baxter Bean, John Bugbee.

Suspension foot bridge on Clearwater River near Dovercourt.

Caroline Traders Store in the process of being moved.

Ricinus Bridge on Clearwater River in flood.

Store being lifted.

Steel bridge on the Clearwater at Ricinus.

Placed across the street.

First Wooden Bridge at Ricinus on Clearwater River 1916-17.

and as it looked in later years.

Across from the Caroline school and the Arena.

Road construction near Dovercourt, 1930.

Brush cutter.

Road construction at Burnt Stick Lake turn off, 1954.

Main Road a mile and a half west of Caroline, 1954.

Power line construction west of Caroline early 1950's.

Agnes, Walt and Jack Schrader.

Clearwater Workers Guild — 1946. Back Row — Mrs. Oper, Lizzie Stewart, Mrs. E. E. Rose, Matilda Rose, Mrs. Knorr, Nellie Kiser, Annie Stewart, Mrs. Frew, Mrs. J. McNutt. Front Row — Chris Raynor, Cynthia St. Denys, Hilda Buckman, Elsie Stewart, Thelma Bean, Mrs. Eustace Rose, Della Stewart, Lillian Knorr, Mrs. Fred Stewart.

Edith Maine 1916.

Caroline Helping Hand Club — back row — Kathleen Chapin, Bryda Myson, Hilda Hickman, Anna Demenuk, Mercedes Dutton, Nellie Carter, Gert Huffman, Jerry Jackins — front row — Mary McLean, Olga Campbell and Elsie Bowden.

Treadmill owned by Robert Miller Sr.

Caroline Sawdust pile.

Al Maine, ?, Edith and Mrs. Maine.

Jim Hamilton driving tractor.

347

Delivering Groceries to the Clearwater.

Oliver Thibedeau's mill on Fred Stewart's place in 1914.

Sawing wood in the early days.

Clark Wren clearing land at Crammond.

Ladies Ball Team — Back Row L.-R. — Laura Clay, Amy Dolphin, Ruth Neal, Agnes LeCerf. Center Row — Myrtle Berry, Lulu Dial, Mae Dezall. Front — Mildred Orcutt and coach Ed Clay.

Stewart's store and fish caught in Alford Creek, 1924.

Construction of road for the M. D. of Raven.

Bill Cross threshing machine in 1928.

Hale Lake 50th Anniversary.

Mr. Fred May on his way to deliver mail via Dovercourt, Butte, Stauffer and Caroline.

Home of the Albert May family.

Frank Ankle and his threshing machine.

Frank Ankle, horse pulled stationary engine for running his thresher.

Hay Sling at Dovercourt.

Altoba Oil Rig — J. Bush, 1938.

Tie McKie, Peg Gordon and Liz McKie on top of rock, Jake McKie, Mrs. Gordon and Isy McKie standing — 1925. This rock went to Expo in 1967.

Building the Sr. Williams' house in 1932.

The log house on the Fred May homestead.

Kenneth Burnes at Chedderville.

Maurice May sweeping hay.

Maurice May with a pack outfit heading for the Brazeau to pan gold with Bill Harbottle.

Supplies going to Joe Bush's oil well on the Clearwater.

351

Bill Harbottle cooking breakfast.

John Moberg sawmill.

Hand feed Moody threshing machine with Joe Wickins feeding and Perry Thompson on stack.

Joe Wickins breaking with a Waterloo-Boy tractor.

1930 on the Prairie — steam locomotive.

Bill Bean pulling stumps and clearing.

Forrest Sr. and Jr. Thacker on 22-36 Hart Parr tractor farming in the Caroline District in 1947.

Jack Bugbee and children — George, Robert, and Sarah — taken at "the Maine place".

Hunting party in 1926 — Bill Bean, Clifford Raynor, two friends, and Baxter Bean.

Mr. McColl breaking land at Big Bend farm.

Chick Demenuk and a load of rabbits 1936.

Curley Fetterly — "Fishing was good."

Stauffer sewing circle in 1940. Left to right — Mrs. Heare, Mrs. May, Mrs. Hankinson, Mrs. Godkin, Mrs. Johnson, Mrs. Lewis, Mrs. Winters, Mrs. Ceasor — children — Jean and Douglas Hankinson, and Phyllis Winters.

Sawing firewood in 1938. Doug and Franklyn Stewart, Alf and Syd Rose.

Alf Rose on binder.

Grandmothers of the Butte district — Mrs. Godkin, Mrs. Lewis, Mrs. Hankinson, Mrs. Stainbrook, Mrs. Buck, Mrs. Ceasor, Mrs. Ray Edmonds, Mrs. Follis and Mrs. Myson.

Stauffer ball team.

Breaking the S.W. field by Alf Rose in 1940.

Almer Pengelly hauling props.

355

The Almer Pengelly homestead at Caroline.

Ed Clay's threshing outfit — 1940.

R. W. Mitten Lumber Yard 1936.

Sawmilling with Steam Power.

Paul Kozlowski's demolished pole truck near the Tay River.

Caroline Hotel 1938.

Bundle teams.

Murray Brothers mill site.

L. to R. — Harvey Buchanan, Elva Mitten, Bob Willsie, Tie McKie, Norma Campbell, Don Dix, John Bucko 1944.

Bob and Bill Murray loading supplies in Calgary.

Bridal shower for Phyl and Ernest Bugbee.

Ivan Graham breaking land.

Curly Wren helping his Dad.

Winter fire wood — Ted Betts and Maurice Carter.

Fawn grows up.

Merle Reese and his dog, 1925.

Sweeping hay.

Ivan Graham and binder.

Mrs. Haney and fawn.

Marriage Certificate.

✠

This is to Certify

That _Charles Augustus Foglesong_

of the _district of Red Deer, Alta; formerly of Wisconsin_

— AND —

Milly Findlay

of the _same district; formerly of Iowa_

were joined together in the Bonds of

* HOLY * MATRIMONY *

according to the Rites and Ceremonies of the Church of

England, on the _21st_ day of _April_

in the year of our Lord _1910_ by me,

CW Gwennap Moore
M.A.

Witnesses:

B P Alford.

Clara Halstead.

Rector of _St Luke's Church_

Red Deer, Alta.

G PARKER & SONS, OXFORD PRESS, 73 ADELAIDE ST. W., TORONTO.

360

"Hard Luck Story"

A farmer who received notice for his MFU fees, replied as follows:

"I wish to inform you that the present condition of my bank account makes it almost impossible. My shattered finanial condition is due to federal laws, provincial laws, liquor laws, mother-in-laws, Brother-in-laws and outlaws. Through these laws I am compelled to pay business tax, head tax, gas tax, oil tax, light tax, water tax, sales tax, carpet tax, poll tax besides excise tax and inome tax. Even my brain has become taxed.

I am required to get a business license, car license, truck license, chauffeur license, driver's license. marriage license and dog license. I am also required to contribute to every society and organization which the genius of man is capable of bringing to life; the Red Cross, the Blue Cross, the purple cross and the double cross. Not to forget the red feather, the anti-red digger, widows' relief, orphans' relief, expectant mothers' relief and the wayward husbands' relief.

For my own safety I am required to carry life insurance, property insurance, liability insurance, fire insurance, burglar insurance, tornado insurance, unemployment insurance, old age insurance, hail insurance and car insurance.

My business is so governed that it is not easy for me to find out who really owns it. I am suspended, expected, suspected, disrespected, rejected, examined, re-examined, informed, summoned, fined, commanded, and compelled until I provide an inexhaustible supply of money to every known need, hope, or desire of the human race. Should I simply refuse to donate to something or other, I am boycotted, talked about, lied about, held up, held down, robbed or ruined.

I can honestly say that, except for a miracle that happened, I could not enclose this cheque. The wolf that comes to many doors nowadays just had pups in my kitchen. I sold the pups and here is the money."

Guide & Outfitter Ball Well Attended At Caroline

A crowd of about 200 turned out on December 1st at Caroline to attend the annual Guides' and Outfitters Ball. A very good time was enjoyed by all in spite of sub-zero weather, and poor road conditions. A raffle for a brand new rifle was won by C. Murray of Caroline.

Conspicuous by their absence, two men were honored, by a district poet, who have gone to happier hunting grounds, Jack Browning and Tan Jameson.

For the Guides and Outfitters Ball, 1961, this special poem was written for the occasion.

"THE OUTFITTERS"

I often sit and wonder
About the days gone by,
About two old outfitters
Who are hunting in the sky.
As I travel through the mountains
Over trails they did blaze,
I see their mark from tree to tree
And I think of the good old days.
I think about the stories
That they have both told me,
About the game that roamed these
    hills
That I will never see.
I've listened to their stories
Of the wolves down in their lair,
About the moose, the big bull elk
And the roar of a wounded bear.
About their days out on the trail
As the snow and rain came down,
About the dude they did guide
From some far eastern town.
About the nights that they spent
    out
Beneath a big spruce tree,
About the night that they made
    camp

When they could scarcely see.
Now the outfitting here is getting
    poor
And poorer, I don't lie,
I hope their hunting's better
In those hills up in the sky.
The day is not forgotten
When they were laid to rest,
So if there is hunting up above
They both deserve the best.
They'll open up new hunting
    grounds
Cut trails through those hills,
They won't be bothered by fores-
    try roads
And the roar of these saw mills.
Now here on earth I wonder
If there will ever be a man,
Who could follow in the footsteps
Of those two Jack and Tan.
—Red Montgomery

BIG HORN STAMPEDE SUCCESSFUL AFFAIR

ROCKY MOUNTAIN HOUSE, July 29 (Special) — The Big Horn Stampede at Jack Browning's ranch on the Clearwater River, thirty miles south of town, was an outstanding success, Thursday. There was a big crowd, many coming for miles to see the first stampede held in the district.

Following were the leading prize winners:

Bronco riding — Don McMurtie, Bearberry; Archie Smith, Bymoor; and Ronald Keen, Eagle Hill.

Steer riding — Don McMurtie, Erick Joist, Arthur Johnstone.

Calf roping, Don McMurtie; stake race, Wes Latham; horseback catch, Archie Smith; maverick catch, Wes Latham.

The best rider of the day was George Bugbee, a young local lad, who gave a fine exhibition of bronk riding, but was disqualified on some technical rule. He just missed what would likely have been a fatal accident when his belt caught on the saddle horn, but luckily the belt broke and he was only bruised.

The stampede proved so successful that a two-day event is planned for next year.

Grandmother's Receet

*Y*EARS AGO when my mother was a bride, my Kentucky grandmother gave her her "receet" for washing clothes. This treasured bit of writing now hangs above my gleaming automatic washer as a grateful reminder of today's mechanical blessings.

1. bild fire in back yard to het kettle of rain water.
2. set tubs so smoke won't blow in eyes if wind is peart.
3. shave 1 hole cake lie sope in bilin water.
4. sort things. make 3 piles. 1 pile white. 1 pile cullord. 1 pile werk briches and rags.
5. stur flour in cold water to smooth then thin down with bilin water. *(STARCH)*
6. rub dirty spots on board. scrub hard. then bile. rub cullord but don't bile just rench and starch.
7. take white things out of kettle with broom stick handel then rench, blew and starch.
8. spred tee towels on grass.
9. hang old rags on fence.
10. pore rench water in flower bed.
11. scrub porch with hot sopy water.
12. turn tubs upside down.
13. go put on cleen dress — smooth hair with side combs, brew cup of tee — set and rest and rock a spell and count blessins.

— Nadine Mills Coleman in *The 65 Magazine*

CAROLINE P. O.
40 MILES WEST OF INNISFAIL

HUNTING AND FISHING TRIPS ARRANGED
TO ANY PART OF CANADIAN ROCKIES

Mr. Fred Stewart and Miss Kathleen Ankle were married in this city Tuesday night by Judge Hovey. The happy twain will make their home on Bad river and the best wishes of one and all in this community for a long life of peace and prosperity.

STEWART & BROWNING
GUIDES and OUTFITTERS

GUIDES TO BEST BIG GAME COUNTRY IN
NORTH AMERICA

FOR INFORMATION
PHONE W. C. BROWNING 71911

EDMONTON
ALBERTA

* * *

Mr. and Mrs. Jack Laidler, Mr. and Mrs. William Laidler and Mr. and Mrs. Gerald Laidler of the city, in company with Mr. and Mrs. Jack Laidler Sr. of Calgary and formerly of Red Deer are leaving Sunday for Victoria to attend the diamond wedding anniversary of Mr. and Mrs. Andrew Laidler. Mr. and Mrs. Andrew Laidler homesteaded in the Caroline district in 1910 and later moved to the Bowden district, where they farmed until they retired in 1946.

---o---

Annual Fair At Caroline

The Caroline Agricultural Society held their 2nd annual fair at the Caroline Community Hall and the grounds adjoining on Sept. 3 Competition seemed to be keener and the exhibits better than the previous year.

Some of the prizewinners for stock were as follows. J. Quinn, mare, first prize, also red ribbon champion. J. Leisk, general purpose team, reserved champion, blue ribbon, Shorty McDermid general purpose team, 2nd prize, T. P beef cow, first prize. and heifer. calf in the champion in the open c . This was a very fine calf and well handled. John is only 7 years old and should make a good stockman some day. He was very proud of his calf, but too shy to tell the judge his own name. He is a cousin of Margaret Roper, who is well known at Lacombe for her calf raising and stock judging. Other prize winners for calves were C. Mason, Shorty McDermid and Mrs. H. Garrett. F. Miller took three first prizes for pigs. Shorty McDermid and H. Garrett took all

School Fair At Caroline

The school fair held at the Caroline community hall on the 3rd of September was a great success

Some of the work in the art corner was beautiful. The visitor could scarcely beleive the posters were hand done. All the school work was highly complimented by the two inspectors, Mr. Gibson, Red Deer, and Mr. Liggett, Olds.

The judges, Miss Coix, for the sewing and Miss King, B.Sc., of the Olds School of Agriculture, spoke highly of the sewing and cooking, also the children's flowers.

The boys had some nice rope work, handy devices and pieces of furniture, which were very nicely put together and painted.

the prizes for the sheep, special prizes included.

Mrs. R. MacLaren, of Rocky Mountain House, as judge spoke very highly of the ladies corner of the fair. The cooking table was treat to see and taste. The embroidery was beautiful. The flowers! One would have to see them to realize what is now grown in the rural districts. There were dahlias, gladiolas, roses, asters, marigolds and mixed flowers, all very large sized.

The two tables of vegetables made a very fine showing and even the non-prize winners were well repaid for the time and labour spent in their gardens by the nice comments of the town visitors.

The keenest competition seemed to be the special prizes given by Mrs. MacLaren, Rocky Mountain House, for the 5 lb. roll of

butter. The judge, in awarding this prize, spoke well of all the butter, but especially of Mrs. J. Leisk's, 1st prize, also Mrs. H Garrett's, 2nd prize.

Mr. Wrigglesworth took the opportunity of the big crowd at the fair to demonstrate his new feed grinder.

A full report of the prize winners will follow in an early issue

Caroline Couple Observe 60th Wedding Anniversary

Mr. and Mrs. O. H. Thibedeau, Caroline district, celebrated their sixtieth wedding anniversary on Sunday, January 27th. Mr. and Mrs. Thibedeau came from Shell Lake, Wisconsin, in 1910, since which time they have lived on their farm near Caroline.

Open house was held at the home of their daughter, Mrs. W. Cross, Caroline. Congratulations were received by telephone from the Hon. J. C. Bowen, Lieut.-govenor of Alberta. Many beautiful flowers were sent, among them being: from Mr. and Mrs. S. Dutton; Mr. and Mrs. M. Benz and family; and the Helping Hand Club. The table was centered with a beautiful 3-tiered wedding cake trimmed with artificial diamonds. Tea was served by Mrs. M. Benz assisted by Mrs. G. Benz. Kitchen arrangments were taken care of by Mrs. W. Cross and Miss L. Cross and Mrs. A. F. Proudler, and tea was served from the bridegroom's mother's teapot, which is over 100 years old and was brought out from old Odtario.

Pictures were taken by the aged couple's grandson, Roy Sawyer.

The afternoon was passed in singing old songs and hymns music being furnished by Mrs B. Harris and S. Dutton. There were 54 guests and 32 relatives present for the occasion.

Mr. and Mrs. Thibedeau's many friends will join with us in wishing them many more happy years. *1946*

PRIZE LIST

CAROLINE SECOND ANNUAL FAIR

DIRECTORS

Mr. Thos. Roper, President.	Mr. James Leask, Vice Pres.
Mr. Wm. Hackett, Sec-Treas	Mr. Melvin Ferguson
Mr. Richard Rhodes	Mr. John Quinn
Mr. Harry Garret	Mrs. H. A. Langley

SPECIAL CONTRIBUTIONS

Municipal District No. 342	$25.00
Killico Store	5.00
Chalmer's Meat Market	5.00
Donald Cameron M.P.P.	5.00
Mrs. MacLaren	5.00
Mr. and Mrs. Linskog	5.00
Innisfail Province	5.00
Mr. and Mrs. Leask	4.00
Mr. and Mrs. Fred Miller	2.00
Mr. and Mrs. Suhr	2.00
Mr. and Mrs. T. Roper	2.00

SPECIAL PRIZES

A. J. Driscoll, Seth Witton, McDermott Hardware, MacLaren Hardware, Rocky Mountain House; Mrs. M. H. Smith, Innisfail Creamery, Bond's Meat Market, Percy's Bakery, Ingham's Jewelry Store, Badcock Drug Store, Innisfail; Mrs. H.A. Langley.

A complete list will be published at a later date including all who have contributed money towards the 1930 Caroline Agricultural Fair. This is our list to date.

The FURROW

A Journal of practical information devoted to the interests of better farming—

JOHN DEERE
HE GAVE TO THE WORLD
THE STEEL PLOW

Editor ~ ~ HOWARD M. RAILSBACK
Associate Editor ~ EDWARD C. RAINEY

PUBLISHED BY

DEERE & COMPANY ~ *Moline, Ill.*

Registered in Canadian Patent Office

VOLUME 36   January—February   1931

THE FURROW is published bi-monthly.

NO SUBSCRIPTION PRICE is charged for *The Furrow.* It is sent free to farmers designated by the John Deere dealer in each community.

IF YOU MOVE from one farm to another in the community, please notify your John Deere dealer so that your change in address may be correctly entered on the mailing list of *The Furrow.*

IF YOU MOVE to a farm in some other community, you can keep on getting *The Furrow* by asking the John Deere dealer in that community to send us your name and your new address.

Caroline Gas Switch-On Ceremony

Mrs. A. Sarc and Mayor M. Carter turn on the gas as M. E. Stewart, Northwestern Utilities' general manager, looks on.

Caroline became the 76th community to be served with natural gas by Northwestern Utilities, Limited following a flare-lighting ceremony in the village Nov. 1.

An oldtimer in the district, 82-year-old Mrs. A. Sarc, who has lived in Alberta since 1912, turned the valve which lit the symbolic flare.

The Hon. A. J. Hooke, Alberta minister of municipal affairs, Murray E. Stewart, Northwestern's general manager, and Mayor Maurice Carter spoke from the flare-lighting platform next to the community hall. Also representing the village were W. Reese and D. Stewart.

Mr. Hooke complimented the community on the important steps that have been made this year in the improvement of community services with the installation of water and sewer lines in the village and the arrival of natural gas service.

Mr. Stewart introduced Northwestern's local agent who will be serving the village Leo McKernan. In welcoming the community to Northwestern's system,

Mr. Stewart noted that the company's policy was to provide each community, regardless of size, and each customer therein "with the best possible gas service at the lowest possible cost, consistent with the highest standards of safety."

Mayor Carter, who has been mayor of the village since its inception in 1952, welcomed the arrival of natural gas which will provide another modern service for the village and encourage its future growth.

Following the lighting of the flare, a reception was held in the community hall for villagers and guests.

Caroline has a potential of 103 services, 82 of which have signed for service to date. The plant was installed at a cost of $29,000.

The village is served from a transmission line west of the village connected to the 36-inch Alberta Gas Trunk Line. Gas rates in the community are $3 for the first 30 therms and 6.7 cents per therm for all additional therms per month.

CARRY YOUR LICENSE WITH YOU

Fee $2.00   1934   N⁰ 4532 Y

Resident's Big Game License

Under and by virtue of the power vested in the Minister of Agriculture under The Game Act, 1932

Mr. _Howard Alstote_, of _Caroline_
(Please Print Name and Address in Block Letters)   (Give Street Address)

Alta. .... Occupation _Farmer_, Age _24_, Colour of Hair _Light_
(Post Office)

is hereby authorized to hunt, take or kill Big Game (including Bear) under the provisions of the law in that respect, in the Province of Alberta, between the _12_ day of _Nov._
(Date of Issue)   (Month of Issue)

and one hour after sunset on the fourteenth day of December, 1934.

Howard Alstote
(Signature of Licensee)

H. Sohn
(Game Guardian or Game License Vendor)

J. F. ANDREW,
Acting Game Commissioner.

N.B.—This License is not valid unless signatures of Game Guardian or Game License Vendor and Licensee appear thereon.

365

GAME REGULATIONS

BAG LIMITS: Mountain Sheep, Deer, Moose and Caribou, one male only; Mountain Goat, one only. Elk, one male with horns of ten points or over. Bear, one of each species. Geese, ten per day, twenty-five for season. Ducks, fifteen per day before October 1st, twenty-five per day thereafter; season, one hundred. Rails, Coots, Wilson Snipe, twenty-five per day; season, one hundred.

Grouse (sharp-tailed), five per day; season, fifty, north of Lacombe-Kerrobert Branch Canadian Pacific Railway and Red Deer River; season, twenty-five south of above line.

Hungarian Partridge, fifteen per day, two hundred for season.

Blue Grouse, Ruffed Grouse, Spruce Partridge and Ptarmigan north of C.P.R. Kerrobert-Coronation-Lacombe Branch five per day and twenty-five per season, of any or all.

(WHITE, CLOSE SEASON; GREEN, OPEN SEASON)

	JAN	FEB	MAR	APR	MAY	JUNE	JULY	AUG	SEPT	OCT	NOV	DEC
MOUNTAIN SHEEP and MOUNTAIN GOAT												
BUFFALO, ANTELOPE, ELK (Wapiti). See Special License.												
DEER, MOOSE, CARIBOU, except in closed areas or with Special Licenses.												
BEAR. Females with cubs and cubs protected at all times												
DUCKS, GEESE, Rails, Coots, Wilson Snipe. Season opens 12 noon, south of Clearwater-Athabasca Rivers												
DUCKS, GEESE, Rails, Coots, Wilson Snipe. Season opens 12 noon, north of Clearwater-Athabasca Rivers.												
ELK (Wapiti) by Special License in Pembina Brazeau Reserve and adjacent areas.												
PHEASANTS, SWANS, CRANES												
GROUSE, Blue Grouse, Ruffed Grouse, Spruce Partridge, Ptarmigan.												
GROUSE, Sharp-tailed (Other species not open season).*												
GROUSE, Sharp-tailed (Known as Prairie Chicken). S. of Lacombe-Kerrobert Br. C.P.R. & Red Deer River.												
HUNGARIAN PARTRIDGE												
Crows, Eagles, Goshawks, Pigeon Hawks, Duck Hawks, Cooper Hawks, Sharp-shinned Hawks, Hawk Owls, Snowy Owls, Horned Owls, Blackbirds, Cowbirds, Grackles, Magpies and House Sparrows												
BEAVER												
FOX												
MINK, FISHER, MARTEN, RED SQUIRREL												
OTTER												
MUSKRAT (North of Township 90).												
MUSKRAT (Between N. Sask. River and Twp. 91).												
MUSKRAT (South of North Saskatchewan River).												

*N. of Lacombe-Kerrobert Br. C.P.R. & Red Deer River.

BIRDS NOT MENTIONED ABOVE MUST NOT BE KILLED OR TAKEN.

Holders of General and Big Game Licenses may secure a Special License to hunt Deer, Moose and Caribou in restricted areas in the Clearwater, Brazeau and Athabasca Forest Reserves, and Special Elk Licenses to hunt Elk in the Pembina-Brazeau Reserve and adjacent areas.

NO OPEN SEASON ON PHEASANTS.

IT IS ILLEGAL FOR ANY PERSON TO HUNT BIG GAME OR GAME BIRDS WITHOUT A LICENSE.

IT IS ILLEGAL FOR ANY PERSON TO REMOVE ALL THE DISTINCTIVE EVIDENCE OF SEX FROM THE CARCASS OF ANY BIG GAME ANIMAL UNTIL THE TRANSPORTATION OF SUCH CARCASS HAS BEEN COMPLETED.

IT IS ILLEGAL TO HUNT BIG GAME UNLESS CLOTHED IN A COAT AND CAP OF SCARLET MATERIAL.

FUR TAX MUST BE PAID ON ALL SKINS OR PELTS OF FUR-PRODUCING ANIMALS TAKEN IN ALBERTA, EXCEPT ON EXEMPTIONS PROVIDED FOR IN THE FUR-FARM REGULATIONS AND SPECIAL BEAVER PERMITS.

IT IS UNLAWFUL:

At any time to have a loaded shot gun or loaded rifle in any vehicle of any kind, or discharge any such shot gun or rifle from any vehicle.

To shoot big game or game birds on Sunday.

To hunt or trap over enclosed lands without obtaining consent of the owner or occupant thereof.

To kill big game animals under one year of age or with horns less than four inches in length.

To buy, sell, deal or traffic in any big game, game bird or part thereof.

To export any animal or bird or part thereof mentioned in The Game Act without a permit from the Minister of Agriculture.

To place the flesh of any big game in cold storage between the 1st day of March and the next following date fixed for the commencement of the open season.

To place the flesh of any game bird in cold storage between the 1st day of March and the following 20th day of September.

To use a dog to hunt big game.

To act as Outfitter or Guide without a license.

To hunt or trap fur-bearing animals without a license (Farmers and members of their families are exempt on their own lands).

To trap any Muskrat or Beaver in their houses or push-ups.

To deal or traffic in skins or pelts of any fur-producing or fur-bearing animal without a license.

To export skins or pelts out of the Province without having paid the royalty on such furs and securing an Export Permit.

Department of Agriculture,
Edmonton, Alberta, August 1st, 1934.

J. F. ANDREW,
Acting Game Commissioner.

1917 1917
GAME REGULATIONS
Sunday Shooting is Prohibited

(WHITE, CLOSE SEASON; BLACK, OPEN SEASON)

Hunting over enclosed lands prohibited without having obtained the consent of the owner or occupant thereof.

The killing of animals under one year of age is prohibited.

	JANUARY	FEBRUARY	MARCH	APRIL	MAY	JUNE	JULY	AUGUST	SEPTEMBER	OCTOBER	NOVEMBER	DECEMBER
Mountain Sheep, Mountain Goats (2 Males only) (3 only)										OCT 14		
Buffalo, Elk, Wapiti												
Antelope												
Deer, Moose, Caribou (1 Male only) (1 only)												DEC 14
Ducks and Geese (Sale or purchase prohibited between March 1 and Sept. 20). Bag limit (ducks) per day 30, season 200.												DEC 14
Swans, Cranes												
Rails, Coots, Black-bellied Plover, Golden Plover, Wilson Snipe and Yellow-Legs												DEC 14
Prairie Chicken, Partridge, etc.												
Hungarian Partridge												
Hungarian Pheasant												
Crows, Eagles, Goshawks, Pigeon Hawks, Duck Hawks, Cooper's Hawks, Hawk-Owls, Blackbirds, Grackels, English Sparrows, Loons, Cormorants, Pelicans and Magpies												
Mink, Fisher, Marten												
Otter, Muskrats												
Beaver												

Birds not mentioned above must not be killed or taken

No duck, geese, snipe, plover, etc., to be placed in cold storage between March 1st and September 20th following.

No person shall export any animal or bird, or part thereof, mentioned in The Game Act without a permit from the Minister of Agriculture.

No person shall wilfully disturb, destroy or take the eggs of any game or other birds protected by The Game Act.

No dog shall be used by any one to hunt big game.

No person shall hunt big game without a License.
No person shall buy or sell any game heads unless branded by the Department.
No person shall buy and sell, deal or traffic in the flesh of any big game or game bird without a License.
No person shall act as guide or camp helper without a License.

BIRDS' EGGS OR NESTS MUST NOT BE TAKEN, DISTURBED OR DESTROYED

LICENSES

NON-RESIDENT		RESIDENT	
General Game Licence	$25.00	Big Game License	$2.50
Bird Game License	5.00	" " " (farmers)	1.00
Trapper's License	25.00	Bird Game	2.25
Guide's License	$2.50		
Camp Helper's License	2.50		
Game Dealer's License	10.00		
Market Hunter's License	5.00		

FINES

Not exceeding $500.00 and costs may be imposed for infractions of The Game Act

Department of Agriculture,
Edmonton, Alta., May 1st, 1917.

BENJ. LAWTON,
Chief Game Guardian

PLEASE POST IN A CONSPICUOUS PLACE
Copies of The Game Act may be had on application.

WORKLESS MUST TAKE JOBS OR LOSE RELIEF

Hon. Dr. Cross Issues Statement on Farm Placement Plan

Edmonton, Oct. 24.—Following a conference with a delegation representing the single unemployed men of this city, at which the men protested their participation in the Dominion-provincial farm settlement scheme should be voluntary, the Alberta Relief commission sent a wire to the Dominion Relief commission and received a wire back that as many men as possible should participate in the scheme, and should be placed before winter sets in.

So far, government officials state several hundred men have been placed under the scheme and they are going out at the rate of 40 a day.

Under this plan the men are paid $5 a month, the farmer is paid $5 a month, and if the men remain on the farm from the time they go until the plan lapses on March 31 next they will receive a monthly bonus of $2.50.

Single unemployed men applying at the soup kitchen for relief and being offered jobs under the Dominion-provincial farm relief scheme must either take those jobs or be struck off relief, Hon. Dr. W. W. Cross, minister of health and in charge of relief, stated. This decision had been made by the government and would be adhered to.

75c lower at $7.35 for selects. Edmonton closed sharply lower at $7.35 for selects. Prince Albert closed 75c lower at $7.25 for selects. Moose Jaw and Regina opened at $8 and closed at $7.25 for selects. Saskatoon opened at $8 and closed at $7.25 for selects. Vancouver paid $8 for slaughter hogs.

Winnipeg Livestock Markets

Winnipeg sold 10,974 cattle and billed through 5,434 head. The market got good support from all quarters, and while there was no substantial upturn, there was a little more strength. However, the combined outlets cannot support much heavier shipments without some price reductions. The weather has turned colder, a favorable factor. A few good strong-weight steers made $5 to $5.25; most of the weighty steers $4 to $4.75; some handyweight killers $4.75, and other suitable kinds $4 to $4.50. Low grades made $2 to $3.75. Some little cattle from the Boissevain Boys' and Girls' club sold from $9 to $11, with the bulk $6 to $8. Butcher heifers improved, with the best $3 to $4. Cows were active from $1.75 to $2.50, and canners and cutters from $1 to $1.50. Stockers and feeders were more active from $2.50 to $3.50, with common stockers $2 down. Winnipeg had 3,837 calves. Good veal active, $5 to odd $6. Heavy, lower, $4 down.

Winnipeg had 8,246 hogs. Prices 75c lower, bacons closing at $7. Lights and feeders increased in volume and selling at $5 to $6.50. Sows $5 to $6. Selects, $1 premium, f. and w.

Winnipeg had 3,650 head of sheep and lambs. Strong loads $7, most of the good lambs $6.75, culls and weighty lambs, $4.50 to $5.75.

St. Boniface Sales
(For Week Ended Oct. 22.)

CATTLE

	Sales	Low	High
Steers up to 1050 lbs.			
Choice	4	$5.00	$5.50
Good	155	4.00	4.75
Medium	315	2.75	3.75
Common	380	2.00	2.50
Steers over 1050 lbs.			
Choice	21	5.00	5.25
Good	199	4.00	4.75
Medium	188	3.00	3.75
Common	45	2.25	2.75
Heifers			
Choice	10	4.00	4.50
Good	417	3.00	3.75
Medium	1166	2.50	2.75
Common	665	2.00	2.25
Fed Calves			
Choice	10	7.00	8.00
Good	20	5.50	6.50
Medium	39	4.00	5.00
Cows			
Good	550	2.25	2.50
Medium	931	1.75	2.00
Common	653	1.50	1.50
Canners and cutters	604	1.00	1.50
Bulls			
Good	40	1.75	2.00
Common	174	1.40	1.50
Stocker and Feeder Steers			
Good	1379	2.50	3.50
Common	2166	1.50	2.25
Stock Cows and Heifers			
Good	386	2.00	2.75
Common	423	1.25	1.75
Milkers and Springers	34	15.00	35.00
Total cattle	10974		

CALVES

Good and choice	766	5.00	5.50
Common and med.	2759	2.00	4.50
Grassers	312	1.50	3.00
Total calves	3837		

HOGS

Select bacon	978	1.00 per head prem.	
Bacon	2724	7.00	7.50
Butchers	868	1.00 per head disc.	
Heavies	109	6.50	7.00
Extra heavies	68	6.00	6.00
Lights and Feeders	2949	5.00	6.50
No. 1 sows	340	5.75	6.00
No. 2 sows	181	5.00	5.00
Roughs	17	4.50	5.00
Stags	12	3.00	4.00
Total hogs	8246		

LAMBS

Good handy weights	2705	6.75	7.00
Good heavies	187	5.75	6.00
Common all weights	478	4.00	5.00
Bucks	23	5.00	5.50
SHEEP			
Good handy weights	195	2.00	2.50
Common	62	1.00	1.50
Total sheep	3650		

BRITISH BACON PRICES

Canadian bacon in Great Britain for the week ended Oct. 23 was quoted at 81s to 84s, Danish at 93s to 94s, Irish at 89s to 94s and Baltic at 81s to 84s.

Livestock Quotations
Winnipeg, Oct. 27.

Steers, up to 1,050 lbs.—		
Good	$4.00	$4.75
Medium	2.75	3.75
Common	2.00	2.50
Steers, over 1,050 lbs.—		
Good	4.00	4.75
Medium	3.00	3.75
Common	2.00	2.75
Heifers—		
Good	3.00	3.75
Medium	2.25	2.75
Common	2.00	2.00
Fed Calves—		
Good	5.50	6.50
Medium	4.00	5.00
Cows—		
Good	2.25	2.50
Medium	1.75	2.00
Common	1.50	1.50
Canners and Cutters	1.00	1.50
Bulls—		
Good	1.75	2.00
Common	1.40	1.50
Stocker and Feeder Steers—		
Good	2.50	2.50
Common	1.50	2.00
Stock Cows and Heifers—		
Good	2.00	2.75
Common	1.25	1.50
Milkers and Springers	15.00	40.00
Veal Calves—		
Good and Choice	5.00	5.50
Common and Medium	2.50	4.50
Grassers	1.50	3.00
Hogs—		
Select Bacon $1.00 per head premium		
Bacon	7.00	7.00
Butchers $1.00 per head discount		
Heavy	6.50	6.50
Extra Heavy	6.00	6.00
Lights and Feeders	5.00	6.25
Sows No. 1	5.50	5.50
Sows No. 2	5.00	5.00
Roughs	4.50	5.00
Stags	3.50	4.00
Lambs—		
Good Handyweight	6.50	6.50
Good Heavies	5.75	6.00
Common	4.00	5.00
Bucks	5.00	5.50
Sheep—		
Good Heavies	1.75	1.75
Good Handyweight	2.00	2.50
Common	1.00	1.25

Ranchers Forced To Reduce Herds

Calgary, Oct. 21.—Ranchers of Alberta's foothills, their pasturage ruined by last summer's drought and an extended Indian summer during September and October, are cutting down their herds to suit their feed supplies.

The "E.P." ranch, owned by King Edward, has proved no exception and the 40-odd head of cattle shipped to Toronto in charge of Donald Carlyle, nephew of Professor W. L. Carlyle, ranch manager, completed another step in this curtailment.

Visitor—"And to what do you attribute your great age and general good health?"
Oldest Native—"Well, I got a good start on most people by being born before them germs was invented."

China Is Real Threat To British Markets

Singapore.—British manufacturers who complain of the effect of cheap Japanese goods on their Far Eastern markets will soon have additional competition to face from a nation which can undercut even the Japanese—that is, China.

Industrial production is developing at a great rate in China, and production costs are lower than in Japan. Recently Kao Shih-heng headed a Chinese trade mission to visit British Malay, Siam and the Dutch East Indies, and in an interview in Singapore said that within five years China would be able to hold her own against Japanese competition, especially in textiles and light manufactured goods.

"We estimate that Chinese production costs are 30 per cent lower than Japanese," he said. "Against this we have to reckon with the Japanese manufacturer's modern machinery, his cleverness in copying other nations' goods and underselling them, and in China itself we have the smuggling menace. But the quality of Chinese goods is constantly improving and Chinese manufacturers are gaining trade which has been held by the Japanese."

Former Sask. Man Missing in Spain

Madrid, Oct. 26.—James Minifie, formerly of Vanguard, Sask., special correspondent for the New York Herald Tribune in Spain, was missing Sunday night following a day of fierce fighting south of Madrid.

Another correspondent, Denis Weaver, of the London News-Chronicle, was missing, and Henry T. Gorrell, of the United Press, was taken prisoner.

Minifie and Weaver had not been heard from since they left Madrid at 2.30 p.m. when they set out by automobile to reach Aranjuez. War ministry officials checked with the Aranjuez general staff, only to learn the missing men had not been seen in that area.

Minifie, born at Boston, England, was educated at the University of Saskatchewan and Oxford. Later he was a teacher at Vanguard, Sask.

New Star Discovered

Cambridge, Mass., Oct. 22.—Harvard observatory announced Wednesday a cable from Copenhagen reported the discovery, on Oct. 7, of another nova, or new star, in the Constellation Aquila.

To all whom it may Concern.

Know ye, That _Garoni Hamilton_
a _Private_ of Captain _H. M. Jenner_
Company, (J) _9th_ Regiment of _Alabama Colored Inf._
VOLUNTEERS, who was enrolled on the _Sixteenth_ day of _February_
one thousand eight hundred and _sixty five_ to serve _Three_ years or
during the war, is hereby **Discharged** from the service of the United States
this _thirty first_ day of _October_, 186_5_, at _Selma_
Alabama by reason of _service no longer needed._
(No objection to his being re-enlisted, is known to exist.*)
    Said _Garon Hamilton_ was born in _____
in the State of _Scotland_ is _thirty six_ years of age,
five feet _five_ inches high, _light_ complexion, _Blue_ eyes,
light hair, and by occupation, when enrolled, _Mining M._
    Given at _Selma Ala_, this _thirty first_ day of
October 186_5_

E.S. Hamm
1st Lt 81st USCI and acm
Commanding the Reg't.

*This sentence will be erased _should there be anything_
in the conduct or physical condition of the soldier
rendering him _unfit for the Army._

[A. G. O., No. 99.]

H. M. Jenner
Capt Co J 9th Us Cear
Colds Co

That section forty-seven hundred and forty-five, title fifty-seven of the Revised Statutes of the United States is hereby amended to read as follows:

SEC. 4745.– Any pledge, mortgage, sale, assignment, or transfer of any right, claim, or interest in any pension which has been, or may hereafter be, granted, shall be void and of no effect, and any person who shall pledge, or receive as a pledge, mortgage, sale, assignment or transfer of any right, claim, or interest in any pension, or pension certificate which has been, or may hereafter be, granted or issued, or who shall hold the same as collateral security for any debt, or promise, or upon any pretext of such security, or promise, shall be guilty of a misdemeanor, and upon conviction thereof shall be fined in a sum not exceeding one hundred dollars and the costs of the prosecution; and any person who shall retain the certificate of a pensioner and refuse to surrender the same upon the demand of the Commissioner of Pensions, or a United States pension agent, or any other person, authorized by the Commissioner of Pensions, or the pensioner, to receive the same shall be guilty of a misdemeanor; and upon conviction thereof shall be fined in a sum not exceeding one hundred dollars and the costs of the prosecution.

Approved February 28, 1883.

UNDER ACT OF FEBRUARY 6, 1907

No. 6764

PENSION CERTIFICATE OF

Gavin Hamilton

Payable Quarterly

by the

U. S. Pension Agent

at Chicago, Ill.

Clerk.

DEATH OF OLD TIMER

On Friday of last week, death removed one of the old timers of the district in the person of Gavin Hamilton, aged 82 years, who died at the general hospital, Calgary, where he had been for some time undergoing an operation.

He was a former resident of Wisconsin, Minnesota and Dakota, and came to Alberta in 1889, settling on a homestead near Hastnattan in the spring of 1890, and was very active in getting and locating settlers in the district, and was ever ready to lend a helping hand to the needy, always remembering any kindness done him. He was an expert judge of timber, having formerly been employed by some of the largest lumbermen in America to locate and estimate timber for them. He had a great memory and could converse intelligently on many, and especially historical subjects. He was a veteran of the Civil War, and for endurance even up to within a year of his death, his equal would be hard to find.

The funeral was held in the Methodist Church, Olds, on Monday, August 21, the service being conducted by Rev. A. E. Argue, and the interment was at Olds cemetery.

He leaves a wife and two daughters, Ina, Barbara, Lillie of Saskatchewan, Mrs. H Lee and Ina Hamilton of Saskatchewan, where he has made his home for the past few years.

FORM 203, (Dept. Form D)

TAX NOTICE

For Sale by Christie's Bookstore, Western Headquarters for School Desks, Maps, Globes, Hyloplate Blackboards, and all School, Local Improvement District and Rural Municipality Supplies, Brandon, Man.

School District of *South Fork*   No. *1803*

To *R R Dial*

Caroline Alta P.O.

You are hereby notified that you are assessed on the Assessment Roll of the above named School District for the year 191*5* , for *160* acres of land the taxes on which at the rate of *2½* cents per acre, amounts $ *12 xx/100* and you are further notified that the arrears of taxes due by you to the said District amount to $ and you are required to pay the same forthwith.

The Land for which you are assessed is

Part of Section	Section	Township	Range	West. Mer.
N E	18	36	5	5

N dis allowed for 30 days

DATED at *Caroline*   *F A Van Arsdale*
                                            Secretary or Secretary-Treasurer.

                              Residence of Secretary or Secretary-Treasurer.

this *29th day of Jan* 191*5*   *Caroline Alta* P.O.

ALL CHEQUES AND DRAFTS MUST BE PAYABLE AT PAR

NOTICE.—In the event of any taxes remaining unpaid after the 31st day of December of the year in which the same are imposed, there shall be added thereto by way of a penalty a sum equal to 5 per centum of such taxes remaining unpaid, and in the event of such taxes or any part thereof still remaining unpaid on July 1st of the year following that during which the taxes were imposed, there shall be added thereto by way of a penalty a sum equal to 5 per centum of such taxes remaining unpaid, and such amount or amounts so added shall form part of the taxes, which to this section are created a special lien upon the land, and such penalty or penalties shall be imposed in the manner aforesaid in each succeeding year during which the said taxes remain unpaid: nothing in this section contained shall be construed to extend the time for payment of the said taxes or in any way to impair the right of distress or any other remedy hereby provided for the collection of the said taxes.

*Receipt for Mr. E. Oliver's
threshing for 1933
Wheat 1446 bu. at 5¢
oats 1134 bu. at 3¢   total $56.32*

*Paid in full.
Ben Harris*

371

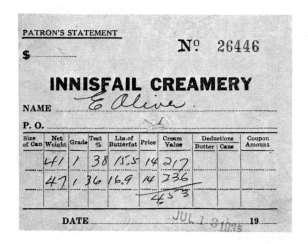

PATRON'S STATEMENT

N°: 26446

$ ....

INNISFAIL CREAMERY

NAME E Oliver.

P.O.

Size of Can	Net Weight	Grade	Test %	Lbs. of Butterfat	Price	Cream Value	Deductions Butter	Deductions Cans	Coupon Amount
41	1	38	15.5	14	217				
47	1	36	16.9	14	236				
					4 53				

DATE JUL 21 1935 19

CANADA REGISTRATION BOARD

This certificate must always be carried upon the person of the registrant

NUMBER
227 216 10

THIS IS TO CERTIFY THAT

Russell Falando Dial

residing at Caroline, Alta.

.... was duly registered for the national purposes of Canada this June day of 22nd, 1918

Mrs Effie Orcutt.
Deputy Registrar

Signature of Registrant Russell H. Dial

Rocky Mountain House, Oct 10 1934
ALBERTA

Imperial Bank of Canada.

IMPERIAL BANK OF CANADA HEAD OFFICE TORONTO

CANADA EXCISE 2 CENTS

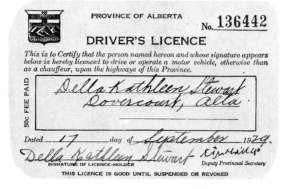

PROVINCE OF ALBERTA

No. 136442

DRIVER'S LICENCE

This is to Certify that the person named hereon and whose signature appears below is hereby licenced to drive or operate a motor vehicle, otherwise than as a chauffeur, upon the highways of this Province.

50c FEE PAID

Della Kathleen Stewart
Dovercourt, Alta.

Dated 17 day of September 1929

Della Kathleen Stewart
SIGNATURE OF LICENCE-HOLDER

Deputy Provincial Secretary

THIS LICENCE IS GOOD UNTIL SUSPENDED OR REVOKED

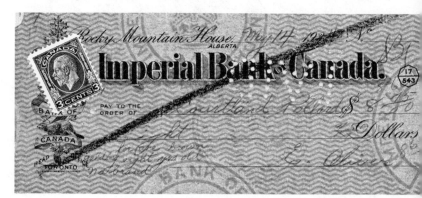

Rocky Mountain House, May 14 193
ALBERTA

Imperial Bank of Canada.

CANADA 3 CENTS

BANK OF CANADA HEAD OFFICE TORONTO

372

Caroline Aug 11 1909

Received from Conrad Schafer

$25.00 Twenty five and 00/100 Dollars

to apply on note

$25.00   Mrs Cynthia Langley

Form No. F 430

$45.00   Raven, Alta. Nov 23 1910

(Town)   (Date)

On or before the first day of Oct 1911, for value received,

I promise to pay to the **International Harvester Company of America**

(A Corporation organized and existing under the laws of the state of Wisconsin)

or order, the sum of Fourty Five 00/100 ——————— DOLLARS

at the office of the Company at Calgary, Alberta, with interest from the date hereof until maturity at 7 per cent. per annum and at 10 per cent. per annum after maturity until paid.

Given on account of price of 1 set Chatham Sleighs Cost Shoe 2½ x 54

The property in and the title to the goods above mentioned, which I hereby agree to buy, shall remain in the Company, and shall not pass to me until full payment of the price thereof, and all obligations given as security therefore.

If I sell or attempt to sell the undermentioned land which I own, or if I make default in payment of this note or any other note or obligation given on account of the said price, or if the Company shall deem itself insecure, the whole amount of the said price and interest thereon and all obligations and notes given therefor shall forthwith become due and payable, and the said Company may forthwith, without making presentment or demand, take action against me therefor; and the said Company may at its option take possession of the said goods and sell the same at private sale or public auction, the proceeds, less expense, to be applied on the debt, all of which shall be without prejudice to the rights of the said Company to collect the balance remaining unpaid which I agree to pay forthwith and for which action may be taken against me by the said Company, I agree that the said goods shall be at my risk as to damage or destruction from any cause, and that I will pay the said price therefor and interest thereon and all obligations given therefor, notwithstanding that the said goods may become damaged or destroyed.

The land above referred to and which I own is S W Sec. No. 10 Township No. 36 Range No. 6 W 5 in the Province of Alberta.

(Insert what part of section)

SIGNED, SEALED AND DELIVERED in the presence of

J A Army ——————— Conrad Schafer.   **SEAL**

Witness to Signature. Post Office Caroline Caroline Alberta   **SEAL**

ALBERTA

30m. 3-08

Fill out all blank spaces except Number.   Signatures by mark must be witnessed.   If name is foreign or illegible write it plainly in margin.

Calgary Number

12013 Year 19 10

[REFER TO THIS NUMBER AND YEAR]

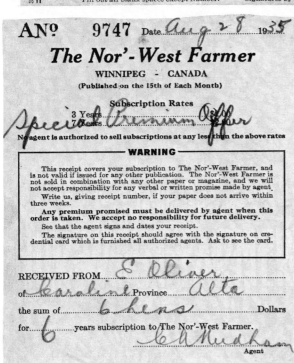

A No. 9747   Date Aug 28 1935

The Nor'-West Farmer

WINNIPEG - CANADA

(Published on the 15th of Each Month)

Subscription Rates

3 Years   Special Premium Offer

5 Years

No agent is authorized to sell subscriptions at any less than the above rates

— WARNING —

This receipt covers your subscription to The Nor'-West Farmer, and is not valid if issued for any other publication. The Nor'-West Farmer is not sold in combination with any other paper or magazine, and we will not accept responsibility for any verbal or written promise made by agent.

Write us, giving receipt number, if your paper does not arrive within three weeks.

Any premium promised must be delivered by agent when this order is taken. We accept no responsibility for future delivery.

See that the agent signs and dates your receipt.

The signature on this receipt should agree with the signature on credential card which is furnished all authorized agents. Ask to see the card.

RECEIVED FROM E Oliver

of Caroline Province Alta

the sum of 6 hens Dollars

for 6 years subscription to The Nor'-West Farmer.

C A Needham

Agent

Mrs. Evelyn M. Graham

announces the marriage of her daughter

Nellie

to

Philip Stewart Kiser

on Friday, January the second

one thousand nine hundred and twenty

at Philip, South Dakota

For Rural Dis...

ASSESSMENT AND

Of the *Chedder*

ASSESSMENT

No. on Roll	Name of Ratepayer [Enter Name of owner and occupant, if any. If owner is unknown, enter unknown.] 1	Post Office Address 2	Description of Property [State Section, Township, Range or Number of Lots, etc., as the case may be.] 3	No. of Acres Assessed 4	Date of Mailing Assessment Notices 5	Secretary's Initials [To be written after each notice mailed] 6	Rate of Taxation on the acre 7	Amount of Taxes for Current Y... 8
							c	$
1	W. G. Ives		NE¼ Sec 6 T37 R6 west of 5th	160	Aug 10th	W R	10	16–
2	Robert Wilson		SE¼ Sec 7 T37 R6	160		"	"	16–
3	Paul Robeck		SW¼ Sec 7 T37 R6	160		"	"	16–
4	John Steward		SW¼ Sec 5 T37 R6	160		"	"	16–
6	William Ives		west ½ Sec 18 T37 R6	320		"	"	32–
7	Harry Wilson		NW¼ Sec 5 T37 R6	160		"	"	16–
8	Raywood Wilson		SE¼ Sec 5 T37 R6	160		"	"	16–
9	D B Wilson		NE¼ Sec 25 T37 R7	160		"	"	16–
10	Mrs D B Wilson		SE¼ Sec 25 T37 R7	160		"	"	16–
11	~~Henry~~ Sid Smith		NE¼ Sec 24 T37 R7	160		"	"	16–
12	Sam Smith		SE¼ Sec 24 T37 R7	160		"	"	16–
14	R S Clarkson		NW¼ Sec 13 T37 R7	160		"	"	16–
15	Mrs E Robinson		S½ Sec 13 T37 R7	320		"	"	32–
16	Wm Robinson		N½ Sec 12 T37 R7	320		"	"	32–
17	Chas Fontaine		S½ Sec 12 T37 R7	320		"	"	32–
18	Sidney S Smith		north ½ Sec 24 T37 R7	320		"	"	32–
19	Hudson Bay Co		Sec 8 and ¾ of 5 in 37-7, Sec 8 in 37-6,	1760		"	"	176–
20	Gilchrist			160		"	"	16–
23	W H Eddleston		SE¼ Sec 14 T37 R7	160		"	"	16–
24	Alexandra		SE¼ Sec 10 T37 R7	160		"	"	16–
25	Rudolph Moberg		NW¼ Sec 10 T37 R7	160		"	"	16–
26	Rex Bancroft		NE¼ Sec 10 T37 R7	160		"	"	16–
27	Pete Olde		SE¼ Sec 15 T37 R7	160		"	"	16–
28	Ray Jones		SW¼ Sec 15 T37 R7	160		"	"	16–
31	C Johnson		SE¼ Sec 16 T37, R7	160		"	"	16–
32	J E Titus		NE Sec 16 T37 R7	160		"	"	16–
33	Mrs Titus		NW¼ Sec 16 T37 R7	160		"	"	16–
34	Ruddleton		SE¼ Sec 21 T37 R7	160		"	"	16–
3[illegible]	Codd		SW¼ Sec 21 T37 R7	160		"	"	16–
	Parker		NE¼ Sec 21 T37 R7	160		"	"	16–
	Lilly		NW¼ Sec 21 T37 R7	160		"	"	16–
	Moberg		SW¼ Sec 20 T37 R7	160		"	"	16–
	Withnall		SE¼ Sec 20 T37 R7	160		"	"	16–
	Gar[illegible]lett		NE¼ Sec 20	160		"	"	16–
			NW¼ Sec 20	160				16–

... information required in columns 1, 3 and 4 is to be filled in by the assessor (*see sections 6 and 7*) after which the roll is to be deli... ...cretary will fill in columns ... and 8 (*see section 13*) and then deliver the roll to the treasurer who will fill in column... ...he duties of ...

TAX ROLL

School District No. 3676 of Alberta   for the year 1919

TAXATION

Arrears of Taxes due from Jan. 1, 1918	Total Taxes Due	Date of Mailing Tax Notice	TREASURER'S INITIALS [To be written after each notice mailed]	PAYMENT OF TAXES		DATE OF POSTING ROLL
9	10	11	12	Amount	Date of Payment	
$ c	$ c					
17-60	33-60	Sep. 10th				
	16-00	"				
17-60	33-60	"				
	16-00	"				
35-20	67-20	"				
	16-00					
	16-00					
	16-00					
	16-00					
~~17-60~~	~~33-60~~					
	16-00					
17-60	33-60					
	16-00					
	32-00					
	32-00					
	32-00					
35-20	67-20					
	176-00					
17-60	33-60					
17-60	33-60					
17-60	33-60					
	16-00					
	16-00					
	16-00					
17-60	33-60					
	16-00					
17-60	33-60					
17-60	33-60					
17-60	33-60					
17-60	33-60					
17-60	33-60					
17-60	33-60					
	16-00					
17-60	33-60					
17-60	33-60					
17-60	33-60					

This Assessment Roll was posted on the .... day of August 1917 .... Secretary

This Tax Roll was posted on the .... day of .... 191.... .... Treasurer

W. Robinson

the secretary who will fill in columns 2, 5 and 6 and then post a copy of the roll and fill in and sign the date of posting (see section 14). The treasurer will also fill in columns

17-60

Ricinus-Dovercourt Mail Route
1927

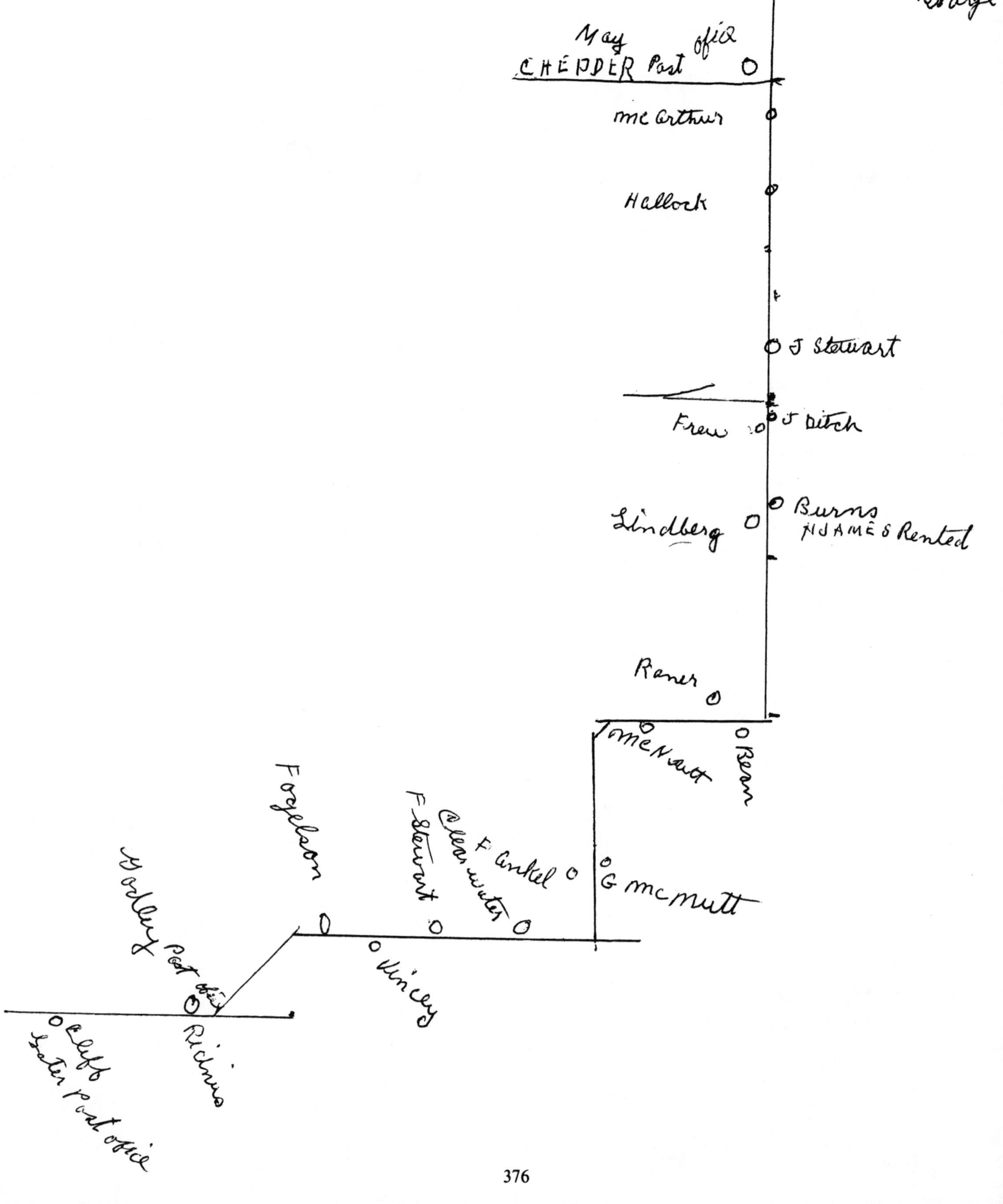

DOVERCOURT PO
Ramsey
Dovercourt Bridge

May
CHEDDER Post office ○

mc arthur ○

Hallock ○

○ J Stewart

Frew ○ ○ J Ditch

Lindberg ○ ○ Burns
N JAMES Rented

Raner ○

○ McNaught ○ Ream

Fogelson ○

F Stewart ○

Clearwater ○

F Unkel ○

○ G mcnutt

○ Kinley

Harley Post office
Ricinus ○

○ Bluff
Crater post office

376

Letter of Appointment to Postmastership.

POST OFFICE DEPARTMENT, CANADA.

Ottawa, 4ᵗʰ November 190 8.

Sir,

I have the honour to inform you that the Postmaster General has been pleased to appoint you to be Postmaster of

Caroline in the Electoral County

of _Strathcona_ in the

Province of _Alberta_ and

Dominion of Canada.

You are, therefore, hereby authorized to exercise all the functions and discharge all the duties appertaining to the said office, according to law.

I am, Sir,
Your obedient servant,

E R Ross
Acting Deputy Postmaster General.

Mr. H. A. Langley,
Caroline.
Alta.

6—1,500-21-6-07.

EARL E. FREEMAN. LL.B.

Barrister, Solicitor, Notary

INNISFAIL, ALBERTA.

CANADA

May 10th 1939

MEMORANDUM OF AGREEMENT made the day above mentioned

Between

GEORGE DANIEL BUGBEE,
hereinafter called the party of

THE FIRST PART

-and-

RAYMOND RICHARD DIAL,
hereinafter called the party of

THE SECOND PART

WITNESSETH:

1.   That party of the First Part does hereby agree to sell to the Party of the Second Part the land described in Certificate of Title No. 220-X-86 at and for the sum of $800.00 represented by the items hereinafter set out.

2.   That the party of the Second Part does hereby agree to pay for said land, the sum of Sixty ($60.00) Dollars in cash; and to deliver Five (5) Head of rising 3-4 year old horses, branded R.D. on Right Shoulder and ⌠ on Left Thigh.   Also to assume all arrears of taxes except as hereinafter mentioned.

3.   Said horses are to be delivered by the 17th day of May 1939.

4.   Party of the First Part agrees with the party of the Second Firs Part that any work already done by the party of the Second Part for the Municipal District of Raven #342 and any money coming to the party of the First Part for said work shall be applied against the taxes now outstanding against the land described in said Certificate of Title.

IN WITNESS WHEREOF the parties hereto have hereunto set their respective hands and seals the day and year first above mentioned.

SIGNED, SEALED AND DELIVERED)   *George D Bugbee*
  in the presence of   )
)
)   *R. R. Dial*

Earl E Freeman

AUD
SANGER
MICKEY
OLLY
LUE
$60.00 cash.

Chedderville   S. D. No. 3676

Attendance for the Month of ....July.... 1927

Teacher: *Phyllis Hunter*

PUPIL'S REGISTER No.	AGE	GRADE	NAMES OF PUPILS	1st Week				2nd Week				3rd Week				4th Week				5th Week					TOTAL
			Day of the Month	4	5	6	7	8	11	12	13	14	15	18	19	20	21	22	25	26	27	28	29			
				MON.	TUES.	WED.	THURS.	FRI.	MON.	TUES.	WED.	THURS.	FRI.	MON.	TUES.	WED.	THURS.	FRI.	MON.	TUES.	WED.	THURS.	FRI.			
2	13	VII	Bancroft Barbara																							14
3	14	VII	Robinson Mary																							13
4	14	VI	Eskdale McKie																							14
5	13	VI	Eror Steve																							7
7	12	V	Anderson Mary																							17
8	12	V	Hodgkinson Fred																							18
9	12	V	May Marjorie																							18
10	12	V	McKie Lizzie																							19
11	11	V	Eror Minnie																							6
12	11	IV	Hutchinson Alex																							17
13	10	III	Anderson John																							18
14	9	III	Bancroft Rex																							20
15	9	III	McKie Dsy																							18
16	11	III	Hallock Mary																							20
17	10	III	Spence Annie																							18
18	9	III	Hallock Vergis																							20
19	11	II	Anderson Gonda																							19
20	8	II	May Alberta																							20
21	8	II	Anderson Lillian																							20
23	7	I	Hallock Vera																							20
24	7	I	McKie John																							19
25	6	I	Hodgkinson Alena																							15
26	6	I	Hodgkinson Donald																							19
27	6	I	Anderson Bill																							20
28	6	I	Anderson Charlie																							15
29	7	I	Eror Wesley																							18
			TOTAL DAILY ATTENDANCE	24	23	22	23	23	23	24	27	27	20	25	26	21	18	20	20	16	19	20	17			431
			NUMBER OF "LATES"	2	6																					

Number of pupils in attendance during the month... 26

I hereby certify that the above record of attendance is correct and does not include any record of teaching on Saturdays or other holidays

Phyllis Hunter
Teacher.

No. of teaching days school was open during the month... 20

Aggregate days' attendance for the month... 431

Average attendance for the month... 21.55

Percentage of attendance for the month... 82.88

NOTE:—At the end of each month transfer each month's attendance to the "Summary of attendance for the term."

STANDARD FORM OF CONTRACT

BETWEEN
TRUSTEES AND TEACHER

This Agreement made in triplicate

BETWEEN:—

The Board of Trustees of _Wooler S.D._

School District No. _297.._ of the Province of Alberta, hereinafter called "the Board"

—and—

Ethel Elizabeth Donovan

of _Innisfail_

the holder of a _first class_
(Insert class of certificate)

Certificate of qualification as a teacher in Alberta, hereinafter called "the Teacher."

WITNESSETH:—

That subject to the provisions of _The School Act, 1931,_ and the Regulations of the Department of Education, the Board hereby employs the Teacher, and the Teacher agrees to teach and conduct school for the Board on the following terms:

1. The annual salary shall be $ _840_ , and subject to the following schedule of increases:

    ....

    ....

    ....

2. The period of employment shall be from and including the _1st Sep_ day of
    .... 193 _1_.

DATED this _twentyninth_ day of _September_ 193_1_.

Signed on behalf of the Board [CORPORATE SEAL].

C. H. Hughes.
Witness to Chairman's signature.

F. G. Garrett
Witness to Teacher's signature.

S. H. Garrett
Chairman.

Ethel Elizabeth Donovan
Teacher.

No. of Teacher's Alberta Certificate _107 - 31_

Innisfail
Teacher's Post Office Address.

NOTE:—For engagement and contract, see Sections 155 to 158 inclusive of The School Act, 1931.

    For minimum salary, see Section 161.

    For method of payment of salary, see Sections 161 to 164 inclusive.

    For method of terminating an agreement, see Section 157.

    For information regarding vacation periods and holidays, see Sections 144 and 145.

    Teacher should sign with Christian names in full.

    In absence of Chairman, any other Trustee may sign (Section 158).

    One copy of this Agreement should be retained by the Board, another by the Teacher, and the third forwarded at once to the Department of Education.

Form 27—45,000-May 1931.

SCHOOL SUPPLIES—SCHOOL DEBENTURES—SCHOOL INSURANCE—TREASURER'S BONDS—SCHOOL PLANS

Long Distance Telephone 4833 | INVOICE SHEET | P.O. Box 1136

Copy. EDMONTON, ALBERTA, June 19, 1913.

Wooler School District, No. 2976,

Per. E. Bell, Esq., Sec. Treas., Caroline, Alta.

BOUGHT OF **The Alberta School Supply Company**

619-621 FOURTH STREET

"The House of Quality"

Invoice No. 3432. How Ordered mail. Sent by mail.

Alberta Agents for

Hero Ventilating Room Heaters

Preston Ball-Bearing School Desks

Johnston Maps always in stock

School Library Books at lowest prices

Milton Bradley's Kindergarten Supplies

Physical and Chemical Apparatus

If it's for a School We Have It

Satisfaction Guaranteed

To:-

1. Rubber Seal	2	00
1. Minute Book		85
1. Cash Book	3	00
1. Assessment & Tax Roll		75
100. Assessment Notices		40
100. Tax Notices		40
100. Tax Receipts		45
100. Ordinary Receipts		45
100. Orders on Treasurer		45
1. File Complete	1	00
1. Carbon Copy Book		50
1. Penhandle & Point FREE		
1. Indelible Pencil "		
1. School Supply Catalogue		
Postage		92
	11	17

Remittances should be made by Bank Draft, Money Order or Postal Note
Add Exchange to Checks

Sole Agents
Preston Ball-Bearing School Desks
Hero Ventilating Room Heater

A. F. CARROTHERS

A. L. GILLIES

Sole Agents
Canadian Phoenix Insurance Co.
London Guarantee and Accident Co., Ltd.

The Alberta School Supply Company

School Supplies, Debentures, Treasurers' Bonds
Insurance, School Plans

Edmonton, Alberta

June 4, 1914.

Melville A. Ferguson, Esq.,

Sec. Treas., Wooler S. D. #2976,

Caroline, Alberta.

Dear Sir:

We enclose herewith invoice and B/L covering your shipment of school supplies. We advise you to have a first class carpenter set up these desks as they will last longer and give better satisfaction if put together rightly at first. These supplies left our warehouse in first class order and should any article be broken or damaged do not give the freight Agent a clear receipt for this shipment.

Appreciating your business, we are,

Yours very truly,

The Alberta School Supply Company,

Per A. F. Carrothers

AFC/HD.

Enc.

COP.

Department of Health.

Dear Sirs:-

        Just a line asking you to have the Wooler
school fumigated -- for two years now there has been
itch in the school. For over two years now my girls
have been off school lots and every time they go back
they get the itch and the other children also even the
teacher gets it.   If the school had been fumigated
two years ago when all the children were sent home with
the itch and closed the school for a week and they did
nothing to it -- so books and everything in the school
has the itch germ on it and when the children touch
anything in school -- its the itch again.   So I
think when school is closed for Easter holidays the
school could be fumigated and perhaps the poor girls
and boys who get the itch will get rid of it.   It is
terrible to see them scratch and scratch till they
are a mass of sores.   I make them bath and rub with
salve and take dope also, and keep there clothes and
bedding washed up :   but it is no good until that
darn school is cleaned up -- see if you can get them
to clean the school.

                    Yours truly.

                        SIGNED........

A. R. GIBSON, M.A., B.PAED.

INSPECTOR OF SCHOOLS

RED DEER, ALBERTA

RED DEER,
ALBERTA

April 29th, 1921.

M.A.Ferguson, Esq.,

    Secy- Wooler S.D.,

        Caroline.

Sir,

    I   am prepared to recommend a permit for Mrs Miller if she
can satisfy the Dept of Education as to her qualifications. I
have phoned them about it but would advise that you send copies
in along with the fee of Five Dollars to the Dept.

                    Your obedient servant,

                    Inspector of Schools.

IN REPLYING GIVE NAME AND NUMBER OF SCHOOL DISTRICT
AND
BE CAREFUL TO REFER
TO

VHS/D.

FILE NO. 7932-23

EDMONTON. **Feb.13,1923.**

Sir:

        In reply to your letter of the 24th ult.,
I beg to say that if the names of Mr.Croke and Mr.
Mann both appeared on the last revised Assessment Roll
of your District and they were both residing within
your District at the time of the election, they were both
properly qualified to vote at that election.

        Your obedient servant,

                J. T. R O S S.

                        Deputy Minister.

                        Per.

Melville A.Ferguson,Esq.,
Sec.Wooler S.D.#2976,
Caroline P.O.Alta.

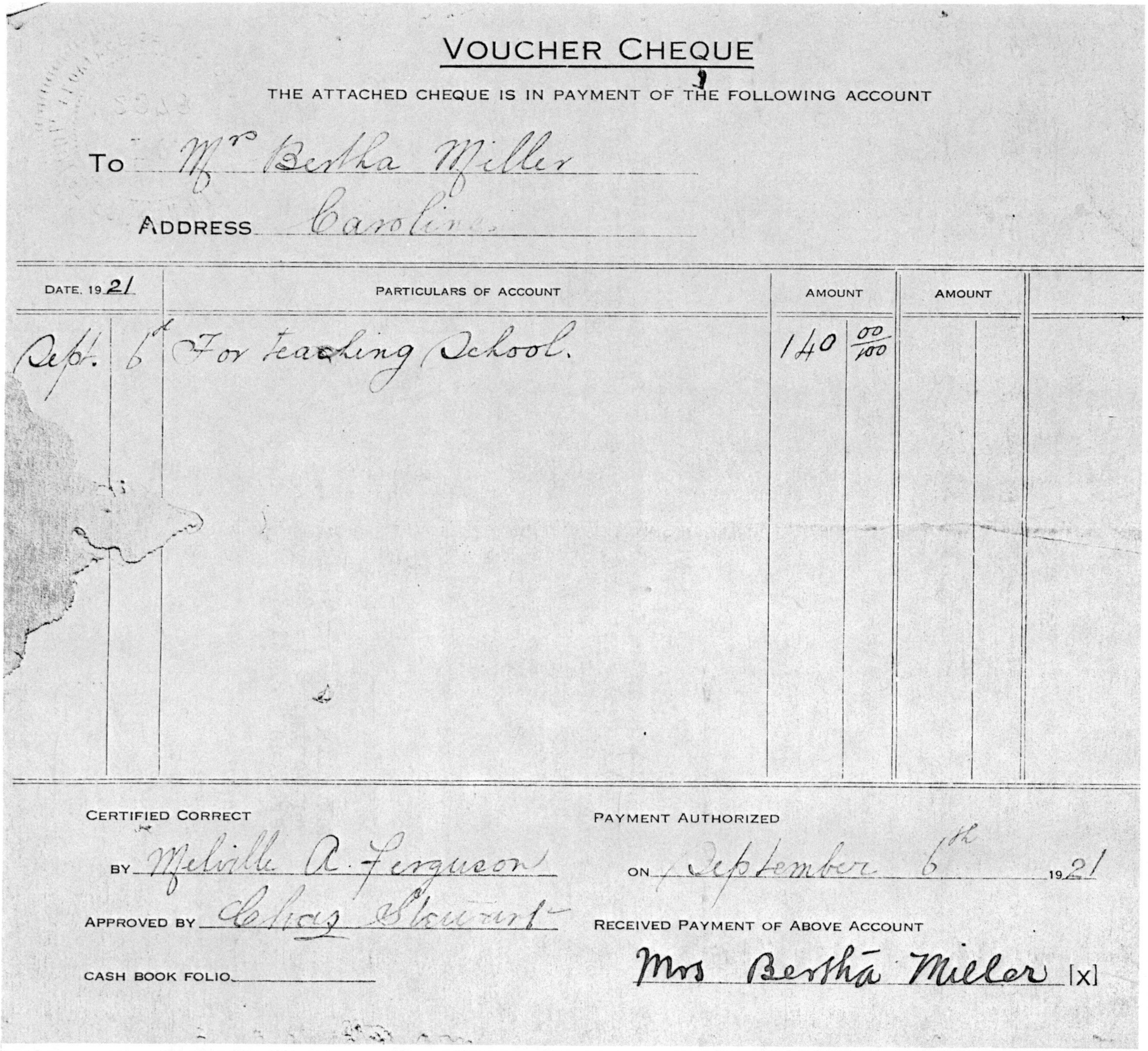

VOUCHER CHEQUE

THE ATTACHED CHEQUE IS IN PAYMENT OF THE FOLLOWING ACCOUNT

To _Mrs Bertha Miller_

ADDRESS _Caroline_

DATE, 19 21	PARTICULARS OF ACCOUNT	AMOUNT	AMOUNT
Apl. 6	For teaching School.	140 00/100	

CERTIFIED CORRECT

BY _Melville A. Ferguson_

APPROVED BY _Wesley Stewart_

CASH BOOK FOLIO

PAYMENT AUTHORIZED

ON _September 6_ 19 21

RECEIVED PAYMENT OF ABOVE ACCOUNT

Mrs Bertha Miller |X|

386

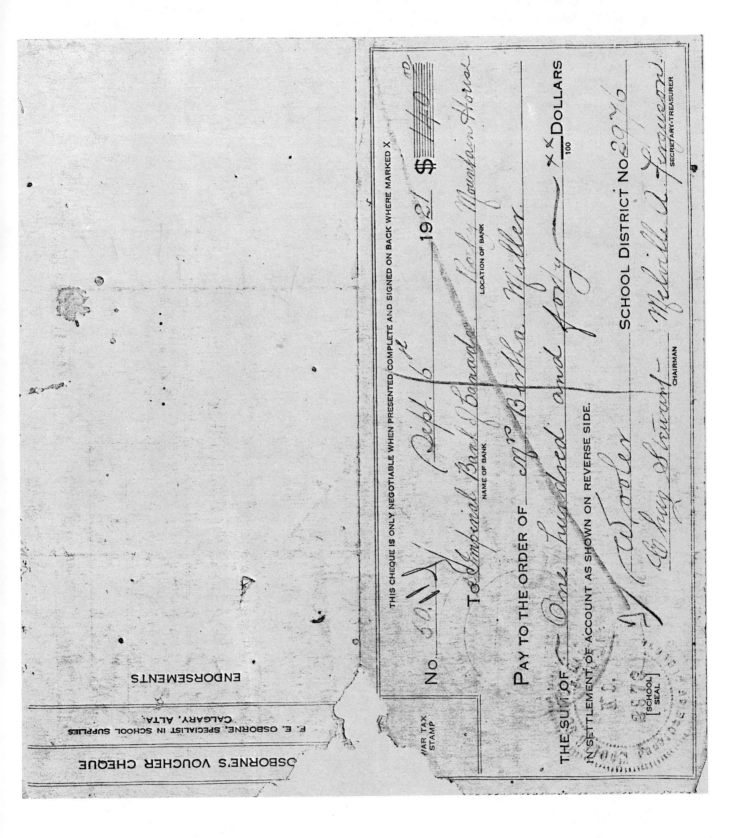

No. 5011

Sept. 6th 1921 $140 00

To Imperial Bank of Canada
Location of Bank   Rocky Mountain House
Name of Bank

PAY TO THE ORDER OF   Mr Botha Miller

THE SUM OF   One hundred and forty   ××   DOLLARS
                                                        100

IN SETTLEMENT OF ACCOUNT AS SHOWN ON REVERSE SIDE.

WAR TAX
STAMP

SCHOOL DISTRICT No 2976

A W Wooler
CHAIRMAN

Melville A Fraser
SECRETARY-TREASURER

[SCHOOL SEAL]

THIS CHEQUE IS ONLY NEGOTIABLE WHEN PRESENTED COMPLETE AND SIGNED ON BACK WHERE MARKED X

ENDORSEMENTS

F. E. OSBORNE, SPECIALIST IN SCHOOL SUPPLIES
CALGARY, ALTA.

OSBORNE'S VOUCHER CHEQUE

387

Caroline Traders
General Trucking - - Anywhere, Anytime
MITTEN & MULLEN
GENERAL MERCHANTS

Caroline, Alta., Aug 29 198

M Ed Oliver

		Account Forward	17	74
1	2 Tobacco		20	
2	papers			15
3	gloves		45	
4	shirts		10	
5	Liberty		05	
6	gas		95	
7			190	
8				
9			1964	
10				
11	Chg			
12				
13				
14	**5**			

WESTERN SALES BOOK CO. LTD., FACTORIES: WINNIPEG AND VANCOUVER

Caroline Traders
General Trucking - - Anywhere, Anytime
R. W. MITTEN, Prop.
GENERAL MERCHANTS

Caroline, Alta., July 8 1937

M Schafer

		Account Forward	1	48
1	shirt		85	
2	Tea		02	
3	Tobacco		70	
4	candy		10	
5			1	67
6				
7			3	15
8	Chg			
9				
10				
11				
12				
13	**18**			
14				

WESTERN SALES BOOK CO. LTD., FACTORIES: WINNIPEG AND VANCOUVER

Caroline Traders
GENERAL MERCHANTS
CROSS & MITTEN, Props.

Caroline, Alta., 194

M

		Account Forward		
1				
2				
3				
4				
5				
6				
7				
8				
9				
10				
11				
12				
13				
14	**7**			

BEDFORM—WESTERN SALES BOOK CO. LTD., FACTORIES—WINNIPEG & VANCOUVER

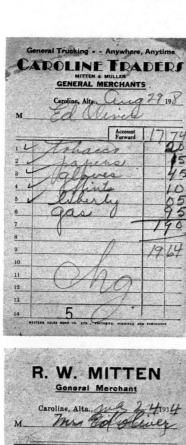

R. W. MITTEN
General Merchant

Caroline, Alta., July 24 1934

M Mrs Ed Oliver

apricot		2	50
comfort			10
paper			05
shuffens			25
Rillys			15
		3	05
charge			70
		3	75
31½ @ 12 gas		3	78
6¢			45
3½			03
31 Credit			

Red Deer Advocate, Red Deer, Alta.

H. A. LANGLEY
GENERAL MERCHANT

Caroline, Alta., May 19 1934

M E Oliver

DOMINION STATIONERS, TORONTO, ONT.

16 d egg		1	12
salt		1	15
tankage		2	10
		3	25
28	Chg		

H. A. LANGLEY
GENERAL MERCHANT

Caroline, Alberta, May 26 1927

M O Schafer

X	butter		70
X	tea		85
X	lemons		50
X	sugar		1 80
X	paper		10
		3	90

Dale Press Ltd. Edmonton, Alta.

DENNIS BROWN

H. E. ROCHE
CAROLINE GENERAL ALTA.

PLEASE KEEP THIS BILL FOR REFERENCE
BOUGHT OF -o-

Date Dec 19th 1935

M Ed Oliver

Address

	Account Forwarded		
Pork liver			62
Coal Oil		1	70
Onions			25
Vinegar			10
Coffee			28
Cocoa			57
Raisins			57
Currants			25
Walnuts			35
soap			20
Currant			15
3 J Po-1 Stir 1 Rasp 1 Plum			15
Do. Lemons			70
Sep 16		6 31	

PLEASE KEEP THIS BILL FOR REFERENCE
BOUGHT OF

R McCandle

Date June 18 1937

M A Oliver hauling

Address hauled by Zimmerman

O		Account Forwarded		
160	1/5 - 10		6	67
113	1/5 - 12		5	65
122	1/5 - 14		7	11
106	1/5 - 16		7	07
			26	50
45				

PLEASE KEEP THIS BILL FOR REFERENCE

Date June 21 1935

M Ed Oliver
To Zel & Bird

Bought of

		Account Forwarded		
1 Piggy Cow				
180 @ 2²⁵			4	05
2 Roller				
270 @ 3⁵⁰			9	45
4 Butcher				
730 @ 3⁷⁵			27	40
1 Bacon				
190 @ 4²⁵			8	05
			48	95
Cheque			48	95
20	Wrigglesworth			

388

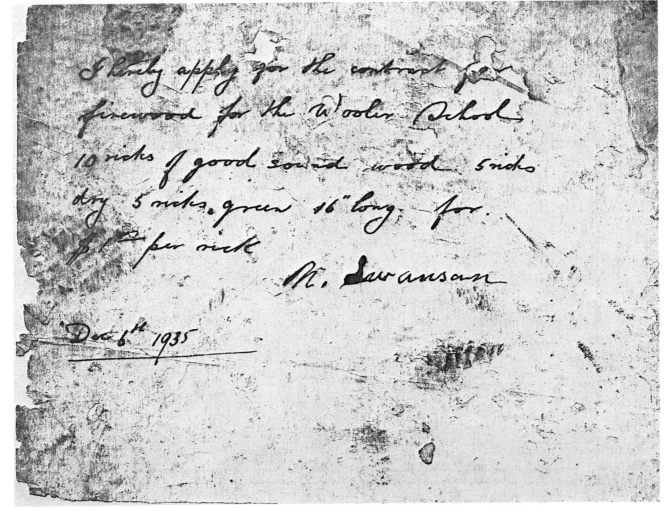

Nov 31st 1919
P Box 67
Hanton
alta

Mr Melville Ferguson

Dear Sir
        I'm writing you about
the School Taxes on SW A 4 Ts 36
Rg 6 ws 5 also on SE A 5 Ts 36 Rg 6 ws 5
for the years 1917 X 18 X 19 due on the
said Land in Wooler School District,
hoping for a reply from you at the
earliest possible Date.

                    yrs Truly
                    H A Garrett

I hereby apply for the contract for
firewood for the Wooler School
10 ricks of good sound wood 5 ricks
dry 5 ricks green 16" long. for
$ per rick
                    M. Swanson

Dec 6th 1935

389

May 12 1926

Received from Mrs. Fergusson

one dollar for scrubbing school

term opening May 12

Mrs Jane Hackett.

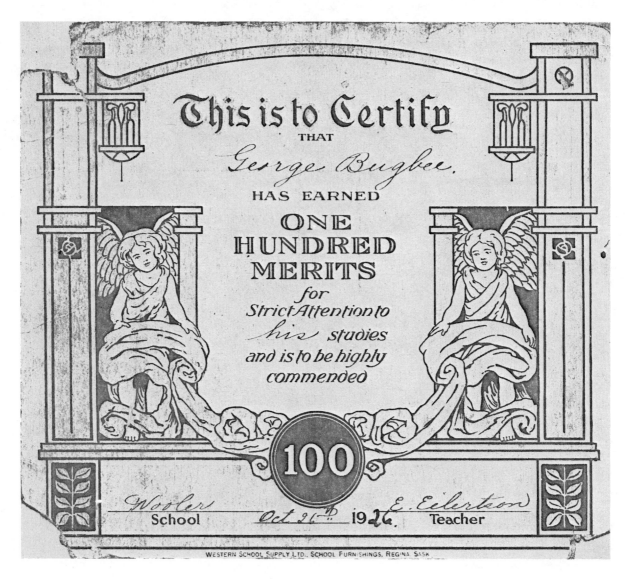

This is to Certify

THAT

George Bugbee

HAS EARNED

ONE
HUNDRED
MERITS

for
Strict Attention to
his studies
and is to be highly
commended

100

Wooler
School

Oct 25th 1926

E. Eilertson
Teacher

WESTERN SCHOOL SUPPLY LTD., SCHOOL FURNISHINGS, REGINA SASK.

390

Index

PRINTED
IN CANADA